God, Meaning and Morality

Third Edition

Edited by

Iain S. Maclean
James Madison University, VA

Diana Edelman
Sheffield University, UK

THOMSON
CUSTOM PUBLISHING

Editor: Nathan Anderson
Production Manager: Staci Powers
Production Coordinator: Brian Schaefer
Marketing Coordinator: Sara L. Hinckley

Printed in the United States of America

Thomson Learning Custom Publishing
5191 Natorp Blvd.
Mason, Ohio 45040
USA

For information about our products, contact us:
1-800-355-9983
http://www.custom.thomsonlearning.com

International Headquarters
Thomson Learning
International Division
290 Harbor Drive, 2nd Floor
Stamford, CT 06902-7477
USA

UK/Europe/Middle East/South Africa
Thomson Learning
Berkshire House
168-173 High Holborn
London WCIV 7AA

Asia
Thomson Learning
60 Albert Street, #15-01
Albert Complex
Singapore 189969

Canada
Nelson Thomson Learning
1120 Birchmount Road
Toronto, Ontario MIK 5G4
Canada
United Kingdom

Visit us at www.e-riginality.com and learn more about this book and other titles published by Thomson Learning Custom Publishing

ISBN 0-759-31183-8

The Adaptable Courseware Program consists of products and additions to existing Custom Publishing products that are produced from camera-ready copy. Peer review, class testing, and accuracy are primarily the responsibility of the author(s).

CONTENTS

SKIP

INTRODUCTION

Humanity by nature desires to know, declared an early Greek philosopher. This desire has led humanity to focus upon the rational dimension of human being and in fact even to argue, as Plato and many since, that the basic reality of all existence is a rational pattern of ideas. Others, from their own experience have reacted to such theories and posited other versions of reality. The debate is ongoing.

This work addresses these philosophical and religious issues raised by human existence. These are not new issues, but rather ones on which many cultures, including the western, have engaged, in generation-long conversations. When these conversations are formally articulated they are described as philosophy. In so doing human reason is employed, This in turn raises the questions of the nature of that reasoning ability, of perception, of knowing, of the nature of humanity, of how then should humanity live, and of the nature of the creative processes.

Philosophy, a word literally translated as "the love of wisdom," is the ongoing attempt by humans as thinkers to analyze and to conceptualize the basic principles by which the universe and indeed all human experience, is organized. However, in the history of human experience, many differing systems, each with their attendant vocabularies, have been produced by individual philosophers, typically responding to specific issues or challenges of their time. Each of these systems with their respective answers to their specific situations, assumes an epistemology (from two Greek words for "knowledge" and "reason" or "system"), or a theory of the nature of knowing. Epistemology is concerned with how and what we know. Do we only know that which we perceive through sense data and upon which our reason functions? Or are there other ways? Or are the two "forms" of knowledge just noted too simplistic an explanation of how perceiving operates? The approach that we only know what we perceive through our senses is called "empiricist," while typically religious, ethical and aesthetic judgments claim other sources of knowing.

The numerous differing philosophical systems in existence arise from differing historical contexts and differing human experiences of nature, others, religion, moral commitments and aesthetics. At the same time such experiences are also deeply influenced by the role and success of technology and the natural sciences in attempting to understand the world. The discovery of the nature of reality (ontology), and theories of the nature of the human person, raise questions as to the purpose of human existence and indeed of human ability to change either themselves or the processes of which they seem to be a part. Is human existence then determined and is humanity less free than it thinks? All these questions in turn raise questions about the nature of ultimate reality.

The numerous philosophical systems can be broadly classified as materialistic, naturalist, idealistic, empiricist, dualistic, or existentialist. Materialist thinkers hold that nature or physical matter is the only reality, all else being but aspects or attributes of this one reality (Heraclites, Democritus, Benedictus Spinoza, Karl Marx). This classical form of materialism has in contemporary times been largely eclipsed by naturalism which holds to an empirical method and the scientific approach to reality. Such an approach would typify many who take a psychological interpretation of human existence and reduce all human endeavors to specific drives or motivations (philosophers such as Ludwig Feuerbach, Karl Marx, and the psychologists Sigmund Freud and B.F. Skinner, or the anthropologist Marvin Harris). These approaches clearly are reductionist in the sense that all of reality is reduced to specific natural, material or psychological forces. Such approaches focus on the contexts or conditioning forces that the role of the mind or ideas is subsumed under some form of determinism. The position that such materialist approaches were reacting to was of course idealism and its classic proponent, Plato (note Alfred Whitehead's comment that all "Western philosophy is but a footnote to Plato"). This position, as its name indicates, prioritizes mind or ideas as primary. While there are of course many differing forms of idealism, philosophers (and theologians) as diverse as Plato, St. Augustine, St. Aquinas, Leibniz, Berkeley, Kant and Hegel can all be considered as idealists.

We return to the issue of epistemology here. While materialism or naturalism begin with the assumption that reality is what appears, empirically to our senses, idealism places the primary emphasis upon the ideas or the rational processes of thought. An alternative approach to these is what might be called dualism, as exemplified by the father of early modern philosophy, René Descartes (1596-1650). Recognizing the great advances in physical sciences in discovering natural laws he saw in these the danger of humanity losing freedom and being reduced to, or understood as controlled by, these self-same laws. He argued that mind and matter are the two basic elements of reality (apart from God, who is above and separate from the created world). The human is thus basically defined as a thinker and as such is free, while at the same time is also a body, which is determined by all the physical laws of nature. Now, in the idealist systems of thought, the so-called objective or empirical realm is reduced to "appearances" or to the idea or concept in the observer's mind. This approach is exemplified in the work of Immanuel Kant (1734-1804), the father of modern philosophy, who argued that the human mind itself was structured in such a way that all our sense experience is shaped by the mind in order to become objects of our knowing. Thus we never actually see or perceive a thing in itself, but only its appearance, (or the concept), in our mind. Thus what we experience empirically is the phenomenon in our mind since we can never actually know the thing in itself or the noumenon. The questions and issues raised by epistemology and perception are admittedly too expansive to be discussed within the limits of this text, so only the most creative period, that of the early Modern period, stretching from Descartes (circa 1650) to Immanuel Kant (1724-1804) is examined in chapter three.

Now, in the idealist systems of thought, the so-called objective or empirical realm is reduced to "appearances" or the idea or concept in the observer's mind. Example of Immanuel Kant (1734-1804), the father of modern philosophy. Kant argued that the human mind itself was structured in such a way that all our sense experience is shaped by them in order to become objects of our knowing. Thus we never actually see or perceive a thing in itself, but only its appearance in our mind. That is what we experience empirically, the phenomenon in our mind, while we never actually can know the thing in itself, the noumenon. The questions and issues raised by epistemology and perception are admittedly too expansive to be discussed here, so only the most creative period, that of the early Modern period stretching from Descartes (circa 1650) to Immanuel Kant (1724-1804) is examined.

These issues naturally lead to the question of the nature of the subject or the self who is doing the perceiving of the reality. Humans have posited a reality that is either beyond, above or under or other than the perceptual one. Of course controversial, but many of these perceptions or understandings of reality are expressed in religious traditions, adhered to by a majority of earth's inhabitants. Here we have to consider not only the numerous and differing claims which religions make concerning knowledge of matters beyond sense perception. How is such knowledge possible and how does it differ from our other sources of knowledge? Each religious tradition presupposes a metaphysical tradition and the ultimate reality posited will depend upon the specific revelation claimed. Thus there are many differing religious views of the world and each claims to offer a complete response to the nature of the world, humanity and salvation and of course, of the question then of truth.

The role of reason is not removed by revelation (as Tertullian [circa 160-220 A. D.] implied in his declaration that: "It is absurd, therefore I believe"), but rather becomes ever more important for a critical and constructive evaluation of such religious claims. Each religious tradition will have specific views of ultimate reality or the divine, reality, the relationship of ultimate reality to reality, humanity, and the world and these, and their interpretations, must all be presented in a rational form. Thus is the divine or god the same as everything, different from everything, related to it in some ways, or not? Answers to these basic questions suggest directions for understanding the questions of the personal nature of the divine, the problems of determinism or predestination and freedom/free will, the problem of evil, personal immortality, the nature of mysticism, etc.

Paul Tillich (1886-1965) described two basic religious approaches to reality, namely the ontological and the cosmological and he argued that both are necessary in a developed philosophy of religion, for to hold to the one without the other would lead to a dichotomy between the secular and religious spheres. The ontological approach is one that addresses the question of Being, for without Being, there would be no things or beings whatsoever. Here a link in contemporary philosophical thought is to be made with the modern existentialist movement in philosophy. Existentialism (a term coined by French philosopher Gabriel Marcel, 1889-1973), like the ontological approach, can be traced back to St. Augustine, and more directly to the works of the 19th century Danish philosopher Søren Kierkegaard (1813-1855), who influenced the late 19th and the 20th century philosophical and religious traditions. While philosophers such as Friedrich Nietzsche (1844-1900) and Jean-Paul Sartre (1905-1980) proposed atheistic existentialist philosophies, others such as Martin Heidegger (1889-1976), and John Macquarrie (1919-) having noted how existentialism points to ontological questions, have advocated theistic positions. Existentialism, in reaction to earlier idealist and materialist positions, emphasizes the role of human decision and the will. Confronted with the myriad possibilities of life, man and woman decide their own "existence" or life that possesses meaning. Put another way then, existentialism is the human search for self-understanding. Religious existentialism holds that authentic existence is that which is decided in the light of God, the ground of being. In this approach to ultimate reality, reason still plays a role, but the emphasis is upon the will, the individual being and self-knowledge, rather than upon rational systems. This latter emphasis is characteristic of the other approach mentioned by Tillich, that of the cosmological. This approach begins with the natural world, rather than with the subjectivity of the individual. Clearly then these approaches correspond to the subjective/objective dichotomy of our knowledge, knowledge that is of ourselves and of the world.

Human pre-conceptions of the above effect how humans then live in the world, and so systems of ethics are developed. These can include approaches based upon conceptions of the self, God, universal law, the principle of utility, or classical and recent virtue theories. Psychological understandings of the self, its development and interactions, also come into play in the twentieth century as the human sciences discover more of how humans function and act. Such numerous starting points were not possible in more traditional societies or even as some maintain, in the West, until the post-Renaissance period opened up more fully the option of not believing in an ultimate reality such as God.

Finally, aesthetics raises questions of what is beauty and related to that, the questions of what then is art? These questions and their respective answers then in turn raise questions of how these conceptions relate to the selves and ontological and cosmological realities raised earlier in this text. If, as many claim, art conveys not just beauty, but values, whose values, in an increasingly pluralist world, are to be expressed and promoted? It is hoped that these issues and the connections between them raised by this text will prompt in turn more questions, both within and beyond the classroom!

—*Iain S. Maclean*

PREFACE

This, the third edition of *God, Meaning and Morality*, has benefited from the comments of colleagues and students in classes. These comments have led to numerous changes for the better in the view of the editors. While the first edition sought a comprehensive overview of the issues involved, this proved to be too ambitious an aim. Thus some judicious pruning has been undertaken, with the omission in this edition of the more technical sections on perception, epistemology, and the theory of aesthetics. In addition, some selections that the editors thought appropriate, but did not have the desired effect for the readers, have simply been omitted.

This edition is not merely a pruned down version though of its predecessor. Some of the colleagues who made critical suggestions, have been the same who came forward with offers to contribute sections, in some cases whole chapters for this edition. Grateful acknowledgment must be made to Dr. Daniel Flage, a past president of the American Philosophical Association (Mid-Atlantic Association), and past Chair of the Department of Philosophy and Religion at James Madison University, for his chapter on perception in pre-modern philosophy. In addition, the two chapters dealing with religious cosmologies are completely new, with all the sections being specifically written for this edition. Our thanks to Dr. Lance Laird of Evergreen State College (Washington) for his contribution on Islam and to Dr. Tim Lubin of Washington and Lee University (Virginia) for the section on Hinduism. Finally, Dr. Mark Liederbach (Southeastern Seminary) contributed the chapters on "Theories of the Self," "The Virtues of Virtue Ethics," and together with John Cunningham (University of Virginia), the chapter on "Conceptions of Beauty."

These changes, as well as the numerous additions, will serve to make this an even more useful teaching resource for undergraduates, particularly in general education courses that seek to provide comprehensive surveys of philosophical and religious understandings of the self, the world, ethics, and aesthetics.

—*The Editors*

PERCEPTION

PERCEPTION

by Ralph Baergen

Direct Realism

Perception is such an important source of beliefs and has played such a prominent role in epistemology that it warrants closer investigation. This examination of perception will follow the trend and focus on vision; many of the things to be said about vision apply to the other sense modalities as well.

The first step in figuring out what epistemology has to say about seeing is to understand what sort of activity seeing is. Seeing something involves, one would suppose, something to be seen along with someone to see it, and this someone would engage in an activity (that is, seeing) that involves the something. Like cutting, eating, and throwing, seeing seems to be an activity that requires an object; just as there can't be cutting or eating without *something* being cut or eaten, there can be no seeing without something's being seen. This way of understanding perception is called the *act/object* approach; perception is regarded as an action of the sort that requires that something be acted upon. What kinds of things can turn up on the object side of perception? In other words, what kinds of things can be perceived? Physical objects spring immediately to mind; we see dogs, pencils, Oldsmobiles, and other pieces of the world's furniture. These, after all, are what confront us when we open our eyes.

If we accept this answer to the above question, it is easy to see how perception can provide us with information about our surroundings. One simply looks around, is aware of objects, and "reads off" their properties from this awareness. If one is aware of something as being warm, stout, and furry, one knows that a warm, stout, furry thing is at hand. Some philosophers claim that all of this puts one in a very strong epistemic position when it comes to finding out about medium-sized objects in the vicinity, for perception provides one with a direct link to them. So long as one is *directly aware* of objects, they say, one needn't worry about whether one's perceptions are accurate; there is no representation mediating between one and the object in question, so there is no opportunity for *mis*representation to creep in.

This talk of direct awareness bears explaining. In sorting this out, though, it's easier to present first the notion of being *indirectly* aware of something. When you look at a photograph of Uncle Wilfred, you are only indirectly aware of Uncle Wilfred; you are aware of him only in virtue of being aware of the photograph. When pilots see blips on their radar screens, they are indirectly aware of other planes; they are aware of them only in virtue of being aware of the blips. When you look at yourself in the mirror, you are only indirectly aware of your face; you are aware of it only in virtue of being aware of its reflection. The basic idea, then, is that in cases of indirect awareness there is always some intermediate thing, and one is aware of the object in question only in virtue of being aware of the intermediate. Of course, for anything to be indirectly perceived, something else (namely, some intermediate object) must be directly perceived. Direct perception is simply perception without any of these intermediates.

This is why it is often claimed that you can be more confident about what something is like if you perceive it directly than if you perceive it indirectly: Indirect perception is accurate—or, to use the philosophers' term, veridical—only if the intermediate passes on the information correctly, but with direct perception there are no intermediates to mess things up. Cameras can have dirty lenses, radar can malfunction, and mirrors can be warped, so if you're aware of something only in virtue of being aware of these you might end up with false beliefs about Uncle Wilfred, air traffic, and your nose. You'd be epistemically much better off to be directly aware of these things.

We have begun with the claim that we are directly aware of our surroundings. When this is conjoined with another claim, one about the nature of those surroundings, the result is called *Direct Realism*. This other claim in question is the immensely plausible one that what is out there to be seen is independent of what anyone says or thinks or believes about it. Actually, it's somewhat more complicated than that; a realist about the external world is one who says (a) our claims about physical objects have truth values (that is, they are the sorts of claims that (unlike imperatives, etc.) are either true or false), (b) a goodly number of these claims are true, and (c) the truth of these claims is independent of what we think or say about the matter. If you are a direct realist, you are in a very good position to form true beliefs about the world around you, for you are in direct perceptual contact with that world. Direct perception "cuts out the middle-man"; it eliminates intermediate stages of awareness in which errors or inaccuracies can be introduced (or so it is often claimed; this will be challenged later on). If you are directly aware *of the object*, and not merely a picture or reflection or some other sort of representation, then the object must be the way it appears to be. After all, the direct realist asks, how could any discrepancy between the object and its appearance arise? Therefore, all your perception-based beliefs about the properties of the objects around you would be true.

Well, everything seems fine so far as our perception-based beliefs about our surroundings are concerned *provided we were right in supposing that we perceive those surroundings directly, and not indirectly*. But one should note an objection often raised against Direct Realism: If we are directly aware of the world around us, why is it that appearances don't always match up with reality? Consider, for example, a stick partly submerged in water. Before sticking one end in the water, you examine the stick and find that it is straight and rigid. But when you partly submerge it, it appears to bend at the waterline. The stick is, in fact, still straight, but it no longer looks that way. In addition to illusions like this one, we may also sometimes experience hallucinations; you, like Macbeth, may seem to see various pieces of dirty cutlery floating about when none are actually present. If our visual experiences provide us with direct access to the world, how could such errors be possible?

One move a direct realist might make in response to this challenge is to say that, although our visual experiences do provide direct access to the world and are always veridical, there are some other experiences—sometimes inaccurate—that only *seem* to be instances of vision. That is, hallucinations (to take one example) might be said to be non-perceptual experiences and thus not a threat to Direct Realism. They would only *seem* to be perceptual, but they wouldn't *really* be perceptual.

Although this might work in the case of hallucinations, the direct realist would have to give us an explanation for illusions, and here this line of argument becomes highly implausible. Go back to our partly submerged stick. The direct realist would, presumably, say that before you stick one end in the water you are directly aware of the stick; after all, this is a perfectly ordinary case of visual perception. To apply this line of argument to the situation in which the stick is partly submerged, our direct realist will have to say that somewhere in the process of dipping one end of the stick in the water your experiences switch from being direct access to the world to being something else (and something that might be inaccurate). But how does this happen? Your visual system doesn't suddenly start doing a different job when the stick is submerged. If you were directly aware of it before getting it wet, you should be directly aware of it afterward. More to the point, if you're not directly aware of it afterward, you weren't directly aware of it before, and if it's possible to be wrong about the shape of the stick at one point there's room for error all along.

Here's another objection sometimes raised against Direct Realism: What we know about the functioning of our perceptual systems seems difficult to square with the claim that we are directly aware of the objects around us. Vision, for example, involves processing the information carried by the light which enters the eye; the patterns of light striking the retina seem to play an intermediary role between the object and our visual experiences. The visual system is, in some respects, like a camera; whether one ends up with an accurate picture depends upon the functioning of the equipment being used (whether it be a camera or a visual system). Altering the conditions of observation will change the character of that observation. This is what is happening with the stick example; light reflected from the submerged part of the stick bends slightly at the waterline, and this accounts for the apparent bend in the stick. That is, our visual awareness seems to be of representations, and not objects; this could not be the case if Direct Realism were correct.

The story is the same with the other sense modalities. Hearing something involves monitoring differences in air pressure; smelling involves detecting the shapes of tiny airborne particles; tasting involves responding to certain chemical structures. In each case, our awareness of external objects seems to be indirect; we are aware of them only in virtue of being aware of something else. This is the case even with the tactile sense, the sense of touch. You place your hand on the table and find that it is cool, smooth, and hard. But the story behind your sensing this involves the stimulation of various nerves in your skin; in spite of the fact that there is direct contact between you and the table, our knowledge of the tactile sense suggests that you are *aware* of the table only in virtue of being aware of a representation of it.

As was mentioned earlier, these objections to Direct Realism hinge on a misunderstanding[1]. Contrary to what has been suggested, the fact that one isn't *aware* of any intermediary in perceiving something does not entail that there are no intermediate *stages* in the perceptual process; all one can reasonably conclude is that one isn't conscious of any intermediate stages. And if there is room for intermediate stages in direct perception, then we have an opening for error and inaccuracy in perception. No thoughtful direct realist would deny that visual processing involves lots of stages (having to do with the retinas, the lateral geniculate nuclei, the occipital cortex, and other parts of the brain); all they deny is that we're aware of what's going on in there. Instead, they say, we're *aware* only of the things out there in front of our eyes that started the perceptual ball rolling.

If this is right, then illusions no longer pose any problem. Go back to the example of the partly submerged stick. According to the direct realist, the object of perception is the stick itself (and not anything going on in the brain). If you're aware of the stick itself, then what you're aware of is *not* bent. Of course, you're not aware of it *as* straight; instead, you're aware of this straight thing as bent. We needn't conclude from this that you're aware of something other than the stick. All we need to say is that your awareness of it doesn't match up with the way it really is; in other words, the properties it seems to have aren't all properties it really has. Thus, the objections listed above have no force against Direct Realism.

It is important to notice, though, that when this confusion about Direct Realism has been cleared up, one of its most attractive features evaporates. The advantage of this theory was supposed to be that when you perceive something you can be confident that it is just as it appears. The idea, you will recall, was that if there are no intermediate stages, then there's no room for anything to go wrong. Well, there *are* intermediate stages in perceptual processing (although we're not aware of them), so we have to leave open the possibility that how things seem differs from how they are. Being directly aware of external objects gives us no guarantee that they are as they seem to be.

Representative Realism

Suppose that, like lots of other people, you thought that Direct Realism was untenable. Clearly, there is *some* sense in which we are aware of the things which surround us; if we're not directly aware of them, we must be *indirectly* aware of them. Our sensory systems, stimulated by objects out in the world, respond by creating representations of these objects; we are directly aware of these representations and are aware of objects "out there" only in virtue of being aware of these representations. This, too, fits with what we know about how our sensory systems work; it differs from Direct Realism in claiming that we are aware of what's going on at some stage of perceptual processing.

Representative Realism also provides us with accounts of illusions and hallucinations. When one sees a partly submerged stick, one is directly aware of the representation and only indirectly aware of the stick itself. This representation will provide an accurate and complete picture of the stick only if it is created in the right way. This means, for one thing, that the visual system must be working properly. Just as flaws in a camera can yield inaccurate photographs, so flaws in one's vision can yield inaccurate visual presentations. In the case at hand, nothing is amiss with the visual system; the explanation for the illusion is found in the external situation. Some of the light reflected from the stick travels only through air, while the light reflected from the submerged part of the stick travels first through water and then through air. Because these media have different indices of refraction, some of the reflected light travels in a straight line, and some of it "bends" at the waterline. Accurate and complete representations, then, require appropriate external conditions as well as properly functioning sensory equipment. When something goes wrong anywhere, errors (like the bent-stick illusion) can arise. The story is very similar for hallucinations. Here we seem to have visual presentations caused, not by the objects around us, but by the improper operation of our visual equipment.

This highlights a reason for uneasiness with Representative Realism: Because things can go awry with sensory systems and with external circumstances, it is difficult—if not impossible—to be sure that the representations of which we are aware accurately depict our surroundings. How can we be sure that the world is the way it seems to be? After all, couldn't we be subject to unremitting illusions and hallucinations? (Although Representative Realism has sometimes been regarded as more epistemically precarious than Direct Realism in this respect, it turns out that these theories are in the same boat so far as the possibility of error is concerned.)

However, there are other questions sparked by Representative Realism, having to do with how the details of the theory are to be worked out. The next section presents one of these.

Sense Data

According to Representative Realism, we are directly aware only of various representations of our world. But what sorts of things are these representations? This difficult question threatens to lead us away from epistemology into the philosophy of mind; in this section, a traditional answer will be considered.

Begin by going back to cases of illusion. When you are aware of the partly submerged stick, it seems bent to you although really it's straight. In order for it to seem bent, though, you must be aware of something that is bent; that is, although the stick itself may not be bent, *something* must be in order for you to have the experiences in question. A quick survey of your surroundings shows that nothing "out there" is bent, so it has been suggested that the bent "something" must be internal to you. Those who make this proposal have called this bent "something" of which you are aware a sense datum. Sense data are said to be the things of which we are directly aware in perception and that have the *apparent* properties of the objects around us. The stick is apparently bent, so the sense datum of which you are aware in perceiving the stick *is* bent, although the stick itself is straight.*

This provides us with an explanation of what sense data are, as well as an explanation of the central supporting arguments for the claim that sense data exist. The idea, of course, is that you're aware of something bent, and if it isn't the stick it must be something else. Here is how C. D. Broad describes it ("sense" is just another term for sense data):[2]

> Under certain conditions I have states of mind called sensations. These sensations have objects, which are always concrete particular existents, like coloured or hot patches, noises, smells, etc. Such objects are called sensa. Sensa have properties, such as shape, size, hardness, color, loudness, coldness, and so on. The existence of such sensa, and their presence to our minds in sensation, leads us to judge that a physical object exists and is present to our senses. To this physical object we ascribe various properties. . . . [A]ll the properties that we do ascribe to physical objects are based on and correlated with the properties that actually characterize our sensa.

Because we are directly aware of sense data, we cannot (it is typically said) be mistaken about what properties they have; error creeps in only when we draw the wrong conclusions about what the external object (the one which brought about my experience of this sense datum) must be like.

A couple of important things can be learned about sense data and perception from this passage. One of them is that sense data have properties; they are hot, or pink, or bitter, or tuneful, and so on. Nevertheless, sense data are not to be found "out there" in the world; they are creatures of a purely mental realm. Their existence lies entirely in their being sensed; a sense datum ceases to be when one ceases to be aware of it. If you find it odd that something purely mental would be said to have such properties as hardness, coldness, blueness, and so forth, remember that sense data are perceived directly, so if they *seem* to have these properties they must really *have* them; after all, direct perception leaves no room for error. (There are no intermediate stages of processing that might introduce inaccuracy.)

There is also a lesson in the above passage about the nature of perception. Broad says that, based on the sorts of sense data we're aware of, we *judge* that the external objects around us are thus and so. What this implies is that our perception of physical objects has two stages, and that these stages have very different characters. The first of these is commonly called *sensation*; it involves the awareness of sense data and nothing more. That is, one is aware of colors, shapes, scents, and so forth, but does not yet draw any conclusions about one's surroundings. Thus, at this first stage, one is aware not of physical objects, but of colored patches, noises, prickly sensations, and the like. Awareness of these is direct; awareness of physical objects, which is indirect, does not come up until the second stage. As was mentioned above, because sensation involves the direct awareness of sense data, one cannot be mistaken about what one senses.

But one can be mistaken about what one perceives. *Perception*, the second stage, begins with the sensations from the first stage and uses them to make judgments or inferences about the external world. These judgments or inferences are typically unconscious; one is generally unaware of having passed through

---

this stage. (One may become conscious of these inferences when they become difficult. For example, when looking at something in poor light or through a thick fog, one may consciously ask oneself what object would have just that shape and color.) Indeed, sense-data theorists typically admit that a great deal of effort and concentration are required if one is to focus on sensation alone (leaving out any judgments about physical objects); many admit that this may be impossible (in some or perhaps even all cases). Nonetheless, sensation is held to be a prior *conscious* stage of perception; the difficulty is in separating this element of consciousness from perception. The judgments we base upon perception draw also upon an (unconscious) stock of generalizations and information; errors in perception are the result of falsehoods in this supplemental material.

Problems with Sense Data

If you're going to be a representative realist, you're probably better off leaving sense data out of your theory. The chief reason for this is that they are Terribly Strange Things. We are told that they have properties such as hardness, coolness, heaviness, and so forth, but that they are ephemeral mental entities. Some sense-data theorists say that they have depth and height and width, but that they are located not in the world around us but in some sort of inner, mental "space." One need hardly say that this is worrisome.

There is a philosophical principle, Occam's Razor, which states, in effect, that, other things being equal, we should prefer theories that posit the existence of fewer sorts of things to those that posit the existence of more sorts of things. There is a continuing debate among philosophers about whether we ought to be guided by this principle (although at present it seems to be widely held), but if it is correct, then a form of Representative Realism that leaves out sense data would (other things being equal[*]) be preferable to one that includes them. You see, sense data are a new sort of thing—they constitute a new ontological[**] category—and if we can find some other sort of thing to play the role of representation we had better leave them alone.

Another difficulty facing sense data is that they do not seem to give us an appropriate account of the vagueness and indeterminacy that we sometimes find in perception. According to sense-data theories, our access to sense data is direct, precise, and unerring. When some external state of affairs generates experiences of an indistinct red patch, it is not that we are only indistinctly aware of a red patch; rather, there is an indistinct red patch (the sense datum), and our awareness of it is flawless. But does this give us an acceptable account of the vagueness and indeterminacy of perception?

In the case of vision, sense data would be similar in some respects to photographs. Now, photos can be vague or indeterminate, but any pictorial property you care to name is either present or absent. This, however, does not seem to be the case with sense data. Here's the standard case used to illustrate this:[3]

---

[*]   This clause has been inserted to remind you that we should prefer forms of Representative Realism that leave out sense data *only if* they are still capable of yielding the results we want. That is, we should make sure that leaving out sense data does not impair the theory's capacity to explain our perceptual experiences and their role in epistemology. If it turns out that Representative Realism requires sense data to account for these. then the simplicity spoken of in Occam's Razor is beside the point. It turns out, though, that sense data are dispensable; no advantage is gained by including them in our account of perceptual knowledge.

[**]   Ontology is that branch of philosophy that concerns itself with what sorts of things there are. Thus, an ontology is a list of the sorts of things to be found in the world. For example, one's ontology might include physical objects, non-physical minds, and abstract objects (such as numbers). Occam's Razor adjures us to keep our ontologies as small as reasonably possible (that is, to have as few ontological categories as possible), and the present point is that it might be better to exclude sense data from our ontology.

> The classic case is that of the speckled hen. I may be able to see that it has quite a number of speckles, but unable to see exactly how many it has. The hen has a definite number of speckles, but the perception is a perception of an indeterminate number of speckles. . . . [T]he difficulty that this indeterminacy of perception creates for a theory of sensory items is that it seems to imply that the items are indeterminate in nature. The non-physical item that exists when we perceive the speckled hen will have to have an indeterminate number of speckles.

A photograph of a speckled hen would, at every point, be brown, or white, or some other shade. When all of this is put together, it might be difficult to sort out where the boundaries of the speckles are (and thus difficult to determine how many speckles there are), but this is vagueness in what counts as a speckle, not in the photograph itself. The problem with vision seems different, though. Here we do *not* seem to have determinate properties at every point; rather, vision seems to be simply "silent" on many points. Your uncertainty about how many speckles you saw on the hen arises, not from uncertainty about what counts as a speckle, but from vagueness or indeterminacy—a kind of "silence"—in vision itself. Thus, sense data cannot be like pictures, but if they're not like pictures what else could they be?

Yet another problem with sense data is that they are designed to fit into the two-stage (sensation and perception) model of perceiving the world, and it turns out that this model is empirically false. This picture of perception suggests that our judgments operate upon a sensory presentation (which was generated without being influenced by our beliefs and so forth), but in fact there is no such untouched sensation with which to work; the influences of cognition reach well down into the visual process.

It has been suggested that we didn't have any really good reasons for supposing that there are sense data in the first place. The argument was, roughly, that we are aware of *something* with various properties, and because that something is not (at least in cases of illusion and hallucination) anything in the world around us, it must be something internal. But why, it has been asked, should we suppose that awareness is always awareness of a *something*; why couldn't it be that we are aware in some *way* or other, without bringing mysterious objects into it? If awareness needn't have an object, then the central motivation for supposing that there are sense data disappears. This is the line of argument taken up in the next section.

Adverbial Theories

Most approaches to perception agree on this fundamental point: Perception is to be understood as a relation between a person (the perceiver) and an object (that which is perceived); this, as was noted at the beginning of the discussion of sense data, is the *act/object* understanding of perception. Anyone who takes this approach will have to figure out whether we are directly or indirectly aware of the external world, what any intermediate objects of perception might be (if perception turns out to be indirect), what we are perceiving in cases of illusion and hallucination, and so forth. These are hard questions, as the previous sections have shown, and a neat way to avoid all of them is to reject the act/object account of perception.

Instead, one might focus on the perceptual experience itself and regard it as a *kind* of experience or a *way* of experiencing. This reflects the suspicion some theorists have that we may have been fooled by the way we talk about perceptions into thinking that perception requires objects of one sort or another to which we might stand in various relations. Here are some analogous cases: Although there are no such things as smiles, limps, and dances, we often talk as though there are. We say that she wore a smile, that he has a limp, and that they returned from Barcelona with a new dance, but there isn't a thing (a smile) that she wears, a thing (a limp) that he has, or a thing (a new dance) that was carried hither from Barcelona in a suitcase. Instead, a smile is a way a face can be, a limp is a way of walking, and a new dance is a pleasurable but inefficient way of locomoting in pairs about a dance floor. We could change the way we talk about smiles, limps, and dances to make more clear that these are events or processes or ways of being rather than objects.

Thus, we could say that she smiled, that he limped, and that they danced. A further modification of this talk would make more vivid the fact that we have here *variations* on certain events or states: She looked smilingly; he walked limpingly; they danced newly. Such statements sound awkward, but they make clear that smiles, limps, and dances are not things. The term "adverbial theory" reflects the fact that adverbs are employed to describe all this (rather than the old, misleading, noun-based approach).

Now, apply all this to perception. Although we talk about perception as though it involves one object or another, the adverbialists say that what we have here are just different ways of perceiving.[4] As in the other cases, this can be reflected in our talk about sensations by using adverbs rather than nouns. Instead of saying that you have a sensation of something blue, say that you are sensing bluely; instead of saying that you seem to see a chair, say that you are appeared to chairly. Admittedly, this sounds odd, but the point is to break us of the habit of thinking of perceptions as involving things and then going on the (alleged) wild-goose chase of trying to figure out what these objects are like.

There is, we are assured, a reward for going the adverbial route. If perceptions aren't things, then we don't need to try to find the differences between these things when we are perceiving these things normally and when we are hallucinating or seeing illusions. For example, when we look at the partly submerged stick we don't have to ask what *is* bent if the stick itself is straight. Or, if we're hallucinating pink armadillos, we needn't wonder what *is* pink and wandering about the room. Instead, we'll just say that one is appeared to bent-slickly or pink-armadilloly, and leave it at that. Along with this, of course, we can say that being appeared to in these ways is *normally* caused by the presence of bent sticks and pink armadillos (respectively), but that in *abnormal* conditions these states might be brought about by any number of things. Furthermore, we can say that the properties of external objects can be determined by examining the ways in which one senses; perceiving bently ordinarily indicates the presence of bent things, for example, and perceiving pinkly ordinarily indicates the presence of pink things.[5]

There are a number of difficulties facing the adverbial approach; only two of them will be mentioned here. The *many property problem* arises when the adverbial theorist tries to give an account of complex sensations.[6] Suppose, to take a common example, that you have an after-image of a blue triangle and a red circle. The adverbial theorist says that you are in a particular experiential state, specifically, the state of sensing blue-triangle-and-red-circlely. (Incidentally, look at this description and then think about how the adverbialist would describe your sensations when you look out the window. Such descriptions would have to be unspeakably ponderous.) Now, either this description is made up of various elements and can be regarded as a composite, or it is a unified whole and irreducible into components. (That is, either this sensory state is analyzable, or it isn't.) The adverbial theorist must go one way or the other, but there seem to be difficulties with each alternative.

Suppose you say that the sensory state just described *is* analyzable; it is a composite of various component states. The components would be sensing bluely and triangularly and redly and circlely. The problem is that this approach seems unable to distinguish between an after-image of a blue triangle and a red circle, and one of a blue circle and a red triangle. Both have the same elements, and this decomposition seems to say nothing about how they are put together. Various attempts have been made to fill in this information about composition, but none of the proposed solutions has become widely accepted.[7]

Suppose, now, that you prefer to regard sensory states as unified and unanalyzable. This avoids the problem just described—one is able to make all the right sorts of distinctions between states—but it runs afoul of another one: It does not seem to preserve the usual relations among claims about sensory states. For example, if you have an after-image of a blue triangle, then you are having an after-image of something blue. This would be perfectly evident if sensory states could be taken apart into components; the blue triangle after-image would have as components sensing bluely and sensing triangularly, and from this it follows that you are sensing bluely. But if sensing blue-triangularly cannot be divided up in this way, there seems to be no clear relation between the claim that you have such an after-image and the claim that you have an after-image of something blue.[8] There may be a way of avoiding these difficulties (and the others alleged to face the adverbial theory), but at this stage more work needs to be done in working out the details.

Phenomenalism

Although there are several alternatives to the accounts of perception presented above, one more will be mentioned: Phenomenalism. It's a bit odd to include this theory here, because it's really a metaphysical theory rather than an epistemological one; rather than explaining how we come to perceive the world, it provides an account of what we mean when we describe the world. This often springs from a despair about answering sceptical objections to the project of bridging the gap between appearance and reality, and the key element lies in dropping Realism. Phenomenalism ensures that the world is the way it appears to be by abandoning the realist claim that the world is independent of the way it appears to us.

According to Phenomenalism, any claim about the world is meaningful only as a shorthand for claims about various actual and possible experiences. For example, consider the claim, "There is a sheet of paper here." The phenomenalist claims that this is equivalent in meaning to something like, "I have a visual experience of something white and rectangular; if I were to give myself experiences of reaching towards it, I would have experiences of feeling something flat and smooth; and if I were to give myself experiences of clutching it with my fingers, I would hear a crinkling sound and the white patch I see would grow smaller." This list of experiences I am now having and those I would have if . . . continues indefinitely and includes every possibility. Because the two claims presented above have the same meaning (according to the phenomenalists), physical objects turn out to be nothing above and beyond our actual and possible experiences; this is sometimes expressed by saying that objects are *logical constructs* out of experiences.

This leaves little room for further sceptical objections, for most sceptics find it hard to deny that we have experiences; if perceiving objects is nothing more than this, then we certainly perceive objects. And if objects are not something "out there" that we might be right or wrong about, then it certainly won't do to say (as sceptics love to do) that all our beliefs about physical objects are (or could be) false. Most sceptics (like most epistemologists) presuppose Realism when they argue, so dropping Realism has the happy effect of disarming their objections.

But this victory over Scepticism is bought at a price: The phenomenalist must abandon a number of claims we want to make about the world of physical objects. For example, we typically claim that it is conceivable that one could have experiences of such-and-such a sort—ones that seem to be experiences of a physical object—even though no object is present. Phenomenalism, however, cannot allow this possibility. If the presence of an object is nothing more than one's having (and being disposed to have) certain experiences, no sense can be made of the object's being absent when one has the experiences. Phenomenalism must also at least revise our understanding of what it is for two or more observers to examine a single object, or for an object to be observed for a second time, or for two objects to have exactly the same appearance. The reader is invited to think about what phenomenalists might say in each of these cases.

Cognitive Influences Upon Perception

The last portion of this discussion of perception will attempt to poke holes in a venerable presupposition, namely, that what we perceive is entirely independent of what we may believe, or expect, or desire, or remember, and so forth. This is related to the sense-data theorist's claim that there is an early, conscious stage in perception—often called "sensation"—that is non-inferential and thus untouched by what may be going on elsewhere in our cognition. This is false. This is not to suggest that perception is always influenced by cognition; the truth lies somewhere between these two views. The purpose of this section is to fill in a few details about how perception can be influenced and to draw out the significance of this to epistemology.[9]

Perception plays a key role in supporting (or defeating) our beliefs and theories, and when we appeal to our perceptions in these contexts we typically assume that those perceptions would have been just the same if our beliefs (and other cognitive elements, such as expectations and desires) had been different; if differences of these sorts would result in different perceptions, the role perceptions can play in epistemically justifying beliefs will have to be re-examined. Given the enormous role perception has traditionally played in theories of knowledge and justification, the matter becomes very significant indeed.

It should be emphasized that the issue at hand extends beyond the influence of *beliefs* upon perception, although this is certainly included in it. There are two reasons for including cognitive elements other than beliefs in an investigation of this sort. First, it is far from clear which of these elements are and which are not beliefs; widening the focus in this way allows one to avoid having to settle the matter. Second, finding that other cognitive elements can influence perception would have much the same implications as finding that beliefs have such an influence. For instance, if our beliefs influence what we see, serious doubts are raised about the support perception can provide for our theories, because which theories we espouse has much to do with which beliefs we hold. Thus, espousing a different theory could lead to having different perceptions, and hence a different evidential position. Similarly, because the theories we espouse and the beliefs we hold have much to do with where we focus our attention and with what we expect in various situations, if cognitive elements such as these influence perception, the support of theories by perception is again called into question. That is, if differences in any of these cognitive elements could yield different perceptions, then we must re-examine how and whether perception can play the roles usually assigned to it.

Returning to the question at hand, either perception is influenced by cognition or it is not, but one must be careful in thinking of the matter in this way. This dichotomy tends to obscure the fact that *the dependence of perception upon cognition admits of degree.* These various degrees could arise in a variety of ways. For example, it might be that only some cognitive elements would influence one's perceptions but others would not. Or it could be that the influence of cognition would have an influence in some circumstances but not others. Or it could be that only some of one's perceptions would be influenced by cognition. Or it could be that cognitive elements could influence where, within a relatively narrow range, the characteristics of a perception would fall, but could not alter it beyond those limits. (For example, it might be that one's expectations could influence whether one sees the spot as red or orange, but that no cognitive state could make the spot appear blue.) And, of course, the influence of cognition upon perception might involve any combination of the above.

The failure to recognize this has led several theorists to present variations on the following claim:

> If cognition influences what one perceives, it is likely to do so in such a way that what one sees will be compatible with what one believes, expects, and so on; for example, it would be difficult to find empirical disconfirmation of one's beliefs and too easy to find (apparent) confirmation of them, even if these beliefs were false.

Some then extend this to include the following:[10]

> But we *can* empirically disconfirm our theories and beliefs; therefore, cognition does not influence what we perceive.

There are a number of serious difficulties with this line of thought, but for present purposes note that the first part would be true only if the influence of cognition upon perception were an all-out affair (although, of course, this alone would not suffice for its truth). However, cognition might have more limited influence, thus allowing for disconfirming observations even when those observations have been shaped in part by the observer's beliefs, expectations, and so forth.

A more significant consequence of this possibility of limited influence, though, is that even cognition-tainted perceptions could still be of value in settling some disputes about beliefs and theories; the extent of this usefulness would, of course, depend upon the nature and extent of the influence. For example, if cognition influenced only the apparent colors of objects, one could still use observation to settle disputes about the masses of objects. Or, if perception is influenced by cognition only in operating on the "assumption" that there are mind-independent physical objects, perception could still be used to adjudicate among theories that agree on this point but differ in their claims about the properties of those objects.

The psychological evidence shows that the operation of the human visual system certainly is influenced by beliefs, assumptions, and expectations. Psychologists sometimes talk of the influence of beliefs upon perception by saying that the processing involved is, to some extent, top-down; that is, instead of being purely driven by information present in the stimulus, various beliefs, expectations, and assumptions, also help determine the character of our visual experiences.[11] The top-down aspects of vision allow us, for example, to recognize objects under poor viewing conditions or when only a small part of them is visible.[12] Also, the assumption that vision involves a top-down element seems to provide the most promising accounts of such phenomena as visual agnosia; apparently, certain forms of agnosia arise when our knowledge about objects is prevented from influencing perceptual processing.[13]

One response to this talk of top-down processing in vision would be to say that although our beliefs about objects and so on influence how we *interpret* what we see, they do not influence the visual presentations themselves. (This is the line taken by sense-data theorists, who distinguish between sensation and perception.) Where and how top-down influences are felt is an empirical question, and several experiments show that there are cases in which our beliefs, expectations, and so on influence our visual presentation, and not merely their interpretation. (Later discussion will point out that an assumption central to responses of this sort is empirically false.) In turning to experimental data, it is important to bear in mind that when one looks at an object, one sees it not only as having a certain shape and color, but also as being at a certain distance. Notice that one does not see everything as "flat" and then make judgments about distance on the basis of various cues present in that picture; the depth, the distance of surfaces from the observer, is part of the visual presentation itself.

There is much to support the suggestion that the apparent depths present in visual experiences can be influenced by a number of things, including the subject's familiarity with that object. Consider, for example, how certain fragmented figures— such as that in Figure 1.1—appear to us. At first these appear as nothing more than a flat arrangement of marks, but

> . . . there is a definite perceptual change that goes along with recognition, when it occurs. Parts that seemed unrelated a moment ago are now grouped together; certain "ground" regions may become figural; and, most important, regions take on particular depth values as the entire array becomes three-dimensional.[15]

Our visual experience changes, not merely our interpretation of the array. As Rock points out, nothing in the stimulus itself could lead us to perceive it as three-dimensional; our visual experience changes because we group certain marks together as figure and others as ground, and because we have various beliefs about (in the case of Figure 1.1) dogs and trees. If we did not recognize dogs, if we lacked these beliefs and so forth, our visual experiences would not undergo this transformation.

Experimental data also suggest that if you have had many experiences with objects of a particular sort (where all objects of that sort are the same size or very nearly so), the information thus acquired will influence this aspect of how you subsequently see that object. In one experiment, playing cards of different sizes were presented to subjects in an environment devoid of other depth or distance cues.[16] When required to

FIGURE 1.1: Fragmented Figure[14]

estimate their size and distance, instead of saying that they had too little information to go on, subjects confidently gave estimates consistent with the card's being of the standard size and at a correspondingly appropriate distance. This suggests that the subjects' familiarity with playing cards is influencing their current perceptions.

Other aspects of what one sees can be influenced in these ways as well. For instance, in some cases the shapes one sees can be influenced by other objects one has seen recently, or even by what one is told before being presented with the target stimulus. One sequence of experiments dealt with subjective contours.[17] A subjective contour is the apparent boundary, usually characterized by an apparent difference in brightness, that is observed in certain arrays. Figure 1.2 is an example of this; it appears that a white triangle has been laid on top of other shapes, partially covering three circles and a black-outline triangle.

In one experiment subjects were presented with an array that might give rise to various subjective contours or to none at all: two collinear horizontal line segments and two collinear vertical line segments arranged so that they form a "plus" sign with the middle missing (Figure 1.3). Before seeing this, some subjects were told that the subjective contour of a circle could be seen in the middle of this array, others were told that the contour of a square could be seen, and still others that the contour of a figure (whose shape was not specified) could be seen. They were then asked to draw any contour they saw.

The results are presented in Table 1.1. Thus, the apparent shape of the illusory figure is significantly influenced by the instructions the subject has received; again, cognitive factors play a significant role in determining the character of one's visual experience. The subjects' "set" may be best characterized in terms other than "belief"—perhaps "expectation" would be more appropriate—but the central point remains: We

FIGURE 1.2: Subjective Contour of a Triangle

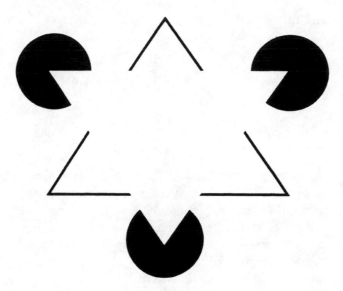

have here another type of case in which the character of one's visual experience is influenced by the subjects' propositional attitudes and so forth.

In the preceding cases the non-visual information that influences visual experiences has been provided by the experimenters in one way or another, but there are other assumptions we all seem to bring with us which can bear upon how we see things. How we interpret ambiguous drawings of three-dimensional objects seems to be influenced by, among other things, how light and shadow are represented. In one set of experiments, the interpretations given to a series of such diagrams were found to be heavily influenced by

FIGURE 1.3: Ambiguous Subjective Contour Stimulus

TABLE 1.1: Subjective Contour Results

	CIRCLE	SQUARE	AMORPHOUS	NO FIGURE
NEUTRAL SET	39%	4%	8%	49%
CIRCLE SET	67%	0%	0%	33%
SQUARE SET	10%	38%	0%	52%

shading.[18] Experienced viewers can "see" certain staircase patterns in two ways, but naive viewers find this virtually impossible. One way of seeing them is as a collection of thin slabs stacked so that those near the center are nearest the observer; the alternative way has the middle slabs farthest from one. (Remember that these differences in depth are differences in the visual presentation itself, and not merely in its interpretation; it is *not* the case that one sees these arrays as "flat" and merely judges surfaces to be at various distances.)

What seems to be at work here are the "assumptions" that only a single light source is present, and that it is shining from overhead. Seeing the figures in different ways requires putting these assumptions aside and supposing instead that there are two light sources; this is rather difficult for us to do. Certain sorts of training can lead viewers to change their expectations about light sources and so arrive at new ways of seeing arrays; naive viewers employ the usual assumptions and so can see arrays only in certain ways. Again, the nature of these assumptions or expectations is hardly clear, and it is likely that they do not fit nicely into the category of beliefs (whatever that turns out to be). But the point I want to make is that we have before us another case in which what one sees depends in part upon cognitive factors of some sort.

The ways in which our beliefs, expectations, and so on influence our perceptions extends also to how objects seem to be moving. Under some circumstances, it can be difficult to tell whether an object is rotating or oscillating, and, if it is rotating, to tell in which direction. In such circumstances, one's familiarity with objects of the relevant sort may influence what one sees. This is what happens when a mask of a human face is rotated about its vertical axis of symmetry (but not when other, unfamiliar objects are rotated thus). Instead of seeing the mask rotate, observers report seeing the mask oscillate (apparently changing direction twice in each rotational cycle); this is called the *rotating-mask illusion*.[19] What is significant about this is that the visual stimulus *does* include information indicating that the mask is rotating rather than oscillating. The pattern of light and shadow, and the various depth cues (such as stereopsis, eye convergence, and lens accommodation) are consistent with rotation, but not with oscillation. However, the visual system ignores this information; this is the case even when the observer knows the actual motion of the mask. Not even the intention to see the mask as rotating can overcome this illusion. An observer may briefly see the mask as rotating before interpreting it as oscillating, but once it is seen as oscillating it can be seen in no other way.

> The susceptibility of perception to cognitive influences undermines its capacity to perform the evidential role epistemologists usually assign it. Foundationalists want to use perceptual experiences as the primary source of basic beliefs in which to ground our inferential beliefs, and BonJour uses perceptual input as a way of anchoring coherent systems of belief to the world. Leaving aside the usual problems facing these theories, explain what effect the results reported above will have on these theories.

Researchers suggest that the reason for this is:

> ... because people are more familiar with convex faces than with concave ones, people interpret the concave projection of the mask as being convex. Presumably, differential familiarity continues to operate when the mask is rotating, overpowering information specifying the mask's true direction of motion as well as the viewer's knowledge that the mask is actually rotating. (p. 523)

The interest of this illusion for our present purposes is heightened by the fact that, unlike some of the cases discussed earlier, this illusion does not require special experimental conditions; the experimenters report that this illusion arises in full force even during informal presentations from the front of a classroom.

Notice also that the role played by cognitive factors is limited; one's familiarity with faces has an influence on what one sees, but one's knowledge that the mask is rotating rather than oscillating does not. This illustrates that although cognition can play a role in determining one's visual experiences, not all visual characteristics can be so influenced, nor is this influence evident in all situations. The dependence of perception upon cognition is a matter of degree (as suggested above), although just how the details work out remains to be seen.

Taken together, these empirical data present us with a picture of a visual system influenced in a number of different ways—and sometimes to significant degrees—by the subject's beliefs, expectations, and other cognitive factors. As mentioned earlier, the greater this influence, the more difficult it will be for perception to play anything like its traditional role in testing theories, justifying beliefs, and so on. Now, think back to a matter mentioned earlier: The attempt to avoid this outcome by distinguishing between our perceptual experiences and our interpretations of them, and claiming that only the latter are influenced by cognition. This might also be put in terms of a distinction between perception and sensation; the idea is that sensation is the raw, uninterpreted output of our sensory organs, while perception is the result of interpreting these data. On this approach, perception might be tainted, but sensation would still provide us with an unsullied source of information that might (somehow) be used in justifying beliefs, settling disputes, and the like. This idea (sometimes with different labels) can be found in a good deal of the philosophical work that has been done on vision; it is perhaps most clearly present in the old sense-data theories.

Although we no longer hold that there are such things as sense or sense-data, the understanding of perception then popular shares an important element with current thought: Many philosophers still seem to think that we introspect uninterpreted visual presentations and then, on the basis of this inspection, form judgments about what is before us. If this is right, one could then go on to say that although our interpretations may be influenced by our beliefs, we may still appeal to uninterpreted sensory presentations in confirming theories, justifying beliefs, and so on.

The experimental results presented above show that cognition influences not only our judgments or interpretations of what we perceive, but also the character of the sensations themselves. The central difficulty with this old way of thinking is an empirical one: Sensory consciousness arises only *after* perceptual information has been interpreted (and hence possibly tainted by one's beliefs, expectations, and so forth).[20] The story about introspective inspection of sensory input and its subsequent interpretation is simply false. The nature and extent of this influence is an empirical matter, requiring a good deal more investigation. Obviously, this prevents the role of perception in justifying beliefs, testing theories, and the like from being simple and straightforward, but it need not preclude perceptions from having such a function. As noted above, if some aspects of perceptual experience are unaffected by propositional attitudes and so on (or if we can isolate situations in which these cognitive influences are absent), there will be room for the usual treatment of evidence. Also, as we discover more about these influences, we may be able to use perceptions in such a way that the effects of cognition are taken into account and thus neutralized.

For Further Reading

David Armstrong, *Perception and the Physical World*. London: Routledge and Kegan Paul, 1961.

Winston Barnes, "The Myth of Sense Data," in *Perceiving, Sensing, and Knowing*, Robert Swartz, ed. Garden City, NJ: Anchor, 1965.

Jonathan Bennett, *Locke, Berkeley, Hume: Central Themes*. Oxford: Oxford University Press, 1971.

Roderick Chisholm, "The Problem of Empiricism." *Journal of Philosophy* 45 (1948).

Roderick Chisholm, *Perceiving*. Ithaca, NY: Cornell University Press, 1957.

James Cornman, *Perception, Commonsense, and Science*. New Haven: Yale University Press, 1975.

C. J. Ducasse, *Nature, Mind, and Death*. La Salle, IL: Open Court, 1951.

R. J. Hirst, Chapters 1 and 2 of *The Problems of Perception*. London: Allen and Unwin, 1959.

Frank Jackson, *Perception: A Representative Theory*. Cambridge: Cambridge University Press, 1977.

C. I. Lewis, *An Analysis of Knowledge and Valuation*. La Salle, IL: Open Court, 1946.

J. L. Mackie, "What's Really Wrong with Phenomenalism." *Proceedings of the British Academy* 55 (1969).

G. E. Moore, "Sense-Data," in his *Some Main Problems of Philosophy*. London: Allen and Unwin, 1953.

G. A. Paul, "Is There a Problem about Sense Data?" in *Perceiving, Sensing, and Knowing*, R. Swartz, ed. Garden City, NJ: Anchor, 1965.

George Pitcher, *A Theory of Perception*. Princeton, NJ: Princeton University Press, 1971.

H. H. Price, *Perception*. New York: McBride, 1933.

W. T. Stace, "Science and the Physical World," in his *Man Against Darkness and Other Essays*. Pittsburgh: University of Pittsburgh Press, 1967.

Notes

1. I want to thank Michael Pendlebury and Mark O. Webb for helping me to see this clearly.

2. "The Theory of Sensa," in *Perceiving, Sensing, and Knowing*, R. Swartz, ed. (Berkeley: University of California Press); pp. 85-129.

3. David M. Armstrong, *A Materialist Theory of Mind* (London: Routledge and Kegan Paul, 1968); pp. 219-220.

4. For prominent examples of the adverbial theory, see C. J. Ducasse *Nature, Mind, and Death*; Carus Lectures, eighth series (LaSalle, IL: Open Court, 1951); and Wilfred Sellars "Seeing, Seeming, and Sensing" in *The Ontological Truth, M. Gram and E. Klemke, eds. (University of Iowa Press. 1974)*.

5. This is developed by Sellars in his "Seeing, Seeming, and Sensing."

6. See Frank Jackson "On the Adverbial Analysis of Visual Experience," *Metaphilosophy*, Vol. 6, No. 2 (April 1975); pp. 127-135; see also Jackson's *Perception: A Representative Theory* (London: Cambridge University Press, 1977); pp. 63 ff.

7. For more details you might look at Michael Tye "The Adverbial Theory: A Defence of Sellars Against Jackson," *Metaphilosophy*, Vol. 6, No. 2 (April 1975); pp. 136-143.

8. Again, Tye claims to have found a way of avoiding this difficulty; see his "The Adverbial Theory: A Defence of Sellars Against Jackson."

9. Material in this section is drawn from my "The Influence of Beliefs upon Perception: The Empirical Story," *Australasian Journal of Philosophy*, Vol. 71, No. 1 (March 1993); pp. 13-23.

10. Something like this is presented in Fodor's *The Modularity of Mind* (Cambridge, MA: Bradford Books, 1983); pp. 37-38.

11. See, for example, Ray Jackendoff's *Consciousness and the Computational Mind* (Cambridge, MA: Bradford Books, 1987); pp. 186-188.

12. See, for example, Irwin Rock, *The Logic of Perception* (Cambridge, MA: Bradford Books, 1983); pp. 307-309.

13. This is pointed out by Martha Farah in *Visual Agnosia: The Disorders of Object Recognition and What They Tell Us about Normal Vision* (Cambridge, MA: Bradford Books, 1990); pp. 149-155.

14. This diagram, designed by R. C. James, is presented in David Marr's *Vision* (New York: W. H. Freeman, 1982); p. 101.

15. Irwin Rock, *The Logic of Perception,* p. 309.

16. V. Fitzpatrick et al., "The Effect of Familiar Size at Familiar Distances." *Perception*, Vol. 11 (1982); pp. 85-91.

17. S. Coren et al., "The Effects of Perceptual Set on the Shape and Apparent Depth of Subjective Contours," *Perception and Psychophysics*, Vol. 39 (1986); pp. 327-333.

18. T. Papathomas and A. Gorea, "Ambiguity in 3-D Patterns Induced by Lighting Assumptions," *Perception*, Vol. 19 (1990); pp. 569-571.

19. D. Klopfer, "Apparent Reversals of a Rotating Mask: A New Demonstration of Cognition in Perception," *Perception and Psychophysics,* Vol. 49 (1991); pp. 522-530.

20. See Jackendoff's *Consciousness and the Computational Mind,* pp. 45-46, 320.

THE NATURE OF REALITY AND PERCEPTION—CLASSICAL ANSWERS ON "WHAT IS REALITY?"

METAPHYSICS: FORM AND SUBSTANCE

by James W. Ward

Introduction

The philosophical pursuit of the nature of reality is known as metaphysics. The philosophical study of the nature of knowledge is known as epistemology. In this essay, I will consider the metaphysics and epistemology of Plato and Aristotle, two of the most influential philosophers in the history of philosophy. The metaphysics and epistemology of Plato and Aristotle has significantly influenced subsequent understanding of many issues in philosophy. I will focus on the following: 1. philosophical method, 2. the nature of universals, 3. the mind/body problem, and 4. the nature of knowledge.

Socrates, Plato, and Aristotle

During the fourth and fifth century B.C.E., Greek civilization established philosophical schools that left indelible marks on Western civilization. The Greek philosopher Socrates (470-399 B.C.E.) is so important that we refer to the philosophers that preceded him, and some that were his contemporaries, as the Presocratics; yet Socrates left us no written record of his own of his thoughts. Most of what we know of the thought of Socrates was recorded by one of his students, Plato.

Plato (427- 348/7 B.C.E) was born into an aristocratic family in Athens. It is likely that his family intended for him to assume a position of social and political prominence. When he was about the age of twenty he began to study with Socrates. As describe by Plato in *The Apology*, in 399 B.C.E., Socrates was tried for impiety and corruption of the youth of Athens and sentenced to death. In the *Phaedo*, Plato wrote of Socrates "of all men of his time whom I have know, he was the wisest and justest and best."[1] Rather than pursue political life, which at this point of his life would have been difficult because of his connection to Socrates and the political fortunes of his own family, after the death of Socrates, Plato would establish his own school, the Academy. Plato's influence on the western philosophy that followed him is so significant that the 20th century Anglo-American philosopher Alfred North Whitehead remarked that "the safest general characteristic of the European philosophical tradition is that it consists of a series of footnotes to Plato."[2]

The most famous student of Plato's Academy was Aristotle (384-322 B.C.E.) Aristotle was the son of the physician to the Macedonian King Amyntas II. Amyntas was the grandfather of Alexander the Great. At the age of 17, Aristotle went to Athens to study in Plato's academy. Aristotle and would remain there until Plato's death. Of Plato, Aristotle wrote that Plato was a man "whom bad men have not even the right to praise, and who showed in his life and teachings how to be happy and good at the same time."[3] Plato described Aristotle as the *nous*, or the intelligence of the Academy personified.

Around 343 B.C.E., Aristotle became the tutor of Alexander, who was then about thirteen years old. Alexander, who would become known as Alexander the Great, became king around 336 B.C.E. Aristotle returned to Athens and founded his own school, the Lyceum. After the death of Alexander in 323 B.C.E., Aristotle fled Athens; reportedly, the reason for this for Aristotle was "lest the Athenians sin twice against philosophy."[4] The influence of Aristotle is such that the Dominican Thomas Aquinas, writing in the mid thirteenth century, referred to him as "the philosopher."

Metaphysics and Epistemology

Though the precise origin of the term metaphysics is unclear, it appears to have been created after the death of the Aristotle (384-322 B.C.E.). One explanation of the origin of the term is that is based on one of the earliest organizations Aristotle's works. Commentators referred to a collection of writings placed after Aristotle's *Physics*, as *meta ta physika* meaning after or beyond the physics. Early commentators on Aristotle interpreted *meta ta physika* as an indication that the metaphysics was a kind of knowledge beyond or higher than the knowledge of physics.[5]

Generally speaking, in the collection of writings now known as the *Metaphysics*, Aristotle considers the question of the nature of being and of wisdom, or knowledge of first principles and causes. The interpretation of this as a higher order kind of knowledge is supported by remarks by Aristotle in this collection. For example, Aristotle described his search in these writings as a search for a "first philosophy."[6]

Aristotle was certainly not the first of the ancient Greek philosophers to ask questions about the nature of being. In fact, as stated above, many describe Aristotle's position as a rejection of the metaphysical position of his teacher Plato. Plato's position in turn can itself be understood as an attempt to synthesize earlier influential Presocratic positions, particularly those of Parmenides, Heraclitus, and Pythagoras.

The major questions considered by these thinkers included questions such as the following: Can we account for all being by positing one kind of being, or is it necessary to recognize many different kinds of being? How can we account for the fact that the world seems to be constantly changing, yet also shows a remarkable unity and stability? Questions such as these are sometimes referred to as the question of the one and the many. Another important question considered by these thinkers was epistemological, or concerned with the theory of knowledge. At the heart of epistemological questions are the following: What is knowledge? Is it possible for us to attain knowledge? If so, how? For example, can we trust our senses to provide us with a reliable understanding of the world, or is the true nature of reality "hidden", so to speak, from our senses and available only to our intelligence or reason, if it is available to us at all?

There will then be two guiding questions to our discussion. What is the nature of being? What is the nature of our knowledge of being? For Plato and Aristotle, metaphysical questions about the nature of being and reality were interrelated with epistemological questions about the nature of knowledge.

Why is it important to have some understanding of Greek metaphysical positions that are more than 2000 years old and, one would think, by now hopeless outdated? A quick response to this question is that the thought of these ancient Greeks established a framework for disciplines as diverse as science, theology, and ethics that was arguably *the* framework for these disciplines for approximately two thousand years. Though the original answers to these questions may no longer be accepted, in many ways this framework is still in place today.

Consider, for example, the current quest of physicists to discover what has been referred to as a theory of everything. This modern scientific search is an attempt to find one theoretical framework from which we can account for all known matter and energy. This could be understood as the modern quest to resolve the question of the one and the many. Assumed in such a pursuit is that what appears as diversity may well be the manifestation of a unity not apparent to us, a unity which we can explain but not directly perceive.

I will now attempt to directly answer the questions posed above. For the first question, that of method, I will consider Plato and Aristotle together. For the other three questions, I will consider Plato and Aristotle separately.

1. Philosophical Method: The Dialectic

What did Plato learn from Socrates that he taught Aristotle? One answer to this question is that Plato acquired a certain kind of understanding of philosophical method, or how to do philosophy. In Plato's dialogues, we find examples of what is now referred to as the Socratic method, in which Socrates, through a series of questions attempts to demonstrate that someone either knows something he thought he did not, or does not know something he thought he did. In Plato's dialogues, a common strategy of Socrates is to urge those in the discussion to create general or universal definitions of the topic being discussed. According to Aristotle, "two things may be fairly ascribed to Socrates, inductive arguments and universal definition..."[7] Socrates referred to the strategy of refuting belief by demonstrating that it led to contradictory or absurd conclusion as *elenchus*. This method of dialogue, logical analysis, and clarification would be described by Plato and Aristotle as the dialectic. From Socrates Plato also acquired a certain understanding of the goal of philosophy as "*psychagogia*, that is, training of the soul for life" which Aristotle also adopted.[8]

2. Plato: The Nature of Universals

2.1. *Rationalism and Realism: Plato's Theory of Knowledge and of the Forms*

How did Plato synthesize these various strands of Greek thought? I ask you to consider for a moment what you mean when you say that something is real. I suspect that one of the understandings you have is that something is real if it endures, if it does not change. Plato used such a definition to distinguish levels of being and truth. Something that remains the same is more real than something that changes. Knowledge that does not change is truer than knowledge that changes.

I would also like you to consider what it is to have an idea of something, such as an idea of this book. It would seem that you have something like the book in your mind, but you do not have the material book in your mind, you have an idea that shares something of the characteristics of the book without being the material book itself. Do all of your ideas have counterparts in the world we encounter with our senses, or do you have some ideas that you cannot see or touch? How do you account for such ideas? Do these ideas correspond to some reality or are they only in your mind?

Using criteria such as the perfection of the unchanging and the distinction between ideas based in sensory experience and those that are not, Plato divided the world into the visible world, the world of change, which is accessible to our senses, and the intelligible world, the world of the forms, which is eternal, unchanging, and accessible only by reason. Metaphysically, this allowed Plato to accommodate the flux described by Heraclitus, the notion of being as eternal and unchanging held by Parmenides, and the notion found in the thought of Pythagoras and Heraclitus that there is an order to the world which is accessible to reason. Epistemologically, this allowed Plato to make a clear distinction between opinion and knowledge. True knowledge is only available to reason. The notion that reason, rather than sensory experience, is the basis of knowledge is known as *rationalism*.

In the *Republic*, Plato described a hierarchy of knowledge and of the objects of knowledge. I will attempt to construct this chart beginning with his description of the visible world.

Visible World Opinions Perceptions	Knowledge Belief
Shadows, reflections	Animals, everything That grows or is made

With the distinctions above, Plato has made a metaphysical and an epistemological distinction. Try to consider a concrete example. Imagine a reflection of a tree in the water. Which is the real tree, the reflection or the tree? Plato argues that the tree is more real than the reflection and that knowledge of the tree is a higher kind of knowledge than awareness of the reflection of the tree. This, I trust, is understandable enough so far.

It may even allow us to make another kind of distinction. Let us call an awareness of the reflection of the tree a perception. This perception is made available to us by our senses. At this level of knowledge, knowledge is opinion. Our perceptions may vary. The reflection of the tree may even be murky enough that we cannot distinguish it as a reflection of a tree.

If we have some knowledge of the tree itself, it is not clear that such knowledge could be perceptual only. Our knowledge of a tree would seem to combine many different perceptions. For the moment then, let us make a distinction between perceptions and beliefs. Thus far I suspect that Plato's position is not that controversial. As we move to the next part of Plato's argument, however, I suspect that more of you will become uncomfortable with Plato's position.

Plato proceeds to outline a similar division for the intellectual world. If we attempt to generally chart this outline, I think it would look something like this.

Intelligible World Opinion	Knowledge
Beliefs about things in the world	Beliefs about our beliefs

The "images" in the intelligible world are our beliefs about the world of our experience. Imagine, for example, that you have now seen two trees. Do the trees look like they are the same kind of tree? How would you attempt to organize the trees that you see? Imagine that you begin to create a taxonomy based on type of bark, type of leaf, etc. Here you have the beginnings of some level of organization, but this organization is still fairly concrete. It should be easy enough to imagine some difference in opinion as to how to distinguish the different kinds of trees. Would it be possible to move from reliance on your "images" of the tree, and to reflect on the idea of the tree itself? This is yet another level of abstraction. You have begun the process of moving from an understanding of the fluctuating nature of experience to some understanding of an order, (or a logos), a unity beyond the apparent diversity of experience.

Let me try to describe this level of abstraction in another way. As we move along Plato's hierarchy of knowledge, what had been assumed as knowledge on one level, perception for example, becomes a basis for knowledge at the next level of abstraction. Plato seems to be saying that it is possible to move from particular perceptions, to beliefs, to understanding, or beliefs about beliefs, to an understanding of the universal itself, or the form. With each level of abstraction we move to more certain knowledge. It is not just our knowledge that is more certain; the object of our knowledge also becomes more certain, more real. Plato, starting with ideas that have some intuitive appeal, has arrived at a conclusion that many of us may find unsettling. The idea, or form of the tree, is more real than the tree we can see and touch. Plato appears to be arguing that the form, or the universal, exists independently both of the particular and of the observer. Such a position is referred to as *realism.*

Unsure that he has made his point clear, Plato makes use of another kind of distinction, a kind of Pythagorean one. In Plato's account, when you draw a triangle on a board, for example, you will not have drawn a perfect triangle. Nonetheless, through the power of reason, you might be able to comprehend the idea, or form, of a perfect triangle. Using the language of geometry you could then explore hypotheses about triangles mathematically. Plato argues that the ideal triangle cannot be realized in the physical world, nor can it be perceived by our senses. The ideal triangle can only be seen by the "eye of the mind."[9] Yet Plato, in contrast to Pythagorean thought, does not describe knowledge of mathematics as the highest form of knowledge.

The highest form of knowledge is completely in the realm of the ideas, or the forms. Even here, Plato admits of distinctions of understanding. The greatest knowledge we can achieve, it would appear, is that of the "first principle of the whole."

Plato concludes this passage of the *Republic* with a description of the four levels of knowledge. Remember, these distinctions are not only epistemological, they are also metaphysical. If we chart this, it would look something like this.

Knowledge	Object of Knowledge (being)
Reason (beliefs about understanding)	The forms, form of the good
Understanding (beliefs about beliefs)	Science, mathematics, logic
Convictions (beliefs about perceptions)	Recognizable perceptions, things in the world
Perceptions (sensory awareness)	Shadows, unrecognizable perceptions

It would appear that Plato recognized that many did not perceive such an order to the world. Plato argued that it took a great deal of effort to comprehend the form of the good. Plato describes this difficulty in a passage from Book VII of Plato's *Republic* commonly referred to as the Allegory of the Cave.

As this is an allegory, it can be interpreted in many ways. Plato offers his own interpretation. Those trapped in the cave are those trapped in their belief that the visible world is the world of truth. We could also read this as a defense of his teacher Socrates. The true philosopher, one freed from the cave, perceives the intelligible world. Notice Plato's contrast between the darkness of the cave and the brightness of the intelligible world. Plato would use this to explain the initial confusion that confronts those who attempt to understand the intelligible world. Our eyes, having adjusted to the darkness of the cave, are blinded by the brightness outside the cave. The prisoner who returned to share this truth with the prisoners in the cave could easily be understood to be Socrates, who was met with ridicule, scorn, and sentenced to death.

2.2. The Mind/Body Problem: Plato on the Immortality of the Soul

> The soul, then, as being immortal, and having been born again many times, and having seen all things that exist, whether in this world or in the world below, has knowledge of them all; and it is no wonder that she should be able to call to remembrance all that she ever knew about virtue, and about everything; for as all nature is akin, and the soul has learned all things; there is no difficulty in her eliciting or as men say learning, out of a single recollection—all the rest, if a man is strenuous and does not faint; for all enquiry and all learning is but recollection.[10]

In the quotation cited above, we see that Plato too held to a doctrine similar to the Pythagorean one, that the soul is immortal and is reincarnated. Plato argues that it is the immortality of the soul that allows us to have knowledge of the forms. Remember that for Plato the highest form of being and knowledge is eternal and unchanging. The highest part of human nature, the soul is also eternal and unchanging. As such our soul participates in the world of the forms and because of this "has knowledge of all things." Thus Plato argued that "all enquiry and learning is but recollection." Plato would appear to be arguing that true knowledge is *a priori*, or prior to experience.

Plato's position also has clear implications for an understanding of the mind/body problem, though not necessarily a clear account of the relationship between mind and body. In the *Laws*, Plato describes the soul as the source of self-initiated motion. Plato clearly distinguishes our soul, also the seat of reason, from the body, and as described above, argued that this soul was immortal. Plato himself is inconsistent in his description of what this means. In places he seems to argue that only our reason is immortal, in others that our entire soul is immortal. This leads us to problem for Plato's understanding of the soul. Plato clearly assumes that each can affect the other, but he offers no explanation of how this could be. How does the body bring about changes in the soul? How does the soul bring about changes in the body? What Plato does not really offer is an account of how the body and soul could be related and interact.

Some Concluding Remarks
A Teleological Worldview

The Greek word for purpose or end is *telos*. Plato argued that the world is not governed by chance. The world is not chaos; it is a cosmos, a world ordered by the Good. The world then does not just have a scientific order; it has a kind of moral order. In a way reminiscent of Pythagorean thought, Plato emphasizes moderation and that the good and just life, both for the individual and for the city-state, is a rational and ordered life. In Book V of the *Republic* Plato states:

> Until philosophers are kings, and princes of this world have the spirit and power of philosophy, and political greatness and wisdom meet in one, and those commoner natures who pursue either to the exclusion of the other are compelled to stand aside, cities will never have rest from their evils, - no, nor the human race, as I believe, - and then only will this our State have a possibility of life and behold the light of day.

I will now turn to a discussion of Aristotle's position on the nature of universals, the mind/body problem, and the nature of knowledge.

3. Aristotle on Universals:

3.1. *Aristotle's Theory of Substance*

A discussion of Aristotle's metaphysics, inevitably involves his discussion of Plato's metaphysics. In what follows, I will use Form to refer to Plato's understanding of the Forms has having some separate reality and form will refer to Aristotle's understanding. Aristotle is typically portrayed as rejecting Plato's theory of the Forms. I will quickly consider two of his criticisms. One is that "Plato is like a man, who, unable to count with a small number, thinks that he will find it easier to do so if he doubles the number."[11] Plato attempts to account for the order we find in the visible world by postulating the existence of the Forms. We can recognize various things in the world as trees because they reflect the Form of a tree. Aristotle's criticizes this by saying that Plato is like someone "unable to count with a small number", i.e. unable to explain or understand a tree without postulating the existence of some other kind of entity, "thinks he will find it easier to do so if he doubles the number." In other words, Plato attempts to account for the existence of the tree by postulating the existence of the Form of a tree, essentially doubling the entities to be explained.

Another criticism Aristotle makes of Plato's theory of the Forms is that it does not offer an account of change. The intelligible world of the Forms is eternal and unchanging. The visible world is supposed to a reflection of the intelligible world. However, the visible world is full of change. In the visible world, things come into being and pass away. Plato's theory of the Forms does not seem to offer us an account of how this is possible.

In the development of his own metaphysical position, Aristotle attempts to find better answers to two major questions. The first is the question of the nature of being. The second is the question of the nature of change. For Aristotle too, metaphysical and epistemological questions are interrelated. A consideration then of Aristotle's metaphysics must inevitably involve some question of Aristotle's epistemology.

3.2. *Aristotle's Metaphysics*

> "And indeed the question which, both now and of old, has always been raised, and always has been the subject of doubt, viz. what being is, is just the question, what is substance?"[12]

Aristotle is often portrayed as emphasizing, against Plato's dualism, the realness the world of our experience, and there is support for such a view. According to Aristotle, for example, "substance is thought to belong most obviously to bodies."[13] Nonetheless, Aristotle considers if there are other possible substances. Here Aristotle would appear to be directly addressing the question of the Forms. According to Aristotle, "Plato posited two kinds of substance – the Forms and the objects of mathematics – as well as a third kind, viz. the substance of sensible bodies."[14]

What then are the status of other "substances" such as Platonic Forms? Aristotle asked the question of what exists primarily. One of the possibilities Aristotle considers as a possibility for primary substance, or the most basic substance, is that of the substratum. By substratum, Aristotle means matter in its most basic sense, unformed matter. This is sometimes referred to as prime matter. It is tempting to describe this material substratum as substance. Aristotle, however, does not. He offers the following argument to support this position: "But this is impossible; for both separability and individuality are thought to belong chiefly to substance. And so form and the compound of form and matter would be thought to be substance, rather than matter."[15]

Aristotle makes an interesting distinction here. Substance is not merely matter. Substance, that which is exists, is matter with a form. Form without matter is potential not actual; matter without form is also potential and not actual. I realize that I have yet to define what Aristotle means by form. In order to do so, it is necessary to introduce another important term for Aristotle, that of essence.

3.3. Aristotle on Essence

"For the essence is what something is…"[16] Essence and substance seem to be related; Aristotle uses both to refer to that which is real, that which exists. However, Aristotle qualifies that "nothing, then, which is not a species of a genus will have an *essence* – only species will have it…"[17] This seems to be another way of saying that in order for us to consider something as a substance, it must have some form. We can see the legacy of Platonic thinking here. Aristotle has asserted that bodies exist, that we are quite right to refer to trees and the like as substances. A tree, however, is just matter; it is matter in the form of a tree.

How then does Aristotle define form? He offers us the following definition: "By form I mean the essence of each thing and its primary substance."[18] On the Aristotelian account, it appears that form is still necessary; the form allows the individual to be an individual and it enables us to acquire knowledge. Again we can see the legacy of Plato here. Knowledge is knowledge of a form. If matter does not have a form, we cannot know it. However, unlike the account of Plato's described above, particulars are not distractions. We encounter forms in our experience of particulars.

This presents us with something of a paradox, namely that, as Aristotle states: "The form has a better claim than the matter to be called nature. For we call a thing something, when it is that thing in actuality, rather than in possibility."[19] Aristotle would appear to be reasserting Plato's position that the Form is more real than the particular. Is Aristotle being inconsistent here? Actually, I think that Aristotle is struggling with a question which is, at first glance, a deceptively simple one and which, upon reflection, is actually a profoundly difficult one, the question of identity. Matter has the potential to be something, but it does not become something until it assumes a form. We could say then that matter individuates form. Let me try to say this in another way. When the form of a tree becomes substantial, when it moves from being potential to being actual, it does so as a particular tree. We do not encounter some generic tree; we encounter a particular tree, with a particular color bark and leaves and all the other characteristics that make this particular tree what it is. Once matter assumes a form, it is not obvious that a change to the matter of the individual necessarily means that the essence of the individual has changed. If a tree loses it leaves, does it cease to be a tree? As long as the essential properties of the individual do not change, it can change in many ways and yet retain its identity, its essence, as a tree. Should the tree die, or lose its form, then the tree will no longer behave as a living tree. It an important sense it is no longer a tree. Once the tree is dead, it becomes wood and begins to act like wood.

Aristotle thus distinguishes *essential* and *accidental* properties and *potential* and *actual* states of being. An acorn, for example, has the potential to be a tree, but in order for this to happen certain conditions have to be met. According to Aristotle, to account for change, we have to posit the following: matter, form, and privation. The acorn, for example, is presently in the form of an acorn, but has the potential to be in the form of a tree. It is deprived of the form of the tree. If it assumes the form of the tree, then it will act to realize this form and grow and mature.

3.4. Aristotle on Primary and Secondary Substance

What is the status of the forms? Do they exist independently somehow of the particular things which reflect them? In Plato's account, at least as depicted above, and as Aristotle appears to have understood it here, a tree, for example, is recognizable as a tree because it participates in the Form of the tree. The individually existing tree is not, however, identical with the Form of the tree. The Form exists separately.

Aristotle argues that such a separation is problematic for several reasons. For Aristotle, to know something is to recognize its essence. On Aristotle's account, our intelligence has the potential to assume multiple forms. We can be said to have a true understanding of something if the form in our mind corresponds to the form of the object. If the essence of an object is separate from the particular object, then knowledge is impossible. Aristotle also argues that this separation also leads to an absurd infinite regress. If a tree is a tree because it participates in the form of the tree, and the reality of the form of the tree is also only participatory or reflective, then we are led to postulate the existence of yet another form, and on and on. Thus Aristotle asserts "clearly, then, each primary and self-subsistent thing is one and the same as its essence."[20]

Aristotle recognizes that we consider the particular individual Socrates, for example, to be a member of a species, human being, and human beings as representative of a genus of animals. Aristotle refers to the particular, Socrates, as *primary substance*, and to all of the abstractions from the particular, such as species and genus, as *secondary substances*. For Aristotle, unlike Plato, the more removed the category is from the particular primary substance, the less real it is.[21]

If you have been paying attention, you will have noticed that in speaking of substances, I have tended to use examples of beings that we would consider alive. This is not accidental. Aristotle makes yet another important distinction about the nature of being. "Some things are due to nature; for others there are other causes."[22] As examples of the former, Aristotle mentions "animals and their parts, plants, and simple bodies like earth, fire, air, and water."[23] As examples of the latter, Aristotle offers things like bed and coat. Artifacts such as beds and coats are dependent on human activity for their creation. According to Aristotle, beds and coats are not properly described as primary substances. It is not in the nature of wood to make itself into a bed, or in the nature of animal hide to become leather for coat.

3.5. Aristotle's Theory of Knowledge

Though Aristotle appeared to reject Plato's metaphysics, he appears to hold something like a Platonic account of knowledge. Aristotle distinguishes between the limited concrete nature of sensory experience and universal nature of reason. Aristotle considers an example from medicine. It is true that a doctor cures a particular man, not some generic man. However, it also the case that the knowledge of having taken a medication for a particular illness does not yet provide us with the knowledge to prescribe the medication properly.

However, Aristotle does not appear to have held to Plato's *a priori* account of knowledge. Aristotle describes the mind as kind of *tabula rasa*, a kind of blank slate. The mind, according to Aristotle, is unformed. When we perceive objects with our senses, our minds assume the form of the object without having to assume the material of the object. Aristotle compares sensory perception to the ability of wax to take the form of a seal without having to become gold. To a certain extent, it makes sense then to say that Aristotle is an empiricist, or one who holds that experience is the basis of knowledge. For Aristotle, as for Plato, knowledge is a movement from particular to universal. However, for Aristotle this movement begins in sensory perception. All higher thought is then based on abstraction from sensory experience.

In as much as Aristotle allows that forms can exist without matter in the mind, Aristotle's position on the status of universals could also be described as that of a *conceptualist*. Aristotle's position could be described as middle ground position between Platonic realism and *nominalism*, which denies the existence of universals altogether asserting that only particulars are real and knowable. The debate over the nature of universals would be one of the most significant philosophical issues of medieval philosophy.

Aristotle argues that though the senses "give us the most authoritative knowledge of particulars...they do not tell us the 'why' of anything – e.g. why fire is hot; they only say that it is hot."[24] Full knowledge then requires not just knowledge of the particular, the what, so to speak, it is also requires knowledge of the why. According to Aristotle, knowledge and understanding require more than knowledge of a particular, it also requires knowledge of cause. It is not enough to know what something is, it is also necessary to know why something is the way it is.

3.6. Aristotle and the Mind/Body Problem

For Aristotle, substance is a combination of matter and form. This means that human beings should be understood as a combination of body and soul. Rather than being a kind of prison for the soul, as Plato seems to have understood it, for Aristotle the body allows the soul to fulfill its functions.

The difficulty Aristotle's thought poses is that of understanding his distinction between passive and active reason. One way to understand this distinction is to see it as a distinction between our ability our passive reception of sensory information and our active manipulation of this information. However, in a passage the interpretation of which is much contested Aristotle describes the active intellect as actual and the passive intellect as potential, the active intellect as unchanging, and the passive intellect as changing, and the active intellect as immortal and the passive intellect as mortal. We forget, Aristotle argues, because the passive intellect is mortal and without the active intellect we cannot think.

Aristotle's position poses yet another difficulty. How is it possible for the form in our mind to correspond to the form of the object? How is this correspondence of internal and external world possible? Ultimately, it could be argued that for Aristotle this correspondence can exist because of the intelligibility of the world, an intelligibility that is itself preserved by an unceasing activity of thought.

In order to explain this, we must first consider Aristotle's understanding of causation.

Aristotle on Causation

Aristotle's uses the term causation in a broader sense than we tend to use it today. Where Aristotle uses the term causation, we would probably use a term like explanation. Aristotle identifies four types of causes. These have come to known as *material, formal, efficient*, and *final*. Properly speaking, these are probably better understood as explanations of change. The material cause is an answer to the question of what something is made. The formal cause is the answer to the question of what something is. The efficient cause is the answer to the question of how something was made. The final cause is the answer to the question of why something is the way it is. Imagine, for example, a marble statue of Aphrodite. The material cause is the marble. The efficient cause is the action of sculpting- the impact of the hammer and the chisel on the marble. The formal cause is an image of Aphrodite. The final cause is the purpose of the statue. Perhaps in this case the statue is to be one of the statues in a temple. According to Aristotle, the formal, the efficient, and the final cause may coincide and often do. For example, we might describe the efficient, the formal, and the final cause of motion in an animal as the soul of the animal.

Aristotle's understanding of substance as a combination of matter and form, his understanding of potential and actual states of being, along with his understanding of causes, allowed him to explain both change and how things can change and yet remain the same. Change can be accidental or substantial. If it is accidental, then the essence of a substance has not changed, only its accidental properties. If I stay in the sun long enough, I will change color, but this is an accidental, not a substantial change. If we cut a tree down, the change to the tree is a substantial one; the wood will begin to behave differently, not as the living wood of a tree, but begin to decompose as dead wood will do.

As Plato before him, Aristotle has attempted to respond to the problems posed by Parmenides. Plato had attempted to do so by distinguishing the knowledge of the change provided by our senses from the knowledge of the eternal provided by reason. With his concepts of potential and actual, and of particulars as substantial forms, Aristotle provided a conceptual framework for accounting for change and stability. Parmenides had argued that change could not occur because it either had to come from something that already existed or from something that did not exist. Change could not take place in that which already exists, because it already is what it is. Change cannot occur from what is not, because something cannot come from nothing. Aristotle's response is that change can occur in those things that have the potential to assume multiple forms.

Aristotle's metaphysics, as was Plato's, was ultimately teleological. Though Aristotle recognized that in certain circumstances, knowledge of efficient cause would be sufficient for our purposes, ultimately the world is understood as the realization of purposes. Things in the world act to fulfill their natures.

Having offered a description of change, Aristotle still has to answer the question of how change is initiated. To answer this question, I turn now to a discussion of Aristotle's prime mover, or first cause. Aristotle's notions of actual and potential and of final cause are key to understanding his notion of the first cause.

Aristotle on the Prime Mover

Aristotle argues that there must be a first cause. Here we have taken yet another paradoxical turn in Aristotle's thought. We began with Aristotle's assertion of the primacy of the sensible world, plants, trees, etc. Yet plants and trees could not have brought themselves into existence. "For substances are the first of existing things, and if they are destructible, all things are destructible. But it is impossible that movement should come into being or cease to be; for it must always have existed."[25]

Aristotle describes change as a movement from potentiality to actuality. He also describes change as a result of privation. Change must either be brought about by something external, or by some kind of internal drive, a movement to realize an end or purpose. If everything is potential, then nothing could have existed to bring it into existence. This means that there must be something that is eternal, immaterial, fully actual, and the first cause. It might be tempting to consider this to be the same as Plato's Form of the Good; Aristotle, however, distinguishes his first cause or prime mover from Plato's Form of the Good.

> Nothing, then, is gained even if we suppose eternal substances, as the believers in the Forms do, unless there is to be in them the principle which can cause movement, and even this is not enough, nor is another substance besides the Forms enough; for if it does not *act*, there will be no movement. Further, even if it acts, this will not be enough, if its substance is potentiality; for there will not be *eternal* movement; for that which is potentially may possibly not be. There must, then, be such a principle, whose very substance is actuality. Further, then, these substances must be without matter; for they must be eternal, at least if anything is eternal. Therefore they must be actuality.[26]

As Aristotle described movement as a movement from potentiality to actuality, the prime mover must move without itself being moved. For if the prime mover was moved, this was imply some lack. The prime mover must be fully actualized. Aristotle then asked what could cause movement without itself moving. "And the object of desire and the object of thought move in this way, they move without being moved... Thus it produces motion by being loved, and it moves the other moving things."[27] Though Aristotle argued that both desire and thought can cause motion without themselves moving, desire can be reduced to thought. It is the object of thought which is the object of desire. For Aristotle then, the first cause is thought; as the greatest good, the thought of the prime mover is directed toward itself. Thus, the first cause is an eternal, unceasing activity of self-reflection.

In Aristotle's cosmology, the earth is a sphere at the center of the universe. The earth is surrounded by water, air, and fire. Beyond the earth are the heavenly spheres. The last of the heavenly spheres is the sphere of the fixed stars. Aristotle believed that the stars were comprised of a fifth material element, the *aether*, and were incapable of any change other than that of circular motion. To account for the movement of the heavens, Aristotle believed that there must multiple spheres.

The prime mover, or first cause, acts as a final cause. The prime mover acts as an object of desire to the intelligence of the first heavenly sphere which responds with circular movement, considered by Aristotle to be perfect movement. This is how Aristotle explained the rotation of the stars around the earth and the origin of all motion.[28] Interestingly, Aristotle offered various at least two possibilities for the number of heavenly spheres, and different numbers of unmoved movers.

In understanding the first cause, it is better to understand the notion of first used by Aristotle not as temporal, but as logical or necessary. Aristotle understood being and motion as having existed eternally.

Though primary substances may come into being and pass away, the secondary substances of species and genera do not. Aristotle's first cause is not properly speaking a creator of the universe. Aristotle's first cause is better understood as that unceasing activity which is at the heart of the activity of the universe.

Conclusion

It is important to note that the positions of Plato and Aristotle are both somewhat "Platonic," in the sense that the positions have been described as unchanging. In actuality, the positions of both Plato and Aristotle developed over time Plato, for example, in his own work presents many of the criticisms of the theory of the Forms we find in Aristotle. Aristotle's positions also changed over time. It was not possible here to share more of Aristotle's empirical work for example. The positions described here, of Platonic Forms, and Aristotelian substance, cannot, and do not, fully reveal the complexity of the thought of either of these philosophers.

Nonetheless, from the metaphysics and epistemology developed by Plato and Aristotle, western philosophy has inherited several philosophical problems which it is still attempting to resolve. One, already discussed, is that of the problem of the nature of universals. Another problem is that of the nature of knowledge. Yet another problem is that of the mind/body problem, or the problem of explaining the relationship of mind, or soul, and body.

For early Christian thinkers, Greek thought posed its own problems, that of reconciling the revealed truth, such as that of the Bible, with the wisdom of the Greeks. This can be seen in Christian understandings of God. Early Christian thinkers such as Augustine would describe the Platonic forms as forms in the mind of God and argue that we can gain access to an understanding of the forms because God reveals their truth to us. Anselm's ontological argument for the existence of God was strongly influenced by Platonic thought. Thomas Aquinas's five ways, or five proofs for the existence of God, would draw strongly on Aristotelian philosophy. Even the Christological controversies can in some ways be understood not just as posing theological problems but metaphysical ones as well. How could God become flesh? How could the created be described as God?

The teleological understanding of the universe also posed its own problems for Christian thinkers. This problem might generally be described in the following way. If the universe is the realization of a purpose, and that purpose is good, how can evil exist? Augustine, for example, would argue that all being is good and that evil is a kind of privation or lack of being. Some have argued that the Greek hierarchy of being has also had problematic consequences contributing to notions of the body as sinful, to the exploitation of the earth, and all those perceived to be less rational.

I suspect that in many ways the legacy of Greek thought is still with us, not perhaps in its specifics, but in its general understandings of perfection as eternal, unchanging, and fully actualized. As did the Greeks, we continue to struggle to resolve questions of the one and the many, the changing and the unchanging. As did the Greeks, we also struggle to offer an account of knowledge as a kind of correspondence between mind and reality.

Additional Reading- Plato's Allegory of the Cave

[Socrates] AND now, I said, let me show in a figure how far our nature is enlightened or unenlightened:—Behold! human beings living in a underground den, which has a mouth open towards the light and reaching all along the den; here they have been from their childhood, and have their legs and necks chained so that they cannot move, and can only see before them, being prevented by the chains from turning round their heads. Above and behind them a fire is blazing at a distance, and between the fire and the prisoners there is a raised way; and you will see, if you look, a low wall built along the way, like the screen which marionette players have in front of them, over which they show the puppets.

[Glaucon] I see.

[Socrates] And do you see, I said, men passing along the wall carrying all sorts of vessels, and statues and figures of animals made of wood and stone and various materials, which appear over the wall? Some of them are talking, others silent.

[Glaucon] You have shown me a strange image, and they are strange prisoners.

[Socrates] Like ourselves, I replied; and they see only their own shadows, or the shadows of one another, which the fire throws on the opposite wall of the cave?

[Glaucon] True, he said; how could they see anything but the shadows if they were never allowed to move their heads?

[Socrates] And of the objects which are being carried in like manner they would only see the shadows?

[Glaucon] Yes, he said.

[Socrates] And if they were able to converse with one another, would they not suppose that they were naming what was actually before them?

[Glaucon] Very true.

[Socrates] And suppose further that the prison had an echo which came from the other side, would they not be sure to fancy when one of the passers-by spoke that the voice which they heard came from the passing shadow?

[Glaucon] No question, he replied.

[Socrates] To them, I said, the truth would be literally nothing but the shadows of the images.

[Glaucon] That is certain.

[Socrates] And now look again, and see what will naturally follow if the prisoners are released and disabused of their error. At first, when any of them is liberated and compelled suddenly to stand up and turn his neck round and walk and look towards the light, he will suffer sharp pains; the glare will distress him, and he will be unable to see the realities of which in his former state he had seen the shadows; and then conceive some one saying to him, that what he saw before was an illusion, but that now, when he is approaching nearer to being and his eye is turned towards more real existence, he has a clearer vision, -what will be his reply? And you may further imagine that his instructor is pointing to the objects as they pass and requiring him to name them, -will he not be perplexed? Will he not fancy that the shadows which he formerly saw are truer than the objects which are now shown to him?

[Glaucon] Far truer.

[Socrates] And if he is compelled to look straight at the light, will he not have a pain in his eyes which will make him turn away to take and take in the objects of vision which he can see, and which he will conceive to be in reality clearer than the things which are now being shown to him?

[Glaucon] True.

[Socrates] And suppose once more, that he is reluctantly dragged up a steep and rugged ascent, and held fast until he's forced into the presence of the sun himself, is he not likely to be pained and irritated? When he approaches the light his eyes will be dazzled, and he will not be able to see anything at all of what are now called realities.

[Glaucon] Not all in a moment, he said.

[Socrates] He will require to grow accustomed to the sight of the upper world. And first he will see the shadows best, next the reflections of men and other objects in the water, and then the objects themselves; then he will gaze upon the light of the moon and the stars and the spangled heaven; and he will see the sky and the stars by night better than the sun or the light of the sun by day?

[Glaucon] Certainly.

[Socrates] Last of he will be able to see the sun, and not mere reflections of him in the water, but he will see him in his own proper place, and not in another; and he will contemplate him as he is.

[Glaucon] Certainly.

[Socrates] He will then proceed to argue that this is he who gives the season and the years, and is the guardian of all that is in the visible world, and in a certain way the cause of all things which he and his fellows have been accustomed to behold?

[Glaucon] Clearly, he said, he would first see the sun and then reason about him.

[Socrates] And when he remembered his old habitation, and the wisdom of the den and his fellow-prisoners, do you not suppose that he would felicitate himself on the change, and pity them?

[Glaucon] Certainly, he would.

[Socrates] And if they were in the habit of conferring honors (conform to American spelling usage) among themselves on those who were quickest to observe the passing shadows and to remark which of them went before, and which followed after, and which were together; and who were therefore best able to draw conclusions as to the future, do you think that he would care for such honors and glories, or envy the possessors of them? Would he not say with Homer, Better to be the poor servant of a poor master, and to endure anything, rather than think as they do and live after their manner?

[Glaucon] Yes, he said, I think that he would rather suffer anything than entertain these false notions and live in this miserable manner.

[Socrates] Imagine once more, I said, such an one coming suddenly out of the sun to be replaced in his old situation; would he not be certain to have his eyes full of darkness?

[Glaucon] To be sure, he said.

[Socrates] And if there were a contest, and he had to compete in measuring the shadows with the prisoners who had never moved out of the den, while his sight was still weak, and before his eyes had become steady (and the time which would be needed to acquire this new habit of sight might be very considerable) would he not be ridiculous? Men would say of him that up he went and down he came without his eyes; and that it was better not even to think of ascending; and if any one tried to loose another and lead him up to the light, let them only catch the offender, and they would put him to death.

[Glaucon] No question, he said.

> [Socrates] This entire allegory, I said, you may now append, dear Glaucon, to the previous argument; the prison-house is the world of sight, the light of the fire is the sun, and you will not misapprehend me if you interpret the journey upwards to be the ascent of the soul into the intellectual world according to my poor belief, which, at your desire, I have expressed whether rightly or wrongly God knows. But, whether true or false, my opinion is that in the world of knowledge the idea of good appears last of all, and is seen only with an effort; and, when seen, is also inferred to be the universal author of all things beautiful and right, parent of light and of the lord of light in this visible world, and the immediate source of reason and truth in the intellectual; and that this is the power upon which he who would act rationally, either in public or private life must have his eye fixed.

Bibliography

J.L. Ackrill, editor. *A New Aristotle Reader.* Princeton: Princeton University Press, 1987.

Frederick Copleston. S.J. *A History of Philosophy, Volume 1 Greece and Rome.* New York: Image Book, 1985.

Paul Edwards, editor in chief. *The Encyclopedia of Philosophy Volume One.* New York: Macmillan Publishing Co., 1967.

James Fieser and Norman Lillegard. *A Historical Introduction to Philosophy: Texts and Interactive Guides.* New York: Oxford University Press. 2002.

Justin Kaplan, editor. *Dialogues of Plato.* New York: Pocket Books, 1950.

Endnotes

[1] *Phaedo*, p. 160.

[2] John Mansley Robinson. *An Introduction to Early Greek Philosophy*, Houghton Mifflin Company, Boston, 1968, p. vi.

[3] Copleston, p. 266.

[4] Copleston, p. 268.

[5] "Aristotle", G.B. Kerferd, *The Encyclopedia of Philosophy Volumes 1 and 2*, Paul Edwards Editor in Chief, Macmillan Publishing Co., New York. 1967.

[6] *Metaphysics* 1026a16

[7] *Metaphysics* 13 1078b

[8] *A Historical Introduction to Philosophy*, p. 37.

[9] Ibid, p. 110.

[10] *Meno*.

[11] Copleston, p. 292.

[12] *Metaphysics*, p. 284.

[13] Ibid, p. 285.

[14] Ibid, p. 285.

[15] Ibid, p. 287.

[16] Ibid, p. 288.

[17] Ibid, p. 288.

[18] Metaphysics, Book VII, Ch. 7, p. 293.

[19] Physics, Book II, Ch. 1, p. 95.

[20] Ibid, p. 292.

[21] *Categories*, Ch. 5, p. 7.

[22]Physics, Book II, Ch. 1, p. 93.

[23]Ibid, p. 93.

[24]Ibid, p. 256.

[25]Metaphysics, Book VII, ch. 6.

[26]Metaphysics, Book XII, ch. 6, p. 346.

[27]Ibid, Book XII, ch. 7, p. 347.

[28]Copleston, p. 315.

THE NATURE OF REALITY AND PERCEPTION—EARLY MODERN PERIOD

THE PROBLEM OF PERCEPTION IN EARLY MODERN PHILOSOPHY

by Daniel E. Flage

Is the world approximately as it appears to the senses? If so, what are our reasons to believe so? If not, can we know how the world is? If so, how do we know it?

In this chapter we examine the answers to these questions posed by the major seventeenth and eighteenth century European philosophers. We begin by looking briefly at the cultural setting that brought the problem of perception to the fore. This was the Renaissance in general and the rise of modern science in particular. Then we shall look at the discussions of perception in the works of René Descartes, Benedict Spinoza, G. W. F. Leibniz, John Locke, George Berkeley, and David Hume.

The Renaissance and the Rise of Modern Science

The rediscovery of the ancients during the Renaissance had a pronounced effect on European intellectual history. In the Christian religion, it was the period when the study of the biblical languages (Hebrew and Greek) was renewed. Erasmus's Greek New Testament was the first Greek New Testament published in Europe. It provided the basis for Luther's German translation of the New Testament. It was a period when the authority of the Roman Catholic Church was called into question. This took the form of the Protestant Reformation on the one hand, and the rise of **humanism**—a system of thought that centers on human beings and their values, capacities, and worth—on the other. While the Renaissance is characterized as the rediscovery of the ancients, in the case of the humanists it was largely a replacement of one ancient system with another. The system of Aristotle—which was "Christianized" by St. Thomas Aquinas in the thirteenth century and attained dominance in European intellectual life (Scholasticism)—was replaced by views closer to those of Plato, Cicero, Seneca, and Epictetus.

In 1562, the writings of Sextus Empiricus were published. Sextus was a second century physician who gathered the writings of and legends about the **skeptics**. A skeptic is a philosopher who holds that knowledge is very limited. The most celebrated skeptic was Pyrrho of Elis (died *c.* 275 B.C.). Like Aristotle, Pyrrho had been a tutor to Alexander the Great. Pyrrho held that if one can neither prove that a given statement is true nor prove that the statement is false, one should simply suspend belief. *Very* few statements could be proven either true or false. It is said that, on a number of occasions, Pyrrho's friends saved him from almost certain death by preventing him from doing such things as stepping out of second-story windows. Such extreme skepticism, which calls for the suspension of beliefs that can neither be known to be true or false, is known as **Pyrrhonian skepticism**.

A less extreme form of skepticism arose in Plato's Academy and became known as **academic skepticism**. This had two elements. (1) The academics developed a sustained, systematic attack on the "dogmatists," the positions of such philosophers as Plato and the Stoics. (2) They developed a detailed doctrine of living among the phenomena. They held that while one can never show that appearance represents "real things," one should continue to act as if they do. Hume was a later champion of academic skepticism, and one can reasonably suggest that academic skepticism is assumed by scientists from at least the eighteenth century to the present.

Sextus' *Outlines of Pyrrhonism* had a profound impact on European—especially French—intellectual activity. The result was a "skeptical crisis" or "Pyrrhonian crisis" (*crise pyrrhonienne*). To see why the skeptic posed a challenge to the belief that the world is as it appears, consider the following discussion:

> THOSE who say that the Sceptics deny appearances seem to me to be ignorant of what we say. As we said above, we do not deny those things which, in appearance with the passivity of our sense-impressions, lead us involuntarily to give our assent to them; and these are the appearances. And when we inquire whether an object is such as it appears, we grant the fact of appearance. Our inquiry is thus not directed at the appearance itself. For example, honey appears to us to have a sweetening quality. This much we concede, because it affects us with the sensation of sweetness. The question, however, is whether it is sweet in an absolute sense. Hence not the appearance is questioned, but that which is predicated of the appearance. Whenever we do expound arguments directly against appearances, we do so not with the intention of denying them, but in order to point out the hasty judgement of the dogmatists. For if reason is such a rogue as to all but snatch even the appearances from under our eyes, should we not by all means be wary of it, at least not be hasty to follow it, in the case of things non-evident?[1]

What's going on here? Sextus draws a distinction between appearance and reality—a distinction that is commonly drawn by philosophers.[2] He is perfectly willing to allow that you can trust appearances. If you eat honey, it appears to be sweet. The apparent sweetness is unquestionable. But we don't say, "I have an appearance of sweetness." We say, rather, "The honey is sweet." Honey is stuff out there in the world. Honey is said to be something distinct from any of our awarenesses. We would be inclined to say that if all humans died off but there were still bees acting the way bees typically act, there still would be honey. What is the *evidence* for this? Don't we see, feel, and taste honey? Sextus' answer is "No." We are aware of a yellow color. We are aware of stickiness. We are aware of a sweet flavor. The honey itself is something distinct from all of our awarenesses. Don't we also know that if we become ill, the honey might appear less sweet? Don't we also know that if seen on a cloudy day, the shade of yellow that we perceive might be different from the shade we perceive on a sunny day? But, surely, the honey's own sweetness or shade of yellow doesn't change, does it? What reasons do we have to say that? Indeed, what reasons do we have to say that the honey is something other than the various properties of which we are aware?

Consider another case. We ordinarily believe that the world is as it appears to us. With our two eyes we see Professor Maclean giving a lecture. There is one person, just as we seem to hear one (distinct and distinctive) voice. Now press your eye with your finger. You now see two Professor Macleans. Does that mean there are now two Professor Macleans lecturing?

Or consider seeing an oar in the water. It appears to be bent. Is it? Or consider looking at a building. From where I sit, I see a hospital. It appears to be 2 ½ inches tall. As I walk "toward" the hospital, it "grows" to a height of some fifty feet. If the world is as it appears, must I say that the hospital is both fifty feet tall and not fifty feet tall, which is a *contradiction*? Contradictory statements, such as "the hospital is fifty feet tall and it is not fifty feet tall" or any conjunction of a statement and its denial,[3] are false if any statements are. Or do an experiment. Bring your shower curtain rod into the kitchen. Fill a pan with cold water and ice. Turn on your stove. Now put your right hand in the ice water and put your left hand over the burner on the stove. After several minutes, grab the shower curtain rod with both hands. To the right hand it will appear warm; to the left hand it will appear cold. Is the rod both warm and cold?

Sextus's work had a significant influence on the sixteenth century French humanist Michel Montaigne (1533-1592). It is Montaigne that generally is taken to provide the skeptical challenge Descartes attempted to answer. Consider some of his remarks on sense perception:

The senses are in some people more obscure and dim, in others more open and acute. We receive things in one way and another, according to what we are and what they seem to us. . . .[4]

What of the fact that our senses interfere with each other? A painting seems to the eye to be in relief, to the tough it seems flat. Shall we say that musk is agreeable or not, which rejoices our sense of smell and offends our taste? There are herbs and unguents suitable for one part of the body which injure another. Honey is pleasant to the taste, unpleasant to the sight.[5]

. . .

Moreover, since the accidents of illness, madness, or sleep make things appear to us otherwise than they appear to healthy people, wise men, and waking people, is it not likely that our normal state and our natural disposition can also assign to things an essence corresponding to our condition, and accommodate them to us, as our disordered states do? And that our health is as capable of giving them its own appearance as sickness? Why should the temperate man not have some vision of things related to himself, like the intemperate man, and likewise imprint his own character on them?

The jaded man assigns the insipidity to the wine; the healthy man, the savor; the thirsty man, the relish.

Now, since our condition accommodates things to itself and transforms them according to itself, we no longer know what things are in truth; for nothing comes to us except falsified and altered by our senses.[6]

. . .

To judge the appearances that we receive of objects, we would need a justificatory instrument; to verify this instrument, we need a demonstration; to verify the demonstration, an instrument: there we are in a circle.

Our conception is not itself applied to foreign objects, but is conceived through the mediation of the senses; and the senses do not comprehend the foreign object, but only by their impressions. And thus the conception and semblance we form is not the object, but only of the impression and effect made on the sense; which impression and the object are different things. Wherefore whoever judges by appearance judges by something other than the object.[7]

Montaigne's point is that since things appear to be different to different people, or the same thing appears to be different to the same person at different times, or the state of our health influences how we perceive things, we cannot take the appearances to be identical with "real objects." These are variations on what is commonly called the **argument from illusion**. So you have to distinguish between appearance and reality. You cannot be wrong about how things *appear to you*. But since there are extraneous factors that seem to account for differences in appearances, there is no reason to believe that real things correspond to any one of your appearances. Indeed, any attempt to provide grounds for claiming that one kind of appearance is privileged—that is gives you an insight into reality—requires circular reasoning. In the seventeenth and eighteenth century philosophers, the argument from illusion provides the basis for distinguishing between **ideas** (appearances) and objects. The **problem of perception** was then understood as seeking grounds for claiming that ideas *can* provide evidence regarding the nature and existence of objects.

Why did this become an acute problem in the sixteenth and seventeenth centuries? The skeptics' arguments go back to ancient times. Why couldn't they claim with the Scholastics (medieval philosophers) that there are intentional forms—what Descartes once called "little pictures"[8]—that go from the object perceived to the perceiver? First, that wouldn't solve the problem. The problem posed by the skeptical arguments was precisely that there might not be any similarity between the "little pictures" one perceives and the object they represent—the *object* might not even exist. (Consider an elephant you "perceive" in a dream.) Second, recall that this was the beginning of the scientific age. Even in its infancy, science placed some credence upon sense perception. If there was no way to establish that there is some definable relation between the way the world appears and the way the world "really is," dropping cannon balls of different weights from the Leaning Tower of Pisa and noticing that they hit the ground at the same time would provide no basis for questioning the Aristotelian (Scholastic) claim that heavier objects fall faster than lighter objects.[9] So, unless it could be shown that perception provides some basis for knowledge of the world outside the mind, the conclusions of science could not be justified.

Before turning to Descartes's celebrated solution to the problem of perception, we should note a movement that grew with the development of the "new science."

Modern science is distinguished from its predecessors on the basis of its "method." You all studied the "scientific method" in your science classes. (If you're a science major, you probably have also noticed that most discussions of "the scientific method" differ in detail from the actual practices of the sciences.) The search for a scientific method was a Renaissance theme. When we look at Descartes and Spinoza, we will notice that they both claim to use a "geometrical method." We also will notice that the methods differ significantly from one another. The expression "geometrical method" had two meanings in the seventeenth century.

When you took geometry in high school, you started with a bunch of definitions, axioms, and postulates, and on the basis of those you proved various theorems. If the postulates had been different, your theorems would have been different. (The fundamental difference between Euclidian geometry and Riemannian geometry—the geometric theory behind Einstein's Theory of Relativity—is alternative statements of the parallel postulate.) Spinoza's *Ethics* is presented geometrically in much the same way Euclid's geometry was presented in your high school class. This is sometimes called *the method of synthesis* or demonstration. It is fundamentally a system in which you reach a number of conclusions on the basis of a set of definitions, axioms, and postulates taken as *given* (taken to be true).

But did you ever wonder how Euclid and his predecessors figured out what those fundamental elements of geometry were? They used "the geometrical method," of course, but this was the method of *analysis*. Descartes claimed to have discovered a universal method of inquiry. He says this is the method of the ancient geometer, Pappus of Alexandra (*c*. A.D. 300), the method of analysis or reduction. It is a search for first principles, such as the fundamental elements of Euclidean geometry. The question is, given that I know, for example, that the interior angles of a triangle are equal to 180°, what general principles will allow me to deduce that? In general, the method of analysis asks, "What must I know in order to know what I know?"[10] Assuming that the world is orderly—in much the same way that geometry is orderly—that there are laws that will allow you to explain phenomena in the way that the laws of geometry allow you to explain why a certain theorem is true, it is simply a search for such laws. The questions are, "What principle, if true, would allow me to explain phenomenon *x*? What principle would allow me to explain the principle assumed to explain *x*?" This is a search for natural laws. It is a method which, with variations, is found in Aristotle's works. It is a method which was discussed in the Italian schools several hundred years before Descartes. It is basically the method Galileo assumed in attempting to describe the universe. And it is not far removed from what occurs in scientific explanation to this day. (Formulate a hypothesis. Test it. See how the hypothesis fits into an on-going scientific theory.) On its face, this is *not* an **empirical** method, that is, a method based on sense experience. In practice, the **verification** of the hypothesis, that is, the evidence tending to show that the hypothesis is true, required empirical observations.

Francis Bacon (1561-1623) developed an empirical theory of scientific method in his *New Organon*. Fundamentally it was a method requiring careful observation and comparison. Consider the case of heat. First, you look for cases in which heat is present. List them. This would include sunlight, fire, fermentation, etc. This he called "the table of presence." Second, you look for cases that are like the first but in which heat is absent. List them. Moonbeams might be an example. This he called "the table of absence." Third is the table of degrees, in which you would list cases producing heat to a greater or lesser degree. Finally, one compares the tables to see "what remains." Light cannot be a sufficient condition for heat, that is, a condition in the presence of which heat always occurs, since heat is absent in moonbeams. Flame cannot be a necessary condition for heat, that is, a condition in the absence of which heat does not occur, since there is no flame involved in fermentation. By a careful comparison of the tables, one should be able to limit one's list of conditions to those in the presence of which heat always occurs, and in the absence of which heat never occurs. The Baconian method, or plain historical method, concerned the correlation of observable properties. As such, it did not sanction hypotheses that went beyond experience. Bacon's method was the official method of the Royal Society of London for the Promotion of Natural Knowledge, a group whose members ultimately included the architect Christopher Wren, the chemist Robert Boyle, John Locke, Isaac Newton, and Stephen Hawking. In practice, the members of the Royal Society were champions of numerous hypotheses that went beyond the observable.

In effect, the "method of analysis" and the Baconian method reflect two aspects of any scientific investigation.[11]

René Descartes (1596-1650)

Descartes was a scientist, a mathematician, and a philosopher. His *Geometry* was an early—though not the first—study of analytic geometry. The Cartesian coordinate system bears his name. His physics was so influential in the later part of the seventeenth century that Newton's physics initially was considered merely a variant on Cartesian physics. His philosophy continues to be influential even today.

Descartes's most famous work is his *Meditations on First Philosophy*. Bothered by the skeptical challenges of Montaigne and others, Descartes claimed, "I realized that it was necessary, once in the course of my life, to demolish everything [I believed] completely and start again from the foundations if I wanted to establish anything at all in the sciences that was stable and likely to last" (*CSM* 2:12). The result was his famous "method of doubt," an attempt to drive skeptical doubts to their ultimate limits and discover truths that are immune from doubt.[12] He began by noting that he had believed that everything he knew was based on sense experience and teaching. But since sometimes his senses had misled him—the building that appears 2 ½ inches tall from my office appears 50 feet tall from its base, and to claim that the building itself is both 50 feet tall and not 50 feet tall is a contradiction—he should not believe that the world is *exactly* as it appears to the senses.[13] But anyone with a bit of experience learns how to "correct" the way things appear. When you were young, you probably "saw" large puddles of water on roads on hot summer days. But you learned that these "puddles" were nothing more than sunlight reflecting from the hot surface of the road, so you are no longer misled. We learn to put our scattered bits of sense experience together so that they yield a coherent and consistent picture of "the world."

But what if you can't tell when you're actually perceiving something? People suffering from various forms of mental illness cannot distinguish the real world from a fantasy world. When you're asleep and having a vivid dream, you cannot distinguish it from a waking experience. You might *believe* you are riding down Main Street on an elephant, while, in fact, you're asleep in bed. Descartes's famous "dream argument"—his version of the argument from illusion—raises the possibility that one never can know that one is perceiving. Does that mean that one can have no knowledge of the world? No. There are certain common elements of one's dreams and one's waking experiences—just as there are common elements to a picture and the world, no matter how abstract the picture might be (the colors are the same, for example)—so one might still know something about the world. At the very least, one might know that the truths of mathematics apply to each. Notice that at this point you might still know things on the basis of perception, although only the most general things. You *cannot* know that the book that *appears* to be in front of you exists.

Descartes carries his skeptical doubts further than any of the earlier skeptics. He raises a series of *hypothetical* doubts. He asks what the consequences would be *if* one makes certain assumptions. *What if* God were a deceiver? If God is all-powerful, a deceiver-God could cause me to believe all sorts of outrageous things. *What if* I were caused by something other than God? Then the less perfect my cause is, the more likely it is that I am defective (prone to err). Any of my beliefs could be false. *What if* there were a powerful evil demon whose sole purpose is to deceive me? I couldn't know that any of my beliefs are true. I might believe that there is a world outside me even if there is none. I might believe that triangles have three sides, even if they actually have four sides. I could not know that *anything* I believe is true.

Does Descartes resolve these doubts? Does he ever reach the conclusion that the world—or some parts of the world—are as they appear to experience? Yes, but the deceiver-God hypothesis requires that Descartes take a major detour. He has to show that God is not a deceiver. He has to consider the implications of that conclusion. So by the time we reach the end of the Sixth Meditation, Descartes is back to his pre-dream doubts. These doubts allow that sense perception provides the basis for claiming the existence of material objects, although it requires that one balance experiences against experiences to develop a *consistent* account of the world. Given this brief look ahead, it's time to return to the road Descartes traveled to that conclusion.

How does Descartes resolve these doubts? He replies, "I think, therefore I am" (*Cogito, ergo sum.*)[14] Just as it is self-contradictory to say, "The building is fifty-feet tall, and it's not fifty feet tall," in a similar way it is self-contradictory to say, "I think, but I don't exist."[15] In the Second Meditation, he follows this with a detailed discussion of his own nature. He concludes that he is a thing that thinks. He reaches this conclusion by starting with a common notion of himself and *eliminating* all those features that could be doubted. He wrote, "Well, the first thought that came to mind was that I had a face, hands, arms and the whole mechanical structure of limbs which can be seen in a corpse, and which I called the body. The next thought was that I was nourished, and that I moved about, and that I engaged in sense-perception and thinking; and these actions I attributed to the soul" (*CSM* 2:17). If there is an evil demon, I can know nothing about my body—it might all be an illusion. So, anything that requires a body, for example, movement and sense-perception, can be eliminated from my known nature. So, I know myself only to be a thing that thinks. This is discovered by *reasoning*.

Descartes concludes the Second Meditation by considering the properties of a piece of wax. Do we know the properties of a piece of wax by sense-perception? No, says Descartes. All the properties we *observe* in observing a piece of wax change under various conditions, even though we believe that the wax itself remains the same. If you take a piece of wax from a beehive, it's yellow, cool, fragrant, sticky, and has a certain size and shape. Sit by a fire with the wax and *all* those properties change: it turns white and hot, it loses its fragrance and stickiness, and the size and shape change. The wax itself can't be both yellow and not yellow, cool and not cool—real things cannot have contradictory characteristics. So, if we eliminate all those properties that change, we discover that there are only three general characteristics that remain: the wax is extended (it takes up some space), it is flexible (capable of taking on various shapes) and movable. These are not discovered by sense experience. These characteristics are discovered by reasoning about what one perceives. Notice that *existence* is not a property of the wax that is known.

At the beginning of the Third Meditation Descartes claims that one can know that clear and distinct perceptions are true. What does that mean? It seems to mean that Descartes can claim to know the natures of things. For example, it would provide the basis for Descartes's claim that God is by nature all-knowing and all-powerful—but the clear and distinct perception *does not* show that God exists.[16] In addition it is presumably on the basis of clear and distinct perception that one knows eternal truths, truths known by the natural light. As we shall see, one of these eternal truths, Descartes's causal principle that there must be at least as much reality in the total and efficient cause as in the effect, plays a significant role in his arguments for the existence of God.[17]

Descartes exists, a point I'm sure Descartes found comforting. But how does he go from the fact that *he* exists to the claim that something else exists? Descartes looks around and considers some possibilities. He says that one has a natural inclination to believe that the world is approximately as it appears to the senses. Is this a ground for claiming that there is a world outside oneself that is approximately as it appears? No. We have two ideas of the sun. One is that of a grapefruit-sized object that we see almost every day; the other is of a huge mass of gases. Astronomical reasoning, based on principles known by the *natural light*, tells us the second is closer to the way the sun is. While the natural light cannot mislead us, we shouldn't put a lot of stock in natural inclinations. So, we still cannot follow sense perception very closely.

How does Descartes come to know of things outside himself? He looks within. He says that he has ideas of himself, God, angels, and ordinary physical objects. He asks whether he can explain the presence of these ideas without assuming something exists outside of himself. He can *construct* ideas of angels and physical objects from the ideas of himself and of God. He introduces his causal principle, that there must be at least as much reality in the total and efficient cause as in its effect on the basis of the natural light.[18] Descartes claimed that it was a corollary of his causal principle that the cause of the idea of something must have at least as much reality as the thing of which it is an idea. On the basis of this principle, he claims that since he is a (finite) **substance**, a thing that does not depend on anything (other than God) for its existence, he is able to form ideas of physical substances. As a finite substance, he has more reality than the properties (modes) of a finite substance, so he himself can cause the ideas of the properties of a physical substance. The only idea he cannot explain by combining other ideas is the idea of God. The idea of God is the idea of an infinite substance. An infinite substance is more real than a finite substance (such as Descartes is). So the only thing that can cause the idea of God is God. So God exists.

Descartes's argument is a form of the **cosmological** argument for the existence of God. A cosmological argument for the existence of God begins with a factual claim—in this case, the claim that I have an idea of God—and argues from that fact to the existence of God.[19] Descartes provides a second cosmological argument for the existence of God in Meditation Three. This begins with the factual claim that I (Descartes) exist as a thing having an idea of God as a perfect being. The question is what could cause me

(Descartes) to exist as something having that idea of God, and the conclusion is that only God could be the cause. While we need not concern ourselves with the details of the argument, it is important to notice that it proves the existence of God *as a perfect being*. Why is that important? If God is perfect, God can have no defects. God would be defective (imperfect) if God were a deceiver. So, God is not a deceiver. Descartes has refuted the fundamental assumption of the deceiver-God argument, the first of his hypothetical doubts.

If God is not a deceiver, doesn't that refute the basis Descartes had for calling the existence of the material world into doubt? Can't we say, *at least*, that we can know mathematical propositions are true, since Descartes claimed you could know *at least* that before he introduced the deceiver-God argument? The answer is, "Sort of." In Meditations Four through Six he traces out the implications of the conclusion that God is not a deceiver, concluding Meditation Six by providing some status to sense-perception.[20]

In Meditation Four, Descartes basically asks whether he has proven too much in proving that God is not a deceiver. If God is not a deceiver, then I cannot make mistakes when I clearly and distinctly perceive something. But since I know myself to occasionally err, wouldn't the fact that God allows me to err sometimes be sufficient to make God a deceiver? Descartes replies that God would be a deceiver only if one has a faculty that causes one to err. He develops a theory of judgment—affirming or denying the truth of a claim—according to which one can (and *should*) withhold judgment except when one clearly and distinctly perceives. When one clearly and distinctly perceives one cannot help but judge that the claim one is considering is true. Descartes's theory of judgment effectively shifts the responsibility for recognizing truth from God back to humans. So long as one uses one's faculties correctly, one cannot err. The fact that one occasionally errs is due to an incorrect use of one's faculties: one judges without sufficient evidence.

In Meditation Five, Descartes turns to mathematics. One clearly and distinctly perceives that the truths of arithmetic and geometry are true. So, those truths apply to something. This does *not* mean that they apply to material objects. As your geometry teacher in high school might have said, geometry applies to "real triangles," not to the poor approximations of them drawn with chalk upon a chalkboard. In Descartes's scheme, the truths of geometry apply to "true and immutable natures" (*CSM* 2:44), which are presumably ideas in the mind of God. But as anyone who has done geometrical proofs will attest, those things can be long and nasty(!). At every stage of the proof we may clearly and distinctly perceive that the next step follows, but how can we be certain that the whole proof holds together? Descartes's answer is that since God is not a deceiver, it cannot happen that every step of the proof would be correct but the proof itself would be defective. As he noted back in the Third Meditation, the sole basis for calling the truths of mathematics into question was the *hypothetical assumption* that God is a deceiver, a "supposition [that] is a very slight and, so to speak, metaphysical one" (*CSM* 2:25). Since he has refuted the possibility that God is a deceiver, the truths of mathematics stand firm.

But what do you obtain when you show that the claims of geometry are true? Geometry provides a description of the world. There is no guarantee that anything in the *material* world corresponds to the truths of geometry. But insofar as our geometrical ideas are clearly and distinctly perceived, it is at least *possible* that there are material objects corresponding to them. This is what is gained in Meditation Five. In Meditation Six Descartes proves that the material world exists. He notes that if he had a body to which his geometrical ideas applied, it would provide an easy explanation of imagination, since the ideas of the imagination *seem* to apply to material objects. This provides some reason to believe—it is probable—that material objects exist. But what takes us from mere probability to certainty that material objects exist? The thesis that God is not a deceiver. God can create anything I clearly and distinctly perceive as I clearly and distinctly perceive it. I can conceive of my mind as only a thing that thinks as distinct from material objects (bodies), which are extended but don't think. So, it's possible for God to create minds and bodies as distinct things. As noted in Meditation Three, one has a disposition to believe that material objects exist. *This alone* does not prove that material objects exist. But, having that disposition, I am aware of no faculty by which I can show that the belief in a material world is false. If I had such a faculty, I would know it. If I do not have a faculty by which I can know that by belief in the material world is false, and if that belief is false, then God would be a deceiver. But God is not a deceiver. So, my belief in the existence of the material world is not false, that is, the material world exists. This, however, does *not* mean the material world is exactly as it appears to the senses—it can be known to be only as it is described by geometry. So, while there is a world, it might not have all the characteristics we normally attribute to it: it might not be colored, it might not be hot or cold, it might not be aromatic, and so forth.

Descartes distinguishes between mind and body. A mind (mental substance) is a thing that thinks but is not extended. A body (material substance) is a thing that is extended but does not think. Humans are composed of a mental substance closely connected to a physical substance. Many of our sensations can be explained on the basis of the relation between a physical substance and a mental substance. If I stub my toe, I feel a sensation of pain. But if a person has lost a leg, he or she might still feel pain "in" the missing limb. How is that to be explained? Bodies are complex machines. If you lose a leg, nerves that were attached to the missing leg are still in place. When some of those nerves are stimulated, you feel the same pains you would have felt had you stubbed your toe. So, it is on the basis of the remaining bodily mechanism and its relation to the mind that "phantom pains" can be explained.

But we still haven't seen Descartes's solution to the problem of perception. To this point we might know that there are bodies, but, you might suggest, we're still not in much better shape than we were just before Descartes introduced the deceiver-God hypothesis. We still haven't dealt with the dream argument, the argument from deception. Recall that the dream argument was fundamentally the problem of being unable to distinguish dreams from waking states. If you could tell when you were awake and you carefully weighed experiences one against another, you could have good reason to believe that the world was approximately as it appeared. Only an insane person—to paraphrase the Descartes of the paragraph before the dream argument in Meditation One—could doubt that he or she is now reading a (dull and long-winded?) discussion of Descartes. In the last paragraph of Meditation Six, Descartes tells how to distinguish between wakeful perception and dreams. Wakeful experiences—genuine cases of sense-perception—"make sense;" they "hang together." If you are asking yourself whether a certain experience was a genuine case of sense-perception or a dream, put it in a context. Does it fit together in a coherent way with the remainder of your experience? Can you tell what happened before it and after it? Does it somehow fit in with ordinary life-experiences? If so, it was (most probably) a genuine case of sense perception. If not, it was (almost certainly) a dream or hallucination.

So, by the end of the *Meditations*, Descartes effectively solves the problem of perception. If what you seem to perceive *coheres* with the remainder of your seeming sense-experiences, it is (most probably) a genuine bit of sense experience. You have very good grounds for claiming that the object exists. Of course, this does *not* mean the world is exactly as it appears: the objects can be said to have only those properties that can be described by mathematics. His route to this point was to doubt all his beliefs presumably based on sense experience and provide a foundation for his claim to sensibly perceive the material world on clear and distinct perceptions of the natures of things and the existence of a nondeceiving God. As we turn now to the later philosophers, we shall discover that they provide alternative answers to the problem of perception.

Benedict (Baruch) Spinoza (1632-1677)

Baruch Spinoza was born in Amsterdam on November 24, 1632. He was the son of Portuguese Jews who had emigrated to Holland to avoid the Inquisition of the Roman Catholic Church in Spain and Portugal. Many Spanish and Portugese Jews had "converted" to Catholicism in the fifteenth and sixteenth centuries, while keeping their Jewish heritage alive. They were known as *marranos*. After the Arabs were driven from the Iberian Peninsula, the Inquisition began an active persecution of the Jews and *marranos*. A significant number emigrated to Holland, which was the most tolerant country in Europe at the time. A fairly large Jewish community was established in Amsterdam.[21]

Spinoza's father, Michael, wanted young Baruch to become a rabbi, and provided him with a good education. Through this, Spinoza became aware of Descartes's philosophy as well as on-going developments in science. Spinoza questioned the Biblical interpretations of the rabbis and was expelled from the synagogue in 1656. He changed his name from Baruch to the Latin equivalent Benedict, and continued his philosophical and scientific studies. He earned his livelihood as a lens grinder. He died on February 21, 1677.

While Spinoza's work was highly regarded by those who understood it—he was offered a professorship at the University of Heidelberg, a position he rejected on the ground of a clause requiring him to avoid religious controversy—only two of his works were published during his lifetime. His *Descartes's "Principles of Philosophy"* was published in 1663, and his *Theological-Political Treatise* was published anonymously in 1670. The *Theological-Political Treatise* is a combination of biblical-criticism and an argument for political tolerance. It was condemned by the Synod of the Reformed Church 1673, and formally banned in 1674. There are two earlier works that were not published during Spinoza's lifetime: *The Emendation of the Intellect* and the *Short Treatise on God, Man, and His Well-Being*. At the time of his death, Spinoza was working on his *Political Treatise*. His greatest and most systematic work—a work that was finished during his lifetime, but which publishers deemed too controversial to publish before his death—is his *Ethics*, a work that includes metaphysics and epistemology as well as moral theory.

Spinoza is sometimes known as the "God-intoxicated" philosopher, since he held that God is the only substance that exists, all other things exist "in" God. If we look at Descartes's definition of substance, we will note that a substance is a thing that can exist by itself.[22] Descartes distinguished between the infinite substance (God), which is wholly independent, and finite substances, which depends solely on God for its existence. Spinoza's definition of 'substance' is similar: "By substance I understand that which is in itself and is conceived through itself, i.e., that whose concept does not require the concept of any other thing, from which it must be formed."[23] If you think about *Descartes's* definition of 'substance' for a time, you'll recognize that if a substance is something that is independent—*completely* independent—then only an infinite substance is a substance properly so called. This was Spinoza's insight, his attempt to make the Cartesian definition of 'substance' consistent. There is only one substance. That substance is God or the world.[24] Everything is "in" God as a **mode** (modification) or as an **attribute** (a general property of a certain kind). Like Descartes, Spinoza recognized that there are at least two attributes, namely, extension and thought, while allowing that there are an infinite number of attributes (I.d6).[25]

Spinoza placed little intellectual faith in perceptual ideas. Contending that his definitions, axioms, and postulates were self-evidently true—known to be true on the basis of reason alone—Spinoza held that the nature of all things in the world follows deductively from the essence of God or nature. The *Ethics* follows the geometrical (synthetic) method. Insofar as the definitions and axioms are self-evident, they indicate the *essence* or inherent nature of the thing defined. Spinoza deemed ideas that correctly represent the essence of something *adequate* (II.d4). Claims that follow by deductive validity from adequate ideas (ideas of the essences of things) are themselves adequate and therefore true. To know something by way of sense perception is entirely different from knowing something by way of deduction from an adequate idea of the essence of a thing. If you have any question about this, consider Descartes's piece of wax argument in Meditation I. What one takes to be essential to the wax on the basis of sense experience alone—its color, determinate shape, size, aroma, temperature, etc.—*cannot* be essential to the wax, since all those properties change while one assumes that the wax itself remains the same and essential properties, by definition, are unchangeable. Since sense perception does not provide insight into the essences of things—what Spinoza calls finite modes of God—sense perception cannot provide adequate ideas.

Gottfried Wilhelm Leibniz (1646-1716)

Leibniz was born in Leipzig in 1646 and attended the University of Leipzig, where he came into contact with the thought of the shapers of modem scientific and philosophical thought, e.g., Galileo, Bacon, Hobbes, and Descartes. He received a doctor of law degree from the University of Altdorf in 1666. Although offered a teaching position at the University of Altdorf, Leibniz went into government service. He was a diplomat for the Elector of Mainz from 1667-1672. In 1676 he became librarian to the Duke of Brunswick in Hanover, a post he held for the remainder of his life. Leibniz's philosophical works—though voluminous—were written in his "spare time." He also, independently of Newton, invented the differential calculus. It is Leibniz's notation, not Newton's, that is used in contemporary calculus books. He died in Hanover in 1716.

Leibniz did not develop a systematic philosophy such as one finds in Spinoza's *Ethics*. The closest he comes to a systematic presentation of his philosophy is his *Monadology*, a short work completed late in his life. His work was fundamentally metaphysical. A monad is a little mind. All things in the world are composed of monads. Each "ordinary thing" has a dominant monad which is its principle of organization. Each monad reflects the entire world from its own perspective. Monads are "windowless": there is no causal interaction among monads. Nonetheless, insofar as a monad reflects the entire world from its own perspective, if one were able to provide a complete analysis of a monad, one would know of all things that exist, although one would not know all the characteristics of those existents. Leibniz draws a distinction between *perceptions* and *apperceptions*. As he writes:

> It is true that animals are sometimes in the condition of simple living things, and their souls in the condition of simple monads, namely when their perceptions are not sufficiently distinct to be remembered, as happens in a deep, dreamless sleep or in a fainting spell. . . . Thus it is good to distinguish between *perception*, which is the internal state of the monad representing external things, and *apperception*, which is *consciousness*, or the reflective knowledge of this internal state, something not given to all souls, nor at all times to the same soul.[26]

Apperception is a state of awareness. It is possible for perceptions to occur in the mind *without* apperception, that is, it is possible for there to be unconscious perceptions, "small perceptions in which nothing is distinct" (*Monadology* §21). Indeed, there are such in a state of deep sleep. This is a point Descartes seemed to deny and which Leibniz considers one of the major shortcomings of the Cartesian philosophy (*Monadology* § 14).

Knowledge is *not* identical with mere apperception or awareness. True reasoning requires knowledge of eternal truths. As Leibniz notes:

> But *true reasoning* depends on necessary or eternal truths, such as those of logic, numbers, and geometry, which bring about an indubitable connection of ideas and infallible consequences. Animals in which these consequences are not noticed are called *beasts*; but those who know these necessary truths are those that are properly called *rational animals*, and their souls are called minds. These souls are capable of performing reflective acts, and capable of considering what is called "I", substance, soul, mind—in brief, immaterial things and immaterial truths. And that is what makes us capable of the sciences or of demonstrative knowledge. (*Principles of Nature and Grace*, §5)

Animals are capable of memory, but they do no have knowledge of causes. Knowledge of causes requires knowledge of eternal truths. These eternal truths are innate in some minds, namely, the minds of rational animals. Leibniz seems to hold—as did Descartes—that innate ideas are dispositions to form ideas with a certain content on specifiable occasions.[27] Among these innate ideas are ideas of eternal truths. These are causal laws specifying that if one event occurs, then another event *must* occur. By understanding an object of apperception within its causal context—by seeing that an object *must* exist given the existence of some other object—one obtains knowledge.

If one looks at the problem of perception in Leibniz's system, one finds that the apperception of an object by itself provides little reason for claiming the existence of that thing as something over and above a mere object of awareness. Indeed, one might suggest that Leibniz's position is a bit unusual. As we noted above, Leibniz's monads are "windowless," that is, there are no causal relations among monads. There is a "harmony of nature," that is, God sets up the entire system of monads in such a way that they *appear* to be causally related to one another, while each actually develops in terms of its own rule. Leibniz claims that a monad is like a seed insofar as, like the development of a plant from a seed, the unfolding of the various stages of a monad are "preprogrammed" (*Principles of Nature and Grace*, §6). A more modern analogy would be to a movie or video tape. If you watch a movie, every "event" is already contained on the reel; it's just a matter of the "plot unwinding" as the movie is shown. Do the characters in the movie cause events to happen? As they are seen, they do not: the "characters" are merely images on celluloid. Nonetheless, the characters are seen *as if* they are causally interacting: you can causally describe the relations among the characters in the film. If Piggy, in *Lord of the Flies*, is hit with a rock, you will predict that he will act as if he is injured (as he does). In Leibniz's case, one discovers causal laws by means of reasoning about the occurrences one apperceives. It is by such reasoning that one becomes aware of eternal truths (including causal laws), and it is by understanding these appearances in terms of causal laws that one comes to know that various objects exist.

So, in Leibniz's case, perceptual awareness alone provides little evidence regarding the existence of the world. Indeed, Leibniz's world could be understood as a large collection of movies—each shot from the perspective of each thing or person in the world—each independent of all the others, although set up in such a way that things appear to causally interact. Perceptual awareness (apperception) alone does *not* tell you how the world is. It is only by discovering the causal laws (necessary and eternal truths) that obtain among the objects in one's appearances that one has grounds for claiming the existence of "ordinary things."

John Locke (1632-1704)

John Locke was the first of three famous British **empiricists**. An empiricist is a philosopher who holds that all ideas (concepts) are derived from sense experience. Unlike Leibniz and Descartes, who maintained that the mind contains "innate ideas" in the sense that the mind is preprogrammed to form certain ideas, for example, the idea of God, and that there are certain eternal truths that are somehow preexistent in the mind,[28] Locke held that while the mind is capable of forming any ideas it actually does form,[29] prior to experience, the mind is a blank tablet (*tabula rasa*).

Locke was born in Wrington, Somerset, on Aug. 29, 1632. The son of a moderate puritan, he was educated at Christ Church, Oxford, where his initial studies were in philosophy and classics, although he had considerable interest in physics and medicine. To avoid taking holy orders—as was customary at the time—he changed his object of study to medicine, in which he received a bachelor's degree in 1674. Locke was a friend of the chemist Robert Boyle and did rounds with the great British empirical physician Thomas Sydenham. Locke devoted much of his life to work the with Anthony Ashley Cooper, 1st Earl of Shaftesbury. Shaftesbury was involved in both colonial affairs—he was one of the proprietors of the Carolinas—and the British government. This was the period of the restoration; Charles II was king. Shaftesbury opposed the Catholic succession, and was involved in various activities that ultimately led to the Glorious Revolution of 1688, although Shaftesbury himself died in 1680. Both for reasons of health—Locke had chronic asthma—and political safety, Locke spent a number of years on the continent, in France and Holland. While in Holland in the 1680s, Locke completed his *Essay concerning Human Understanding*, which was published anonymously in 1690, as was his *Two Treatises of Government*. From his return to England in 1689 until his death in 1704, Locke held various government posts and wrote on topics ranging from epistemology to education to religion.

The *Essay* is Locke's principal work in epistemology, a work that went through four editions during Locke's lifetime.[30] The structure of the *Essay* is quite straightforward. Locke begins with a criticism of the doctrine of innate ideas. *Some* proponents of innate ideas held that innateness is the mark of truth. Lord Herbert of Cherbury was one such, and is the only proponent of innate knowledge Locke mentions by name (see *Essay* 1.3.15). Locke argued on empirical grounds that there are no innate ideas of either speculative principles such as "It is impossible for something to both be and not be at that same time" or moral principles, since there is no agreement among all persons of their truth. The same holds for ideas such as the idea of God. Since there is no agreement among all persons regarding the truth of such propositions or the components of ideas, there is at least good reason to believe that there are no innate ideas. The remainder of the *Essay* is devoted to showing that everything that allegedly can be known on the hypothesis of innate ideas can be known without that hypothesis, that is, on the basis of an empiricist hypothesis, so, since the empiricist hypothesis is simpler—even the most ardent devotee of innate ideas held that *some* ideas are derived from experience—his empiricist hypothesis is more probably true.

In Book II of the *Essay* Locke concerns himself with the origin of ideas. All *simple* ideas are derived from sense experience or experience of the states of one's mind (reflection). By sight one obtains simple ideas of color, shape, extension, and motion. By touch one obtains simple ideas of extension, texture, and motion. Aromas are known by the sense of smell, flavors by taste, and sounds by hearing. One is similarly aware of the several kinds of mental states—perceiving, remembering, imagining, and the various emotions, for example. By combining and rearranging these ideas, one can form complex ideas of those things of which one has not been aware in experience or reflection. For example, although I have never seen a fuscia-colored computer, I can imagine what one would look like by recombining simple ideas I have had on other occasions to form the idea of a fuscia-colored computer.

Like Descartes, Locke accepted a representative theory of perception: ideas are mental states and some of them represent objects in the world. Ideas represent objects on the basis of resemblance or similarity. Not all ideas of objects resemble the objects themselves, however. Recall that Descartes claimed that only geometric properties represent material objects as such; colors, heat and cold, sounds, flavors, and so forth are not found in material objects as such, rather, it is on the basis of the geometric properties of material objects that one's ideas of color and so forth are causally explained. Locke drew a similar distinction, although, unlike Descartes, he did not he did not emphasize geometric properties. The **primary qualities** of objects are those qualities in virtue of which an object is a material object. The primary qualities are solidity, extension, figure, and mobility (*Essay* 2.8.9), to which list he sometimes adds texture (*Essay* 2.8.14), bulk, and number (*Essay* 2.8.17). All material objects of any size, including material atoms or **corpuscles**, possess the first four qualities; combinations of corpuscles possess all seven qualities. The ideas of primary qualities resemble "Patterns [that] do really exist in the Bodies themselves" (*Essay* 2.8.14, p. 137). In contrast to the primary qualities are **secondary qualities**, which include colors, heat and cold, sounds, flavors, and so forth. Ideas of secondary qualities do *not* resemble properties in the objects themselves; rather, they are caused by combinations of objects having only the primary qualities (*Essay* 2.8.10). Objects having a certain texture reflect certain light rays and absorb others, and, given the way our senses operate, we see an object as red, even though the "redness" of the object *as such* is nothing more than a power to produce a certain idea in us.

Locke was an empiricist; he held that all knowledge of objects is based upon experience. So, when he talks about knowledge of kinds of ordinary objects (kinds of substances), he maintains this can be known only by experience. Consider a substance such as gold. When one was a child, one might have held that it was a shiny, heavy, yellow, metal. These are the ideas that came together to form your idea of gold. As you grew older, you might have added ideas of additional properties to your idea. You might now characterize gold as a shiny, heavy, yellow, metal that is malleable and fusible. If you're a chemist, you might add certain chemical properties. If you're a fan of the commodities market, you might add that it's "costly" (about $280 per ounce as of this writing). Your idea of gold as a kind of thing and mine might not be the same. Each of our ideas provides the basis on which we name something "gold;" each of our ideas is what Locke calls a **nominal essence** or an **abstract idea**. An **essence** is that in virtue of which something is a thing of a certain kind.[31] The nominal essence of a thing is *only* an idea used to classify a thing as a thing of a certain kind. Locke contrasts this with the **real essence** of a thing. The real essence of a material object consists of the arrangement of corpuscles that causes one to perceive those ideas one actually perceives. Locke was skeptical about the ability to have knowledge of the real essences of particular kinds of material objects. He contended that even if one were able to develop microscopes powerful enough to perceive the surface characteristics of material objects, there would be no way to know that the properties one perceives are the most fundamental properties of an object of a kind.

Locke contrasts ideas of kinds of substances with ideas of kinds of modes. A mode is a property of a thing or action. While ideas of substance are taken to represent objects—objects that are generally assumed to exist (although the idea of unicorn would be an exception)—ideas of modes need not represent things we assume to exist as represented. On the one hand, there are ideas of the secondary qualities, which do not resemble their causes, although in some sense they might represent their causes. On the other hand there are ideas of mathematical objects, such as triangles, which are generally not taken to represent ordinary objects. Triangles have whatever properties they have necessarily: the properties of a triangle follow with necessity (deductively) from the definitions and postulates of Euclid. Similarly, Locke claimed that ideas of mixed modes—ideas that provide the meaning of terms in ethics, law, politics, and so forth—represent nothing apart from themselves. So, as in the case of mathematics, conclusions in areas such as ethics and law are merely a matter of what follows from the ideas (terms) used. Returning to the language of real and nominal essences, the idea of a mode is both the real and nominal essence of the kind of thing in question.

So far, this really tells us little about what exists. Locke's ideas of substances are merely a means of classifying objects. In the case of ideas of modes, nothing is assumed to exist apart from one's ideas or concepts. What exists, and how does one know that which exists?

Locke defined 'knowledge' as "*the perception of the connexion and agreement, or disagreement and repugnancy* [inconsistency] *of any of our Ideas*" (*Essay* 4.1.2, p. 525). The "connections" with which he is concerned are conceptual connections, that is, deductively necessary connections. For example, from the concept of gold as a shiny, heavy, yellow, metal, it follows that gold is yellow.[32] Similarly, if I perceive something that is gray, dull, heavy, and metallic, I can know that it is *not* gold, since the grayness and dullness are *inconsistent with* my idea of gold, that is, the statement, "This substance is both shiny and yellow all over and dull and gray all over" is a contradiction, it is impossible that the statement is true. In the case of knowledge of modes, it is a matter of deduction: anything that is true of the mode follows with necessity (deductively) from the idea (concept), and any claim that does not follow deductively from the idea (concept) is false of the mode. Still, this does not tell us what exists.

Locke distinguished between one's knowledge of one's own existence, one's knowledge of God's existence, and one's knowledge the existence of ordinary objects. He claimed that one has intuitive (immediate) knowledge of the existence of ideas in one's own mind and of one's own existence. Like Descartes, Locke seemed to hold that there is a contradiction in claiming, "I think, but I don't exist." He claimed one has demonstrative knowledge of the existence of God, that is, the existence of God follows by a deductive argument from principles that are necessarily true (whose denial is a contradiction). His argument in *Essay* 4.10.2 goes like this:

> ... Man knows by an intuitive Certainty, that *bare nothing can no more produce any real Being, than it can be equal to two right Angles*. If a Man knows not that Non-entity, or the absence of all Being, cannot be equal to two right Angles, it is impossible he should know any demonstration in *Euclid*. If therefore we know there is some real Being, and that Non-entity cannot produce any real Being, it is

an evident demonstration, that from Eternity there has been something; Since what was not from Eternity had a Beginning; and what had a Beginning, must be produced by something else.

The proof rests on the assumption that there cannot be an infinite series of causes of a thing that now exists—which is questionable.

Knowledge of the material world is had by sensation. "... no particular Man can know the *Existence* of any other Being [than God], but only when by actual operating upon him, it makes it self perceived by him. For the having the *Idea* of any thing in our Mind, no more proves the Existence of that Thing, than the picture of a Man evidences his being in the World, or the Visions of a Dream make thereby a true History" (*Essay* 4.11.2, p. 630). How does perception differ from mere thought? If I think of an angry dog, this does not provide reason for me to believe that there is an angry dog corresponding to my idea—I've dreamed of angry dogs or imagined angry dogs when there were none. How does perception differ? In the case of perception, the idea one has (in seeing a dog, for example) is caused by something outside of oneself. Locke held that there is a necessary connection between cause and effect, so it is possible to pick out an object as the cause of an idea. He also held that, in the case of primary, but not secondary qualities, there is a resemblance between the idea and the object it represents. Ideas of sensation are taken to be caused by external (material) objects. So, the issues are: (1) Why should I believe that the ideas of sensation are caused by and represent external objects? (2) How can I distinguish ideas of sensation from other kinds of ideas?

Locke's answer to the first question—not unlike Descartes's—rests upon God's goodness. Locke writes, "As to myself, I think GOD has given me assurance enough of the Existence of Things without me: since by their different application I can produce in myself both Pleasure and Pain, which is one great Concernment of my present state. This is certain, the confidence that our Faculties do not herein deceive us is the greatest assurance we are capable of, concerning the Existence of material beings" (*Essay* 4.11.3, p. 631). He then goes on and to give four grounds for claiming that the ideas of sensation are caused by external objects:

First, 'Tis plain those Perceptions are produced in us by exterior Causes affecting our Senses: Because *those that want the Organs of any Sense, never can have the* Ideas *belonging to that Sense* produced in their Minds. This is too evident to be doubted: And therefore we cannot but be assured, that they come in by the Organs of that Sense, and no other way. (*Essay* 4.11.4)

Secondly, Because *sometimes I find that I cannot avoid the having those* Ideas *produced in my Mind.* For though when my Eyes are shut, or Windows fast, I can at Pleasure re-call to my Mind the *Ideas* of *Light*, or the *Sun*, which former Sensations had lodg'd in my Memory; so I can at pleasure lay by that *Idea*, and take into my view that of the *smell* of a Rose, or *taste* of Sugar. But, if I turn my Eyes at noon towards the Sun, I cannot avoid the *Ideas*, which the Light, or Sun, then produces in me. So that there is a manifest difference between the *Ideas* laid up in my Memory; (over which, if they were there only, I should have constantly the same power to dispose of them, and lay them by at pleasure) and those which force themselves upon me, and I cannot avoid having. And therefore it must needs be some exteriour cause, and the brisk acting of some Objects without me, whose efficacy I cannot resist, that produces those *Ideas* in my Mind, whether I will, or no. (*Essay* 4.11.5, p. 632)

Thirdly, Add to this, *that many of those* Ideas *are produced in us with pain, which afterwards we remember without the least offence.* (*Essay* 4.11.6, p. 633)

Fourthly, our *Senses* in many cases bear *witness* to the Truth of each other's report, concerning the Existence of sensible Things without us. He that sees a *Fire*, may, if he doubt whether it be any thing more than a bare Fancy, feel it too; and be convinced by putting his Hand in it. (*Essay* 4.11.7)

Some evidence that the ideas of sensation are caused by external material objects is provided by the fact that those lacking an organ of sense—those who are blind or deaf, for example—do not have ideas of the requisite types. Further evidence is provided by the fact that the mind is passive in perception. There is some kind of mental activity involved in forming ideas of the memory and imagination—one recognizes that there is some kind of mental effort involved in forming the requisite ideas—but this activity is not found in forming an idea of sensation. On a sunny day, all I need do is open my eyes to see the sun; indeed, I cannot prevent myself from seeing the sun *unless* I close my eyes. Third, if I see myself stepping on a nail, I feel a sensation of pain; I do not have the same kind of sensation if I remember stepping on a nail—even if I remember the pain, there is not the same intensity as I experienced when I stepped on the nail. Similarly, if I dream that I am on fire, there are not the sensations of pain that accompany actually being on fire (*Essay* 4.2.15). Finally, there is a coherence among one's several senses: I not only see the fire, I feel the fire's heat. Notice that the first two considerations tend to provide evidence that there are external causes of ideas of sensation. The second and third provide a basis for distinguishing ideas of sensation from ideas of other kinds. The fourth tends to support the claim that ideas of sensation represent existent, external things.

Locke recognized that the evidence for the existence of external objects provided by the senses is weaker than that either for his own existence or for the existence of God. Regarding the existence of any particular object, it is possible that one is deceived. The existence of an external world, or any object in the external world, is merely *probable*, rather than certain.

What is one to make of Locke's position? Given that Locke held there is a necessary connection between cause and effect, the existence of the effect (the idea of sensation) is sufficient to show that there is *some* cause of the idea. Given his primary/secondary qualities distinction, there is reason to believe that *some* of the qualities in the ideas of sensation resemble the qualities in the idea, for example, there is a resemblance between the idea of extension and the extension in the object, although there is no such resemblance between the color in the idea and the object. All this *assumes* that there is a distinction between and idea and the object perceived. The idea of sensation is taken to represent an object in much the way a photograph represents its object. It *assumes* that one does not perceive physical objects directly, that is, it rejects what ordinary people assume all the time. Ordinarily, if someone asks me why I believe there is a desk in front of me, I respond, "I see it"; I don't say, "I am immediately aware of an idea which is caused by and resembles a desk."

In the next two sections, we shall examine Berkeley, who rejects the representative thesis while retaining the causal thesis, and Hume, who raises doubts regarding the claim that there is a necessary connection between cause and effect, thereby casting doubt on the claim that perception can provide any grounds for claiming the existence of *anything* beyond the domain of perception.

George Berkeley (1685-1753)

George Berkeley was born on March 12, 1685 near Kilkenny, Ireland. He was educated at Trinity College, Dublin. His first book, *An Essay towards a New Theory of Vision* was published in 1709. His *Principles of Human Knowledge* was published in 1710, and a popularized version of his doctrine, *Three Dialogues between Hylas and Philonous*, was published in 1713. Berkeley as ordained as an Anglican minister in 1710. He taught philosophy for a time at Trinity College. In 1728, he left for America, intending to establish a college for children of colonists and Native Americans in Bermuda. He never went to Bermuda, rather, he spent four years near Newport, Rhode Island—the house he built, Whitehall, is still in existence. When it became clear that the promised funds for his college would not be forthcoming, he returned to England in 1732. He was ordained an Anglican bishop in 1734, and lived the last years of his life in Cloyne, Ireland. He retired in 1752 and moved to Oxford, ostensibly to supervise the education of his son George. He died on January 17, 1753 and is buried in Oxford.

Berkeley claimed to be a defender of religion and common sense. One element of common sense that he defended was the contention that what one perceives immediately—which he called ideas or objects of knowledge[33]—exists. In one respect this is not odd: all his predecessors had held that ideas exist as modes of minds. Berkeley, however, identified collections of ideas with ordinary objects and argued that the notion of matter is unintelligible, so there is no reason to introduce matter into one's philosophical theory. Ideas depend for their existence on minds, so ordinary objects, as collections of ideas, also depend for their existence on minds. Insofar as only the only things that exist are minds and things that depend for their existence on minds, Berkeley was an **idealist**. Insofar Berkeley identified ordinary objects—tables, chairs, deer, and so forth—with collections of ideas, he was a **phenomenalist**.[34] In what follows, I sketch Berkeley's defense of his position in the opening sections of the *Principles of Human Knowledge*, Part I.[35] My approach to Berkeley will be epistemic—in terms of a theory of knowledge—over which an ontology—an account of the nature of reality—is laid.[36]

Berkeley begins the *Principles* by saying, "It is evident to any one who takes a survey of the objects of human knowledge, that they are either ideas actually imprinted on the senses, or else such as are perceived by attending to the passions and operations of the mind, or lastly ideas formed by help of memory and imagination, either compounding, dividing, or barely representing those originally perceived in the aforesaid ways" (*PHK* §1). This suggests that Berkeley, like Descartes (*CSM* 2:26), distinguished between ideas as modes of a mind and ideas as things known (as having a certain cognitive content). The opening suggests that he is concerned with the latter, as does his remark later in the section that "a certain colour, taste, smell, figure and consistence having been observed to go together, are accounted one distinct thing, signified by the name *apple*. Other collections of ideas constitute a stone, a tree, a book, and the like sensible things" (*PHK* §1). In claiming that collections of ideas *constitute* things, one is reminded of Locke's accounts of the ideas of substance and nominal essence, which are conceptual or epistemic constructs, that is, they reflect what we know a thing to be on the basis of the ideas of which we are aware in experience. Taken as an epistemic claim, the identification of objects with collections of ideas is reasonable; taken as a claim regarding the nature of objects it is, dubious at best—especially since Berkeley provides no argument in support of the claim.

If there are ideas as things known, then there also must be something that knows or perceives them, which Berkeley calls "*mind, spirit, soul* or *my self* . . . for the existence of an idea consists in being perceived" (*PHK* §2). The existence of a sensible object is to be perceived, or as Berkeley famously says, its *esse is percipi* (*PHK* §3). The word 'perceive' has several meanings. It can be understood as the relation between a mind and an object in sense perception. It can be understood as the relation of inherence between an idea (as a mode) and a mental substance. And it can be understood as synonymous with 'to know'. We shall understand it in this final sense. There are several reasons for this. (1) It is consistent with Berkeley's original introduction of ideas as objects of human knowledge. (2) There are several places where Berkeley uses forms of 'know' and 'perceive' as synonymous (see, for example, *PHK* § §2 and 6). (3) In *PHK* §49 he writes, "those qualities are in the mind only as they are perceived by it, that is, not by way or *mode* or *attribute*, but only by way of *idea*," a claim that makes little sense if one identifies ideas with modes and perception with inherence in a substance.

Things become interesting in Section 4, where Berkeley argues that the common view that "houses, mountains, rivers, and in a word all sensible objects have an existence natural or real, distinct from being perceived" is not merely false but self-contradictory. As he writes:

> whoever shall find in his heart to call it in question, may, if I mistake not, perceive it to involve a manifest contradiction. For what are the forementioned objects but the things we perceive by sense, and what do we perceive besides our own ideas or sensations; and is it not plainly repugnant that any one of these or any combination of them should exist unperceived? (*PHK* §4)

If we take the word 'idea' to be shorthand for 'object of human knowledge,' we may restate Berkeley's argument as follows:

    (1)   All ordinary objects (mountains, etc.), if known, are objects known by sense.

    (2)   All objects known by sense are objects of human knowledge.

    (3)   So all ordinary objects, if known, are objects of human knowledge.

    (4)   No objects of human knowledge can exist unknown.

    (5)   So, no ordinary objects, if known, can exist unknown.

    (6)   According to the common view, some ordinary objects, (even) if known, can exist unknown.

    (7)   The common view expressed in (6) is inconsistent with (5).

    (8)   Therefore, the common view is "a manifest contradiction," "plainly repugnant."

Contradictions describe impossible situations. So, if the common description of houses, mountains, rivers, etc., as things that can exist unperceived (unknown) is self-contradictory, then it is impossible for such objects so to exist. Hence, *esse is percipi* must be true. But as *we* are reading Berkeley, this is only an epistemic claim: it is impossible for something to be known and unknown at the same time.

After noting that "From what has been said, it follows, there is not any other substance than *spirit*, or that which perceives" (*PHK* §7), Berkeley introduces his likeness principle, the principle that only an idea can be like an idea. His argument is as follows:

> If we look but ever so little into our thoughts, we shall find it impossible for us to conceive a likeness except only between our ideas. Again, I ask whether those supposed originals or external things, of which our ideas are the pictures or representations, be themselves perceivable or no? If they are, then they are ideas, and we have gained our point; but if you say they are not, I appeal to any one whether it be sense, to assert a colour is like something which is invisible; hard or soft, like something which is intangible; and so of the rest. (*PHK* §8)

The gist of Berkeley's argument is that there is no evidence, or anything that could count as evidence, that an idea can be similar to or resemble anything that is not an idea. The only things of which we are aware are ideas. If external objects are composed of ideas, there is no problem. If external objects are composed of something distinct from ideas, there is no way to make a comparison. So, if we are concerned with ideas as objects of knowledge, we cannot know that there are resemblances between ideas and things that are not objects, so there is no reason to assume that there are such resemblances.[37]

The likeness principle is introduced, at least in part, to provide a piece of conceptual ammunition in arguing against the primary/secondary qualities distinction. Berkeley attacks that distinction and the traditional theory of material substance to show that there are no grounds for claiming that there are *material* objects. If one accepts the likeness principle, there is no ground for claiming that the primary qualities *resemble* qualities in ordinary objects. Further, he argues that, as a matter of fact, one cannot form an idea of visual extension, for example, without also forming an idea of color—one recognizes the limits of a piece of visual extension only on the basis of a change in color—and since color is granted to exist only in the mind, extension must also so exist (*PHK* §10). So, there is no reason to accept the existence of *material* objects as described by the primary/secondary qualities distinction. But there is an older theory of material substance that takes substance to be a substratum that "lies under" the qualities one perceives. In considering that account of substance, Berkeley argues: (1) one cannot form an idea of such a substance (*PHK* §§ 16-17), (2) material substance has no explanatory value (*PHK* §§ 18-20), and (3) it is impossible to so much as conceive of the possibility that objects exist unperceived (unknown, *PHK* §§22-23). If there are no grounds for knowing material substance, there is no reason to assume such things exist. Assuming that all substances are either material or immaterial (spiritual, mental), only immaterial substances exist.

Berkeley continues by arguing that only spiritual substances can be causes. He starts by arguing that ideas cannot be causes. "All our ideas, sensations, or the things which we perceive, by whatsoever names they may be distinguished, are visibly inactive, there is nothing of power or agency included in them. So that one idea or object of thought cannot produce, or make any alteration in another" (*PHK* §25). But since we perceive a continual succession of ideas, there must be a cause of them. Since this cannot be any idea or combination of ideas, and since it cannot be a material substance—since there are no grounds for admitting material substance into one's philosophical theory—it must be an immaterial or spiritual substance (*PHK* §26). "A spirit is one simple, undivided, active being: as it perceives ideas, it is called the understanding, and as it produces or otherwise operates about them, it is called the will. Hence there can be no idea formed of a soul or spirit: for all ideas whatever, being passive and inert, *vide Sect*. 25, they cannot represent unto us, by way of image or likeness, that which acts. . . . Such is the nature of *spirit* or that which acts, that it cannot be of it self perceived, but only by the effects which it produceth" (*PHK* §27).

Berkeley concludes the opening sections of the *Principles* by providing a brief argument for the existence of God and the basis of distinctions between ideas of sensation and ideas of the imagination, and between real things and imaginary things. His argument for the existence of God is quite straightforward. I am aware that I am not the cause of all the ideas of which I am aware. "When in broad day-light I open my eyes, it is not in my power to choose whether I shall see or no, or to determine what particular objects shall present themselves to my view; and so likewise as to the hearing and other senses, the ideas imprinted on them are not creatures of my will. There is therefore some other will or spirit that produces them" (*PHK* §29). This *has to be a spirit*, since only spirits can be causes, and Berkeley's various remarks suggest that only God is the cause of those ideas we do not cause ourselves. Notice that this appeal to the passivity of the mind in sense perception parallels one of Locke's grounds for claiming the existence of material objects (*Essay* 4.11.5). Like Locke, Berkeley held that the immediate objects of knowledge are ideas. Unlike Locke, however, he held that there are no grounds for claiming the existence of material objects as things distinct from ideas: the theory of materiality cannot be made cogent and nothing can be like an idea except an idea. Like Locke, Berkeley held that at least some ideas do not resemble their causes—and he argued that *no* ideas can resemble their causes, since only a spirit can be a cause and there can be no ideas of spirits. So, Berkeley has taken the basis for one of Locke's arguments for the existence of material objects—the passivity of perception—and used it as the basis for an argument for something that is *not* a material entity, namely, God.

In Sections 30-33, Berkeley distinguishes between ideas of the imagination and ideas of sense. "The ideas of sense are more strong, lively, and distinct than those of the imagination; they have likewise a steadiness, order, and coherence, and are not excited at random, as those which are the effects of human wills often are, but in a regular train or series, the admirable connexion whereof sufficiently testifies the wisdom and benevolence of its Author" (*PHK* §30). On the basis of ideas of sense, one can make predictions regarding what one will see at some point in the future. They follow *laws of nature*, that is, the constant patterns by which God causes ideas in us (*PHK* §§30 & 62). These laws concern, among other things, the ways in which the ideas of the several senses are coordinated in experience. So while the Locke of *Essay* 4.11.7 takes the "agreement" of the senses as a mark of the material objects that cause them, Berkeley can argue that this is nothing more than the lawful correlation of ideas. And just as Locke can claim that knowledge based upon ideas of sensation is sufficient for our needs as humans (*Essay* 4.11.3 & 8), Berkeley notes, "This gives us a sort of foresight, which enables us to regulate our actions for the benefit of life. And without this we should be eternally at a loss: we could not know how to act any thing that might procure us the least pleasure, or remove the least pain of sense" (*PHK* §31). Finally, while Locke's ideas of sensation supposedly provide us with knowledge of real things that cause the ideas and resemble them, in Berkeley's case the ideas themselves are real things. As he writes:

> The ideas imprinted on the senses by the Author of Nature are called *real things*: and those excited in the imagination being less regular, vivid and constant, are more properly termed *ideas*, or *images of things*, which they copy and represent. But then our sensations, be they never so vivid and distinct, are nevertheless ideas, that is, they exist in the mind, or are perceived by it, as truly as the ideas of its own framing. The ideas of sense are allowed to have more reality in them, that is, to be more strong, orderly, and coherent than the creatures of the mind; but this is no argument that they exist without the mind. They are also less dependent on the spirit, or thinking substance which perceives them, in that they are excited by the will of another and more powerful spirit: yet still they are *ideas*, and certainly no *idea*, whether faint or strong, can exist otherwise than in a mind perceiving it. (*PHK* 33)

For Berkeley, the objects of perception are nothing other than ideas. Ordinary objects are nothing but combinations of ideas. There is no "veil of perception," there is nothing "outside" that is represented by the ideas. The common sense view that what we immediately perceive are real things is upheld—but at the price of sacrificing what seems to be a common sense view that there is a distinction between things in the mind and objects.

In summary, Berkeley identifies ideas with objects of knowledge. This sets up a distinction between the thing known (the idea) and the knower (the mind or spirit). For an idea of sense, to be is to be perceived, that is, the object of knowledge and the object perceived by sense are one and the same. Do these ideas represent objects that are not ideas? Berkeley's likeness principle claims that since there is no way to know that they represent objects that are not ideas, there are no grounds for claiming that they represent nonideas. The various versions of the theory of material objects are examined and found wanting: there is no reason to accept any of them, since they cannot be made intelligible and they cannot explain the phenomena perceived by sense. All the eighteenth century proponents of material substance took the existence of God as given. God allows Berkeley to explain the origin of those ideas he does not himself cause. Berkeley's theory explains everything that could be explained by the eighteenth century proponents of material substance *without* introducing material substance. Berkeley's theory is simpler. Assuming that the simplest theory is most probably true—that "God does nothing in vain," as it was often said at the time—there is good reason to believe that the world is as it is known, that is, that ordinary objects are nothing but collections of ideas and that the only substances are minds (spirits).

David Hume (1711-1776)

David Hume was born in Edinburgh, Scotland on April 26, 1711 (according to the Julian calendar). He was educated at the University of Edinburgh and engaged in independent research in France in the middle 1730s. His *Treatise of Human Nature* was published in three books in 1739 and 1740. The main doctrines of the *Treatise* were revised for popular consumption and published as *An Enquiry* [originally *Essays*] *concerning Human Understanding* and *An Enquiry concerning the Principles of Morals* in 1748 and 1752. He was most noted in his own time for his *History of England*. Hume never held an academic position. As the second son of a Scottish landholder, he received an allowance of £50 per year and supplemented that with jobs including librarian for the Advocates Library in Edinburgh and chargé d'affaires at the British embassy in Paris. He died in August 1776 after wishing his friend Benjamin Franklin and the colonists well on their revolution.

Hume was a skeptic: he held that the domain of knowledge is very limited. He is most noted for his attack on the assumption that there are objective necessary connections among objects causally related to one another. We will look briefly at Hume's distinction between impressions and ideas and his critical examination of causation before turning to the implications of that critique on the possibility of knowledge based on sense perception.

Hume was clearly in the Lockean empirical tradition. He drew a distinction, however, that is not found in Locke. Hume begins the *Treatise* with these words:

> All the perceptions of the human mind resolve themselves into two distinct kinds, which I shall call IMPRESSIONS and IDEAS. The difference betwixt these consists in the degrees of force and liveliness, with which they strike upon the mind, and make their way into our thought or consciousness. Those perceptions which enter with most force and violence, we may name *impressions*; and, under this name, I comprehend all our sensations, passions, and emotions, as they make their first appearance in the soul. By *ideas*, I mean the faint images of these in thinking and reasoning; such as, for instance, are all the perceptions excited by the present discourse, excepting only those which arise from the sight and touch, and excepting the immediate pleasure or uneasiness it may occasion.[38]

Like Locke, he distinguished between perceptions (impressions and ideas) of sensation and perceptions of reflection, the latter pertaining to states of the mind and emotions. Like Locke, he distinguished between simple and complex ideas, contending that all simple ideas are in their first instances caused by and perfect copies of simple impressions. His arguments for this consist of an appeal to the seeming fact that one can always trace one's simple ideas back to simple impressions—together with a challenge to find an exception—and the fact that persons with defective organs of sense do not have the ideas corresponding to those organs of sense.[39] This copy theory of ideas is taken to be a contingent truth (a factual claim), *not* a necessary truth, as is shown by Hume's claim that it is possible to imagine a situation that would constitute an exception to the principle (see *T*, pp. 5-6, *EHU*, pp. 20-21).

Hume claimed that "All objects of human reason or inquiry may naturally be divided into two kinds, to wit, *Relations of Ideas*, and *Matters of Fact*" (*EHU*, p. 25). In the domain of relations of ideas one finds all the truths of mathematics. The truths of mathematics, for example, cannot be denied without resulting in a contradiction. In the case of matters of fact, the denial of a claim does *not* result in a contradiction. Many of our beliefs in the factual domain are based on causal reasoning. How are causal relations known? On the basis of experience. As he wrote:

> I shall venture to affirm, as a general proposition, which admits of no exception, that the knowledge of this relation is not, in any instance, attained by reasonings *a priori*; but arises entirely from experience, when we find, that any particular objects are constantly conjoined with each other. Let an object be presented to a man of ever so strong natural reason and abilities; if that object be entirely new to him, he will not be able, by the most accurate examination of its sensible qualities, to discover any of its causes or effects. Adam, though his rational faculties be supposed, at the very first, entirely perfect, could not have inferred from the fluidity, and transparency of water, that it would suffocate him, or from the light and warmth of fire, that it would consume him. No object ever discovers, by the qualities which appear to the senses, either the causes which produced it, or the effects which will arise from it; nor can our reason, unassisted by experience, ever draw any inference concerning real existence and matter of fact. (*EHU*, p. 27)

If causal relations were known *a priori*, apart from experience, then one would be able to infer what effect would occur by considering nothing more than the cause. This cannot be done. "The mind can never possibly find the effect in the supposed cause, by the most accurate scrutiny and examination. For the effect is totally different from the cause, and consequently can never be discovered in it" (*EHU*, p. 29). If, as was held from at least the Middle Ages, a cause is something distinct from its effect, then it is impossible to infer the effect given nothing more than the cause. To understand this, contrast the case of mathematical truths. The statement "2+2 = 4" is true and necessary. It would be a contraction to claim that the addition of two things to two other things results in anything other than four things. Anything that represents two plus two things also represents four things: the expression "2+2" means the same thing as the expression "4." The same cannot be said about causal claims. I might be very certain that if the cue ball on a pool table rolls toward and hits the 8-ball, the 8-ball will roll away. But while I cannot so much as imagine what it would be like for the addition to two things and two other things to be equal to anything other than four things, I have no trouble imagining that the course of nature would change. When the cue ball hits the 8-ball, I can imagine that the 8-ball would divide in two and the cue ball would continue on its merry way; I can imagine that the 8-ball would turn into a brass band, or that the room would undergo a change of color, or that the world would end, or . . . Assuming that whatever is imaginable is possible, anything could happen when the cue ball hits the 8-ball. So, knowledge of causal relations is not *a priori*; there are no necessary connections between a cause and its effect. Causal relations are known only on the basis of experience.

But don't we know by experience that if the 8-ball has always rolled away when hit by the cue ball in the past, that the 8-ball will roll away the next time that it is hit by the cue ball? This is an *inductive* inference. It rests upon what is sometimes called the **Principle of the Uniformity of Nature**, the principle that causal relations in the future will resemble (be of the same kinds as) causal relations that have held in the past. Given this principle, we can construct a nice deductive argument:

> All times in the past are times when the cue ball hitting the 8-ball caused the 8-ball to roll away.

> All causal relations in the future are causal relations that have held at all times in the past.

> All times in the future are times when the cue ball hitting the 8-ball will cause the 8-ball to roll away.

Is the second premise—the principle of the uniformity of nature—true? Perhaps. Can one know that it is true? You cannot know that it is true *a priori*, since you can imagine a case in which the principle does not hold. You cannot know it *a posteriori*, that is, from experience, because all reasoning from experience *assumes* that the principle of the uniformity of nature is true: any argument from experience **begs the question**, that is, it assumes what it sets out to prove (*EHU*, pp. 35-36).[40] Everything that is known is either known *a priori* (by relations of ideas) or *a posteriori* (from experience). The principle of the uniformity of nature cannot be known in either way. So, there is no way to *know* that the principle of the uniformity of nature is true. Hence, properly speaking, there is no knowledge of future causal relations.

Yet "It is certain that the most ignorant and stupid peasants—nay infants, nay even brute beasts—improve by experience, and learn the qualities of natural objects, by observing the effects which result from them" (*EHU*, p. 39). Hume's answer to his skeptical problem—his "skeptical solution" to the doubts—is that human beings develop habits of expectation. If I have seen the normal relation between a moving cue ball and an 8-ball several times, I will come to expect the 8-ball to behave as it has in the past—if asked "What will happen next?" when seeing a video of a cue ball crashing into an 8-ball, I'll answer, "Why the 8-ball will roll away, of course." Of course, such *habits* do not constitute knowledge. Psychological habits may explain why peasants, infants, and the rest of us actually make the causal inferences we make, but they do not allow us any advance in knowledge.

What is the impact of Hume's skepticism regarding causal relations on claims of perceptual knowledge? Hume provides a general summary early in his discussion of causation in the *Treatise*. Where an impression is taken as what is immediately given in sense experience, he notes:

> As to those *impressions*, which arise from the *senses*, their ultimate cause is, in my opinion, perfectly inexplicable by human reason, and it will always be impossible to decide with certainty, whether they arise immediately from the object, or are produced by the creative power of the mind, or are derived from the Author of our being. (*T*, p. 84)[41]

Why could he say that? Consider the common sense view that we perceive the world directly. You still have the problem that if you press your eye with your finger the number of things perceived doubles, but no one assumes that the number of objects in the world also doubles (cf. *T*, pp. 210-211). Or consider an oar that appears to be bent when it is in the water, but which appears to be straight when taken out of the water. *Berkeley* could explain the different appearances in either case on the basis of natural laws describing how God causes ideas. But the skeptical arguments regarding our knowledge of laws of nature—our knowledge of the ways in which objects two kinds of objects are causally related to one another at all times and in all places—blocks that move. Hence, the common sense view cannot provide knowledge of the world outside the mind.

The representative view proposed by Descartes and Locke is in even worse straights. This assumes that the impression is something distinct from but caused by and resembling (to at least some degree) a material object. But since one is never aware of the material object itself—since one can never be aware of anything other than an impression or idea—there is no way to know that the presumptive cause resembles the impression of which one is aware. Further, since doing away with the presumption of an objective necessary connection between cause and effect implies that "Any thing may produce any thing" (*T*, p. 173), there is no guarantee that what causes an impression of a certain kind at one time is the same kind thing that produces an impression of the same kind at another time—for example, two impressions of your dog Spot. Finally, since causal relations, to the extent they can be known at all, are known on the basis of a constant conjunction of two kinds of objects (seeing one kind of object always followed by some other kind of object), the fact that one's sense perceptions are limited to the domain of impressions—one cannot in principle be directly aware of the alleged material object presumed to stand in a causal relation to an impression—not even the ordinary grounds upon which one's belief in a causal relation between two kinds of objects can hold. Hence, there is *no* ground for claiming that there are objects that cause and resemble impressions.

Thus, it seems that the kinds of skeptical arguments that led Descartes to attempt to push skeptical doubts to their limits, and thereby over come them, resurface *with a vengeance* in Hume. What is one to do?

Skepticism is not a popular philosophical view. As Hume noted, it is a characteristic of skeptical arguments "*that they admit of no answer and produce no conviction*" (*EHU*, p. 155n). In concluding this discussion, we shall look briefly at Immanuel Kant's reply to Hume at the end of the early modern period.

Immanuel Kant (1724-1804)

Immanuel Kant was born in Königsberg, East Prussia (now part of Poland) on May 8, 1724. He studied at the University of Königsberg. He taught philosophy at the University of Königsberg. He is said to have spent all of his life within fifty miles of Königsberg. His early writings were in the natural sciences. In 1781 he published his *Critique of Pure Reason*, which was his attempt to answer Hume's skeptical doubts.

Kant is a watershed figure in the history of philosophy, since all philosophers after him had to take his views into account. Kant changed the questions. While earlier philosophers asked *whether* one could have knowledge of the world, Kant asked *how* one had such knowledge. Kant *assumed* that the world is inherently subject to mathematical description (cf. Hume, *EHU*, pp. 31-32), and he assumed that there are necessary connections among objects in the world. The world to which mathematical description and necessary connections apply, however, is the world of sense experience—not some world beyond experience (the world of things in themselves or noumena)—and he provided a theory to explain how such knowledge was possible.

Kant's contention is that the mind (what he called "the transcendental unity of apperception") imposes certain structures upon experience, thereby transforming it from what William James later called a "blooming, buzzing confusion" to a world of objects. Unlike earlier philosophers, Kant claimed that the truths of mathematics are synthetic *a priori* truths. As *a priori* truths, they are known before experience. As synthetic truths, they increase what we know. He claimed that in knowing that $7 + 5 = 12$, we discover that two numbers can be united to form a single number. He suggests that one learns this by counting. But it will not do to count apples or oranges, for then you would simply discover that every time you had seven oranges and counted five more you had twelve, which is known only through experience and *could* (?) turn out differently on a later occasion. What is "counted" must be *a priori*, that is, given prior to experience. He argues that what one counts are bits of space and time—time in the case of arithmetic, space in the case of geometry. Space and time are not things like tables and chairs. If you take away all the objects of which you are aware in experience, space and time remain. These Kant called **pure intuitions**. They are necessary conditions for experience to be as we are aware of it. The mind structures experience in terms of space and time. Space and time are prior to experience in the sense that they are imposed on appearances and are the first ordering that transforms appearances into the ordered structure we discover in experience.

Similarly, Kant suggests that there is a second-order structuring of experience. This ordering is done in terms of twelve **categories**, which include causation and substance. Why is it true that every event has a cause? Because the mind imposes causal structures on experience, that is, it orders it in such a way that every event has a cause. Why are there substances, that is, things that persist through time? Because the mind so orders experience.

It is on the basis of the pure intuitions and the categories that the mind transforms raw appearance into what Kant calls **phenomena**. The world of natural science is the world of phenomena, that is, strictly ordered appearance. It is on the basis of the pure intuitions and the categories that raw appearances are transformed into objects. The domain of knowledge properly so called is limited to phenomena.

Are there things *beyond* immediate experience, as Descartes and Locke suggested? Kant held that it is natural to believe that there are, but they cannot properly be known. They are the objects of metaphysical discussion.

We've looked at seven philosophers. They developed seven accounts of the world and one's knowledge of it. Each is distinct. No two are wholly compatible with one another. So they can't all be right. The question you will naturally ask is, "Yeah, but *who's* right?" It is *your* job as a philosopher to examine these systems, to raise questions regarding them, and to attempt to come up with the most plausible and coherent account of perceptual knowledge. The problem of perception has not been solved. The fun is in attempting to answer the question, "What can be known?"

Notes

[1] Sextus Empiricus, *Selections from the Major Writings on Scepticism, Man, & God*, translated by Sanford G. Etheridge, edited by Philip P. Hallie (Indianapolis: Hackett Publishing Company, 1985), p. 38.

[2] You might recall, for example, that Plato held his Forms to be real or "more real" than the objects that participate in them. An ordinary table is a table because it participates (imperfectly) in the form Table.

[3] Or, as the logicians would say, where *p* is a variable that can be replaced by any statement whatsoever, any statement of the form "*p* and *not-p*" is a contradiction.

[4] Michel Montaigne, *Apology for Raymond Sebond*, in *The Complete Essays of Montaigne*, translated by Donald M. Frame (Stanford: Stanford University Press, 1976), p. 452.

[5] *Ibid.*, pp. 453.

[6] *Ibid.*, p. 453-4.

[7] *Ibid.*, p. 454.

[8] René Descartes, *The Optics*, in *The Philosophical Writings of Descartes*, translated by John Cottingham, Robert Stoothoff, and Dugald Murdoch, 2 volumes (Cambridge: Cambridge University Press, 1985 and 1984), volume 1, p. 165. Further references to *The Philosophical Writings of Descartes* will be abbreviated *CSM* and will be made by volume and page.

[9] There apparently is no factual basis for the story that Galileo dropped cannon balls from the Leaning Tower of Pisa, but it still works for purposes of illustration.

[10]Before you declare this utterly strange, it is the basic procedure you used in geometry to find a triangle similar to a given triangle but with a side of a given length—there was a bit of cross-multiplication.

[11]Even Descartes recognized the value of the Baconian method. As Descartes wrote Marin Mersenne on May 10, 1632, "You once told me that you knew some people who were so dedicated to the advancement of science that they were willing to make every kind of experiment at their own expense. It would be very useful if some such person were to write the history of celestial phenomena in accordance with the Baconian method and to describe the present appearances of the heavens without any explanations or hypotheses, reporting the position of each fixed star in relation to its neighbours, listing their differences in size and colour and visibility and brilliance and so on." René Descartes, *The Philosophical Writings of Descartes: The Correspondence*, translated by John Cottingham, Robert Stoothoff, Dugald Murdoch, and Anthony Kenny (Cambridge: Cambridge University Press, 1991), p. 38.

[12]It should be noted that the "method of doubt" is *not* the same as his method of analysis. While analysis is the general method Descartes uses in all his writings, the "method of doubt" is found only in his philosophical writings. What follows is a very general account of Descartes's philosophy. For a very good general introduction to Descartes's philosophy, the reader is encouraged to read Anthony Kenny, *Descartes: A Study of his Philosophy* (New York: Random House, 1968). For a detailed discussion of the *Meditations* seen from the perspective of the Cartesian method of analysis, see Daniel E. Flage and Clarence A. Bonnen, *Descartes and Method: A Search for Method in Meditations* (London: Routledge, 1999).

[13]The very fact that Descartes can doubt assumes that no statement can be true and false at the same time—the principle of contradiction—which is something that cannot be known on the basis of sense experience.

[14]He does not say this in so many words in the *Meditations*, although what he says leads to the same conclusion. He does say this in his *Principles of Philosophy*, Part 1, Section 10, and there is the French equivalent in Part IV of his *Discourse on Method*.

[15]The perceptive reader will notice that claiming, "I think, but I don't exist" is *not* a case of joining a statement with its denial, as in the case of the building that both is and is not fifty feet tall. Something more is needed. *One* way to read "I think, therefore I am" is as an argument that assumes the (unstated) premise "Everything that thinks, exists." From this it follows that "I exist." Whether that was *Descartes's* understanding of "I think, therefore I am" is a very controversial issue.

[16]At least it is not taken to do so in the Third Meditation. There is an argument in the Fifth Meditation—a so-called **ontological** argument for the existence of God—that is based only on an idea of God as a perfect being and makes *no* appeals to factual claims. The soundness of the argument and why Descartes introduces it are controversial issues. We shall not discuss the argument.

[17]Various commentators have grumbled about Descartes's causal principle. For what it is worth, it was *assumed* in raising the second hypothetical doubt that the less perfect my cause is, the more likely it is that I would fall into error.

[18]Many people find his appeal to the natural light problematic, but it has at least some plausibility. In the preface to the French edition of his *Principles of Philosophy* (1644), he talks about four levels of knowledge: (1) notions that are so clear that they can be recognized as true without meditation, (2) sense experience, (3) education and hearsay, and (4)—which is little more than a variation on (3)—books, at least, books written by competent writers (*CSM* 1:181). Virtually everyone before Descartes claimed that there were some truths known apart from experience, or known *a priori*. We already have seen that the process of doubting takes the principle of contradiction for granted. While one might question some of the principles Descartes claims to know by the natural light, it is at least not completely mad to claim that *some* principles are so known.

[19]More common factual claims providing the basis for a cosmological argument are the world exists, or there are motions in the world, or there are causes in the world. Perhaps the most famous versions of the cosmological argument are presented by St. Thomas Aquinas in his *Summa Theologica*, Book 1, Question 2, Article 3.

[20]If one looks at the deceiver-God argument in Meditation One, one will notice that there are three distinct doubts that fall under that argument. (1) If God is a deceiver, I cannot know that the material world exists. (2) If God is a deceiver, I cannot know the truths of mathematics. (3) If God is good, isn't the fact that I can be deceived even occasionally inconsistent with God's goodness? See *CSM* 2:14.

[21]For an extensive discussion of the Jewish community in Amsterdam and its impact on Spinoza, see Yirmiyahu Yovel, *Spinoza and Other Heretics: The Morrano of Reason* (Princeton: Princeton University Press, 1989).

[22]Descartes, *Principles of Philosophy* Part 1, Section 5 1.

[23]Benedict Spinoza, *Ethics*, Part 1, Definition 3, in *The Collected Works of Spinoza*, edited and translated by Edwin Curley (Princeton: Princeton University Press, 1985), p. 408. Further references to the *Ethics* will be to the Curley translation and will be provided in accordance with standard practice among Spinoza scholars in terms of part (by Roman numeral), definition (d followed by an Arabic numeral), axiom (a followed by an Arabic numeral), proposition (p followed by an Arabic numeral), corollary (c followed by an Arabic numeral if there is more than one corollary), and scholium (s). So the reference, "I.p13.c.s.", refers to the scholium to the corollary to Proposition 13 of Part 1.

[24] If you want to come at this in a different way, consider the common philosophical definition of 'God' as a being that is all-powerful, all-knowing, etc. You and I have *some* powers; you and I know *some* things. If God is all-powerful, then some of our powers—however limited—must be God's powers as well, not in the sense of in some way *depending upon* God, but in the sense of being *identical* with God's powers. Short of this, God would not *have* all powers. And the same goes for knowledge, goodness, etc.

[25] Whether Spinoza held that there are an *infinite number* of attributes is a matter of some controversy. (See Jonathan Bennett, "Spinoza's Metaphysics," in *The Cambridge Companion to Spinoza,* edited by Don Garrett [Cambridge: Cambridge University Press, 1996], pp. 61-88, especially pp. 64-66; Roger Scruton, *Spinoza,* Past Masters [Oxford: Oxford University Press, 1986], pp. 44-47.) Since this is irrelevant to the problem of perception, however, we may ignore the problem.

[26] G. W. Leibniz, *Principles of Nature and Grace, Based on Reason,* §4, in G. W. Leibniz, *Philosophical Essays,* translated and edited by Roger Ariew and Daniel Garber (Indianapolis: Hackett, 1989), p. 208. Cf. *Monadology* §14.

[27] See G. W. Leibniz, *New Essays on Human Understanding,* translated and edited by Peter Remnant and Jonathan Bennett (Cambridge: Cambridge University Press, 1981), p. 52. Cf. René Descartes, *Comments on a Certain Broadsheet, CSM* 1:304.

[28] Descartes, Spinoza, and Leibniz are often called "rationalists." The term 'rationalist' is anything but precise, but it is commonly taken to refer to any philosopher who holds that there are innate ideas, particularly innate ideas of eternal truths.

[29] John Locke, *An Essay concerning Human Understanding* (hereafter *Essay*), edited by P. H. Nidditch (Oxford: Clarendon Press, 1975), Book 1, Chapter 2, Section 5, p. 50.

[30] In addition to the *Essay*, Locke wrote three successive replies to criticisms of the work by Edward Stillingfleet, Bishop of Worcester. In addition, his *Of the Conduct of the Understanding* was published posthumously.

[31] Recall that Descartes had held that extension is the essence of matter and thought is the essence of mind.

[32] This is what Immanuel Kant later called an analytic truth.

[33] George Berkeley, *A Treatise concerning the Principles of Human Knowledge,* Part 1, § 1. Since all editions of the *Principles (PHK)* are uniformly divided into sections, all references will be by section number.

[34] Phenomenalism and, particularly, idealism are seen by some to test the extent to which Berkeley was a champion of common sense. What ordinary people would claim that ordinary objects depend for their existence on minds? My suspicion is that Berkeley would reply that ordinary people do not have a considered account of the nature of objects.

[35] Part I is the body of the *Principles* as it has come down to us. Originally Berkeley intended to publish several additional parts in which he developed his philosophy further. He apparently abandoned that plan in about 1716. In the second edition of the *Principles* (1734), he dropped "Part I" from the body of the work.

[36] This is not the only way to read Berkeley's arguments. It is quite common to suggest that the ontology is primary, that the notion of an idea is fundamentally the notion of a mental entity. See, for example, I.P. Tipton, *Berkeley: The Philosophy of Immaterialism* (London: Methuen, 1974).

[37] For an alternative reading of the likeness principle, see Phillip D. Cummins, "Berkeley's Likeness Principle," in C. B. Martin and D. M. Armstrong, editors, *Locke and Berkeley: A Collection of Critical Essays* (Garden City, NY: Doubleday Anchor Books, 1968), pp. 353-363.

[38] David Hume, *A Treatise of Human Nature* (hereafter *T.*), edited by L. A. Selby-Bigge, 2nd edition revised by P. H. Nidditch (Oxford: Clarendon Press, 1978), p. 1.

[39] The second is at *T*, p. 5; both are in David Hume, *An Enquiry concerning Human Understanding* (hereafter *EHU*), in David Hume, *Enquiries concerning the Human Understanding and concerning the Principles of Morals* edited by L. A. Selby-Bigge, 3rd edition revised by P. H. Nidditch (Oxford: Clarendon Press, 1975), pp. 19-20.

[40] And the first premise does not fare much better, since there is no way to determine whether at *all* times in the past when the cue ball hit the 8-ball, the 8-ball rolled away. Should you challenge that claim—should you claim there is a perfectly complete history of pool written by a person of unimpeachable authority (God, perhaps) and found in the library—consider the same situation regarding subatomic particles.

[41] For Hume's complete discussion of knowledge by way of the senses, see *T*, pp. 187-218.

TRUTH

THE SEARCH FOR TRUTH

by Robert C. Solomon

> It is now some years since I detected how many were the false beliefs that I had from my earliest youth admitted as true, and how doubtful was everything I had since constructed on this basis: and from that time I was convinced that I must for once and for all seriously undertake to rid myself of all the opinions which I had formerly accepted and commence to build anew.
>
> — Descartes, *Meditations*

What is True?

> One unerring mark of the love of truth is not entertaining any proposition with greater assurance than the proofs it is built upon will warrant.
>
> —John Locke, *Essay on Human Understanding*

No matter what particular metaphysical view of the world we support: What is it for a set of beliefs to be true? How will we know when our beliefs are true? Sometimes this seems to be **obvious** (**self-evident**): but what if the "obvious" is not always so? These questions are the basis of the discipline called **epistemology** the theory of *knowledge*.

The question "What is it for our beliefs to be true?" has a seductively easy answer: A belief is true if (and only if) it corresponds to the facts. Thus my belief that I have at least 75 cents in my pocket is true if and only if I do *in fact* have 75 cents or more in my pocket. Your belief that the Philadelphia Phillies will win the

World Series is true if and only if, *in fact*, the Phillies do win the World Series. The great astronomer Galileo's belief that Jupiter has four moons is true if and only if in fact Jupiter has four moons, and so on. A belief is true if it corresponds to the facts. But that turns out, you will see, not to help us at all.

First, consider the statements "75 x 3 = 225" and "The cube root of 64 is 4." Are these statements true if and only if they correspond to the facts? What facts? Suppose it happens to be the case that there are not, in fact, any actual combinations of three sets of seventy-five things in the world: would that make the statement "75 x 3 = 225" false, at least for the moment? Of course, you might say that *if* there were three sets of seventy-five things in the world, *then* they would add up all together to 225 things. But it is also true that *if* the Phillies were to win the World Series, then indeed they would win the World Series. But suppose they do not win; the "if" doesn't make it true. But "75 x 3 = 225" seems to be true even if there are no facts in the world for the statement to correspond to. Therefore, presumably, there are true statements that do not (or need not) correspond to any facts.

Second, consider the status of a great many statements of "common sense." For example, going out in cold, damp weather causes us to "lower our resistance" and get sick. Doctors dispute this on the basis of scientific evidence, and yet we hold to such beliefs until they are *conclusively* refuted—some continuing to hold on to them even then. How do we know that what we believe as a matter of common sense is in fact justified and not just a set of plausible falsehoods that have been handed down, uncritically from person to person, generation to generation?

Third, compare such statements as "there is a coffee cup here on the table," which is the report of an immediate and particular perception, and the natural law in science that "there is gravity between any two masses." Both statements claim to be based on experience, but the latter obviously involves a much more complicated process of confirmation than the former. Between the two there are any number of generalizations based on experience—of *hypotheses*—that are formulated and confirmed by inductive argument, such as "water freezes at 32°F" and "cats run away when you wave a German shepherd in front of them." But must all statements in science be confirmed by experience? Could it be that two very general theories might have no observation or experiment that could distinguish between them and verify one while refuting the other? And what about religious truths—not only "God exists" but such claims as "Moses parted the Red Sea with the help of God"? Are these true because they "correspond to the facts"? Because they can in any sense be verified? Or is there a kind of truth that depends on faith and is very different from scientific truth?

Finally, what about very general truths or truisms, such as "all things will pass" and "boys will be boys"? Tautologies are true, even though they don't seem to tell us anything about the world. And what are we to make of those grand statements uttered by the philosophers: "It is the Forms that are most real" and "There is only one substance"? Are they true or not? Are any of them true? How can we tell? What does our knowledge of such matters ultimately depend upon? What is truth, and how will we know it when (or if) we find it?

Two Kinds of Truth

It has been suggested that true statements (or, simply, truth) might be divided into two separate categories: (1) true because of the facts; and (2) true because of reasoning. Examples of the first would be the true statement that there is no change at all in my pocket, the true statement that Switzerland has not fought in a war in this century, and the true statement that water boils at less than 100°C on the top of a mountain. Examples of the second would be the true statement that 2 + 2 = 4, the true statement that A + B = B + A, and the true statement that no bachelor is married. These "truths of reason" are called **necessary truths** for they could not possibly be false.

Empirical Truth

A statement that is true because of the facts is called an **empirical truth**—that is, true because of experience. (The word "empirical" means having to do with experience.) Empirical truths can only be known to be true once we have actually looked at the world. (Of course, we don't always do this ourselves; most of our empirical knowledge depends upon the observations and experiments carried out by other people. We take their word for it.) But since an empirical truth can be known only by looking at the facts of the world, a statement such as "There are no trees on the University of Texas campus" might—for all we know before we actually go out and look around—be false. Philosophers refer to such a statement (and the circumstances to which it refers) as **contingent** or as a **contingent truth** (if it is true; if it is false, it is a **contingent falsehood**). Thus the statement that there are no trees on the University of Texas campus happens to be false, but it is contingently so. We can *imagine* what it would be like otherwise; if someone were to cut down the few remaining trees, then the statement would become true, but only contingently true, since there might someday once again be trees on the campus. As a general rule in philosophy, all empirical statements are, if true, only contingently true.

Necessary Truth

A statement that is true because of reason, on the other hand, is *necessarily* true; it is a necessary truth. "Necessary" is here the opposite of "contingent": We can always imagine what it would be for a contingent truth not to be true (or a contingent falsehood not to be false). We cannot even make sense out of the suggestion that a necessary truth might not be true (or that a necessary falsehood might not be false). "2 + 2 = 4" is a necessary truth, in that we cannot imagine—no matter how imaginative we happen to be—what circumstances might make that statement false. (Suppose I add together two drops of ink, and they combine to form one drop; would this prove the statement to be false? Why not?) For example, the necessary falsehood "1 + 1 = 1" cannot be imagined to be true under any circumstances. Necessary truths can be said to be true, accordingly, *prior to* experience or (in Latin) *a priori*. (It is important to note again that *a priori* does not mean "before" in the sense of temporally "before any experience"—that is, it does not mean that we know these things before we were born. Some philosophers do believe that there are ideas "born into" us or *innate*. Nevertheless, we must come to recognize these truths after we have learned a language and presumably, acquired considerable intellectual sophistication.)

So long as we restrict ourselves to a limited number of standard examples—the statement that there is so much change in my pocket or the statement that "2 + 2 = 4"—the distinction between empirical, contingent truths, on the one hand, and what some philosophers call "truths of reason," or necessary truth, on the other, seems adequately clear. Does God exist? What is reality? And, looking ahead, is there a meaning to human life? Are the answers to these questions empirical or necessary truths, and should we appeal to our experience or reason (or both, or neither) to answer them?

Believing in the existence of God, for example, would seem to be a belief in a fact; indeed, many philosophers have argued that the existence of God is the ultimate fact. But suppose we imagine an argument between a theist (who believes in the existence of God) and an atheist (who does not). What facts can the theist show the atheist which would compel the atheist to believe in God? The theist can show the atheist one of the many passages in the Bible in which the existence of God is forcefully asserted; but of course the atheist will not accept this as evidence, since an atheist does not believe that most of the Bible is true. A few theists may even be able to claim that they have direct evidence of God's existence, since He has actually talked with or presented Himself to them. But, again, the atheist will not think anything of this alleged evidence either, since he or she will dismiss such experiences as mere delusions. The theist brings up the miracles that have been recorded in history as evidence of God's presence on earth; the atheist dismisses these as accidents or as unexplained (but not unexplainable) occurrences. The theist points to the intricacy of the world (by way of the "argument by design" as evidence that there must be a God to create such a

What Facts Will Prove The Existence of God?

Theist's Proof	Atheist's Reply
Stated in the Bible	Not all statements in the Bible are true.
Experiences God in a vision	Mere hallucination, doesn't prove anything.
Miracle of the Red Sea	Geophysical quirk, not a miracle.
Delicate order of nature	Product of natural selection and chance occurrences.
The existence of the world	Just happened, otherwise, we wouldn't be here to discuss it.
The victory of the good over evil (in World War II for instance.)	Superiority of Allied forces and a few lucky turning points.

masterpiece; the atheist insists that it is all chance, and, anyway, the world isn't such a "masterpiece" after all; it all depends on how you look at it.

The futility of this debate shows us that believing in God is not simply a matter of accepting the facts, but of something more. What more? "Faith" is one traditional answer, but faith is not so much a claim to know the truth as it is a matter of *hoping* that what one believes is true. It has been argued, however, that believing in the existence of God is perfectly rational and demonstrable, not as a matter of fact but through abstract reasoning. If such an argument is successful, then "God exists" is a necessary truth.

Consider in the same way a statement about the meaning of life—whether life is meaningful or not and what that meaning might be. Suppose I insist, without going into details, that human life is meaningful. What facts make this true? I point out the pleasures of love, the joys of knowledge, the thrills of skiing, the delights of a good glass of wine in front of a fireplace. "Life is good," I conclude, as if I've proved it. But you, who think life is absurd, disagree with me. "Love never lasts," you insist; statistically, at least, you are certainly right. You point out the futility of knowledge, the number of broken legs among skiers, the cost of decent wine and firewood. You go through the crudest facts of human history, the atrocities of war, the cruelties and the dead ends, even in those societies that lived under the illusion that life was "getting better all the time." You point out the tragedies in life and in any case, how short life is. You conclude, "Life is no good." We each have facts on our side. Who is right? Well, once again, it is clear that the facts won't tell us. I can insist that even wars and tragedies serve their purpose, to remind us of the value of life and to give us something to fight for. I can insist that life is intrinsically meaningful no matter how long it lasts or how many misfortunes should befall us. In other words, it is the **interpretation** of the facts that matters, not the facts themselves.

Finally, consider the statement that what is most real are Plato's Forms, not the things and facts of everyday experience. If this is true, is it true because it corresponds to the facts? No, since the theory itself says that the facts of everyday life are not the basis of truth. Could you say that this theory in turn does—or does not—correspond to the facts? If you do, then you generate a paradox—namely, that the theory is true because it corresponds to the facts which it denies are the basis of truth. Once again, we can see that this philosophical statement, if it is true, must be true in such a way that the facts are not the central consideration. It, too, perhaps, is defensible through pure thinking and without regard for whether the apparent facts of the world support it. Indeed, most philosophers would say straight out that the facts of ordinary experience (or, for that matter, the facts of extraordinary experience) may have very little to do with philosophical truth. But then are all philosophical truths necessary truths—the product of reasoning? Can reason deliver such an enormous promise? Some philosophers have certainly thought so; others have denied it. But almost all of them (until recently) thought that if there was an answer to any philosophical question (or any other question of knowledge), it would have to be *either* an empirical truth based on experience *or* an *a priori* truth that was both necessary and a product of reason.

It is one thing to say that a statement is true or false and something else to say what *kind* of truth it is and how we would know that it is so. Recent philosophers have argued that knowledge is "justified true belief." Truth is only one of the necessary conditions of knowledge. It is also necessary to be able to *justify* our belief. And it is the attempt to justify philosophical beliefs that has given rise to the single biggest split in modern philosophy.

Rationalism and Empiricism

In the past three hundred years, two schools of philosophy have come to dominate much of the discussion of these questions about the kind of truth to be found in philosophy. They are usually given the names

Rationalism: Knowledge is based on reason

The Continental rationalists:

René Descartes (France)

Benedict Spinoza (Holland)

Gottfried Wilhelm Leibniz (Germany)

Nineteenth century:

Immanuel Kant (Germany)

G. W. F. Hegel (Germany)

Empiricism: Knowledge is based on experience

The British empiricists:

John Locke (England)

Bishop George Berkeley (Ireland)

David Hume (Scotland)

Nineteenth century:

John Stuart Mill (England)

Twentieth century:

Bertrand Russell (England)

rationalism and **empiricism**. The names alone should give you a good indication of the positions they represent.

Rationalism is a broad designation for a variety of theories, all of which have in common the confidence that human *reason* can provide the final answers to the most basic and essential philosophical questions. Furthermore, these answers will all be necessary truths. Great rationalists in modern times include the philosophers Descartes, Spinoza, Leibniz, Kant, and Hegel; in ancient and medieval times, most of the great philosophers were rationalists, including Plato, Aristotle (with qualifications), Saint Augustine, and Saint Thomas Aquinas (with qualifications). They all believed—in one way or another—that philosophical reasoning can give us the answers, and that these answers are all necessary truths and are to be found within our thinking processes themselves—whether inspired by God, or radiated by "Forms," or built into the structure of our minds, or "born into" our brains (or "innate"). Experience might provide some of the material for our thinking, as well as some clues and perhaps the trigger to the answer, but experience cannot by itself, according to the rationalists, teach us anything at all. Truth is not subject to the vicissitudes of experience.

Empiricism, on the other hand, is a philosophical method which rejects this conception of "innate ideas" and insists, in the words of John Locke, that "all knowledge comes from experience." According to Locke, the human mind at birth is a "blank tablet" (*tabula rasa*), on which experience writes the general principles as well as the details of all our knowledge. Other empiricists include David Hume, the nineteenth-century thinker John Stuart Mill, and the twentieth-century philosopher Bertrand Russell.

Empiricists still believe in *reason*, of course, but only in the well-defined activities of calculation and logic—as in mathematics, for example. But they do not believe that reason has anything of importance to say about the big philosophical questions; indeed, the most radical empiricists of this century have even insisted that reason can tell us nothing about the world, but only about the structure of our own language.

The rationalists, on the other hand, do not reject the testimony of the senses either, but they do insist that observation and experiment—in short, *experience*—cannot give us philosophical truths. Both rationalists and empiricists would agree that the question "How much change do you have in your pocket?" is to be answered only by appeal to experience, and that the statement "If A is a B and all Bs are Cs, then A is a C" is a necessary truth by virtue of reason. What they disagree about is how the fundamental questions of philosophy are to be answered, and whether they can be answered. The rationalists believe that they can be answered, and answered with certainty—that is, as necessary truths. The empiricists generally believe that if they can be answered at all, they will have to be answered either as trivial statements about the meaning of our words (for example, the word "reality" simply *means* "that which is material and sensible") or as generalizations based on extensive experience (for example, the empiricist John Stuart Mill thought that even such statements as "$2 + 2 = 4$" were in fact very general claims about experience, and not "truths of reason" at all). Since, for the empiricists, all knowledge is based on experience (and inductive arguments), knowledge is (at best) highly probable and not certain. Not surprisingly, many empiricists have argued that some of the big questions of philosophy are not answerable, and much of empiricism has been a reexamination of the questions themselves, an attempt to show that they cannot be answered and, perhaps, that they do not make much sense in the first place.

One of the main points of debate between the rationalists and the empiricists—both in the seventeenth century and today (for instance, in the debate between linguist Noam Chomsky and such contemporary empiricists as Nelson Goodman)—concerns the existence of innate ideas. We have already seen that innate ideas are those "born into" us, but this does not mean (what would be absurd) newborn infants already "know" that 437 multiplied by 73 equals 31,901 (as if he or she just hasn't yet acquired the language to express this). Briefly put, the rationalists generally accept the idea of innate ideas; the empiricists usually reject it. Descartes, a rationalist, tried to begin with such intuitively certain truths as the idea that God is a perfect being, and then tried to deduce from this other truths that would (by virtue of a valid deduction) be equally certain. John Locke, an empiricist, rejected this idea of innate ideas and insisted that the mind is at birth a blank tablet (*tabula rasa*). All of our ideas must therefore be derived from experience, for none of them are innate.

The problem here is that much of our knowledge does not consist of individual perceptions ("Here is a coffee cup.") but rather is made up of universal statements such as "every action has an equal and opposite reaction." How do we get from the individual perceptions and our limited experience to such universal claims? The rationalists insist that it is only by way of some innate ideas or rational intuitions that this is possible—and that the most necessary truths about the world (the statements of mathematics) could not possibly be based on experience, but must be based on innate ideas.

The Presuppositions of Knowledge

> Reason already persuades me that I ought no less carefully to withhold my assent from matters which are not entirely certain and indubitable than from those which appear to me manifestly to be false, if I am able to find in each one some reason to doubt.

> — Descartes, *Meditations*

We have seen that there are two kinds of truth; we have also seen that it is not at all clear which (if either) kind of truth we will find in philosophy. But at this point in our discussion we should also point out that there are other principles which share this problematic status with such big questions as the existence of God, the meaning of life, and the nature of reality. Unlike the big questions of philosophy, these principles are not usually considered a matter of debate; they are rarely, if ever, suggested to be a matter of mere opinion, or faith, and so they are often not thought of as principles of philosophy at all. But they are. These are philosophical principles that lie at the foundations of virtually all of our knowledge and beliefs. They are the **presuppositions** of our thinking, without which we could believe nothing, know nothing, think nothing else.

For example, the basic philosophical belief that the *world exists* is the presupposition of anything that any scientist wants to say about the world. It is presupposed, too, in our most ordinary statements, such as "We ought to paint the door of the house green instead of red," since that presupposes that there is a door, a house, paint, and the world. Similarly, one of the philosophical principles that has long been discussed and debated is the principle that *everything that happens has a cause* (sometimes called the **principle of universal causality**). We cannot imagine chemistry without this principle, in fact, and we cannot imagine even the most everyday occurrences without it. Consider what you would think of a garage mechanic who told you, when your car wouldn't start, "Nothing's wrong: this is one of those events without a cause." You wouldn't call into question the principle that everything that happens has a cause; you would go to another mechanic.

In moments of uncertainty, most of us wonder whether there is a God or whether life has meaning. Many people wonder from time to time—though only rarely to the extent of the philosophers—what the world is really like. But no one in his or her right mind ever really wonders whether the world exists; indeed, when philosophers debate such curious topics, it is usually only to test out a theory they have about truth or reality, not to see whether in fact the world exists. But however obvious these principles may seem to us, their status as knowledge is in question in much the same way that the status of our big philosophical questions is in question. These statements are not clearly about matters of fact. They are not provable through experience. (That is why we know *before* we go to the garage, or *a priori*, that something must be the cause, though we do not know what.) Neither are they evidently true by virtue of reason. It is not contradictory to think that the outside world might not exist. Yet surely the existence of the world is not a

Are There Innate Ideas?

THE EMPIRICISTS VIEW

It is an established opinion among some men, that there are in the understanding certain innate principles, some primary notions, stamped, as it were, upon the mind of man which the soul receives in its very first being, and brings into the world with it. It would be sufficient to convince unprejudiced readers of the falseness of this supposition, if I should only show how many men obtain to all the knowledge they have, without the help of any such innate impressions . . . . Let us suppose the mind to be a blank tablet; how comes it to be furnished? To this answer in one word, from experience.

—Locke, *Essay Concerning Human Understanding*

THE RATIONALIST REPLY

Is the soul empty, like a tablet upon which nothing has been written? Does all truth depend on experience, that is to say, on induction? . . . The senses, although necessary for all our actual knowledge, are not sufficient to give us the whole of it, since the senses never give anything but examples. And it would seem that necessary truths, such as are found in pure mathematics and especially in arithmetic and geometry, must have principles the proof of which does not depend on examples, nor, consequently, on the testimony of the senses, although without the senses it never would have occurred to us to think of them.

—Leibniz, *New Essay on Human Understanding*

mere matter of opinion. So what are we to say about philosophical truth? How can we prove, beyond a doubt, that these obvious truths are indeed true?

Skepticism

Nothing exists. If anything did exist, we couldn't know it. If we could know it we couldn't communicate it.

— Plato, *Gorgias*

It may not be a question we ever ask in real life, but suppose someone were to ask you how you know that you're not dreaming right now. Suppose the same person—a friend taking his or her first philosophy course, perhaps—were to ask you how you know that the world even exists or has ever existed, how you know that everything you have ever experienced, from your mother's breast to the car you call your own, has not been just ideas in your own mind. How would you answer? What would you say?

It is important to notice the assumption lying behind these questions, not necessarily because the assumption is false, but rather because it is indeed the assumption of most of our metaphysical thinking, as well as our way of talking about ourselves. The assumption is that there are two distinct realms of reality, one "outer"—the physical world—and one "inner"—the world of our experience. The physical world would exist, presumably, even if we were not here to experience it, but the world of our experience might be the same, according to this assumption, even if we were just dreaming about it, and even if, as Leibniz suggested, each of us were nothing but a mind, programmed by God to have certain experiences at certain times, *as if* there were a physical world "outside" us.

How do we get into this rather odd and troubling assumption? It seems rather obvious, given the way we have been talking—that each of us knows the world, from our own perspective, through our own personal experience. Both the empiricists and the rationalists would agree that what we know directly (whether through reason or experience) is first of all our own ideas and sensations. But these ideas and sensations are "in our minds." The world, obviously, is "outside" of our minds, an "external" world. We assume, naturally, that our ideas or "representations" correspond to the things in the world, but how do we know this? Many empiricists, following John Locke, would argue that the things in the world affect our sense organs in certain ways that cause us to have certain sorts of experiences, and that we infer from the nature of these experiences what the things that caused them must be like. Rationalists, on the other hand, might assume that there is some inherent connection between our ideas and the world—perhaps, as Descartes argued, guaranteed by God. But then, we might wonder, why do the rationalists disagree among themselves?

The two-world assumption, however, leads us into a serious dilemma. We can see the nature of the problem if we restate our assumption in the form of two apparently reasonable claims: (1) there is an "external" world—that is, a world beyond our beliefs and experiences, which is not affected by what we happen to believe about it, and (2) we cannot ever make direct contact with the world itself, but only with the contents of our own minds—with our ideas, our beliefs, our various experiences, and the principles which we find to be necessary truths (such as the principles of logic and arithmetic).

The two statements above have been accepted by a great many thinkers of the past several centuries (though the second would not have been acceptable to most philosophers in ancient times). And they are still accepted by a great many philosophers today. Indeed, we seem to accept both of them, too; the idea that the world actually exists seems so obviously true that, except in a philosophy class, we wouldn't even think of questioning it. And the idea that what we know directly are our own experiences also seems indisputable; don't we often have experiences without knowing whether they are true? And we sometimes have experiences which do not in fact match up (or "correspond") to the world (hallucinations, for example, as well as dreams). Could we know anything whatsoever about the world if we did not first experience it in some way? But however reasonable these two statements may be, together they give rise to an intolerable conclusion: namely, that we can never know—or at least we can never be sure that we know—the world at all.

What we know are our own opinions, ideas, and experiences; what we cannot know is whether those opinions, ideas, and experiences match up to the world as it really is. The world we thought we knew so intimately suddenly seems far away from us, unreachable by either thought or experience.

Now if anything is to be true, it must be true by reference to the facts and objects of the world, or it must be true as a "truth of reason." But according to the two-world assumption, what we know directly are our own ideas and experiences, not the physical world itself. This is why it is possible for us to imagine, without changing anything in our experience, that the world might not exist, or that we are now dreaming. Furthermore, we might raise the question whether the principles we believe *a priori*—our necessary truths— might in fact be true only of our way of thinking, or true of our language, but not true of the world itself—in other words, not true. But now we have raised an embarrassing set of questions, for could it be that the world of our ideas, beliefs, and experiences, no matter how certain we are of them, is not at all like the physical world "outside" of us? This set of doubts that we might not actually know the world at all is generally referred to as **skepticism**. In the sections that follow, we will see how two of the great philosophers of modern times, the rationalist René Descartes and the empiricist David Hume, used this set of doubts as the engine of their entire philosophical enterprise.

Descartes and the "Method of Doubt"

> The first rule is to accept nothing as true which I do not clearly recognize to be so; that is to say, carefully to avoid precipitation and prejudice in my judgments, and to accept in them nothing more than what was presented to my mind so clearly and distinctly that I could have no occasion to doubt it.

—Descartes, *Meditations*

The philosopher best known for his deliberations about all of this is the French philosopher **René Descartes** (1596-1650). He wrote a series of essays, the *Meditations*, generally considered to be the foundation of modern philosophy. Descartes accepted both of the statements above; in fact, he considered them both to be obviously true. But Descartes was a rationalist. He insisted on proof. Descartes was so concerned with *proving* his beliefs to be true, in separating his true beliefs from his opinions and false beliefs, that he decided, as a matter of method, to suspend his belief in everything. Doubt everything, Descartes decided; assume that everything one believes is false until one can prove it to be true. Indeed, one of the things Descartes doubted was the very existence of the external world. "Suppose I am now dreaming," we might paraphrase him. "After all, I have found myself dreaming before, when I thought (in the dream) that I was awake. Could I not possibly be dreaming all of the time? In fact, probably not. But if I cannot know this for certain, then I must doubt it, for until I can prove that a belief *must* be true, I do not have the right to believe it at all."

Now you might think that once one has made such a drastic move, there is nothing in the world which cannot be doubted. But this is not the case. It is our second statement, in fact, which provides Descartes with his first absolutely **indubitable** belief (that is, beyond doubt or unquestionable): What we know directly are the contents of our own minds. "Suppose," we might paraphrase him again, "I try to doubt the existence of my own mind. What I find is that I doubt that I am now doubting. But if I doubt that I am doubting, then, as a matter of necessity, I must indeed be doubting." Descartes' conclusion: "I cannot doubt that I'm doubting." More generally he concluded, "I cannot be wrong about the fact that I'm thinking, for the fact that I'm thinking about thinking already proves that I'm thinking." And from this simple logical principle emerges Descartes' most famous statement, "I think, therefore I am" (in Latin "*Cogito ergo sum*"). Here is a statement that cannot be doubted. Here, therefore, is a statement which can be used as a premise with which to prove beyond a doubt the objective truth of other beliefs, too, including our belief in the existence of the external world.

The rest of Descartes' proof remains one of the most heatedly debated arguments in the history of modern philosophy. In brief, it is this: Given the certainty of the statement "I think, therefore I am," Descartes then proved (or tried to prove) the existence of God, by way of one version of the ontological argument. That is, from the fact that I exist and can think and have an idea of God, it must be the case that God exists. So now Descartes had two **certain** statements: "I exist" and "God exists." But God, we know, is by definition a perfect being, who includes within His perfections perfect goodness. And if this is so, God would not allow us to be fooled about the existence of the world. Therefore, since God exists, the world must exist, for otherwise "I do not see how He could be vindicated from the charge of deceit, if in truth (my experiences) proceeded from any other source or were produced by other causes than corporeal things." So, too, Descartes could now argue that all of the beliefs of which I seemed so certain can now be shown to be true, necessarily. "God would not fool me; so I can know that I know the world, after all."

David Hume's Skepticism

A very difficult conclusion emerges from the deliberations of the Scottish empiricist **David Hume**. Hume accepted the two statements—that there is an "external" world existing independently of us, and that each of us is only in direct contact with the contents of our own mind—as obviously true, but he, too, insisted on proof of them. As an empiricist, he accepted John Locke's principle that "all knowledge comes from experience"; so for him the question was whether our belief in the existence of the external world could be proven to be true by appeal to experience. Or, if not, could it be shown to be true as a "truth of reason"? And this would be true of all our other philosophical questions, too, about the principal of universal causality, the existence of God, and the nature of reality. But whereas Descartes emerges from his *Meditations* with the positive conclusion that we *can* know the answers to these questions, and know them with certainty (that is, *a priori*, or as necessary truths), David Hume emerges from his study with the most negative of conclusions—that we cannot know the answers to any of these questions, that the most basic principles of our everyday knowledge as well as the most important guiding principles of our lives are without justification.

Hume's argument was elegantly simple, and philosophers have been trying to refute it ever since. (Bertrand Russell once wrote that in his opinion no one had yet succeeded, and that "Hume's conclusions . . . are equally difficult to refute and to accept.") Hume's position is skepticism, and it amounts to the negative claim that we cannot know the answers to questions to which we once thought the answers were obvious. The argument simply presses home the idea that there are two (and only two) kinds of truth, "matters of fact" and "truths of reason," and any belief which cannot be proved one way or the other is therefore without justification. So Hume asked, with regard to any belief, "Is this a matter of fact, to be defended by appeal to experience or experiment? Or is this a truth of reason, the truth of which can be demonstrated by an abstract calculation of the kind we find in mathematics or logic?" If the answer is "Neither," then Hume insisted that the judgment in question had no grounds for our continued belief, since it was without rational justification.

Hume's skepticism began, as Descartes' rationalist proofs had begun, by accepting the second of our two statements. He might doubt the existence of the world, but he did not for a moment doubt that our knowledge begins with experience, and that what we know directly are our own ideas and experiences (or what Hume called "impressions"). From this starting point, Hume shows us why we are not justified in believing principles that no sane person would actually doubt (except in philosophical investigations). Let's look first at his argument against the principle of universal causality, then at his argument against our supposed knowledge of the external world.

Is the principle of universal causality a "matter of fact," known through experience? Or is it a "relation of ideas" known through calculation and logic? Let's take the second possibility first: The principle of universal causality essentially says that everything that happens has a cause. Can we imagine a world in which everything that happens does not have a cause? Seemingly so; physicists talk quite frequently about

Hume's Strategy ("Hume's Fork")

Every justifiable true statement is either a
"truth of reason" (*a priori*)   or   "matter of fact" (empirical)
       "**2 + 2 = 4**"   "**There are tigers in India.**"

Which are the following philosophical statements?
       "God exists."
       "Life has meaning."
       "Everything that happens has a cause."

subatomic emissions which have no cause (not simply no *known* cause, but *no* cause). We can imagine a particle in space, significantly isolated from all other particles, simply shooting off in one direction with no cause whatsoever. And regarding all particular causes, this is certainly not a matter of reason. We know, for example, that the collision of one moving billiard ball with another causes the second to move; but this, Hume argued, we learn entirely from experience, not on the basis of reason. The first human being, Hume suggested, could not possibly have figured out that water would drown him, or that fire would burn him, until he actually had the experience of trying (unsuccessfully) to breathe under water, or the painful experience of putting his hand in the fire. Knowledge of causes and effects is a matter of experience, not reason. And so, we presume, is our knowledge that everything that happens has a cause. But this, it turns out, is not the case either.

In our example with the metaphysically perverse garage mechanic, the key to our illustration was the fact that we knew before we entered the garage that something had to be the cause of the car's failure. (In other words, we knew it, or thought we knew it, *a priori*). But this means that we do not learn the principle of universal causality *from* experience but in some sense carry it *to* experience. No number of unexplained events in the world would ever lead us to give up this principle, and in fact it is only because we already expect a cause that we know how to look for and find one.

One of the presuppositions of knowledge is that there are *causes*. What is a *cause*? We might say that one event causes another if the first event brings about the second. But if you look at the above sentence, we see that it is an utterly trivial statement; "brings about" is just another phrase for "causes," so we have not yet explained what a cause is. Let's take a particular example: the example of the two colliding billiard balls. The movement of the first causes a certain movement in the second. (If we know the speed and direction of the first, we can calculate in advance the speed and direction of the second.) But what we actually see, Hume pointed out, is not the cause at all. What we see are just the two events— (1) the movement of the first ball, and (2) the movement of the second ball. Indeed, the first time (or first several times) we watch, we may have no way of predicting the movement of the second ball at all. We might expect the first ball to come to a complete stop, or bounce backward, or we might expect both balls to break, or explode. This means that knowledge of causes is not a matter of reason. But no matter how many times we watch, all that we ever actually see are the two events— the movement of the first ball, the movement of the second ball—and we never see the connection between them, the actual *cause* of the second event, at all. Hume concluded that we never actually see the cause of events at all, but only that two events are regularly found together, in "constant conjunction." Here, too, Hume's conclusion is skeptical: Something we thought we knew for sure turns out not to be justifiable through experience or reason.

Regarding the existence of the external world, Hume's argument is equally devastating and of much the same form. Can our belief in the external world be shown to be a matter of logic? Clearly not, since we can imagine what it would be for the world not to exist, and we can imagine ourselves simply dreaming, as Descartes suggested. Is it a matter of experience? No, for just the same reason that pinching yourself to see if you are dreaming doesn't tell you if you are dreaming. Any experience is itself a part of that world of experience. So long as we accept the two-world assumption, which seems quite irrefutable, it surely is possible that the world of our experience exists but the physical world does not, and that within that world of experience there is no experience by which we can tell that this is not so.

When we run over libraries, persuaded of these principles, what havoc must we make? If we take in our hand any volume of divinity or school metaphysics, for instance, let us ask. Does it contain any abstract reasoning concerning quantity or number? No. Does it contain any experimental reasoning concerning matter of fact and existence? No. Commit it to the flames, for it can contain nothing but sophistry and illusion.

—David Hume, *A Treatise of Human Nature*

The Resolution of Skepticism: Kant

Skepticism has been a powerful philosophical position ever since ancient times. It is not an answer to the big questions of philosophy so much as the disturbing reply that there are no answers. Where the basic questions of knowledge are concerned, this does not seem tolerable. Can we really doubt that the world exists or the ordinary presupposition that everything that happens has a cause? For this reason, skepticism has usually been considered more of a problem to be avoided or a challenge to be answered than a philosophical position to be accepted for its own sake. In your own thinking, it is a signal of danger that should keep you on your toes and wary of too easy, dogmatic answers which in fact you can't defend. Indeed, what makes Descartes' method of doubting everything and Hume's skeptical conclusions so valuable to us is, more than anything else, the fact that they make us so aware of how easily we simply presume that the obvious is objectively true. And the point of philosophy, in answering the big questions, is precisely to allow us to go beyond what we first think is obvious, and think things through to the point where we can actually defend what we believe—even against so brilliant a skeptic as Hume. How much of what we believe is merely personal opinion? How many of our beliefs do we share only with our family or our friends but not with the larger community? Which of our beliefs might be generally accepted by everyone in our society but not at all by people in other societies? Which of our beliefs might in fact be built into our language but not into other languages? Are there beliefs which are built into the human mind as such but which may nonetheless be false, beliefs which other intelligent creatures—perhaps highly intelligent beings from another planet—would know to be based on faulty evidence and misleading ideas which for some reason seem to be particularly prevalent on earth? To ask such questions is not to reject any possibility of our knowing the truth, any more than Descartes' method of doubt was an admission on his part that he could never know anything. But it is to make us more sensitive to the limitations of our knowledge, and the need to support our beliefs on more solid footing than the fact that we, personally, find them to be "obvious."

We end our discussion of skepticism, however, not with Hume and the apparent victory of the skeptic, but with Hume's greatest successor, the German idealist Immanuel Kant. Kant read Hume's arguments in defense of skepticism and was deeply shocked—"awakened from his dogmatic slumber," as he put it. He considered Hume's "fork" and realized that so long as one accepted the exclusivity of the "matters of fact"—"relations of ideas" dichotomy and, even more, so long as one accepted the seemingly innocent "two-world assumption," there would be no getting around skepticism—and that meant no way of justifying those basic presuppositions upon which all our knowledge is based. So what Kant does, put simply, is to deny the two-world assumption. We already saw that Kant insisted that we "constitute" or "set up" the world according to *a priori* rules. But then it is not true, he says, that we first of all and "directly" know only our own experiences, and only secondarily or by inference the things of the world. To the contrary, the world *is* just the world of our experience, nothing "beyond" or "external" to it. The mind, Kant suggests, imposes its forms and categories on our experience, and among these forms and categories are those that provide the presuppositions of our knowledge (for example, "causality" and "substance"). These presuppositions, accordingly, are neither empirical truths nor "relations of ideas," but a special and new kind of truth that Kant calls "*synthetic apriori.*" The truths are synthetic because they are not mere tautologies, not merely trivially true. They are *a priori* because, like all necessary truths, they are "prior" to experience. What would our experience of the world be like if we didn't impose these forms on it? The answer is that we would not have anything we could really call "experience." We would not be able to identify objects, recognize similarities or differences between our sensations, or even have any sense of self as the subject of different experiences succeeding one another in time. Thus, the presuppositions of our knowledge can be said to be necessarily true because they are the rules according to which any experience at all is possible. And since they are *our* rules, skepticism about them—or whether they "correspond" with the world they constitute—is utterly pointless. Or so Kant argued, and after him Hegel.

Knowledge, Truth, and Science

Many people and most philosophers today look for the truth—they look to **science**. For several centuries, science and its methods have been the royal road to finding out how the world really is. Empiricists and rationalists both tended to be scientists or to have great admiration for scientists. Skeptics often tended to defend their skepticism as "scientific." Educated religious critics of science did not usually reject science, but only questioned some particular scientific theory or the intrusion of science into some concern where it was inappropriate. One need not attack science, for example, to reject Darwin's theory of evolution, or to insist that the experience of love is not something that social scientists should try to study. On the other hand, science does presume a certain worldview that may well be judged to be too limiting or too impersonal for many questions about human life. Nevertheless, this much seems undeniable: Science is today our touchstone of truth. To say that something is "scientifically established"—whether it is a theory about the surface of the planet Saturn or the effectiveness of a new, improved brand of toothpaste—is to say that we have come as close to the truth as we can expect to get.

"Science" has been a word filled with praise for several centuries. The German equivalent, *Wissenschaft*, was used by such figures as Kant and Hegel to emphasize the seriousness and thoroughness of their thinking about all sorts of matters, from physics to metaphysics. Today, however, the term "science" tends to be limited to those questions that can and must be answered by reference to **experience** and extrapolations from experience. Thus it might be said that science is an **empirical** discipline—as opposed to logic and mathematics, for example. Physics, chemistry, geology, and biology—the natural sciences—are the standard examples. Somewhat more controversial are the social sciences—psychology, sociology, anthropology, and economics—but there is no doubt that, whatever else they may be, they are also empirical disciplines based on observation and, to a more limited extent than physics and chemistry, on experiment. (There are no moral restrictions on chemical compounds, but there are all sorts of ethical limits to the ways in which one can experiment with people.) To say that a science is empirical is to insist that its theories and hypotheses must be tested in experience and can be shown to be true or false by way of experience. Our measure of truth is largely a matter of whether or not this can be done, and many philosophers—called **logical positivists**—once argued that any statement that could not be so tested was simply "meaningless" (unless, of course, it was a trivial truth or a statement in mathematics or logic).

It would be a mistake, however, to think of science as nothing but the gathering and testing of facts through experience. It would be a very limited and boring science indeed that did nothing more than collect large numbers of facts. Chemistry would be nothing but an enormous laboratory and catalogue filled with specimens and names of different substances. Biology would be nothing but garden-tending and zoo-keeping. But these are not chemistry or biology, and never were. Chemists since the ancient Babylonians—and probably long before that—operated not only with observed facts but with hypotheses and theories. The facts served the theories by *confirming* them—showing them to be probably true—or by disproving them—showing them to be probably false. A caveman searching for a mammoth, and trying to avoid a saber-toothed tiger, is operating with hypotheses about where each of those creatures should be (behind the bushes, in the swamp, asleep in the cave), and his experience had better confirm his hypotheses. Modern chemists do not just collect chemicals but formulate hypotheses about how different chemicals relate to one another, how one is produced from another, why some chemicals cannot be further broken down, and so on. To do this, they need a whole language of chemistry that is not merely descriptive of what we can see, touch, and pour into bottles. In addition to such a descriptive **observational** language ("a fine red powder that easily bursts into flame"), chemists also need a **theoretical** language ("atoms," "molecule," "element," "chemical bond," "oxidation"). Strictly speaking, no one has ever seen an electron. Yet electrons are among the most important particles ever discussed by chemists, and it is by talking about electrons (and kindred subatomic particles) that chemists can describe most of what they know about the world.

Science is an empirical discipline, but like metaphysics, it involves speculation, imagination, the specification of things unseen. In addition to the observation of facts and the carrying out of experiments, the scientist or the science student needs to *think* to formulate theories, to go beyond what can be observed and suggest what might explain it. Mathematical models, for example, play a central role in many sciences—physics and economics, for example. Truth in science is not just the truth of facts. It is also the truth of theories. A scientist without a theory and without a hypothesis for guidance would not have anything to do. Like a child with a new chemistry set, of course, a chemist could just throw together one substance after another and see what happens. But in addition to being dangerous, this would be an aimless activity and as unlikely to produce an insight into truth as a monkey at the word processor is to produce a novel.

Hypotheses and theories guide observation and experiment. A scientist might notice something by accident that leads to the formulation of a hypothesis and a sketch of a theory, but this is possible only after the scientist has been thinking about and working with the same subject for some time. A hypothesis tells us what facts to look for. A theory tells us how to understand these facts. The hypothesis that water is a combination of oxygen and hydrogen tells us what kind of experiments to perform (those that combine the two elements, those that divide water molecules into its components). It is atomic theory, however, that tells us how to interpret such results. Indeed, without atomic theory it is not even clear how we would interpret the idea that water is a "combination" of anything—much less the combination of two gases that cannot even be seen.

The importance of hypotheses and theories in science raises enormous problems about truth. We are not very confused about what is meant by "truth" when the claim is observationally straightforward: "The frog is sitting on the stone," for example, or "The powder just changed to blue." But when a large theory is under consideration, its truth, by its very nature, cannot be simply discerned. Darwin's theory is a complex and ingenious scheme for describing an enormously wide variety of observations—many of them not yet made. It is not the only scheme that explains these observations, even within the realm of evolutionary theory. So what does it mean to say that it is "true"? It might be shown that it is the simplest, the most far-reaching, the best-confirmed theory. Nevertheless, we want to say that "truth" means something more than "very well confirmed"; it means "the way the world really is." Are we ever justified in saying this of a theory?

Indeed, are we justified even in saying that a particular fact is true? We have seen how the skeptic tries to throw into doubt *all* our knowledge of the world, except, perhaps, the most basic facts of our senses ("I am seeing green right now"). The importance of theories in science points to a different way in which the truth of science might be doubted. Facts get gathered in order to confirm or disprove a hypothesis; the selection of hypotheses, in other words, determines what we will look for. But observations in general get made in the light of theories. To call something a "sunset" is to see it in the light of a certain astronomical theory—a false theory, in fact. To call a streak of a cloud in a chamber an "electron" is to interpret what we see in the light of a certain theory. One might say, "There are no electrons; they are only postulations of a theory." But so, too, one might object, "There are no sunsets; there is only a certain position of the earth vis-à-vis the sun, with some peculiar refractions of light as the result." Facts get interpreted according to theories. Without a theory, there would not even be certain facts. Some philosophers of science, on the basis of such considerations, have argued that there are no facts as such only facts as viewed in the light of theories. Every observation in science presupposes a theoretical framework, just as every theory presupposes some facts to make it empirically plausible. But suppose, as we look through the history of science, we find that scientists have held very different theories, and interpreted the same facts in very different ways. What, then, are we to say about truth in science? How do we compare theories to tell which, if any, are true?

The question here is whether science really does give us the truth, or perhaps only a truth of its own making. For example, many scientific observations are possible only by means of specially invented scientific equipment—a telescope, a microscope, a cloud chamber, or a cyclotron. Could it be that the truth we discover is in fact the creation of the implements we use? Imagine yourself in Galileo's laboratory several hundred years ago, looking through some weird-looking invention called a "telescope." Through this strange tube, you see what look like moons around the planet Jupiter, and you see what look like mountains on the face of the moon. Do you trust your eyes? If you were living at the time, you might well refuse to accept what you saw, on the grounds that the tube distorted your vision, much as a red-colored lens will make the world look red. What would convince you that the tube really had improved your vision rather than distorted it? Or could it be that any implement in science, even while it allows us to learn something, nevertheless interferes with and distorts precisely the subject it seeks to study? (Imagine a traffic cop—in uniform—studying the ordinary behavior of drivers. What the cop sees, for the most part, is not the ordinary behavior of drivers at all, but the behavior of drivers when they are in the presence of a police officer.)

Why do we take science as a paradigm of truth? Isn't it possible that the results of science can be doubted? Isn't it possible that even the facts described by science can be doubted? The answer to both questions is "yes," but nevertheless science has two impressive claims in support of its current status as the road to truth:

1. Science has been highly successful in predicting nature and in giving us the ability to invent instruments to alter nature to our will. One might question whether science has allowed us to understand nature better than ancient religious or Renaissance artists, but one can hardly question the success of science in predicting how hitherto-unknown chemicals will react, or in putting a man on the moon.

2. Science has both empirical and intellectual integrity. Scientific hypotheses can be and must be tested and tested again. No scientific theory is ever simply accepted; it must be supported over and over with new research. It must always stand up to new questions, new challenges. No one ever has the authority to force a theory on science against the evidence, and no opinion is considered influential enough to reject a theory that better explains the evidence. Any scientist will admit that these standards are sometimes violated; scientists are only human, after all. But the ideals remain and are accepted by everyone. Because of the rigor of these ideals, science has earned, and keeps, its place in our philosophy.

Even if we accept all this, however, we can still ask whether science deserves what often looks like an *exclusive* right to the honorable word "truth." What about human feelings—are they "true" or not? What about art and beauty—how do they fit into the scientific world? What about human relationships and international politics—are they made better through science? When we pride ourselves on approaching all questions "scientifically," is it possible that we are harming more than helping ourselves?

Consider one of the most controversial debates of our decade: the debate between the theory of evolution (not necessarily Darwin's) and the creationist view of the world based on Genesis. To their discredit, the evolutionists have sometimes dismissed the religious view of creation altogether, not even trying to see how the two views might be fitted together, even if the words in Genesis are taken more or less literally. To their discredit, the creationists have sometimes argued some appallingly bad science in trying to refute the evolutionists, and they, too, have not always been willing to see how the two antagonistic views might be put together. One could interpret evolution as God's means of creation; one can invoke God as the explanation of how the whole process got started. But without entering into the tangled web of emotions and beliefs that make this controversy so intractable, we can make two points in favor of a cease-fire:

1. Whatever the plausibility of creationism as a scientific hypothesis, it must be understood that the thrust behind creationism is not scientific curiosity; it is an attempt to stop science and its exclusive claim to truth from encroaching on territory where it has no business—the domain of religion. The origin of species is the border between the two domains.

2. Whatever one might think of any particular theory of evolution, science is nothing if it is not empirical. A theory must be confirmed by observed facts, not just based on authority. A theory must be falsifiable by facts; that is, we must at least be able to say what kinds of findings would undermine the theory. On the basis of its importance as a religious viewpoint, creationism may have as convincing grounds for belief as evolutionary theory has. But it is not, and should not claim to be, a *scientific* theory. (If the existence of fossils doesn't undermine it, what could?) Indeed, given the importance of the first point, why would creationism prefer to compete as bad science rather than as solid and established religious doctrine?

The Nature of Truth

> To say of what is that it is not, or of what is not that it is, is false, while to say of what is that it is, or of what is not that it is not, is true.
>
> Aristotle

We have already seen that some statements are true whether or not they correspond to the facts. We have also seen that the principles of philosophy are of this sort; they are not "matters of fact," but something else—perhaps (according to the rationalists) "truths of reason," perhaps (according to the skeptics) mere matters of opinion which cannot be justified at all. But in either case, what has become clear to us is that our initial conception of truth is inadequate. Let us give it a name: It is called the **correspondence theory of truth**—that is, a statement is true if and only if it corresponds to the facts. But there are other kinds of truth, as we have seen, such as the true statements of mathematics and logic. We need a more general theory which will include them as well as the true statements (if there are any) in philosophy.

So far we have talked primarily about truth, setting aside the question how we might come to know the truth. But the statement of the correspondence theory of truth, and its presupposed two-world view, forces us to take this secondary question much more seriously. Indeed, what good is a theory of truth if it gives us no indication how—or even whether—we can ever *know* the truth? With that in mind, philosophers have often shifted their attention from a statement or belief *being* true to our *reasons* (or justification) for accepting it *as* true. And what has happened, with this shift in emphasis, is that the search for reasons for accepting a statement or belief as true has come to encroach upon the question of truth itself; in other words, the reasons for believing that something is true have now been suggested to *be* truth.

Consider this. In a detective story, a man is murdered out in the country on a dark and cloudy night. There are no witnesses, only a small scattering of clues (a footprint, some fabric from a raincoat made in Transylvania, some suspicious marks on the neck of the accused). Now, if you are the detective investigating the case, or if you are a member of the jury at the trial, it won't help much to be told that you know that D is the killer if and only if you know that the statement that D is the killer is true. What interests you are the *reasons* for believing that D is the killer—the perfect match of the footprints, the fact that D has recently "lost" his raincoat, the curious toothy smile D occasionally displays in the prisoner's box. But such reasons never add up to a complete picture. They are always no more than evidence, which point to a conclusion but never actually reach it. (This is so even if D confesses; that is sometimes an excellent piece of evidence, but it is not in itself the truth we are looking for.) The truth itself is in the past; all we have now is the evidence.

Now, given the fact that the truth itself seems lost to us, a number of very different conclusions follow from this. Suppose that you, as detective, have developed an airtight case against D. What does this mean? Not that it could not possibly be false (since it is, in any case, a *contingent truth* that D is the killer), but that the alibis that D would need to convince anyone that he was not the killer would seem so ridiculous and so unreasonable that no one would believe them; for example, stories to the effect that he has a twin brother who is always getting him into trouble, or that he is the victim of a collective conspiracy on the part of you, the police, and all the witnesses. The evidence still adds up to less than the truth, but can we say that we *know* that D is the killer, that this is an objective truth instead of a merely subjective opinion? Some people would say, "Yes, of course; all you need to claim that your belief is true is the best available set of reasons; there is nothing else you can have." But others would say, "No, you never actually know what is true; at most, you have the best belief under the circumstances, and you have to make do with that." In the first claim, we still have objective truth, but it now depends not on a property of the object but on the reasons we provide for our beliefs. In the second view, there is no objective truth at all; it is simply a matter of competing opinions, some of which are more persuasive than others.

Now this is even more difficult with philosophical truths. If we are concerned with the existence of God, for example, it is clear that the same problem exists. If He appears directly to us, perhaps that would seem to settle the question. (But even then, how do we know that He is God, as opposed to a delusion, or as opposed to the Devil who is trying to fool us?—only by appeal to the *reasons* for believing one interpretation rather than another.) We claim to have some evidence that God exists (the existence of the Bible, for instance, the existence of the world as a designed masterpiece). But the evidence never adds up to God. To say that one *knows* that God exists is to say that one's belief is both justified and true. But we have already seen that there are serious questions about what should *count* as a justification for belief in God. It seems that one must accept the truth of God's existence not because of, but rather prior to any evidence or argument that would confirm His existence. This is why Kierkegaard holds that all belief in God requires a "leap of faith."

But this apparent need to have the truth *before* one collects adequate evidence and argument is not just a problem with the very special belief in God's existence. It would seem that any claim to know the truth—whether coming from a rationalist or an empiricist—requires that we know the facts *independently* of our claim to know the truth in order to justify our claim to the truth. But this would mean, according to the correspondence theory of truth, that we first need the truth (the facts) in order to justify our claim to the truth. In other words, we can't say that a statement is true without having justifying reasons—but this would seem to suppose (on the correspondence theory) that we can know the world apart from our own knowledge.

And here we meet the skeptic face to face: Is it the case that we can't know the truth because we can never be certain, because there is always a leap from our evidence and our reasons to the "facts"? Or is it even worse, that we can never know the truth because we have to somehow know the truth before we can have any reasons for claiming to know the truth? But perhaps the problem isn't truth but rather this particular, seemingly obvious theory of truth—the correspondence theory. Perhaps there are other conceptions of truth, which have the twin virtues of both accounting for the various kinds of truth we have discussed and of answering the skeptic?

Two such theories have predominated in the past few centuries. They both shift the emphasis away from the "facts" toward the *reasons* for accepting a certain belief. One is called the **coherence theory of truth**, the other is called the **pragmatic theory of truth**.

The Coherence Theory of Truth

The coherence theory begins by rejecting the correspondence theory, insisting that the very notion of correspondence to the facts not only fails to account for truth in mathematics and logic but even fails (as our detective story example showed) to account for ordinary factual truth. All we have are reasons for believing—evidence, arguments, principles, and our various beliefs themselves. But why do we need anything more? Indeed, when we talk about truth, what we mean is simply this: What is true is simply that statement or belief which best *coheres* with, or fits into the overall network of our experience and beliefs. We accept a principle as true because it fits with our other principles. We accept an argument because it follows from what we believe and leads to conclusions we can accept. We agree on the evidence because it fits into our hypotheses, because it fits together, because it adds up to a coherent picture. Nothing else is needed to give us the truth. Of course, our evidence is always incomplete, and the beliefs that we already accept are not always sufficient to allow us to know with certainty whether some new belief should be accepted. In fact, there may be occasions (for instance, a religious conversion) in which the whole network of our beliefs exhibits a significant shift or turnaround or disruption. But this is not to be taken as our inability to ever reach the truth; quite to the contrary, what it means is that the truth is within our grasp, and that with experience we change our beliefs precisely to grasp it more exactly.

The Pragmatic Theory of Truth

> Grant an idea or belief to be true, what concrete difference will its being true make in anyone's actual life? . . . What, in short, is the truth's cash-value in experiential terms?

> —William James, *Pragmatism*

The pragmatic theory supplements the coherence theory with a practical proviso—namely, that among the reasons for accepting a statement or a belief as true is whether it allows us to function better, whether it suggests fruitful lines of inquiry to be pursued in the future—whether it "works," in the words of the most famous defender of the theory, the American pragmatist, William James. One hypothesis in science, for instance, may not have any more evidence for it than another, and it may fit into our overall beliefs no better than do a number of others; but it may well be more easily testable, encourage further experimentation in the same field, suggest interesting possibilities not suggested by other hypotheses. To say that a view is true, therefore, is to say that it is the most valuable, the most promising explanation available to us But the value of a view is not just its scientific promise. It might be its social or spiritual value as well—for example, in our views of morality and religion.

Rationality

With the shift of attention to reasons for believing something to be true, the virtue of having good reasons, or what we call **rationality** has become increasingly important. Throughout most of the history of philosophy, from Plato to the modern rationalists, rationality and the search for truth were considered absolutely identical. But where truth seems to refer only to the "way the world is," without any reference to our ways of knowing it, rationality clearly refers to our activities, to our methods of finding the truth, and so provides us with a much more tangible and less evasive topic of discussion.

Rationality means "thinking and acting in accordance with reason"; rationality is thinking with reasons, good reasons. What is a "good reason"? If thinking is based on "facts," then the facts must be well confirmed, not simply hearsay or wild guesses. (We do not have to say that the facts must be "true" in the correspondence sense; someone might have very good reason to accept them but, by some twist of circumstances, they turn out not to be true.) If thinking is based upon deductive reasoning, then the reasoning must be valid. Of course, a "good reason" must make sense; appeals to mysterious forces or mystical insights will not do in rational argument. And a good reason must be relevant to the case at hand; a brilliant argument and a number of facts do not constitute rationality if they are not directed at the matter under consideration. But this last point is derived from the most important general characteristic of rationality: Rationality depends most of all upon coherence. To be rational is to think of as many reasons, dig up as many facts, and call up as many beliefs as are necessary to provide a comprehensive logical web in support of any given belief.

Since Kant, this ideal of rationality has ruled philosophy in place of the traditional ("correspondence") notion of truth. But what is the relationship between rationality and truth? In one sense, it is important that we insist that rationality does not require that our beliefs be true. For example, you might think that the belief that the earth is flat, or motionless, or made of water, is a false belief, and, in terms of the system of beliefs which we all share today, any of these beliefs certainly is not *rational*. But had you lived in earlier times, in ancient Greece for example, these would not have seemed false at all, but completely rational. And in the context of their system of beliefs, what you now believe would have been utterly

THEORIES OF TRUTH

Correspondence theory: *True beliefs (or sentences) correspond to the facts.*

"The cat is on the mat."

Coherence theory: *True beliefs (including beliefs about experience) and sentences cohere to each other.*

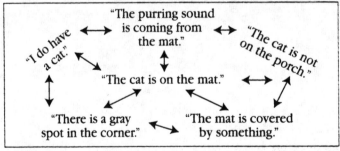

Pragmatic theory: *True beliefs (or sentences) are those that "work."*

"It's time to feed the cat."
"Get the cat off the mat."
"Why can't we burn the mat?"
"Why is the mat so heavy?"

irrational. This does not mean that it is always rational to believe what everyone around you believes and irrational not to; it *is* possible that everyone's beliefs are irrational, founded on bad reasons, lack of evidence, refusal to think about them clearly or carefully, and unspoken prejudice or superstition. But this is not always or even usually the case. In the above example, we may suppose that the Greeks had the best of reasons for believing what they did about the earth. Rationality, therefore, does not require truth; it requires only that a person make the best possible use of all of the information and "reason" at his or her disposal.

What, then, are we to say about the commonsense idea that truth is "correspondence to the facts"? We don't want to deny this. It is hard to deny that what makes my statement "the cat is on the mat" true is just that the cat is in fact on the mat. But what the preceding considerations and arguments suggest is that we can't simply take this "correspondence" of statement to fact at face value. What lies behind it is the entirety of our language and our ways of conceiving and referring to the world. In isolation, the words (or more properly, the sounds or the scribbles) "the cat is on the mat" mean nothing at all, refer to nothing at all, and are neither true nor false. And what justifies the statement or belief that the cat is on the mat is not "the fact" but the array of evidence, both visual and from the other senses—the coherence of that statement or belief with all manner of other statements and beliefs and the implications for various practical concerns. In other words, even if one wants to insist that what makes the statement true is the relevant fact, we can say that we *know* that the cat is on the mat only because it is the most rational thing to believe. So although we can distinguish between rational thinking and truth in some particular cases, the truth is that which is most rational to believe at a given time and in a given situation, on the basis of the best available evidence and the most careful thinking possible. According to many philosophers, there is no other sense to be given to the words "true" and "truth," unless we are to fall back again into the intolerable and absurd doubts of Hume's skepticism.

Why Be Rational?

By now, you might well ask, why be rational? First, we have to distinguish several conceptions of rationality (just as we distinguished several conceptions of truth). Sometimes, "rational" has a familiar negative connotation, such as when you accuse a friend or lover of "being too rational," meaning insensitive, not in touch with his or her emotions, or abusing thought as a way of escaping from an emotionally charged situation. In this sense, we can quickly agree that there is good reason not to be rational. Similarly, if you think of rationality as "thinking something into the ground" so that you never act upon it at all, or always too late, then we can willingly give up rationality in that sense, too.

The answer to the philosophical question "Why be rational?" is simply this: Rationality is the most efficient way to comprehend the world, and the best guarantee that you know what is going on around you. But if this answer isn't convincing to you, the following should be: It is a mistake to talk about "rationality" as purely a matter of understanding. It is also a matter of action and of living—acting rationally and living rationally. And as soon as we add this pragmatic dimension, the answer to the question "Why be rational?" becomes extremely persuasive. To act rationally is to act in such a way that you are more likely to get what you want (including knowledge as well as enjoyment, satisfaction, and an occasional ego boost). The best way to get something is not always the most "rational" in the narrow sense of "most efficient." In this machine-and-consumer society, it is often more efficient to buy something than to make it with your own hands; that doesn't make it more rational. And it is not necessarily rational to think everything out and plan ahead, for sometimes what we want is novelty and adventure, in which case it may be most rational not to think it all out and plan ahead. But, in any case, rationality, in this sense, is hardly objectionable.

Rationality is trying our knowledge and our lives together in the most coherent and effective way. But here we come back to the dilemma facing philosophy since Kant. If we have separated truth and rationality from the question of the "way the world really is," it is apparent that different societies and even different individuals can tie their experiences and their lives together in very different ways. According to our account of rationality, are we going to be forced to accept any system, no matter how bizarre, as rational and even true, just because it is coherent and satisfies the person or the people who believe in it?

Subjective Truth: Any Truth at All?

What is Truth but to live for an idea? /It is a question of discovering a truth which is truth for me, of finding the idea for which I am willing to live or die.

—Kierkegaard, *Journals*

The objective accent falls on WHAT is said, the subjective accent on HOW it is said.

—Kierkegaard, *Concluding Unscientific Postscript*

As our conception of truth moves further away from the "way the world really is" and correspondence with the facts, it moves nearer and nearer to the subject, to the person trying to learn the truth. In other words, we move further from **objective truth** (that is, truth independent of our personal opinions) toward what has sometimes been called **subjective truth**, truth *dependent on the subject* and his or her beliefs. We might say that the paranoid's view of the world is a subjective truth; true for him, but not objectively true—that is, not true of the world. We might say that an entire society's view of the world is subjectively true for that society, even if we know that its view is objectively false. The problem is that with this conception of subjective truth, we have moved far away from the concept of truth—that is, that there is but one truth, one true set of facts which is true for everybody whether they know it or not. Subjective truth seems to allow for a different truth, a different set of facts, for everyone. But isn't this just saying that *nothing* is true?—that there is no truth but only different perspectives and different ways of looking at the world? In other words, can we call anything "true" if it is true only for one person or one society? Doesn't truth, if it is truth at all, have to be objective?

The most outspoken champion of subjective truth, Soren Kierkegaard, was exceedingly cautious when he defended his notion of a personal truth "for which I am willing to live or die." He insisted that this kind of truth—personal, subjective truth—is the most important kind of truth, the kind of truth that makes life meaningful, the kind of "true commitment" to God or other people that gives life a direction it otherwise would not have. But, at the same time, he did not try to extend his conception of subjective truth to the entire realm of knowledge, only to those areas he called "objective uncertainties." In other words, he also believed in objective truth—in science, for example—and his theory of subjective truth therefore is this: In those areas of human life where science cannot give us the answer, such as in ethics and religion, subjective truth—passionate personal commitment—is necessary. But this still left open the question of the nature of so-called objective truth, which is not denied but simply supplemented by another notion of truth which Kierkegaard thought was more important. (It is worth noting that Kierkegaard also thought that the search for subjective truth is **irrational** that it follows no rules and often requires blind faith rather than careful thinking and planning.) The ultimate question is: Could it be that objective truth is itself subjective?

Where are we to find truth, that is, objective truth? Current thinking on this issue is both confusing and exciting: On the one side, philosophers are generally agreed that subjective truth is, in the realm of science, for example, not sufficient. Truth, if it is truth at all, must be generally believable, confirmable by any number of persons, true not just for someone but true even in spite of what people believe about it. But on the other hand, the arguments of the skeptics and the alternative theories of truth—the coherence theory and the pragmatic theory—have made philosophers (and scientists, too) more humble than they used to be, no longer so sure that they are finding out the facts of the "world as it really is," and wondering just how many of their "discoveries" are indeed the product of an order which they themselves have imposed on nature, through their theories, their concepts, and their experiments. Does this mean that we shall never know the "way the world really is"? Does this mean that two alternative ways of looking at the world might both be *equally* true? However we answer these very difficult questions, our conclusion cannot be, "It's all subjective," which is more often than not a sign of lazy thinking or of a refusal to answer the hard questions at all. The answer is, rather, that whatever the claims we make for truth, the rules of rationality retain a persistent hold on us. We might have a powerful insight or mystical vision; we might be suddenly inspired or emotionally moved. But what we say and believe nevertheless requires something more: It requires *reasons*. It requires working out. It requires development into a systematic understanding of what this insight, vision, inspiration, or emotion amounts to.

And that's the truth.

Bibliography and Suggested Readings

Bertrand Russell's *The Problems of Philosophy* (Oxford University Press, 1912) is a short classic and an excellent introduction to the problems of "appearance and reality" that have occupied so much of modern philosophy. David Hume's theory of knowledge is summarized in his *Enquiry Concerning Human Understanding* (Oxford University Press, 1955); the more complete argument is his *Treatise on Human Nature*, ed. L. A. Selby-Bigge (Oxford University Press, 1980). The main works of the British empiricists John Locke, Bishop George Berkeley, and David Hume can be found together in *The Empiricists* (Doubleday, 1960). The best general study of the history and strategy of skepticism is Richard Popkin, *A History of Skepticism: From Erasmus to Descartes* (Harper & Row, 1964); and a good study of Descartes and his methods is Anthony Kenny, *Descartes* (Random House, 1968). A short treatment of the various problems of truth is Alan R. White, *Truth* (Doubleday, 1970). Two very good general discussions of the problems of knowledge are Bruce Aune, *Rationalism, Empiricism, Pragmatism* (Random House, 1970) and Adam Morton, *A Guide Through the Theory of Knowledge* (Wadsworth, 1977). A classic study in the philosophy of science is C. G. Hempel, *Philosophy of Natural Science* (Prentice-Hall, 1966). For a modern, though controversial, view of science, see Thomas S. Kuhn, *The Structure of Scientific Revolutions* (University of Chicago Press, 1970). For a detailed study of the creationism-evolution debate, see Philip Kitcher, *The Abuse of Science* (MIT Press, 1983). For a challenging defense of modern skepticism, see Peter Unger, *Ignorance* (Oxford University Press, 1979). A creative approach to these problems can be found in Arthur Danto, *Connections to the World* (New York: Harper & Row, 1989).

THE SELF

CONCEPTIONS OF THE SELF

by Mark Liederbach & John Cunningham

Know thyself

—Socrates

Without knowledge of self there is no knowledge of God . . .
Without knowledge of God there is no knowledge of self.

—John Calvin, The Institutes of the Christian Religion 1. 1. 1, 2.

I. Introduction: Who Are You?

At first blush a question like "what is the self?" may seem esoteric or irrelevant to the daily life of a college student. However, with just a little thought it is easy to discover not only how frequently the question arises, but also how relevant it is to many of the central issues our society faces today.

Consider the following scenarios that might play out in life of an average college student:

A sophomore calls home for some advice about choosing a major. Afterward, she confides in her friend. "I'm not sure what do," she sighs, "My dad wants me to be an engineer, but my real love is music. I think it will really make him mad if I decide on a music major, *but I just have to be true to myself.*"

Two students are out on their third date when the guy begins making sexual advances. Unfortunately, even after the girl indicates she is uncomfortable with his advances, he continues to press the issue. Finally, she explodes, *"Who do you think you are? I said no!"*

A freshman considers pledging a fraternity, but after attending a party where most of the fraternity brothers were smoking dope he decides to drop his bid. When asked about this by a friend he replies, "*That's just not me.*"

Or suppose you are interviewing for admission to a prestigious college or university and the interviewer says to you, "Tell me about yourself." What kind of answers would you give? Most of us, I presume, would give answers that reflect our activities and achievements.

Now suppose you were setting up the meeting place for a blind date and your future date asks you to describe yourself so that he or she can identify you. Most of us would give answers that describe our physical characteristics.

Finally, suppose you have an appointment with a counselor or psychologist in order to work through some disturbing issues in your past. The counselor begins the time together by saying "I need to get to know you first, what can you tell me about yourself?" Most of us, I believe, would give answers that reveal some of our inner qualities—our longings, beliefs, hurts, and desires.

Which answer reflects the "real" you? The self defined by externalities like majors, jobs, status, titles? The self defined by physical characteristics like hair color, gender, height, weight? Or is the real self defined by some internal quality like virtues, beliefs, ideas?

Obviously, questions about the self abound. But in addition to the frequency of its occurrence, the question of self-identity also relates to some of the most difficult circumstances of life. Consider the following as a case in point.

> Several years ago while flying from Washington D.C. to Denver, Colorado, I was seated next to a recent college grad named Jim. After a few minutes of chit- chat, I asked Jim if he was married. This seemingly innocuous question took the discussion in a more serious direction. The question seemed to make Jim nervous, then he turned pensive, and finally his mood became sad and dark. Finally, after a few minutes of silence, he related what was obviously a very personal and difficult story.
>
> Two years prior, he and his fiancé were in a terrible automobile accident. He emerged relatively unscathed, but his fiancé suffered irreversible brain damage. She was now in a semi-vegetative state undergoing long-term care. Doctors offered little hope of her ever regaining most of her mental faculties. Indeed, while she is able to recognize Jim, she is unable to remember much of their history.
>
> Jim finds himself alternately confused, mad, and simply sad. Each day he goes to visit his fiancé with the hopes of finding some improvement. Each day a little more of that hope dies.
>
> After two long years of uncertainty Jim finds himself at a loss with how to go on with his life. At 34,000 ft. somewhere between Washington and Denver, Jim turned to me with the following questions: "What do you think, is she still the same person I was going to marry? What should I do?"

Is she the same person? Why or why not? How was Jim to know?

A striking thing about this case, is the intensity of feeling and opinion it evokes from students. Most of my philosophy and religion students have some immediate opinion about what Jim should do. However, when pushed to explain why, few are able to give clear justification for their opinions. Most have never been forced to carefully articulate what it is they actually believe about the self.

In addition, the diversity of opinions about the case reveals further confusion. Some students believe Jim's fiancé is still "present" in her body and should be cared for like this was any other accident—with loyalty and patience. Others have argued that her "real self" is "trapped" in a broken body. The right thing to do, they argue, is to "free the self" from the body through some form of euthanasia. Others believe that Jim's fiancé is "no longer present in the body anyway," so Jim's only concern now is for himself.

While few college freshman have ever been pushed to wrestle with the questions about the self at this level, there are plenty of theologians and philosophers who have. Throughout the history of philosophy "knowing oneself" has been a concern of central importance. The simple reason for this is that answers to so many other questions of life (like those of God, personal meaning, and reasons to be moral) depend upon what one believes the self to be. The task of this chapter is to explore the ideas of several influential thinkers regarding the nature of the self in hopes of shedding some light on this elusive issue.

By way of procedure, then, the remainder of the chapter will focus on various influential conceptions of the self in the history of philosophy. Rather than attempting to give an exhaustive survey of conceptions of the self (such a task would require volumes in itself!), this chapter seeks to give the reader a selection of tastes from the smorgasbord of ideas about the self in western culture.

Ultimately, the purpose of this approach is not only to expose the reader to a wide selection of ideas regarding the self, but to provide a basic foundation from which to understand many of the issues behind questions of both meaning and morality. The question "what is the self?" bears heavily on everything from being made fun of as a child for having freckles to questions about the morality of abortion or euthanasia.

We will begin, as do most issues in Western philosophy, with Plato and Aristotle. Next we'll consider Augustine's thinking which influenced the West for the next 1,500 years. Then we'll move into modernity with David Hume's skeptical views, Kierkegaard's religious existentialism, and Freud's psychological determinism. Finally, we'll look at Sartre's existential absurdist notions, which are the forerunners of many contemporary postmodern perspectives.

II. Views of the self

Plato

Understanding Plato's view of the self requires some basic knowledge of his metaphysics. Plato begins with the observation that human beings tend to judge or evaluate the things they encounter. Usually, this evaluation takes the form of comparison between what something is and what it ought to be. He argues that in order for such a comparison to be possible, there must be some ideal concept or perfect pattern against which things in our experience can be compared. For example, Plato challenges us to consider what actually takes place when an event is judged to be unjust or when a piece of art is described as beautiful. How is such an evaluation of justice made, against what standard of beauty is the art work compared to? Plato's answer is that we use as our standard an ideal, perfect pattern, or "Form" of justice or beauty. For Plato, these Forms or Ideas actually exist apart from that thing or event we are evaluating.

Now while these Forms do not exist in space or time, nor are they directly perceivable to human senses, Plato argues that they really exist. In fact, he argues that these Forms are actually "more real" than the ordinary objects compared to them. The reason they are more real is that while the objects we actually perceive are always changing, the Forms do not change. They remain stable and consistent and without decay, and thereby provide a fixed point or standard by which to compare all things.

To substantiate his theory Plato uses geometric proofs to show that while no physical object is perfectly straight or round, theorems and proofs show that perfect lines or circles actually are a reality and that by which we judge all others lines or circles. The circles and lines that we actually see and experience are known to be circle or lines only in that they resemble those perfect forms or patterns. We judge circles and lines in light of those perfect forms.

What emerges from this theory is a *dualistic* understanding of the nature of reality. Based on this theory of Forms, Plato concluded that reality consists of two realms: that world in which we live (the world of *Becoming*), and the realm of the Forms (the world of *Being*). The only access to knowledge of the realm of Forms, for those existing in the world of Becoming, is through the rational soul. It is the soul which acts as a sort of bridge between these two Worlds enabling the self to evaluate to what degree things in this world of Becoming actually "participate" in the Forms.

Plato's dualistic understanding of the nature of the reality relates directly to his understanding of the self. Plato maintained that the human soul is a very real, albeit immaterial, entity. The existence of the soul is independent from the existence of the material body. In addition to being immaterial, the soul is also immortal and indestructible.[1] It existed prior to the birth of the human body that it inhabits and it will continue to exist after the body perishes. The material body, on the other hand, is both mortal and destructible. The body then, acts almost like a cage or jail that impedes the soul's understanding of the Forms that comprise the world of Being. Thus, freeing the soul from the hindrance of the body is a goal for those who would be all that they can be. Plato tells us that his hero and mentor, Socrates, faced death with peaceful anticipation, knowing that ultimately, his soul would be freed from the body to return to the realm of the Forms. In Platonic thought, the soul comprises the essential nature of the self.

While Plato conceives the nature of the self in a dualistic manner (body and soul), he also maintains that there are three distinct parts that make up the soul. The three parts are the *appetite*, the *spirit*, and *reason*. To explain the functioning of the soul, Plato uses the metaphor of a chariot being pulled by two winged horses.[2] One of these horses, representing the appetitive part of the soul, is brutish and poorly bred. Its main concern is the pursuit of bodily gratification such as sex, food and drink or other bodily pleasures. The other horse, representing the spirited part of the soul, is noble, well bred, and honorable. This horse represents what we might term the "psychological" human drives such as ambition or anger.

Obviously, if these two horses pull in an unrestrained manner they will become unruly and lead the soul astray. Thus, it falls to the charioteer to properly restrain and guide the horses, channeling their energies in the right direction. Whereas the horses represent the appetites and spirit, the charioteer, represents the *rational* part of the soul. In this way Plato maintains that reason is the highest part of the soul. Reason must be nurtured and developed above the others for when nurtured correctly, it recollects the World of Being, its true home, and regains true knowledge of the Forms.

The implications of Plato's conception of the self are striking. He likens the human condition to that of prisoners chained deep within the walls of a cave. Without a developed rational soul and without proper skills, people perceive only shadows of the true nature of things.[3]

Plato's view of the self carries with it an implicit ethical program. He views life as a long and sometimes arduous journey out of the cave, culminating in our emergence into the blinding light of the real. Consequently, the more the soul progresses, the less hold this shadow-world has on it. In order to progress in the journey, however, one's reason must foster the development of four basic virtues: temperance, courage, prudence, and justice. Temperance is consistent and enduring self-control in relation to the passionate part of the soul. Courage is the consistent enduring willingness to face adversity and relates primarily to the spirited part of the soul. Prudence relates to the consistent, enduring wisdom in choosing the right direction toward the world of Being, and justice relates to the overall disposition of the virtuous person who embodies the other three Virtues.

As the soul employs these cardinal virtues, it aligns itself increasingly with the realm of the Forms, thereby rising to its rightful heights. Eventually the true self, the soul, leaves this world of illusion behind.

Aristotle

Whereas Plato's conception of the self is dualistic, his most famous pupil, Aristotle, had a very different view. In fact, Aristotle flatly rejected many of Plato's metaphysical and ontological assumptions. In particular, he opposed Plato's belief in the actual existence of a "realm of Forms." For Aristotle, such a notion creates more philosophical problems than it solves. Furthermore, he questioned exactly how things in this world of becoming "participated" in the Forms existing in the world of Being. Instead, he argued that forms do indeed exist, but that they are not separate from the things of this world. For Aristotle, the forms are the actual properties of things in this world. Plato believed that experiences in this world should lead us to contemplate a higher, truer reality. Aristotle argued that such experiences should lead us to ponder the actual nature of the particular thing. Forms for Aristotle do not exist in some separate realm of reality, they are essential parts of particular things experienced in this reality.

This rejection of Plato's dualism lead Aristotle to develop a different conception of the self. As a result, Aristotle argued that there is no radical distinction existing between body and soul. Instead, he held that human beings are unified entities—psychosomatic unions—whose bodies and souls are both necessary parts of one whole being. Aristotle's view is bound up in his understanding of *substances*.

Aristotle describes substances as any thing that actually exists, or has being. He argues that substances are comprised of properties that can be divided into two categories: accidental and essential. By accidental properties, he means characteristics that are not an essential part of the substance. These qualities could be removed from the substance and the substance would still exist as that substance. For example, a person doesn't cease to be a person if he or she gains 50 pounds when they stop exercising or loses hair due to chemotherapy treatment. These occurrences do not change persons into something else (a non-person). These characteristics (portliness or baldness) are unessential or *accidental* to the nature of the person existing as a person.

Essential properties, on the other hand, are those characteristics that if lost, will cause that substance to cease to exist as the same substance. According to Aristotle, the soul is that "essential property" of the human person. It is important, however, to understand that Aristotle has a different conception of the soul than did Plato. For Plato, it is possible for the soul to exist apart from the body. Aristotle's notion of the soul, however, is that which animates or brings the person to life in the body, *but cannot exist apart from the body.* Thus, body and soul are interrelated parts of one united whole.[4]

Whereas Plato sees the ultimate aim of the soul to be participation in the realm of the Forms by releasing the soul from the constraints of the body, Aristotle finds the highest purpose of the human being in the embodied soul. When a person pursues the highest aim of the soul, he or she begins to lead an excellent life or a life of highest possible happiness. The Greek term Aristotle used to describe this kind of life was *eudaemonia* which, when translated to English means, "a life of flourishing" or "well being." For him, when the soul functions properly, *eudaemonia* results. The obvious question for Aristotle, then, is "What is it that is the highest purpose of the soul? What is it that when it is pursued will give a person the highest possible fulfillment of self?"

To reach a conclusion Aristotle reasons that there are many functions humans share with plants and animals. All three (plants, animals, and humans) perform essential life functions, like absorbing nutrition. Both humans and animals can move and have the ability to sense things, but only humans have a particularly important ability that plants and animals do not. The unique human capacity that sets humans apart is the ability to reason.

Since *reasoning* is the highest function of the essential quality of the human, it follows then that *reasoning well* is the highest purpose or highest end toward which the self can strive. Aristotle's conception of the self, then, includes the idea that when a person lives a life constituted by excellence in reasoning, then he or she will live a life of true happiness, a life of flourishing.

For Aristotle, human maladies are traceable to a failure to act in light of the highest human end. Because humans are social beings, in order for society to truly flourish, then it must be comprised on people who are flourishing. To accomplish this, people must develop the skills necessary to live a flourishing life. The development of personal virtues and, in particular, the ability to use practical reason in the circumstances and dilemmas of life are essential in determining a course of action that leads to human flourishing.

In the end, Aristotle looks for a society built of people who embrace an ethical approach to all of life. These people live (and raise their children) in a virtuous manner, learning how to develop the skills to avoid excess or deficiency in actual behavior and thereby building a society exhibiting the same qualities.

Augustine

The influence of St. Augustine's (354-430 CE) work is immeasurable due to the scope and depth of his writings. Not only do his theology and philosophy serve as a link between the great classical thinkers (particularly Plato) and the doctrines of Christianity, but the trajectory of his thinking profoundly shaped Roman Catholic and Protestant theology and aimed the trajectory of philosophical inquiry for the next thousand years.

The influence of Platonism on Augustine is unquestionable. He links his own conversion to Christianity to reading "some books of the Platonists." However, it would be a mistake to suggest that Augustine merely "baptized" the philosophy of his day. On the contrary, while the early Augustine undoubtedly stands in the tradition of "Christian Platonism," his philosophical theology grew and changed throughout his career to the point that he reworked almost every major tenet of the tradition he inherited. His methodology of "faith seeking understanding," and his commitment to Biblical revelation led him to new theological formulations that are unrivaled in their influence on the history of Christian thought, and which hold tremendous purchase for many even today.

Augustine develops a rich and influential concept of the self that coopts and adapts many stock platonic ideas. He revises Plato's theory of the Forms, turns the notion of the ascent of the soul on its head, and mitigates the radical separation of body and soul.

Whereas Plato argued that the Forms exist independently in a separate realm, Augustine suggested that the Forms are immutable, eternal ideas that exist in the mind of God. As divine ideas, they function as Forms or patterns of all reality, and are, therefore, the blueprints by which the entire created universe came into existence. Thus, similar to Plato, he argued that these divine eternal forms are the criteria by which all things are compared for evaluation. But how does a person gain knowledge of these divine forms that exist in the mind of God?"

Until Augustine, Platonic philosophy of all types advanced the idea that the soul progresses through stages in its quest for union with Divinity. According to this model of "the ascent of the soul," when a person has been purified of worldly attachments, that person can look within him or her self where he or she will see a divine essence. The early Augustine declares, "Wherever you turn, by certain traces with which wisdom has impressed on her works, she speaks to you, and *recalls you within*, gliding back into *interior things* by the very forms of exterior things."[5] For Augustine the soul is created in God's image, therefore one may see God by contemplating his own soul. Nothing else is closer to God.[6]

However, when Augustine looked within he did not find divinity. On the contrary, the more he introspected the more he found in himself an irrational inclination toward sin. No matter how much he desired to follow God, he became increasingly aware of another, contrary impulse. Even when he restrained himself, in keeping with the Platonic program, he suspected that the reason he wasn't sinning was just because he lacked opportunity, not because he was becoming more divine. He once observed that a manure pile doesn't stink until it is stirred up. Likewise the human heart may not commit a particular sin until the opportunity presents its self.

After studying the Bible in light of his own introspection, Augustine came to believe that humans aren't born with a natural inclination toward the higher forms of reason, and an ever-improving impulse toward virtue. Quite the opposite. He read passages in the Bible like "THERE IS NONE RIGHTEOUS, NOT EVEN ONE; THERE IS NONE WHO UNDERSTANDS, THERE IS NONE WHO SEEKS FOR GOD; ALL HAVE TURNED ASIDE, TOGETHER THEY HAVE BECOME USELESS; THERE IS NONE WHO DOES GOOD, THERE IS NOT EVEN ONE,"[7] and concluded that his experience was the norm. People have an inborn propensity to evil that can't be shaken by will power. Augustine's formulation of these ideas culminated in his doctrine of Original Sin. To view the self not as good and not in complete control of its own inclinations was, of course, a radical shift in the conception of the self. As was his understanding of "grace." For Augustine, God helps those who can't help themselves. Humility, then, comes to the fore as a virtue. For the self to achieve its desired end, it must seek help from above.

So then, while Platonism suggests humans have the innate ability to ascend toward knowledge of the Forms through the cultivation of a wise and just character, Augustine came to believe something very different. He argued, instead, that humans are dependent upon *divine illumination* for knowledge of the divine forms. We subsist in darkness until God graciously "turns on the lights" as it were so that we can behold Him. The vision of God (*visio Dei*) became for Augustine, and the tradition that followed in his wake, the highest good of the human soul.

So then, Augustine's reworking of his Christian Platonist heritage forged a new view of the self. The first component of his mature theory of self is the assertion that humans are created beings. Augustine taught the doctrine of creation *ex nihilo* meaning the creation of matter out of nothingness. There was no pre-existing matter that existed from which God made persons. Instead, the creation was special not only in the form it took, but in the very fact that it exists at all. For this reason, it was possible for Augustine to affirm not only the matter of creation as valuable but, more to the point, he was able to affirm the value of the *material* nature of the human person.

In addition to an affirmation of the physical nature of the self, there is also a strong emphasis on the spiritual or immaterial aspect of human nature. Following the Biblical account of Genesis 2:7, Augustine maintained that the human person has been endowed with a divinely created soul[8] that includes the reason, the will and the emotions. In a manner similar to Plato, Augustine argues that it is in the soul that a person comes to true understanding of ultimate reality. According to Augustine, however, the soul has two capacities: a lower reason and a higher reason. The lower reason is that which relies primarily on the data of the senses which yields *knowledge* of things in the created universe. It is the function of this lower reason that enables humans to come to scientific knowledge of the universe. The higher reason is superior to the lower in that it appeals to higher sources of data (divine illumination) and leads not just to knowledge, but to *wisdom* and understanding of Truth. Its goal is not just knowledge for knowledge's sake, but rather seeks to order all things under the highest end—God. In this light, then, the real self, according to Augustine, is an embodied self (both body and soul) that comprises the reflection of the image of God in self asserted in the Biblical record.[9]

Because of the effects of sin, the self no longer has its higher reasoning ability to come to ultimate, eternal Truth or knowledge of God. The soul, due to sin's effects, became dull, blinded, and "enfeebled by infirmity" leaving the person unable to see God.[10] In addition, the will is no longer guided toward its proper end and it is unable to follow the precepts of God when unaided by grace. "A man's free will," Augustine argued, "avails is for nothing, except to sin, if he knows not the way of truth."[11] Finally, sin leaves the appetitive desires and emotions to run amuck so that the self can now only yearn for the temporal and fleeting pleasures of the world, not the higher ends for which he or she was ultimately created.

Based on this idea of self as sinner, some have interpreted Augustine's perspective of the self as having a primarily negative tone. However, it is the fourth aspect of the self that not only offers another radical departure from Platonism, but provides a basis from which to argue that Augustine's view of the self is in fact an extremely elevated one. And that is the argument he made, that in addition to being a created self, and image-bearing self, and a sinful self, humans are also recipients of grace.

Thus through a full reading of Augustine one can see that he assigns a high value to the self both because the self is the object of divine creation and the object of divine redemption. The former places an inherent worth or value on every human life, the latter offers hope of reaching the vaunted end or purpose for existence initially offered by the Creator.

Hume

David Hume's (1711-1776) theory of the self is a radical departure from the conceptions surveyed up to this point. Regarded by many as the most influential empiricist of the 18th century European Enlightenment, this Scottish philosopher and historian was known for his skeptical views about metaphysics. Hume argued that human perceptions of the nature of the universe relied solely upon sense data gathered through experience—this is the characteristic feature of empiricism. However, because of the limitations of human sense ability and the inability to apprehend the "causal links" between causes and effects, any assertions about reality must be held with a heavy dose of skepticism and uncertainty.

Hume's skepticism also played an important role in regard to the question of self-identity and attempts to define the self. Plato, Aristotle, and Augustine all described the self in terms of a permanent core or essential self around which every changing and new experience took place. Hume, however, rejected this notion. It was his contention that we can have no perception of a self that exists apart from fallible sense experience, and therefore we can have no sure conception of the self.

In his 1739 work *A Treatise on Human Nature,* he argued that it is impossible for a person to fully experience and know the self in a simple and enduring manner. To support his conclusion he reasoned that if a substance "is more than the sum of its perceptible parts, the substance must really be something extra, and in that case we ought to have a separate impression of it. "But," he argues, "we have no such impression."[12] Our inward glances can only attach themselves to specific ideas or feelings and are, therefore, unable to uncover an essential self. What we consider to be an actual self is really only a "fictitious, second best substitute for genuine identity."[13]

Hume reached this conclusion by arguing that if any idea of the mind is to be more than an empty abstraction, it must be linked to a corresponding sensual perception (such as an emotion, feeling, etc.). He bases this conclusion on his empiricist assumptions that all ideas come from the world of experience and are, therefore, dependent upon sense impressions. But what kind of sense impression would lead to an idea of self? He concludes that because there is no adequate form of sense impression to give us adequate basis for a theory of self, the most we can assert is that the true nature of the self is simply a conglomeration of many perceptions. That is, all we can know of the self is merely a "bundle of perceptions" in a state of constant flux. The most we can assert is that the self is a collection of perceptions derived through experience. He first asks, "What then give us so great a propension to ascribe an identity to these successive perceptions, and to suppose ourselves possest of an invariable and uninterrupted existence thro' the whole course of our lives?" Hume's answer is "I may venture to affirm . . . that they are nothing but a bundle or collection of different perceptions, which succeed each other with an inconceivable rapidity, and are in a perpetual flux and movement."[14] Hence, in stark contrast to Plato, Aristotle and Augustine, Hume maintained that we can have no knowledge of an essential, self-conscious self that remains constant over time.

Kierkegaard

Soren Kierkegaard (1813-1855), a Danish philosopher and Christian thinker regarded by many as the father of modern existentialism, attempted to provide a Christian response to skepticism and enlightenment rationalism. In addition, it was his chief desire to bring the Christian faith out of the realm of abstraction and into the realm of actual experience. To this end he attempted to describe the self in a way that linked one's outward behavior in public life to one's inward beliefs and convictions. His concern was to draw a distinction between the self of genuine faith and true belief, and the apathetic, inauthentic traditionalism he believed to be rampant in the Church.

In this context Kierkegaard's discussion of the nature of the self begins with the argument that while an individual is born a *human being* made up of body and soul, such a description is inadequate to describe what is means to be a *self*.[15] It was his contention that a human being only truly *becomes* a self through subjective and inward awareness of the intentions, actions, attitudes and dispositions that take place in one's life. This is the process of self-realization.

To support this conception of the self, Kierkegaard argued that in addition to the physical and the soulish aspects of the self, there is a third component which he calls the *Spirit*. In *The Concept of Dread* he comments "Man is a synthesis of the soulish and the bodily. But a synthesis is unthinkable if the two are not united in a third factor. This third factor is the spirit."[16] Kierkegaard described this spirit as *potentiality* present in all human beings and related it to the idea of human possibility and the freedom to determine one's future self Therefore, the spirit, is not so much an anthropological description of an actual part of the self, as much as it is a vision of a possible reality of self-determination present in the individual and which pushes towards true selfhood. Thus, like Hume, and in opposition to a fixed essential self seen in the earlier figures, Kierkegaard offers a non-substantial conception of the self that exists in a state of movement. Individual experience and freedom of choice both play a key role in the progression and development of the human being into true selfhood. According to Kierkegaard, the human being is free to choose his or her own direction of life. But within each person there is an internal spirit that drives one toward a future mode of self-determination. In essence, there is an ongoing tension between the current individual and the potential future self waiting to be determined. In this process of self-determination, Kierkegaard distinguishes three particular modalities of existence that reflect differing stages along the path to becoming a self. The three are: the *aesthetic*, the *ethical*, and the *religious*. Each of these three stages has its own distinguishing marks and the former stages must be undergone before an individual can move to the next.

The *aesthetic* self, Kierkegaard claims, pursues pleasure and enjoyment. Feeling is the standard by which existence and the self are judged. The chief enemy of the aesthetic self is boredom. Therefore, in an attempt to avoid this enemy the aesthetic self constantly shifts in its pursuits of pleasures. Kierkegaard argues that this boredom leads to despair and a realization that the self chosen at this point is not the self one can be. In fact, he argues, until one reaches the mode of the religious self, despair is the reality of the human self that we try to mask through pursuits of pleasure. Eventually, however, individuals will come to the realization of this underlying reality of despair and will attempt to find a different mode of existence that might assuage the despair. Because the person cannot be sure if the new mode of existence will cure the despair, the person has no alternative than to make a leap of faith to the new mode. Thus, a leap is made from the aesthetic to the ethical.

The *ethical* self judges life and existence in light of the value system of the society or tradition one finds oneself in. In this stage Kierkegaard describes an individual who is increasingly becoming aware of an eternal stage of existence as well as his or her own inability to reach it. The ethical self interprets the despair of existence in terms of guilt and inability to keep moral standards. Thus, the attempt made by the individual is to lessen this guilt through obedience to law. Again, however, Kierkegaard argues that such efforts can only result in despair as one realizes he or she cannot assuage the feelings of despair through personal effort. The spirit of the person drives toward a higher level of existence, but the self knows it is too weak to make it happen. Ultimately, Kierkegaard argues, it is only through the promise of forgiveness offered in Christ that one can find the solution to the despair and the inability to keep the law. For this reason a person will make a leap of faith to a religious mode of existence.

The *religious* self, then, is the mode of existence in which a person knows that she cannot assuage the despair on her own, nor can she live in light of an eternal reality. Yet the spirit drives toward fulfillment of a desire to exist in that mode. Kierkegaard maintains that in Jesus Christ one finds forgiveness and alleviation of despair. When embraced through a leap of faith, the self exists in a mode of being which is the true goal of human existence and provides the full realization of self. Because it cannot be reached by self-effort or moralism, the only recourse is a leap of faith, freely chosen, into the arms of God. Only in this way can the self reach the highest mode or stage of existence and escape the despair that plagued it in the earlier stages, for now it exists in the reality of the eternal.

Sigmund Freud

Known popularly as the father of modem psychiatry, Sigmund Freud (1856-1939) first pioneered an understanding of the self primarily in terms of psychological categories. Foundational to his theories of psycho-analysis and the self are Freud's atheistic and materialist assumptions about the nature of the universe. Based on this perspective Freud maintained that "all phenomena are determined by the laws of physics and chemistry, and even man himself is a product of natural evolution, ultimately subject to the same laws."[17]

These assumptions had a direct impact on his view of the self. Freud maintained that because all things, including persons, are subject to the laws of cause and effect, it would be wrong to describe any thought, feeling, action or behavioral event occurring in the life of a person as random. Thus, the first element of the self, according to Freud, is that the self is subject to cause and effect relationships. Every event of the self is ultimately determined by causal influences.

In this light, Freud reasoned that if all causes could be discovered, then proper treatment solutions for the all the psychological problems that ail people could be discovered. The problem, however, is that it is so difficult to discover all the causes. Indeed, both the experiences and the individual make-up of each person is so complex that discovering all causes is impossible. However, it is through the discovery and identification of causes, and redirection of their effects that psychological healing can take place.

Part of Freud's ground-breaking work in understanding human nature came as a result of trying to discover and reveal the basic nature of the mind in order to understand and trace causes leading to unreasonable or unhealthy behavior. This pursuit resulted in the second aspect of his theory of the self. the tripartite view of the mind.

Freud posited that the human mind consists of far more than that which people hold consciously in their memory or active thinking process. In fact, there are many things that are unconsciously held and cannot be brought forth by an individual under any normal circumstances. Thus, "the mind is not co-extensive with what is conscious or can become conscious, but includes items of which the person can have no ordinary knowledge at all."[18]

What then does Freud believe to be the structural make-up of the mind? The three major parts that make up the human mind are the *id*, the *ego*, and the *super-ego*. The *id* consists of the permanently unconscious appetitive, instinctual, or primal passions that call out for immediate satisfaction and often conflict with one another causing internal turmoil. The *ego* is the conscious self "occupying a beleaguered middle ground between the disreputable demands of the id, and the repressive discipline of the super-ego."[19] The *super-ego* is that part of the mind that sets itself over and above the rest of the self.[20] It is the part of the mind to which we ascribe the function of conscience and which "consists in keeping a watch over the action and intentions of the ego and judging them, in exercising a censorship."[21] It is, in essence, an internal authority that exerts mental pain upon the ego in an attempt to prevent the self from following a course that would lead to either a loss of love or to actual physical punishment.[22]

In addition to positing a deterministic self following the laws of cause and effect, and a tripartite self in regard to the make-up of the mind, a third aspect of Freud's conception is the idea that the self is instinctual and driven by mental forces energizing actions and choices. In particular he argued that the basic instinct for self preservation and especially the sexual instinct were the fundamental driving forces of human nature.[23]

While it may be a "vulgar misinterpretation of Freud to say that he traced all human behavior to sexual motivations," it is true that he "gave sexuality a much wider scope in human life than had formerly been recognized."[24] For example, Freud put forth the idea that the infant or young child has a varied array of wants and desires, chief among which are the sexual and life preserving instincts. These drives not only call out for satisfaction, they also initiate internal conflicts as the child wrestles with them. Ultimately, if the child perceives that his or her wants or desires run contrary to those of his or her father (representative of external authority figures), the child will try to repress the desires to avoid any form of punishment the father might inflict. This, obviously, reveals an internal conflict of desires and drives. As a result, Freud argues that in order to avoid conflicts and the infliction of pain from the father, the child eventually develops a super-ego to watch over the actions and desires of the ego.

In light of this idea it is easy to see how Freud also argued for a fourth important element in understanding self-hood. That is, the self must be understood as a developing self. There are many stages in life and many corresponding stages in personal development.[25] Examples of these developmental stages in children include the oral stage, the anal stage, and the phallic stage. Each of these stages Freud believed to be important developmental stages, in particular regard to the basic drive of sexuality and centering on gratification.

It was Freud's contention that in order for a person to function in a mentally healthy, well balanced manner he or she must establish a healthy interaction between the internal parts of the mind and development in a manner, that adequately deals with the basic drives and impulses of the self. It is primarily the role of the ego to establish this balance. "The ego has to reconcile the id, super-ego, and external world, perceiving and choosing opportunities for satisfying the instinctual demands of the id without transgressing the standards required by the super-ego."[26]

Neurosis, then, results when these opposing forces in the self are unable to be reconciled in the ego. This primarily results from unhealthy repression of basic desires through externally imposed forces or the hyper-diligence of the super-ego which can become increasingly harsh as a personality develops to the point where Freud can even describe it as "sadistic."[27] At such points, it is expedient for the individual to actively oppose the super-ego to lessen its demands and help a person become, as it were, "less moral."[28]

Freud's conception of the self, then, asserts that the self is deterministic, subconscious, driven and developing. His views were not only groundbreaking in terms of offering a view of the self not previously explored, but his ideas of the self provided the basis for all modern psychoanalysis.

Sartre

French Philosopher, playwright, and novelist Jean-Paul Sartre's (1905-1980) conception of the self became popularly accessible not only through his philosophical treatise *Being and Nothingness,* but also through his famous dramas *Flies* and *No Exit.* Through such works he adopted an existentialist foundation similar to that of Kierkegaard, yet merged it with an assumption of the non-existence of God. Thus, whereas the existentialist views of Kierkegaard led him to an ultimate ground in the religious leap of faith, Sartre's atheistic assumptions led him to ask whether life is ultimately absurd.

Sartre's atheistic assumptions did play an important role in his philosophy. He reasoned, for example, that without God there are no limits to what is permitted. The self is totally free, as if "abandoned," to find meaning only in completely free individual choices. Perhaps the quintessential idea that captures Sartre's idea of the self more than any other is the assertion that *existence precedes essence.* By this Sartre asserts that humans have no end goal, purpose, or externally given *telos* that defines, drives, or focuses the agenda of life. Instead, it is the choices, experiences, and desires of the individual that define the self. The self is historically situated and is responsible for his or her own existence in light of the intentionality of the choices one makes. In other words, the self one becomes, is the self one chooses to become throughout the span of life. There is no moral or religious "meaning to life" that one must discover in order to be whole.

In this light, in addition to being a free self, Sartre maintains that individuals are "future selves." That is, the self is not a static entity, but is in a constant state of becoming. Self-identity is something that is earned over the course of life, always in the future based on the decisions made and responses given.

For this reason, not only is the self completely free, and a future self, but one is also a responsible self. What one is becoming depends upon an individual's own choices. In this light Sartre introduces two ideas about existence that relate to the self as responsible. First, there is the "facticity" of life. That is, there are certain things that are simply true about the nature of our existence and experience that we have little or no control over. For example, the kind of family a person is born into, what race a person is, what height he or she grows to are all facts of life that result from a natural lottery. The agent has no say over these facts of life.

On the other hand, the way a person reacts or responds to these facts of existence are the responsibility of the person alone and will determine who one will become. Thus, the second factor in understanding the nature of the responsible self is that Sartre argues that an individual can "transcend" the facts of his existence at every turn and respond to them in the matter of his or her choosing. For example, in the course of life a man might lose his wife to a tragic case of cancer. He can respond to her loss by slipping into a state of utter depression or by becoming a spokesperson for a foundation dedicated to wiping out that form of cancer. In either case, the response chosen is up to the individual. He is totally free to decide how to respond and can choose to transcend the circumstances.

However, because individuals are free, and therefore responsible to transcend the facticity of life, when they do not, Sartre argues, they act in "bad faith." That is, according to Sartre "bad faith involves the deliberate creation in myself of the appearance of a belief which I in fact know to be false." The reason behind this type of action is to deny, at some level, responsibility action and "to avoid facing up to painful facts about the ourselves."[29]

The self, then, is free and developing. The self is a future self responsible for its actions and status in light of the ability of the human person to transcend the facts and circumstances of life and avoid acting in bad faith through a denial of intentionality and responsibility.

IV. Conclusion

What is the Self? When left unexamined, the answer to the question seems simple and self evident. Daily we refer to the self on many levels, and certainly function as if the self actually exists. However, when confronted by tough ethical situations about life and death, or when attempting philosophical analysis, one quickly realizes the complexity of the question. Philosophers and religious figures through the ages have attempted to lay out conceptions in order to explain not only who we are, but also why we are here or what we are to live for. In this chapter we have examined the views of several thinkers whose perspectives have had, to varying degrees, significant impact on both individuals and society as a whole.

Who is right? Is the self an unchanging core essence shared by all humans beings and about which experiences and perceptions revolve or cling to? Or is the self merely an unstable, fluctuating bundle of perceptions or an ever developing future self? Is the self driven by reason and rationality or are humans primarily driven by subconscious passions? Is the self innately social and interactive or are we innately egoistic, alone, and autonomous? Is the self determined either by God or law of cause and effect or is the self free to choose whatever end it desires? Finally, is there reason for the self to have a hope in an objective purpose or is the self adrift in the universe making the question of meaning or purpose simply absurd?

As evidenced from the cases presented at the beginning of the chapter, working through questions about the nature of the self is of paramount importance. Through exploring differing conceptions of the self put forth by influential philosophers and theologians, it is also evident that there are many different notions about what the solutions to life's ailments are. Simply put, the more difficult realities of life push us to find answers and to make hard decisions, and the differing views of the self provide different answers. In either case, the answers given in regard to the question "what is the self," will go a long way to determining other related and more immediately felt questions like "What is the meaning of life?" and "Why should I be moral?"

Endnotes

[1] Plato, *Republic* 608-611.

[2] Plato, *Phaedrus* 254-526.

[3] Plato, *Republic*, 515.

[4] For more discussion of this see, Ron Nash, *Life's Ultimate Questions* (Grand Rapids, Mi.: Zondervan Publishing House, 1999), 99-100.

[5] Augustine *De Lib. Arb.* II. 16

[6] Augustine *De Q.* 77.

[7] Rom. 3:11-12

[8] "Then the Lord God formed man of dust from the ground, and breathed into his nostrils the breath of life; and man became a living being" (Genesis 2:7 NASB).

[9] "And God created man in His own image, in the image of God He created him; male and female he created them." (Genesis 1:27 NASB).

[10] Augustine, *Sermons on the New Testament*, 67.15.

[11] Augustine, *On the Spirit and the Letter*, 5.

[12] David Pears, *Hume's System: An Examination of the First Book of his Treatise*, (Oxford: Oxford Univ. Press, 1990), 125.

[13] *Ibid.*

[14] Hume, *Treatise on Human Nature*, l.iv.6.

[15] Soren Kierkegaard, *Sickness unto Death* (Garden City, N.Y.: Doubleday & Co., Anchor Books, 1954), 146.

[16] Soren Kierkegaard, *The Concepts of Dread* (Princeton: Princeton University Press, 1957), 39.

[17] Leslie Stevenson, *Seven Theories of Human Nature* (Oxford: Oxford University Press, 1974), 64.

[18] Stevenson, 65.

[19] Simon Blackburn, *The Oxford Dictionary of Philosophy* (Oxford: Oxford University Press, 1994), 114.

[20] Sigmund Freud, *Civilization and its Discontents* (W.W. Norton and Company 1961), 84.

[21] *Ibid.*, 100.

[22] *Ibid.*, 85, 89.

[23] Sigmund Freud, *Two Short Accounts of Psycho-Analysis*, translated and edited by James Strachey (Penguin, London, 1962), 69.

[24] Stevenson, 67.

[25] Sigmund Freud, *Two Short Accounts of Psycho-Analysis*, 73, 12 1.

[26] Stevenson, 68.

[27] Sigmund Freud, *Civilization and its Discontents*, 100.

[28] *Ibid.*, 108.

[29] Thomas Baldwin, "Bad Faith" in *The Oxford Companion to Philosophy*, Ed. by Ted Honderich (Oxford: Oxford University Press, 1995), 76.

MEANING IN LIFE AND CONCEPTIONS OF THE DIVINE

THE MEANING OF LIFE

by Robert C. Solomon

> "Maybe I did not live as I ought to have done," it suddenly occurred to him. "But how could that be, when I did everything so properly?" he replied, and immediately dismissed from his mind this, the sole solution of all the riddles of life and death, as something quite impossible.
>
> —Leo Tolstoy, *The Death of Ivan Ilych*

The Meaning of Meaning

For most of us, the question about the meaning of life is most likely to arise in a time of confusion, when we are depressed, or when some incident has upset our values and expectations. In everyday life, when we aren't studying philosophy or thinking in general about things, life seems crammed full of meanings—there's a term paper to write, an oil filter in the car to change, a good party to look forward to or remember, the prospect of an important job interview sometime in the next few weeks. But when we begin to think abstractly, as we inevitably do at times, it becomes obvious to us that none of these small goals and expectations could possibly count as the meaning of life. And so we look at bigger things—happiness in general, doing well in life, success, influence, love. But then the ominous message of Ecclesiastes hits home: "All is vanity," and soon to pass away. And so we begin to look beyond life itself for the meaning of life—the ultimate question of philosophy.

What is the meaning of life? First we should ask, what is the meaning of "meaning" in this question? Sometimes, the meaning of something (a sign, a word) is what it refers to, something beyond itself. Thus the sign "Beware of the dog" presumably refers to some dog, probably unseen, presumably large and possibly ferocious. The name "Socrates" is the name of Socrates. Thinking of meaning this way, we would say that the meaning of each of our lives is whatever our individual lives refer to. But what would this be? One might say that each of our lives in some sense refers to other people around us—family, friends, associates—so that the meaning of life is other people. Or one might say that each of our lives refers to the larger community, to the nation, or to humanity as a whole. Or one might say that our lives refer to our Creator, so that the meaning of life is God. But the concept of "reference" becomes stretched very thin here, and one might well object that a life doesn't refer to anything at all. It just *is*. However, this seems to leave us without an answer to the question of the meaning of life, but perhaps the problem is with the notion of meaning as reference.

We can say that particular words and signs refer, but they do so only within the context of a language, a community of shared meanings. The written word *pepino* doesn't mean anything to a person who doesn't speak Spanish. The word *fore!* may be meaningless to someone who doesn't play golf. Reference is a contextual affair, and so it is in life, too. The meaning of our particular acts can be explained by reference to goals and conventions ("He did that in order to impress the recruiter" or "He did that in order to signal a lefthand turn"). But can we similarly explain the meaning of our whole lives? A rare person does dedicate his or her entire existence to a single goal—winning the revolution or finding a cure for cancer—but most people are not so singleminded and their lives don't have a meaning in this easy-to-define sense. But this doesn't mean that their lives lack meaning. In linguistics, we can ask the meaning of the word *pepino*, but we cannot intelligibly ask for the meaning of the whole language. The question "What is the meaning of Spanish?" is nonsense. So, too, we might say, asking for the meaning of life *as a whole* is nonsense. But this seems to deprive us of any possible answer to our all-important question.

When people ask about the meaning of life, however, they often have in mind just such reference to something beyond them, something outside of their lives. These references may be extremely important. They may even be the most important things *in* life. But it is worth pointing out that, in a sense, they do not fully answer the question; they only postpone it. There are four such answers worth mentioning: thinking of one's children as the meaning of one's life, thinking of God as the meaning of one's life, thinking of an afterlife as the meaning of one's life and, in despair, concluding too quickly that life has no meaning.

Children as Meaning

Many people would say that the meaning of life lies in their children and their children's children. But this answer has an odd consequence, as soon as you start to think about it. If the meaning of life lies not in their own lives, but in someone else's life, what is it that makes *their* lives meaningful? *Their* children. But what makes their *children's* lives meaningful in turn? Their children, and so on. In this way people have always tended to project abstractly into the future, to a place of total peace and happiness—what philosophers call a utopia. And this is how they would like their children, or their children's children, or their children's children's children, to live. But how does this make their *own* lives meaningful? And what is the meaning of life for those distant relatives happily living in Utopia? The question remains for them. Successful couples often look back to their years of struggle together and agree that *those* were the best years of life. And is simple happiness itself so obviously the meaning of life?

God as Meaning

A traditional answer to the question of the meaning of life is: God. In fact, it has often been suggested that for people who believe in God the question does not even arise, and that in the days before people doubted His existence, the meaning of life was never in question. But this simply is not true. The great philosopher Saint Augustine, the most devout of Christians, asked that question more persistently than any atheist. So did

Martin Luther and an enormous number of Christian thinkers before him and since. To think that believing in God by itself *answers* the question of the meaning of life only pushes the question back one step further. *Why* has God created us? What does He expect from us? Why did He create *us*? Some people think that God created us as something special, not only "in His own image" but with a mission to accomplish for Him here on earth. But why would He do that, since he can do anything? To prove a point? (To whom?) To satisfy His vanity? (The Jehovah of the Old Testament was, after all, a jealous God: perhaps a vain God, too.) Why should we think that we have been created for a special mission or purpose? And if so, what is that mission? What is that purpose? The question thus repeats itself, as the great thinkers of Christianity have long recognized; what is the meaning of our lives? Belief in God seems only to make the question more urgent; belief does not solve it.

Afterlife as Meaning

People also believe that the meaning of life is to be found in another life that is our reward or punishment for this one. But whether or not you believe in such an "afterlife," this answer to the question is odd, too; to say that this life has meaning only by reference to the next one is to say, as Ecclesiastes openly argues, that this life itself is insignificant, meaningless. But what is it that we are to do in this insignificant life so that we will be rewarded in the next one? Simply have faith? Do good works? Live life to the fullest? Realize our artistic or social potential? Convert the heathens? Learn to cook? Again the question repeats itself, and one might also ask: If this life is so insignificant, what would make the next one any more meaningful? Is it the fact that this one is so short and the next one is so long? But if life—even a few minutes of life—has no significance in itself, then what significance can eternal life have? If you're bored by sitting in a class for an hour, it won't make you any less bored if you are told that the class will be extended for ten more hours. On the other hand. Christian thinkers, especially in the past several centuries, have often argued that the rewards of the next life will be available only to those who live *this* life to the fullest. And there is our question again: What is it to live life to the fullest? What is it to find this life meaningful?

No Meaning at All

On the other side of the question, there are those philosophers—and a large portion of today's students—who would say that life has no meaning at all. The word that is often used to express this view is **absurd**. "Life is absurd," they say, which means that it has no meaning. Again, this is a view that has been held both by people who believe in God and by people who don't, although it is clear that the most troubling and final statements have come from those who do not. For example, the French philosopher **Albert Camus** said in his book *The Myth of Sisyphus* that the absurd had become a widespread sensibility in our times.

> At any streetcorner the feeling of absurdity can strike any man in the face. . . .
>   It happens that the stage sets collapse. Rising, streetcar, four hours in the office or the factory, meal, streetcar, four hours of work, meal, sleep, and Monday Tuesday Wednesday Thursday Friday and Saturday according to the same rhythm—this path is easily followed most of the time. But one day the "why" arises and everything begins in that weariness tinged with amazement.

It is important to emphasize that each of these answers may have extreme importance in a person's life. One can certainly dedicate oneself to one's children, and many people have always done so. It is possible (though more rare than people usually say) to devote one's life to God, and many people do. But it is just as important to realize that these noble answers leave open our question, for they just transfer the question one step down the line. What is the meaning of our children's lives? What is the kind of life to live in service of God? We need an answer *in* our lives, not just beyond them.

The same might be said of the reply that life has no meaning, that it is all absurd. Camus sometimes argues that position on the basis of his atheism; if there is no external meaning, then there can be no meaning at all. But external meanings may not be the meaning of life, and it does not follow from the absence of God (if in fact He does not exist) that life is without meaning.

It is worth noting that linguists now insist that meaning must be found *within* the context of language. A word has meaning not just because of its reference but, more important, because of its sense in the language. Thus we might say, by way of analogy, that the meaning of life is to be found in the context of our lives—the sense they make and the sense we give to them—rather than in reference to anything outside of life. Devotion to God answers the question of the meaning of life insofar as one actually *lives for* God. Children answer the question insofar as one actually lives for one's children. Ironically, **nihilism**—the view that life has no meaning—can also provide life with a meaning, if one actually dedicates one's life to the proposition that life has no meaning, and deflating the false and sometimes self-righteous and vicious meanings that people think it has. Camus seemed to have lived his life that way.

The Meanings of Life

Life is like the Olympic games; a few strain their muscles to carry off a prize, others sell trinkets to the crowd for a profit; some just come to look and see how everything is done.

—Pythagoras

Life is like playing a violin in public and learning the instrument as one plays.

—Samuel Butler

Life is just a bowl of cherries.

—Anonymous

Life is a bowl of pits.

—Rodney Dangerfield

The question of the meaning of life is not one of those questions that require or allow for a specific answer. Indeed, it is more of a metaphor that is required, an image, a vision of life in which you can see yourself as having a definite role, a set of reasonable expectations, and—what makes this so important—your vision in many ways determines the life you will lead. For example, suppose you go into business, or perhaps to school, with the attitude that life is "dog eat dog" and everyone for himself. You will greet everyone as a threat and a rival; you will not be wholly honest, and in any case you will not generally enjoy others' company. People will begin to sense your competitive hostility and distrust you, perhaps even testing your intentions with small acts of provocation. And soon you will find yourself indeed in a "dog eat dog" atmosphere—one that you have largely created yourself. So the question of the meaning of life is not just a matter of discovery; it is also an important act of creation. Your own philosophy is only in part the expression and clarification of the view you already have of the world, for the philosophy you formulate will also be an instrument for forming that view. Thus some philosophers who have had a gloomy or pessimistic temperament have willfully formulated rather cheerful and optimistic philosophies, not in order to deceive themselves but in order to *change* themselves, and some of them have succeeded remarkably well.

The images we use to talk about life define the meaning we find, or don't find, in it. Thus your answers to opening questions 1 and 4 in particular should give you a fairly clear indication about the general view of life you seem to accept, even if your answer is playful or poetic. (It is in play and poetry, as well as in doing serious philosophy, that our views become clear to us.) If you stated that "Life is a game," for example, then you said that you think life shouldn't be taken very seriously (whether or not you yourself do take it seriously), that it doesn't add up to anything in the end and that the best way to live is to enjoy it. On the other hand, if you stated that "Life is a gift from God, to be used wisely," you said that you think life is indeed serious, with a more or less definite mission (which you have to learn) and a fairly clear-cut sense of success and failure (in God's judgment). In what follows, I have listed and briefly described a number of grand images of life and its meaning (or lack of it) that have appeared in history and in students' papers. Of course, the list is not at all complete; you may well want to add some images of your own, which may be even better than the ones I have listed here.

Life as a Game

If life is a game, it is not to be taken so seriously, as we said above. A game is a self-contained activity, and even if it does add up to something (as playing basketball increases your coordination, or as running track increases your endurance), the significance of the game lies in the playing itself. ("It's not whether you win or lose, but how you play the game.") But then again, some people see games as fiercely competitive. (Thus Vince Lombardi's famous line, "Winning isn't everything; it's *the only thing!*") And to see life that way is to see it as a perpetual contest in which you win or lose. If you think life is a game, therefore, it is also important to ask what kind of game. Some games are played for fun alone. Some games are played to prove your superiority (arm wrestling); others are played to kill time (solitaire). Some games are distinctively social (bridge); some are intentionally anxiety-producing (poker for high stakes); some are aimed at hurting the opponent (boxing); and some are aimed at helping others (turning charity into a game, for example, to see who can collect the most money for the cause). The notion of life as a game has been used by many writers: two decades ago, for example, the most popular book on the best-seller list was Eric Berne's *Games People Play* and some philosophers have suggested that language, economics, and philosophy itself are games. To think of life as a game is to put it in a certain perspective, in order not to take it *too* seriously, in order to emphasize the importance of obeying the rules and, perhaps, the centrality of being a "good sport," enjoying oneself and, if possible, winning. But we tend to use the words "winner" and "loser" in a dangerous way. For example, what kind of standards are we setting for ourselves when we declare that the second-best football team *in the world*—the team that just lost the Super Bowl—"is a bunch of *losers*"?

Life as a Story

"Life imitates art," wrote the British dramatist and essayist Oscar Wilde, twisting around Plato who wrote that art is an imitation of life. It is obvious that we live, not just moment to moment or (most of us) for some single great goal, but rather we follow a rather detailed script, a story, a narrative, which (to at least some extent) we make up as we go along. The outlines of the story and our roles in it are probably provided by our culture, first our families, then by the circumstances in which we find ourselves. To think of life as a story is to think of life in a particular temporal way, as a plot unfolding, as the development of character and personality. (The German philosophers of the nineteenth century talked about life as a *Bildungsroman*, a story of personal development as a young person goes through the various quests, disappointments, and discoveries of life.) We often find ourselves making decisions about our lives using the standards we also use in evaluating literature or a movie: Is it interesting? Is it boring? Does it have enough suspense? Is it in good taste? Is it well-timed? Is it carried out dramatically, or overdramatically, "overacted"? Is this action in line with the character of the hero (namely, *you*). The American novelist John Barth (in *The End of the Road*) suggested that each of us is the hero of his or her own story: "The character Polonius," he writes, "did not consider himself a minor character in *Hamlet*." One could rewrite *Hamlet* from Polonius' point of view (as, indeed, playwright Tom Stoppard has wonderfully rewritten Hamlet from the point of view of two even more minor characters, Rosenkrantz and Guildenstern, in his play, *Rosenkrantz and Guildenstern Are Dead*). *Hamlet*, of course, is a tragedy. But some people live their lives as comedies, as farce, others as adventure stories—choosing glamorous jobs or dangerous hobbies—and do whatever is dramatically required to add to their list of swashbuckling episodes. According to this view, it is not the end goal or outcome of life that gives life meaning but rather the quality of the story, the quality with which one lives out and develops his or her role or roles. To choose the wrong role (one for which one is unsuited and untalented) or not to recognize one's role—or to have too many roles or incoherent roles—is to damage the meaning that one finds in life.

Life as Tragedy

One incontrovertible fact is that we all die. But this fact can be ignored; or death can be viewed as an inconvenience, as a passage to another life, or as ultimate disaster. If we look at our lives as less dramatic and less well written versions of *Hamlet, Macbeth, Othello,* or *Faust,* we can indeed find the crucial ingredients of tragedy in every one of us—some tragic flaw, some error in judgment, some fatal contradiction—that get played out through life until everything ends in death. The philosopher Camus ends his novel *The Stranger* with a character declaring, "All men are brothers, and the same end awaits them all—death." Opposed to the game metaphor, the tragedy metaphor makes life into a serious and unhappy process, punctuated by pleasures, perhaps, but ultimately an inevitable progression of a tragic plot that can have only one end. To live well, in this view, means to play one's tragic role well—to bear it heroically, perhaps making some grand soliloquies along the way.

Life as Comedy

"Life is a joke." Well, perhaps not, but it may be refreshing to think of life that way in contrast to the idea that life is tragic. Laughter is too often ignored as an essential ingredient in life, perhaps, even, as *the* essential ingredient in the good life. Plato does not write much about laughter, but he certainly displays a profound sense of humor throughout his Socratic dialogues. The sixteenth-century Dutch philosopher Erasmus wrote one of the most profound books about human life, which he called *In Praise of Folly*, a celebration of human foolishness. Nietzsche's fictional prophet Zarathustra is taught (by his animal friends) not to be so serious, to enjoy laughter and levity. Of course, there are many kinds of humor. There are jokes, including both good and bad jokes, offensive jokes, and "shaggy dog" (tediously protracted) jokes. Some thinkers would emphasize the importance of sophistication in humor, but others would say that laughter itself is what is important, not what the laughter is about. (Offensive jokes, as opposed to merely bad or silly jokes, on the other hand, perhaps should not count as "humor" at all.) Jokes, however, tend to be rather contrived and limited in time, and a person who spends all of his or her time playing or telling jokes (a "jokester") too easily becomes a tedious and pathetic person to have around. But then there are more serious comedies, not one-line stand-up humor but a protracted story of ambition and frustration, desire and disappointment, all treated not in terms of what Camus called The Absurd but rather as absurdity in a humorous sense. Tragedy and comedy can be combined, in "black humor" or in irony. At the end of a great Humprey Bogart-John Huston movie, *The Treasure of Sierra Madre*, the old man (played by Walter Huston, John's father) has lost everything, but he breaks out in uproarious laughter and encourages the others to do the same. It provides the only possible "happy ending" to a story of greed, disappointment, and death. It is hard to deny that all of us could use a little more humor, not only in our lives (television provides more than enough of that) but *about* our lives, in the way we see our own faults and foibles.

Life as a Mission

Christianity has often taught that life is a mission, the mission being to get others to become Christians, too. But not only Christians accept this view of life as a "calling." The German poet **Wolfgang von Goethe**, for example, described his mission in life as the creation of poetry to give the German people a sense of cultural identity, and the philosopher Hegel took it as his mission (about the same time as Goethe) to use philosophy to clarify for everyone the meaning of the world following the French Revolution. Political radicals often talk of their life as a mission—to liberate oppressed people or to get rid of tyranny in their homeland. Scientists sometimes feel they have a mission to fulfill in the expansion of knowledge or the development of a cure for some dread disease, and people with children often feel that their mission is to raise their children well and do what they can to make the world a better place for them to live in. If one's mission is primarily moral, it will vary according to one's moral philosophy. A utilitarian like Bentham would aim to change things in order to promote the greatest happiness of the greatest number. An ethical rationalist like Kant would urge that our goal should be to cultivate our moral personality and make the world a better place by practicing our duty as prescribed by reason.

Life as Art

"Live your life as a work of art," wrote the German philosopher **Friedrich Nietzsche**. But he did not have a story in mind, more an art like sculpture, in which one lives by creating a shape for oneself, "building character," developing what we call "style." The German philosopher **Friedrich von Schelling** saw the whole of life as God's work of art. (We are, in effect, His apprentices.) Artists often describe their sense of mission in life as simply "to create," but it is the activity itself that counts for them as much as the results of their efforts. The ideal of this view is, appropriately, to live *beautifully*, or if that is not possible, to live at least with style, "with class" we might say. From this view, life is to be evaluated as an artwork—as moving, inspiring, well designed, dramatic, or colorful, or as clumsy, uninspired and uninspiring, or easily forgettable.

Life as an Adventure

Life as a story, life as art—these are inspiring images, but the virtues of life then become the virtues of literature or sculpture: their shape and timing, their appeal to onlookers. But life can be aesthetic and exciting without being like art, without the necessity of always thinking about the shape of the whole or what it looks like to an observer. There is also the thrill of living "to the fullest," taking chances, enjoying challenge and the rush of adrenalin. Seeing life as an adventure is like that. It is living life by taking risks, even risking life, and thrilling in that sense of skill and uncertainty. It is certainly not an image for everyone. (There is an old Chinese curse: "May you live in interesting times!") But for those who see life this way, there may be no other way to live. Everything else is boring and tedious. And unlike life as art or as literature, life as adventure never plans a proper ending. When it's over, it's just—over.

Life as Disease

Life viewed as tragedy has a sense of grandeur about it; life viewed as a disease is rather pathetic. Sigmund Freud, for example, said several times that "the goal of all life is death," a view that has been around since ancient times. Not many years ago, the neo-Freudian American philosopher Norman O. Brown wrote that "man is a disease" and in the early 1980s, a large number of books were published describing the "disease" of modern life, of Western civilization, of capitalism, and so on. But to be "sick" presupposes some sense of what it is to be well, and the all-important question for anyone who uses this metaphor is: What would count as a *healthy* life? Immortality? A life of antlike social productivity? A life of unblemished happiness? A life of continuous love without a hint of hostility? These may all be desirable, or course, but to desire them does not mean that not to have them makes life a disease. And yet, much of our language these days is caught up in such "health" metaphors. (Another word for much the same view is the word "natural"; natural is healthy, unnatural means disease or deformed.) We talk about a "healthy economy" and we think of what we used to call games now as "exercise" to promote health. And life itself, viewed through the health metaphors, is bound to seem like a fatal disease, at least ultimately, since there seems to be no cure for it.

Life as Desire

This view is often linked to the Sisyphus myth of life as constant frustration. The Greek allegory in this case is **Tantalus** (from whose name we get the word "tantalizing"), who was condemned by the gods to be tied just out of reach of a bunch of grapes; he spent all eternity reaching for the fruit, but never managed to get any. The modern version of this story is *Faust*, which has been written into some of the most brilliant plays of modern times, one (*Dr. Faustus*) by the English writer Christopher Marlowe in 1589, another (*Faust*) by Goethe, already mentioned. Faust lived for his desires; when one was satisfied, it was immediately replaced by another. The image of life is that of continuous wanting, one thing after another, with no end in sight. A person wants to earn "just enough money to support myself," and does so, only to find that now he or she wants something more, which becomes the focus of life until it is acquired, but then it, too, is not enough. What one wants is something else. And so on and so on. This is not to say that life is frustration, for such desires can usually be satisfied. It is rather the life of desire after desire, in which nothing is ever ultimately satisfying. It is desire, as well as the satisfaction of desire, that gives life meaning. Not to desire, on the other hand, is to be already dead.

Life as Nirvana

The opposite view of life as desire is life as *not* desiring, the overcoming of desire. Freud called this the "constancy principle" in his early psychoanalytic works, the "nirvana principle" later on. In his view the goal of life is to attain as restful a state as possible, without tension or desire. The word nirvana comes from Buddhism and means "at peace" in Sanskrit; the goal of Buddhism is to loosen the hold of our desires and reach a state of tranquility where nothing bothers us. The Buddhists even say that nirvana and death are very similar (and thus nirvana includes an equanimity toward death), and Freud, too, sometimes referred to his principle as the "death wish." In Western philosophy, the sense of peace is sometimes promoted as the goal of philosophical activity or **contemplation**.

Life as Altruism

Altruism is acting for the benefit of others, even if there is no benefit whatsoever to oneself. Some people see themselves as being here on earth to help others less fortunate than they are. It is a view of life that has a very definite sense of mission, as well as quite clear-cut views of success and failure and of what ought to be done. For some people, life as altruism is a one-way enterprise; they help others in order to give their own lives meaning, but they expect nothing in return. For other people, life as altruism is a *general* ideal, and their hope is that, some day, everyone will selflessly help everyone else.

Life as Honor

It is a concept that has changed over time, but for the Greeks in Homer's *Iliad*, for instance, life was essentially a matter of living up to the expectations of your community, of proving yourself in battle and not disgracing yourself in any way. This was not to say that you couldn't behave badly: Achilles went sulking in his tent like a child when the king took one of his favorite slave girls away from him. But he established his honor again when he returned to the field of battle to avenge the death of his best friend. For the Greek heroes, honor was more important than life itself, and given the choice between death with honor and life without it, they would not have hesitated for a moment. But the concept of honor has not been limited to military heroes. Socrates died for his honor, too, not in battle but in a prison cell, in order to show that he valued his principles more than life itself. Our own concept of honor is not so clear, however; American soldiers have died with honor, of course, but the more general sense of honor—as the guiding principle of life—is surely not so evident in daily American life as it supposedly was in ancient Athens. But we do have a sense of *duty*, and many people would say that, whatever else, the meaning of life is doing your duty—to God, country, family, friends, and employer.

Life as Learning

A common image is the view of life as a learning experience. Of course, *why* we are learning all of this is an open question; but some learning, at least, is satisfying for its own sake. This satisfaction, presumably, is what the learning of life is all about. We have a bad experience (being walked out on by a boyfriend or girlfriend, being thrown out of school for smoking) and we "chalk it up to experience." Some people feel compelled to experience as much as possible, to "try everything at least once," just in order to know what it is like. For them, "living life to the fullest" means doing everything. But notice that the same expression means something very different from other viewpoints: The person who sees life as a mission lives life to the fullest by taking every opportunity to carry out his or her mission, and the person who sees life as tragedy takes that phrase to mean to suffer dramatically. A popular metaphor today is that life is a "growth experience" and that living is a matter of "developing your human potential." This view of life was also popular in Germany almost two hundred years ago, and it can be found, too, in Greek philosophy—for example, in Aristotle. Does it make sense to ask what we are learning *for*? The age-old answer is that learning leads to **wisdom**, and accordingly, the life of **contemplation** (continual learning and thinking) has been the suggestion of philosophers ever since ancient times.

Life as Suffering

Here we can raise again the vision of Sisyphus pushing his rock up the mountain only to have it fall back again. We sometimes look at life as just one repetition after another, ultimately adding up to nothing. A character in one modern novel commits suicide when she looks at her toothbrush and realizes that she will have to brush her teeth again and again for the rest of her life, a prospect that, when thought of all at once, indeed seems pointless. Sometimes you fix something, knowing that it will only break again soon; you learn how to do something for the seventeenth time, knowing that you will have forgotten it in a week. You get a high school diploma just in order to go to college, just in order to get a B.A., just in order to get into medical school, just in order to get an M.D., just in order to intern, just in order to study surgery, just in order to practice surgery, just in order to live the good life you wanted to live while you were in high school, but then you are too old and too busy to enjoy it. Some people would say that this is absurd, in just the same way. But it is worth mentioning that Camus thought that Sisyphus' life was meaningful, despite the absurdity of his task, because he reacted to his frustration with a kind of defiance. Is there anything analogous to this in our

"Four Noble Truths" of Buddhism:

1. Life is suffering.
2. Suffering arises from desire.
3. Desire can be eliminated.
4. One can eliminate desire by following the "right way."

lives? The great pessimist Arthur Schopenhauer also thought that life is frustration. Our desires are ultimately irrational and pointless, he says. The answer, he proposes, is **detachment** through either aesthetic contemplation or ascetic self-denial. Schopenhauer's answer is similar to that of the ancient philosophy called **Stoicism**, which also teaches that most of our passions are irrational and are best ignored through the detached wisdom of reason.

Life as an Investment

Since we live in a society in which business plays such a major role, it is natural that we should sometimes think of life as business. ("The business of America is business," said Calvin Coolidge, a businessman who happened also to be president.) To think of life this way is to think of the years of our lives as so much capital, which we invest in various enterprises—a career, a particular school, marriage and children—in order to get a certain return. What it is that is returned is never all that clear, and so the standards for a good investment versus a poor one are a matter of considerable dispute. A father might consider his son to have "wasted his talents" (that is, to have made a poor investment) because he decided to be a poet, while the son may accuse the father of having "sold out" for going into business as he did. It is fairly easy to confuse the metaphor with its most prominent manifestation, and think of the actual money a person earns in life and the estate he or she accumulates as a test of success. A moment's reflection, however, will prove that this is not always a dependable measure, and if a good investment is measured by what one has at the end, there is a very real question about how this, rather than the activity of living itself, is the meaning of life.

Life as Relationships

We have said too little directly about love and marriage and friendship, but it has been obvious to many people that the most important thing in their lives, and what gives their lives meaning, is human relationship—not the grand and abstract sense of being part of humanity or a citizen of a great nation but the very particular relationship one has with another person or a few other persons. Thus people say that what really counts in life is friendship, or the most important thing in life is love. But it is worth pointing out a curiosity about the metaphorical term "relationship"; why do we describe something so important with a word that is so bland? Why do we think of the union of two people as a "relating" of one separate being to another, rather than thinking in terms of a union to begin with? Indeed, much of our language about "relationships" presents us with this unflattering picture of two lonely souls trying to "get through" to one another, trying to "communicate" or "break down the barriers." But then, on the other hand, there is a much more inspiring picture of all of us already connected, perhaps—as Hegel argued—in one all-embracing Spirit. In this view, it is the distance between us, not intimacy, that is the aberration. The meaning of our lives is our network of relations with other people; ideally, the meaning of life is **love**.

Aristotle, On Friendship and the God

The excellent person is of one mind with himself, and desires the same things in his whole soul. The excellent person is related to his friend as he is to himself. The friend is another himself. Hence friendship seems to be one of the features of the good life.

Bibliography and Suggested Readings

Ecclesiastes is in the Old Testament; I have used the King James Version. Johann Wolfgang von Goethe's *Faust* has been translated many times, recently by Walter Kaufman (Doubleday, 1961). Nietzsche's view of life as art begins with his study of the Greeks in *The Birth of Tragedy*, trans. Walter Kaufman (Random House, 1967); his attack on Socrates and the life of reason is best summarized in *The Twilight of the Idols in The Viking Portable Nietzsche*, trans. Walter Kaufman (Viking, 1954). Albert Camus' *Myth of Sisyphus*, trans. Justin O'Brien (Vintage, 1955), is one of the classic books of the absurdist tradition in modern literature, and should profitably be read along with Camus' powerful short novel *The Stranger*, trans. Stuart Gilbert (Vintage, 1946). Arthur Schopenhauer's pessimism is exemplified and expounded in his *Studies in Pessimism* translated by Thomas Bailey Saunders (Macmillan, 1908). Sigmund Freud's vision of life is perhaps best argued in his classic *Civilization and Its Discontents*, trans. James Strachey (Norton, 1962). For a variety of views on the meaning of life, see David R. Cheney and Steven Sanders, *The Meaning of Life* (Prentice-Hall, 1980). See also, for a good popular approach, Thomas Moore, *Care of the Soul* (HarperCollins, 1992).

THE DIGNITY OF HUMAN LIFE

by David F. Swenson

I. The Need for a View of Life

Man lives forward, but he thinks backward. As an active being, his task is to press forward to the things that are before, toward the goal where is the prize of the high calling. But as a thinking, active being, his forward movement is conditioned by a retrospect. If there were no past for a man, there could be no future; and if there were no future and no past, but only such an immersion in the present as is characteristic of the brute which perisheth, then there would be nothing eternal in human life, and everything distinctively and essentially human would disappear from our existence.

As a preparation for an existence in the present, the youth of a nation are trained in various skills and along devious lines, according to their capacities and circumstances, for the parts they are to play in existence; their natural talents are developed, some by extended periods of intellectual training, others for participation in various forms of business or technical training; but whatever be the ultimate end of the training, its purpose is to develop those latent powers they possess which will eventually prove of benefit to themselves or to others. But, in addition to this, which we may call a preparation for the external life, a something else is urgently needed, a something so fundamentally important that in its absence every other form of preparation is revealed as imperfect and incomplete, even ineffective and futile.

This so particularly indispensable something is a *view of life*, and a view of life is not acquired as a direct and immediate result of a course of study, the reading of books, or a communication of results. It is wholly a product of the individual's own knowledge of himself as an individual, of his individual capabilities and aspirations. A view of life is a principle of living, a spirit and an attitude capable of maintaining its unity and identity with itself in all of life's complexities and varying vicissitudes; and yet also capable of being declined, to use the terminology of the grammatical sciences, in all the infinite variety of cases that the language of life affords. Without this preparation the individual life is like a ship without a rudder, a bit of wreckage floating with the current to an uncomprehended destiny. A view of life is not objective knowledge, but subjective conviction. It is a part of man's own self, the source whence the stream of his life issues. It is the dominant attitude of the spirit which gives to life its direction and its goal. This is why it cannot be directly communicated or conveyed, like an article of commerce, from one person to another. If a view of life were a body of knowledge about life, or a direct and immediate implication from such knowledge, it would be subject to objective communication and systematic instruction. But it is rather a personal expression of what a man essentially is in his own inmost self, and this cannot be learned by rote, or accepted at the hands of some external authority. Knowledge is the answer or answers that things give to the questions we ask of them; a view of life is the reply a person gives to the question that life asks of him. We begin life by scrutinizing our environment, ourselves playing the role of questioners and examiners and critics; but at a later moment, when the soul comes of age and is about to enter upon its majority, it learns that the tables have been turned and the roles reversed; from that moment it confronts a question, a searching and imperative question, in relation to which no evasion can avail, and to which no shifting of responsibility is possible.

In discussing the problem of *a view of life which can give it meaning and dignity and worth*, I am well aware that no one can acquire a view of life by listening to a speech.[1] Nevertheless, a speech may serve the more modest purpose of stimulating a search, perhaps a more earnest search; and may render more articulate possibly the convictions of those who have already won some such conception, having made it their own by a heartfelt and spontaneous choice.

II. One Approach

All men are endowed by nature with a desire for happiness—a principle so obvious as scarcely to need any explanation, and certainly no defense. A human life without happiness or hope of happiness is not a life, but rather a death in life. Happiness is life's vital fluid and the very breath of its nostrils. Happiness and life are so much one and the same thing that the more profoundly any life discovers happiness, the more significant and abundant is that life itself. . . .

But for a thinking human being—and God made every man a thinker, whatever may be our estimate of that which men make of themselves—for a thinking human being, happiness cannot consist in satisfaction of momentary impulse, of blind feeling, of brute immediacy. A pleasant absorption in the present, oblivious of prospect or retrospect, careless of the wider relation or the deeper truth of life, can be called happiness only on the basis of frivolity and thoughtlessness. Just as life is not life unless it is happy, so happiness is not happiness unless it can be justified. In order really to be happiness it requires to be interpenetrated with a sense of *meaning, reason,* and *worth.*

For the quest of happiness, like every other human quest, faces a danger. The danger that confronts it is the possibility of error: the error of permitting oneself to be lured into promising paths that lead to no goal, and the error of coming to rest in hollow satisfactions and empty joys. It is possible to believe oneself happy, to seem happy to oneself and to others, and yet in reality to be plunged in the deepest misery; just as, on the other hand, it is possible to stand possessed of the greatest treasure, and yet, in thoughtlessness, to imagine oneself destitute, and through that very thoughtlessness not only neglect and ignore but actually deprive oneself of what one already has. The basic problem of life, the question in response to which a view of life seeks to propound an answer, may therefore be formulated as follows: What is that happiness which is also a genuine and lasting good? In what does it consist, and how may it be attained?

There exists an ancient handbook, an *Art of Rhetoric,* compiled for the guidance and information of orators and other public speakers, written by one of the greatest of Greek philosophers. In this handbook the author formulates the commonly prevailing conceptions of happiness as among the things useful for public speakers to know. . . . Happiness is said to be commonly defined as independence of life, as prosperity with virtue, as comfortable circumstances with security, or as the enjoyment of many possessions, together with the power to keep and defend them. Its constituent elements are noble birth, wealth, many good and influential friends, bodily health and beauty, talents and capacities, good fortune, honors, and lastly virtue.

We readily perceive how strange and old-fashioned these conceptions are, how foreign to all our modern and enlightened notions. I shall therefore subjoin a more up-to-date consideration of the same subject, derived from a very modern author writing in a journal of today. The author raises the question as to what circumstances and conditions have the power to make him feel really alive, tingling with vitality, instinct with the joy of living. He submits a long list including a variety of things, of which I shall quote the chief: the sense of health; successful creative work, like writing books; good food and drink; pleasant surroundings; praise, not spread on too thick; friends and their company; beautiful things, books, music; athletic exercises and sports; daydreaming; a good fight in a tolerably decent cause; the sense of bodily danger escaped; the consciousness of being a few steps ahead of the wolf of poverty. . . . So speaks our modern writer. And now that I have juxtaposed these two accounts, I have to confess to the strange feeling that, despite the interval of more than two thousand years between them, they sound unexpectedly alike. . . . How strange to find such a similarity! Can it be that after all that has been said and written about the revolutionary and radical changes introduced into life by modern science, modern invention, and modern industry, the influence of the steam engine and the printing press, the telegraph and the radio, the automobile and the airplane, together with the absolutely devastating discoveries of astronomers—can it be, in spite of all this, that the current conceptions of life and its meaning have remained essentially unchanged? . . .

III. Problems with that Approach

However that may be, I do not think that anyone will deny that such views as these are widely held, and constitute the view of life perhaps of the majority of men. . . . But there are serious difficulties in the way of constructing a view of life out of such considerations.

[1.] The constituents of happiness are in both cases a multiplicity of things. . . . But the self which sets its heart upon any such multiplicity of external goods, which lives in them and by them and for them, dependent upon them for the only happiness it knows—such a self is captive to the diverse world of its desires. It belongs to the world and does not own itself. It is not in the deepest sense a self, since it is not free and is not a unity. The manifold conditions of its happiness split the self asunder; no ruling passion dominates its life; no concentration gives unity to the personality and single mindedness to the will. Its name is legion, and its nature is doublemindedness. . . .

[2.] Reflection discovers yet another difficulty in connection with such views of life. Whoever seeks his happiness in external conditions, of whatever sort, seeks it in that which is in its essential nature precarious. He presumes upon the realization of conditions which are not intrinsic to him, or within his control. This happiness is subject to the law of uncertainty, to the qualification of an unyielding, mysterious *perhaps*. Here lurks the possibility of despair. Give a man the full satisfaction of his wishes and ambitions, and he deems himself happy; withdraw from him the smile of fortune's favor, and disappoint his expectation and his hope, and he will be plunged into despair. The shift from happiness to unhappiness in such a life is every moment imminent. . . .

[3.] A third consideration. Wealth and power and the like, even bodily health and beauty of person, are not in the strictest sense intrinsic values, but rather representative and comparative, conditional and hypothetical. Money is good—if I have learned how to use it; and so with power and influence, health and strength. But in themselves these things are abstract and neutral, and no man can truthfully say whether the acquirement of them in any individual case will work more good than harm. . . .

[4.] Lastly, it must be pointed out that the conditions of happiness as conceived in all such views of life, inevitably imply a privileged status for the happy individual. They rest upon differential capabilities and exceptionally fortunate circumstances. To choose them as the end and aim of life constitutes an injury to the mass of men who are not so privileged. This one thought alone is of so arresting a quality as to give the deepest concern to every man who has the least trace of human sympathy and human feeling. I hope I have a soul not entirely a stranger to happy admiration; I know I feel moved to bend low in respect before exceptional talent and performance, and that I am eager to honor greatness and genius wherever I have the gift to understand it. And I am not so unfeeling as to refuse a tribute of sympathetic joy to those who rejoice in fortune's favors and bask in the smiles of outward success. But as the fundamental source of inspiration of my life, I need something that is not exclusive and differential, but inclusive and universal. I require to drink from a spring at which all men may refresh themselves; I need an aim that reconciles me to high and low, rich and poor, cultured and uncultured, sophisticated and simple; to the countless generations of the past as well as to the men and women of the future. I need a spiritual bond that binds me to all human beings in a common understanding of that which is fundamental and essential to human life. To have my life and happiness in that which is inaccessible to the many or to the few, seems to me an act of treason to humanity, a cowardly and pusillanimous attack upon the brotherhood of man; for without the inner spiritual tie of an essential aim which all can reach and all can understand, the concept of the human race as a spiritual unity is destroyed, and nothing is left of mankind but a biological species, only slightly better equipped than the other animals to cope with the present state of their physical environment.

The differences between man and man are indeed inseparable from this our imperfect temporal existence; but I cannot and will not believe that their development constitutes the perfection of life itself. Rather is this to be found in the discovery and expectation of *something underlying and absolute*, something that can be found by all who seek it in earnest, something to which our lives may give expression, subordinating to its unifying principle the infinite multitude of ends, reducing them to their own relative measure and proportion, and refusing to permit the unimportant to become important, the relative to become absolute. The possibility of making this discovery and of giving it expression is, so it seems to me, the *fundamental meaning of life, the source of its dignity and worth*. The happiness that is found with this discovery is not invidious and divisive, but unifying and reconciling; it does not abrogate the differences, but it destroys their power to wound and to harm, the fortunate through being puffed up in arrogance and pride, the unfortunate through being depressed in envy and disappointment. For this happiness is not denied to any man, no matter how insignificant and humble.

IV. The Ethico-Religious View of Life

Our criticism has brought us to the threshold of an ethical view of life. That the essence of life and its happiness is to be sought in the moral consciousness alone is the conviction that animates this address, and gives it its reason for being. This view holds that *the individual human self has an infinite worth, that the personality has an external validity, that the bringing of this validity to expression in the manifold relations and complications of life is the true task of the self, that this task gives to the individual's historical development an infinite significance*, because it is a process through which the personality in its truth and depth comes its own. "Find your self," says the moral consciousness; "reclaim it in its total and in so far unworthy submergence in relative ends; dare to think the nothingness, the hollowness, the relativity, the precariousness, the lack of intrinsic meaning of that which constitutes the entire realm of the external and the manifold; liberate yourself from slavery to finite ends; have the courage to substitute the one thing needful for the many things wished for, and perhaps desirable, making first things first, and all other things secondary—and you will find that these other things will be added unto you in the measure in which you require them and can use them as servants and ministers of your highest good."

So speaks the voice within us, a still small voice, a soft whisper easily overwhelmed by the noise and traffic of life, but a voice, nevertheless, which no one can permit to be silenced except at the cost of acquiring restlessness instead of peace, anxiety instead of trust and confidence, a distracted spirit instead of harmony with one's self. The moral spirit finds the meaning of life in choice. It finds it in that which proceeds from man and remains with him as his inner essence rather than in the accidents of circumstance and turns of external fortune. The individual has his end in himself. He is no mere instrument in the service of something external, nor is he the slave of some powerful master; nor of a class, a group, or party; nor of the state or nation; nor even of humanity itself, as an abstraction solely external to the individual. Essentially and absolutely he is an end; only accidentally and relatively is he a means. And this is true of the meanest wage slave, so called, in industry's impersonal machine—precisely as true of him as it is of the greatest genius or the most powerful ruler.

Is there anyone so little stout-hearted, so effeminately tender, so extravagantly in love with an illusory and arbitrary freedom, as to feel that the glorious promise of such a view of life is ruined, its majestic grandeur shriveled into cramped pettiness, because the task which it offers the individual is not only an invitation, but also an obligation as well? Shall we confess that we cannot endure this "Thou must" spoken to ourselves,[2] even when the voice proceeds from no external power but from our inmost self, there where the human strikes its roots into the *divine*? Truly, it is this "Thou must" that is the *eternal* guarantee of our calling, the savior of our hope, the inspirer of our energy, the preserver of our aim against the shiftings of feeling and the vicissitudes of circumstance. It steels the will and makes it fast; it gives courage to begin after failure; it is the triumph over despondency and despair. For *duty is the eternal in a man, or that which he lays hold of the eternal; and only through the eternal can a man become a conqueror of the life of time*. It is in the moral consciousness that a man begins truly to sense *the presence of God*; and every religion that has omitted the ethical is in so far a misunderstanding of religion, reducing it to myth and poetry, having significance only for the imagination, but not for the whole nature of man as concrete reality. The moral consciousness is a lamp, a wonderful lamp; but not like the famous lamp of Aladdin,[3] which when rubbed had the power to summon a spirit, a willing servant ready and able to fulfill every wish. But whenever a human being rubs the lamp of his moral consciousness with moral passion, a Spirit does appear. This Spirit is God, and the Spirit is master and lord, and man becomes his servant. But this service is man's true freedom, for a derivative spirit like man, who certainly has not made himself, or given himself his own powers, cannot in truth impose upon himself the law of his own being. It is in the "Thou must" of God and man's "I can" that the divine image of God in human life is contained, to which an ancient book refers when it asserts that God made man in his own image. That is the inner glory, the spiritual garb of man, which transcends the wonderful raiment with which the Author of the universe has clothed the lilies of the field, raiment which in its turn puts to shame the royal purple of Solomon. The lilies of the field[4] cannot hear the voice of duty or obey its call; hence they cannot bring their will into harmony with the divine will. In the capacity to do this lies man's unique distinction among all creatures; here is his self, his independence, his glory and his crown.

I know that all men do not share this conviction. Youth is often too sure of its future. The imagination paints the vision of success and fortune in the rosiest tints; the sufferings and disappointments of which one hears are for youth but the exception that proves the rule; the instinctive and blind faith of youth is in the relative happiness of some form of external success. Maturity, on the other hand, has often learned to be content with scraps and fragments, wretched crumbs saved out of the disasters on which its early hopes suffered shipwreck. Youth pursues an ideal that is illusory; age has learned, O wretched wisdom! to do without an ideal altogether. But the ideal is there, implanted in the heart and mind of man by his Maker, and no mirages of happiness or clouds of disappointment, not the stupor of habit or the frivolity of thoughtlessness, can entirely erase the sense of it from the depths of the soul. . . .

Let us but learn to perceive that no differential talent, no privileged status, no fortunate eventuality, can at bottom be worthwhile as a consummation; that all such things are quite incapable of dignifying life; and when the misunderstandings with respect to the nature of a moral consciousness have been cleared away, the road will be open to the discovery of man as man. A preoccupation with the secondary thoughts and interests of life is always exhausting and trivializing, and in the end bewildering. Our true refreshment and invigoration will come through going back to the first and simplest thoughts, the primary and indispensable interests. We have too long lost ourselves in anxious considerations of what it may mean to be a shoemaker or a philosopher, a poet or a millionaire; in order to find ourselves, it is needful that we concentrate our energies upon the infinitely significant problem of what it means simply to be a man, without any transiently qualifying adjectives. When Frederick the Great asked his Court preacher if he knew anything about the future life, the preacher answered, "Yes, Your Majesty, it is absolutely certain that in the future life Your Highness will not be king of Prussia." And so it is; we were men before we became whatever of relative value we became in life, and we shall doubtless be human beings long after what we thus became or acquired will have lost its significance for us. On the stage some actors have roles in which they are royal and important personages; others are simple folk, beggars, workingmen, and the like. But when the play is over and the curtain is rolled down, the actors cast aside their disguises, the differences vanish, and all are once more simply actors. So, when the play of life is over, and the curtain is rolled down upon the scene, the differences and relativities which have disguised the men and women who have taken part will vanish, and all will be simply human beings. But there is this difference between the actors of the stage and the actors of life. On the stage it is imperative that the illusion be maintained to the highest degree possible; an actor who plays the role of king as if he was an actor, or who too often reminds us that he is assuming a role, is precisely a poor actor. But on the stage of life, the reverse is the case. There it is the task, not to preserve, but to expose, the illusion; to win free from it while still retaining one's disguise. The disguising garment ought to flutter loosely about us, so loosely that the least wind of human feeling that blows may reveal the royal purple of humanity beneath. This revelation is the moral task; the moral consciousness is the consciousness of the dignity that invests human life when the personality has discovered itself, and is happy in the will to be itself.

Such is the view of life to which the present speaker is committed. He has sought to make it seem inviting, but not for a moment has he wished to deny that it sets a difficult task for him who would express it in the daily intercourse of life. Perhaps it has long since captured our imaginations; for it is no new gospel worked out to satisfy the imaginary requirements of the most recent fashions in human desire and feeling; on the contrary it is an old, old view. But it is not enough that the truth of the significance inherent in having such a view of life should be grasped by the imagination, or by the elevated mood of a solemn hour; only the heart's profound movement, the will's decisive commitment,[5] can make that which is truth in general also a truth for me.

LIVING WITHOUT APPEAL: AN AFFIRMATIVE PHILOSOPHY OF LIFE[6]

by **E.D. Klemke**

I.

From time to time, philosophers get together at congresses and symposia in which some philosophers read papers and others criticize and raise questions. To the layman, I am sure, the topics which are discussed seem highly technical and inaccessible, and the vocabulary used is, doubtless, unintelligible. Indeed, if the ordinary man were to drop in on such meetings, he would, I suspect, find the proceedings to be either totally incomprehensible or the occasion for howling laughter. To give some indication of what I am referring to, I shall list the titles of some recent philosophical papers, many of which are acknowledged to

> The meaning of a word
> Performative—constative
> Negative existentials
> Excluders
> Reference and referents
> Proper names

On referring
Parenthetical verbs
Bare particulars
Elementarism, independence, and ontology
The problem of counterfactual conditionals
Is existence a predicate?
Etc.

Upon hearing (or reading) papers such as these, the ordinary man would probably exclaim "What's this all got to do with philosophy?" And he would, no doubt, be in agreement with Kierkegaard, who once wrote:

> What the philosophers say about Reality is often as disappointing as a sign you see in a shop window which reads: Pressing Done Here. If you brought your clothes to be pressed, you would be fooled; for the sign is only for sale. (*Either*/Or, v. 1, p. 31.)

Now I have no quarrel with what goes on at these professional gatherings. I engage in such activities myself. I believe that most philosophical problems are highly technical and that the making of minute distinctions and employment of a specialized vocabulary are essential for the solution of such problems. Philosophy here is in the same boat as any other discipline. For this reason, there is (and perhaps always will be) something aristocratic about the pursuit of philosophy, just as there is about the pursuit of theoretical physics or Peruvian excavation. The decriers of philosophy often overlook the fact that any discipline which amounts to more than a type of verbal diarrhea must proceed by making subtle distinctions, introducing technical terminology, and striving for as much rigor and precision as is possible. And the critics fail to see that, in philosophy as in other fields, by the very nature of the discipline, some problems will be somewhat rarified, and of interest mainly to the specialist.

On the other hand, I am inclined to think that the philosopher ought occasionally to leave the study, or the philosophical association lecture hall, or even the classroom, and, having shed his aristocratic garments, speak as a man among other men. For the philosopher is, after all, human too. Like other men, he eats, sleeps, makes love, drinks martinis (or perhaps cognac), gets the flu, files income tax, and even reads the newspapers. On such more democratic occasions, he ought to employ his analytical tools as diligently as ever. But he should select as his topic some issue which is of concern to all men, or at least most men, at some time in their lives. It is my hope that I have chosen such a topic for this essay.

The problem which I wish to discuss has been formulated in a single sentence by Camus (in *The Myth of Sisyphus*), which I take as a kind of "text." The sentence to which I am referring is: "Knowing whether or not one can live *without appeal* is all that interests me."[7] I say that I take this as a *kind* of text because, as so often, Camus overstates the point. Thus I would not—and perhaps most of us would not—say that, knowing whether or not one can live without appeal is *all* that interests me. But I believe that most of us would say that it certainly is one of those crucial problems which each man must confront as he tries to make sense of his life in this wondrously strange existence.

II.

Prophets of doom and redemption seem to exist in almost every age, and ours is no exception. It is commonly held by many present-day thinkers, scholars, and poets, that the current state of the world and of many of the individuals within it is one of disintegration and vacuity. As they see it: Persons of our age grope for disrupting principles and loyalties, and often reveal a destructive tension, a lack of wholeness, or an acute anxiety. Whether or not this is a unique situation in history, as an account of the present state of things, such disintegration is commonly mentioned. And theorists in almost every discipline and pursuit have given analyses of the current predicament and offered solutions. For example, philosophers and theologians (Jaspers, Marcel, Swenson, Tillich, Schweitzer, Niebuhr), scientists and scientific writers (Einstein, DeNuoy), sociologists (Sorokin), historians (Butterfield), among others, have waved warning signs, sometimes in a last effort to "save civilization from utter destruction. "I would like to consider some points which are held in common by many of these writers (and others whom I have not indicated) and then to comment about those views. In this section. I shall state the common core of this position. In the next section, I shall make my comments and show that there is another genuine alternative.

According to many of the above writers (and others whom I have not mentioned), our age is one in which a major catastrophe has taken place. This has been designated as an increasing lack of a determining principle, the severing of a determining bond, the loss of a determining passion, or the rejection of a determining ultimate. What is the nature of this ultimate? It has been described as a principle by which finite forces are held in equilibrium, a bond which relates all horizontally functioning powers vertically to a realm beyond the finite. It is said to be a unifying and controlling power by which the varied inclinations, desires, and aims of an individual may be kept in balance. It is characterized as an agency which removes those oppositions and dichotomies which tend to destroy human selfhood. It has been held, by writers such as the above, to be a *transcendent* and *unconditional ultimate*, the one indispensable factor for the attainment of a *meaningful* and *worthwhile* existence. In their view, in order to prevent the destruction of individuals and cultures, and to provide a sense of direction and wholeness, the awareness of and relationship to such an ultimate are absolutely necessary.

Many of the writers have noted that, not only in intellectual circles, but at a much wider level, many individuals are increasingly refusing to accept the reality of this controlling ultimate. As they see it, such individuals have either remained content with a kind of vacuum in "the dimension of the spiritual, " or they have "transvaluated and exalted immanent, finite forces" into a substitute for the transcendent. Men have tried—say these writers—to find equilibrium and unity through "natural", nonauthoritative, self-regulating, temporal aims and principles, which they hold to be capable of an innate self-integration which requires no outside aid. According to these writers, this hope is futile, for as soon as reliance upon the transcendent ultimate ceases, disintegration results. Only when finite relationships, processes, and forces are referred back to a transhistorical order can integration, wholeness, meaning, and purpose be achieved. As long as men lack confidence in, or sever the bond to, the transcendent, their accomplishments and goals, no matter how noble or worthy, can have no final consistency or solidity. Rather, their efforts are mere remnants of an "atrophied world," shut up within the realm of immanence, intoxicated with itself, lured by "phantasms and idolatrous forces."

According to this view, the integrity of the individual is today threatened by the loss of belief in the transcendent ultimate and its replacement by a "devitalized" and "perverse" confidence in the all-sufficiency of the finite. The only remedy, we are told, is the recognition of the determining regulation of a dimension beyond the fleeting pace of the temporal world, by which alone existence can have worth and value.

At this point, one might be tempted to ask several questions of these writers:

(1) "Even if the above characterization of the world has some truth, must one look to transcendentalism as the remedy? Cannot a 'natural' philosophy or principle help us?"

The usual answer is: No. All naturalistic views reduce existence to mere finite centers and relationships. But all of these finite agencies are conditioned by others. All are therefore transitory and unstable. None can become a determining ultimate. Only a transcendent ultimate is capable of sustaining the kind of faith which gives human existence meaning and value.

(2) "But isn't this supernaturalism all over again? And doesn't it (as usual) imply either an unbridgeable gulf between the finite and the infinite or an external control or suppression of the finite by the so-called infinite?"

The customary reply is that this view may indeed be called supernaturalism. But (we are told) this does not imply the impossibility of any association of the finite and the infinite. For the ultimate, according to these writers, is not transcendent in the sense of being totally isolated from the finite, but, rather, is operative within the natural world. Furthermore (so the reply goes), the existence of a transcendent order does not entail either external control or suppression of the finite. It merely implies a human receptivity to a non-natural realm. That is, human achievement and value result from the impingement of the infinite upon the finite in moments of *kairos*,[8] providing fullness and meaning but not at the price of denying the human activity which is involved. There always remains the awareness that the human subject is in a personal relation to another subject, a relation of supreme importance.

(3) "And how does one come to this relation?"

Perhaps mainly (say many of these writers) through suffering and sorrow, through a sense of sin and despair. When an individual sees that all finite centers and loyalties are fleeting and incapable of being lasting objects of faith, then he will renounce all previous efforts in despair, repent in humility, and gratefully make *the movement of faith* by which alone his life can become meaningful and worthwhile.

This, then, is the view which I propose to comment on. It is an all-or-nothing position. Its central thesis is that there exists a transcendent ultimate of absolute supremacy, which reigns over all finite things and powers, and *which alone is capable of providing meaning and worth to human existence*. Finite, historical centers can at best bring temporary assistance. They all wither with time and circumstances. Only when men turn from the finite to the infinite can they find (in the words of Kierkegaard) a hope and anticipation of the eternal which holds together all the "cleavages of existence."

III.

I shall refer to the above view (which I have tried to portray justly) as transcendentalism. It contains three component these. These are:

(1)   There *exists* a transcendent being or ultimate with which man can enter into some sort of relation.
(2)   Without such a transcendent ultimate, and the relation of faith to it, human life lacks *meaning, purpose,* and *integration*.
(3)   Without such *meaning, purpose,* or *integration*, human life is not *worthwhile*.

It is necessary to comment upon all three of these points.

(1) First, the thesis *exists* such a transcendent ultimate or power. I assume that those who assert the existence of a transcendent being intend their assertion to be a *cognitive* one. That is, they claim to be saying something which states a fact and which is capable of being either true or false. Thus they would not admit that their claim is merely an expression of feelings or attitudes. I also assume that those who make this assertion intend their statement to be interpreted *literally*. That is, they mean to say that the transcendent *really exists*. The transcendent presumably does not exist in the same sense in which Santa Claus may be said to "exist." These persons would, I assume, hold that the transcendent exists in actuality, although it may not exist in any empirical sense.

I ask: What *reasons* are there for holding that such an entity as the transcendent exists? I take it that I do not have to linger on such an answer as the testimony of a sacred book. The fact that the Bible or any other sacred writing asserts the existence of a transcendent is no more evidential to the existence of such a being than it is to the non-existence. All that a scriptural writing proves is that someone *believed* that a transcendent ultimate exists. And that is not at all the same as showing that such a being actually exists. The same may be said for the testimony of some unusual person—Moses, Jesus, Mohammed, etc. Furthermore, the fact that the testimony is made by a large number of persons does not substantiate the view. An impartial reading of history often shows that, on major issues, the majority is almost always wrong.

I also shall not linger on the traditional arguments for the existence of a god: The ontological, cosmological, teleological arguments, etc. Many theologians themselves now acknowledge that these are not so much arguments for the existence of such a being as they are explications of the affirmation of faith. Therefore, the fact that a certain segment of the universe is orderly, that it exhibits beauty, that it shows an adaptation of means to ends does not in any way provide evidence that there is one who orders, beautifies, and adapts, etc.

Arguments from religious experience are also unconvincing. Due to their lack of intersubjective testability, the most that such arguments can demonstrate is that someone has had an unusual experience. They do not provide any evidence that the *object* of such an experience exists. That object may, of course, exist. But the occurrence of such an experience does not verify the existence of an actual, rather than imaginary, object. Suppose that, while a dentist is drilling my tooth, I have an experience of a blinding light or an unusual voice. I do not take this to be an adequate reason for saying that I *know* that I have now communed with the Absolute. I trust that you do not do so either.

What evidence, then, is there for the existence of a transcendent? I submit that there is *none*. And my reading of religious writings and my conversations with many of those who maintain the existence of the transcendent lead me to affirm that they also would agree that there is none. For they hold that the existence of the transcendent (although a cognitive claim) is apprehended, *not* in a cognitive relationship but in the relationship of *faith*.

Thus in the usual sense of the term 'evidence,' there seems to be no evidence for the existence of a transcendent ultimate. Why, then, should I accept such a claim? After all, throughout the rest of my philosophical activity *and* throughout my normal, everyday activities, I constantly rely upon criteria of evidence before accepting a cognitive claim. I emphasize that this holds for my *everyday* life and not merely for any philosophical or scientific beliefs which I may entertain. Not only do I accept or reject (say) the Principle of Rectilinear Propogation of Light because of evidence. I also ask for evidence in order to substantiate such simple claims as 'The stylus in my stereo tone arm is defective,' or 'Jones eloped with his secretary.'

It is clear that both believers and non-believers share this desire for evidence with me. At least, believers agree up to the point of the transcendent-claim. If I reject this claim because of lack of evidence, I do not think that I can be justly accused of being an extremist. Rather, I should be commended for my consistency!

The transcendentalist will reply: "But the usual criteria do not apply in this case. They work only for natural entities. The transcendent is not a natural being." I answer: Then the only reasonable procedure seems to be that of suspending my judgment, for I do not know of any non-natural criteria. The transcendentalist replies: "No, merely suspending your judgment implies that you think that some evidence might eventually be found. We are in a different dimension here. An act of *faith* is required."

I reply with two points: (a) In its normal usage, the term 'faith' still implies evidence and reasons. Why do I have faith in Smith, but not in Jones? Obviously because of *reasons*. I do not have faith in people haphazardly and without evidence. (b) If I am told that faith in the transcendent is not faith in the normal sense, but a special act of commitment, then I can only honestly reply: *I have no need for such faith.* The transcendentalist retorts: "Ah, but you do, for only through faith in the transcendent can life have meaning; and surely you seek a life that is significant and worthwhile." And this leads us to the second thesis.

(2) The transcendentalist claims that without the transcendent and faith in the transcendent, human existence is without *meaning, purpose, integration.* Is this true? And if true in some sense, what follows?

(A) Let us take *meaning* first. Is there any reason to believe that without the existence of the transcendent, life has no meaning? That is, does the existence of meaning presuppose the existence of the transcendent?

It is necessary to distinguish between *objective* meaning and *subjective* meaning. An objective meaning, if there were such, would be one which is either structurally *part of* the universe, apart from human subjective evaluation; or dependent upon some *external agency* other than human evaluation. Two comments are in order: (i) *If* the notion of objective meaning is a plausible one, then I see no reason why it must be tied up with the existence of a transcendent being, for it certainly is not self-contradictory to hold that an objective meaning could conceivably exist even though a transcendent being did not. That is, the two concepts of 'transcendent being' and 'objective meaning' are not logically related in the way in which the two concepts 'three' and 'odd' (for example) are related. (ii) But, more fundamental, I find the notion of an objective meaning as difficult to accept as I do the notion of a transcendent being. Therefore I cannot rely upon the acceptance of objective meaning in order to substantiate the existence of the transcendent.

Further comment is needed on this point. It seems to me that there is no shred of evidence for the existence of an objective meaning in the universe. If I were to characterize the universe, attempting to give a complete description, I would do so in terms of matter in motion, or energy, or forces such as gravitation, or events, etc. Such a description is *neutral*. It can have no non-descriptive components. The same holds for a description of any segment of the universe. Kepler, for example, was entitled to say that the paths of the planets are elliptical, etc. But he was not entitled to say that this motion exhibits some fundamental, objective purpose more so than some other type of motion would. From the standpoint of present evidence, evaluational components such as meaning or purpose are not to be found in the universe as objective aspects of it. Such values are the result of human evaluation. With respect to them, we must say that the universe is valueless; it is *we* who evaluate, upon the basis of our subjective preferences. Hence, we do not discover values such as meaning to be inherent within the universe. Rather, we "impose" such values upon the universe.

When the transcendentalist holds that, without the transcendent, no objective meaning for human existence is possible, he assumes that the notion of an objective meaning is an intelligible one. But if one can show, as I believe one can, that the idea of objective meaning is an implausible one, then his argument has no point. In no way does it give even the slightest evidence for the existence of a transcendent ultimate.

However, it is possible that some transcendentalist would want to take a different position here. There are at least two alternatives which he might hold.

(i) The transcendentalist might *agree* that there is no *objective* meaning in the universe, that meaning is a function of human subjectivity. His point now is that *subjective* meaning is found if and only if there exists a transcendent. I reply with two points (1) This is a grandiose generalization, which might wow an imbecile but not anyone of normal intelligence, and, like most such generalizations, it is false. (I shall return to this point in connection with the transcendentalist's third thesis.) (2) The meaning which the transcendentalist here affirms cannot be subjective meaning, for it is dependent upon some external, non-human factor, namely, the existence of the transcendent. This sort of meaning is *not* a function of human subjectivity. Thus we are back where we were. The transcendentalist's views about meaning do not provide any evidence at all for the existence of a transcendent ultimate.

(ii) I mentioned that the transcendentalist may take a second alternative. He might want to hold: "Of course, the fact of meaning in human existence does not in any way prove, demonstratively or with probability, that there *is* a transcendent being. Therefore, I won't say that meaning in life is impossible unless the transcendent exists. I will merely say that one cannot find meaning unless *one has faith* in the transcendent. The fact of meaning testifies to the necessity of *faith*."

I reply again with two points. (1) This generalization is also false. I know of many humans who have found a meaningful existence without faith in the transcendent. (2) However, even if this statement were true—even if heretofore not a single human being had found meaning in his life without faith in the transcendent—*I should reject such meaning and search for some other kind.* To me, the price which the transcendentalist pays for his meaning is too dear. If I am to find any meaning in life, I must attempt to find it without the aid of crutches, illusory hopes, and incredulous beliefs and aspirations. I am perfectly willing to admit that *I may not find any meaning at all* (although I think I can, even if it is not of the noble variety of which the transcendentalist speaks). But at least *I must try* to find it on my own. And this much I know: I can strive for a meaning only if it is one which is within the range of my comprehension as an inquiring, rational *man.* A meaning which is tied to some transcendent entity—or to faith in such—is not intelligible to me. Again, I here maintain what I hold throughout the rest of my existence, both philosophically and simply as a living person. I can accept only what is comprehensible to me, i.e., that which is within the province of actual or possible experience, or that for which I find some sound reasons or evidence. Upon these grounds, I must reject any notion of meaning which is bound with the necessity of faith in some mysterious, utterly unknowable entity. If my life should turn out to be less happy thereby, then I shall have to endure it as such. As Shaw once said: "The fact that a believer is happier than a skeptic is no more to the point than the fact that a drunken man is happier than a sober one. The happiness of credulity is a cheap and dangerous quality."

(B) I shall not say much about the transcendentalist's claim that, without the transcendent, or without faith in it, human existence is *purposeless.* For if I were to reply in detail, I should do so in about the same manner as I did with respect to the matter of meaning. An objective purpose is as difficult to detect in the universe as an objective meaning. Hence, again, one cannot argue that there must be a transcendent or that faith in such is necessary.

(C) What about the transcendentalist's claim that, without the transcendent, or, without *faith* in the transcendent, no integration is possible?

(i) In one sense of the term, this assertion, too, is obviously false. There are many persons who have attained what might be called psychological integration, i.e., self-integration, integration of personality, etc., without faith in the transcendent. I know of dozens of people whose lives are integrated in this sense, yet have no transcendental commitments.

(ii) But perhaps the transcendentalist means something much more fundamental than this psychological thesis by his claim. Perhaps he is making some sort of metaphysical assertion—a statement about man and his place in the universe. Thus his assertion must be taken to mean that metaphysical integration is not achievable without the transcendent or without faith in it. Like Kierkegaard, he holds that the cleavages of existence cannot be held together without the transcendent. What shall we say to this interpretation?

I am not sure that I understand what such integration is supposed to be. But insofar as I do, it seems to me that it is not possible. I am willing to admit that, if such integration were achievable, it might perhaps be attained only by virtue of something transcendent. But I find no conclusive or even reasonable evidence that such integration has been achieved either by believers in the transcendent or by non-believers. Hence one cannot infer that there is a transcendent ultimate or that faith in such an entity is necessary.

What about the mystics? you ask. It would be silly for me to say that the mystics have not experienced something very unusual which they have *interpreted* as some sort of unity with the universe, or whatever it may be. They may, indeed, have *felt* that, at rare moments, they were "swallowed up in the infinite ocean of being," to quote James. But again, peculiar and non-intersubjectively testable experiences are not reliable evidence for any truth-claim. Besides, suppose that the mystics *had* occasionally achieved such unity with the universe. Still, this is somewhat irrelevant. For the point is, that *I*, and many beings like myself (perhaps most of you), have not been favored with such experiences. In fact, it appears that most people who have faith in the transcendent have not had such experiences. This is precisely *why* they have faith. If they had complete certainty, no faith would be needed. Thus faith itself does not seem to be enough for the achievement of integration; and if integration were obtained, faith would be unnecessary. Hence the transcendentalist's view that integration is achieved *via* faith in the transcendent is questionable.

But even if this last thesis were true, it does me no good. Once again, I cannot place my faith in an unknown X, in that which is incomprehensible to me. Hence I must accept the fact that, for me, life will remain without objective meaning, without purpose, and without metaphysical integration. *And I must go on from there.* Rather than crying for the moon, my task must be, as Camus said, to know whether or not one can live *without appeal*.

(3) This leads us to the transcendentalist's third (and most crucial) thesis: That without meaning, purpose, and integration, life is not *worthwhile*. From which he draws the conclusion that without a *transcendent* or *faith* in it, life is not worthwhile. I shall deal only with the claim that without *meaning*, life is not worthwhile. Similar comments could be made regarding purpose and integration.

If the transcendentalist's claim sounds plausible at all, it is only because he continues to confuse objective meaning with subjective meaning. It is true that life has no objective meaning. Let us face it once and for all. But from this it does not follow that life is not *worthwhile*, for it can still be subjectively meaningful. And, really, the latter is the only kind of meaning worth shouting about. An objective meaning—that is, one which is inherent within the universe or dependent upon external agencies—would, frankly, leave me cold. It would not be *mine*. It would be an outer, neutral thing, rather than an inner, dynamic achievement. I, for one, am *glad* that the universe has no meaning, for thereby is *man all the more glorious.* I willingly accept the fact that external meaning is non-existent (or if existent, certainly not apparent), for this leaves me free to *forge my own meaning*. The extent of my creativity and thereby my success in this undertaking depends partly on the richness of my own psyche. There are some persons whose subjectivity is poor and wretched. Once they give up the search for objective meaning, they may perhaps have a difficult time in finding life to be worthwhile. Such is the fate of the impoverished. But those whose subjectivity is enlarged—rationally, esthetically, sensually, passionally—may find life to be worthwhile by means of their creative activity of subjective evaluation, in which a neutral universe takes on color and light, darkness and shadow, becomes now a source of profound joy, now a cause for deep sorrow.

What are some ways by which such worthwhileness can be found? I can speak only for myself. I have found subjective meaning through such things as *knowledge, art, love, and work*. Even though I realize that complete and perfect knowledge of matters of fact is not attainable, this does not lessen my enthusiasm to know and to understand. Such pursuits may have no practical utility; they are not thereby any less significant. To know about the nature of necessary truth or the probable structure of the atom is intrinsically fascinating, to me. And what a wealth of material lies in the arts. A Bach fugue, a Vlaminck painting, a Dostoevsky novel; life is intensely enriched by things such as these. And one must not neglect mention of one's relationships of friendship and love. Fragmentary and imperfect as these often are, they nevertheless provide us with some of our most heightened moments of joy and value. Finally, of all of the ways which I listed, none is more significant and constantly sustaining to me than work. There have been times when I, like many others, no doubt, have suffered some tragedy which seemed unendurable. Every time, it has been my work that has pulled me through.

In short, even if life has no meaning, in an external, objective sense, this does not lead to the conclusion that it is not worth living, as the transcendentalist naively but dogmatically assumes. On the contrary, this fact opens up a greater field of almost infinite possibilities. For as long as I am *conscious*, I shall have the capacity with which to *endow* events, objects, persons, and achievements with value. Ultimately, it is through my *consciousness* and it alone that worth or value are obtained. Through consciousness, the scraping of horses' tails on cats' bowels (to use James' phrase) become the beautiful and melodic lines of a Beethoven string quartet. Through consciousness, a pile of rock can become the memorable Mount Alten which one has climbed and upon which one almost perished. Through consciousness, the arrangements of *P*s and *Q*s on paper can become the symbols of the formal beauty and certain truth of the realm of mathematical logic. Through consciousness, the gift of a carved little piece of wood, left at one's door by a friend, can become a priceless treasure. Yes, it is a *vital* and *sensitive consciousness* that counts. Thus there is a sense in which it is true, as many thinkers and artists have reminded us, that everything begins with my consciousness, and nothing has any worth except through my consciousness.

IV.

I shall conclude with an ancient story. "Once a man from Syria led a camel through the desert; but when he came to a dark abyss, the camel suddenly, with teeth showing and eyes protruding, pushed the unsuspecting paragon of the camel-driving profession into the pit. The clothes of the Syrian were caught by a rosebush, and he was held suspended over the pit, at the bottom of which an enormous dragon was waiting to swallow him. Moreover, two mice were busily engaged in chewing away the roots of the already sagging plant. Yet, in this desperate condition, the Syrian was thralled to the point of utmost contentment by a rose which adorned the bush and wafted its fragrance into his face."[9]

I find this parable most illuminating. We are all men hanging on the thread of a few rapidly vanishing years over the bottomless pit of death, destruction, and nothingness. Those objective facts are starkly real. Let us not try to disguise them. Yet I find it marvelously interesting that man's *consciousness*, his reason and his passion, can elevate these routine, objective, external events, in a moment of lucidity and feeling, to the status of a personally appropriated ideal—an ideal which does not annul those objective facts, but which *reinterprets* them and clothes them with the apparel of *man's subjectivity*.

It is time, once again, to speak personally. What your situation is, I cannot say. But I know that I am that Syrian, and that I am hanging over the pit. My doom is inevitable and swiftly approaching. If, in these few moments that are yet mine, I can find no rose to respond to, or rather, if I have lost the ability to respond, then I shall moan and curse my fate with a howl of bitter agony. But *if* I can, in these last moments, respond to a rose—or to a philosophical argument or theory of physics, or to a Scarlatti sonata, or to the touch of a human hand—I say, if I can so respond and can thereby transform an external and fatal event into a moment of conscious insight and significance, then I shall go down *without hope or appeal yet passionately triumphant and with joy*.

Notes

1.   This essay was originally presented as an address to an audience.—E.D.K.

2.   Suggested by Emerson's "So nigh is grandeur to our dust." *Voluntaries*.—D.F.S.

3.   S. Kierkegaard, *Postscript*, p. 124.—D.F.S.

4.   S. Kierkegaard, *The Gospel of Suffering*, pp. 174-177.—D.F.S.

5.   *Postscript*, p. 226.—D.F.S.

6.   This essay was first read in the Last Lecture Series, at DePauw University, and was repeated, by request three times. In a revised form, it was read as the Top Prof lecture at Roosevelt University. It was again revised for this volume.—E.D.K.

7.   A. Camus, *The Myth of Sisyphus*. Tr. by J. O'Brien (New York: Vintage Books, 1959), p.45.—E.D.K.

8.   In theology a special event in which a transcendent being is said to make itself manifest to humans.—E.D.K.

9.   R. Hertz, *Chance and Symbol* (Chicago: University of Chicago, 1948), pp. 142-143.—E.D.K.

THE SELF IN RELATION TO ULTIMATE REALITY: JUDAISM, CHRISTIANITY, AND ISLAM

JUDAISM

by Diana Edelman

Judaism is the earliest of the three monotheistic faiths found in western tradition. It is the parent of Christianity and is seen within Muslim tradition to be an earlier form of the divine revelation that was subsequently revealed again in Christianity and then revealed yet again in Islam.

The time period in which Judaism first emerged is not known for certain. Scholars tend to use the term to refer to the faith of the descendants of the people who formerly lived in the kingdom of Judah. Their ancestors were sent into exile by the Babylonians in 598 and 586 BCE and settled in areas along the Tigris River. In 538 BCE, after the Persians had conquered the Babylonians and become the world rulers of their day, descendants of those exiled earlier were allowed to return to the former region of Judah, now a Persian province called Yehud, and mingle with the descendants of those who had never gone into exile. Monotheistic Judaism is thought to have emerged either among those who went into exile, or in Yehud after the intermingling of the two communities, either under Persian rule (538-333 BCE) or during the subsequent Greek rule (333-33 BCE). This is the "outsider" view; the "insider" view of members of the faith community is that Judaism began with the patriarchal father of the nation of Israel, Abraham.

The roots of Judaism trace back to the national religion of the kingdom of Judah, which existed from about 975 BCE to 586 BCE. This religion, which scholars call Yahwism, was not monotheistic, but polytheistic. There was a divine pantheon, or hierarchy of gods, that was headed by the divine couple, Yahweh and Asherah. Traces of this older, pre-Jewish religion are found in the Bible.

Forms of Judaism Today

There is no single form of Judaism whose adherents share a common creed or set of dogmas. It is difficult to provide an easy definition of what makes a person a Jew, particularly since the term goes beyond being a strictly religious label to one that has an ethnic dimension. Some people who are born to one or more Jewish parents are agnostic or atheist in their religious outlook but still consider themselves to be Jewish because of their cultural heritage.

> . . . Judaism . . . is an indefinite manifold. Its existence consists of the coming together and the moving apart of great numbers of diverse and contradictory items of thought, feeling, and conduct. Each and every one of these items has a claim upon the consideration of any person endeavoring to establish what Judaism is or what Judaism is not. . . . The definition which any citizen gives Judaism depends on his loves and hates, on his wishes and frustrations. Those cause him to react selectively to the entire shifting aggregate of which living Judaism is composed. They will lead him to affirm qualities that others deny, and deny qualities which others affirm.[1] There is not *a* Jewish view of life. There are Jewish *views* of life.[2]

To call Jews "people of the Book" as sometimes is done does not allow them to be distinguished from other religions whose faith is centered around divine revelation that is contained in sacred Scripture, such as Muslims, Christians, and Hindus. The same problem inheres in labeling them monotheists who espouse the unity of God, since Muslims, Christians, and many Hindus share this same belief.

More accurately, Jews are "the people of the covenant." Jewish Scripture defines a series of covenants that God has entered into with humanity, beginning with Noah on behalf of all life on earth in perpetuity (Genesis 9:8-17), moving on to Abraham, the forefather of Israel (Genesis 12:1-3; 13:14-17; 15:1-20; 17:1-14; 22:15-18), to Israel itself and its descendants at Sinai (Exodus 19-24), to David, to have a descendant on the throne in Jerusalem forever (2 Samuel 7), and finally, to a new covenant with descendants of Israel and Judah upon whose hearts God will write His law directly (Jeremiah 31:31-34; variant versions, Isaiah 55; 61).

The stipulations for the Sinai covenant include the ten commandments as a summary of the divine will and revelation for moral human behavior. Thus, Judaism understands God to be the source of morality and sacred Scripture the vehicle through which the divine will has been made known to humanity.

The concept of covenant also reflects the general view that God has selected a particular group of humans and their descendants with whom to have a special relationship. A universal God, all of humanity will benefit from God's grace and favor through the example set by the Jews.

Over time, different forms of Judaism have developed and today, one can speak of six general branches. These include Orthodoxy or Torah-True, Kabbalah, the mystical form of the faith, Hasidism, Reform, Conservatism, and Reconstructionism. In practical terms, these six branches can be grouped under two main headings: traditional Judaism, which would include Orthodoxy, Kabbalah, Hasidism, and traditionally leaning Conservative Jews, and liberal, which includes Reform, Reconstructionism, and liberally leaning Conservative Jews.

Orthodox or Torah-True Judaism is the direct descendant of ancient Pharisaic Judaism, which became prominent after the destruction of the temple in Jerusalem in 70 CE by the Romans. Once the temple ceased to exist, God could no longer be worshipped through the old sacrificial cult, which traced back to Yahwism. Instead, worship shifted to a study of God's revealed word in sacred Scripture, or Torah. Individual and communal thanksgiving, repentance, and prayer continued, however, from the earlier period. Torah-centered study had emerged centuries earlier, perhaps as early as the exile, and had already become a favored form of worship in communities outside of Yehud, where sacrificial worship was not possible because Jerusalem had emerged as the only legitimate place to offer such sacrifice.

Orthodox Judaism is rabbinic Judaism; it centers on scholars, called *rabbis*, making explicit what is implicit in the 613 commandments found in the Jewish Bible.[3] Understanding the Bible to contain direct divine revelation of norms of human behavior, these scholars set about to clarify the parameters of observance. So, for example, the Fourth Commandment orders humans to remember and sanctify Shabbat. But when does sundown begin, signalling the beginning of Saturday and when does Saturday officially end? How does one remember the day and how does one sanctify it? Work is prohibited. What constitutes work?

Different Rabbis gave and continue to give different answers to these questions. Eventually, the answers of particularly well-respected rabbis were gathered together in two versions of a written commentary on the Torah called the Talmud. One was produced in Palestine and one in Babylonia. Today, Torah-True boys and men spend a large portion of their lives studying and debating the different rabbinical views found in the Talmud.

For Orthodox Jews, the Talmud is oral Torah ("teaching") that was revealed to Moses at Mt. Sinai alongside the written Torah, the first five books of Moses. This view encapsulates the belief that the *rabbis* are not adding to the original Torah in any way but merely making explicit parts of the original revelation. They firmly believe that "all is contained within Torah."

The Talmud does not provide a practical code for Jewish conduct; it leaves the range of opinions side by side with no final ruling. Since the goal of Torah study is ultimately to understand the divine will and put it into action, a short-hand guide was needed. The *Shulhan Arukh*, written in 1555 CE by Joseph Karo and expanded by Rabbi Moses Isserles, serves as the authoritative code for Torah-true Jews today.

Within Orthodoxy, it is the duty of a Jew to observe all 613 commandments found in the Torah to his or her best ability; all the commandments are seen to be eternal in duration and not culturally specific in their scope. Many of the commandments are understood literally rather than figuratively. For example, the command in Deuteronomy 6:8 to "bind these words as a sign upon your hand and as an emblem on your forehead" is fulfilled at morning prayer by observant male Jews who don the *tefillin*. These are little cubes held in place by leather straps. One goes on the forehead and the other on the arm. Inside each cube is a piece of parchment onto which the words have been copied.

Similarly, the command in 4:9 to "write them on the doorposts of your house" is fulfilled by the placing of *mezuzoth*, small cases inside of which the words have been copied onto parchment, on the right side of the doorframe of every room in a Jewish house that is used as living space (not closets, toilets, or bathrooms). The command to put fringes on the hems of one's clothes has led to the practice of men wearing a vest with fringes called a *tallit qatan* underneath their regular clothes during the day and the command not to cut a male's sideburns is kept literally, leading to the long sidecurls or earlocks, so characteristic of orthodox men.

Kabbalah

Every form of organized religion has a mystical branch and Judaism is no exception. The desire to know and encounter God directly is a strong urge in humanity. Kabbalah, meaning "tradition" or "reception of orally transmitted teachings," focuses on the big unknowns in life: the nature of God, the creation of the universe, the purpose of human life, and the nature of evil, adding a specifically Jewish concern, the ultimate meaning of the Torah. Over time, a coherent, though not uniform system of thought and action has developed and been written down in a series of books.

According to Kabbalistic teaching, God is beyond all existence and can only be described by negative terms since to assign any positive attribute would limit the limitless Divine. The name that is given to this Eternal Source is *En Sof*, which means "without end or limit." The physical world and universe is the result of a long chain of emanation from *En Sof*, in which the invisible and limitless Divine is made manifest and limited, though it remains infinite and unlimited. The closer along the chain of emanation an object is to the Source, the greater is the concentration of divine within it.

En Sof produces the first emanation, called Crown, which then in turn produces Wisdom, which produces Intelligence. These first three spheres, which are closest to God, represent the domain of reason. Intelligence then emanates Greatness, Greatness Strength, and Strength Beauty. The second triad of spheres represents the domain of feeling and perception. Beauty emanates Firmness, Firmness Splendor, and Splendor Foundation, the third and final domain of nature that governs the visible world. Finally, Foundation emanates Kingdom, which is a gateway to the next lower world and, at the same time, an upward connector to the highest world. These ten comprise the *Sefirot*, or spheres, which comprise the World of Emanation, closest to *En Sof*. It is to this world that all souls go after their successful testing on earth.

Kingdom, the last *sephirah*, continues the emanation process into a new world, that of Creation, which contains the throne of glory, seven heavenly places, and the emanated souls before they are incarnated. This world also contains ten spheres that mirror the ten *sephirot*, but which have less of the pure spirit in them, and so are called the *kelippot*, or "shells." The chain of emanation continues through a third World of Formation comprised of ten spheres, where most angels live and the seven heavenly halls exist, to the final world of Making, which is our universe. It is inhabited by the lower angels who combat evil and receive human prayers as well as humans and all of life as we know it.

Humans, though very distant from *En Sof* along the chain of emanation, still contain within them a tiny spark of the divine. It is mostly matter, which is a lack of pure spiritual being—not an independent substance. The Torah reveals that humanity's task is to observe all 613 commandments and so generate positive pulsations or energy that are sent back along the chain of emanation to the Source, repairing any breaks along the way. This process is called *tikkun olam*, or repair of the universe. Once these weak impulses return "home," they release a flood of positive divine energy back down the chain, benefitting all links in all worlds. We can never understand God's true nature or join with *En Sof*, but we can observe the Divine indirectly through the visible, emanated universe, through the goodness of which human beings are capable, and in the hidden meanings in Torah.

According to Kabbalistic teaching, all souls were created at the same time and are born into human bodies to be tested. Any which remains pure in spite of the temptations and polluting influences of the body in the physical world as we know it go upon death to the World of Emanation for eternity. Those that become contaminated or impure are reborn in another human body at death to try to remove the impurity during the subsequent life. Transmigration or reincarnation continues through as many lives as its takes for the soul to resist temptation, purify itself, and earn a place in the World of Emanation.[4]

The origins of Kabbalah are debated. Some early works appeared in the 7th-9th centuries CE, but the primary work, the *Zohar*, was written at the close of the 13th century, with another period of Kabbalistic flourishing and further elaboration in the 16th century, associated with Rabbi Isaac Luria in the town of Safed, in the Galilee. Within Orthodox circles, no one under 40 is supposed to study Kabbalah because of its theology that is in some ways at odds with normative orthodox doctrine. Its doctrine of transmigration of the soul, for example, is very unorthodox, as is its reading of a number of Torah passages.

Most of those who choose to study Kabbalah are drawn from the ranks of Orthodoxy. Today, there is no Kabbalistic community with its own synagogue and separate form of worship. If a Jew becomes interested in embarking on a mystical path to God, he will find a teacher who knows the Kabbalistic literature and study with him, putting into practice the beliefs set forth in the writings. He will remain a member of his home Jewish community and continue his family obligations and attendance at his local place of worship.

Hasidism

In Poland in the first half of the 18th century CE, a Torah-True Jew with little formal schooling in Torah and Talmud named Israel ben *Eliezer* began to teach to surrounding communities of Jews a new approach to God that did not stress Torah learning as the primary way to communicate with God. Instead, he explained that God is everywhere and in everything of the universe and one simply needs sincerity, honest prayer, joy, and the ability to live life totally dedicated to God to experience the divine. His message was gladly embraced by thousands of Jews for whom Talmudic study was too demanding and lacked spiritual vitality. In addition, his positive message struck a chord with many in eastern European Jewish communities whose relatives and immediate ancestors had experienced severe persecution during the Cossack massacres in the 17th century and had also experienced extreme disappointment when the long, hoped for messiah did not turn out to be Shabbetai Tzevi, in spite of such claims on his behalf. Israel ben *Elizer* became known as the Baal Shem Tov, Master of the Good Name, or Besht for short. This title was bestowed on any Jew who could perform healings and other wonders by invoking "the good name" of God in one of its many forms presented in Kabbalistic writings.

Hasidic teaching has "democratized" Kabbalistic teaching, making it accessible to the masses instead of the learned few. In the process, it has also altered some of its original teachings. An important change involves the amount of divinity within the manifest world; Kabbalah teaches that it diminishes the farther along the chain of emanation one progresses away from *En Sof*, but Hasidism argues that the manifest divine substance is equally present everywhere and in everything in the visible and invisible emanated worlds.

The goal of humans is to realize that God is the only true reality and nothing exists apart from God; all things are in God. As a result, humans must strive to attain *shiflut*, "humility," and not claim to the highest life form and masters of life on earth. At the same time they must cultivate *devekut*, "cleaving or attachment," in which they focus their mind in every waking hour on God, dedicating all actions, however mundane, to Him and recognizing simultaneously that He is the source of the universe and master of all life, material and immaterial. By devoting oneself to these two ideals as well as the keeping of the 613 commandments as conveniently codified in the *Shulhan Arukh*, Hasidic men can effect the repair of the universe, *tikkun olam*.

Nevertheless, it is recognized that *devekut* in particular is extremely difficult and the belief developed that only a few extremely spiritual men, called *Zaddiks*, are able to achieve this goal. As a result, ordinary Hasidic followers attach themselves to a *Zaddik*, who then prays on their behalf, heals them as necessary, and gives spiritual counsel and wisdom, particularly on Shabbat and at festivals, when the followers eat at the *zaddik's* table and receive sermons from him. Pronouncements by a *zaddik* are written down for the benefit of the group and passed on from generation to generation.

The extra spiritual qualities of *zaddiks* are believed to be handed down genetically within families, resulting historically in dynasties of religious leaders among Hasidic groups. They are as close as one comes to an official clergy as it is conceived in Christianity, where a leader can serve as an intermediary between a follower and God and be an instrument for conveying divine blessing and grace.

Reform

This form of Judaism arose in the early 1800s in Germany in response to the Enlightenment and the extension of the right of citizenship to Jews within modern states for the first time. This momentous development led to a number of different reactions within the Jewish community at large. Many Torah-True did not want to embrace the offer of citizenship but preferred to continue to live as a minority community without rights under the limited protection of the host state and powers that be. At the other extreme were those who abandoned Judaism altogether, either converting to Christianity or simply becoming secular citizens wishing to be totally assimilated into the majority. An intermediate position led to the creation of the Reform and, in reaction to it, the Conservative and Neo-Orthodox movements.

A number of Jews wanted to embrace citizenship while continuing to be Jews, but wanted to remove from Judaism practices that set them apart from their Christian neighbors. In particular, the dietary laws that made it virtually impossible to eat with non-Jews, the old-fashioned dress that distinguished them, the earlocks, the wearing of the *tallit qatan*, the separating of men and women during worship, the failure to use musical accompaniment during worship, the use of Hebrew for worship, the restriction of women from serving as rabbis, the strict observance of no work or riding on Shabbat, the use of *tefillin* and prayer shawls during worship, the need to recite prayers three times a day, the use of *mezuzot* in the home, and the wearing of a *yarmulke* or skull cap on the head were thought no longer to have meaning or relevance to the modern world and so should be abandoned.

Underlying these changes was the belief that Torah/Tanak was not direct divine revelation but rather, the attempts of humans in certain times and places to understand the divine. As a result, it was argued that the 613 commandments were not eternal and changeless revelations of the divine will but were culturally specific practices that developed in particular historical circumstances that had now changed and were no longer relevant in many cases. Most reformers attempted to make Judaism strictly a religion and to remove from it any ethnic dimension.

Although initiated in Germany and established by the 1850s in France, Hungary and England, Reform found its largest group of adherents in America. Many German Jews with Reform leanings emigrated to America in the mid 1830s-50s. The majority of Jewish congregations became Reform, in part because of the lack of a strong Orthodox presence that could try to assert adherence to traditional practices.

Neo-Orthodoxy

In reaction to the development of Reform congregations in Germany, a new form of Orthodoxy developed in Germany and Austria that embraced citizenship and limited secular learning alongside traditional Torah study but which upheld at the same time the status of Torah and Talmud as direct divine revelation and the need for change to develop naturally from within the community, based on rabbinic principles of Torah interpretation. Thus, none of the 613 Commandments was to be eliminated, but new explicit meanings could be embraced that were more in harmony with the times.

Conservatism

In reaction to the Reform movement, there emerged a group of Jews who did not embrace neo-Orthodoxy but who also felt that Reform had gone too far in abandoning traditional Jewish faith, principles, and practices. Known as "positive (meaning scientific) historical Judaism" because of a key phrase used by its earliest advocate Zechariah Frankel, the chief rabbi of Dresden, to try to articulate a middle-road position between Reform and Neo-Orthodoxy, this new movement argued that any change made to tradition needed to be based on both scientific history and a majority expression of popular will. Frankel's writings found concrete expression in America, where a new movement with its own seminaries and synagogues was born as a mid position between neo-Orthodoxy and Reform.

Accepting the Reform position that Torah is a humanly produced, culturally bound artifact that contains the accumulated responses of generations of Jews to particular historical circumstances, it disagreed about the ease with which large portions of the tradition could be discarded suddenly. The tradition, which had evolved slowly over time, should be retained unless found no longer to be a meaningful vehicle for expressing the Jewish spirit by a majority of the community—not just the educated rabbinical elite as in orthodoxy. It advocated gradual adaptation and innovation.

Specifically, when the movement got underway in America in the 1880s, its synagogues encouraged the observance of Shabbat, of dietary laws, and of the maintenance of Hebrew instruction in Jewish education. Use of the prayer shawl was continued but the separation of men and women was generally, although not universally, abandoned. Some prayers were translated into English and the sermon was given in English, as in Reform. Nevertheless, the movement also emphasized that every Jew had the right to decide personally what practices and beliefs would be followed. This is why some Conservative Jews are virtually Orthodox and why others are virtually Reform.

Conservatism might not have survived as an independent movement were it not for the emigration of mass numbers of eastern European Jews of Orthodox and Hasidic backgrounds in the last decades of the 19th century and the early decades of the 20th century. Leaders of established Reform congregations were not anxious to be associated with the impoverished and barely literate Jews and did not want them joining their synagogues. Most would not have been interested in Reform congregations anyway since they were too foreign to their traditional set of beliefs.

To deal with the new arrivals and acculturate them as quickly as possible so that all Jews were not looked down upon by other non-Jewish Americans as ignorant peasants, a number of wealthy Reform Jews poured money into the development of the Conservative Seminary and new Conservative synagogues. Their plan worked. Conservatism's embracing of many traditional practices made these Jews feel comfortable, while their lack of Hebrew skills and absorption in Torah study apparently made the rather radical change in stance on Torah as divine revelation less heretical. In addition, the ability of the movement to embrace a wide set of beliefs could have minimized this issue, once the newcomers fully understood it, and there were so few orthodox synagogues or Hasidic *zaddiks* available that by default, Conservatism became the form of organized Judaism that was closest to what they were familiar with back home. Today in America, the majority of self-declared Jews with official affiliation belong to the Conservative Movement.

Reconstructionism

The most recent form of Judaism to gain recognition as an official movement with its own synagogues and seminary is called Reconstructionism, which has its origin in the writings of Mordecai Kaplan (1881-1983). This movement originated in America but has spread worldwide. Its founder remained an avowed Conservative until his death, not wanting to fragment Judaism any further, but during his tenure as a professor at the Conservative Jewish Theological Seminary of America, many of his pupils, who became rabbis, tried to get him to repudiate Conservatism and establish Reconstructionism as a new movement. A Reconstructionist seminary was opened in 1968 in spite of Kaplan's attempt to forestall a split with Conservatism.

Kaplan was one of the strong advocates of individual choice within Judaism and may have made this emphasis more prominent within Conservatism over time. While Conservatism's original and primary stance was that modification of aspects of tradition that were deemed no longer to be applicable to the modern situation was to be done by a majority vote of members, Reconstructionism leaves it to individual conscience and reason to decide what parts of tradition a person finds meaningful and decides to follow and which he or she discards as no longer relevant.

The movement places a strong emphasis on the deliberate and self-conscious "updating" or "reimaging" of traditional concepts like God, Torah, Israel, and the synagogue to conform to and reflect contemporary thought and society. Kaplan was the first to advocate the equal status of women, which eventually was embraced by the Conservative movement as well. Jews work together to improve the world in voluntary groups called *havurot* or fellowships, where decisions are reached by consensus and the rabbi is not looked to as a leader but rather as a resource person.

Kaplan considers Judaism to be a religious civilization, not just a religion and not just a nationality. It is a way of life in which all aspects—religion, language, literature, customs, folkways, music art, and communal organization—should be informed by and permeated with modernized Jewish ideals and ethics. For Kaplan, contemporary Jewish identity is to be grounded on the sense of belonging to a people whose salvation is linked with individual self-fulfillment, rather than belief.[5] At the same time, however, Jews are to live as citizens of democratic societies; they are to live simultaneously in two societies.

Reconstructionism alone among Jewish movements rejects the idea of God's chosen people as being elitist and offensive, substituting for it the idea of Israel's vocation. All references to the desire for the restoration of animal sacrifice in a rebuilt temple in Jerusalem, physical resurrection, God's rewarding and punishing Israel by granting or withholding rain, disparaging references to women, slaves, and Gentiles, and anthropomorphic representations of God have been removed from the liturgy.

God

Judaism refers to the limitless, eternal source of life and reality as God or Lord. It has inherited from earlier Yahwism the name YHWH to designate this formless being, even though within Yahwism the name had been used to represent a human-like divinity who ruled the heavenly realm and was king of a heavenly court.

YHWH is the old name or title of the head of the pantheon. It consists of four consonants, whose vocalization is not absolutely certain because in ancient Hebrew vowels were not written out when spelling a word, only consonants. The consonants represent a verb whose basic meaning is "to be, to become, to cause to be/become."

The name is considered so sacred in Torah-True Judaism that it is blasphemous to speak it and other terms are substituted for it, like *hasshem*, "the name," or *Adonai*, "Lord." As monotheistic Judaism replaced the older polytheistic Yahwism, a more abstract concept of the divine developed, rejecting that of a god with human characteristics in favor of a reality that is beyond human limits and the physical laws of nature.

In mystical Judaism, this abstract concept of the divine came to be called *En Sof*, "without end/limit," which attempts to define the divine or Other by stating what it is not so as not to limit it in any way by placing upon it finite, positive attributes.

Today in Judaism there is no single formulation of God/ godhead/the divine that is authoritative for all Jews.

> Just as the God-idea progressed from a perceptual image to a conception like the one which identifies God as the sum of all those factors and relationships in the universe that make for unity, creativity and worthwhileness in human life, so can the attributes of God, which once were externalized and concrete, be translated into modern terms and made relevant to modern thinking and living. Men attributed to God their own highest desires and aspirations. They called him creator, protector, helper, sovereign, and redeemer. These terms can now be identified with the highest and most significant aims of human existence, and achieve a new force and vitality through this conscious process of identification. We can no longer believe that God is a mighty sovereign, or that the universe is the work of his hands. In the light of the present development of the God-idea, however, we can see that God is manifest in all creativity and in all forms of sovereignty that make for the enhancement of human life.[6]

Purpose of Life

Genesis 1:26-28 defines the purposes of human life to be fruitful, to multiply, to replenish and subdue the earth and to dominate the other life on earth. The subsequent covenant or treaty established between God and Israel at Sinai in the Book of Exodus adds to this list of commands the further one of being obedient to the terms of the pact that God revealed to Moses as the representative of the people on Mt. Sinai, so that Israel can be a nation of priests holy to God. These terms are summarized in the Ten Commandments. Throughout the Hebrew Bible or Tanak there are 613 divine commands or *mitzvot* that are placed upon Israel and its descendants.

Orthodox Judaism teaches that the purpose of life is to try to live in accordance with these 613 divine commandments to the best of one's abilities, thereby conforming one's human will to the divine will and making humanity holy. So central is the Torah for Orthodoxy that Rabbi Johanan ben Zakkai claimed that humans were created for the purpose of studying Torah. Since Torah is viewed as the literal, revealed word of God, its study allows one to experience "communion with God, as though one were present at Sinai when God revealed himself to all Israel."[7]

The specifics of how to observe the commandments revealed in Torah are elaborated in a set of writings called the Talmud. What, for example, does the divine command not to boil a kid in its mother's milk mean? The Talmud presents a range of opinions by rabbis on how to answer this set of questions. While it is recognized that no human is perfect and all will fail in keeping the *mitsvot*, those who do a good job, who succeed more than fail, will be resurrected at the Final Judgment Day and will be restored to eternal life in a new Israel that will rule a new earth in a new universe under the guidance of a descendant of King David. Those who fail more than succeed will simply cease to exist for eternity. For the Torah-True, suffering that is endured in this world is seen as divinely planned, to allow a person to enter the next world with a "clean bill of spiritual health"[8] and with an increased ultimate reward. The good fortune that the wicked enjoy is in payment for the little good they might do in this world,[9] but they will not realize eternal life after death because of their wickedness during life.

In dialogue with Aristotelian philosophy, Maimonides (1135-1204) argued that God created the universe by His will for differing purposes: "some things of their own sakes, some for the sake of other beings, which include their own purpose in themselves. The universe does not exist for man's sake; just as the divine will created man, so it also willed the existence of the heavens and stars and angels, each of which has its own purpose of existence. When something can only exist provided that something else has previously existed, God caused the latter to precede it, as for example, sensation preceded comprehension.[10] Thus, everything exists because the divine will choose to allow it to be created and so all is dependent on the divine will.

Hasidic Judaism has a slightly different understanding of the purpose of life. It teaches that humans must achieve a unity with God without compromising or destroying either. We must try to integrate what our senses tell us is an independent, earthly reality with God's all-encompassing, absolute reality. Once we begin to discern the divine in our world and strive to move closer to it, humans play a vital role in keeping the emanated universe sound and healthy. By keeping all 613 mitzvot and doing all actions with a knowledge that God is the source of all reality and we are not, in spite of what our senses suggest, we send good impulses back along the chain of emanation to *En Sof* and repair breaks that develop in the chain through sin. At the same time, in some Kabbalistic traditions, it is thought that we can raise god's glory, or *shekinah*, which has been banished to the created world, back to unite with God.

Within the Hasidic worldview, humans have the rather heavy burden of helping to maintain and highlight the chain of emanation through actions done with the proper intent, which is the realization that all the created world is indeed divine. By using our godlike mental abilities to understand and make manifest the divine nature in every thing, which otherwise lies concealed due to the use of our normal senses that perceive the world as separate from God, we individually and collectively determine God's destiny. We either make

God immanent, by seeing the divine in everything, or we make God transcendent by failing to perceive the divine in all created substance.

Martin Buber (1878-1965) explains this situation in the following way:

> . . . the divine is dormant in all things. . . . Corporeal reality is divine, but it must be realized in its divinity by him who truly lives it. The shekinah is banished into concealment; it lies, tied, at the bottom of every thing, and is redeemed in every thing by man, who, by his own vision or by his own deed, liberates the thing's soul. Thus, every man is called to determine, by his own life, God's destiny.[11] True human life is conceived to be a life lived in the presence of God. . . . He who turns toward the world and desires to see God in all things does not truly live in His presence. God may be seen seminally in all things, but He must be realized between them. Just as the sun's substance has its being among the stars yet beams its light into the earthly realm, so it is granted to human creatures to behold in their midst the radiance of the ineffable's glory. It glows dimly in all human beings, every one of them; but it does not shine in its full brightness within them—only between them. In every human being there is present the beginning of universal being (Allsein); but it can unfold only in his relatedness to universal being, in the pure immediacy of his giving and taking, which surrounds him like a sphere of light, merging him with the oneness of the world. The Divine may come to life in the individual man, may reveal itself from within individual man; but it attains its earthly fullness only where, having awakened to an awareness of their universal being, individual beings open themselves to one another, help one another; disclose themselves to one another, help one another; where immediacy is established between one human being and another; where the sublime stronghold of the individual is unbolted, and man breaks free to meet other man. Where this takes place, where the eternal rises in the Between, the seemingly empty space: that true place of realization is community, and true community is that relationship in which the Divine comes to its realization between man and man.[12]

Chief Rabbi Abraham Isaac Kook (1865-1935), who combines aspects of Orthodoxy, Kabbalah and liberal Judaism in his thought, sees the purpose of life to be the perfection of the world.

> The more clearly one studies the character of individual human souls, the more baffled one becomes over the great differences between personalities. . . . It is, however, precisely through their differentiations that they are all united toward one objective, to contribute toward the perfection of the world, each person according to his special talent. Surely one must marvel at the higher wisdom wherein by an inner, mysterious power known only to God, these opposites are integrated and related one to the other, so that through the fusion of all the diverse minds and physiognomies, there emerges a unified structure of consummate harmony.[13] Every act carried out in sanctity—that is, with God-oriented intent—is a road to the heart of the world. There is nothing that is evil in itself; every passion can become a virtue, every inclination 'a vehicle of God.' It is not the matter of the act that is decisive but its sanctification. Every act is hallowed, if it is directed toward salvation. The soul of the doer alone determines the character of his deed. With this, the deed does in truth become the life-center of religiosity. Simultaneously, the fate of the world is placed in the hands of the doer. The fallen divine sparks, the erring souls dispersed in things and beings, are liberated through the deed that is sanctified by its intention. By his acts man works for the redemption of the world. Indeed, he works for the redemption of God himself, for, through the supreme concentration and tension of this deed, and for an unfathomable instant's period of grace, he can cause the exiled glory of God [shekinah] to draw closer to its source.[14]

In liberal forms of Judaism, strict adherence to all 613 *mitzvot* is not considered the main requirement in life. These Jews feel that any of the *mitzvot* that are no longer relevant to modern life no longer need to be kept. Liberal Jews, for example, tend not to keep Shabbat strictly, usually do not observe the kosher laws for food preparation and eating, and do not wear any form of distinctive clothing to identify them as Jews. They tend to view the purpose of life to become the best human one possibly can by living ethically and in accordance with the spirit of the Ten Commandments, so developing the intellect and having it control the passions.

The concept of a final judgment day after death and a new universe ruled by a descendant of David is downplayed considerably. The idea of the Messianic world is not projected to a new universe in the eternal future but rather, is seen to be a reality obtainable here in this world by humans who strive to perfect themselves and society.

> The kingdom of God is a paradox, an inner contradiction that must somehow be resolved. For ages men have put their faith in conformity and obedience to authority. In the eighteenth century, a reaction set in and men began to look upon the absolute freedom of the individual as the chief end.[15] Humans must learn to act both interdependently and independently to achieve the world to come by balancing individualism and collectivism.[16] The world to come is none other than this world redeemed from slavery and war, from want and suffering, from disease and crime. . . . Every human being is both an *ego* and an *alter*, a self and an other. The *ego* or self hungers for the satisfactions that yield individuality and selfhood. The *alter*, or other, yearns for absorption in a larger self, in an enveloping permanence and order and meaning. This polarity is an inescapable part of the nature of things. Human life is most complete when it reckons with its double aspect. Then it approximates a mode of life which is in accord with the law of God as writ in the nature of man.[17]

Tanak is not seen to be the revealed will of God or the divine but rather, a human attempt to understand the relationship between the divine and human realms of reality.

Relationship of Human to the Divine

In the Tanak, humanity is made in the image of the divine and so is the highest form of creation in the visible world. The three traits that set us apart from other animals within creation are our ability to reason, our ability to speak, and our possession of free will. The latter is necessary in order for us to be rational and decide between different possibilities that our brains can perceive in any given situation. This explains why humans are made rulers of the earth. At the same time, it is these three traits that allow us to apprehend the existence of God beyond the created realm as well as within us and other elements of creation, to express it to others, and to choose to devote our lives to the divine, rather than the corporeal.

Humans are routinely spoken of as the "children of God" and the relationship between God and the individual is most often conceived of as that of parent/child. There is a bond between the two that is physical and emotional. God is a loving, kind, forgiving, and patient parent who is responsible for teaching his offspring correct values and behavior in life. At the same time, he is a disciplinarian who becomes angry and punishing when crossed or repeatedly disobeyed. This parental image tends to emphasize the immanence of the divine, in spite of its otherness. Less frequently relationship is expressed in terms of master/slave, when God's otherness, remoteness, and transcendent nature is emphasized.

Judaism takes over this sense of closeness or connectedness to God, even when God becomes an impersonal, abstract reality, by making God the expression of perfection and ideals that we strive to emulate. At the same time, the transcendent, otherness of the divine is emphasized since we can only aspire to such perfection, but never fully achieve it.

Although Tanak does not contain any reference to the existence of a soul that survives death, all forms of Judaism believe that humans have within their mortal bodies an immortal soul, which is a small spark of divinity. In this way, too, then, humans are children of God, since they contain divine essence within them.

Free Will

Judaism does not have any concept of original sin, which was developed by the Christian church. We are all born sinless, with the potential to live a perfect life. However, it is also readily admitted that no human ever manages to succeed in living the perfect life because as beings endowed with free will, we inevitably make bad choices. According to Genesis 6:5, these bad choices begin already during childhood, as we begin to exercise our intellects but when our senses tend to drive our decisions more than reason and we often give in to natural urges and desires. Thus, Torah-True Jews understand the giving of the law at Mt. Sinai to be God's attempt to help humanity overcome the bodily urges and let the intellect rule life. When we do this, we are emphasizing our unique human traits that reflect the way we are made in the image of God. By conforming our wills to the divine will through the exercise of free will, we are teaching our divine souls to rule over our perishable bodies, so making ourselves a nation of priests holy to God (Exodus 19:6).

Hasidic Judaism views free will as a trait that God made part of the human character so that once our minds discern that the earthly world we inhabit is connected directly to *En Sof* through the chain of emanation, we will choose to clarify the connection and amplify it. We will use our minds to discern the patterns in nature and life that point to the existence of another reality beyond the one our senses discern, which is the source of our limited world.

> He [God] endowed our earthly reality with a seemingly independent existence that appears to mask G-d's absolute reality, with the distinct objective that we would ultimately use our free will to access our innate desire to unite with G-dliness. As our eyes and hearts and minds grow more knowledgeable about our physical reality, we begin to see, like scientists or engineers, that there is indeed an unshakable and divine unity that underlies and gives meaning to everything we do.[18] By creating our world so that the outermost layers peel away to reveal successively more abstract and spiritual layers, G-d provided us with an opportunity to understand our creator. Just like the student, we gain knowledge of our universe step by step, metaphor by metaphor.[19] . . . We inhabit a finite reality which, by definition and nature, precludes contact with anything truly infinite or transcendent. But in creating us, G-d also imbued within us channels of awareness that allow us to breach the outer fragmented layers of our physical world, the 'container,' and glimpse the pure essence of G-d's unifying 'light' within.[20] Our perception of the "light" continues to be heightened as our 'containers' continue to be widened, as we approach ever nearer to the perspective of the creator, our divine guide and teacher: G-d.[21]

Liberal Jews emphasize the human possession of free will and see it as a primary aspect in our development of ideals and drive toward the perfection of the world and our individual selves. Having rejected the view that Torah is the direct revelation of the divine will for humans, free will plays an even larger and more central role in the setting up of ethical norms of behavior and personal decisions about what aspects of Jewish tradition are to be meaningful to the individual. At the same time, however, the de-emphasis on the omnipotence and omnipresence of the divine in human affairs lessens the traditional tension between divine foreknowledge and human free will, making it a less important issue. Like traditional Jews, however, liberal Jews would see the positive exercise of free will to lead to the heightening of the spiritual over the corporeal and the striving for more perfect knowledge and self-improvement.

Selection on free will:

> Traditional theology is a diluted version of medieval Jewish philosophy . . . Traditional Jewish theology is vulnerable because of its indissoluble connection with the presently discarded Aristotelian philosophy.

Aristotle's philosophy emphasizes the static, self-contained character of substance at the expense of *process*, *temporality*, and *relativity*, which typifies modern thought . . . If the modern Jew clings to this view, he will be confused about his Judaism—if not indeed, alienated from it.

The problem of freedom concerns itself with an attempt to reconcile God's *omnipotence* with *human responsibility*. To say that God is omnipotent—in the traditional sense—means that God has all the power possible. But if God has all possible power, and all possible knowledge, then God must not only *direct* all that happens, but must *know* all that has happened, is happening, or ever will happen.

Such a view of God makes it impossible for man to have any genuine freedom or capacity to create. For how can he affect the process of creation at all—either positively or negatively—if God has all power?

. . . To state this argument technically:

If God is all-powerful, then there can be no power other than God's.
If there is no power other than God's, then man can have no power.
If man has no power, then man can have no responsibility.

Traditionalists have affirmed that man has freedom in spite of the omnipotent character of God. Surely this is based on a confusion, which can readily be seen. *It stems from the belief that responsibility can be divided between God and man without, at the same time, dividing power between God and man.*

To have genuine responsibility, man must have genuine power. For traditional theology this means an intolerable assault on God's omnipotence . . . Such a belief is based on a misunderstanding. Omnipotence means the greatest possible power for any single being. It does not and cannot mean all possible power in general.

. . . Medieval philosophy generally recognized logical limits to God's power. For instance, it affirmed that God could not do what is logically impossible, like square a circle, or create a stone so heavy that He could not lift it. What has not been seen clearly is that there are certain limits in terms of real being to God's omnipotence. These do not detract from that omnipotence. On the contrary, they render it intelligible. The ontological limit of God's omnipotence is the reality of man and creation. Once God creates the world, a real element is introduced that has being and power and which demands its due. God then has maximum power, but He cannot have all possible power if His creation *really* is to exist. . . .

Maimonides' doctrine of negative attributes makes it unnecessary to define God's omnipotence since one can only speak of God in terms of what He is not and not in terms of what He is. Maimonides also makes a distinction between his relational attributes (goodness, power, etc.) and His essential attributes (infinitude, unity) which further resolves this dilemma. . . .

If God is defined as omnipotent and omniscient in the traditional sense, then man's freedom is limited to a re-enacting of a pattern already in God's mind. This means that man does not genuinely create or decide anything. Creativity and freedom mean the capacity to decide what is really undecided. They imply an open future with real alternative possibilities; the real determination of what is essentially indeterminate.

Judaism affirms that man has a real choice and is responsible for that choice; it affirms that his choice makes a difference for good or for ill to man himself and to the universe in which man lives. . . . In order to vindicate the power and creativity of man, . . . omnipotence cannot mean all possible power other than purely logical ones. There are limits in terms of *what exists*.

. . . There is a genuine difference before and after creation. After creation man and nature have being and power, and all the attributes of God have to be redefined so as to account for the being and power of creation. Once we affirm that not only God but creation also has being, power, and goodness, then one major consequence follows. God is not the sole cause of the continuing process of the world. He is the major cause in sustaining, ordering, and actualizing the world but not the *only* cause, and hence, cannot be *solely responsible* for actuality. Other beings make a genuine difference in this process. This allows for a genuine freedom. It vindicates both man's power and man's responsibility.[22]

Reality

All forms of Judaism see God as the source of reality. In the book of Genesis, he is seen as the active creator of the visible and invisible universe and establisher of the physical laws of motion. Creation takes place by dividing primeval waters in half and creating dry land between them. One set of waters is then held above the dry land by a giant metal barrier to create heaven, and the other set is restricted under the earth, to create the subterranean waters (Genesis 1: 1 -10). Judaism does not embrace the idea of creation from nothing; creation takes place out of primeval waters that already exist and no explanation is given in Tanak about where they came from. Judaism emphasizes God's invisible nature and his limitless qualities, which go beyond what our human sense scan perceive, resulting in a twofold reality: the created, visible world we can experience through our senses, and an invisible world that we cannot experience directly through regular human perception.

The process of creation and the dual nature of reality is more fully elaborated within mystical forms of Judaism. In Kabbalistic thought, God is called *En Sof*, which means "without end or limits." As the ultimate source of all reality, *En Sof* is beyond revealed reality and our ability to perceive through our senses. At the same time, however, *En Sof* is present in the material world and all of the universe though a chain of emanation that links back directly to it and is simply the divine made visible or manifest, yet is not coterminous with it the visible world. Thus, reality as we know it through our five senses is the visible form of the divine, but there exists in addition to this reality an invisible reality, which is the source of the visible reality. The process of creation in this system consists of a continuous chain of emanation leading out from the core of *En Sof*. It consists of ten *sefirot* that constitute the building blocks of four worlds; we live in the fourth world, which contains both invisible and visible reality; there are believed to be three additional worlds that are invisible, but which also are emanations from *En Sof* that exist outside of the core. In mystical Judaism, then, the apparent dual reality is resolved into unity; there is only one reality, which has an invisible aspect as well as a visible one.

In liberal Judaism, Jewish philosophers have embraced the full range of traditional philosophical explanations for the nature of reality: idealism, materialism, and pragmatism. As individuals, they are free to decide what makes the most sense to them and are not bound by tradition to accept the materialistic view of creation as set forth in Tanak. Since Tanak is not considered to be divine revelation but the work of humans writing in ancient cultures that had very different presuppositions about the nature of the world and how things operate than we do today, individuals are free to allow newer evidence, knowledge and theories to influence their final understandings.

Knowledge

Although our ability sets us apart from other animals and is one of the three ways in which we are made in the image of the divine, all forms of Judaism recognize that human knowledge is imperfect in comparison with divine knowledge. All Jews recognize that our knowledge of the physical world is limited by the ability of our senses to function properly and by our brains to interpret sense input by comparing and contrasting it with past sensory experiences stored in our memories and identified in a particular way. At the same time, it is recognized that perfect knowledge exists beyond the realm of imperfect knowledge in the created world, in the eternal, or God.

Jews who profess religious faith, whether Orthodox, Hasidic, or liberal, would agree that our imperfect senses, detecting imperfect reality, nevertheless receive clues that point to the existence of an unlimited reality and perfect knowledge. These clues are evident in the larger harmony of the universe and the workings of its physical elements, which our minds perceive through rational thought. They also are evident in phenomena that stir our souls and hearts to seek the source and light of all creation.

For Torah-True and Hasidic Jews, the Torah also contains direct revelations of the existence of this perfect knowledge and its will for humanity; God has given humanity the Torah to serve as a guide for perfection in this imperfect world. Nevertheless, in order for us to understand Torah, it must be presented in a way that our senses can process and interpret. For the latter groups, the Torah provides all the information humans need to come to know that our knowledge is limited but that we are created, limited, flawed extensions of the eternal, perfect, limitless divine. By ceasing to view ourselves as the center of the universe and trusting in the reality we construct according to our limited knowledge, we will be able to gain true knowledge about the relationship between the created universe and its source, *En Sof* / God. The realization that divine knowledge is not tied to limited human reasoning or logic is driven home particularly in the book of Job.

Liberal Jews also recognize the limits of human knowledge, but they tend to derive this insight from our relative insignificance in relation to the larger universe, the inexplicable larger harmonies within nature and the laws of nature, scientific observations, and the stirrings of the soul. They do not consider Torah to be a revelation of this knowledge to humanity from the divine source; instead, they would argue that where Torah recognizes and expresses the idea of limited human knowledge, it is a result of deductive or inductive human insight based on human experience.

All knowledge blurs the object of knowledge even as it clarifies it, because all human knowledge is blurred, as it is the knowledge of every finite creature that began its existence in time. The essence of life is rooted in the relationship of God to existence, and this is part of the unknown, which can be discerned only by the most hidden love in the heart. It cannot be defined in precise terms, because it will become blurred through limitation, thus obscuring the continuity of existence. It is for this reason that no finite being can comprehend the divine being. This would contradict the divine existence. The ultimate goal of knowledge is to discern the continuity of life, that there be no veil separating it from the source of life and existence, and this can only be in the confession of our not knowing. In other words, it is not in the characterization of our lack of knowledge, but in the very negation of knowledge, in the higher darkness, that the essence of true knowledge is present, without any touch by a finite hand, which would diminish its stature. "Do I not fill heaven and earth? says the Lord."[23]

Our knowledge of God is determined by our knowledge of reality. As our knowledge of reality is enlarged, our knowledge of God is deepened. Today we find it possible for a civilization to express itself spiritually and to feel the sense of destiny without claiming to have experienced theophany, without resorting to a conception of direct cause-and-effect relationship between obedience to God and the fortunes of the individual, and without having to assume that the only way a new world will ever emerge out of the present chaos will be through some supernatural cataclysm.[24]

Origin of Evil

Torah/Tanak does not expressly state how or where evil originated, but links its continuing existence and propagation to the human intellect and, by implication, to human free will. While Genesis 8:21 claims that the human imagination/mind is evil from its youth, which is logical in terms of human free will, no direct statement is made that God created humans this way, or even in what way humans are made in the image of the divine. There are plenty of references to evil behavior in Tanak, so its existence is never doubted, but there is no systematic attempt to define its ultimate source of origin.

Three possible positions about the origin of evil are reflected in the Tanak. The first is that evil results from the exercise of human free will, when a person makes a bad choice. Evil is the necessary punishment for human sin and so is created by humans rather than God, who must uphold divine justice. This view is found, for example, in Leviticus 26:14-17, 20 and Deuteronomy 11:13-17, 28.

A second position is voiced in Lamentations 3:8 and Isaiah 45:7. Evil exists because the material world consists of opposites: good, evil, light, darkness, truth, falsehood. According to this view, God has created evil so that good can be known; without its opposite, we cannot know good since it is only by experiencing its absence or opposite that we can firmly understand the meaning of a thing. Evil is a necessary part of creation, but not a characteristic of the divine itself, which lies beyond the limited, finite world of duality.

The final possible position on the origin of evil is reflected in Exodus 4:24, which can be understood to state that the divine itself must include within its very essence good and evil, and other opposites; that duality is not limited to the physical created world but is part of the very nature of the divine.[25]

Orthodox Judaism teaches that humans are born with an inclination or impulse for good as well as one for evil and that it is the duty of all humans to acquire the knowledge to develop the first and to harness the second. This is best done through the study of Torah. The impulse toward good is one of recognizing truth and spirituality, whereas the impulse toward evil is not bad in itself, but rather, an orientation toward the physical, which can have positive overall effects in life. Without it, for example, there would be no passion, no marriage, no ambition, and no civilization.

The concept of Satan as a fallen angel who is the source of evil in rebellion against God is not specifically Jewish. In the Tanak, there is no Satan *per se*; there is the *satan*, or "the adversary," in the book of Job, who challenges God to test Job's righteousness and faith by piling upon him unearned misery. This "adversary" is not described as a fallen angel, however. It is merely a member of the heavenly court who waits upon God. There are a few references to the existence of such a court scattered throughout Torah: Genesis 1:26; 1 Kings 22:19; Psalm 29: 1; Isaiah 6:6-8, Job 1:6.

All uses of "the satan" in Tanak come from the latest strata of the writings and seem to reflect a new concept that emerges during the Persian period (535-333 BCE), probably under the influence of the empire religion of Zoroastrianism, which argued that there was a cosmic battle underway between the forces of good and the forces of evil. Out of this concept, "the adversary" eventually develops into Satan, or evil personified.

As Judaism encountered philosophy and was challenged to develop a systematic theology that answered specific questions about reality, knowledge, the existence of God, free will and the source of evil, arguments were advanced to account for the origin of evil. Moses Maimonides specifically tackled this issue, arguing that evil is a necessary consequence of corporeal or created matter, which once given reality, has the potential for negation or absence of certain traits, which yields evil. Creation is good in itself, but since the created world consists of opposites in balance, it carries the seeds of evil because of the ability of things to fall out of balance, creating negations.

> ... Evils are evils only in relation to a certain existing thing, and that which is evil in reference to a certain thing, either includes the non-existence of that thing or the non-existence of some of its good conditions. The proposition has therefore been laid down in the most general terms, "All evils are negations." Thus for man death is evil; death is his non-existence. Illness, poverty, and ignorance are evils for man; all these are privations of properties. If you examine all single cases to which this general proposition applies, you will find that there is not one case in which the proposition is wrong except in the opinion of those who do not make any distinction between negative and positive properties, or between two opposites, or do not know the nature of things—who, e.g., do not know that health in general denotes a certain equilibrium, and is a relative term. The absence of the relation is illness in general, and death is the absence of life in the case of any animal. The destruction of other things is likewise nothing but the absence of their form.
>
> After these propositions, it must be admitted as a fact that it cannot be said of God that He directly creates evil, or He has the direct intention to produce evil; this is impossible. His works are all perfectly good. He only produces existence, and all existence is good; whilst evils are of a negative character, and cannot be acted upon. Evil can only be attributed to Him in the way we have mentioned. He creates evil only in so far as He produces the corporeal element such as it actually is; it is always connected with negatives, and is on that account the source of all destruction and all evil. Those beings that do not possess this corporeal element are not subject to destruction or evil; consequently, the true work of God is all good, since it is existence. The book which enlightened the darkness of the world says therefore, "And God saw everything that He had made, and behold, it was very good" (Gen. i.3 1). Even the existence of this corporeal element, low as it in reality is, because it is the source of death and all evils, is likewise good for the permanence of the Universe and the continuation of the order of things, so that one thing departs and the other succeeds. Rabbi Meir therefore explains the words, "and behold it was very good"; that even death was good in accordance with what we have observed . . . ; all that the prophets and Sages remarked about the perfect goodness of all the direct works of God. In *Bereshit Rabba* (chap. 1.) the same idea is expressed thus: "No evil comes down from above."[26]

For Maimonides, there were three kinds of evils: 1) those caused to man because he is mortal and possesses a body that decays, such as great deformities or paralysis of a specific organ. This is the least frequent kind. 2) The second most numerous are evils people cause each other, which originate in us although the sufferer cannot avert such sin; and 3) the most numerous are those we cause to ourselves by our own actions. All the evils that we cause in class two and three are due to non-existence since they originate in ignorance, which is the absence of wisdom. They arise from certain intentions, desires, opinions, and religious principles, all of which are forms of non-wisdom.[27]

Mystical or Kabbalistic Judaism also offered specific solutions to the origin of evil. Like Maimonides, the work called the *Bahir* denies that God deliberately created evil. It asserts that sin or evil arose during the process of emanation, from an imbalance between the *sephirot* Strength and Beauty where Strength overflowed. Thus, evil is an unintentional consequence of the chain of emanation, due to the nature of reality that balances opposites but which can become imbalanced. It was not directly created by God but instead, was an unintended side-effect produced by one of God's emanated attributes or *sephirot*.

A second proposed source of origin for evil is seen to be matter that remained in the universe from an earlier aborted chain of emanation. This material was not fully reabsorbed into the godhead and so floated around like plaque or barnacles that glommed onto the new chain of emanation as an encrustation that hindered the smooth flow of energy.

Martin Buber, a representative of liberal Judaism, sees evil to arise from inertia; "inertia and indecisiveness are called the root of all evil; sin is basically nothing more than inertia. . . . Sin means not to live in freedom, that is, decision-making, but in bondage, that is, being acted upon, conditioned."[28] In the act of teshuva, or turning to God, where humans let their mental abilities dominate their physical perceptions and they are able to perceive the divine nature of things and view the world from this new perspective, instead of trusting their senses to determine the nature of the world, humans exercise their freedom of will. "The man who 'returns' rises to freedom; he rises from conditionality into unconditionality; he is, as the Zohar calls it, 'alive all around, at one with the tree of life.' "[29]

Ethics

Orthodox Judaism views ethical standards of human life to have been divinely revealed in the Torah. Hence, God is the ultimate source of authority for ethical behavior, and such behavior is specifically demanded of humans as part of their conforming their human wills to the divine will.

A distinction is made between behavior enjoined upon Jews and non-Jews. The former are to keep all 613 revealed *mitzvot* to the best of their abilities, while the latter need only observe the seven laws of Noah. These include 1) not to worship idols, 2) not to commit adultery or incest; 3) not to commit murder, 4) not to steal, 5) not to blaspheme, 6) to practice justice, and 7) not to be cruel to animals. Those who do this are considered members of the righteous and are to enjoy eternal bliss in the World to Come.

Within the Torah-True view, it is not enough simply to act ethically by following the "letter of the law" and doing what is commanded. A person's intentions and frame of mind while carrying out an action determine whether they are fulfilling "the spirit of the law," which is more important. In the case of giving charity, for example, there are eight levels of giving that have been distinguished. The lowest is when one gives charity grudgingly, fulfilling the letter of the law. The seventh is when a person gives less then they should, but does so in a cheerful frame of mind, not grudgingly. Sixth is when one gives to the poor after being asked directly, while fifth is when one gives alms to the poor without being asked. Fourth is indirect giving, when the recipient knows the donor but the donor does not know the recipient. Third is indirect giving when the recipient does not know the identity of the donor but the donor knows the identity of the recipient. The second highest level of charity is double-blind giving, when neither donor nor recipient knows the identity of the other. Finally, the highest form of charity is when a person helps another before impoverishment sets in by offering a substantial gift in a dignified way or extending a loan or helping the other to find employment to forestall financial ruin and dependency.[30]

In contrast to classical Greek philosophy, whose four cardinal virtues were courage, justice, wisdom, and temperance, Jewish tradition encouraged the cultivation of generosity, compassion, sympathy, and mercy as exemplary human traits that imitated divine qualities.[31] These virtues were to be exercised in interactions between humans and other humans, Jewish and non-Jewish, between humans and animals, and between humans and God.

For Rabbi Isaac Kook, ethics are part of the fabric of the universe, the natural order, which our souls respond to through our hearts and recognize as yet another example of the created world that links back to *En Sof.*

Morality, the impulse for equity and good, represents the central direction of the will of existence. This center, in the particularization of life, must conform to all the surrounding reality, to all existence, in its inner essence as well as its outer expression. Through the inner perception deep in the heart of what is equitable and good one recognizes the action of the moral law that pervades all existence, in the form of a vital, vibrant idealism. In the Torah this moral conformity in all its manifestations is represented in the light of holiness, adapted to each community according to its stature, and to the Jewish people in its most authentic form.[32]

For liberal Jews who do not consider Tanak to be divine revelation, norms of ethical behavior are still central to one's identity as a Jew. Instead of appealing to God as an ultimate source and authority, however, liberal Jews base ethical norms and sanctions on principles deemed to be normative of all human relationships, and on past Jewish tradition. In the first case, for example, all humans are to be treated as ends in themselves, not means to be used to accomplish one's own objectives. In the latter case, the appeal to the past prevents the ethics from becoming dogmatic without any rationale or basis, and at the same time, can show that ethical norms are in line with the "tendencies inherent in the very nature of man, and in keeping with that character of the world which expresses itself as the power that makes for righteousness."[33]

The Jewish philosopher Achad Ha'am (1856-1927) considered the core of Judaism to be its ethical monotheism and Israel's specific "mission" as the chosen people was to spread the ethical doctrines throughout the world and humanity. Focusing on the prophetic literature, he argued, "The essential thought of Hebrew prophecy was the reign of absolute justice in all creation; above—through the 'Righteous One of the Universe,' who holds in his hand the category of Justice and judges all his creatures with righteousness; below—through man, who was created in the image of God and who is obligated to imitate his Creator and to help him, as it were, in the conduct of the world in the ways of righteousness. . . . Righteousness is beauty, is good, is wisdom and truth and without it—all is vanity."[34] For Ha'am, Jewish ethics are based on justice, not love, although the latter is to supplement the former. Justice is an objective concept that can be concretized in universal laws, while love is subjective and so cannot serve as the basis of any lasting society. The goal of Torah is the salvation and perfection of the totality—not just the individual, but also the nation, and all of humanity.[35]

Selected Bibliography

General Guides to Judaism:

Donin, Rabbi Hayim Halevy. *To Be A Jew: A Guide to Jewish Observance in Contemporary Life.* New York: Basic Books, 1972.

Jacobs, Louis. *The Book of Jewish Belief.* West Orange, NJ: Behrman House, 1972.

Solomon, Norman. *Judaism: A Very Short Introduction.* Oxford: Oxford University Press, 1996.

One-Volume Encyclopedias:

Bridger, David, ed. *The New Jewish Encyclopedia.* New York: Behrman House, 1962.

Wigoder, Geoffrey, ed. *The New Standard Jewish Encyclopedia.* New York: Facts on File, 1992.

The History of Judaism in America:

Raphael, Marc Lee. *Profiles in American Judaism: The Reform, Conservative, Orthodox, and Reconstructionist Traditions in Historical Perspective.* San Francisco: Harper & Row, 1984.

Rosenthal, Gilbert S. *Contemporary Judaism: Patterns of Survival.* 2nd edition. New York: Human Sciences Press, 1985.

Anthologies of Jewish Thought:

Cohen, Arthur A. and Mendes-Flohr, Paul, eds. *Contemporary Jewish Religious Thought: Original Essays on Critical Concepts, Movements, and Beliefs.* New York: The Free Press, 1987.

Glatzer, Nahum N., ed. *Modern Jewish Thought: A Source Reader.* New York: Schocken Books, 1977.

Endnotes

[1]Horace M. Kallen, "A Jewish View of Life," in *Modern Jewish Thought: A Source Reader* (ed. N.N. Glatzer; New York: Schocken Books, 1989) 158-61, esp. 159.

[2]*Ibid.*, 161.

[3]The Jewish Bible is referred to within the faith as TANAK, which is an acronym summarizing the three main grouping of books under Torah (Teaching) (first five books of Moses: Genesis, Exodus, Leviticus, Numbers, and Deuteronomy) Nevi'im (Prophets) and Ketuvim (Writings). Sometimes the term "Torah" is used to describe the entire collection covered by Tanak, as an extension of the most sacred core, the first five books, to cover the entire set of writings.

[4]Erich Bischoff, *The Kabbala: An Introduction to Jewish Mysticism and its Secret Doctrine* (York Beach, ME: Samuel Weiser, 1993) 39-49.

[5]H. Schulweis, "Reconstructionism," in *Contemporary Jewish Thought*, 755-59, esp. 757.

[6]Mordecai M. Kaplan, *Judaism as a Civilization* (New York: Schocken Books, 1967) 400.

[7]*Ibid.*, 377.

[8]*Ibid.*, 373.

[9]*Ibid.*

[10]Moses Maimonides, *The Guide for the Perplexed* (trans. from Arabic by M. Friedlander; New York: Dover Publications, 1956) 274.

[11]Martin Buber, *On Judaism* (ed. Nahum N. Glatzer; New York: Schocken Books, 1967) 106.

[12]*Ibid.*, 109-110.

[13]Abraham Isaac Kook, *The Lights of Penitence, the Moral Principles, Lights of Holiness, Essays, Letters, and Poems* (trans. from Hebrew by Ben Zion Bokser; The Classics of Western Spirituality; New York: Paulist Press, 1978) 6.

[14]*Ibid.*, 48.

[15]Kaplan, *Judaism as Civilization*, 403.

[16]*Ibid.*

[17]*Ibid.*

[18]Menahem Mendel Schneerson, *Toward a Meaningful Life: The Wisdom of the Rebbe* (adapted by S. Jacobson; New York: William Morrow and Company, 1995) 238.

[19]*Ibid.*, 240.

[20]*Ibid.*, 238-39.

[21]*Ibid.*, 240.

[22]Rabbi Jack Bemporad, "Toward a New Jewish Theology," in *The American Jewish Reader: essay, fiction and poetry from the pages of American Judaism* (ed. Paul Kresh; New York: Abelard-Schuman, 1967) 38-43.

[23]Kook, *Lights of Penitence*, 162-63.

[24]Kaplan, *Judaism as a Civilization*, 405.

[25]These three options have been outlined by B.L. Sherwin ("Theodicy," in *Contemporary Jewish Religious Thought: Original Essays on Critical Concepts, Movements, and Beliefs* [ed. A.A. Cohen and P. Mendes-Flohr; New York: Macmillan, 1987] 959-79).

[26]*The Guide for the Perplexed*, 266-267.

[27]*Ibid.*, 267-70.

[28]Buber, 82.

[29]*Ibid.*

[30]Hayim Halevy Donin, *To Be A Jew: A Guide to Jewish Observance in Contemporary Life* (New York: Basic Books, 1972) 50.

[31]Jacobs B. Agus, *The Vision and the Way* (New York: Frederick Ungar, 1966) 10.

[32]Kook, *Lights of Penitence*, 86.

[33]Kaplan, *Judaism as a Civilization*, 463.

[34]Jacob B. Agus, *Modern Philosophies of Judaism: A Study of Recent Jewish Philosophies of Religion* (New York: Behrman's Jewish Book House, 1941) 46, translating from "Al Porashat D'rochim," I, p. 182.

[35]*Ibid*, 47.

CHRISTIANITY

by Iain S. Maclean

1. Introduction

Christianity is one of the two religions that stem from Judaism (the other, also from Christianity, being Islam) and together with Judaism and Islam, recognizes one God, the God of Abraham, and the Jewish Scriptures (Tanakh, Hebrew Bible, or Old Testament). Christianity differs from both however in claiming that Jesus was the Messiah, or in Greek, the Christ. Further, it claims that Jesus is the incarnation of God, sent to humanity to make atonement for sin, to overcome evil and to usher in the beginnings of the final or messianic age, all in accordance with Jewish Scripture.

Christianity like Judaism, practices prayer, the study of Scripture, fasting, almsgiving or tithing, and care for the poor and disadvantaged. While these can be performed at any time, specific days are set aside for communal worship, in particular Sunday, the 8th day of first day of the (originally) Jewish week. Sunday is the perpetual feast day commemorating the resurrection of Jesus the Christ from the dead on the first day of the week. There are two specific rituals that are performed, replacing the Jewish rituals of circumcision and the Passover, namely baptism and the Eucharist (Lord's Supper, the Breaking of Bread, Mass, or Communion), called dominical (of the Lord) because they are specifically commanded by Jesus Christ. The early Church developed, largely within a pastoral context, further rituals, finally standardized in the Middle Ages (together with the two dominical institutions) as the Seven Sacraments, now including penance, extreme unction, confirmation, ordination and marriage. The great Christian festival is that of Easter, celebrating the resurrection of Jesus from the dead, occurring roughly at the same time as the Jewish Passover (differences in timing occur as the former is dated on a solar calendar, the latter on a lunar one). Two lesser festivals are the feat of Pentecost, (occurring seven weeks after Easter and ten days after the Ascension) and Christmas (replacing an earlier Roman celebration of the Sun). The Eastern Churches celebrate the birth of Christ somewhat later on the feast of the Epiphany or Manifestation of Christ to the Gentiles on January 6th.

2. Brief Historical Overview

Emerging then in the first century A.D. within the Greco-Roman world as an offshoot of Judaism, Christianity initially grew slowly under the pressures of persecution, first from Jews and then from the Roman Empire. However by the time it was decreed the official religion of the empire in 381 A.D. by Theodosius I, its adherents were to be found in and beyond the imperial frontiers. It spread throughout the Middle East, East towards India, and through Southern Europe and North Africa, reaching as far as Ethiopia in the South East. While its growth in the Middle East and in North Africa was checked by the rise of Islam in the seventh century, it continued to spread into Western and Northern Europe and with the European discovery of the Americas in 1492, was also brought there. Nineteenth century European and then American missionary movements, both Roman Catholic and Protestant, brought Christianity to other regions of Africa as well as to South, South East, and East Asia. During the twentieth century Christianity has experienced decline in its traditional strongholds in Europe, though it continues to grow rapidly elsewhere with most Christians concentrated in areas outside of Europe and North America, with Africa now surpassing Europe as the continent with the greatest number of Christians.

While the details are controverted, it seems that the earliest Churches were organized around local overseers or bishops, organized into regional areas called dioceses and local congregations were led by priests assisted by deacons. The bishops were regarded as final authorities within their dioceses, with final authority resting in ecumenical councils comprised of all bishops. Gradually in the West the bishop of Rome came to hold the position of "first among equals," as the pope, a development never accepted by the Eastern Churches. Differences, particularly over the precise understanding of how the union of the divine and the human in the one man, Jesus Christ, led to divisions. The Eastern Orthodox Churches, largely organized on ethnic or national or cultural lines, were to be distinguished from those churches that either did not recognize these Christological formulations or had failed to be present at the ecumenical Councils where they were defined. These included the Coptic (largely Egyptian), Ethiopian, Mar Thomas (North Indian), Syrian and Armenian Orthodox Churches. The Eastern Churches, both Orthodox and others, all rejected the Bishop of Rome's claim to be the supreme bishop or patriarch of the whole universal Church. Rather they recognized as final authorities either a regional archbishop or Patriarch, such as the bishop of Constantinople, Antioch, Cilicia, Van, Alexandria, or, a council comprising all the bishops of the Church (such a council has not been held since the Seventh Ecumenical Council, 781 A.D.)

In the eleventh century major schism in the Church occurred when, due to numerous political and theological differences, sharply exacerbated by the crusades, the Patriarch of Constantinople, the ecumenical leader of Eastern Christendom, and the Bishop of Rome, the Pope, mutually excommunicated each other (excommunications lifted only after Vatican Council II, 1963-1965). This division between East and West was reinforced when Constantinople fell to Muslim Turkish armies in 1453, further isolating the Eastern from the Western Church.

Then in the period 1517-1521 A.D. in the West, the actions of the German Augustinian monk, Martin Luther, led to further division as most of the far Western and Northern lands separated from the Roman Church, resulting in the formation of national churches such as the Lutheran (German states, Northern Europe), the Anglican (England), the reformed or Presbyterian (in France, Switzerland and Scotland), and more radical separatist communities such as the Mennonites and Anabaptists. In the following centuries, as members of these Churches emigrated to the United States after the American Revolution and as in many (ex-colonial) states the Episcopal (Virginia), Roman Catholic (Maryland) or Puritan (Congregational/Presbyterian, Dutch Reformed) churches were now dis-established, there arose the completely state-independent and peculiarly American phenomenon of denominationalism. As noted above, during the nineteenth century great missionary activity by both Protestants and Roman Catholics spread Christianity into non-Western regions with such effect that Africa is now the continent with the largest number of Christians and Christianity itself is the largest world religion, there being more Roman Catholic Christians alone than any other religion (100 millions), with Orthodox Christians next with about 330 millions and then 260 million Protestants.

3. Main Events in Life of Founder

In terms of the wealth of information offered by modern biographies, far less is presented in the Gospels about the life and self-awareness of Jesus. In addition the material is presented in the New Testament in four Gospels, each with differing target audiences, a fact that leads to rather differing portraits. This knowledge, ever since the question of the sources and origins of the synoptic problem (why more than one Gospel and how are Matthew, Mark and Luke related to each other?) became an issue, has forced the recognition that the Gospels are not so much biographies as statements of faith, designed to bring others to faith (John 20:31).[1]

This issue has led to three distinct phases in the "search for the historical Jesus," begun in 1906 (ET, 1910) with Albert Schweitzer's, epochal study *The Search of the Historical Jesus* and continued in the nineties of this past century with the radical conclusions of the "Jesus Seminar" led by Robert Funk and others.[2] Despite the more radical results of the last-mentioned group, largely based on debatable dating techniques and assumptions, certain valuable lessons has been gained. For prior to Schweitzer's work, the "search for the historical Jesus" had been an attempt to separate out what was unique in the teaching of Jesus. Thus anything that sounded like it was rabbinical or could be paralleled in the rabbi's was regarded as "secondary" or as a "borrowing." The problem with this method was its arbitrariness. Surely Jesus used the idiom, the ideas and the topics of his time? Just because these were common "stock-in-trade" terms or expressions does not mean they are not original to Jesus. Schweitzer's work in the Jewish background revealed that apocalyptic language about the "end" and the coming "kingdom of God" were not part of some assumed "primitive" worldview, but were views actually held by Jesus. A corollary of this was the rediscovery that the NT does in fact present Jesus largely in terms of Jewish expectation. This had been obscured by later, dogmatic interpretations which had so stressed the divinity and "otherness" of Jesus as the Christ, that his humanity and with that, his Jewishness, had been obscured. Thus such historical research shifted the focus from the "Christ of dogma" to the "Jesus of History."

This has resulted in most significant results for contemporary Christianity. The most critical affirmation of such research has been the assertion that (obvious as it might sound now), that Jesus was Jewish and needs to be understood within the context of Second Temple Judaism, rather than from the perspective of much later credal formulations. From such historical study it becomes clear that the period in which Jesus lived was one of chaos, on both the social, political and religious levels. There were also competing Jewish parties, teachings and movements. Much of this social and political detail is brought out in the works of scholars such as Richard Horsley and John Dominic Crossan, while the religious practical implications are brought out in Albert Nolan's concise work.[3]

Briefly stated, after the Jewish revolt led by Judas Maccabeus against the Hellenistic ruler Antiochus Epiphanes, was successfully concluded in 164 B.C., his successors ruled until they were overtaken by Herod the Great. In 63 B.C. the Romans took over the region, but ruled indirectly through the Herods. The indigenous Jewish population was sharply stratified in what was in effect a colonial situation, with indirect rule, harsh taxation, and military occupation. Society was also sharply divided especially between the Galilee and Jerusalem areas. Jewish response to such occupation was diverse, ranging from accommodation (Herodians and Sadducees), through passive pietism (Pharisees), to radical options including withdrawal from society (Essenes) and armed revolt (Zealots).

In this historical context, Jesus thought of his own life and ministry in terms of that of a Jewish prophet, calling an erring Israel back to God and his law. Modern historical research such as noted above, by taking the context of Jesus' ministry into account, means that the effects of later western—and false—dichotomies such as individual versus social, material versus spiritual, or political versus religious, need to be taken into account when interpreting the message of Jesus. Jesus by taking upon himself the mantle of the end-time or eschatological prophet who was to appear at the end of the age, addressed the Judaism of his time in all its dimensions (as the Law itself did). Thus the central burden of his message was that of the coming Kingdom of God (or in more contemporary idiom, the "rule of God") in which a New Israel would be restored out of the old. Such a rule involved all dimensions of life, the personal, social, economic and political. Such a rule was to be accomplished through accepting the message of repentance and believing in the Gospel (Mark 1:1-2).

This basic message and mission centered then around the concept of the rule of God, a theme that runs through both major periods of Jesus' ministry in the Synoptic Gospels. The first period, called the Galilean ministry, is presented in the Gospels as occupying the bulk of his ministry, three years in and around the area of Lake Galilee. The teaching is marked by the frequent use of parables whose concern is with the coming, indeed present, Kingdom of God. The second period, that marked by Jesus' entry into Jerusalem (remembered on Palm Sunday), comprises but one week from that entry through to the events of the Last Supper, the betrayal, the arrest, trial and crucifixion. That this chronologically brief time is significant should be recognized from the fact that the narration of this last week of Jesus' life, together with the accounts of his resurrection, comprise fully one third of the Gospel materials and was probably the earliest section of the Gospel to be written down. This conclusion receives support from the earliest New Testament documents, some of the letters of Paul (I Thessalonians and I Corinthians), which describe the earliest Christian message (or "kergyma") as one of belief in the one who died and rose again.

4. Sacred Scriptures

The account of the formation of the Canon (from the Greek word for "measuring rod") of the Sacred Scriptures is too complex to go into here, suffice it to say that it must be recognized that the Scriptures themselves cannot be simply understood as "bare words" but rather as interpretations of the meaning of the person Jesus Christ for the earliest Christian communities.

The earliest Christians were Jews and accepted the Jewish Scriptures in their Greek translation, known as the Septuagint ("version of the Seventy"), to which twenty-seven additional books were added to form the Christian Canon. While the reasons for this are not clear, it is suggested that in the case of the gospels, that as the apostles died they committed their memories of Jesus to written form and thus created a new literary genre, the gospel. Other suggestions are that they were written as apologies, to defend the new religion against charges of opponents, to show the Roman authorities that Christianity was a law-abiding religion, and to reject false ideas concerning Jesus. These were common, including he was a magician (see Acts 8:7-19), or a new teacher of philosophy (see Acts 17:16-20). Probably the gospels all shared the intent clearly expressed at the end of the Gospel of John, that they were written to call readers/ hearers to faith (John 20:31). The basic structure of the first three (or synoptic) gospels follow that of Mark. There is an introduction, followed by a description of Jesus' ministry in Galilee (3:7-6:6), then of his journey to Jerusalem (6:7-8:21), of his teaching of his disciples (8:22-10:51, including the confession of Peter) and finally the section called the "Passion Narrative." (11:1-16:8). This last section comprises at least one third of the content of the gospels and scholars consider it the earliest section to have been committed to writing.

The earliest written New Testament book is in fact not a Gospel, but a letter of Paul, that of the first letter to the Thessalonians, followed by others in the early sixties. The Gospel of Mark became the first Gospel to be written, and provided the written outline for two later gospels, Matthew and Luke, which in addition, had a "sayings source" nicknamed "Q" as well as their own specific materials (called "M" and "L" respectively). The last Gospel to be written was that of St. John, dated anywhere from before 70 A.D. to after the turn of the century. While different regions had slightly differing collections of documents (apart from the Old Testament in Greek, the Septuagint), by the time of the early Councils, the basic Canon List of the 27 New Testament books had been recognized by the church on the fourfold grounds of their authorship (by an apostle), agreement with previous revelation, use by the churches, and their spiritual usefulness.

5. Beliefs about Knowledge, Self, and the World

Christianity in accepting the Jewish Scriptures, accepted also the Genesis account (Genesis 1-3) of the creation of the world. While there have been differences in interpreting these chapters (the early Church Fathers of Alexandria, well-versed in Greek natural science, held the accounts to be mythic or, utilizing the doctrine of accommodation, taught that the events were so described in order that Moses and the Israelites might understand) the fullest and earliest interpretation was provided by St. Augustine (354-430 A.D.). It was Augustine in fact who provided the basic theological structures that have moulded western theology and culture to this day. He developed a theology or systematic interpretation of creation. His theology stressed the initiative of God, the creation *ex nihilo* ("out of nothing"), the fact of the initial goodness of matter, and the freedom of human will.

Augustine, by training a Roman philosophy teacher, had before his conversion been deeply attracted to the teachings of the Persian sage Mani (whose teachings are known as Manicheanism) who had taught that the world was eternal and that there exist only two eternal elements, matter and spirit, the one evil, the other good. Augustine, who confessed to much struggle against the attractiveness of this dualism long after his conversion, rejected such teaching in the light of Christian revelation. He argued, against much Eastern and Greek thought, that the world was not eternal. To hold this position, he declared, would make the world or matter divine and thus make it God or a second god. So he argued that the doctrine of creation *ex nihilo* not only emphasized the createdness of matter, but the distinction between it and God. Further, according to Scripture, and against Manichaeanism, Augustine stressed that when God created the world, the Scriptures state that God repeatedly declared of the world that "it was good." Certainly Augustine recognized the fact of sin, both in this "good" world and in humanity. He was the first theologian to fully develop the doctrine of original sin along biological lines, that is, to argue that by the act of procreation, the fault of Adam and Eve is linearly transmitted to future generations. Stated in another way, it could be argued that this was his way of declaring the universality of sin. However this sin, this imperfection in a world originally created good, was not—as the Manicheans claimed—to be attributed to the world or to matter or to the body. Rather it lay in a human will that congenitally refused to obey the divine will to love God and others. The human will, instead of being directed to obeying and loving God's commandments, was "incurvatus in se" or curved in upon itself in self-love.

For Augustine all rested upon a correct estimation of the human self. Here he utilized the expression from Genesis that Adam ("humanity" in the Hebrew) was created from the earth in the "image and likeness of God" (Genesis 1:26-27). This phrase had radical political implications for its time and of course later in the progress of Western history. In the ancient Middle East, only the king or royalty were regarded as divine or as offspring of the gods. To claim then, as the Scriptures did, that every human was "in the image of God" was thus a challenge to absolutist power and to allegedly absolute distinctions between peoples. Of course, this phrase did not mean that humanity is created after a physical likeness, for to so claim is to raise problematic questions about God's omniscience, omnipotence and omnipresence. What then does this phrase "the image of God," or in technical theological Latin "Imago Dei," mean?

Christianity understood the Imago Dei as expressing the essence of human nature. However, this does not encompass the totality of humanity, but only the soul, or more specifically the mind ("nous" in Greek), its highest part, and the site of intelligence, knowledge, freedom, the will, and virtue. While this image tended to be understood as both a natural endowment and as a supernatural gift, it was damaged, but not lost through sin, or to be specific, it was held that the supernatural gift was lost, but not the natural one. Thus common interpretations of this phrase have included the following: that it refers to the human soul; to the human ability to reason, or to the ability to relate to others, and to God.

The dominant understanding in the west was the last-mentioned, most fully developed by Augustine, who argued that the doctrine of God as Trinity is by analogy seen in the Imago Dei in humanity. He described three sets of analogies, the first two (the mind, knowledge, and love and memory, intelligence, and will) describing the relation of the soul to itself, while the third analogy (memory of God, intelligence and love) describe the relation between the soul and God. Love was the bond which united not only individual psychology, but also the soul to God. In so doing, by analogy, the Imago Dei points to the eternal relations of love that bind the persons of the Trinity.[4] This stress on love-as-relation as integral to understanding the nature of humanity continued through western history, and was notably developed by the 20th century Protestant theologian Karl Barth (described by Pope Pius XII the greatest theologian since Thomas Aquinas) who even described the marriage bond as a reflection of that relational love that bound the persons of the Trinity.

How then was the Imago Dei affected by the Fall? Was it purely at the moral or ethical level, or was human reason also affected? Clearly it was at the ethical and relational levels, as these can be immediately perceived and evaluated. The question remained if the effects of sin are understood as touching even reason itself. This was later to become a point of division between Roman Catholics and Protestants, as the former held that natural reason could still attain some knowledge of God, while the latter held that rationality, as well as morality, had fallen. The doctrine of total depravity states then that all dimensions of human existence are affected by the fall. This doctrine is often misunderstood as teaching that there is no good in non-Christians. This is incorrect, rather the doctrine refers to the inability of humanity, without God's aid, to employ their reason, emotions, or will, to effect their own salvation.

6. Christian Understandings of Ethics

Christianity, though in many respects the most confessional or doctrinally-oriented of all world religions, is primarily to be understood as a way of life and in fact the first followers of Jesus were simply called "the way" until they received the Roman nickname of "Christians" (Acts 11:26). The diversity of cultures in which Christianity took root led to much greater diversity in liturgy, ethos, and in the relation to culture and ethics than would be apparent from its doctrinal uniformity. Despite the diversity of Christian communions and Churches, there are certain central themes of both personal and social ethics that unite this diversity. These fall into three basic paradigms, namely that of the imitation of Christ, and flowing from that, the primacy of love, or of the law, as ethical norms.

From its inception, Christianity has to greater or lesser extent, understood the human life of Jesus Christ as an example to be followed. This approach is founded on passages in Scripture such as Matthew 11:29 ("Take my yoke upon you, and learn from me; for I am gentle and humble-hearted and my yoke is light and you shall find rest for your souls.") and Matthew 16:24 ("Then Jesus said to his disciples, 'if anyone desires to come after me, let him deny himself, and take up his cross and follow me.'"). However, what precisely this imitation comprised has never been fully determined, but rather is expressed in the lives of those who have struck their contemporaries as exemplifying some aspect of the life of Christ. Thus early (and in fact all later) monastic traditions see themselves as following the example of Christ as summed up in the monastic vows of poverty, chastity and obedience. Later, and most famous, examples would include St. Francis of Assisi, St. Clare and the late Mother Teresa of Calcutta. This tradition is perhaps best summed up in the second most circulated book apart from the Bible itself, the *Imitation of Christ* by St. Thomas à Kempis (1380-1471). This tradition is by no means restricted to the Roman Catholic, Anglican or Orthodox monastic traditions, but continues to be expressed in the more radical and pacifist Protestant traditions and reappears in the nineteenth century in America not only in communal and millennialist movements, but in works such as the (still in print) *In His Steps* by the Methodist minister Charles Sheldon, and has re-appeared in the recent phenomenon of the "WWJD" (for "What would Jesus do?") movement among younger evangelical Christians. A modern theologian often taken as exemplifying this "imitation" approach to the ethical life, is the German Lutheran martyr, Dietrich Bonhoeffer (1906-1945).

A problem with this approach is that of the extent to which the imitation is to be followed. Of course certain events in the life and ministry, such as the Baptism of Jesus (as identification with the sins of the world) and the Crucifixion and Resurrection are inimitable. Yet, even St. Francis at the end of his life revealed the stigmata or marks of the crucifixion on this hands, feet and side. Does the imitation go this far? What of the "hard sayings" of Jesus concerning those with wealth, of obeying every "jot and title" of the (Jewish) law, or of "making oneself an eunuch" for the sake of the Kingdom? Were these sayings meant to be taken literally? If not, and they were only meant to be taken allegorically, then why stop at these examples?

Another approach, which was to become a dominant one in the twentieth century, was that which sought the core and indeed, the essence of Christian living and relationship to others, in the "greatest commandment," that of love (John 13:33). Whether expressed in Jesus' summary of the law as "You shall love the Lord your God with all your heart, with all your soul, with all your strength, and with all your mind, and your neighbor as yourself" (Luke 10:27) or in the great passages on love in John's Gospel (John 13:14-16), the Johannine epistles, and in I Corinthians 13, love has become a central focus of much modern ethical theory, as it seems to avoid the complexities of interpreting the law in radically different (and non-theocratic) contexts as well as appealing directly to autonomous individuals. At its best, this approach comes close to the sacrificial loving others almost at the expense of one's self (an emphasis sharply critiqued by feminists in the Seventies) in the imitation of Christ, while at its least useful it tends to an antinomian ("no-law") extreme where no ethical norms seem possible.

The greatest modern exponent of love as the central focus of Christian ethics was the Lutheran Anders Nygren, following on a long Lutheran tradition rooted in earlier Augustinian themes. Here the influence of the classical Greek and later Roman tradition of the virtues merged with Christian convictions about the ethical life. In adapting the philosophical tradition of virtues to Christianity, St. Augustine added to the traditional (or as later Christians described them, the "cardinal") four virtues of courage, prudence, temperance, and fortitude, the three "theological virtues" of faith, hope and love (from St. Paul, I Corinthians 13:13). The cardinal virtues were attainable by all persons on the natural human level, by virtue of their being created in the image of God, while only God could grant, on the supernatural level, through grace, the last three. These seven virtues comprised the focus of Christian living right through the history of the western world until the Renaissance (1400-1600) and Enlightenment (circa 1800) periods.

The role of the law brings us back to the imitation of Christ approach. This approach in addition implies that the individual Christian should strive not only to follow the example of Christ, but like Him, strive to keep the Mosaic Law. This approach to the ethical life drew on the example of Jesus in claiming not to have abrogated the Mosaic law, but indeed even heightened or sharpened its demands in his Sermon on the Mount (Matthew 5-7). A problem with this approach is that it faces the ambiguity of the New Testament itself over the place of the Law in the Christian life. Thus while Jesus himself in the Sermon on the Mount claims not only to be the fulfillment of the Law but warns against those who "suppose that I have come to abolish the law and the prophets" (Matthew 5:17), Paul elsewhere claimed that Jesus is "the end of the Law" (Romans 10:4). This ambiguity continues throughout Christian history, with Christians claiming both adherence to the Decalogue, as well as to the claim that true Christian freedom is found in the power of the Holy Spirit working in individuals' lives. Thus for instance St. Augustine called for adherence to the Ten Commandments and stated: "Love God and do what you like." Of course, such ambiguity can be traced back not only to Christ, to Paul and to the New Testament writings, but also to later diverging Christian interpretations of the role of the Jewish, or Mosaic, law in Christian life. Thus in the Protestant tradition, Martin Luther (1483-1546) argued that the Mosaic law has but two purposes for the church: first it reveals God's standards by which individual failure or sin is sharply revealed, second, it serves as a compendium of laws for the state or civil authorities. The Christian by contrast, lives by the law of the Spirit that is the domain of the Christian Church. This is what has been called Luther's "Zweireichlehre" or theory of the two kingdoms. According to this theory, the Christian is simultaneously a member of the kingdom of the Church (ruled by the Spirit and grace) and of the kingdom of the state (and is simultaneously there ruled by law). The reformed tradition, stemming from the teaching of John Calvin and Ulrich Zwingli, argues that there is a "third use of the law," namely its use as a guide for Christian living and makes no separation between Church and world.

The implications of these differing understandings of the law for the Christian are quite momentous in their practical outworking. The Lutheran teaching of the two kingdoms has led to latter generations positing a sharp separation between the "spiritual" and the "physical" or the social and political realms of life. This separation tends to leave the Church with no right to critique the social order or the "earthly kingdom" as this is understood as an independent sphere. The reformed position on the role of the law enables the Church or individual Christian to critique the social and political orders as they, like the Church, are both subject to the one law of the one God. The Lutheran tradition was sharpened in the later Pietist movements, and their institutional expressions in the Moravians, and then in the Methodist, Baptist and other Pietist, and later in America, in the twentieth century Fundamentalist and Evangelical Churches. The Calvinist or Reformed tradition with its acceptance of the Mosaic law as a guide for Christian life, did not separate life into different spheres, but regarded all areas of life—the personal, familial, social and political—as under the law of God. Such churches tended towards a theocratic vision of life and produced in turn Cromwell in England, and theocracies in Geneva, Scotland, and in the New England colonies. While the theocratic concept has been abandoned today (except for extremely radical Calvinist groups) its influence remains in mainline Protestant Churches' leveling critiques against current political and social arrangements and assumptions.

The practice of the virtues and the application of the Mosaic and the Law of Christ were understood, for most of western history, as applying both to individuals as well as to the social and political realms. This was how both the Western and in fact the Eastern Churches understood the second petition of the Lord's Prayer, that "Thy kingdom come, thy will be done, on earth as it is in heaven" (Matthew 6: 10). The political powers were thereby responsible for the application of and enforcement of divine law. This understanding or rather cooperation of the state with the church (though the institutions were distinguished) lasted in the form of "Christendom" until the time of the Reformations of the 16th century. While this approach was maintained by Roman Catholics, and especially Calvinism and the Puritans, into the pre-modern and modern period the continuing emergence of several national Protestant Churches led to a gradual relativization of this approach. Finally, in the Constitution of the United States in the late 18th century, the individual states were granted the right to either sustain a state Church or to disestablish the existing one. This process of separation of Church and state, or secularization has led to crisis in the twentieth century as many societies pay little attention to Church institutions. Among Protestants the attempts to address a rapidly changing and culturally pluralist social order led to numerous forms of accommodation of traditional categories to new realities, the most influential being the "Social Gospel" propounded by the Baptist Professor Walter Rauschenbusch (1861-1918) in Rochester, New York as an attempt to address the needs of newly urbanized industrial workers. This approach, with modifications to address its overly optimistic stance, was continued in the "Christian Realism" of the Congregationalist Reinhold Niebuhr (1892-1971) who balanced this optimism with an Augustinian emphasis on human finitude or sin. A recent phenomenon has been the politicization of the American Fundamentalist and Evangelical Churches, initiated the Reverend Jerry Falwell of Liberty Baptist Church in Lynchburg, Virginia.

The Roman Catholic Church was to develop a powerful set of principles in the late nineteenth century by which to address the modern world. In so doing it became a leader in the development of social and political principles for the emerging new nation states in Europe and Latin America. These principles were first enunciated in the justly famous encyclical letter of Pope Leo XIII (1810-1903) entitled *Rerurm Novarum* (encyclicals are named after their first Latin words) or "New Things" (1891) which laid out the Catholic response to modernity. Modernity, with its great social and political issues such as industrialization, a living wage for workers, and the threat to the Church of atheism, capitalism, and socialism, led the Church to propose an alternative. The alternative, taking the middle path between the evils of both capitalist individualism and socialist communism, lay in establishing Catholic parties and workers unions on Catholic ethical principles, to represent Catholic interests in the political and social spheres. Such an approach, later developed as the principle of subsidiarity by Pope Pius XI, had the advantage of rejecting the conflictual assumptions about society inherent in both capitalist and socialist systems. This "third way" approach between capitalism and socialism, ultimately based on the Augustinian conception of love, was to characterize Roman Catholic social ethics through the twentieth century.

ON FREE CHOICE OF THE WILL, BOOK II
By St. Augustine

WHY DID GOD GIVE FREEDOM OF THE WILL TO MEN, SINCE IT IS BY THIS THAT MEN SIN?

EVODIUS. Now, if possible, explain to me why God gave man free choice of the will since if he had not received it he would not be able to sin.

AUGUSTINE. Are you perfectly sure that God gave to man what you think ought not to have been given?

EVODIUS. As far as I seem to understand the discussion in the first book, we have freedom of will, and could not sin if we were without it.

AUGUSTINE. I, too, remember that this was made clear to us. But I just asked you whether you know that it was God who gave us that which we possess, through which it is clear that we commit sin.

EVODIUS. No one else. For we are from Him, and whether we sin or whether we do right, we earn reward or punishment from Him.

AUGUSTINE. I want to ask, as well: do you know this clearly, or do you believe it willingly without really knowing it, because you are prompted by authority?

EVODIUS. I admit that at first I trusted authority on this point. But what can be more true than that all good proceeds from God, that everything just is good, and that it is just to punish sinners and to reward those who do right? From this it follows that through God sinners are afflicted with unhappiness, and those who do right endowed with happiness.

AUGUSTINE. I do not object, but let me ask another question: how do you know that we are from God? You did not answer that; instead, you explained that we merit punishment and reward from God.

EVODIUS. The answer to *that* question, too, is clear, if for no other reason than the fact that, as we have already agreed, God punished sins. All justice is from God, and it is not the role of justice to punish foreigners, although it is the role of goodness to bestow benefits on them. Thus it is clear that we belong to God, since He is not only most generous in bestowing benefits upon us, but also most just in punishing us. Also, we can understand that man is from God through the fact, which I proposed and you conceded, that every good is from God. For man himself, insofar as he is a man, is a good, because he can live rightly when he so wills.

AUGUSTINE. If this is so, the question that you proposed is clearly answered. If man is a good, and cannot act rightly unless he wills to do so, then he must have free will, without which he cannot act rightly. We must not believe that God gave us free will so that we might sin, just because sin is committed through free will. It is sufficient for our question, why free will should have been given to man, to know that without it man cannot live rightly. That it was given for this reason can be understood from the following: if anyone uses free will for sinning, he incurs divine punishment. This would be unjust if free will had been given not only that man might live rightly, but also that he might sin. For how could a man justly incur punishment who used free will to do the thing for which it was given? When God punishes a sinner, does He not seem to say, "Why have you not used free will for the purpose for which I gave it to you, to act rightly?" Then too, if man did not have free choice of will, how could there exist the good according to which it is just to condemn evildoers and reward those who act rightly? What was not done by will would be neither evildoing nor right action. But punishment and reward would be unjust if man did not have free will. Moreover, there must needs be justice both in punishment and in reward, since justice is one of the goods that are from God. Therefore, God must needs have given free will to man.[6]

To Americans, the most familiar version of belief in predestination comes from that school of Protestant Christianity called Calvinism. In the following passage, the famous American Calvinist theologian, Jonathan Edwards (1703-1758), gives a defense of his belief in predestination.

From **"FREEDOM OF THE WILL,"**
By Jonathan Edwards

WHEREIN IT IS CONSIDERED WHETHER THERE IS OR CAN BE ANY SUCH SORT OF FREEDOM OF WILL, AS THAT WHEREIN ARMINIANS[7] PLACE THE ESSENCE OF THE LIBERTY OF ALL MORAL AGENTS; AND WHETHER ANY SUCH THING EVER WAS OR CAN BE CONCEIVED OF. . . .

First, I am to prove, that God has an absolute and certain foreknowledge of the free actions of moral agents.

One would think, it should be wholly needless to enter on such an argument with any that profess themselves Christians: but so it is; God's certain foreknowledge of the free acts of moral agents, is denied by some that pretend to believe the Scriptures to be the word of God; and especially of late. I therefore shall consider the evidence of such a prescience in the Most High, as fully as the designed limits of this essay will admit of; supposing myself herein to have to do with such as own the truth of the Bible.

ARG I. My first argument shall be taken from God's *prediction* of such events. Here I would, in the first place, lay down these two things as axioms.

(1.) If God does not foreknow, he cannot foretell such events; that is, he cannot peremptorily and certainly foretell them. If God has no more than an uncertain guess concerning events of this kind, then he can declare no more than an uncertain guess. Positively to foretell, is to profess to foreknow, or to declare positive foreknowledge.

(2.) If God does not certainly foreknow the future volitions of moral agents, then neither can he certainly foreknow those events which are consequent and dependent on these volitions. The existence of the one depending on the existence of the other; the knowledge of the existence of the one depends on the knowledge of the existence of the other; and the one cannot be more certain than the other.

Therefore, how many, how great and how extensive soever the consequences of the volitions of moral agents may be; though they should extend to an alteration of the slate of things through the universe, and should be continued in a series of successive events to all eternity, and should in the progress of things branch forth into an infinite number of series, each of them going on in an endless line or chain of events; God must be as ignorant of all these consequences, as he is of the volitions whence they take their rise: all these events, and the whole slate of things depending on them, how important, extensive and vast soever, must be hid from him.

SECTION XII.

God's certain Foreknowledge of the future Volitions of moral Agents, inconsistent with such a Contingence of those Volitions as is without all Necessity.

Having proved that God has a certain and infallible prescience of the act of the Will of moral agents, I come now, in the *second* place, to show the consequence; to show how it follows from hence, that these events are *necessary*, with a Necessity of connection or consequence.

The chief Arminian divines, so far as I have opportunity to observe, deny this consequence; and affirm, that if such Foreknowledge be allowed, it is no evidence of any Necessity of the event foreknown. Now I desire, that this matter may be particularly and thoroughly inquired into. I cannot but think that, on particular and full consideration, it may be perfectly determined, whether it be indeed so or not.

In order to a proper consideration of this matter, I would observe the following things.

I.   It is very evident, with regard to a thing whose existence is infallibly and indissolubly connected with something which already hath or has had existence, the existence of that thing is necessary. Here may be noted:

1.   I observed before, in explaining the nature of Necessity, that in things which are past, their existence is now necessary: having already made sure of existence, it is too late for any possibility of alteration in that respect: It is now impossible that it should be otherwise than true, that that thing has existed.

2.   If there be any such thing as a divine Foreknowledge of the volitions of free agents, that Foreknowledge, by the supposition, is a thing which already has, and long ago had, existence; and so, now its existence is necessary; it is now utterly impossible to be otherwise than that this Foreknowledge should be, or should have been.

3.   It is also very manifest, that those things which are indissolubly connected with other things that are necessary, are themselves necessary. As that proposition whose truth is necessarily connected with another proposition, which is necessarily true, is itself necessarily true. To say otherwise, would be a contradiction: it would be in effect to say, that the connection was indissoluble, and yet was not so, but might be broken. If that, whose existence is indissolubly connected with something whose existence is now necessary, is itself not necessary, then it may possibly not exist, notwithstanding that indissoluble connection of its existence.— Whether that absurdity be not glaring, let the reader judge.

4.   It is no less evident, that if there be a full, certain, and infallible Foreknowledge of the future existence of the volitions of moral agents, then there is a certain infallible and indissoluble connection between those events and that Foreknowledge; and that therefore, by the preceding observations, those events are necessary events; being infallibly and indissolubly connected with that whose existence already is, and so is now necessary, and cannot but have been.

To say the Foreknowledge is certain and infallible, and yet the connection of the event with that Foreknowledge is not indissoluble, but dissoluble and fallible, is very absurd. To affirm it, would be the same thing as to affirm that there is no necessary connection between a proposition's being infallibly known to be true, and its being true indeed. So that it is perfectly demonstrable, that if there be any infallible knowledge of future volitions, the event is necessary; or, in other words, that it is impossible but the event should come to pass. For if it be not impossible but that it may be otherwise, then it is not impossible but true. But how absurd is that, on the supposition that there is now an infallible knowledge (i.e. knowledge which it is impossible should fail) that it is true. There is this absurdity in it, that it is not impossible but that there now should be no truth in that proposition which is now infallibly known to be true.

II. That no future event can be certainly foreknown, whose existence is contingent, and without all necessity, may bc proved thus; it is impossible for a thing to be certainly known to any intellect without evidence. To suppose otherwise, implies a contradiction: because, for a thing to be certainly known to any understanding, is for it to be evident to that understanding: and for a thing to be evident to any understanding, is the same thing as for that understanding to see evidence of it: but no understanding, created or uncreated, can see evidence where there is none: for is the same thing as to see that to be which is not. And therefore, if there by any truth which is absolutely without evidence, that truth is absolutely unknowable, insomuch that it implies a contradiction to suppose that it is known . . . .

III. To suppose the future volitions of moral agents not to be necessary events; or, which is the same thing, events which it is not impossible but that they may not come to pass; and yet to suppose that God certainly foreknows them, and knows all things, is to suppose God's knowledge to be inconsistent with itself. For to say, that God certainly, and without all conjecture, knows that a thing will infallibly be, which at the same time he knows to be so contingent that it may possibly not be, is to suppose his knowledge inconsistent with itself; or that one thing that he knows, is utterly inconsistent with another thing that he knows.[8]

Brief Bibliography

Augustine, Saint Aurelius. *The City of God.* New York: Penguin edition, 1960.

Augustine, Saint Aurelius. *Confessions.* New York: Penguin edition, 1984.

Calvin, John. *Institutes of The Christian Religion.* Edited by John T. McNeill, (Library of Christian Classics) 2 volumes. Philadelphia: Westminster Press, 1960.

Maritain, Jacques. *Moral Philosophy.* New York: Charles Scribners, 1960.

Niebuhr, Reinhold. *The Nature and Destiny of Man.* New York: Harpers Brothers, 1946.

Pelikan, Jaroslav, *Portraits of Jesus,* 2nd edition, New Haven: Yale University Press, 1997.

Leo XIII, Rerum Novarum, in *Catholic Social Thought. The Documentary Heritage,* edited by David J. O'Brien and Thomas A. Shannon. Maryknoll, NY: Orbis Books, 1992.

McGrath, Alistair. *History of Christian Theology.* Cambridge, MA: Blackwells, 1998.

Rauschenbusch, Walter. *A Theology for the Social Gospel.* New York: Macmillan, 1917.

Endnotes

[1] On the whole "Synoptic Problem" the classic work is B.H. Streeter, *The Four Gospels,* London: Macmillan, 1924.

[2] Albert Schweitzer, *The Search of the Historical Jesus.* New York: Macmillan, 1910. This was followed in the Fifties with another attempt, pioneered by J. Robinson to further discern the "Jesus of history." This search, like others, as Schweitzer had predicted, failed as researcher's presuppositions inevitably "colored" what they sought and indeed found. Schweitzer put it this way: "The researcher is like man who looks down a well, and in the water sees reflected back a pale reflection of himself." For works that deal with the most recent "search" largely focused upon "Q" and the "Gospel of Thomas," see *The Jesus Quest. The Third Search for the Jew of Nazareth,* by Ben Witherington III (Downers Grove, ILL: Intervarsity Press, 1995 and most recently, the two volume *Christian Origins and the Question of God* Vol. 1, *The People of God* and Vol. II, *Jesus and the Victory of God.* Minneapolis: Fortress Press, 1992, 1996.

[3] Richard Horsley and John Hanson, *Bandits, Prophets and Messiahs: Popular Movements in the Time of Jesus.* New York: Winston Press, 1985; John Dominic Crossan, *The Historical Jesus. The Life of a Mediterranean Jewish Peasant.* New York: Harpercollins Publishers, 199 1; Albert Nolan, *Jesus Before Christianity.* Maryknoll, NY: Orbis Books, 1987.

[4]St. Augustine, *De Trinitate* ("Concerning the Trinity"); *The City of God* XI, 10,3; and, more accessibly, in his *Confessions*, chapter 13:22,23.

[5]Barth, Karl. Church Dogmatics Volume III, part 1.

[6]*St. Augustine, On Free Choice of the Will*, trans. Anna S. Benjamin and L.H. Hackstaff. (Indianapolis: Bobbs-Merrill, 1964).

[7]Jacobus Arminius (1560-1609) was a Dutch theologian who claimed that although God has foreknowledge of our actions, human beings nonetheless act freely. Edwards aims his arguments against Arminius' followers throughout.

[8]Jonathan Edwards, "Freedom of the Will," from *The Works of President Edwards, In Four Volumes*, Vol. 2 (New York: Leavitt and Allen, 1856).

ISLAM

by Lance D. Laird

Introduction

With well over one billion Muslims worldwide, Islam is the majority religion in about 50 nations, and Muslims form a significant minority in dozens more. The most populous Muslim countries are Indonesia and Pakistan; those whose native language is Arabic make up less than one-tenth of the total Muslim population. Estimates of the Muslim population in the United States range from six to ten million, and many scholars project that Muslims will outnumber Jews in this country in the next decade. Despite the rich intellectual, artistic, scientific and cultural heritage of the Islamic world, to which Western civilization is greatly indebted, Islam has served as the quintessential Other for Christians and others in the West for over a millennium. Perceived political and religious threats to European or American cultural interests have generated negative images of Muslims in the writings of Dante and Luther, Western academics and contemporary popular media.

Seeking to provide their own account, many Muslims who encounter Western notions of religion as "belief systems" or "institutions" in the West claim that "Islam is a way of life, not a religion!" The claim finds support in the word *Islam* itself. Arabic words generally have three letter roots, and the root of the word *islam* is S-L-M. The word for peace, *salam* (cf. Hebrew, *shalom*) shares this root. "Islam" is the active participle form, and thus it means "submitting" (making peace). The person who does the act of submitting is called a *muslim* (note the root S-L-M). Muslims are thus those people who actively submit their personal wills to the will of the one God. Islam, then, is something one does.

For Muslims, Islam is not a new religion. According to Islamic understandings of sacred history, the first man Adam was the first Muslim and the first messenger of God. Subsequent messengers of Islam, the way of submitting to God, include Noah, Abraham, Moses, David, and Jesus, among many others. The prophet Muhammad is the "seal" or the final prophet in a long line of God's messengers to humanity, not the "founder" of Islam. Muslims recognize in Judaism and Christianity a shared heritage of the one God who is revealed through acts in human history. The message of the Qur'an and the life of Muhammad represent both a continuation and a corrective to the religious beliefs and institutions of Christians and Jews.

Diverse cultures and nationalities, languages and political systems, economic and social conditions have created a rich tapestry of particular Muslim beliefs and practices. Muslims worldwide, however, share a "way of life" that provides some normative patterns of belief and devotional practice, social relations, economic duties, political ideals, and community loyalties. These derive from, and continually interact with, the story of God's revelation of the Qur'an to Muhammad and of the people who originally gathered in response to its message.

Historical overview

The life and career of the Prophet Muhammad take shape against the backdrop of a culture in transition. By the sixth century CE, the city of Mecca in the west central Arabian peninsula had a growing settled merchant class, thriving on the long-distance caravan trade between Yemen and the Mediterranean and on the religious sanctuary that attracted pilgrims. The desert pastoralists and the settled townspeople shared no political unity, though common values of manliness, martial valor, hospitality and generosity linked them in defense of family, clan and tribal honor and provided forms of alliance. Accounts of blood feuds and unreasoned violence led many later Muslims to label this culture barbaric, ignorant of the virtues of the true religion. They label the period prior to the revelation of the Qur'an the period of *jahiliyyah*, ignorance.

Pre-Islamic Arabs did not share a uniform set of religious beliefs and practices. Mecca's central shrine, a cubical structure known as the Ka'bah, reportedly contained 360 idols representing various divinities or spirits. The name "Allah" referred to a high god, though this god seems to have had little significance in the ritual life of the community. More popular deities included the three daughters of Allah and a war god, whose cult was prominent among powerful Meccans. Christians and Jews may also have inhabited Mecca at this time, though little is known of them, and a small group of believers known as *hanifs* apparently worshipped the One God.

The prophet Muhammad was born in 570 CE as a member of the Banu Hashim clan, the branch of the dominant Quraysh tribe responsible for administering the pilgrimage sites. Orphaned early in life, his uncle Abu Talib raised him and later protected him from opposition. Muhammad married the widow Khadijah, an older woman who employed him to run her caravan trade. He earned the appellation al-Amin (the trustworthy one) as a merchant in Mecca.

Muhammad often retreated to a mountain cave outside Mecca for devotional and meditative practice. During one such retreat in the month of Ramadan, 610 CE, Muhammad reported a strange encounter with an angel who commanded him, "Recite!" After asking three times what he must recite, Muhammad heard the angel say, "Recite! In the name of thy Lord and Cherisher Who created, created man out of a clot of congealed blood: Proclaim! And thy Lord is Most Bountiful, He Who taught (the use of) the Pen, Taught man that which he knew not" (Surah 96:1-5). After reciting this, Muhammad awoke with the strange feeling of these words being written on his heart. Running down the mountain, he heard a voice call out, "Muhammad, you are the Messenger of God, and I am Gabriel": he looked up to see an angelic form standing on the horizon.

Disturbed by this message, Muhammad confided in his wife Khadijah, who reassured him. As further revelations came, he recited them to family and friends and soon developed a small group of believers in Mecca. The early messages warned of divine judgment and invited people to return to the ways of earlier prophets, including Abraham, Moses, and Jesus. These revelations of God's unity (*tauhid*) threatened the pilgrimage economy of Mecca. The message of a new universal community, the *ummah*, also challenged the social structure dependent on tribal bonds and blood feuds. Muhammad's message that God demanded social justice and reform, care for the poor and weak, confronted the growing wealth of prominent merchants in the urban economy.

The small band of Muhammad's followers faced hostility and resistance from powerful members of Meccan society, especially after Abu Talib died. In 622 CE, Muhammad and a group of followers emigrated northward to Yathrib, where Muhammad was invited to make peace between feuding tribes. This event marked the beginning of the Muslim calendar, as Muhammad began the process of shaping a new community based on the revelations he had received. The city was later renamed Madinat an-Nabi, "the city of the Prophet," and is known today as Madinah (Medina).

After a series of battles with the Meccans, Muhammad and his followers returned to subdue Mecca in 630 CE, cleanse the Ka'bah of idols, and establish a society based on the revelation and his own example. During this time, Muhammad used diplomatic and military means to unite Arab tribes around the Peninsula, who joined with the Muslim *ummah* by alliance or conversion. Muhammad performed a "farewell pilgrimage" in 632 CE, establishing the rites of the *hajj* and exhorting his followers to maintain the *ummah*. He died that same year.

The death of the prophet, lawgiver, governor and judge put the young religious community in a quandary. Who could possibly succeed the prophet and assume authoritative leadership of the Muslim ummah, now that God's messenger and guide had gone? Would the allied tribes and clans remain loyal to this new community without direct access to divine revelation? Abu Bakr al-Siddiq, a pious elder, proclaimed to those in disbelief, "Whoever worships God, God is alive and immortal; whoever worships Muhammad, Muhammad is dead!" A group of the prophet Muhammad's closest companions in Madinah chose Abu Bakr to be the *khalif'ah* (deputy) of the prophet. The new caliph assumed leadership of Friday prayers and temporal governance of the community as "commander of the faithful".

A faction of the *ummah*, however, asserted that the prophet Muhammad had designated his successor to be his cousin and son-in-law `Ali ibn Abu Talib. Known as the *shi`at `Ali* (the partisans of `Ali), they recalled the event at the Ghadir of Khumm when Muhammad reportedly said, "surely I leave among you such that, if you hold fast to it, you will never stray: the Book of God and my family, the People of my House, who will never be separated until both join me at the Pool of Paradise."[1] This faction, which claimed that the prophet's authority rightly belonged to his family, eventually became the known as the *Shi`ah*. Though their differences with other Muslims were originally political, they later developed a special doctrine of spiritual leadership and recognized the Imams as heirs of Muhammad's spiritual and temporal authority, endowed with esoteric knowledge of the divine revelation.

Tensions between the partisans of `Ali and the rest of the Muslim community continued under the caliphates of Abu Bakr (632-634), `Umar ibn al-Khattab (634-644), and Uthman ibn`Affan (644-656). Abu Bakr's armies pacified rebellious Arab tribes and began to challenge Byzantine and Sassanian control in Iraq and Syria. `Umar entered Jerusalem in victory, established Muslim garrison towns Iraq, Syria, and Egypt, and mortally weakened Persia. He appointed judges to put Qur'anic guidance into public policy. `Uthman, a Meccan aristocrat and early convert, established governors for the new territories, and he is credited with producing the first official recension of the Qur'anic text. Upon `Uthman's murder, the community selected `Ali as the fourth caliph, though his rule was marred by major political trouble with his predecessor's Umayya family. Mu`awiyah, a powerful governor and relative of`Uthman, challenged `Ali's authority with military force. `Ali's decision to arbitrate differences with Mu`awiyah cost him the support of the Kharijites. With the subsequent assassination of `Ali, the period Sunni Muslims regard as the golden age of "the rightly guided caliphs" came to an end, and the Umayyad dynasty was established in Damascus.

Mu`awiyah suppressed Shi`i dissenters, and his son and successor Yazid eventually squelched a rebellion of Shi`i supporters of `Ali's youngest son, Husayn. The martyrdom of Husayn at Karbalah in Iraq in the year 680 would provide the central motif of Shi`i piety as well as of opposition political mobilization. The Umayyads ruled from Damascus until 750, extending Arab Muslim military control to Spain and North Africa, Persia and parts of the Indian subcontinent. The pious opposition to the Umayyads took many forms, developing different criteria for legitimate Islamic leadership. The collection and study of *hadith* literature began during this period, and certain pious figures began to use ascetic and meditative practices to achieve an inner knowledge of God, developing a tendency that would eventually be known as Sufism, or Islamic mysticism.

The Abbasid revolt against the Umayyads began in Persian territory under the banner of Shi`i protest. The new dynasty, which was to found the city of Baghdad and foster the flowering of high culture in Islam, soon abandoned the Shi`ah for a majoritarian policy. Under the early Abbasids, the loosely defined group known as *ahl al-sunnah wa al-jama`ah* ("the people of the sunnah and communal unity", shortened to *Sunni*) began to take shape over against the Shi`ah. The recognition of the authority of the community experience itself, and not the following of the prophet's sunnah (discussed below) was the distinguishing factor. The formation of schools of law, the development of educational institutions, the patronage of the visual and literary arts, philosophy and theology, and scientific advances, are among the achievements of the Abbasid period, which lasted until the Mongol invasion in 1258.

Even before the thirteenth century Mongol invasion, various smaller dynasties had assumed control of territories nominally controlled by the Abbasid caliphs. In the wake of the Mongols, however, the Muslim world eventually splintered into a number of different political entities, the chief among which were the empires of the Ottomans in the Mediterranean, the Safavids in Persia, and the Mughuls in India, each of which lasted into the modern period. Developing unique architectural, cultural and administrative forms, each witnessed the rise of professional guilds, educational institutions for the study of Islamic law and theology, and the spread of Sufi orders.

The pilgrimage to Mecca, trade routes, travel for religious education, and the Sufi orders provided unifying links among the far-flung Muslim territories. Undue attention to the role of military conquest in the spread of Islam has prevented many from seeing the important role of indigenous Christians and Jews under Muslim rule and the gradual conversion over centuries of the majority of the populations in these lands. In the middle periods, from the 13th through the 18th centuries, the word of Islam spread to sub-Saharan Africa and Southeast Asia primarily through Muslim merchants and Sufi missionaries.

Sources of Religious Authority

Inasmuch as this world civilization can claim to be "Islamic", it draws on authoritative religious sources for its legitimacy. The most obvious source is the central historical event of the revelation of the Qur'an. As an oral recitation, it is the living word of God, available to the human heart through the sense of hearing. Many have compared the theological significance of the Qur'an with the *logos* doctrine in Christianity; instead of becoming flesh, the Word became recited words. Devotional listening to a Qur'an recitation involves for Muslims a sense of communion with God and participation in the prophetic event. When the Prophet Muhammad repeated the portions revealed to him, his companions memorized and transcribed them, and they became an authoritative source of spiritual truth and practical guidance for life.

Muslims relate a traditional story of how the various *surahs* (chapters) and *ayahs* (lit., "signs", cf verses) were arranged into the text now known as the Qur'an. The early companions of Muhammad maintained the Qur'anic revelation in memory and passed it on orally in recitations. According to tradition, the third caliph, `Uthman ibn `Affan (reigned 644-656) authorized the collection and arrangement of all the transcribed and memorized portions of the Qur'an. The "Uthmanic recension" was distributed as authoritative, though various vowelings and recitative traditions continued to flourish in different regions. The Qur'an was not edited or arranged thematically, and the surahs are ordered generally from longest to shortest. The non-Muslim reader may experience the text as disjointed and episodic, though many Muslims see even this arrangement as divinely inspired.

Western scholars have argued widely divergent historical scenarios for the collection of the Qur'an, based on the textual evidence and the development of early commentarial traditions. They have concluded, on one extreme, that the present text of the Qur'an was available before Muhammad's death, and on the other extreme, that the present text was not fully formed until the third century A.H. (9th c. CE). As with any historical text, other scholars raise questions about cultural influences, particularly in terms of stories and practices that resemble Christian and Jewish sources. For Muslims, however, the similarities result from a common divine source, while differences indicate where previous communities have strayed from their original revelation.

As divine revelation and a continuance of the Prophet Muhammad's authority, the Qur'an is the authoritative source for legal and theological norms. In Muslim life, the Qur'an holds a primary place in everyday practice. Muslims treat the physical text itself with great reverence, and copying the text in rich

Arabic calligraphy is a devotional act. Listening to the Qur'an recited by specialists or meditative reading before the five daily prayers makes the revelation available to Muslims, and Qur'anic phrases provide the fundamental vocabulary of everyday Muslim piety, from greetings and salutations to prayer and popular poetry.

The major themes of the Qur'an include the justice and mercy of God, the guidance God gives to humanity, the responsibility of human beings to God and to one another. The Qur'an contains numerous psalms of praise and thanksgiving to God—creator, sustainer, giver of guidance, the merciful and compassionate judge—repeatedly calling attention to the "signs" of God's unity, character and action in nature and in human history. Warnings and encouragement about the day of judgment, the division of believers and unbelievers (or those grateful and ungrateful to their Lord), eternal reward and punishment, accompany pleas for repentance and right action. Though the Qur'an contains few extended narratives, the text alludes to and comments on the stories of previous prophets, through whom God's guidance has come, who faced resistance from their communities, and whom God strengthened to be faithful messengers of God's mercy and judgment. These stories provide a model for the Prophet Muhammad and for the community of listeners. Texts addressing practical legal concerns make up only about one-tenth of the entire corpus.

Hadith and Sunnah

The second major source of religious authority for Muslims is the *sunnah* of the Prophet Muhammad. *Sunnah* was an Arabic term referring to the "custom, practice" of one's elders, which formed the basis of social norms in a community. During Muhammad's lifetime, and even after his death, the community of Muslims looked to Muhammad as the authoritative model of right practice. As the messenger of God, his *sunnah* (his words, actions, and decisions in community matters) demonstrated how to five out the divine revelation (Aishah quote). The prophet's *Sunnah* is known through the *hadith* (lit., "report"; pl., *ahadith*) passed down from his wives and companions to the following generations.

In the decades after the death of the Prophet, these *hadith* circulated among the community orally. As the time of the Prophet receded into the past with the death of companions and their followers, the growing Muslim community faced significant challenges in developing normative legal patterns for its increasingly diverse population. Scholars traveled around the Muslim world to receive *hadith* from acknowledged authorities, who often issued a certificate (*ijazah*) to those who successfully memorized the corpus of hadith they held. Legal scholars in the ninth century acknowledged that the fabrication of reports about the Prophet was a real threat, and they developed a system of *hadith* criticism based on the *isnad*, the chain of transmitters of the report. Scholars compiled biographies of the companions and their successors and evaluated the general reliability of their transmission based on moral character and the likelihood of an authentic *ijazah* from an authoritative transmitter in their generation. By the tenth century six collections of *ahadith* found general acceptance as "canonical" among legal scholars.

The content of *hadith* reports ranges from divine words (known as *hadith qudsi*) apart from the Qur'anic revelation to biographical details about events in the Prophet's life or the life of the Companions; elaboration of stories like Muhammad's famous "night journey and ascension," briefly mentioned in the Qur'an (17:1) to practical instructions given by the Prophet; from his response to questions or controversial situations to details of Muhammad's personal hygiene practices. The *hadith* have been useful for Qur'an commentators to determine how the Prophet understood the implications of a particular portion of the revelation, or to locate the revelation in the context of an event in Muhammad's life. Biographies of Muhammad rely on *hadith* literature in their construction of a hagiographical narrative, while modern historians depend on and debate the reliability of the *hadith* as historical documents. Muslim legal scholars have turned to *hadith* reports to determine elements of the Prophet's *sunnah* that are normative for the whole Muslim community, even in the midst of changing circumstances and conditions.

Imamate

The Shi`ah have developed an additional source of religious authority in the notion of the Imamate. Building on the political struggle over succession to the Prophet Muhammad, the Shi`ah continued to recognize only direct descendants of `Ali as rightful rulers and guides for the Muslim ummah. The Imam became the authoritative interpreter of the meaning of the Qur'an, and the Shi`ah believe that the Imams are gifted with special insight into the esoteric meanings of the revelation. Their words and deeds are also recorded in hadith collections and become part of the sunnah and a source of law.

The largest group of Shi`ah are called Twelvers, because they recognize twelve Imams in succession. The last Imam disappeared in his infancy in 873, beginning what is known as the "lesser occultation". Representatives of the Imam communicated with him until 941, when the "greater occultation" began. Twelver Shi`ah still await the return of the twelfth Imam as the *Mahdi*, the "guided one" who will restore true religion to the Muslim community. Though not official doctrine in Sunni Islam, the idea of a Mahdi has inspired popular movements of political revolt, for instance in the 19th century Sudanese Mahdist movement. Twelver Shi`ah have held sway in a number of Muslim dynasties, particularly in the tenth century and in the 16th century Safavid empire, and are now most numerous in Iran and Lebanon.

The Imamate is significant for other groups as well. The Fivers or Zaydi Shi`ah split with the main body in the eighth century over the rightful succession of a grandson of Imam Husayn. The Zaydis remained a significant moderate force in the middle periods and maintained a small state in the Yemen as late as the 20th century. The Ismailis, or "Sevener" Shi`ah, likewise broke away from the main group over the succession of the seventh Imam. Insisting on the authority of the esoteric knowledge of the Imam over the external forms of Qur'an, hadith, and shari`ah, the Ismailis aggressively pursued propaganda, educational, and military missions challenging the authority of Sunni rulers. The Fatimids, an Ismaili dynasty, ruled North Africa in the 10th-12th c. and established the famous Al-Azhar, later to become the center of Sunni scholarship and one of the first universities in the world. Today Ismaili communities in India, East Africa, Yemen, Europe and North America, under the leadership of the Aga Khan, use their considerable business success to support global relief efforts as well as university research in Islamic studies and architecture.

Ulama

Islam has no priesthood. This statement holds true, when one contrasts authority figures in the Islamic community with the sacerdotal and mediating functions of a priest in the Jewish or Christian traditions, or the hierarchical arrangement of bishops, cardinals and popes. Muslims have, however, recognized the authority of educated or informed members of their communities and the role of these figures in preserving the *sunnah* of the Prophet among them.

Traditional Islamic education begins at an early age, when children memorize and learn to recite the Qur'an. Today, many children attend Qur'an schools as part of their elementary education. Older students learn the hadith, Arabic grammar, Qur'an interpretation; and some may then pursue more specialized education in the roots of Islamic law and its application according to particular schools of *fiqh* (jurisprudence). A traditional education also involves the study of at least some *kalam* (theology). Those recognized by the community as authoritative custodians of traditional learning are known as `ulama (singular, `alim). They may serve as Qur'an reciters, Islamic schoolteachers, imams (prayer leaders) and *khatibs* (preachers) in a local mosque, and professors of law or theology in a university.

In Sunni Islam, by and large, the `ulama have no formal hierarchy or institutional structure. Their religious authority derives primarily from an ability to achieve consensus among themselves and to communicate to the larger community the relevance of Islamic tradition to the needs and concerns of the day. Some are appointed to official positions as *qadi* (judge) or as *mufti* (one who delivers legal opinions) for a particular jurisdiction, though the relationship of `ulama to the governing power has often been ambiguous. In some historical situations, for example the Ottoman Empire, they formed a distinctive class, hierarchically arranged by the ruling authorities. Sunni Muslims have also rejected the authority of the 'ulama on various occasions in Islamic history, either because of their scholasticism, their lack of piety, or their unwillingness to accommodate social change. In some societies, the Sufi *pir* or *shaykh* has assumed authority in the community, based on a different form of authoritative knowledge.

In Shi'i Islam, the 'ulama assume greater importance and hierarchical organization. The higher-ranking Twelver Shi'i 'ulama are called *ayatollahs* (lit., "signs of God"), and they lead the community in the absence of the Imam, who remains in occultation. Individual Shi'i Muslims must choose an *ayatollah* whose interpretation of the tradition is authoritative for their lives, though they may change allegiances as well. Periodically, one *ayatollah* may be designated the supreme living authority. Despite differences in hierarchical structure though, Shi'i 'ulama generally serve in the same occupations as their Sunni counterparts.

The 'ulama thus link Muslims with the prophet's time by guarding the interpretation of the revelation and prophetic example. They help to define the meaning of religious action (*islam*) as well as the content of faith (*iman*).

Religious Duties

Scholars usually categorize Islam and Judaism, in contrast to Christianity, as "orthoprax" religious traditions. That is, in their emphasis on legal prescriptions for communal and individual life, one sees less emphasis in these traditions on "correct belief" (*ortho-doxy*) and theological formulation, and less prominence given to theologians, than one finds in the Christian tradition. The chief concern of the 'ulama is the elaboration of the "straight path" to which God guides human beings to live.

Shari'ah, Sources and Role

The preserve of the 'ulama is known as *shari'ah*. The term *shari'ah*, often translated loosely as "Islamic law", literally means "broad path leading to water". The shari'ah thus elaborates the path of responsible action a Muslim follows to achieve success in this world and the next.

The first source of shari'ah is the Qur'anic revelation itself. As the early Muslim community organized around religious authority instead of tribal custom the Qur'an provided ethical norms and confirmed some customary laws. In situations about which the Qur'an is silent, the Prophet Muhammad's teaching, practice, and legal judgment provided direction. Both Qur'an and prophetic sunnah, therefore, derived their authority from the divine lawgiver. These are the two primary sources of the early shari'ah.

With the expansion of Islam over vast territories after the death of the Prophet, however, local Muslim rulers found it necessary to preserve existing administrative structures and customary laws of the conquered land in areas about which the Qur'an was silent. Umayyad judges also ruled on the basis of their own opinions, and hadith collection was not yet regarded as an authoritative source of law. Frustrations over Umayyad legal and political abuses, however, led eventually to the formation of major legal schools in Medina and Kufah under Abbasid rule.

The concept of *sunnah* became a cornerstone of these schools, and the ascription of traditions to the Prophet became an important practice. The Medinan school of Malik ibn Anas (d. 795), culturally near to the Prophet's milieu, ascribed additional legal authority to the consensus of the local community (ijma'). The Kufan school under Abu Hanifah (d. 767) in the Iraq allowed broader acceptance of foreign customs from the environment. Jurists developed a fourth source in *qiyas*, reasoning by analogy from the text of the Qur'an or hadith to a contemporary situation. The learned Muhammad ibn Idris al-Shafi'i (d. 820) is credited with systematizing the science of Islamic jurisprudence (*fiqh*). Al-Shaffi'i elaborated four sources or roots (*usul*) for deriving authoritative Islamic law: Qur'an, sunnah, ijma', and qiyas. Ahmad Ibn Hanbal (d. 855), known as a strict traditionist among the "people of hadith", rejected the principle of qiyas, while the Maliki school continued to emphasize ijma`, and the Hanafis added the principle of discretion (*istihsan*). These four legal schools were accepted as the authoritative interpreters of divine law by the tenth century CE. While some Western scholars and many Sunni Muslims have claimed that the "gate of *ijtihad*" (independent reasoning) was closed upon the death of these four founding imams, leading to stagnation and blind imitation in Islamic law, many reformers through the centuries often claimed such authority for themselves and enriched the tradition. modern revivalists have likewise proclaimed the gate open again.

Shi`i jurisprudence developed along a slightly different path. The Ja`fari school, named after the sixth Imam Ja`far al-Sadiq (d. 765), recognized the authority of legal opinions and interpretations of the Imams as an additional source of law and gives less authority to the hadith of the early Muslim community after Muhammad. After the 9th century, with the occultation of the 12th Imam, Shi`i jurisprudence developed along similar lines. Shi`i `ulama, however, have always maintained the right to exercise *ijtihad*. Shi`i law differs only slightly from Sunni practices, for instance in the provision for the practice of temporary marriage (*mut`ah*).

The content of the shari`ah can be divided into two major categories: the obligations owed to God (`*ibadat*) and the obligations between human beings (*mu`amalat*). The `ibadat include such things as the regulations pertaining to ritual purity and the performance of acts of devotion beyond the required "five pillars" discussed below. The mu`amalat include everything having to do with life in the world. Acts are not simply required or prohibited, however, and the jurists of Islam elaborated a classification of all acts in five categories: obligatory, recommended, permissible, reprehensible, and forbidden. The different law schools may disagree on the category applied to a certain act, for instance the use of gold and silver or the consumption of milk from a donkey.

Five Pillars

The set of practices known as the "five pillars of Islam" are a good example of duties prescribed in the *shari`ah* and shared by all Muslims. In an important hadith, the angel Gabriel asks Muhammad to define *islam*. The prophet responds, "Submission means that you should bear witness that there is no god but God and that Muhammad is God's messenger, that you should perform the ritual prayer, pay the alms tax, fast during Ramadan, and make the pilgrimage to the House if you are able to go there".[2]

In order to join the fold of Muslims, one has merely to utter with sincerity in the presence of witnesses the *shahadah*, the testimony: "I bear witness that 'there is no god but God'; I bear witness that 'Muhammad is the messenger of God.' " All other duties follow from this confession, out of gratitude and obedience to the one God and in recognition of the authoritative revelation given to the prophet Muhammad.

The most regular devotional duty of Muslims, required five times daily, is the ritual of formal worship, *salat*. The *salat* consists of a precise, formalized cycle of spoken formulas, Qur'an recitation, and bodily postures, performed alone or in a congregation, facing towards Mecca. Muslims must purify themselves with ritual ablutions (*wudu'*) before performing the *salat*. Friday midday worship is the only required gathering for the community at a *masjid* (Eng., "mosque"; lit., "place of prostration"), and this worship includes a sermon along with regular *salat*.

Zakat, or almsgiving, is a required religious tax on property and wealth for all Muslims of means; it is considered an act of service to God, not a charitable gift. The act of giving a portion purifies the remainder for the one who gives it. Various official Islamic institutions, depending on the country, distribute the annual *zakat* collection to needy or suffering Muslims or for those serving the community in propagation or maintenance needs.

For the entire lunar month of Ramadan, Muslims are obliged to perform a daily fast, known as *sawm*. Fasting means abstinence from food, drink, sexual relations, smoking, and unhealthy habits of mind and speech from daybreak to nightfall. It is a season of reflection and increased self-discipline. During the evening, Muslims gather as families and communities to break the fast, to hold special prayer gatherings, and to celebrate the auspicious month of Ramadan, during which the first Qur'anic revelation came down to Muhammad. The month of fasting concludes with the "Feast of Fast-Breaking" (*`Id al-Fitr*), which usually includes greeting cards, special foods and travel to visit distant family members.

The *hajj* or pilgrimage to Mecca during the special period of the year is obligatory only upon those Muslims whose financial and family situation permits it. Pilgrims travel from around the world to visit the *Kàbah*, the sacred center of the Muslim world, toward which Muslims face during everyday *salat*. According to Muslim traditions, the prophets Abraham and Isma`il erected the *Kàbah* as the first house of worship for the one true God, on the site where Adam and Eve had lived. Male pilgrims enter into a ritually pure state and wear two pieces of seamless white cloth, while women may choose to wear modest national clothing or a full white garment. Pilgrims follow the practice of Muhammad and early monotheistic Arabs by circumambulating the *Kàbah* seven times on three occasions. They ritually reenact events from the life of Abraham, Hagar and Ishmael, including the sacrifice of a consecrated animal in commemoration of Abraham's willingness to sacrifice his son. Muslims not on pilgrimage also perform this "Feast of Sacrifice" (*`Id al-Adha*), the second major festival of the liturgical calendar. The *hajj* represents an important rite of passage for the pilgrim, and he or she takes the title *hajji(ah)*.

Some Muslims have considered the practice of *jihad* to be a "sixth pillar" of Islam. While often associated today with the "holy war" conducted by radical Islamist groups against Western institutions or fellow Muslims, the term in its most basic sense means "exertion, struggle" in the way of God. Though Muslims differ on whether *jihad* may be applied beyond defense against enemies of Islam to aggressive warfare for the spread of Islam, one of Muhammad's famous teachings calls such external struggle the "lesser *jihad*". The "greater *jihad*" is the spiritual struggle with one's own sin, repentance, faith and discipline. *Jihad*, regulated by specific standards, is thus integral to the concept of worship or service to God in the world.

The five pillars of Islam certainly do not exhaust the Muslims' duties to God or encompass the variety of devotional practices Muslims perform. Recitation of the Qur'an plays a prominent role in acts of *salat* as well as the public celebration of the two major, and other minor, annual festivals. More informal, petitionary prayer (*du`a*) often follows the performance of formal *salat* during the day as well. The five pillars provide a framework for Muslim worship through acting out beliefs and values in submission to God's will (*islam*).

The Shari`ah provides the ideal code of conduct for both individuals and society, and one may say that Islam recognizes no real separation between the secular and the religious, between "church" and "state". In practice, however, caliphal grievance courts, the application of customary laws, and compromises with alternate (e.g., European colonial) legal systems have supplemented the shari`ah in most historical Muslim societies. modern experiments in Pakistan, Iran, Saudi Arabia, and Sudan represent attempts to apply shari`ah in various ways to the radically new situation of nation-states.

Theological and Philosophical Understandings of God and World

In the hadith of Gabriel, Muhammad also defines faith (*iman*): "Faith means that you have faith in God, His angels, His books, His messengers, and the Last Day, and that you have faith in the measuring out, both its good and its evil". Reflection on the meaning of *iman* is the purview of theology or *kalam* (theology, lit., "speech"). This discipline developed out of Qur'anic interpretation, political conflict, dialogue with Jews and Christians, and the influx of Greek philosophical ideas. Major theological debates centered on the nature of God, the nature of the Qur'an and prophecy, the relationship of faith and works, free will and determinism. In discerning the content of *iman* theologians gave primary authority to revelation; philosophers, to Reason; and theosophical Sufis, to "unveiling" or experiential knowledge of God.

The first sentence of the shahadah, "There is no god but God", is the central affirmation of Islamic theology. According to the Qur'an, God has sent all prophets with this same message: "There is no god but I, so worship Me" (21:25). Radical affirmation of the unity of God (the concept of *tauhid*) and the prohibition of "associating" (*shirk*) anything with God (i.e., an idol, a person, one's own desire) are the dual implications of this confession. To surrender one's will to anything other than the God who reveals himself in the Qur'an is *shirk*, a violation of original human nature.

The Qur'an continually directs the reader, or the hearer, to examine the "signs" of God. The very words of the Qur'an, God's speech, are called "signs" of God: "These are the signs of the manifest book. We have sent it down as an Arabic Qur'an" (12:1-2). Signs or messages of God also appear in nature (e.g., 17:12; 36:33), in the miracles of the prophets and scriptures given to them (12:7; 28:36), and in historical events. Beginning with the confession that God is one, Muslims seek to discern the attributes of God through the created world around them.

Theological reflection on the nature of God begins with the names of God in the Qur'an. Muslim theologians often speak of the "most beautiful names" of God (*al-asma` al-husna*), of which a hadith claims there are ninety-nine. For instance, the first verses of the Qur'an identify God as "Lord of the universe", "the Compassionate", "the Merciful", "Owner of the Day of Judgment". Other names include the Permanent, the Independent, the All-Knowing, the Almighty, the Just, Creator, Slayer, the Forgiver, and the Real (*al-Haqq*). Muslim theologians have frequently divided all of these names into those that refer to God's essence (what God is not), God's attributes (what God is), and God's acts (how God relates to the universe).

The names of God's essence indicate that God is unlike anything known to human beings. God is the Holy, the Glorified, the Independent, and the Permanent, none of which can be applied to humans or other created beings. The names of God's attributes, however, compare the ultimately Real (God) with the relatively real qualities of creatures. Thus, God is Alive, Knowing, Seeing, and Hearing, though in each of these attributes God is infinitely more so than human beings are. The names of God's acts identify God in terms of how God interacts with the universe in different ways and at different times, and these names often involve opposites. God is thus the Lifegiver and the Slayer, the Forgiver and the Avenger, the Merciful and the Wrathful.

The ideas that God is both wrathful and merciful, and that God is both totally unlike human beings and yet similar to some degree, lead to the paradox of distance and nearness. While God is distant and unchanging, God is also "closer than the jugular vein". God is the ultimately Real, in contrast to which everything else is unreal; the more distant things are from manifesting the qualities of God, the more unreal they are. Hell is the extreme image of this distance from God. At the same time, God's Reality encompasses and embraces all that is relatively real. Inasmuch as human beings or other things in the universe exhibit the faintest qualities of God, they are close to God and thus are becoming more real. Paradise is depicted as a place where these qualities are fully realized. According to a hadith, the Prophet said that upon God's throne is the inscription, "My mercy takes precedence over my wrath". God's mercy, in drawing near to what is only relatively real, takes precedence over the wrath manifest against those whose actions and thoughts reflect a preference for unreality.

The mark of God's sovereignty is that only God "measures out" to created things their range of potentialities, the limits within which they operate (54:49). God's "measuring out" is known as *qadar*, sometimes translated as "fate" or "predestination". God created the world out of nothing, and ordered laws that determine the behavior and nature of all parts of creation are the chief "signs" of God. The Qur'an mentions angels and jinn as creatures likewise endowed with both will and responsibility, though of a different order than human beings. God in wisdom also "measures out" to human beings their own powers, abilities and limitations, but also freedom and guidance. God is thus the source of all loss and gain, benefits and suffering, and human beings are still responsible for what they do with what is given them. These doctrines of God's attributes, and particularly God's measuring out, are central concerns of centuries of Islamic theology.

The mid-seventh century transition between the caliphate of the "four rightly guided caliphs" and the Umayyad caliphate in Damascus spurred the rise of political factions with theological concerns. The Kharijites ("those who leave") rejected both the caliph `Uthman's nepotism and caliph `Ali's decision to arbitrate with the Umayyad contender, Mu`awiyah; they claimed that grave sinners could not be Muslims, and certainly not the rulers of Muslims. The majority Murji`ites ("those who postpone judgment") answered that God alone could judge deeds and intentions, that a statement of faith was enough to qualify one as a Muslim, and that God had predetermined the present regime to rule. This situation raised the theological question of whether God, who "measures out" all things, was the source of evil and injustice.

Critics of the Umayyad regime, later known as the Mu`tazilites ("those who stand aloof"), challenged the majority opinion on God's predestination. Developing a theological school in the Abbasid period, they employed Greek rationality, logic, and natural law philosophy to analyze Qur'anic statements about human responsibility and the Last Day. God could not require human beings to follow a way and judge them for their response if they were incapable of making a free choice. The Mu`tazilites called themselves "the people of (divine) justice and unity" (*ahl al-`adl wa al-tauhid*). God's justice meant for them that God could only command what is just and good, while creatures alone could take responsibility for injustice and evil acts.

The Mu`tazilites also challenged majority notions of the nature of the Qur'an and God's attributes. They insisted that God's qualities of seeing, hearing, knowing, willing, etc., could not be eternal attributes of the one, transcendent God. To see these attributes as eternal would be to compromise the *tauhid* of God. The same applied to the Qur'an as God's speech. The majority of Muslims had developed the idea that the Qur'an was preexistent and uncreated (cf. Christian doctrine of *Logos*), written before time on the "Heavenly Tablet", but the Mu`tazilites insisted that the Qur'an, like all things other than God, must be created and not eternal alongside God. While Mu`tazilites enjoyed the support of some Abbasid caliphs, they were ultimately displaced in Sunni theology. Their emphasis on the unity and justice of God, the use of reason, and on the responsibility of Muslims to "command the good and forbid the evil" has continued to influence the development of theology in the Shi`i world

Sunni theologians turned toward the synthesis of reason, revelation and tradition achieved by Abu al-Hasan al-Ash`ari (d. 935). Al-Ash`ari reasserted doctrines of God's omnipotence, God's attributes, the uncreatedness of the Qur'an, and predestination. He used reason and logic to explain and defend belief, though Qur'an and hadith remained for him superior to reason. God in al-Ash`ari's theology was transcendent and omnipotent, capable of intervening at any moment and interrupting the usual laws of cause and effect. God willed and created all actions and events new each moment, though human beings could by "voluntary acquisition" (*kasb*) assume responsibility and accountability for their actions. The Ash`arite school had by the 11th century become a major stream in Islamic theology alongside Shafi`i jurisprudence, and the Persian theologian Abu Mansur al-Maturidi (d. 944) developed a more rationalistic version of Sunni theology that became influential in the eastern Islamic empires where Hanafi jurisprudence prevailed. Conservative traditionists such as Ahmad Ibn Hanbal (d. 855) still suspected orthodox scholastic theology for its use of reason.

Islamic philosophy arose with the translation of classical Greek works into Arabic during the early Abbasid period. Perhaps the most systematic of medieval Muslim philosophers was the Persian physician Ibn Sina (Avicenna, d. 1037). In contrast to orthodox theologies of creation, he developed a doctrine of the eternity of the world, which emanated from God. His related concept of God as "necessary Being" in relation to which the world is "contingent" fit well with orthodox theology of God's signs and human dependency, though theologians rejected the idea of an eternal world. Ibn Sina interpreted, through the lens of Aristotle and Plotinus, the Mu`tazilite doctrine of God's Pure Being, existent but without essence or attributes. As ultimate cause, God could know all particulars; thus Ibn Sina transformed Greek thought to support Islamic revelation. While Ibn Sina rejected bodily resurrection, since only the soul survived, the Aristotelian philosopher Ibn Rushd (Averroes, d. 1198) later argued that a *simulacrum* of the human body could be resurrected. Ibn Rushd defended his path of reason and science in pursuit of the "real" as a path alongside that of revelation. The `ulama rejected such rational philosophy primarily for this, because it judged "religion" to be a "philosophy for the masses" symbolically articulated by a Prophet of supreme intellect and spirit. Thus the philosophers regarded revelation and the *shari`ah* as unnecessary for the intellectual elite, who could realize truth independently.

Many regard the great theologian, mystic and legal scholar Muhammad al-Ghazah (d. 1111) as a pivotal figure in Islamic history. He criticized philosophers for the "incoherence" of their doctrines and their misapplication of reason to metaphysical speculation. He also found traditional theology, with its use of reason in defense of doctrine and tradition, to be deficient. Al-Ghazali argued that a reformed Sufism, with an emphasis on experiential testing of truth and the "life of the heart", was the real basis for "revivifying" theology and law. Al-Ghazali established Sufism as compatible with orthodox *shari`ah* piety and theology, paving the way for the rise and spread of Sufi orders in subsequent centuries. Sunni theology and philosophy would continue in combination after al-Ghazah, for instance in the rationalist Ash'ari theologian Fakhr al-Din al-Razi (d. 1209).

Other theologians integrated Sufi concepts of "gnosis" and "unveiling" with the philosophical insights of Ibn Sina and Ibn Rushd. Shihab al-Din Suhrawardi (d. 1191) articulated a "philosophy of illumination" in which he synthesized ancient Persian sages, Greek philosophy, and the Sufi notion of the Light unveiled. Reviving Ibn Sina's doctrine of emanation, he saw reality arrayed according to "grades of being". Cognition of that Being, achieved through philosophical training combined with spiritual gnosis, meant direct awareness and immediate presence of the self-luminous Light. Ibn al-`Arabi (d. 1240) developed a theoretical Sufism that conceived of "the unity of being" (*wahdat al-wujud*), which emanates into the many forms perceived in the external world. The human being is for Ibn al-`Arabi a mirror of God's attributes. Mulla Sadra of Shiraz (d. 1640) later synthesized these philosophical, theological, and mystical trends in Islamic thought. Illuminationist ideas provided significant themes for Sufi literature and Shi`i theology, especially in the esoteric Ismaili sects. The more traditional `ulama often reacted against Sufi and philosophical forms of theological speculation, insisting on measuring orthodoxy by the Qur'an and Sunnah of the Prophet.

The debate over the relationship of reason, revelation, and traditional legal authority in Muslim life has continued into the modern period. Modernist intellectuals like Jamal al-Din like al-Afghani (d. 1897), Muhammad `Abduh (d. 1905), and Muhammad Iqbal (d. 1938) have argued for educational reforms, the cultivation of science and reason to recover the lost intellectual heritage of Islamic civilization. Revivalists or "Islamists" like Sayyid Qutb (d. 1966) have called for a return to fundamentals of the Qur'an and Sunnah as a solution to modern problems. The `ulama are often the conservative traditionists, maintaining their authority to interpret Qur'an and Sunnah according to the accepted schools of law. Finally, secularist Muslims argue for a separation of Islam from modern science, technology, and social institutions.

Understanding of Human Self

According to the Qur'anic account of creation, God molded Adam out of baked clay and breathed His own spirit into him (15:26ff.), and thus the human self (*nafs*) is a non-dualistic union of material and spiritual elements. God created the human being to be "a vicegerent (*khalifah*) on earth" (2:30 ff.), though the angels protested that this new creation would "make mischief" and "shed blood". God demonstrated the superiority of the human being by teaching him the names of all things, and all the angels and jinn but Iblis bowed before Adam. Iblis thus became Satan, the adversary and tempter of human beings, and was cast from heaven.

Human beings are God's highest creation, endowed not only with knowledge but also with free choice to carry out the Trust (*amanah*) as deputies of God on the earth: "We did indeed offer the Trust to the heavens and the earth and the mountains, but they refused to undertake it, being afraid: but the human being undertook it; he was indeed unjust and foolish" (33:72). In addition to this Trust, humans are likewise bound by a primordial covenant, described in 7:172—

> "When your Lord took the progeny of the children of Adam from their loins, he made them bear witness concerning themselves, saying: 'Am I not your Lord?' They said: 'Yes indeed! We bear witness to it!—this, lest you should say on the Day of resurrection: 'We had not known it to be so,' or lest you should say: 'It was our ancestors who went after false gods, and we are only their descendants after them. Will you then destroy us for the deeds of those strangers to the truth?' "

Thus the Qur'an establishes the basic outlines of the essential nature of human beings. They are created in the image (or form) of God as both a microcosmic reflection of God's attributes and God's servants, entrusted with establishing a just order on the earth as God's vicegerents. God subjected all nature to the *khalifah* (14:32-34), and God will hold human beings accountable for their success or failure in this mission. In this struggle, however, God will measure out to each person and community the knowledge, guidance, and protection (*taqwa*, or "God-wariness") necessary for success. Human beings must recognize God through God's signs, respond to God's guidance, and follow God's commands to walk the "straight path", in order to fulfill their true nature as *muslim*. During regular daily *salat*, Muslims recite the *Fatiha* or "Opening" chapter of the Qur'an:

> In the name of God, the Compassionate, the Merciful
> Praise be to God, Lord of the universe,
> The Compassionate, the Merciful,
> Owner of the Day of judgment;
> You alone we serve,
> To you alone we come for help;
> Guide us in the straight path,
> The path of those upon whom your favor rests,
> Not of those who have earned your wrath,
> Nor of those who go astray.

As in Jewish and Christian tradition, the problem is that human beings do "go astray" from the path God has set out for them. The Qur'anic version of Adam's disobedience in the Garden, however, ends with Adam's repentance and God's forgiveness, after which God sends Adam and Eve "down" from the Garden (apparently located above) to the earth to be vicegerent, as God intended from the time of the human's creation. God then "chooses" Adam as the first prophet and protects him from further error. Contrary to the Christian "original sin" doctrine, such a "fall" provides a model for human repentance, divine forgiveness and guidance, rather than imputing a sinful nature to all subsequent humanity.

So human beings are born *muslim*; they inherit from Adam the primordial covenant and retain the divine *fitrah* or innate disposition; and God's measuring out of *taqwa* protects them. But the Qur'an repeatedly emphasizes that human beings are prone to disobey God's commands. They are "petty", "heedless", "ignorant", "weak", and "forgetful": "We had already made a covenant beforehand with Adam, but he forgot; and We did not find in him firm resolve" (20:115). Human beings fail to see God's signs, to recognize God's prophets, or to understand God's command. Rather, human beings see only what is in front of them, making gods out of elements of nature or their own "caprice". They live without regard to the transcendent Reality and without thought of the eternal consequences of their actions. As the proper relationship of human beings to God is one of gratitude and submission, the word for unbelief, *kufr*, means both "covering up" and "ingratitude" toward God. The unbelievers thus cover up the plain truth and ignore their debt to the sovereign source of all that is.

The Qur'an speaks both of human free will and God's "hardening" of the hearts of those who reject him. Though theological debates, mentioned above, have highlighted the extremes of human responsibility and divine sovereignty, the Qur'an seems to balance the roles, with God responding to human action: God "leads astray" those who have already left the path or denies guidance to "the unjust" (e.g., 2:26, 258; 3:86); while God guides those who turn to God and do what is beautiful and good (5:16; 42:13). "God will not change the way of a people until they change it themselves" (13:11). The Qur'anic vocabulary of "sin" refers to "disobedience", "mistake", "slip"; all refer to wrong activity, actions that deviate from the path of obedience known as *shari`ah*.

Human nature may become distorted almost beyond recognition. Human beings are accountable for the path they choose, and their choice and degree of God-wariness is evident in their deeds. The ultimate, unforgivable sin is idolatrous association of something with God (*shirk*), which means denying the truth about God *and* about oneself. The consequence of sin is that one forgets one's own self (59:19), becoming alienated not only from God but also from one's true nature, the *fitrah* with which each human being is endowed.

The remedy for forgetfulness is, of course, a reminder. The Qur'an calls itself a *dhikr*, a "reminder, remembrance" of God. The merciful God sends prophets, some with Books (Torah, Gospel, Qur'an), to the forgetful human race to remind them of their true nature and of the straight path that will allow them to fulfill their mission as God's vicegerents. The Prophet Muhammad is the Seal, the last of God's many messengers; and the Muslim *ummah* is called to spread news of God's guidance to the world. The Qur'an warns that every individual and community must take responsibility for the consequences of their own actions, and so Muslims reject the Christian idea that one person may "redeem" or bear punishment for another, or even intercede between a human being and God. Sincere repentance and an established pattern of good works remove the consequences of sins on the Day of Judgment.

Since a Muslim is one who declares the unity of God and recognizes the prophethood of Muhammad, the straight path is to obey the word of God and to follow the command and example of the Prophet. Surah 3:31-32 delineates the choice clearly: "Say: 'If you love God, follow me: God will love you and forgive you your sins; for God is ever forgiving, most merciful.' Say: 'Obey God and His messenger. If you turn away—God has no love for unbelievers'." The broad path of salvation is available to Muslims in the *shari`ah*. Submission to the will of God takes concrete form in the commands and prohibitions that regulate both divine-human and human-human relations.

The Sufi stream within Islam places particular emphasis on extending the *shari`ah* into the inner dimensions of one's life, designating the narrower path of spiritual development as *tariqah*. Using categories drawn from the Qur'an, Sufi writers speak of taming the *nafs* (self, soul), which is of course the "greater *jihad*". The first stage is the *nafs* "which commands to evil (12:53), the lower self or base instincts. With discipline, one develops a more active conscience, the "blaming" *nafs* (75:2). The highest level of purification is then the *nafs* "at peace" (89:27), which returns home to God. Sufi masters describe this discipline of the *nafs* in many different ways as a process involving both practices and spiritual gifts. It is the process by which *islam* (in the sense of right action) becomes *ihsan* (doing what is beautiful, assuming the qualities of God), and thus is the beginning of ethics. The way of salvation thus purifies the human self and restores it to right relation with God, both in this world and the next.

Lest we assume that the human self in Islam is merely concerned for individual salvation, however, we should remember that one of the profound results of living life in obedience to God and the Prophet is the creation of a new people, the Muslim *ummah*. Not only the individual Muslim, but also the *ummah*, is promised "success" in earthly existence and in the hereafter. Such earthly success includes physical, emotional, and spiritual security (*salam*, cf Heb. *shalom*), while Paradise is the final reward and goal.

Ethics and Judgment

As discussed above, the human being in Islamic perspective is entrusted with profound responsibility as God's vicegerent and servant. The *shari`ah* defines these responsibilities, and the five pillars represent merely the chief outward forms of submission or obedience to God. The true Muslim, however, is one whose submission to God's will arises from a realization of one's inward nature; the Qur'an speaks of "true religion" as living according to the "patterns by which God has created humankind" (30:30). In the hadith of Gabriel, the Prophet Muhammad also defines *ihsan*: "Doing what is beautiful means that you should worship God as if you see Him, for even if you do not see Him, He sees you."[3] God judges human beings for what they do but also for what is in their hearts (5:7; 29:10; 33:51), and God loves specifically those who "do what is beautiful" (2:195; 5:13). Though Sufi writers developed most fully the notion of *ihsan* ("doing what is good, beautiful") as "qualifying oneself with the qualities of God", all Islamic discussions of ethics focus on the relationship between right action and this deeper level of human character, intentionality.

The five pillars, though primarily outward obligations toward God, have an inward and ethical dimension. The Pakistani revivalist, Abu A`la Mawdudi (d. 1979), speaks of the five pillars as "a course of training" that allows the Muslim to harmonize ideals (e.g., *tauhid*) and practices. For instance, the regular prayer renews the covenant with God, keeps life's object and mission focused, and creates a bond of love, unity, and equality among Muslims. Fasting develops patience and self-control, while almsgiving curbs selfishness and promotes sacrifice while providing for the needs of the poor. The hajj concentrates consciousness of God and affirms the unity and solidarity of Muslims. These acts of worship thus internalize the values and principles of the *shari`ah*, the central code of conduct for Muslims.[4]

The concept of "doing what is beautiful" involves an integration of right action, thought and intentions. The development of *ikhlas* (sincerity, pure intention) focuses one's intention on God alone and away from the fulfillment of personal desires or pleasing others. The cultivation of *taqwa* (god-wariness) means protecting oneself from dangerous temptations and taking moral responsibility in view of God's reward and punishment. The perfection of character traits (*ikhlaq*) involves, for the Muslim, conforming to the model of the Prophet Muhammad. Especially in Sufi circles, he became known as the Perfect Man.

Medieval Islamic education extended beyond knowledge of the rules of *shari`ah* to the cultivation of *adab* (manners). Works on *adab* in classical Islam included not only customary hospitality toward strangers but spiritual discipline, knowledge of poetry, and activities appropriate to professions and behavior in public and private spaces, all deriving from the example of the Prophet. Sufi poets speak of the Muslim following the beautiful example of the Prophet in order to prune and polish the soul, that the latent divine qualities might manifest themselves from the inside out. The polished soul then produces acts of humility, compassion, generosity, love, and fairness.

Far from being a guide merely for individual ethics, the aim of the shari`ah is to establish a just social order. The Qur'an speaks of the Muslim community as one that "enjoins the good and forbids what is evil" (3:104, 110; 9:7 1). The Qur'anic message condemns competition over wealth and the neglect of the poor, prohibits usurious lending and fraudulent contracts, establishes property and inheritance rights for women and men, mandates dispute arbitration, sets rules for the just use of force, and prohibits the exploitation of weaker members of society (e.g., encouraging the care of widows and orphans, and the principle of "no compulsion in religion", 2:256). The scholars of *fiqh* developed over the centuries a variety of social structures and institutions to apply these commands and prohibitions in new situations.

Classical scholars divided the world into two realms or "abodes": *dar al-Islam* ("the abode of Islam") and *dar al-harb* ("the abode of war"). The abode of Islam, for most Sunni scholars, was a political entity in which Islamic values are supreme. The knowledgeable Muslim ruler can judge effectively on the basis of Qur'an and hadith, he consults with religious scholars (ulama) on policy matters, and he does not command anything opposed to Islamic values.[5] While realistic about the ways in which actual Muslim rulers have fallen short of such ideals, many Muslims today feel that the formation of an Islamic state is the only way to guarantee lasting peace with justice. The wide variety of movements today indicates considerable debate about the actual form of such a state and the means by which it might be achieved.

Ultimately, living one's life as if one sees God means living life, individually and socially, in view of the next life. All human beings return to God for judgment. On the Last Day, God will raise the dead, weigh their individual deeds and judge them according to the revelations given their communities, resolve their disputes, and determine their final destiny. Those who are near to God—sincere in their worship, god-wary in their moral responsibility, acting with wholesome intent, enjoining on others what is good and beautiful—will enjoy God's love and mercy and enter Paradise. On the other hand, those who are hypocrites—"gone astray", forgetting God, choosing ignorance, practicing corruption—will feel God's wrath, judgment, and enter the Fire. The Qur'an describes Paradise in rich imagery of gardens, clear flowing rivers, plentiful fruit and beautiful maidens, culminating in the vision of God. Images of hell speak of fire and molten metal, physical torment, anguish and spiritual separation from God.

Aesthetics

The prophetic message of divine unity invites human beings not only to realize the goodness of God in their activity and moral character, but also to realize beauty in the realm of forms. Since the primary form of God's communication with humanity is the revealed Word, the arts of Islamic civilizations developed out of attempts to "beautify" the recitation, writing, and ritual use of the Qur'an. The Prophet's prohibition of representational images to avoid idolatry may seem a limitation, but it has produced arts of recited poetry and music, calligraphy, and mosque architecture that express the central Islamic notion of *tauhid*, and the balance and harmony of the divine order in the world.

The beautiful speech of Qur'anic recitation flows from the intersection of Arabic, Persian, and South Asian cultures of reciting poetry with the beautiful word that represents God's manifest presence among believers. The Qur'an is first and foremost a "recitation", and Muslims have developed rich and intricate rules for the impeccable pronunciation of each consonant and vowel, the articulation of phrases, the modulation of the voice unaccompanied to convey the word. The trained Qur'an reciter at a festival, a funeral service, or in the local mosque, invites devotional participation in the event of revelation and invites the listener to comprehend the message on a level deeper than the language of intellect. The rhythmic sound, harmony and balance of Qur'an recitation extend further into the highly nuanced sound of classical Arabic and Persian as well as vernacular poetry accompanied by musicians of the caliphal court, the Sufi *dhikr* ceremony, or the roadside singer.

Perhaps the most well known form of Islamic art is calligraphy. Muslim calligraphers have for many centuries elaborated the Arabic script of the Qur'an in linear, interlocked, and flowing patterns to invite imaginative reflection on the symbolic textures of the divine word. The simple or intricate patterns, many of which are difficult to read even for educated Arabs, embellish the lamps and furnishings, niches, doorways, and ceilings of Muslim homes, public buildings, and places of worship as a reminder of God's speech in the world. Abstract calligraphic patterns blend together with the winding, curving arabesques to convey a sense of growth and change, while linear, geometric shapes lend a sense of order and stability to the art and architecture of Islam.

The beautiful recitation and the beautiful visual forms demand a beautiful space for the seeing and hearing of the divine word. While any clean area on earth may be a *masjid* (place of prostration for prayer), richly variegated mosque architecture developed in various regions of the Muslim world by incorporating some basic features into increasingly elaborate local architectural forms. Most mosques have a small niche, the *mihrab*, in the wall facing Mecca to mark the *qiblah* (direction of prayer); an ablution (*wudu`*) area; a *minbar* or raised pulpit for the Friday sermon; and some type of tower or *minaret* from which the call to prayer is issued. The physical forms of these basic features vary widely. From the square arches and courtyard of the prophet Muhammad's house in Medina to the great mosque in Cordoba; to the blue-tiled honeycombed archways around a Persian-style courtyard in Isfahan; to the large Ottoman-style domes flanked by thin minarets in Istanbul or Cairo; to the elaborate mud-and-beam structures of West Africa, mosques exhibit the ideals of beautiful symmetry, and open, intentionally ordered space. Great tombs and shrines, as well as palaces and public buildings, demonstrate the immense flexibility of Muslim expressions of unity and beauty.

Islamic visual arts also include an immense variety of other forms. In decorative art on pottery, carpets, and household items displayed privately, especially among the aristocracy, representational human and animal forms mingle with vegetal and geometric patterns. Persian miniature paintings in illuminated manuscripts flourished after 1300 in lands under the rule of the Mongols and their successors. Though calligraphy and Qur'anic recitation, the "arts" of the word, remain the preeminent vehicles for manifesting the fundamental truth of divine unity, Muslims have recognized a variety of formal expressions of the divine attribute of beauty in the lived environment.

Extracts on Predestination and Free Will

Qur'an

"God does not disdain to make comparison with a gnat or with a larger creature. The faithful know that it is the truth from their Lord, but the unbelievers ask: 'What could God mean by this comparison? By such comparisons God confounds many and enlightens many. But He confounds non except the evil-doers, who break His covenant after accepting it, and put asunder what He has bidden to be united, and perpetrate corruption in the land. These will surely be the losers." (2:26, tr. N.J. Dawood)

"Such is God's guidance; He bestows it on those of His servants whom He chooses. Had they served other gods besides him, their labours would have been vain indeed" (6:88, tr. Dawood)

"He knows the unknown and the manifest. He is the Supreme One, the Most High. It is the same whether you converse in secret or aloud, whether you hide under the cloak of night or walk about in the light of day. Each has guardian angels before him and behind him, who watch him by God's command. God does not change a people's lot unless they change what is in their hearts. If God seeks to afflict them with a misfortune, none can ward it off. Besides Him, they have no protector. . . . The unbelievers ask: 'Why has no sign been sent down to him by his Lord?' Say: 'God leaves in error whom He will, and guides to Himself those who repent and have faith; whose hearts find comfort in the remembrance of God. Surely in the remembrance of God all hearts are comforted." (13:9-11, 27-8, tr. Dawood)

"Is he whose foul deeds seem fair to him [like the man who is rightly guided]? God leaves in error whom He will and guides whom He pleases. Do not destroy yourself with grief on their account: God has knowledge of all their actions." (35:8, tr. Dawood)

Theologians

Baghdadi Shi`i theologian al-Sharif al-Murtada (d. 1044):

"The following answer may be given to one who asks, 'Do you say that good and evil both come from God Most High?'

If you mean that God is the source of well-being and affliction, of poverty and riches, of health and sickness, of fertility and barrenness, of hardship and ease, then it is granted that all of this comes from God. The misfortunes of life are called evil, whereas in reality they are wise, reasonable, true and just.

But if you mean that God is the source of immorality, depravity, lying, deceit, oppression, unbelief, crime and shameful deeds, then God forbid that we should say that. Rather, oppression comes from oppressors, and lying from liars, immorality from immoral people, and polytheism from polytheists. Justice and equitable dealings issue from the Lord of the Worlds."[6]

Iranian Shi`i scholar `Aflamah Sayyid Muhammad Husayn Tabataba'i on free will and predestination:

"The necessity of the action in relation to all of the parts of the complete cause is not contradictory to the possibility of the relation of the action with respect to man, who is one of the parts of the complete cause. Man has the possibility of free will (ikhtiyar) to perform the act. The necessity existing in the relation between the action and all of the parts of the cause does not mean that the relation of the action to some of the parts of the cause, of which man is one, should also be that of necessity and determinism. . . . ". . . according to the instruction of the Household of the Prophet, which is also in conformity with the literal instructions of the Qur'an, man is free (mukhtar) in his actions but not independent (mustaqill). Rather, God the Almighty through his free will has willed the act. According to our previous analysis, God the Exalted has willed and made necessary the act through all of the parts of the complete cause, of which one is the will and free choice of man. As a result of this kind of Divine will, the action is necessary but in it man has also free will, that is, the action is necessary with respect to all the parts of its cause, and possible and free in choice with respect to one of those parts which is man. The sixth Imam—upon whom be peace—has said, 'It is neither determination nor free will but something between the two.' "[7]

Abu al-Hasan al-Ash`ari (d. 935) on acquisition of acts:

"*Question*: Why do you assert that the acquisition of God's servants are created by Him?
Answer: Because God has said: 'God has created you and what you make' [Qur'an 37:96].

The rational indication for the [divine] creation of people's acts is that we find that rejection [kufr] is repugnant, wrong, vain, inconsistent, and contrary, while faith is good, troublesome, and painful. If the matter is thus, rejection must have a producer who produces it intentionally as rejection, vain and repugnant. Its producer could never be the unbeliever, who desires that rejection be good, right, and reality, when it is the contrary of that. Similarly faith must have a producer who produces it as it really is, troublesome, painful, and vexatious, who is other than he person of faith, who, though he or she strives that faith be the contrary of its actual pain, trouble, and vexatiousness, has no way to effect it. So if the one who produces rejection as it really is cannot be the unbeliever, and the one who produces faith as it really is cannot be the faithful, then the intentional produces of both must be God Most High, Lord of the Worlds. For no body could produce these, since bodies can effect nothing in things distinct from themselves."[8]

From the school of Abu Mansur al-Maturidi (d. 944), Sunni theologian and Hanafi jurist:

"The sins of humankind occur by God's wish [irada], will [mashi`a], ordaining [qada'], and power [qadr], but not by His good pleasure [rida], love [mahabba], and command [amr], according to His World, 'One whom God wills to send astray, He makes the bosom close and narrow' [6:125], and His Word, 'You wish nothing, unless God wishes it' [76:3 1]. If the creature were able to act by its own will, then it could prevail over the will of God, be He exalted. The Mu`tazila have held that God does not will to prevail over Humankind, according to His word, 'I have only created humans and Jinn that they might serve Me' [51:57]: meaning 'I have not created them to reject Me,' so that He does not will it. We reply, the meaning is: 'He orders them to serve Him,' and He has so ordered. The meaning is not: 'God does not will injustice to His servants' [40:3 1]. That is true, but this is not the context, and it does not apply here, nor does their saying that in causing sin God is doing what He Himself reproves: acting lightly. We say to this that it would only be fight behavior if there occurred no proof that God is free of that. Also their statement that if God wills sin people are compelled to commit it does not apply. Just as humankind cannot escape God's will, it cannot escape God's omniscience, and it constitutes no excuse for sin. If they ask, 'What does it mean then when God says, 'Whatever of ill befalls you is from yourself [4:73]?' We reply: it means that evil cannot be attributed to God outrightly, for considerations of decency, just as one cannot invoke Him as 'Creator of swine!' but must be attributed to him in a more general way, as He says, 'Say, all comes from God' [4:78].

"God created rejection and willed that it should exist, but He did not order people to commit it; rather, He ordered the rejected to have faith, but He did not will that one must do it. If anyone asks, 'Is God's will pleasing to Him or not?' we say, it is pleasing. If they then ask, 'And why should He punish what pleases Him?' we reply: He punishes what is *not* pleasing. For His will and His providence, and all His attributes are pleasing to Him, but the act of the rejecter is *not* pleasing to Him. It is hateful to Him, and it is punished by Him."[9]

Bibliography

Esposito, J. L. (1998). *Islam: the straight path.* 3d ed. New York, Oxford University Press.

Murata, Sachiko and William C. Chittick, *The Vision of Islam* (New York: Paragon House, 1994).

Endnotes

[1]Quoted in John Alden Williams, ed., *The Word of Islam* (Austin: University of Texas, 1994), p. 171.

[2]Quoted in Sachiko Murata and William C. Chittick, *The Vision of Islam* (New York: Paragon House, 1994), p. xxv.

[3]Chittick, p. xxv.

[4]Abu A`la Mawdudi, *Towards Understanding Islam* (Lahore: Idara Tarjuman-ul-Qur'an, 1988), 87-94.

[5]John Kelsay, *Islam and War: A Study in Comparative Ethics* (Louisville: Westminster/John Knox, 1993), 33-4.

[6]Al-Sharif Al-Murtada, *Inqadh Al-Bashar min Al-Jabr wa-l-Qadar (The Deliverance of Mankind from Predestination and Fate),* translated and quoted in K. Cragg, and M. Speight, *Islam from within: anthology of a religion* (Belmont, CA: Wadsworth, 1980), p. 128.

[7]A. S. M. H. Tabataba`i,), *Shi`ite Islam* (Albany: State University of New York Press, 1977), pp. 134-5.

[8]From Ash`ari's Kitab al-Luma', translated and quoted in J. A. Williams, *The word of Islam* (Austin: University of Texas Press, 1994), p. 152.

[9]Quoted in J. A. Williams, *The word of Islam* (Austin: University of Texas Press, 1994), pp. 147-8.

THE SELF IN RELATION TO ULTIMATE REALITY: HINDUISM & BUDDHISM

HINDUISM

by Tim Lubin

The Religions of South Asia

The Indian subcontinent has had an enormous impact on world religious history, an impact that reaches far beyond its own borders. Besides being home to Hinduism, it was the birthplace not only of numerically small traditions like those of the Sikhs and the Jains, it also provided a haven for Zoroastrians (known in India as Parsis) fleeing religious persecution in Persia. Christians (2½% of Indians today) lay claim to a history of more than a millennium and a half in India. Muslims began arriving— as conquerors, merchants, and preachers—a thousand years ago. With the decline of the Persian empire, India under the Mughals for a time became a world center of Islamic culture. Muslims now make up 14% of the population of independent India, and around 30% of South Asians as a whole. It is natural that the Hindu tradition bears the imprint of its interactions with these religions over the centuries.

Hinduism itself is difficult to quantify, because it is not clear what this label should cover. The name "Hindu" has been applied since antiquity by outsiders, and was in essence a geographical marker applied initially to those who live near (and later beyond) the Sindhu (= Persian Hind, Latin Indus) and thus was like saying "Indian." Other indigenous traditions were (and still are) identified by reference to legendary teachers: followers of the Buddha ("Enlightened One") were called Bauddhas (Buddhists); those of the Jinas ("Conquerors [of the passions]") were the Jainas. But there was no one, agreed-upon teacher who was recognized as central among the people known today as Hindus. When we use the term "Hindu" we generally mean all South Asians who do not belong to one of the other religions mentioned above. This includes a cluster of traditions with long histories and classical sacred texts as well as traditions of regional or even local character that are preserved in customary practices and oral lore. As diverse as these can appear—innumerable deities with different names, distinctive modes of worship, village legends, street theater, and bardic poetry—there are some unifying factors that can be identified. We can trace the development of these ideas far back through 3000 years of Sanskrit literature.

The Religion of the Veda

The vast majority of religious texts that have been preserved from ancient and classical India are the work of an elite caste of priests and scholars who called themselves brahmins (*brahmanas*), a label that points to their supposedly innate connection with a mysterious principle called *brahman*. In by far the oldest works, the hymns collected in the *Rig Veda* (ca. 1200 BCE), the word *brahman* often means the verses themselves, but over time it comes to denote the power of the well-turned word, a power only the inspired poet-sage (*rishi*, *vipra*) is able to tap. Most of the 1028 hymns of the *Rig Veda* praise or beseech a range of loosely personified divine powers who presided over various natural phenomena and spheres of life, as well as over human beings. The warlike Indra, wielder of the lightning-bolt, is said to have defeated the serpent Vritra, who had imprisoned the waters in a mountain cave. Thus the waters were released to make the earth fruitful, an event reenacted every time the monsoon rains arrive. Indra's heroism was the model for the Vedic warrior, who mimicked him in partaking of the invigorating nectar of the Soma plant, which itself was treated as a god.

What we might call Vedic ethics was the province of Varuna and the other Adityas. They not only ordained the structure of the universe and of society, but supervised human conduct and punished people for misdeeds. The sun, as the eye of Varuna and Mitra, "observes all beings, and perceives the thought among mortals" (*RV* 7.61.1); they know all secrets and punish falsehood (*anrita*). Each individual stands subject to the will of the gods, which takes the form of ordinances (*vratas, dhamans*); those who wish to please the gods strive to live in accordance with these rules. Divine favor takes the form of concrete blessings (*svasti*) such as long life, health, burgeoning herds, fruitful crops, and male offspring. Material prosperity is seen as confirmation of the gods' approval. Although in succeeding ages many aspects of Vedic piety were to be displaced or overlaid by other sets of ideas and practices, this sense that moral and ritual scrupulousness is naturally rewarded with material success remains a prominent part of the ethos of the Indian man-in-the-world.

The Vedic hymns were compiled for use in complex worship rites called *yajna*, in which individual verses or entire litanies were made to coincide with libations of melted butter, Soma juice, and various other food offerings deposited in an array of ritual fires. Agni, the god who manifests himself in the fires, was said to convey these offerings to the other gods, who were invisibly present. Agni was said to be present "in the three worlds" (earth, heaven, and the space in between), to be ever-young because reborn at every kindling. He is divine priest, model for the ritualist, overseer of men's adherence to the rules (*vratas*) of ritual piety. When an observant sacrificer died, Agni was invoked as the cremation fire to carry him to the "world of the fathers" presided over by Yama. Yama's world was envisioned sometimes as a southern or underground palace, sometimes as a realm at the base of heaven; either way, the departed was said to live there in comfort, as in a sort of retirement community, enjoying the merit which he had stored up during a pious life, and receiving periodic offerings from his dutiful male descendants.

Common Assumptions of Classical Hinduism

The Vedic culture was carried throughout the region over the centuries by its brahmin exponents, but the old mythology and sacrificial system gradually gave way to the constellation of ideas and practices that have come to be distinctive of South Asian religiosity. With a very few exceptions, all of the traditions that have arisen since late Vedic times accept as axiomatic the idea that each individual is animated by an immortal soul (*atman*, 'self'), which takes birth repeatedly in different bodies. The various possible births (human in various rankings, but also as animals, denizens of hells and heavens, and even gods) are the natural result of the operation of *karma*, which is at once action and its residual effects on a person: a preponderance of good deeds leads to a better birth; bad deeds lead to a worse one. This basic "law of *karma*" is the primary Indian explanation for the often seemingly unjust distribution of fortune and misfortune in the world (although Hindus in some contexts will have recourse to the concepts of fate, divine dispensation, or simple luck). *Samsara*, the cycle of deaths and rebirths, provides the basic problem of the human condition. Once born, all beings are subject to emotional attachments and cravings arising from the embodied condition. There has been a very strong tendency to view *samsara*—by which is meant all of worldly life—as a source of unavoidable unhappiness (*duhkha*). This can be avoided only by systematically cultivating an attitude of detachment to things of this world, which is said to lead, if pursued fully, to a state of freedom from desires and aversions that is called *moksha* (liberation) or *nirvana* (extinguishing [of desire]).[1]

So far as the precise mechanics of the operation of *karma* and the means to religious attainment are concerned, a number of doctrinal systems have offered various explanations. These systems differ in how they answer the following questions: What is the nature of the world of experience, and how does it impinge on the soul? What is the relationship between the soul and the deity? What are the appropriate aims of life? How should one live if one is to attain those aims? Here we can consider only a few of the most prominent examples.

The Upanishads

Although the success to which the ancient Vedic sacrificer aspired was one of earthly prosperity followed by heavenly rewards, the *brahmana* literature that arose to expound the inner meaning of Vedic worship developed a mystical dimension represented by the *Upanishads*. Although referred to collectively by this title, which denotes "secret teachings," these were short works originally appended to the separate canons of the various Vedic lineages, and only later compiled together; they include anecdotes, didactic dialogues, symbolic accounts of creation and divine powers, and a body of versified "wisdom literature." Hence, the *Upanishads* do not have a single doctrine to convey, but rather offer a series of individual reflections on the nature of the "self" (atman), the divine reality, the mechanics of consciousness, and the aims of human life. Nevertheless, they have long been regarded as embodying the "ultimate degree of wisdom" (*vedanta*), that is, the essence of the Veda, and many of the great figures of Brahmanical thought took them as an indispensable point of reference and source of authority.

The Upanishads often take the form of parables and didactic dialogues between famous sages and those who put questions to them; others presented maxims in verse. What distinguished them from the earlier Vedic literature is that the Vedic rites become just a starting point for reflections directly on the nature of the world and of individual existence in it. While the subject necessarily leads beyond the realm of what can be directly perceived, the method of argument is to begin from what is known from the testimony of the senses—the outward characteristics of the world and the human person—and to extrapolate by means of analogy and inference to postulate the hidden order behind all things, and the existence of a changeless essence behind the apparent plurality and mutability of the world.

The *Mundaka Upanishad* begins by distinguishing a lower from a higher wisdom. The lower wisdom turns out to include not only the main texts of the Vedas but all the spheres of earthly knowledge, including grammar, prosody, astronomy, and so forth. The higher wisdom is defined simply as "that by which one grasps the imperishable." Over and over, the *Upanishads* approach this subject from many angles, striving to indicate through words what they themselves assert to be inconceivable and inexpressible: the true nature of the self or the true nature of a universal essence simply called *brahman*, which are directly equated on many occasions. *Brahman* in the *Rig Veda* denoted the words of an inspired poet-sage, and later, the same words treated as revelation; in the Upanishads, *brahman* is nothing less than the single, invisible, eternal basis of everything in the visible world. While it is recognized that *brahman* cannot be grasped directly by the senses or the mind, it is assumed that a direct awareness of it can be provoked through the roundabout method of progressive approximation and the use of multiple analogies from everyday life: *brahman* is the salt that pervades salt water, the tiny germ within the seed from which the tree grows, the loom on which the world is woven, the thread on which things are strung together as so many pearls. Just as it is the basis of everything "out there," it is also the basis of each individual. So Uddalaka Aruni, giving his son Svetaketu one illustration after another of *brahman's* hidden presence in the empirical world, concludes each time: "You are that," (*tat tvam asi*, in Sanskrit).

The *Upanishads* in places also personify this universal essence, giving it a number of names. First the grammatically neuter word *brahman* is treated as a masculine name, Brahma, also called Prajapati (Lord of Creatures), is presented as the father of the gods themselves, who are thus demoted to the status of mere celestial creatures. The positing of a supreme deity beyond the Vedic gods honored in the sacrificial service (Indra, Agni, Soma, et al.) begins with a doubt voiced repeatedly in a hymn of the *Rig Veda* (10.121): "Who (*ka*) is the god we should worship with our offering?" In the final stanza, the poet answers himself by invoking Prajapati, and ever after, Ka has been one of his names. In the *Isha Upanishad*, he is addressed as *ish* (Lord). The *Shvetashvatara Upanishad* calls him Rudra, the awesome archer of the mountains who is approached as Shiva, "the benign"; this Upanishad identifies him with the Purusha of *RV* 10.90 and with Agni, the god of the ritual fire. This Self (*atman*), in turn, is personified as the "thumb-sized person in the heart" and the "inner controller." In other cases, the vital airs (*prana*) or faculties (*indriya*) are venerated as divinities, and are said to compete with each other to prove who is the most important, with a form of breath prevailing.

The *Upanishads* emphasize the importance of attaining insight (*jnana* or *vijnana*) into the nature of *brahman* and the *atman* (which ultimately seems to amount to the same thing). The frequent use of paradox and negative characterizations (*brahman* is "not this, not that") indicates that conventional modes of thought are inadequate. Moreover, the identity of *atman* and *brahman* implies a parallelism between the cosmos and the person as microcosm, which the earlier Upanishads spend much time demonstrating; indeed this provides palpable evidence for the essential link between these two spheres, which is not graspable directly. These texts insist that the rewards of Vedic ritual performance accrue only to "him who knows this" (*ya evam_veda*). The later Upanishads go so far as to dismiss actual ritual practice and material aims as superfluous; insight alone, perhaps together with recitation of the Vedic mantras or minimal rites, is all that is necessary to enjoy true immortal bliss.

There are some scattered remarks of an ethical nature. "The good and the pleasant come before man; the wise man reflects and chooses between them; for the wise man prefers the good to the pleasant, while the stupid man chooses the pleasant over exertion and rest" (*Katha Upanishad* 1.2.2). The precocious boy Nachiketas and Yajnavalkya's reflective wife Maitreyi turn down material gifts to press for the wisdom by which one passes beyond death. The virtues of truthfulness, generosity, and faith are praised repeatedly. When Satyakama ("He who desires truth") is asked his family background by a potential teacher (who will only accept those of high birth), he admits that his father is unknown; his truthfulness is taken as sufficient proof of true brahminhood (*Chandogya Up.* 4.4.1 5). We also can find allusions to a sort of judicial law. A man wrongly accused of theft, when tried by the ordeal of grasping a red-hot axe blade, "covers himself with truth" and thereby is not burnt (*Chandogya Up.* 6.16.1 2). Elsewhere, *dharma* is praised as "that by means of which the weaker man prevails over the stronger."

It is only in these late Vedic texts that the idea of rebirth and the decisive role of all kinds of action (*karma*) appear in the Brahmanical literature. As the genre develops there is a trend toward rejecting worldly pleasures and material aspirations in favor of cultivating dispassion and self-control. Later Brahmanical tradition will view the Upanishads as the *jnana*-oriented perspective superseding the more limited *karma*-oriented portions of the Veda; the contrast comes to be embodied in the world-renouncing ascetic (the sannyasi), who abandons the short-sighted and undisciplined life of the householder.

Aside from guided reflection on the nature of the self and the world, a method of self-cultivation is also proposed. *Yoga* literally means "yoking" or "harnessing" in the sense of bringing something under control for a useful purpose. While it earlier denoted the activities of Vedic adventurers seeking wealth and glory, in the *Upanishads* the word refers to some sort of inward undertaking, a spiritual exercise aimed at harnessing the mind and subduing the senses. The clearest description comes in the *Katha Upanishad*, where it involves control of breathing and sense faculties, and mental focus.

Patanjali's Yoga System

Sometime in the early centuries of the Common Era, the *yoga* ideal received a definitive treatment that would be a point of reference for many later teachers. The *Yoga Sutra* (1.2) begins by defining *yoga* as "the suppression of thought-activity," as a result of which the soul's true nature is no longer obscured by mental and physical distractions. This Yoga system built upon the cosmological theory of the Samkhya school, according to which the world arises out of a primordial essence, *prakriti*, which, though dimensionless and undifferentiated to begin with, evolves first into consciousness (*buddhi*) and eventually into mind, the five senses, and at last the concrete objects of sense, that is, the elements of the empirical world. Note that all the mental faculties are conceived of as having nothing to do with the soul (*purusha*), which stands aloof from this evolutionary process and is unaffected by it. The aim of the Samkhya was to extricate the spirit from the material world by arousing a correct knowledge of *prakriti* in all its forms. Patanjali's Yoga introduces a new element, which might be called God, which the Samkhya does not recognize. The *Yoga Sutra* defines "the Lord" (*ishvara*) as "a special soul" that has never been affected by *karma* or its results, nor by the afflictions of ignorance, egoism, longing, aversion, and craving for existence (*YS* 1.24, 2.3). This Lord was the "teacher of the ancients," and dedication to him is a part of the yogic method (*YS* 2.1, 2.32, 2.45).

As in the Samkhya, the focus is on the mental dimensions of experience, and the overcoming of the material world's detrimental effects is to be accomplished ultimately by gaining control over and modifying the processes of thought. This same insistence on the role of cognition and thought in making human beings who they are, and the corresponding emphasis on reforming these processes in order to overcome human misery and limitation, is found in Buddhist thought as well, especially in meditation-oriented schools such as the Yogachara.

Moral perfection is seen not as the aim of *yoga* practice, but as its prerequisite. The objective is liberation of the spirit through absolute mental self-control, but such control could not be possible without discipline of the body and its behavior. The entire regimen is divided into eight stages (*YS* 2.29 3.7). The first calls for five restrictions (*yamas*: abstinence from causing harm, lying, stealing, sexual activity, and possessions), which when observed in all contexts is deemed "the great rule."[3] Next, there are five positive moral prescriptions (*niyamas*: purity of body and mind, contentment, ascetic fervor, recitation of holy texts, and devotion to the Lord). When this moral discipline has been established, one can turn to preparing the body for meditation: by adopting a stable, relaxed posture (*asana*) that will not call attention to the body, by regulating and gradually attenuating the breathing (*pranayama*), and by withdrawing the senses from the outer domains (*pratyahara*). One who can do this is ready for the last three steps, which confer total self-control (*samyama*): focusing the mind on one point (*dharana*), holding it steady from one moment to the next (*dhyana*), and thus entering into a state of concentration (*samadhi*) devoid of any discursive thinking. This exquisite state is by definition inconceivable, but in it the soul is able to "assume its own form" rather than being shaped by thoughts based on experience of the material world (*YS* 1.3 4). This spiritual independence (*kaivalya*) is beyond the sphere of social values, but presupposes that the yogi has overcome all base (this-worldly) impulses and passions. But as a fundamentally ascetic exercise, it poses a challenge to the values of worldly life.

The Dharmashastra

From the time of the Upanishads, many of the religious movements that arose in India—including Patanjali's Yoga, but also Buddhism, Jainism, and many Brahmanical groups—were conceived and developed by ascetics. Yet this tendency was at odds with the world-affirming spirit of Vedism, as it would later clash with the *bhakti* sensibility. During the last few centuries BCE, the expanding brahmin community sought to establish a consistent set of standards of religious practice in a series of codes called *sutras* and *shastras*. At first these focused on the mechanics of ritual observance, but they became broader and broader in scope until they were defining general principles of *dharma*, the ideal of upright conduct and proper social roles, which was meant to cover every aspect of life. The righteous life was essentially that of the married householder, who had completed a period of Veda study with a teacher in youth, and who had then consecrated himself to fulfilling his debts (*rina*) of offerings to the gods, Veda-recitation to the Sages, and sons to the ancestors. The authorities on *dharma* were hesitant to recognize ascetic ways of life as fully legitimate alternatives to the life of the householder (*grihastha*), but eventually the paths of the perpetual student (a celibate who lives in the service of a teacher), the hermit, and the wandering mendicant were accepted as occupations (*ashramas*) compatible with *dharma*.

There remained a tension, though. *Moksha*, the aim of the professional ascetic, seemed the inverse of a householder's aspiration to live the good life, seeking wealth and long life, begetting children, and hoping for a pleasant situation in the next life (whether in heaven, or in a higher rebirth). A solution to this dilemma was finally found with the compilation of the *Manava Dharma Shastra*, or "Laws of Manu" (ca. 2nd c. BCE). This massive code presented the *ashramas* not as alternate choices for the young man finishing his studies, but as stages of life incumbent (in theory) upon all males of the three higher classes (brahmin, kshatriya, and vaishya). Celibate studentship (*brahmacharya*, lit. pursuit of *brahman*) was prescribed for youth, beginning with the initiation that served as the second birth for members of these "twice-born" classes. The prime of life, beginning with the marriage, was to be devoted to worldly ventures and the paying of the "debts." This is the time when one may properly pursue the first three "human aims" (*purusha-arthas*): *dharma* (what is right), *artha* (what is profitable), and *k__ma* (what gratifies the desire for pleasure), the last two insofar as they do not violate *dharma*. Then, when one has become a grandfather, he should retire to the forest to live simply and soberly, disciplining body and mind with austere regimens. The final stage comes late in life, when the ritual fires are symbolically internalized, home is abandoned for good, and all ties of kinship broken, so that true desirelessness and escape from the round of births—*moksha*, the final and highest human aim—can be attained.

Together with elaborate rules about the separateness and proper behavior of castes, this " *dharma* of classes and life-stages" (*varna-ashrama-dharma*) was meant to preserve a harmonious and balanced society to mirror the divine order of the natural world. The *Manava* code presents itself as of divine authorship; it commences with an account of the creation of the world (including the disposition of society into four classes with divinely ordained functions), and of the transmission of the text. The second chapter broaches the question, How is *dharma* to be ascertained? The formula proposed is a sequence of authorities, of descending weight: the Vedic texts are the first recourse, for they embody *shruti*, divine wisdom that is still to be heard recited verbatim by learned brahmins; where this leaves some doubt, one may turn to the *smriti*, the classic works of human authorship that are based on authentic Vedic wisdom (the epics and the Dharmashastra itself are generally placed in this category). Beyond this, the conduct of good people may be taken as a model. Otherwise, one should do "what is satisfactory to oneself," that is, rely on one's conscience. Thus, textual authority is paramount, but conventional standards and even individual judgment are sanctioned insofar as people of good faith are presumed to be able to recognize what is *dharma*.

Many of Manu's prescriptions, especially those on the sequence of *ashramas*, were abstract ideals that must rarely have been lived out in practice. But it did provide a rational basis for reconciling, or at least accommodating, the contrasting values of the householder and the ascetic. Yet there are respects in which the tension between the two ideals remains unresolved. At the start of the second chapter, Manu declares that there can be no action with *kama*, desire. From the Vedic householder s point of view there is no problem with this: desire is both natural and necessary. But the ascetic sees desire as the source of all suffering, and seeks to extinguish it altogether, or anyway to desire only *moksha*, which is the end of all desires. So Manu is left in a quandary. By and large, married life is praised as the most important of the *ashramas*, and is the one in which *artha* and *kama* may legitimately be pursued. Yet Manu constantly warns the householder to suppress desire, avoid passion, and seek equanimity, and *kama* come in for much more blame than praise. One comes away with the sense that the fulfillment of desires is virtually a duty of the householder's *ashrama*, pleasant though it may be, and all men are ultimately advised to renounce such pleasures in later life as an impediment to spiritual self-realization.

The Bhagavad Gita

One other solution was found to this dilemma, around the same time. The mammoth Sanskrit epic poem, the *Mahabharata*, took shape over some centuries around the beginning of the Common Era. It tells the story of a conflict between two sets of cousins over the succession to the Kuru throne. The story celebrates the values of a warrior culture (which are not much different from the ethos of early Vedism), but it is also permeated with Brahmanical priestly lore. From the point of view of ethics, the overriding theme in the epic is the complexity and ambiguity of *dharma*: how can one know what is ultimately right in a messy world? All the characters in the story have strengths and failings, and none—including the Pandava brothers, the ostensible heroes—is devoid of faults. Again and again in the story, evil comes when good sense is overcome by greed, anger, pride, or fear. When battle is imminent, and brave Arjuna stands on his chariot with his friend and advisor Krishna at the reins, he despairs as he sees he will be fighting elders of his own family and former teachers—people to whom he should show honor and respect. True, his enemies have overturned *dharma* by cheating the Pandavas of their rightful throne and by ruling unjustly, and it is Arjuna's own duty (*sva-dharma*) as a kshatriya (warrior-prince) to fight. Yet he feels that no good can come of such a war, that the glory he would win would be hollow, the spoils bitter: "... with my mind in a muddle about *dharma*, I ask you, What is better? Tell me the what is right for sure..." (*BhG* 2.7). But when he lets the bow slip from his hands, Krishna rebukes him, and preaches the sermon embodied in eighteen chapters of book six of the *Mahabharata*, which have since been known and handed down independently as the *Bhagavad Gita*, the "Song of the Lord."

The *Gita* begins by reviewing Upanishadic arguments for the importance of both *jnana* (wisdom) and *karma* (action) in this world. When Arjuna points out that they seem to contradict one another, Krishna proposes the importance of *yoga* (self-discipline), by which action in the world is informed and shaped by true insight. Krishna's ideal person is a *karma-yogin*, one adhering to the discipline of action, which means giving up any interest in the fruits (*phala*) of one's actions. One should act according to *dharma* dispassionately and with self-control. In this way, one cultivates the yogi's freedom from attachments and desires, but without withdrawing from everyday life to become a hermit or wandering mendicant. Even living the life of a married householder, even as a warrior, one can rise above pleasure-seeking and distraction. The contemplative life of withdrawal (*jnana-yoga*) may also lead to liberation, but since absolute inaction is impossible, it is here deemed inferior to disciplined engagement in the world, which is said ultimately to yield *jnana* as well.

Krishna's *karma-yoga* thus reconciles the Vedic ideal of a prosperous life of action in accord with *dharma* with the Vedantic ideal of liberation through absolute self-discipline. The result has sometimes been compared with the Protestant Christian ideal of "this-worldly asceticism." The *Bhagavad-Gita* adds another dimension to this idea, though. Krishna gradually discloses that he is the bodily avatar of the supreme God, *brahman* in a personal form, culminating in an overwhelming vision of his inconceivable divine nature. So not only should Arjuna perform all his actions for their own sake, for *dharma* (rather than out of self-interest), but he should make an offering of their "fruits" to God, just as one might bring actual fruit or other food as an offering in the temple. Likewise, all people should live their lives in every moment in an attitude of worshipful devotion (*bhakti*), remembering that all things have their origin and end in Krishna. In this way, *karma-yoga* becomes *bhakti-yoga*—not the esoteric technique taught by Patanjali, nor the strenuous ascetic regimens described in the Dharmashastra, but a simple rule of life that follows naturally and easily from a sincere, loving self-dedication to God. And whereas the earlier yogic paths were available only to those of high caste, deep learning, and specialized training, *bhakti-yoga* is accessible equally to all.

Debates over the Meaning of the Vedanta

While the *Upanishads* offer a wealth of evocative reflections on the nature of the self and its relation to an ultimate universal principle, they do not constitute a systematic treatment of the question. The *Bhagavad Gita* clearly aimed to harmonize Vedantic ideas and produce a synthesis of them with the idea of *bhakti*. Besides this, there were in later centuries various projects aimed at systematizing the Vedanta, which are remembered today as the schools of Vedanta-*darshana* (theory). All of these begin from the Upanishads and Bhagavad Gita, along with an aphoristic summary of Vedantic ideals in 555 sentences called the *Brahma Sutras* (or *Vedanta Sutras*) of Badarayana. The various systems that developed differed in important ways, but all were able to find ample support for their positions in this core literature, while apparently contradictory passages had to be interpreted nonliterally.

The first major thinker in this tradition was Shankara (8th c.), who composed commentaries on these works (as well as some independent treatises). Shankara's school comes to be known as Advaita Vedanta since he deemed the unmanifest *brahman* to be the sole reality, "without duality" (*advaita*). This view entails not only that the whole empirical world lacks reality, but that the soul (*jiva*) within people is nothing but *brahman* itself present in the intellect. Suffering in *samsara* is caused not by the effects of matter on the soul, but by soul's being prevented from recognizing its own freedom by a power called *maya*. *Maya* is *brahman's* capacity to raise an illusory edifice of mental constructs that seem real to the "person" who is himself illusory. The result is a state of *avidya* (ignorance) that veils the true nature of the soul. Shankara illustrates this process of error by calling attention to the process of cognition and the many ways in which it can go awry. Thus, to use famous examples, one may see a shiny shell and mistake it for silver, or a coil of rope on the path may be mistaken for a serpent. In these cases, the mind "superimposes" upon one thing the mental image of another; likewise, we superimpose the idea of self on that other things such as body, mind, and experiences. The thoughts and emotions that result—desire and attraction, or fear and aversion—ensnare us ever tighter in a world of unreal but persuasive experiences, for all thoughts and perceptions are equally unfounded, including the very mind itself. Liberation comes through recognizing the process of misapprehension, and gaining an intuitive experience of the soul's infinite consciousness and joy.

Shankara himself avoids personifying *brahman* as a deity, but many subsequent theologies have been founded on the Advaita theory, such as the Pratyabhijna school of Shaivism (Shiva theology). From such perspectives, the inconceivable supreme deity takes various "lower" forms in order to become intelligible to humanity. The world arises out of the deity's "self-recognition" (*pratyabhijna*), which creates the subject-object dichotomy and set the creation of a seemingly manifold reality in motion. The aim of such theologies is to recognize God in oneself; *moksha* consists in removing the mistaken sense of separateness and merging back into the spiritual unity.

In the 11th century, Ramanuja, a south Indian imbued in local traditions of devotional piety, proposed—in commentaries on most of the same texts, and in other works—a modified form of the Advaita.

He asserts that *brahman*, the Supreme Soul (*purushottama*), possesses auspicious qualities (rather than being quality-less, as Shankara argued), and he pervades the (real) universe, which is his body. Contrary to Shankara's view, there is some distinction (*vishesha*) between *brahman* and the soul—hence this school is known as the Vishishta-Advaita. Ramanuja resorts to a paradox to explain this distinction: based on the testimony of the *Upanishads*, individual souls are both different and not different (*bheda-abheda*) from *brahman*. By this he means that although souls are uncreated and coeternal with *brahman*, at the time of creation (when the material elements begin to undergo changes), the souls expand from *brahman* like sparks from a flame. Thus they are parts of *brahman* in substance, but differ in their attributes of tiny size and separateness. But like *brahman*, souls have intelligence and will, and agency. Besides the souls, Ramanuja (as all the Vedantins except Shankara) treats *prakriti* as a real substance, eternal but mutable; it is the permutations of this material nature in which souls come to be bound, and which they must escape by means of meditation on God (which Ramanuja explains as constant, loving remembrance of God).

The Vishnu-devotee Madhva (14th c.) makes *brahman* a fully personal God, Lord Vishnu. Souls are reflections of God, as in a mirror, taking their form and nature from Him, and dependent upon his grace. Madhva alone among Vedantists regards *prakriti* as a separate but dependent power, personified as the female divinity, Lakshmi. Vishnu sets creation in motion by his will, but Lakshmi is the material source of all insentient things. Souls are eternal but limited in their knowledge. *Moksha* is not merely relief from suffering and bondage, but a blissful state of closeness to God.

For all their difference, the Vedanta schools agree that *brahman* is the cause of the empirical world; that knowledge of *brahman* leads to *moksha* (although not knowledge alone, according to Ramanuja and Madhva), and that reason alone is inadequate to attain that knowledge: one must look to revealed wisdom (the *Vedas*, *Upanishads*, and *Bhagavad Gita*).

The Medieval Agamic and Tantric Sects

During the same centuries when the Vedanta doctrines were developing, a number of theologies (both Shaiva and Vaishnava) with a Samkhya-based dualist cosmology and an emphasis of ritual performance were being promulgated in Sanskrit works called *Tantras* and *Agamas*. These were produced by sects which one joined by undergoing one or more levels of initiation (*diksha*). The initiations are said to be the direct mechanism of liberation, insofar as they evoke a "descent of divine power" (*shakti-pata*), the direct manifestation of God's grace (*anugraha*). Tantric *yoga*, a secret technique learned under the guidance of a guru, is believed to activate the latent divine energy of *prakriti* itself (personified as the Goddess) in such a manner that the body and mind are purged of impurity and the visualized coupling of God and Goddess at the top of the skull confers a taste of the bliss of liberation. Liberation itself is understood in such sects as the release of the individual soul from material bonds of *maya* (the manifold physical world), *karma* (invisible traces of past action that adhere to the soul), and *mala* (the intrinisic impurity that affects an embodied soul, and the last defect to be removed). The liberated soul ascends to a celestial realm to reside for eternity with God (or, in Advaita terms, the soul that has recognized its own divinity merges fully with the highest *brahman*).

The Vernacular Bhakti Movement

Over against this complex ritualism and the theoretical debates on the nature of God, the soul, and world carried on over the millennia in Sanskrit, a piety of a very different character began to emerge from around the 6th century in south India, spreading gradually northward until it had permeated the entire subcontinent by the 15th century. This piety was a passionate, even ecstatic love of God expressed not in the refined and formal measures of a classical language but in the spoken language. Whereas the Sanskrit literature was the province of brahmin scholars, these voices came from all walks of life: many women and members of low castes are represented among the revered figures of the tradition, and the hagiographies of these figures (often composed by brahmins) tell how the high would bow to the low-born saint. In fact, aside from Shankara, all the Vedantic thinkers as well as the Agamic and Tantric teachers were influenced by this new *bhakti* spirit and its assumptions about the nature of the religious life.

For all its diversity, this movement has several common tendencies. Direct experience of God in this world is sought, whether through the medium of the outward image or in the inner realm of the heart. Simple faith and spontaneous love are deemed more pleasing to God than punctilious, orthodox ritual observance— hence even the lowest and humblest may reach God more quickly than a haughty or hypocritical brahmin. The core texts of the tradition are the lyrics of God-obsessed devotees, who sang of the bitter-sweet pain of longing for God and the joy of reuniting with Him. The motifs are drawn to begin with from the poetry of love and heroism in Old Tamil, transferred from human objects to divine, but in later centuries regional folk genres entered as the movement spread, and the unifying trait is the confessional tone of the songs, in which the singers tries to convey their innermost feelings and observations about God and the world. These singers came to be regarded as exemplary devotees, even as embodiments of the deity, and thus come to be treated as saints, receiving worship in their own right and interceding with God on behalf of their petitioners. The central message of the tradition is that God responds to true devotion, whatever form it may take, and no special training or authority in necessary to approach God directly. Hence, the movement in its origins is deeply suspicious of religious institutions, although it inevitably evolved institutions of its own.

Despite its popular, sometimes even anti-brahmin character, the *bhakti* movement soon drew in the vast majority of brahmin intellectuals, who, tapping their Sanskrit learning (including earlier Sanskrit reflections on *bhakti*, such as the *Bhagavad Gita*), were inspired to produce systematic theologies in the new *bhakti* vein, both in Sanskrit and in other languages. This confluence of Sanskritic and non-Sanskritic ideas threw into relief the disparity between their outlooks on the nature of the religious life. Traditional Sanskritic and vernacular *bhakti* assumptions about the nature of the religious life, drawn together with Brahmanical conceptions of religion: the joining of vivid outpourings of devotion and erudite scholasticism led to some interesting debates about the nature of religious life. There was general agreement that human beings yearn to overcome human limitations and to reach God somehow, and while the particulars had been debated in Sanskrit (and, one presumes, in general society), in Tamil Vaishnavism, two points of view emerged: the Vadagalai ("northern school") and the Tengalai ("southern school"). The Tengalai held to the "cat doctrine," that the devotee is as utterly dependent upon divine grace for salvation as a kitten carried helplessly in its mother's mouth. No human effort can avail to bring about liberation; one loves God simply because He is God. The Vadagalai's "monkey doctrine" left room for human initiative: the devotee must seek God out in order to receive grace, just as the baby monkey clings to its mother as she carries it.

On the other hand, the *bhakti* spirit is hard to reconcile with the yogic asceticism of a Shankara or even a Patanjali, for whom correct knowledge or rigorous practice is adequate to bring about *moksha*. The ascetic has been made acceptable in *bhakti* terms only by representing his discipline as an expression of earnest devotion. Conversely, the passionate love of the *bhakti* saints for their personal God has been termed a form of *yoga*. Mirabai, for instance, a 16th-c. Rajasthani princess, was said to have been so enrapt in love of Krishna that she refused to accept her human husband, earning the ridicule of society and the fury of her in-laws. In one of her hymns she presents herself as adhering to a yoga of devotion. Many of these singer saints speak of the social alienation, self-abnegation, self-denial of personal needs, and mental focus on God that arise in the life of a true devotee as the purest form of yogic discipline.

Just as in ascetical and meditative traditions, the transmission of divine wisdom from guru to pupil is found also in the *bhakti* movements. In fact, the guru or swami (spiritual master) has always played a key role in Hindu religiosity. Intiation with a teacher is called a rebirth in a higher condition, and is a necessary step toward eventual *moksha*. But while the *bhakti* guru is simply a window on God, a living embodiment of the divine presence, there are no special techniques or arcane texts to be transmitted (besides perhaps a simple mantra for use in focusing the mind on God), rather it is the direct relationship with the pupil that awakens love or insight.

The Sant Movement

By the 14th century, the new devotionalism was sweeping north India, and devotional songs in Marathi, Hindi, Bengali, and other languages were being collected. Many of these addressed the personal gods Shiva and Vishnu (the latter especially in his human avatars Krishna and Rama), but there was also a trend toward devotion to an abstract supreme deity devoid of material attributes (that is, *nirguna*) and thus inconceivable in terms of human qualities or temple images. This trend echoed the abstract mystical language of Shankara's Advaita, but the words were heard now from the lips not of brahmin scholars but of unlearned, often low-caste singers (called Sants, "the holy ones") drawing on their own reflections and experience. Vedantic ideas were doubtlessly circulating orally in North Indian in this period, and Sufi Muslim preachers were also active under the auspices of Islamic rule. Thus Kabir, born into a weaver caste that had converted to Islam, drew on ideas both Islamic and Hindu, while being sharply critical of the authority figures and orthodox practices of both traditions, which he saw as encouraging parochialism and hypocrisy. Ravidas, whose caste-occupation as a tanner placed him in the lowest ranks of Indian society, exulted that God comes even to those whom the sanctimonious brahmins despise as impure. What is true purity? "That family which has in it a true devotee is pure."

How does one encounter a God who cannot be seen in the temple or even envisioned? The Sants advised their listeners to look within the heart, where the *sadguru*, the True Teacher, ever resides. Guru Nanak of the Punjab called upon his disciples to listen inside themselves for the unceasing sound of God, the divine Word (*sabad*). This group, continues as the Sikhs, "the pupils," a group recognized as an independent religion today, under the guidance of the Guru Granth Sahib, a collection of the lyrics of Nanak, Kabir, Ravidas, and other singer-saints. For all the Sants, the simple utterance of the name of God is a means of direct approach, a radically simple meditative act, accessible to all who would hear it.

Elements of an Ethics

With a history spanning more than three millennia, India has proposed a wide range of nuanced perspectives on the nature of divinity and the soul, the human condition, and the appropriate means of overcoming human limitations to reach God. Broadly speaking, there is consensus (at least since the *Upanishads*) that the empirical world throws up impediments to religious self-realization, and that knowledge of and access to God (in whatever way it may be acquired) is essential to this purpose. Beyond this rather bland observation, there are important differences with regard to conceptions of the nature of God and the world, the scope of individual human intiative in seeking God (are we entirely dependent upon grace, or can salvation be actively pursued?), the nature of the ideal religious life (the relative merits of ascetic withdrawal, training in yogic techniques, ritual observance according to dharma, scriptural inquiry, and simple faith), and attitudes to conventional society (as divinely ordained and good; as something to be transcended; or simply as irrelevant to the life of faith).

For all the deep reflection and sophisticated theorizing the tradition includes, there is nothing quite corresponding to a philosophical ethics. Morality was a topic addressed incidentally, in the context of some other concern: as conformity to a divinely ordained world-order, as a preliminary stage of a spiritual training, or as a by-product of sincere faith. It is addressed for its own sake mainly in collections of wisdom-verses and in the large fable literature, where it is illustrated in anecdotes and crystalized in maxims. It is treated most systematically in the Dharmashastra, but without real theorizing: righteousness is simply prescribed on the basis of revelation above all; convention is recognized and approved; the dictates of conscience are the last resort. On the other hand, in philosophical works, notions of the good are always subordinate to the purpose of individual salvation: moral virtue is advised because it is conducive to spiritual liberation. The whole *karma* theory, which explains the unequal distribution of fortune in the world and is meant to provide a motivation for good conduct and to dissuade from wickedness, comes closest to providing an analysis of what makes good actions good, and vice versa. But even here, most of the attention focuses on the mechanics and economics of the effects of *karma*, rather than on the criteria for evaluating particular actions in moral terms. This is not to say that Hinduism lacks a notion of morality. But those who wish to make a comparison of Western ideas of morality with Hindu ones must take the trouble to cull and assemble material on moral issues from diverse sources in which they come up. On the other hand, Hinduism offers a rich and diverse literature on the nature of God and the human being, the relationship between them, and the means of attaining knowledge about these things.

Brief Bibliography

Flood, Gavin. *An Introduction to Hinduism.* Cambridge: Cambridge University Press, 1996.

Hawley, John Stratton, and Mark Juergensmeyer, *Songs of the Saints of India.* New York: Oxford University Press, 1988.

Miller, Barbara Stoler, translator. *The Bhagavad-Gita: Krishna's Counsel in Time of War.* New York: Bantam Books, 1986.

Miller, Barbara Stoler, translator. *Yoga: Discipline of Freedom.* New York: Bantam Books, 1998 (1996).

Olivelle, Patrick, translator. *Upanishads.* London: Oxford University Press, 1996.

Notes

[1] Although the former term is usually associated with Hindu viewpoints and the latter with Buddhist, the words are often used virtually synonymously in Hindu texts (e.g., *BhG* 2.72).

[2] The Buddhists (discussed in ch. 8b) were some of the first systematically to explain these matters, although they had been addressed already in the Upanishads and other ancient Sanskrit texts.

[3] These likewise constitute the basic Buddhist "fivefold rule of conduct."

BUDDHISM

by Iain S. Maclean

1. Introduction

Buddhism has fascinated the West ever since its teachings and way of life began to be disseminated in the West during the Nineteenth century. This was largely accomplished through the popularity of travelogues and the writings of for instance the American Lafcadio Hearn (1850-1904) and the German-British scholar Max Müller, the translator of Pali Buddhist texts Mrs. Rhys Davids, and others.[1] The Nineteenth century saw numerous absorptions of Buddhist ideas into Western culture, most specifically in the religious and literary spheres. For example we might mention the works and influence of Mary Baker Eddy (1821-1910) the foundress of Christian Science, Madame Helena Petrovna Blavatsky who with Henry Steel Alcott founded the Theosophical Society in New York (1875), Alice A. Bailey (1880-1949), and Annie Besant (1847-1933) who were prominent figures in theosophy movements in England and in Europe.

Indeed recently *Time Magazine* ran a front cover story on Buddhism entitled, "America's Fascination with Buddhism," and featuring reviews of recent successful movies with Buddhist themes, such as *Kundun* and *Golden Child*, and an interview with Brad Pitt, star of *Seven Years in Tibet*. The article notes the rise in Buddhist meditation centers and monasteries in the USA, and the increasing number of books on Buddhist thought, meditation, and understandings of the human situation.[2] Buddhism is perhaps most well-known today in its Tibetan expression through the peace work of the 14th Dalai Lama (Tibetan for "religious teacher of profound knowledge"), Bstan-'dzin-ryga-mtsho, at present an exile from the Chinese occupation of his homeland,

Buddhism as a religion arose as a reform movement from within Hinduism. This reform was initiated and led by a Khyshitriya nobleman Siddartha ("wish-fulfilling") Gautama, son of the rajah of the Sakya clan in Magadha, of (now Kapilavastu, Bihar state of modern Nepal) born circa 563 B.C. Recognized by his followers as the "enlightened one" or Buddha, his life and teaching represent a radical rejection of traditional Hindu teaching and its replacement by what is in effect a radical humanism, teaching that one attains Nirvana ("extinguishing of the flame") through one's own perception, volition and effort, without the assistance of any mediators or divinity. Thus Buddhism in its original form was a rejection of Hindu theologies and speculative metaphysics. It offered access to Nirvana in this life, (not through successive re-incarnations) to everyone and anyone regardless of caste (directly through the experience of true awareness).

The original core of Buddhist teaching and practice derives from the example set out by the Buddha himself, who after an ascetical six-year quest, and after his enlightenment after meditating under the Bo ("Bohdi" or "knowledge") tree (still surviving at Bodh-Gaya, Bihar, in India), set out his principles for enlightenment in the famous "Deer Park Sermon," in the summary known as the *Four Noble Truths*. This sermon led to the conversion of his five ascetic companions, and so to the established monastic communities (called Sanghas) for monks to live together in community, and later similar establishments from women.

True to his calling and sense of compassion that had led him to renounce entering Nirvana, but had led to him to return in order to tell others of the path to enlightenment, the Buddha spent the rest of his forty-five years as a monk, preaching to all the basic message of the *Four Noble Truths*. He died at the age of eighty years at Kusinara, Oudh, in 483 B. C.

Originating then in India, Buddhism spread Westwards to the Hellenistic kingdoms of the Eastern Mediterranean, Southwards to the tip of the Indian sub-continent, and across to Ceylon (Sri Lanka) and from there to the Indonesian archipelago, North to Tibet and into Mongolia, and Eastwards through China to Korea and Japan (by 552 A. D.) Today the majority of Buddhists still live in these regions (over 300 million), with about another 900,000 in North America.

2. A Brief History

In 480 B.C., shortly after the death of the Buddha, the monks gathered at the First Council of monks at Rajagaha and accepted what have remained as the three basic principles of Buddhist life, called the "three baskets" (the *Tipitaka*). These "three baskets" summarized Buddhism as primarily a discipline for the Sangha, a way of life, and as a philosophy or interpretation of human existence. A century later in 380 B.C. the Second Council at Vaisali was marked by division over the question of conformity to the strict monastic code, a requirement that seemed to exclude the laity from attaining Nirvana. This division marked the beginnings of the split between the Theravada (Hinayana) and Mahayana streams of Buddhism. Eventually, over the next three hundred years, these basic divisions were to lead to the growth of sixteen further Buddhist schools.

The critical event for the spread of Buddhism was the reign of King Asoka. In 273 B.C. King Asoka ascended to the throne of Magadha, then dominating most of India. Deeply convicted by Buddhist principles, he renounced his warlike past and vigorously propagated Buddhist ideals, even to the extent of prohibiting the killing of many classes of animals and inscribing up to thirty-five edicts on mountain sides that dictated how his peoples should live in peace. These "Asoka Inscriptions" mark the earliest record of religious toleration, as these edicts advocated peace towards Jains and Hindus. He convened the Third Council in 240 at Paliputra, which re-organized the Sanghas, and also sent out missionaries East and West. In fact his son (or perhaps his brother) went to Sri Lanka and established Buddhism there from whence it spread to most of South-East Asia. Buddhism however, died out in its motherland by the 12th century, through the combined effects of the resurgence of Hinduism and the Northern invasions of Islam and only returned to India in the nineteenth century during a revival of the religion itself.

Two distinct groupings emerged and survive to this day, namely Mahayana ("broad vehicle") and Theravada ("narrow vehicle"). Adherents of the latter regard this as a somewhat derogatory term and prefer the term Hinayana or "Teachings of the Elders." These two basic traditions differences remain to the present. The Hinayana tradition is dominant in Ceylon, Burma, and South East Asia. It remains a strictly ascetic, monastic tradition with extensive moral guidelines. In effect, one really has to become a monk/nun, either now or in another lifetime, to actually reach Nirvana. In all this the pattern set by the example of the Buddha himself provides the paradigm. Scriptures are only the ancient Pali canon. In addition, it is held that the Buddha is not there to help as the Buddha has entered Nirvana, and so one must help oneself achieve Nirvana.

After the death of Emperor Asoka, through to the second century A.D. Northern India was conquered by a succession of Hellenistic invaders who assimilated Buddhist teachings and prepared the way for the other major Buddhist tradition, that of Mahayana. While this was no doubt a complex process, the following stages seem clear: First, Gautama was elevated to a divine position, and became the object of bhakti ("devotion'), complete with the development of an elaborate mythology surrounding his previous incarnations as a Boddhisattva. Thus this explains the quick spread and popularity of Mahayana Buddhism, for the doctrine of past and future Buddhas opens the way to many enlightened individuals and their ways of salvation. These can assist individuals in attaining Nirvana and can be divided into three classes of supernatural beings who hold extra merit and thus can be worshipped and to whom prayer is directed. Manushi Buddhas, Boddhisattvas, Dhyani Buddhas, all out of compassion (a pure altruism) seek to assist mortals in reaching Nirvana. In addition this form of Buddhism offers a way to Nirvana that is open to all, not just to the religious specialist or monastic. Thus the ideal for Mahayana, instead of the arhat ("perfected one") of Hinayana, is the Boddhisattva ("one whose essence is perfected wisdom"), the one who having reached the threshold of Nirvana, renounces it out of compassion to tell the world. In summary it could be said that for Mahayanas, the Buddha is interpreted as placing compassion above self salvation, and the Buddha is understood not so much as a saint but as a savior.

3. Main Events in the Life of the Buddha

Siddartha ("Wish-Fulfilling") Gautama was born in 563 B.C in Magadha (state Bihar, now in Nepal) in the Himalayan foothills, of the Khshitriya caste. Many tales and legends, such as recounted in the 550 Jataka tales are related of the events that surrounded and marked his birth. The most critical one is that of the prophesy of the "four passing sights" in which an old monk warns Siddartha's father that if his new-born son and heir were ever to see the "four passing sights," that is, an old man, a sick man, and a dead man, symbolizing the change and suffering of the human condition, followed by the "fourth passing sight," a monk, symbolizing the solution, then he would never inherit his father's estate. Thus his father kept him from the world and the face of human misery. The legends relate in fabulous detail the luxury in which he was kept, far from any possibility of seeing any old, ill or dying person. At the age of nineteen, he married his first cousin Yashodara who bore him a son, named Rahula.

At age 29 however, despite all precautions, he saw the "four passing sights," the first three revealing the misery of life, the last the route to emancipation. This revelation led to Siddartha leaving his family, position and wealth (called in Buddhism the "Great Renunciation") and embarking on a seven year quest for salvation. He sought Nirvana through the traditional Hindu paths of first knowledge and then through bodily asceticism. Near death after extreme ascetic practices, he settled himself at the end of this period under a Pipal tree, later of course to become famed as the "Bo" (wisdom) tree, at Bodh-gaya, near modern Bihar on the Neranjara river. After meditating for a total of forty-nine days, resisting in the process the numerous temptations of the tempter Mara, who sent his "daughters" Discontent, Delight and Desire to distract Siddartha, he reached enlightenment. This came about after he had moved through the four stages of meditation: namely 1] detachment from sensory objects, 2] the move from discursive to intuitive thinking, 3] the shift from vitality to blissful peace, and finally 4] the move beyond opposites to pure awareness, whereby he learned of the "six super knowledges" and the "three, cognitions," which included the memory of past incarnations, and the extinction of desire.

This achievement led to the knowledge of the *Four Noble Truths*. This the core of the now Buddha's experience, comprised knowledge of the following four facts of human experience. First the fact or truth of universal human suffering ("dhukka"). According to Buddhist tradition, such suffering can be understood as encompassing the following three aspects, first that of ordinary suffering, including imperfection, second that of suffering produced by change, or third, as that suffering occasioned by conditioned states.

The second Noble Truth describes the source of suffering ("trishna") as human desire, while the third Noble Truth addresses the fact that there is the cessation of suffering ("niradha"), and the fourth Noble Truth provides the noble eight-fold path as the therapy to this end ("mayga"). The eight-fold path comprised the following intellectual, moral and volitional dimensions: 1] right understanding, 2] right-mindedness, 3] right speech, 4] right action, 5] right livelihood, 6] right effort, 7] right meditation, and 8] right emancipation.

The goal of this is Nirvana (from the image of a candle flame "blowing out") or the cessation of suffering, of striving, desiring, and becoming. However, the Buddha out of his great compassion for the suffering of others, decides not to attain Nirvana now, but to tell others and returns to his five ascetical companions to give the "Deer Park Sermon" in the Deer Park at Isipatana near Benares. His five friends are converted and form the nucleus of the first Sangha or monastic community. United by their desire to seek Nirvana the monks (and later nuns) are united in the simple monastic vow of "I take refuge in the Buddha, the Dharma and the Sangha." The Buddha died at eighty years of age at Kusinara in Uttar Pradesh (India) in 483 B.C.

4. Sacred Scriptures

While tradition relates that the monks at the First council (480 B.C.) recited the whole of the present contents of the Tripitaka, this is unlikely. Rather several centuries were to pass before the books were gathered that became known as the Pali Canon. Finally compiled in India circa 80 B.C. in written form these books, in three divisions, or the "three baskets" ("Tripitaka") as they are known, comprised the Monastic Rules ("Vinaya Pitaka"), the Discourses ("Sutta Pitaka"), and the Supplement to the Doctrines ("Abhidhamma Pitaka"). The second of these, the Discourses, is the central writings, as it relates the teachings of the Buddha himself. Comprising numerous discourses, the most significant being the "Longer" and "Shorter" Discourses and the fifteen book "Small Book Collection" which contains a life of the Buddha ("Buddha Vamsa"), the moral tract the Dhammapada ("Verses on the Law"), the Hymns of the elder Monks and nuns ("Therigatha" and "Theragatha"), and the story-poems of the Buddha ("The Jataka Tales"). There is no one canonical selection of sacred books in Buddhism, but rather a vast collection of saying and commentaries.

5. Beliefs about Knowledge, Self, and the World

It is somewhat of a conundrum to address a subject such as "Buddhist views of self, the world" and so forth, as the Buddha repeatedly rejected philosophical speculation about the nature of these entities. He considered such speculation as irrelevant to the human situation and the practical quest for salvation. Indeed, so were the many divinities and gods that inhabited the Hindu cosmologies. These he regarded as but finite, created beings, and in the absence of an absolute being who directed human destinies then prayer and intercession were of little use. Thus the sacred Vedas, the Brahmin priests and their sacrifices were likewise of little help. The Buddhist disciple must depend upon him or herself.

Buddhism as it developed divided into many traditions beyond the Theravadan and Mahayanan, with numerous differences of interpretation, belief, ritual and practice. Thus only the broadest outlines of the Theravadan tradition, being that one that has adhered more closely to the Buddha's teaching, will be given in this section. In addition to differences within Buddhism, there are also differences in the manner in which certain elements (such as beliefs about, pre-existence, the soul, the self and re-incarnation) from Hinduism are retained.

Like Hinduism, Buddhism teaches that all knowledge and being (except Nirvana) is in varying states of impermanence. Human existence itself can be characterized by three basic factors: that it is impermanent; that it is unsatisfactory, and that it is soulless. These ideas were developed by the Buddhist teacher Nagarjuna (first Century A. D.) who concluded that all views of and about reality are contradictory. Reality is thus a void or "empty." However this refers to the world of sensory perception. It is thus only present life (subject to Samsara) that is described as subject to impermanence and is thereby ultimately illusory. Thus sense perception is illusory. Only thought and contemplative experience enable humanity to reach unchanging reality beyond the realm of the sensory. Latter schools of Buddhism were to argue that Nirvana and the absolute were the same. Thus when one reaches Nirvana, the "one" or "self" disappears and becomes the same as being, as the Absolute.

In fact the Buddha himself had stressed correct understanding of reality and existence and so sought to show the failure of traditional understanding of life. This he accomplished by examining in turn three traditional, that is, Hindu conceptions of life: those respectively of suffering, of the nature of the human self, and of the soul. By examining the impermanence ("annica") of life, the Buddha pointed out not just the transitory nature of life, which was a Hindu commonplace, but in addition, the impermanence of the pleasures of life. Ultimately they all failed to bring fulfillment to the seeker. By "dukkha" the Buddha sought to warn humanity against placing their trust in human desires and emotions, based upon this transitory existence. These are ever changing and so a life dominated by emotion will inevitably lead to sorrow. Finally the Buddha taught the doctrine of "anatta" (from the negative "a," connective "n," and the term for soul "atta") or no-soul. The difficulty with this teaching lies not only in translation, but also in the differences within different schools of Buddhism on this issue. Basically, the word "atta" has two meanings. The first meaning is its everyday usage (no philosophical connotations) as a reflexive pronoun ("one" or "oneself"). The second meaning is found in the term's philosophical usage. In this sense the meaning is restricted to what we might call the "soul" and thus implies "individuality" or the whole "body-soul" unit. The problem here is that the term refers to something that cannot be discerned empirically. It is thus an abstract category. Hence the differing interpretations given to this concept. This has led to two specific schools: the one teaching that the human has no soul (Theravada) and that only the body is real, with no underlying element or soul that holds its constituent parts together. The other, associated with the Mahayana school, is that everything is empty. According to this theory, humans have neither souls nor bodies.

The sermon "On the Anatta Characteristics" (Anatta Lakkhana Sutta), delivered almost immediately after the Deer Park Sermon to the same group of the Five Ascetics is a primary source of the Buddha's teaching on the self. This sermon is based on the reality of the five components or "Five Aggregates" (matter/body, sensations/feelings, perceptions, mental formations/ emotional reactions and consciousness), all of these together composing what we would understand as a self, I, or being. However this is not to be understood as an *essentia*, but rather as referring to a being in continual flux. This is the doctrine of "no-soul" or anatta. Remember also, that one cannot separate "soul -matter" or "self -body/ matter" but rather recall that these are to be regarded as a "bundle" or aggregate of attributes. This theory of the "Five Aggregates" was common in Indian society. It was meant to explain the emotion-led life of humans on the level of Samsara only. This is not an essential conception as the Greek one. The "no self" doctrine then stands for the life dominated by the "Five Aggregates." Such a "self" is not to be considered as our real self because it is not under our control (when led by emotions). The (false) "self" that the Buddha so clearly rejects is the one ruled by the "Five Aggregates."

In addressing this issue of the nature of the "self" in Buddhism, care must be taken not to confuse it with Western categories. The Greek and Christian concepts are really descriptions of how the soul is or is composed, whereas the Buddhist one is an attempt to explain the appetitive or emotional nature of the self. Further, it seems that when Buddha used this term, he was not referring to ideas of "mortality" or "immortality." This was realm of metaphysical speculation that he rejected as unprofitable.

The Buddha did retain belief in two distinctive Hindu doctrines, namely the Law of Karma and rebirth. The Law of Karma still held inflexible rule over those who failed to control their will and emotions. However, the person—of whatever calling or caste—who experienced a complete change through following the teaching of the *Four Noble Truths*, and became an Arahat, was freed from the rule of Karma. Old Karma was destroyed and no new Karma produced in such a case. As the cause of their existence, desire, is destroyed, they as beings are destroyed at death like a "lamp being extinguished" (Nirvana). Those however who are still controlled by desire will in fact be subject to the Law of Karma and will be reborn. The Buddha's teaching on rebirth (re-incarnation or transmigration) has raised many questions, as he taught that there is no soul, and consequently, what then is re-incarnated? No substantial being or entity such as a soul was transmigrated, but rather a karma-bearing structure. The example given is that of an impression that is impressed upon soft wax. Only the impression or character is transmitted to the wax, not the seal itself, or again, in another example, that of a flame passing from one candle to another.

6. Ethics—T*he* D*hamma*

The dhamma (or dharma), according to the Buddha, is not simply a system of ideas to be understood intellectually, but primarily a path, or a movement towards Nirvana. Thus in a common image, it has been said that the Buddha is to be viewed as a physician rather than a metaphysician. He understood his own task as that of a healer rather than that of developing elaborate theologies or metaphysical systems. This focus is graphically illustrated in the parable told by the Buddha to a future disciple, Malunkyaputta. In discussing the human condition of suffering and its cure, the Buddha related a story of a man shot with an arrow who, while being treated, insisted in knowing everything about the arrow before it is extracted, things that it was impossible to know, such as who had manufactured it and who had shot it. The wounded man the Buddha declared, would, if he insisted on knowing everything, probably die before the arrow was extracted and certainly without the answers to his questions. According to the Buddha, the point is to heal the man's wound, not to know all the social and personal details of the one who fired the arrow. Thus the Buddha's teaching advocated an empirical, pragmatic, and individual approach to the human situation. As it has been summed up:

> the theory that the world is eternal (or that it is non-eternal) is a jungle, a wilderness, a puppet-show, a writhing and a fetter, and is coupled with misery, ruin, despair and agony and does not tend to aversion, absence of passion, cessation, quiescence, knowledge, supreme wisdom and Nirvana.[3]

Further, we must recall that for the Buddha the truth of his dhamma must be discovered and realized by each individual him—or herself. Thus the individual cannot depend on the teaching or life of a Brahman, a priest, or even a monk—let alone doctrines, dogmas etc. . . . . The central features of the Buddhist ethical system are found in the contents of the Buddha's first sermon ("Deer Park Sermon") specifically in the section entitled, "Setting in Motion of the Wheel of Dhamma" which enumerate the *Four Noble Truths* in turn as: Dukka, the arising of Dukka, the ending of Dukka, and the path which leads to that ending. Thus the First Noble Truth declares that:

> this is the noble truth of dukka: birth is dukka; decay and old age is dukka, disease is dukka; death is dukka; association with what is unpleasant is dukka; separation from what is pleasant is dukka.- failure to obtain what one wants is dukka; briefly stated, the five groups of physical and mental processes that make up the individual, are due to grasping, and are the objects of grasping, these five groups of grasping are dukka.[4]

This stresses that all, including the individual self are not static entities but are in continual flux or process of becoming. Thus the conglomeration of the "four aggregates" (matter, sensations, perceptions and consciousness) is in continual process of formation and deformation into new formations. Thus the actions or sensations of the present are the efflux of such past sensations, thoughts etc. Hence the image used by the monk Nagasena of the chariot, comprised differing parts in relation to each other—but when examined individually, there is no chariot.[5] It should be noted that the concept of dukka is not limited to "suffering" as a pessimistic description of human life, but rather as an analysis that includes deeper philosophical meanings. It also includes ideas such as imperfection, impermanence, emptiness, and insubstantiality.

The second Noble Truth declares:

> It is this craving which produces re-existence and re-becoming, and which is bound up with passionate greed, and which finds fresh delight now here and now there, namely in 1] craving for sense pleasures 2] craving for continued becoming [existence] and 3] craving for self-annihilation.[6]

It is desire which gives rise to one's sense of self. This desire or craving is described variously as a monkey as in the statement: "the thirst of a thoughtless man grows like a creeper; he runs from life to life like a monkey seeking fruit in the forest." In another well-known image, human becoming is likened to a raging fire, seen as a combination of greed, hate, and delusion. Indeed the Buddha described this becoming in terms of a twelvefold chain of causations or cause and effect ("Dependent Origination"). The first two causes or links arise from a previous existence, the next eight from present existence and the last two with future existence.

The Third Noble Truth declares that where there is no desire there is no suffering. The cessation of desire (nirodha) is the truth of Nirvana ("blowing out"). Thus when the Buddha was asked where the enlightened one goes after death, he replied, "Where does a fire go after it has been deprived of fuel? It goes out."[7]

Finally, in expounding the Fourth Noble Truth, the Buddha clearly sought the middle road, out of his own experience, between the two extremes of indulgence in pleasures and its opposite, extreme mortification. This middle road he decided is comprised in the "Eightfold Path" of 1] right views 2] right intents 3] right speech 4] right conduct 5] right means of livelihood 6] right endeavor 7] right mindfulness 8] right meditation. This eight-step program involved the basic components of right thought, action, and livelihood. The key to this is "mindfulness" or *sati* or the "fourfold setting up of mindfulness." This places the role of right thinking in the center, and this involves the two elements of simple awareness and comprehension. The former comprises the ability to objectify and to consider the self as "body, feelings, thoughts and ideas." Thus mindfulness to the body requires attention to breathing, to the composition and to the decomposition of the body. This further involves attention to the activities of the body. This all enables one to "objectify" the body, its internal processes, and external activities. In turn, this enables one to comprehend the "impermanence" of the self by noting its continual changes. Likewise one must develop awareness of feelings of pleasure and of pain as well as of ideas. This mindfulness is supported by and enables at the same time the *Four Great Efforts* to restrain unprofitable states of mind, to abandon unprofitable states of mind, and positively to develop and to maintain the profitable states.

Now one's "becoming" in birth and re-birth is conditioned by Kamma or Karma of which there are three types, namely right, wrong, and neutral karma. The "Eightfold Path" is a means of burning up or destroying accumulated demerit and of accumulating merit. Rebirth can occur at the human or at one of thirty other levels. In Buddhism these rebirths can be understood as *depth* of perception (i.e. subjectively) or objectively as places of residence (heaven, hell etc). That is, the same reality is perceived differently by different levels of self-consciousness. Thus the sophisticated or educated practitioner will understand that ghosts, gods and demons are but personifications of desires, anxieties, fears and ignorance etc. Thus Gautama's struggle with himself before Enlightenment is personified as a struggle between Gautama and Mara (the evil one).

It can be seen that in Buddhism the intellectual and ethical are closely related and interdependent. These are usually summed up as wisdom and compassion. This does involve the correct relation existing between ethics, mental training and wisdom. This is summed up in the *Dhammapada* in this verse:

> Not to commit any sin, to do good, and to purify one's own mind, that is the teaching of all the Buddhas.

The disciple who has reached the end of the eightfold path has achieved the status of Arahat or of one who has awakened. This is the Buddhist equivalent of a saint. One who has attained wisdom, the "Six Perfections" (wisdom, morality, charity, patience, striving, and meditation), has conquered the "three intoxications" (sensuality, ignorance and thirst leading to rebirth) and participates in the higher vision or "sambodhi." This is understood as a state just preceding Nirvana. The Arahat then is no longer concerned about a "self." From this follows the great compassion or benevolence for all creation, though some have argued, inconsistently, given the Theravadan focus on self-liberation. In fact this issue was the major reason for the division between Theravadan and Mahayanan Buddhism. Both traditions though held to the ideal of a universal, disinterested love, an ideal expressed in the opening verses of the *Dhammapada*:

> If a man speaks or acts with a pure thought, happiness follows him, like a shadow that never leaves him. "He abused me, he beat me, he defeated me, he robbed me"—in those who harbor such thoughts hatred will never cease—in those who do not harbor such thoughts hatred will cease. For hatred does not cease by hatred at any time; hatred ceases by love-this is an old rule.

Brief Bibliography

Conze, Edward, editor and translator. *Buddhist Scriptures*. New York: Penguin, 1959.

Conze, Edward. *Buddhism: Its Essence and Development*. New York: Harper and Row, 1959.

Rahula, Walpola. *What the Buddha Taught*. New York: Grove Weidenfeld, 1959.

Rhys Davids, Mrs. *Buddhist Birth-Stories* (Jataka Tales). New York: Routledge, 1868.

Streeter, Burnett H. *The Buddha and the Christ*. New York: Macmillan, 1932.

Notes

[1] See Lafcadio Hearn, *Gleanings in Buddha Fields.* Ayer Publishers (reprint of 1890 ed.), 1974; Max Müller, an anglicized German and Oxford professor who initiated a massive translation of *Sacred Books of the East*, Mrs Rhys Davids who with her husband T.W. Rhys Davids, translated many Buddhist texts into English. For example see *Buddhist Birth-Stories* (Jataka Tales) London: Routledge, 1878.

[2] "America's Fascination with Buddhism" and "Buddhism in America" by David van Biema, *Time Magazine*, (October 13, 1997), front page, 72-84.

[3] Majjhima-Nikaya. See also the Sutta Pitaka.

[4] First Noble Truth. See the "Deer Park Sermon."

[5] Visuddmiagga (Pali Text Society), pp. 594-595.

[6] Second Noble Truth. See the "Deer Park Sermon."

[7] See Rahula, *What the Buddha Taught,* page 43.

THE SELF IN RELATION TO THE UNIVERSE: EXISTENTIALISM, ATHEISM AND HUMAN FREEDOM

RELIGION DEBUNKED

by Albert Camus

Areligious Existenialism

From *The Myth of Sisyphus and Other Essays* by Albert Camus, Justin O'Brien, translator, 1955

The French existentialist, Albert Camus (1913-1960), a novelist as well as an essayist, won the Noble Prize for Literature. Along with Jean-Paul Sartre, Camus led the existentialist movement in the forties and fifties until his death in a car accident.

Camus's existentialist themes are revolt and freedom within an absurd universe, the social universe as well as the natural. He stresses the radical contingencies of life and a presumed inability of science and philosophy to explain human awareness. He is skeptical of any externally imposed system of values, and attacks science, as well as religion, when either would tell us who or what we are or what should be our values. Sartre insists that each of us makes our own meaning, and Camus views this as part and parcel of freedom. Choice is central in the existentialist view; it is our existence. Thus the existentialist slogan, "Existence before essence," means choice over idea—personal, arbitrary, individual choice before any explanation or imposed set of ideas or values.

Camus sees atheism as a matter of deep honesty and good faith. Near the end of his first novel, The Stranger, *the central character, Meursault, who is about to be executed, dramatically banishes a priest from his cell, refusing an offer of spiritual expiation. Camus sees the religious existentialist, who like himself views the world as absurd, but who unlike himself makes a leap of faith, as selling out, as abandoning the existentialist attitude because absurdity is too hard to live with. Camus's counsel is instead: "Everything considered, a determined soul will always manage."*

The selection here is excerpted from Camus's essay, The Myth of Sisyphus, *and is mainly occupied with what is wrong with the so-called religious existentialist, who arbitrarily leaps to God. For Camus, the titan Sisyphus of Greek mythology, condemned to push a rock up a hill only to have it roll back and to have to do it all over again, for an unforeseeable eternity, is the model of the true existentialist who triumphs in an inner attitude against the absurdity of his/her situation.*

If I accuse an innocent man of a monstrous crime, if I tell a virtuous man that he has coveted his own sister, he will reply that this is absurd. His indignation has its comical aspect. But it also has its fundamental reason. The virtuous man illustrates by that reply the definitive antinomy existing between the deed I am attributing to him and his lifelong principles. "It's absurd" means "It's impossible" but also "It's contradictory." If I see a man armed only with a sword attack a group of machine guns, I shall consider his act to be absurd. But it is so solely by virtue of the disproportion between his intention and the reality he will encounter, of the contradiction I notice between his true strength and the aim he has in view. Likewise we shall deem a verdict absurd when we contrast it with the verdict the facts apparently dictated. And, similarly, a demonstration by the absurd is achieved by comparing the consequences of such a reasoning with the logical reality one wants to set up. In all these cases, from the simplest to the most complex, the magnitude of the absurdity will be in direct ratio to the distance between the two terms of my comparison. There are absurd marriages, challenges, rancors, silences, wars, and even peace treaties. For each of them the absurdity springs from a comparison. I am thus justified in saying that the feeling of absurdity does not spring from the mere scrutiny of a fact or an impression, but that it bursts from the comparison between a bare fact and a certain reality, between an action and the world that transcends it. The absurd is essentially a divorce. It lies in neither of the elements compared; it is born of their confrontation.

In this particular case and on the plane of intelligence, I can therefore say that the Absurd is not in man (if such a metaphor could have a meaning) nor in the world, but in their presence together. For the moment it is the only bond uniting them. If I wish to limit myself to facts, I know what man wants, I know what the world offers him, and now I can say that I also know what links them. I have no need to dig deeper. A single certainty is enough for the seeker. He simply has to derive all the consequences from it.

The immediate consequence is also a rule of method. The odd trinity brought to light in this way is certainly not a startling discovery. But it resembles the data of experience in that it is both infinitely simple and infinitely complicated. Its first distinguishing feature in this regard is that it cannot be divided. To destroy one of its terms is to destroy the whole. There can be no absurd outside the human mind. Thus, like everything else, the absurd ends with death. But there can be no absurd outside this world either. And it is by this elementary criterion that I judge the notion of the absurd to be essential and consider that it can stand as the first of my truths. The rule of method alluded to above appears here. If I judge that a thing is true, I must preserve it. If I attempt to solve a problem, at least I must not by that very solution conjure away one of the terms of the problem. For me the sole datum is the absurd. The first and, after all, the only condition of my inquiry is to preserve the very thing that crushes me, consequently to respect what I consider essential in it. I have just defined it as a confrontation and an unceasing struggle.

And carrying this absurd logic to its conclusion, I must admit that struggle implies a total absence of hope (which has nothing to do with despair), a continual rejection (which must not be confused with renunciation), and a conscious dissatisfaction (which must not be compared to immature unrest). Everything that destroys, conjures away, or exorcises these requirements (and, to begin with, consent which overthrows divorce) ruins the absurd and devaluates the attitude that may then be proposed. The absurd has meaning only in so far as it is not agreed to.

There exists an obvious fact that seems utterly moral: namely, that a man is always a prey to his truths. Once he has admitted them, he cannot free himself from them. One has to pay something. A man who has become conscious of the absurd is forever bound to it. A man devoid of hope and conscious of being so has ceased to belong to the future. That is natural. But it is just as natural that he should strive to escape the universe of which he is the creator. All the foregoing has significance only on account of this paradox. Certain men, starting from a critique of rationalism, have admitted the absurd climate. Nothing is more instructive in this regard than to scrutinize the way in which they have elaborated their consequences.

Now, to limit myself to existential philosophies, I see that all of them without exception suggest escape. Through an odd reasoning, starting out from the absurd over the ruins of reason, in a closed universe limited to the human, they deify what crushes them and find reason to hope in what impoverishes them. That forced hope is religious in all of them. It deserves attention.

I shall merely analyze here as examples a few themes dear to Chestov and Kierkegaard . . . .

. . . To be sure, it is hard to outline clear propositions in so elusive a writer [as Kierkegaard]. But, despite apparently opposed writings, beyond the pseudonyms, the tricks, and the smiles, can be felt throughout that work, as it were, the presentiment (at the same time as the apprehension) of a truth which eventually bursts forth in the last works: Kierkegaard likewise takes the leap. His childhood having been so frightened by Christianity, he ultimately returns to its harshest aspect. For him, too, antinomy and paradox become criteria of the religious. Thus, the very thing that led to despair of the meaning and depth of this life now gives it its truth and its clarity. Christianity is the scandal, and what Kierkegaard calls for quite plainly is the third sacrifice required by Ignatius Loyola, the one in which God most rejoices: "The sacrifice of the intellect."[1] This effect of the "leap" is odd, but must not surprise us any longer. He makes of the absurd the criterion of the other world, whereas it is simply a residue of the experience of this world. "In his future," says Kierkegaard, "the believer finds his triumph."

It is not for me to wonder to what stirring preaching this attitude is linked. I merely have to wonder if the spectacle of the absurd and its own character justifies it. On this point, I know that it is not so. Upon considering again the content of the absurd, one understands better the method that inspired Kierkegaard. Between the irrational of the world and the insurgent nostalgia of the absurd, he does not maintain the equilibrium. He does not respect the relationship that constitutes, properly speaking, the feeling of absurdity. Sure of being able to escape the irrational, he wants at least to save himself from that desperate nostalgia that seems to him sterile and devoid of implication. But if he may be right on this point in his judgment, he could not be in his negation. If he substitutes for his cry of revolt a frantic adherence, at once he is led to blind himself to the absurd which hitherto enlightened him and to deify the only certainty he henceforth possesses, the irrational. The important thing, as Abbé Galiani said to Mme d'Epinay, is not to be cured, but to live with one's ailments. Kierkegaard wants to be cured. To be cured is his frenzied wish, and it runs throughout his whole journal. The entire effort of his intelligence is to escape the antinomy of the human condition. An all the more desperate effort since he intermittently perceives its vanity when he speaks of himself, as if neither fear of God nor piety were capable of bringing him to peace. Thus it is that, through a strained subterfuge, he gives the irrational the appearance and God the attributes of the absurd: unjust, incoherent, and incomprehensible. Intelligence alone in him strives to stifle the underlying demands of the human heart. Since nothing is proved, everything can be proved.

Indeed, Kierkegaard himself shows us the path taken. I do not want to suggest anything here, but how can one fail to read in his works the signs of an almost intentional mutilation of the soul to balance the mutilation accepted in regard to the absurd? It is the leitmotiv of the *Journal*. "What I lacked was the animal which *also* belongs to human destiny. . . . But give me a body then." And further on: "Oh! especially in my early youth what should I not have given to be a man, even for six months . . . what I lack, basically, is a body and the physical conditions of existence." Elsewhere, the same man nevertheless adopts the great cry of hope that has come down through so many centuries and quickened so many hearts, except that of the absurd man. "But for the Christian death is certainly not the end of everything and it implies infinitely more hope than life implies for us, even when that life is overflowing with health and vigor." Reconciliation through scandal is still reconciliation. It allows one perhaps, as can be seen, to derive hope of its contrary, which is death. But even if fellow-feeling inclines one toward that attitude, still it must be said that excess justifies nothing. That transcends, as the saying goes, the human scale; therefore it must be superhuman. But his "therefore" is superfluous. There is no logical certainty here. There is no experimental probability either. All I can say is that, in fact, that transcends my scale. If I do not draw a negation from it, at least I do not want to found anything on the incomprehensible. I want to know whether I can live with what I know and with that alone. I am told again that here the intelligence must sacrifice its pride and the reason bow down. But if I recognize the limits of the reason, I do not therefore negate it, recognizing its relative powers. I merely want to remain in this middle path where the intelligence can remain clear. If that is its pride, I see no sufficient reason for giving it up. Nothing more profound, for example, than Kierkegaard's view according to which despair is not a fact but a state: the very state of sin. For sin is what alienates from God. The absurd, which is the metaphysical state of the conscious man, does not lead to God.[2] Perhaps this notion will become clearer if I risk this shocking statement: the absurd is sin without God.

It is a matter of living in that state of the absurd. I know on what it is founded, this mind and this world straining against each other without being able to embrace each other. I ask for the rule of life of that state, and what I am offered neglects its basis, negates one of the terms of the painful opposition, demands of me a resignation. I ask what is involved in the condition I recognize as mine; I know it implies obscurity and ignorance; and I am assured that this ignorance explains everything and that this darkness is my light. But there is no reply here to my intent, and this stirring lyricism cannot hide the paradox from me. One must therefore turn away. Kierkegaard may shout in warning: "If man had no eternal consciousness, if, at the bottom of everything, there were merely a wild, seething force producing everything, both large and trifling, in the storm of dark passions, if the bottomless void that nothing can fill underlay all things, what would life be but despair?" This cry is not likely to stop the absurd man. Seeking what is true is not seeking what is desirable. If in order to elude the anxious question: "What would life be?" one must, like the donkey, feed on the roses of illusion, then the absurd mind, rather than resigning itself to falsehood, prefers to adopt fearlessly Kierkegaard's reply: "despair." Everything considered, a determined soul will always manage. . . .

All Sisyphus' silent joy is contained therein. His fate belongs to him. His rock is his thing. Likewise, the absurd man, when he contemplates his torment, silences all the idols. In the universe suddenly restored to its silence, the myriad wondering little voices of the earth rise up. Unconscious, secret calls, invitations from all the faces, they are the necessary reverse and price of victory. There is no sun without shadow, and it is essential to know the night. The absurd man says yes and his effort will henceforth be unceasing. If there is a personal fate, there is no higher destiny, or at least there is but one which he concludes is inevitable and despicable. For the rest, he knows himself to be the master of his days. At that subtle moment when man glances backward over his life, Sisyphus returning toward his rock, in that slight pivoting he contemplates that series of unrelated actions which becomes his fate, created by him, combined under his memory's eye and soon sealed by his death. Thus, convinced of the wholly human origin of all that is human, a blind man eager to see who knows that the night has no end, he is still on the go. The rock is still rolling.

I leave Sisyphus at the foot of the mountain! One always finds one's burden again. But Sisyphus teaches the higher fidelity that negates the gods and raises rocks. He too concludes that all is well. This universe henceforth without a master seems to him neither sterile nor futile. Each atom of that stone, each mineral flake of that night-filled mountain, in itself forms a world. The struggle itself toward the heights is enough to fill a man's heart. One must imagine Sisyphus happy.

Philosophical Atheism

From "Philosophical Concepts of Atheism" by Ernest Nagel in *Basic Beliefs*, Johnson E. Fairchild, editor, 1959

Ernest Nagel (born 1901), editor of the prestigious Journal of Philosophy *for almost twenty years, presents positive philosophic commitments or at least tendencies and themes that unite philosophical atheists beyond their opposition to theism and other religious points of view. These are three: first, a materialist tendency, materialist in the sense of a denial of incorporeal agencies and disembodied spirits or minds; second, empiricism, with controlled sensory evidence (i.e., the scientific experiment) viewed as the final court of appeal for any factual question; and third, a moral dimension of utilitarianism and libertarianism.*

The moral dimension of philosophical atheism is not usually brought out. Here Nagel shows moral parameters provided by atheism, and, perhaps more profoundly the temperament of the philosophical atheist's approach to moral issues and human values. Nagel eloquently expresses his sense of the philosophical atheist's typical courage and serene resignation in the face of a nature hostile to many a "legitimate desire." It is interesting to compare such sentiment with that of probably the most famous philosophical atheist of the twentieth century, Bertrand Russell.

. . . [I] will show how atheism belongs to the great tradition of religious thought. Needless to say, this expectation is difficult to satisfy, and did anyone succeed in doing so he would indeed be performing the neatest conjuring trick of the week. But the expectation nevertheless does cause me some embarrassment, which is only slightly relieved by an anecdote Bertrand Russell reports in his recent book, *Portraits from Memory*. Russell was imprisoned during the First World War for pacifistic activities. On entering the prison he was asked a number of customary questions about himself for the prison records. One question was about his religion. Russell explained that he was an agnostic. "Never heard of it," the warden declared. "How do you spell it?" When Russell told him, the warden observed "Well, there are many religions, but I suppose they all worship the same God." Russell adds that this remark kept him cheerful for about a week. Perhaps philosophical atheism also is a religion. . . .

. . . the question [arises] whether, apart from their polemics against theism, philosophical atheists have not shared a common set of positive views, a common set of philosophical convictions which set them off from other groups of thinkers. In one very clear sense of this query the answer is indubitably negative. For there never has been what one might call a "school of atheism," in the way in which there has been a Platonic school or even a Kantian school. In point of fact, atheistic critics of theism can be found among many of the conventional groupings of philosophical thinkers—even, I venture to add, among professional theologians in recent years who in effect preach atheism in the guise of language taken bodily from the Christian tradition.

Nevertheless, despite the variety of philosophic positions to which at one time or another in the history of thought atheists have subscribed, it seems to me that atheism is not simply a negative standpoint. At any rate, there is a certain quality of intellectual temper that has characterized, and continues to characterize, many philosophical atheists. (I am excluding from consideration the so-called "village atheist," whose primary concern is to twit and ridicule those who accept some form of theism, or for that matter those who have any religious convictions.) Moreover, their rejection of theism is based not only on the inadequacies they have found in the arguments for theism, but often also on the positive ground that atheism is a corollary to a better supported general outlook upon the nature of things. I want therefore to conclude this discussion with a brief enumeration of some points of positive doctrine to which by and large philosophical atheists seem to me to subscribe. These points fall into three major groups.

In the first place, philosophical atheists reject the assumption that there are disembodied spirits, or that incorporeal entities of any sort can exercise a causal agency. On the contrary, atheists are generally agreed that if we wish to achieve any understanding of what takes place in the universe, we must look to the operations of organized bodies. Accordingly, the various processes taking place in nature, whether animate or inanimate, are to be explained in terms of the properties and structures of identifiable and spatio-temporally located objects. Moreover, the present variety of systems and activities found in the universe is to be accounted for on the basis of the transformation things undergo when they enter into different relations with one another—transformations which often result in the emergence of novel kinds of objects. On the other hand, though things are in flux and undergo alteration, there is no all-encompassing unitary pattern of change. Nature is ineradicably plural, both in respect to the individuals occurring in it as well as in respect to the processes in which things become involved. Accordingly, the human scene and the human perspective are not illusory; and man and his works are no less and no more "real" than are other parts of phases of the cosmos. At the risk of using a possibly misleading characterization, all of this can be summarized by saying that an atheistic view of things is a form of materialism.

In the second place, atheists generally manifest a marked empirical temper, and often take as their ideal the intellectual methods employed in the contemporaneous empirical sciences. Philosophical atheists differ considerably on important points of detail in their account of how responsible claims to knowledge are to be established. But there is substantial agreement among them that controlled sensory observation is the court of final appeal in issues concerning matters of fact. It is indeed this commitment to the use of an empirical method which is the final basis of the atheistic critique of theism. For at bottom this critique seeks to show that we can understand whatever a theistic assumption is alleged to explain, through the use of the proved methods of the positive sciences and without the introduction of empirically unsupported *ad hoc* hypotheses about a Deity. It is pertinent in this connection to recall a familiar legend about the French mathematical physicist Laplace. According to the story, Laplace made a personal presentation of a copy of his now famous book on celestial mechanics to Napoleon. Napoleon glanced through the volume, and finding no reference to the Deity asked Laplace whether God's existence played any role in the analysis. "Sir, I have no need for that hypothesis," Laplace is reported to have replied. The dismissal of sterile hypotheses characterizes not only the work of Laplace; it is the uniform rule in scientific inquiry. The sterility of the theistic assumption is one of the main burdens of the literature of atheism both ancient and modern.

And finally, atheistic thinkers have generally accepted a utilitarian basis for judging moral issues, and they have exhibited a libertarian attitude toward human needs and impulses. The conceptions of the human good they have advocated are conceptions which are commensurate with the actual capacities of mortal men, so that it is the satisfaction of the complex needs of the human creature which is the final standard for evaluating the validity of a moral ideal or moral prescription.

In consequence, the emphasis of atheistic moral reflection has been this-worldly rather than other-worldly, individualistic rather than authoritarian. The stress upon a good life that must be consummated in this world, has made atheists vigorous opponents of moral codes which seek to repress human impulses in the name of some unrealizable other-worldly ideal. The individualism that is so pronounced a strain in many philosophical atheists has made them tolerant of human limitations and sensitive to the plurality of legitimate moral goals. On the other hand, this individualism has certainly not prevented many of them from recognizing the crucial role which institutional arrangements can play in achieving desirable patterns of human living. In consequence, atheists have made important contributions to the development of a climate of opinion favorable to pursuing the values of a liberal civilization and they have played effective roles in attempts to rectify social injustices.

Atheists cannot build their moral outlook on foundations upon which so many men conduct their lives. In particular, atheism cannot offer the incentives to conduct and the consolations for misfortune which theistic religions supply to their adherents. It can offer no hope of personal immortality, no threats of Divine chastisement, no promise of eventual recompense for injustices suffered, no blueprints to sure salvation. For on its view of the place of man in nature, human excellence and human dignity must be achieved within a finite life-span, or not at all, so that the rewards of moral endeavor must come from the quality of civilized living, and not from some source of disbursement that dwells outside of time. Accordingly, atheistic moral reflection at its best does not culminate in a quiescent ideal of human perfection, but is a vigorous call to intelligent activity—activity for the sake of realizing human potentialities and for eliminating whatever stands in the way of such realization. Nevertheless, though slavish resignation to remediable ills is not characteristic of atheistic thought, responsible atheists have never pretended that human effort can invariably achieve the heart's every legitimate desire. A tragic view of life is thus an uneliminable ingredient in atheistic thought. This ingredient does not invite or generally produce lugubrious lamentation. But it does touch the atheist's view of man and his place in nature with an emotion that makes the philosophical atheist a kindred spirit to those who, within the frameworks of various religious traditions, have developed a serenely resigned attitude toward the inevitable tragedies of the human estate.

Radical Freedom: Existenialism

Kant's suggestion has been taken up in a very different way in European philosophy, particularly by the existentialists. Like Kant, they accept (or at least do not bother to reject) determinism in science. But they insist that even if determinism is true, one must always view *him* or *herself as agent* as necessarily free. When you have to decide what to do, all the knowledge of the possible factors determining your decision are not sufficient to cause you to decide. For you cannot predict your own decision without at the same time making it.

Jean-Paul Sartre, the late French existentialist, has defended the Kantian claim for human freedom as far as it can possibly be defended. In his mammoth book *Being and Nothingness*, Sartre argued that we are, always, absolutely free. This means, as Kant had insisted, that insofar as we act (and Sartre says that we are always acting) our decisions and our actions cannot be viewed as having any causes whatsoever. We must make decisions, and no amount of information and no number of causal circumstances can ever replace our need to make them. We can, of course, refuse to make decisions, acting as if they were made for us, as if circumstances already determined them, as if the fates had already established the outcome. But even in these cases, we are making decisions, "choosing not to choose," in a classic Sartrian phrase. We are "condemned to be free," he says, in a phrase that has since become famous. Again, desires may enter into consideration, but only as "consideration." We can always act against a desire, any desire, no matter how strong, if only we are sufficiently decided that we shall do so. A starving man may yet refuse food if, for example, he is taking part in a hunger strike for a political cause to which he is dedicated. A mother may refuse to save her own life if it would be at the expense of her children. A student may miss his favorite television show if he has resolved to study for tomorrow's test. Whether trivial or grandiose, our every act is a decision, and our every decision is free. Even if we fail to live up to them or find that we "cannot" make them, we are responsible nevertheless. There is no escape from freedom or responsibility.

"ABSOLUTE FREEDOM"

by Jean-Paul Satre

Although the considerations which are about to follow are of interest primarily to the ethicist, it may nevertheless be worthwhile after these descriptions and arguments to return to the freedom of the for-itself and try to understand what the fact of this freedom represents for human destiny.

The essential consequence of our earlier remarks is that man being condemned to be free carries the weight of the whole world on his shoulders; he is responsible for the world and for himself as a way of being. We are taking the word "responsibility" in its ordinary sense as "consciousness" (of) being the incontestable author of an event or of an object." In this sense the responsibility of the for-itself is overwhelming since he is the one by whom it happens that *there is* a world; since he is also the one who makes himself be, then whatever may be the situation in which he finds himself, the for-itself must wholly assume this situation with its peculiar coefficient of adversity, even though it be insupportable. He must assume the situation with the proud consciousness of being the author of it, for the very worst disadvantages or the worst threats which can endanger my person have meaning only in and through my project; and it is on the ground of the engagement which I am that they appear. It is therefore senseless to think of complaining since nothing foreign has decided what we feel, what we live, or what we are.

Furthermore this absolute responsibility is not resignation; it is simply the logical requirement of the consequences of our freedom. What happens to me happens through me, and I can neither affect myself with it nor revolt against it nor resign myself to it. Moreover everything which happens to me is *mine*. By this we must understand first of all that I am always equal to what happens to me *qua* man, for what happens to a man through other men and through himself can be only human. The most terrible situations of war, the worst tortures do not create a non-human state of things; there is no non-human situation. It is only through fear, flight, and recourse to magical types of conduct that I shall decide on the non-human, but this decision is human, and I shall carry the entire responsibility for it. But in addition the situation is *mine* because it is the image of my free choice of myself, and everything which it presents to me is *mine* in that this represents me and symbolizes me. Is it not I who decide the coefficient of adversity in things and even their unpredictability by deciding myself?

Thus there are no *accidents* in life; a community event which suddenly burst forth and involves me in it does not come from the outside. If I am mobilized in a war, this war is *my* war; it is in my image and I deserve it. I deserve it first because I could always get out of it by suicide or by desertion; these ultimate possibles are those which must always be present for us when there is a question of envisaging a situation. For lack of getting out of it, I have *chosen* it. This can be due to inertia, to cowardice in the face of public opinion, or because I prefer certain other values to the value of the refusal to join in the war (the good opinion of my relatives, the honor of my family, *etc.*). Any way you look at it, it is a matter of choice. This choice will be repeated later on again and again without a break until the end of the war. Therefore we must agree with the statement by J. Romains, "In war there are no innocent victims." If therefore I have preferred war to death or to dishonor, everything takes place as if I bore the entire responsibility for this war. Of course others have declared it, and one might be tempted perhaps to consider me as a simple accomplice. But this notion of complicity has only a juridical sense, and it does not hold here. For it depended on me that for me and by me this war should not exist, and I have decided that it does exist. There was no compulsion here, for the compulsion could have got no hold on a freedom. I did not have any excuse; . . . the peculiar character of human-reality is that it is without excuse. Therefore it remains for me only to lay claim to this war.

But in addition the war is *mine* because by the sole fact that it arises in a situ ation which I cause to be and that I can discover it there only by engaging myself for or against it, I can no longer distinguish at present the choice which I make of myself from the choice which I make of the war. To live this war is to choose myself through it and to choose it through my choice of myself. There can be no question of considering it as "four years of vacation" or as "reprieve," as a "recess," the essential part of my responsibilities being elsewhere in my married, family, or professional life. In this war which I have chosen I choose myself from day to day, and I make it mine by making myself. If it is going to be four empty years, then it is I who bear the responsibility for this.

Finally, . . . each person is an absolute choice of self from the standpoint of a world of knowledges and of techniques which this choice both assumes and illumines; each person is an absolute upsurge at an absolute date and is perfectly unthinkable at another date. It is therefore a waste of time to ask what I should have been if this war had not broken out, for I have chosen myself as one of the possible meanings of the epoch which imperceptibly led to war. I am not distinct from this same epoch; I could not be transported to another epoch without contradiction. Thus *I am* this war which restricts and limits and makes comprehensible the period which preceded it. In this sense we may define more precisely, the responsibility of the for-itself if to the earlier quoted statement, "There are no innocent victims," we added the words, "We have the war we deserve." Thus, totally free, undistinguishable from the period for which I have chosen to be the meaning, as profoundly responsible for the war as if I had myself declared it, unable to live without integrating it in *my* situation, engaging myself in it wholly and stamping it with my seal, I must be without remorse or regrets as I am without excuse; for from the instant of my upsurge into being, I carry the weight of the world by myself alone without anything or any person being able to lighten it.

Yet this responsibility is of a very particular type. Someone will say, "I did not ask to be born." This is a naïve way of throwing greater emphasis on our facticity. I am responsible for everything, in fact, except for my very responsibility, for I am not the foundation of my being. Therefore everything takes place as if I were compelled to be responsible. I am *abandoned* in the world, not in the sense that I might remain abandoned and passive in a hostile universe like a board floating on the water, but rather in the sense that I find myself suddenly alone and without help, engaged in a world for which I bear the whole responsibility without being able, whatever I do, to tear myself away from this responsibility for an instant. For I am responsible for my very desire of fleeing responsibilities. To make myself passive in the world, to refuse to act upon things and upon Others is still to choose myself, and suicide is one mode among others of being-in-the-world. Yet I find an absolute responsibility for the fact that my facticity (here the fact of my birth) is directly inapprehensible and even inconceivable, for this fact of my birth never appears as a brute fact but always across a projective reconstruction of my for-itself. I am ashamed of being born or I am astonished at it or I rejoice over it, or in attempting to get rid of my life I affirm that I live and I assume this life as bad. Thus in a certain sense I choose being born. This choice itself is integrally affected with facticity since I am not able not to choose, but this facticity in turn will appear only in so far as I surpass it toward my ends. Thus facticity is everywhere but inapprehensible; I never encounter anything except my responsibility. That is why I can not ask, "*Why* was I born?" or curse the day of my birth or declare that I did not ask to be born, for these various attitudes toward my birth—i.e., toward the *fact* that I realize a presence in the world—are absolutely nothing else but ways of assuming this birth in full responsibility and of making it *mine*. Here again I encounter only myself and my projects so that finally my abandonment—i.e., my facticity—consists simply in the fact that I am condemned to be wholly responsible for myself. I am the being which *is* in such a way that in its being its being is in question. And this "is" of my being is as present and inapprehensible.

Under these conditions since every event in the world can be revealed to me only as an *opportunity* (an opportunity made use of, lacked, neglected, etc.) or better yet since everything which happens to us can be considered as a *chance* (i.e., can appear to us only as a way of realizing this being which is in question in our being) and since others as transcendences-transcended are themselves only *opportunities* and *chances*, the responsibility of the for-itself extends to the entire world as a peopled-world. It is precisely thus that the for-itself apprehends itself in anguish; that is, as a being which is neither the foundation of its own being nor of the Other's being nor of the in-itselfs which form the world, but a being which is compelled to decide the meaning of being—within it and everywhere outside of it. The one who realizes in anguish his condition as *being* thrown into a responsibility which extends to his very abandonment has no longer either remorse or regret or excuse; he is no longer anything but a freedom which perfectly reveals itself and whose being resides in this very revelation. But as we pointed out . . ., most of the time we flee anguish in bad faith.[3]

Sartre's position is the culmination of a full century of existentialist thought, beginning with Soren Kierkegaard in the 1840s. Kierkegaard too argued that one is responsible for whatever one is and that self-conscious choice and commitment were the factors that made a person most human. Sartre's very strong sense of responsibility goes even so far as to ascribe an act of choice to those situations in which we seem clearly to be only victims, for example, in war. "There are no accidents in life," he argues. It is always my choice as to how I shall act in and deal with a situation. One can always complain, "I didn't ask to be born," Sartre says, but this is only one of many ways we have of trying to avoid responsibility. Given the fact that we have been born, raised in certain conditions, and so forth, it is now entirely up to us as to what we shall make of all this. Instead of looking at the events of the world as problems and intrusions, Sartre ultimately says, we should learn to look at everything as an opportunity. Here is the optimistic note to his very strong defense of human freedom.

What all of these arguments demand is the following: In one's own case, in making your decision, there can be no appeal to determinism even if determinism is true. Whatever might be theoretically determined, in practice, you must choose. Since freedom is the key to our self-esteem and our pride in ourselves, some people will demand it at any cost.

The most brilliant, if bizarre, example of this existentialist demand is formulated by the strange character in Dostoyevski's short novel *Notes from the Underground*. The argument is simple. Any prediction can be thwarted as long as you know about it. If they say, "you'll do *x*"; do *y*. Now, suppose that determinism is true. In particular, suppose that psychological determinism is true and that its basic law is this: "people always act to their own advantage." Now, what does this have to do with the predictability of a person's actions? Absolutely nothing, if you are sufficiently determined not to be predictable. Accordingly, the character in this novel is, more than anything else, spiteful. His main concern is not being predictable, in proving his freedom even if it means making himself miserable. Now you might say that his spite itself is the determinant of his behavior, and of course it is. But the very point of the argument is that causes and explanations of any kind are simply beside the point. Let the underground man know what you expect him to do, and he'll do precisely the opposite. If you predict he'll act spiteful, he'll be as agreeable as can be—just out of spite!

THE CREATION OF MORALITY: NIETZSCHE AND EXISTENTIALISM

by Robert H. Solomon

There are crucial differences between ancient and modern moral perspectives; the most striking is the difference in the scope of their applicability. In Aristotle's moral philosophy, only a small elite is thought to be capable of true happiness (*eudaimonia*) through virtuous action and contemplation. Other people (women, slaves, noncitizens) may live comfortably enough and do their duties and chores efficiently, but they cannot be called "happy." The elite, however, are characterized by their excellence, by their individual achievements, including wealth, power, honor, intelligence, wit, and all of those rewards that come with an aristocratic upbringing, the best of education and a life that is guaranteed in basic comforts from birth. In Kant's conception of morality, by contrast, all people who are rational (that is, everyone except morons, very young children, and popular musicians) are to be judged by the same moral standards, the standards of duty. There are no elites. And since the judgments of moral worth are made solely on the basis of good intentions, no "external" advantages are relevant to a person's goodness or badness. In fact, it is possible that a perfectly "good" person would, with only the best intentions, cause chaos and unhappiness around him wherever he goes. And the harder he tries to make amends, the more he fouls them up. Dostoyevski wrote one of his greatest novels, *The Idiot*, about just this—a perfectly good man, with all the right intentions, causes suffering and even death every time he tries to do good. Yet the point is, he is, by this modern conception, still the perfectly good man. Aristotle would find this laughable. How could we call a man virtuous just because of his intentions? How can a perfect failure be an example of ideal goodness?

In Aristotle's morality, the only people who operate on the basis of duty are those who are incapable of being truly good and truly happy. Duty is a morality for women and servants. For the elite, it is rather a question of personal excellence—in battle, in games, in business, in love, in debate, and in all things, especially philosophy. And where Kant's morality mostly consists (like the Ten Commandments) of "thou shalt not . . ." Aristotle's morality appropriately consists of personal desires and ambitions, not commands to achieve, and certainly not negative commands. The key element of Kant's philosophy, duty, is treated minimally in Aristotle, where the emphasis is on personal growth and achievement. On the other side, the image of the well-rounded, successful man, excellent in all things and the envy of his fellow men, plays only a secondary role in Kant's philosophy (for example, in his *Doctrine of Virtue*, the second part of the *Metaphysics of Morals*). For him, what is important is the person who does what he or she is supposed to do. For Aristotle, the ideal is to strive for personal excellence, and doing what a person is supposed to do is simply taken for granted along the way.

Now notice that both moralities have many of the same results. Aristotle's morality will praise many and condemn most of the same acts as Kant's morality: Killing needlessly and stealing are wrong; telling the truth and keeping promises are right. But their conceptions of morality, and consequently, their conceptions of people are distinctively different. As we appreciate the nature of this difference, we will be in a position to understand one of the most dramatic moral revolutions of modern times, initiated by Friedrich Nietzsche. Nietzsche called himself an **immoralist**, and he attacked morality as viciously as he attacked Christianity. But though he has often been interpreted as saying that we should give up morality and feel free to kill, steal, and commit crimes of all kinds, his moral philosophy does not in fact say that at all. What he did was to attack modern morality, as summarized by Kant and Christianity, and urge us to return to ancient Greek morality as summarized by Aristotle. He also attacked utilitarianism, which he considered "vulgar." Like a great many philosophers of the nineteenth century (particularly German philosophers: Fichte, Hegel, Marx), Nietzsche saw in the ancient Greeks a sense of personal harmony and a sense of excellence that had been lost in the modern world. Nietzsche, like Aristotle, saw the concept of duty as fit for servants and slaves, but such a morality was wholly inadequate to motivate us to personal excellence and achievement. And Nietzsche, like Aristotle, was an unabashed elitist. Only a few people were capable of this "higher" morality. For the rest, the "slave morality" of duty would have to suffice. But for those few, nothing was more important than to give up the "thou shalt not . . ." of Judeo-Christian morality and seek out one's own virtues and abilities. This does not mean that such a person need ever violate the laws of morality although it must be said that Nietzsche's belligerent style and often warlike terminology certainly suggests that his master morality will include a good amount of cruelty and immorality. But it is clear that Nietzsche does not consider obedience to laws as the most important thing in life. Nor does this mean that Nietzsche is (as he is often thought to be) an ethical egoist. To say that a person should develop his or her own virtues and become excellent in as many ways as possible is not at all to say that one must act only in one's own interests. As in Aristotle, the excellence of the individual is part of and contributes to the excellence of mankind as a whole.

Nietzsche takes his central project as a philosopher to be what he calls "the creation of values." In this he is rightly listed as one of the existentialist philosophers, or at least as one of their most important predecessors. The phrase is perhaps misleading, however. What Nietzsche is doing is not inventing new values so much as reasserting very old ones. Furthermore, Nietzsche, like Aristotle, takes ethics to be based solely upon human nature, and so it is not a question of "creating values" so much as finding them in oneself. But where such a philosophy for Aristotle was in agreement with most of the thinking of his times, Nietzsche's thought was a radical disruption of the usual Kantian style of thinking of the modern period and so takes on the tone of violent destructiveness rather than—as in Aristotle—the self-satisfied tones of a gentleman. Since Nietzsche, unlike Aristotle, did not believe that every human "nature" was the same, he taught that different individuals would most assuredly find and follow different values, different conceptions of excellence and thus have different moralities. For this reason, students who read Nietzsche looking for concrete moral advice, a set of principles to act on, are always disappointed. His central teaching is rather "follow yourself, don't follow me." Consequently, he can't— and won't—try to tell you how to live. But he does tell you to live and to give up the servile views that we have held of ourselves for many centuries.

Nietzsche's moral philosophy is largely critical, and most of his efforts have gone into the rejection of Kant's conception of morality in order to make room for individual self-achieving as found in Aristotle. His argument, however, is not a refutation in the usual sense. Instead, he undermines morality by showing that the motivation behind it is decrepit and weak. Categories of Nietzsche's philosophy are strength and weakness, and he considers the Greek tradition of personal excellence a source of strength, the modern conception of morality a facade for weakness. Accordingly, he calls the first a "master morality," the second, a "slave morality" or, with reference to modern mass movements, a "herd instinct." The excerpts that follow, therefore, illustrate Nietzsche's general attack on morality. But never forget that his purpose is not merely destructive but, in his eyes, creative, and the point is to get us to look to ourselves for values and to excel, each in our own ways (the phrase "will to power" refers to just this effort to excel as individuals).

ON "MASTER AND SLAVE MORALITY"
By Friedrich Nietzsche

What does your conscience say? "You should become him who you are."

Herd-Instinct.—Wherever we meet with a morality we find a valuation and order of rank of the human impulses and activities. These valuations and orders of rank are always the expression of the needs of a community or herd: that which is in the first place to *its* advantage—and in the second place and third place—is also the authoritative standard for the worth of every individual. By morality the individual is taught to become a function of the herd, and to ascribe to himself value only as a function. As the conditions for the maintenance of one community have been very different from those of another community, there have been very different moralities; and in respect to the future essential transformations of herd and communities, states and societies, one can prophesy that there will still be very divergent moralities. Morality is the herd-instinct in the individual.[4]

Apart from the value of such assertions as "there is a categorical imperative in us," one can always ask: What does such an assertion indicate about him who makes it? There are systems of morals which are meant to justify their author in the eyes of other people; other systems of morals are meant to tranquillise him, and make him self-satisfied; with other systems he wants to crucify and humble himself; with others he wishes to take revenge; with others to conceal himself; with others to glorify himself and gain superiority and distinction;— this system of morals helps its author to forget, that system makes him, or something of him, forgotten; many a moralist would like to exercise power and creative arbitrariness over mankind; many another, perhaps, Kant especially, gives us to understand by his morals that "what is estimable in me, is that I know how to obey—and with you it *shall* not be otherwise than with me!" In short, systems of morals are only a *sign-language of the emotions.* . . .

In a tour through the many finer and coarser moralities which have hitherto prevailed or still prevail on the earth, I found certain traits recurring regularly together and connected with one another, until finally two primary types revealed themselves to me, and a radical distinction was brought to light. There is *master-morality* and *slave-morality;*—I would at once add, however, that in all higher and mixed civilisations, there are also attempts at the reconciliation of the two moralities; but one finds still oftener the confusion and mutual misunderstanding of them, indeed sometimes their close juxtaposition—even in the same man, within one soul. The distinctions of moral values have either originated in a ruling caste, pleasantly conscious of being different from the ruled—or among the ruled class, the slaves and dependents of all sorts. In the first case, when it is the rulers who determine the conception "good," it is the exalted, proud disposition which is regarded as the distinguishing feature, and that which determines the order of rank. The noble type of man separates from himself the beings in whom the opposite of this exalted, proud disposition displays itself: he despises them. Let it at once be noted that in this first kind of morality the antithesis "good" and "bad" means practically the same as "noble" and "despicable";—the antithesis "good" and "*evil*" is of a different origin. The cowardly, the timid, the insignificant, and those thinking merely of narrow utility are despised; moreover, also, the distrustful, with their constrained glances, the self-abasing, the dog-like kind of men who let themselves be abused, the mendicant flatterers, and above all the liars:—it is a fundamental belief of all aristocrats that the common people are untruthful. "We truthful ones"—the nobility in ancient Greece called themselves. It is obvious that everywhere the designations of moral value were at first applied to *men*, and were only derivatively and at a later period applied to *actions*; it is a gross mistake, therefore, when historians of morals start questions like, "Why have sympathetic actions been praised?" The noble type of man regards *himself* as a determiner of values; he does not require to be approved of; he passes the judgment: "What is injurious to me is injurious in itself"; he knows that it is he himself only who confers honour on things; he is a *creator of values*. He honours whatever he recognises in himself: such morality is self-glorification. In the foreground there is the feeling of plenitude, of power, which seeks to overflow, the happiness of high tension, the consciousness of a wealth which would fain give and bestow:—the noble man also helps the unfortunate, but not—or scarcely—out of pity, but rather from an impulse generated by the super-abundance of power. The noble man honours in himself the powerful one, him also who has power over himself, who knows how to speak and how to keep silence, who takes pleasure in subjecting himself to severity and hardness, and has reverence for all that is severe and hard. "Wotan placed a hard heart in my breast," says an old Scandinavian Saga: it is thus rightly expressed from the soul of a proud Viking. Such a type of man is even proud of *not* being made for sympathy; the hero of the Saga therefore adds warningly: "He who has not a hard heart when young, will never have one." The noble and brave who think thus are the furthest removed from the morality which sees precisely in sympathy, or in acting for the good of others, or in *désintéressement*, the characteristic of the moral; faith in oneself, pride in oneself, a radical enmity and irony towards "selflessness," belong as definitely to noble morality, as do a careless scorn and precaution in presence of sympathy and the "warm heart."—It is the powerful who *know* how to honour, it is their art, their domain for invention. The profound reverence for age and for tradition—all law rests on this double reverence,—the belief and prejudice in favour of ancestors and unfavourable to newcomers, is typical in the morality of the powerful; and if, reversely, men of "modern ideas" believe almost instinctively in "progress" and the "future," and are more and more lacking in respect for old age, the ignoble origin of these "ideas" has complacently betrayed itself thereby. A morality of the ruling class, however, is more especially foreign and irritating to present-day taste in the sternness of its principle that one has duties only to one's equals; that one may act towards beings of a lower rank, towards all that is foreign, just as seems good to one, or "as the heart desires," and in any case "beyond good and evil": it is here that sympathy and similar sentiments can have a place. The ability and obligation to exercise prolonged gratitude and prolonged revenge—both only within the circle of equals,—artfulness in retaliation, *raffinement* of the idea in friendship, a certain necessity to have enemies (as outlets for the emotions of envy, quarrelsomeness, arrogance—in fact, in order to be a good *friend*): all these are typical characteristics of the noble morality, which, as has been pointed out, is not the morality of "modern ideas," and is therefore at present difficult to realise, and also to unearth and disclose.—It is otherwise with the second type of morality, *slave-morality*. Supposing that the abused, the oppressed, the suffering, the unemancipated, the weary, and those uncertain of themselves, should moralise, what will be the common element in their moral estimates? Probably a pessimistic suspicion with regard to the entire situation of man will find expression, perhaps a condemnation of man, together with his situation. The slave has an unfavourable eye for the virtues of the powerful; he has a scepticism and distrust, a *refinement* of distrust of everything "good" that is there honoured—he would fain persuade himself that the very happiness there is not genuine. On the other hand, *those* qualities which serve to alleviate the existence of sufferers are brought into prominence and flooded with light; it is here that sympathy, the kind, helping hand, the warm heart, patience, diligence, humility, and friendliness attain to honour for here these are the most useful qualities, and almost the only means of supporting the burden of existence. Slave-morality is essentially the morality of utility. Here is the seat of the origin of the famous antithesis "good" and "evil":—power and dangerousness are assumed to reside in the evil, a certain dreadfulness, subtlety, and strength, which do not admit of being despised. According to slave-morality, therefore, the "evil" man arouses fear; according to master-morality, it is precisely the "good" man who arouses fear and seeks to arouse it, while the bad man is regarded as the despicable being. The contrast attains its maximum when, in accordance with the logical consequences of slave-morality, a shade of depreciation—it may be slight and well-intentioned—at last attaches itself to the "good" man of this morality; because, according to the servile mode of thought, the good man must in any case be the *safe* man: he is good-natured, easily deceived, perhaps a little stupid, *un bonhomme*. Everywhere that slave-morality gains the ascendancy, language shows a tendency to approximate the significations of the words "good" and "stupid."—At last fundamental difference: the desire for *freedom*, the instinct for happiness and the refinements of the feeling of liberty belong as necessarily to slave-morals and morality, as artifice and enthusiasm in reverence and devotion are the regular symptoms of an aristocratic mode of thinking and estimating.— Hence we can understand without further detail why *love as a passion*—it is our European specialty—must absolutely be of noble origin.

And on the philosopher:

> The philosophical workers, after the excellent pattern of Kant and Hegel, have to fix and formalise some great existing body of valuations—that is to say, former *determinations of value*, creations of value, which have become prevalent, and are for a time called "truths"—whether in the domain of the *logical*, the *political* (moral), or the *artistic*. It is for these investigators to make whatever has happened and been esteemed hitherto, conspicuous, conceivable, intelligible, and manageable, to shorten everything long, even "time" itself, and to *subjugate* the entire past; an immense and wonderful task, in the carrying out of which all refined pride, all tenacious will, can surely find satisfaction. *The real philosophers, however, are commanders and law-givers*; they say: "Thus *shall* it be!" They determine first the Whither and the Why of mankind, and thereby set aside the previous labour of all philosophical workers and all subjugators of the past—they grasp at the future with a creative hand, and whatever is and was, becomes for them thereby a means, an instrument, and a hammer. Their "knowing" is *creating*, their creating is a law-giving, their will to truth is—*Will to Power*.—Are there at present such philosophers? Have there ever been such philosophers? *Must* there not be such philosophers some day?[5]

Nietzsche is often viewed as the most extreme of the antimoralists, those who attack the traditional duty-bound Kantian-Christian conception of morality. In fact, he is but one among many philosophers who have rejected that morality in exchange for a more personal and individual set of principles. Given his emphasis on human "nature," we can say that even Nietzsche is much more traditional than is usually supposed (though it is the Aristotelian, not the Kantian tradition). In the past few decades, however, morality has become far more personalized than even Nietzsche suggested. In Anglo-American philosophy, largely in the wake of logical positivism, ethics has been reduced to a matter of emotions, prescriptions, and attitudes rather than principles and rational laws. (Ironically, Nietzsche has always been in extreme disfavor among such philosophers while Kant has been considered with extreme favor.)

The attack on the absolute moral principles of reason, which are the same for everyone, has been one of the most vigorous philosophical movements of the twentieth century, so much so that many philosophers, religious leaders, and moralists have become alarmed at the destruction of uniform moral codes and have attempted to reassert the old moral laws in new ways. The problem is one of relativism. Is there a single moral code? Or are there possibly as many moralities as there are people? There are intermediary suggestions, such as relativizing morals to particular groups or societies, but the question is still the same: "Is there ultimately any way of defending one moral code against any other?"

The most extreme relativist position of all has emerged from Nietzsche's existentialist successors, particularly Jean-Paul Sartre. In Sartre's philosophy, not only the idea of a uniform morality but the idea of a human nature upon which this morality might be based is completely rejected. Not because different people might have different "natures," as in Nietzsche, but because for Sartre our values are quite literally a question of creation, of personal commitment. In answer to any question about morality, the only ultimate answer is "because I choose to accept these values." But what is most fascinating about Sartre's conception of morality as choice is that he does not therefore abandon general principles as Nietzsche does. Quite the contrary, he adopts an almost Kantian stance about the need to choose principles for all mankind, not just oneself. The difference is that Sartre, unlike Kant, makes no claims about the singular correctness of these principles. All he can say is "this is what I choose mankind to be." Thus Sartre's moral philosophy is a curious mixture of the most radical relativism and the most traditional moralizing.

From "EXISTENTIALISM,"
By Jean-Paul Sartre

Man is nothing else but that which he makes of himself. That is the first principle of existentialism. And this is what people call its "subjectivity," using the word as a reproach against us. But what do we mean to say by this, but that man is of a greater dignity than a stone or a table? For we mean to say that man primarily exists—that man is, before all else, something which propels itself towards a future and is aware that it is doing so. Man is, indeed, a project which possesses a subjective life, instead of being a kind of moss, or a fungus or a cauliflower. Before that projection of the self nothing exists; not even in the heaven of intelligence; man will only attain existence when he is what he purposes to be. Not, however, what he may wish to be. For what we usually understand by wishing or willing is a conscious decision taken—much more often than not—after we have made ourselves what we are. I may wish to join a party, to write a book or to marry—but in such a case what is usually called my will is probably a manifestation of a prior and more spontaneous decision. If, however, it is true that existence is prior to essence, man is responsible for what he is. Thus, the first effect of existentialism is that it puts every man in possession of himself as he is, and places the entire responsibility for his existence squarely upon his own shoulders. And, when we say that man is responsible for himself, we do not mean that he is responsible only for his own individuality, but that he is responsible for all men. The word "subjectivism" is to be understood in two senses, and our adversaries play upon only one of them. Subjectivism means, on the one hand, the freedom of the individual subject and, on the other, that man cannot pass beyond human subjectivity. It is the latter which is the deeper meaning of existentialism. When we say that man chooses himself, we do mean that every one of us must choose himself; but by that we also mean that in choosing for himself he chooses for all men. For in effect, of all the actions a man may take in order to create himself as he wills to be, there is not one which is not creative, at the same time, of an image of man such as he believes he ought to be. To choose between this or that is at the same time to affirm the value of that which is chosen; for we are unable ever to choose the worse. What we choose is always the better and nothing can be better for us unless it is better for all. If, moreover, existence precedes essence and we will to exist at the same time as we fashion our image, that image is valid for all and for the entire epoch in which we find ourselves. Our responsibility is thus much greater than we had supposed, for it concerns mankind as a whole. If I am a worker, for instance, I may choose to join a Christian rather than a Communist trade union. And if, by that membership, I choose to signify that resignation is, after all, the attitude that best becomes a man, that man's kingdom is not upon this earth, I do not commit myself alone to that view. Resignation is my will for everyone, and my action is, in consequence, a commitment on behalf of all mankind. Or if, to take a more personal case, I decide to marry and to have children, even though this decision proceeds simply from my situation, from my passion or my desire, I am thereby committing not only myself, but humanity as a whole, to the practice of monogamy. I am thus responsible for myself and for all men, and I am creating a certain image of man as I would have him to be. In fashioning myself I fashion man . . . .

. . . Who can prove that I am the proper person to impose, by my own choice, my conception of man upon mankind? I shall never find any proof whatever; there will be no sign to convince me of it . . .

If I regard a certain course of action as good, it is only I who choose to say that it is good and not bad . . . . nevertheless I also am obliged at every instant to perform actions which are examples. Everything happens to every man as though the whole human race had its eyes fixed upon what he is doing and regulated its conduct accordingly . . . .

As an example by which you may the better understand this state of abandonment, I will refer to the case of a pupil of mine, who sought me out in the following circumstances. His father was quarrelling with his mother and was also inclined to be a "collaborator"; his elder brother had been killed in the German offensive of 1940 and this young man, with a sentiment somewhat primitive but generous, burned to avenge him. His mother was living alone with him, deeply afflicted by the semi-treason of his father and by the death of her eldest son, and her only consolation was in this young man. But he, at this moment, had the choice between going to England to join the Free French Forces or of staying near his mother, and helping her to live. He fully realized that this woman lived only for him and that his disappearance—or perhaps his death—would plunge her into despair. He also realized that, concretely and in fact, every action he performed on his mother's behalf would be sure of effect in the sense of aiding her to live, whereas anything he did in order to go and fight would be an ambiguous action which might vanish like water into sand and serve no purpose. For instance, to set out for England he would have to wait indefinitely in a Spanish camp on the way through Spain; or, on arriving in England or in Algiers he might be put into an office to fill up forms. Consequently, he found himself confronted by two very different modes of action; the one concrete, immediate, but directed towards only one individual; and the other an action addressed to an end infinitely greater, a national collectivity, but for that very reason ambiguous—and it might be frustrated on the way. At the same time, he was hesitating between two kinds of morality; on the one side the morality of sympathy, of personal devotion and, on the other side, a morality of wider scope but of more debatable validity. He had to choose between those two. What could help him to choose? Could the Christian doctrine? No. Christian doctrine says: Act with charity, love your neighbour, deny yourself for others, choose the way which is hardest, and so forth. But which is the harder road? To whom does one owe the more brotherly love, the patriot or the mother? Which is the more useful aim, the general one of fighting in and for the whole community, or the precise aim of helping one particular person to live? Who can give an answer to that *a priori*? No one. Nor is it given in any ethical scripture. The Kantian ethic says, Never regard another as a means, but always as an end. Very well; if I remain with my mother, I shall be regarding her as the end and not as a means: but by the same token I am in danger of treating as means those who are fighting on my behalf; and the converse is also true, that if I go to the aid of the combatants I shall be treating them as the end at the risk of treating my mother as a means.

If values are uncertain, if they are still too abstract to determine the particular, concrete case under consideration, nothing remains but to trust in our instincts. That is what this young man tried to do; and when I saw him he said, "In the end, it is feeling that counts; the direction in which it is really pushing me is the one I ought to choose. If I feel that I love my mother enough to sacrifice everything else for her—my will to be avenged, all my longings for action and adventure—then I stay with her. If, on the contrary, I feel that my love for her is not enough, I go." But how does one estimate the strength of a feeling? The value of his feeling for his mother was determined precisely by the fact that he was standing by her. I may say that I love a certain friend enough to sacrifice such or such a sum of money for him, but I cannot prove that unless I have done it. I may say, "I love my mother enough to remain with her," if actually I have remained with her. I can only estimate the strength of this affection if I have performed an action by which it is defined and ratified. But if I then appeal to this affection to justify my action, I find myself drawn into a vicious circle. . . .

In other words, feeling is formed by the deeds that one does; therefore I cannot consult it as a guide to action. And that is to say that I can neither seek within myself for an authentic impulse to action, nor can I expect, from some ethic, formulae that will enable me to act. You may say that the youth did, at least, go to a professor to ask for advice. But if you seek counsel—from a priest, for example—you have selected that priest; and at bottom you already knew, more or less, what he would advise. In other words, to choose an adviser is nevertheless to commit oneself by that choice. If you are a Christian, you will say, Consult a priest; but there are collaborationists, priests who are resisters and priests who wait for the tide to turn: which will you choose? Had this young man chosen a priest of the resistance, or one of the collaboration, he would have decided beforehand the kind of advice he was to receive. Similarly, in coming to me, he knew what advice I should give him, and I had but one reply to make. You are free, therefore choose—that is to say, invent. No rule of general morality can show you what you ought to do.

To say that it does not matter what you choose is not correct. In one sense choice is possible, but what is not possible is not to choose. I can always choose but I must know that if I do not choose, that is still a choice. This although it may appear merely formal, is of great importance as a limit to fantasy and caprice. For, when I confront a real situation—for example, that I am a sexual being, able to have relations with a being of the other sex and able to have children—I am obliged to choose my attitude to it, and in every respect I bear the responsibility of the choice which, in committing myself, also commits the whole of humanity . . . . Man finds himself in an organized situation in which he is himself involved: his choice involves mankind in its entirety, and he cannot avoid choosing. Either he must remain single, or he must marry without having children, or he must marry and have children. In any case, and whichever he may choose, it is impossible for him, in respect of this situation, not to take complete responsibility. Doubtless he chooses without reference to any pre-established values, but it is unjust to tax him with caprice. Rather let us say that the moral choice is comparable to the construction of a work of art.

No one can tell what the painting of tomorrow will be like; one cannot judge a painting until it is done. What has that to do with morality: We are in the same creative situation. We never speak of a work of art as irresponsible; when we are discussing a canvas by Picasso, we understand very well that the composition became what it is at the time when he was painting it, and that his works are part and parcel of his entire life.

It is the same upon the plane of morality. There is this in common between art and morality, that in both we have to do with creation and invention. We cannot decide a priori what it is that should be done. I think it was made sufficiently clear to you in the case of that student who came to see me, that to whatever ethical system he might appeal, the Kantian or any other, he could find no sort of guidance whatever; he was obliged to invent the law for himself. Certainly we cannot say that this man, in choosing to remain with his mother—that is, in taking sentiment, personal devotion and concrete charity as his moral foundations—would be making an irresponsible choice, nor could we do so if he preferred the sacrifice of going away to England. Man makes himself; he is not found ready-made; he makes himself by the choice of his morality, and he cannot but choose a morality, such is the pressure of circumstances upon him.[26]

Sartre says that "man makes himself." He believes this to be true both individually and collectively. It is through my actions that I commit myself to values, not through principles I accept a priori or rules that are imposed upon me by God or society. If you accept the voice of some authority, you have chosen to accept that authority rather than some other. If you appeal for advice or help, you have chosen to seek that kind of advice rather than some other kind. If you refuse to choose between alternatives, then you are responsible for neglecting both or all the alternatives, for "copping-out." In any case, you must do something, even if what you do is "doing nothing" (that is, not taking one of the important alternatives before you).

Here is Sartre's reply to his predecessors: We are no longer in the position of Aristotle, in which morality appears to us as a given, as "natural," and without alternatives of the most irresolvable kind. We can no longer trust our "sentiments," as Hume did, for we now find ourselves torn with conflicting sentiments of every kind. We can no longer accept the a priori moralizing of Kant, for we now see that the circumstances in which we must act are never so simple that they will allow for a simple "categorical" imperative. And even "the greatest good for the greatest number" no longer provides a guide for our actions, for we no longer pretend that we can calculate the consequences of our actions with any such accuracy. Besides, who is to say what "the greatest good" or, for that matter, "the greatest number" is today? Against all of this, Sartre argues that there is simply our choice of actions and values, together with their consequences, whatever they are. There is no justification for these and no "right" or "wrong." But this does not mean that we need not choose or that it is all "arbitrary." To the contrary, the upshot of Sartre's thesis is precisely that we are always choosing and that morality is nothing other than our commitments, at least for the present, to those values we choose to follow through our actions.

PHILOSOPHICAL CONCEPTS OF ATHEISM

by Ernest Nagel

I.

I must begin by stating what sense I am attaching to the word "atheism," and how I am construing the theme of this paper. I shall understand by "atheism" a critique and a denial of the major claims of all varieties of theism. And by theism I shall mean the view which holds, as one writer has expressed it, "that the heavens and the earth and all that they contain owe their existence and continuance in existence to the wisdom and will of a supreme, self-consistent, omnipotent, omniscient, righteous, and benevolent being, who is distinct from, and independent of, what he has created." Several things immediately follow from these definitions.

In the first place, atheism is not necessarily an irreligious concept, for theism is just one among many views concerning the nature and origin of the world. The denial of theism is logically compatible with a religious outlook upon life, and is in fact characteristic of the great historical religions. . . . Early Buddhism is a religion which does not subscribe to any doctrine about a god; and there are pantheistic religions and philosophies which, because they deny that God is a being separate from and independent of the world, are not theistic in the sense of the word explained above.

The second point to note is that atheism is not to be identified with sheer unbelief, or with disbelief in some particular creed of a religious group. Thus, a child who has received no religious instruction and has never heard about God, is not an atheist—for he is not denying any theistic claims. Similarly, an adult who has withdrawn from the faith of his fathers without reflection or because of frank indifference to any theological issue is also not an atheist—for such an adult is not challenging theism and is not professing any views on the subject. Moreover, thought the term "atheist" has been used historically as an abusive label for those who do not happen to subscribe to some regnant orthodoxy (for example, the ancient Romans called the early Christians atheists, because the latter denied the Roman divinities), or for those who engage in conduct regarded as immoral, it is not in this sense that I am discussing atheism.

One final word of preliminary explanation. I propose to examine some *philosophic* concepts of atheism, and I am not interested in the slightest in the many considerations atheists have advanced against the evidences for some particular religious and theological doctrine—for example, against the truth of the Christian story. What I mean by "philosophical" in the present context is that the views I shall consider are directed against any form of theism, and have their origin and basis in a logical analysis of the theistic position, and in a comprehensive account of the world believed to be wholly intelligible without the adoption of a theistic hypothesis.

Theism as I conceive it is a theological proposition, not a statement of a position that belongs primarily to religion. On my view, religion as a historical and social phenomenon is primarily an institutionalized *cultus* or practice, which possesses identifiable social functions and which expresses certain attitudes men take toward their world. Although it is doubtful whether men ever engage in religious practices or assume religious attitudes without some more or less explicit interpretation of their ritual or some rationale for their attitude, it is still the case that it is possible to distinguish religion as a social and personal phenomenon from the theological doctrines which may be developed as justifications for religious practices. Indeed, in some of the great religions of the world the profession of a creed plays a relatively minor role. In short, religion is a form of social communion, a participation in certain kinds of ritual (whether it be a dance, worship, prayer, or the like), and a form of experience (sometimes, though not invariably, directed to a personal confrontation with divine and holy things). Theology is an articulated and, at its best, a rational attempt at understanding these feelings and practices in the light of their relation to other parts of human experience and in terms of some hypothesis concerning the nature of things entire.

II .

As I see it, atheistic philosophies fall into two major groups: (1) those which hold that the theistic doctrine is meaningful, but reject it either on the ground that (a) the positive evidence for it is insufficient or (b) the negative evidence is quite overwhelming; and (2) those who hold that the theistic thesis is not even meaningful, and reject it (a) as just nonsense or (b) as literally meaningless, but interpreting it as a symbolic rendering of human ideals, thus reading the theistic thesis in a sense that most believers in theism would disavow. It will not be possible in the limited space at my disposal to discuss the second category of atheistic critiques; and in any event, most of the traditional atheistic critiques of theism belong to the first group.

But before turning to the philosophical examination of the major classical arguments for theism, it is well to note that such philosophical critiques do not quite convey the passion with which atheists have often carried on their analyses of theistic views. For historically, atheism has been, and indeed continues to be, a form of social and political protest, directed as much against institutionalized religion as against theistic doctrine. Atheism has been, in effect, a moral revulsion against the undoubted abuses of the secular power exercised by religious leaders and religious institutions.

Religious authorities have opposed the correction of glaring injustices, and encouraged politically and socially reactionary policies. Religious institutions have been havens of obscurantist thought and centers for the dissemination of intolerance. Religious creeds have been used to set limits to free inquiry, to perpetuate inhumane treatment of the ill and the underprivileged, and to support moral doctrines insensitive to human suffering.

These indictments may not tell the whole story about the historical significance of religion; but they are at least an important part of the story. The refutation of theism has thus seemed to many an indispensable step not only toward liberating men's minds from superstition but also toward achieving a more equitable reordering of society. And no account of even the more philosophical aspects of atheistic thought is adequate which does not give proper recognition to the powerful social motives that actuate many atheistic arguments.

But however this may be, I want now to discuss three classical arguments for the existence of God, arguments which have constituted at least a partial basis for theistic commitments. As long as theism is defended simply as dogma, asserted as a matter of direct revelation or as the deliverance of authority, belief in the dogma is impregnable to rational argument. In fact, however, reasons are frequently advanced in support of the theistic creed, and these reasons have been the subject of acute philosophical critiques.

III.

One of the oldest intellectual defenses of theism is the cosmological argument, also known as the argument from a first cause. Briefly put, the argument runs as follows. Every event must have a cause. Hence an event A must have as cause some event B, which in turn must have a cause C, and so on. But if there is no end to this backward progression of causes, the progression will be infinite; and in the opinion of those who use this argument, an infinite series of actual events is unintelligible and absurd. Hence there must be a first cause, and this first cause is God, the initiator of all change in the universe.

The argument is an ancient one . . . and it has impressed many generations of exceptionally keen minds. The argument is nonetheless a weak reed on which to rest the theistic thesis. Let us waive any question concerning the validity of the principle that every event has a cause, for though the question is important its discussion would lead us far afield. However, if the principle is assumed, it is surely incongruous to postulate a first cause as a way of escaping from the coils of an infinite series. For if everything must have a cause, why does not God require one for His own existence? The standard answer is that He does not need any, because He is self-caused. But if God can be self-caused, why cannot the world be self-caused? Why do we require a God transcending the world to bring the world into existence and to initiate changes in it? On the other hand, the supposed inconceivability and absurdity of an infinite series of regressive causes will be admitted by no one who has competent familiarity with the modern mathematical analysis of infinity. The cosmological argument does not stand up under scrutiny.

IV.

The second "proof" of God's existence is usually called the ontological argument. It too has a long history going back to early Christian days, though it acquired great prominence only in medieval times. The argument can be stated in several ways, one of which is the following. Since God is conceived to be omnipotent, he is a perfect being. A perfect being is defined as one whose essence or nature lacks no attributes (or properties) whatsoever, one whose nature is complete in every respect. But it is evident that we have an idea of a perfect being, for we have just defined the idea; and since this is so, the argument continues, God who is the perfect being must exist. Why must he? Because his existence follows from his defined nature. For if God lacked the attribute of existence, he would be lacking at least one attribute, and would therefore not be perfect. To sum up, since we have an idea of God as a perfect being, God must exist.

There are several ways of approaching this argument, but I shall consider only one. The argument was exploded by the 18th century philosopher Immanuel Kant. The substance of Kant's criticism is that it is just a confusion to say that existence is an attribute, and that though the *word* "existence" may occur as the grammatical predicate in a sentence, no attribute is being predicated of a thing when we say that the thing exists or has existence. Thus, to use Kant's example, when we think of $100 we are thinking of the nature of this sum of money; but the nature of $100 remains the same whether we have $100 in our pockets or not. Accordingly, we are confounding grammar with logic if we suppose that some characteristic is being attributed to the nature of $100 when we say that a $100 bill exists in someone's pocket.

To make the point clearer, consider another example. When we say that a lion has a tawny color, we are predicating a certain attribute of the animal, and similarly when we say that the lion is fierce or is hungry. But when we say the lion exists, all that we are saying is that something is (or has the nature of) a lion; we are not specifying an attribute which belongs to the nature of anything that is a lion. In short, the word "existence" does not signify any attribute, and in consequence no attribute that belongs to the nature of anything. Accordingly, it does not follow from the assumption that we have an idea of a perfect being that such a being exists. For the idea of a perfect being does not involve the attribute of existence as a constituent of that idea, since there is no such attribute. The ontological argument thus has a serious leak, and it can hold no water.

V.

The two arguments discussed thus far are purely dialectical, and attempt to establish God's existence without any appeal to empirical data. The next argument, called the argument from design, is different in character, for it is based on what purports to be empirical evidence. I wish to examine two forms of this argument.

One variant of it calls attention to the remarkable way in which different things and processes in the world are integrated with each other, and concludes that this mutual "fitness" of things can be explained only by the assumption of a divine architect who planned the world and everything in it. For example, living organisms can maintain themselves in a variety of environments, and do so in virtue of their delicate mechanisms which adapt the organisms to all sorts of environmental changes. There is thus an intricate pattern of means and ends throughout the animate world. But the existence of this pattern is unintelligible, so the argument runs, except on the hypothesis that the pattern has been deliberately instituted by a Supreme Designer. If we find a watch in some deserted spot, we do not think it came into existence by chance, and we do not hesitate to conclude that an intelligent creature designed and made it. But the world and all its contents exhibit mechanisms and mutual adjustments that are far more complicated and subtle than are those of a watch. Must we not therefore conclude that these things too have a Creator?

The conclusion of this argument is based on an inference from analogy: The watch and the world are alike in possessing a congruence of parts and an adjustment of means to ends; the watch has a watch-maker; hence the world has a world-maker. But is the analogy a good one? Let us once more waive some important issues, in particular the issue of whether the universe is the unified system such as the watch admittedly is. And let us concentrate on the question of what is the ground for our assurance that watches do not come into existence except through the operations of intelligent manufacturers. The answer is plain. We have never run across a watch which has not been deliberately made by someone. But the situation is nothing like this in the case of the innumerable animate and inanimate systems with which we are familiar. Even in the case of living organisms, though they are generated by their parent organisms, the parents do not "make" their progeny in the same sense in which watchmakers make watches. And once this point is clear, the inference from the existence of living organisms to the existence of a supreme designer no longer appears credible.

Moreover, the argument loses all its force if the facts which the hypothesis of a divine designer is supposed to explain can be understood on the basis of a better supported assumption. And indeed, such an alternative explanation is one of the achievements of Darwinian biology. For Darwin showed that one can account for the variety of biological species, as well as for their adaptations to their environments, without invoking a divine creator and acts of special creation. The Darwinian theory explains the diversity of biological species in terms of chance variations in the structure of organisms, and of a mechanism of selection which retains those variant forms that possess some advantages for survival. The evidence for these assumptions is considerable; and developments subsequent to Darwin have only strengthened the case for a thoroughly naturalistic explanation of the facts of biological adaptation. In any event, this version of the argument from design has nothing to recommend it.

A second form of this argument has been recently revived in the speculations of some modern physicists. No one who is familiar with the facts can fail to be impressed by the success with which the use of mathematical methods has enabled us to obtain intellectual mastery of many parts of nature. But some thinkers have therefore concluded that since the book of nature is ostensibly written in mathematical language, nature must be the creation of a divine mathematician. However, the argument is most dubious. For it rests, among other things, on the assumption that mathematical tools can be successfully used only if the events of nature exhibit some *special* kind of order, and on the further assumption that if the structure of things were different from what it is, mathematical language would be inadequate for describing such structure. But it can be shown that no matter what the world were like—even if it impressed us as being utterly chaotic—it would still possess some order, and would in principle be amenable to a mathematical description. In point of fact, it makes no sense to say that there is absolutely *no* pattern in any conceivable subject matter. To be sure, there are differences in complexities of structure, and if the patterns of events were sufficiently complex we might not be able to unravel them. But however that may be, the success of mathematical physics in giving us some understanding of the world around us does not yield the conclusion that only a mathematician could have devised the patters of order we have discovered in nature.

VI.

The inconclusiveness of the three classical arguments for the existence of God was already made evident by Kant, in a manner substantially not different from the above discussion. There are, however, other types of arguments for theism that have been influential in the history of thought, two of which I wish to consider, even if only briefly.

Indeed, though Kant destroyed the classical intellectual foundations for theism, he himself invented a fresh argument for it. Kant's attempted proof is not intended to be a purely theoretical demonstration, and is based on the supposed facts of our moral nature. It has exerted an enormous influence on subsequent theological speculation. In barest outline, the argument is as follows. According to Kant, we are subject not only to physical laws like the rest of nature, but also to moral ones. These moral laws are categorical imperatives, which we must heed not because of their utilitarian consequences but simply because as autonomous moral agents it is our duty to accept them as binding. However, Kant was keenly aware that though virtue may be its reward, the virtuous man (that is, the man who acts out of a sense of duty and in conformity with the moral law) does not always receive his just desserts in this world; nor did he shut his eyes to the fact that evil men frequently enjoy the best things this world has to offer. In short, virtue does not always reap happiness. Nevertheless, the highest good is the realization of happiness commensurate with one's virtue; and Kant believed that it is a practical postulate of the moral life to promote this good. But what can guarantee that the highest good is realizable? Such a guarantee can be found only in God, who must therefore exist if the highest good is not to be a fatuous ideal. The existence of an omnipotent, omniscient, and omnibenevolent God is thus postulated as a necessary condition for the possibility of a moral life.

Despite the prestige this argument has acquired, it is difficult to grant it any force. It is enough to postulate God's existence. But as Bertrand Russell observed in another connection, postulation has all advantages of theft over honest toil. No postulation carries with it any assurance that what is postulated is actually the case. And though we may postulate God's existence as a means to guaranteeing the possibility of realizing happiness together with virtue, the postulation establishes neither the actual realizability of this ideal nor the fact of his existence. Moreover, the argument is not made more cogent when we recognize that it is based squarely on the highly dubious conception that considerations of utility and human happiness must not enter into the determination of what is morally obligatory. Having built his moral theory on a radical separation of means from ends, Kant was driven to the desperate postulation of God's existence in order to relate them again. The argument is thus at best a *tour de force*, contrived to remedy a fatal flaw in Kant's initial moral assumptions. It carries no conviction to anyone who does not commit Kant's initial blunder.

One further type of argument, pervasive in much Protestant theological literature, deserves brief mention. Arguments of this type take their point of departure from the psychology of religious and mystical experience. Those who have undergone such experiences often report that during the experience they feel themselves to be in the presence of the divine and holy, that they lose their sense of self-identity and become merged with some fundamental reality, or that they enjoy a feeling of total dependence upon some ultimate power. The overwhelming sense of transcending one's finitude, which characterizes such vivid periods of life, and of coalescing with some ultimate source of all existence, is then taken to be compelling evidence for the existence of a supreme being. In a variant form of this argument, other theologians have identified God as the object which satisfies the commonly experienced need for integrating one's scattered and conflicting impulses into a coherent unity, or as the subject which is of ultimate concern to us. In short, a proof of God's existence is found in the occurrence of certain distinctive experiences.

It would be flying in the face of well-attested facts were one to deny that such experiences frequently occur. But do these facts constitute evidence for the conclusion based on them? Does the fact, for example, that an individual experiences a profound sense of direct contact with an alleged transcendent ground of all reality, constitute competent evidence for the claim that there is such a ground and that it is the immediate cause of the experience? If well-established canons for evaluating evidence are accepted, the answer is surely negative. No one will dispute that many men do have vivid experiences in which such things as ghosts or pink elephants appear before them; but only the hopelessly credulous will without further ado count such experiences as establishing the existence of ghosts and pink elephants. To establish the existence of such things, evidence is required that is obtained under controlled conditions and that can be confirmed by independent inquirers. Again, though a man's report that he is suffering pain may be taken at face value, one cannot take at face value the claim, were he to make it, that it is the food he ate which is the cause (or a contributory cause) of his felt pain—not even if the man were to report a vivid feeling of abdominal disturbance. And similarly, an overwhelming feeling of being in the presence of the Divine is evidence enough for admitting the genuineness of such feeling; it is no evidence for the claim that a supreme being with a substantial existence independent of the experience is the cause of the experience.

VII.

Thus far the discussion has been concerned with noting inadequacies in various arguments widely used to support theism. However, much atheistic criticism is also directed toward exposing incoherencies in the very thesis of theism. I want therefore to consider this aspect of the atheistic critique, though I will restrict myself to the central difficulty in the theistic position, which arises from the simultaneous attribution of omnipotence, omniscience, and omnibenevolence to the Deity. The difficulty is that of reconciling these attributes with the occurrence of evil in the world. Accordingly, the question to which I now turn is whether, despite the existence of evil, it is possible to construct a theodicy which will justify the ways of an infinitely powerful and just God to man.

Two main types of solutions have been proposed for this problem. One way that is frequently used is to maintain that what is commonly called evil is only an illusion, or at worst only the "privation" or absence of good. Accordingly, evil is not "really real," it is only the "negative" side of God's beneficence, it is only the product of our limited intelligence, which fails to plumb the true character of God's creative bounty. A sufficient comment on this proposed solution is that facts are not altered or abolished by rebaptizing them. Evil may indeed be only an appearance and not genuine. But this does not eliminate from the realm of appearance the tragedies, the sufferings, and the iniquities which men so frequently endure. And it raises once more, though on another level, the problem of reconciling the fact that there is evil in the realm of appearance with God's alleged omnibenevolence. In any event, it is small comfort to anyone suffering a cruel misfortune for which he is in no way responsible to be told that what he is undergoing is only the absence of good. It is a gratuitous insult to mankind, a symptom of insensitivity and indifference to human suffering, to be assured that all the miseries and agonies men experience are only illusory.

Another gambit often played in attempting to justify the ways of God to man is to argue that the things called evil are evil only because they are viewed in isolation; they are not evil when viewed in proper perspective and in relation to the rest of creation. Thus, if one attends to but a single instrument in an orchestra, the sounds issuing from it may indeed be harsh and discordant. But if one is placed at a proper distance from the whole orchestra, the sounds of that single instrument will mingle with the sounds issuing from the other players to produce a marvellous bit of symphonic music. Analogously, experiences we call painful undoubtedly occur and are real enough. But the pain is judged to be an evil only because it is experienced in a limited perspective— the pain is there for the sake of a more inclusive good, whose reality eludes us because our intelligences are too weak to apprehend things in their entirety.

It is an appropriate retort to this argument that of course we judge things to be evil in a human perspective, but that since we are not God this is the only proper perspective in which to judge them. It may indeed be the case that what is evil for us is not evil for some other part of creation. However, we are not this other part of creation, and it is irrelevant to argue that were we something other than what we are, our evaluations of what is good and bad would be different. Moreover, the worthlessness of the argument becomes even more evident if we remind ourselves that it is unsupported speculation to suppose that whatever is evil in a finite perspective is good from the purported perspective of the totality of things. For the argument can be turned around: What we judge to be a good is a good only because it is viewed in isolation; when it is viewed in proper perspective, and in relation to the entire scheme of things, it is an evil. This is in fact a standard form of the argument for a universal pessimism. Is it any worse than the similar argument for a universal optimism? The very raising of this question is a *reductio ad absurdum*[7] of the proposed solution to the ancient problem of evil.

I do not believe it is possible to reconcile the alleged omnipotence and omnibenevolence of God with the unvarnished facts of human existence. In point of fact, many theologians have concurred in this conclusion; for in order to escape from the difficulty which the traditional attributes of God present, they have assumed that God is not all-powerful, and that there are limits as to what He can do in his efforts to establish a righteous order in the universe. But whether such a modified theology is better off is doubtful; and in any event, the question still remains whether the facts of human life support the claim that an omnibenevolent Deity, though limited in power, is revealed in the ordering of human history. It is pertinent to note in this connection that though there have been many historians who have made the effort, no historian has yet succeeded in showing to the satisfaction of his professional colleagues that the hypothesis of a Divine Providence is capable of explaining anything which cannot be explained just as well without this hypothesis.

VIII.

This last remark naturally leads to the question whether, apart from their polemics against theism, philosophical atheists have not shared a common set of positive views, a common set of philosophical convictions which set them off from other groups of thinkers. In one very clear sense of this query the answer is indubitably negative. For there never has been what one might call a "school of atheism" in the way in which there has been a Platonic school or even a Kantian school. In point of fact, atheistic critics of theism can be found among many of the conventional groupings of philosophical thinkers—even, I venture to add, in recent years among professional theologians, who in effect preach atheism in the guise of language taken bodily from the Christian tradition.

Nevertheless, despite the variety of philosophic positions to which atheists have subscribed at one time or another in the history of thought, it seems to me that atheism is not simply a negative standpoint. At any rate, there is a certain quality of intellectual temper that has characterized, and continues to characterize, many philosophical atheists. (I am excluding from consideration the so-called village atheist, whose primary concern is to twit and ridicule those who accept some form of theism, or for that matter those who have any religious convictions.) Moreover, their rejection of theism is based not only on the inadequacies they have found in the arguments for theism but often also on the positive ground that atheism is a corollary to a better supported general outlook upon the nature of things. I want therefore to conclude this discussion with a brief enumeration of some points of positive doctrine to which by and large philosophical atheists seem to me to subscribe. These points fall into three major groups.

In the first place, philosophical atheists reject the assumption that there are disembodied spirits, or that incorporeal entities of any sort can exercise a causal agency. On the contrary, atheists are generally agreed that if we wish to achieve any understanding of what takes place in the universe, we must look to the operations of organized bodies. Accordingly, the various processes taking place in nature, whether animate or inanimate, are to be explained in terms of the properties and structures of identifiable and spatio-temporally located objects. Moreover, the present variety of systems and activities found in the universe is to be accounted for on the basis of the transformations things undergo when they enter into different relations with one another—transformations which often result in the emergence of novel kinds of objects. On the other hand, though things are in flux and undergo alteration, there is no all-encompassing unitary pattern of change. Nature is ineradicably plural, both in respect to the individuals occurring in it as well as in respect to the processes in which things become involved. Accordingly, the human scene and the human perspective are not illusory; and man and his works are no less and no more "real" than are other parts or phases of the cosmos. At the risk of using a possibly misleading characterization, all of this can be summarized by saying that an atheistic view of things is a form of materialism.

In the second place, atheists generally manifest a marked empirical temper, and often take as their ideal the intellectual methods employed in the contemporaneous empirical sciences. Philosophical atheists differ considerably on important points of detail in their account of how responsible claims to knowledge are to be established. But there is substantial agreement among them that controlled sensory observation is the court of final appeal in issues concerning matters of fact. It is indeed this commitment to the use of an empirical method which is the final basis of the atheistic critique of theism. For at bottom this critique seeks to show that we can understand whatever a theistic assumption is alleged to explain, through the use of the proved methods of the positive sciences and without the introduction of empirically unsupported *ad hoc* hypotheses about a Deity. It is pertinent in this connection to recall a familiar legend about the French mathematical physicist Laplace. According to the story, Laplace made a personal presentation of a copy of his now famous book on celestial mechanics to Napoleon. Napoleon glanced through the volume, and finding no reference to the Deity asked Laplace whether God's existence played any role in the analysis. "Sire, I have no need for that hypothesis," Laplace is reported to have replied. The dismissal of sterile hypotheses characterizes not only the work of Laplace; it is the uniform rule in scientific inquiry. The sterility of the theistic assumption is one of the main burdens of the literature of atheism both ancient and modern.

And finally, atheistic thinkers have generally accepted a utilitarian basis for judging moral issues, and they have exhibited a libertarian attitude toward human needs and impulses. The conceptions of the human good they have advocated are conceptions which are commensurate with the actual capacities of mortal men, so that it is the satisfaction of the complex needs of the human creature which is the final standard for evaluating the validity of a moral ideal or moral prescription.

In consequence, the emphasis of atheistic moral reflection has been this-worldly rather than other-worldly, individualistic rather than authoritarian. The stress upon a good life that must be consummated in this world has made atheists vigorous opponents of moral codes which seek to repress human impulses in the name of some unrealizable other-worldly ideal. The individualism that is so pronounced a strain in many philosophical atheists has made them tolerant of human limitations and sensitive to the plurality of legitimate moral goals. On the other hand, this individualism has certainly not prevented many of them from recognizing the crucial role which institutional arrangements can play in achieving desirable patterns of human living. In consequence, atheists have made important contributions to the development of a climate of opinion favorable to pursuing the values of a liberal civilization, and they have played effective roles in attempts to rectify social injustices.

Atheists cannot build their moral outlook on foundations upon which so many men conduct their lives. In particular, atheism cannot offer the incentives to conduct and the consolations for misfortune which theistic religions supply to their adherents. It can offer no hope of personal immortality, no threats of Divine chastisement, no promise of eventual recompense for injustices suffered, no blueprints to sure salvation. For on its view of the place of man in nature, human excellence and human dignity must be achieved within a finite life-span, or not at all, so that the rewards of moral endeavor must come from the quality of civilized living, and not from some source of disbursement that dwells outside of time. Accordingly, atheistic moral reflection at its best does not culminate in a quiescent ideal of human perfection, butts a vigorous call to intelligent activity—activity for the sake of realizing human potentialities and for eliminating whatever stands in the way of such realization. Nevertheless, though slavish resignation to remediable ills is not characteristic of atheistic thought, responsible atheists have never pretended that human effort can invariably achieve the heart's every legitimate desire. A tragic view of life is thus an uneliminable ingredient in atheistic thought. This ingredient does not invite or generally produce lugubrious lamentation. But it does touch the atheist's view of man and his place in nature with an emotion that makes the philosophical atheist a kindred spirit to those who, within the framework of various religious traditions, have developed a serenely resigned attitude toward the inevitable tragedies of the human estate.

Notes

1. It may be thought that I am neglecting here the essential problem, that of faith. But I am not examining the philosophy of Kierkegaard or of Chestov or, later on, of Husserl (this would call for a different place and a different attitude of mind); I am simply borrowing a theme from them and examining whether its consequences can fit the already established rules. It is merely a matter of persistence.

2. I did not say "excludes God," which would still amount to asserting.

3. Jean-Paul Sartre, *Being and Nothingness*, trans. Hazel E. Barnes (New York: Philosophical Library, 1956).

4. Friedrich Nietzsche, *Joyful Wisdom*, trans. Thomas Common, in Complete Works of Friedrich Nietzsche, Oscar Levy, gen. ed. (1909-11) (New York: Russell & Russell, 1964).

5. Friedrich Nietzsche, *Beyond Good and Evil*, trans. Helen Zimmern, in *Complete Works of Friedrich Nietzsche*, Oscar Levy, gen. ed. (1909-11) (New York: Russell & Russell, 1964).

6. Jean-Paul Sarutre, *Existentialism As a Humanism*, trans. Philip Mairet (New York: Philosophical Library, 1949).

7. A reduction to absrdity.—E.D.K.

THE SELF IN RELATION TO ULTIMATE REALITY: MYSTICISM

LANGUAGE, EPISTEMOLOGY, AND MYSTICISM

by Steven T. Katz

I should like to start by raising several standard elements in the discussion of mysticism and mystical experience in order to dispose of them at the outset. This will leave us free to concentrate on our main epistemological concerns. The first such feature is actually not one issue but a set of related issues having to do with the nature and referent of claimed mystical states. The easiest way to introduce these concerns is by referring to the terms' 'interpretation' and 'verification' and all that these notions suggest to the philosophically perceptive reader. Let us first deal with the issue of verification. There are major, perhaps insuperable, problems involved in the issue of trying to verify mystical claims, if by verification we mean the strong thesis that independent grounds for the claimed event/experience can be publicly demonstrated. Indeed, it seems to me, though I will not try to justify this position here, that it is not possible to provide 'verification' of this sort. As a corollary of this view it also seems correct to argue that no veridical propositions can be generated on the basis of mystical experience. As a consequence it appears certain that mystical experience is not and logically cannot be the grounds for *any* final assertions about the nature or truth of any religious or philosophical position nor, more particularly, for any specific dogmatic or theological belief. Whatever validity mystical experience has, it does *not* translate itself into 'reasons' which can be taken as evidence for a given religious proposition. Thus, in the final analysis, mystical or more generally religious experience is irrelevant in establishing the truth or falsity of religion in general or any specific religion in particular.[1]

Despite the strict limitation being placed on the justificatory value of mystical experience, it is *not* being argued either that mystical experiences do not happen, or that what they claim may not be true, only that there can be no grounds for deciding this question, i.e. of showing that they are true *even* if they are, in fact, true. Moreover, even this disclaimer requires the further declaration that, though no philosophical argument is capable of proving the veracity of mystical experience, one would be both dogmatic and imprudent to decide *a priori* that mystical claims are mumbo-jumbo, especially given the wide variety of such claims by men of genius and/or intense religious sensitivity over the centuries as well as across all cultural divisions. Nor does it seem reasonable to reduce these multiple and variegated claims to mere projected 'psychological states' which are solely the product of interior states of consciousness.

The related topic of 'interpretation' also needs brief mention both because the ordinary sense in which this notion is taken in relation to our subject is *not* our direct concern, and also because the work done here seems to me, despite the beginnings of some valuable investigations in this area, to be still preliminary in terms of its methodology as well as its results. When I speak of 'interpretation' here I mean to refer to the standard accounts of the subject which attempt to investigate what the mystic had to say *about* his experience. This interpretative enterprise is, of course, carried on at several different removes and in several different ways. Among these are: (*a*) the first-person report of the mystic; (*b*) the mystic's 'interpretation' of his own experience at some later, more reflective, and mediated, stage; (*c*) the 'interpretation' of third persons within the same tradition (Christians on Christian mysticism); (*d*) the process of interpretation by third persons in other traditions (Buddhists on Christianity); and so on. In addition, all these forms of interpretation can be highly ramified or not as the case may be.[2] Though all these stages in the 'interpretation' of mystical experience are of importance, and in the later parts of this paper we shall have occasions to return to certain aspects of them they are, for the most part, only tangential to our essential, still more basic, 'preinterpretive' concern.

The issue of 'interpretation', however, raises another standard feature of the analysis of mystical states which does move us directly to where we want to concentrate our epistemological attentions. Here I have in mind the almost universally accepted schema of the relation which is *claimed* to exist between one mystic's experience (and his report of the experience) and the experience of other mystics. This schema takes three forms, one less sophisticated, the other two, in differing degrees, often highly sophisticated. The less sophisticated form can be presented as follows:

(I)   All mystical experiences are the same; even their descriptions reflect an underlying similarity which transcends cultural or religious diversity.

The second, more sophisticated, form can be presented as arguing:

(II) All mystical experiences are the same but the mystics' *reports about* their experiences are culturally bound. Thus they use the available symbols of their cultural-religious milieu to describe their experience.

The third and most sophisticated form can be presented as arguing:

(III) All mystical experience can be divided into a small class of 'types' which cut across cultural boundaries. Though the language used by mystics to describe their experience is culturally bound, their experience is not.

A word has to be said about each of these. Thesis I is more commonly found in the early literature on the study of mysticism, much of it having been generated by missionary and related activity which sought to find some common denominator among people of widely diverse religious backgrounds. This ecumenical desire coloured much of the early investigation of the subject as well as being responsible for making it a popular subject of study. Again, a second less ecumenical feature, also at least in part tied to the early missionary enterprise; which often prompts this sort of argument is the dogmatic consideration, i.e. all religions, even if appearing different, really teach x - the definition of x being variously supplied on the basis of the particular dogmatic beliefs the given interpreter happens to hold, e.g. the Christian finds the x to be the Christian God.[3] Among the results of this paper one will be to show that Thesis I is mistaken. There is no *philosophia perennis*, Huxley [4] and many others notwithstanding.

Thesis II, though more sophisticated than I, can also be made for the same ecumenical and dogmatic reasons as I, as it also supports such enterprises. The ecumenicist or dogmatist is still able to argue on the basis of II that underneath or above all differences there is one common Truth, and this is what he is after in any case. That this sort of essentialist reductionism, i.e. reducing all reports of *x* to one claimed essence *y*, is usually not open to falsification, nor to any clear hermeneutical, methodological, or metaphysical procedure is of little account to well-meaning ecumenicists or dyed-in-the-wool dogmatists. If one differs with the essentialist over the meaning of a specific mystical report or mystical reports in general, for example, by pointing to variations between them, one is dismissed as not understanding them, and all disagreement is accounted as the result of such 'misunderstanding'. There is, however, something more to say about Thesis II for it has also come into prominence for at least one good reason, i.e. the more, if still not completely, dispassionate study of the relevant mystical data. To serious academic students of the subject who owed some allegiance to the academy as well as to a given tradition it became unavoidably obvious that not all mystical experience was *reported* in ways that easily suggest that they are all reports of the same experience. Despite this last virtue Thesis II is also to be rejected as inadequate for dealing with all the relevant evidence.[5]

Thesis III is more sophisticated still, recognizing a disparity both of content and of form in mystical reports. The best recent studies of mysticism belong under this rubric, as, for example, the work of R. C. Zaehner,[6] W. T. Stace,[7] and N. Smart.[8] It is to their credit to have recognized the deep problems involved in trying to classify various mystical experiences as the same. Yet even the positions of Zaehner,[9] Stace,[10] and Smart[11] are unsatisfactory because they try to provide various cross-cultural phenomenological accounts of mystical experience which are phenomenologically as well as philosophically suspect. The positive position argued later in the present paper will materially bear on this topic of cross-cultural phenomenological categorization for it will try to demonstrate that even these comparatively sophisticated accounts have remained too close to Thesis II which will be shown, as noted, to be unacceptable, even if a marked improvement over Thesis I. By way of anticipation and as an interim conclusion, it will suffice here to suggest that, for example, the phenomenological typologies of Stace and Zaehner are too reductive and inflexible, forcing multifarious and extremely variegated forms of mystical experience into improper interpretative categories which lose sight of the fundamentally important differences between the data studied. In this sense it might even be said that this entire paper is a 'plea for the recognition of differences'.

II

Our interest, however, is only incidentally concerned with the adequacy of framing a typology for the study of mystical experience for this, despite its occupying the centre stage of almost all the important research on mysticism from William James's classic *Varieties of Religious Experience*, through the work of Underhill, Inge, Jones, Otto, Zaehner, and Stace, is a second-order inductive procedural concern. It is a second-order concern to the more basic inquiry into why the various mystical experiences are the experiences they are.[12]

To get a clearer conception of what this paper is after when it speaks of the issue of 'Why mystical experiences are the experiences they are', let me state the single epistemological assumption that has exercised my thinking and which has forced me to undertake the present investigation: *There are* NO *pure (i.e. unmediated) experiences.* Nether mystical experience nor more ordinary forms of experience give any indication, or any grounds for believing, that they are unmediated. That is to say, *all* experience is processed through, organized by, and makes itself available to us in extremely complex epistemological ways. The notion of unmediated experience seems, if not self-contradictory, at best empty. This epistemological fact seems to me to be true, because of the sorts of beings we are, even with regard to the experiences of those ultimate objects of concern with which mystics have intercourse, e.g. God, Being, nirvana, etc. This 'mediated' aspect of all our experience seems an inescapable feature of any epistemological inquiry, including the inquiry into mysticism, which has to be properly acknowledged if our investigation of experience, including mystical experience, is to get very far. Yet this feature of experience has somehow been overlooked or underplayed by every major investigator of mystical experience whose work is known to me.[13] A proper evaluation of this fact leads to the recognition that in order to understand mysticism it is *not* just a question of studying the reports of the mystic after the experiential event but of acknowledging that the experience itself as well as the form in which it is reported is shaped by concepts which the mystic brings to, and which shape, his experience. To flesh this out, straightforwardly, what is being argued is that, for example, the Hindu mystic does not have an experience of *x* which he then describes in the, to him, familiar language and symbols of Hinduism, but rather he has a Hindu experience, i.e. his experience is not an unmediated experience of *x* but is itself the, at least partially, pre-formed anticipated Hindu experience of Brahman. Again, the Christian mystic does not experience some unidentified reality, which he then conveniently labels God, but rather has the at least partially prefigured Christian experiences of God, or Jesus, or the like. Moreover, as one might have anticipated, it is my view based on what evidence there is, that the Hindu experience of Brahman and the Christian experience of God are not the same. We shall support this contention below. The significance of these considerations is that the forms of consciousness which the mystic brings to experience set structured and limiting parameters on what the experience will be, i.e. on what will be experienced, and rule out in advance what is 'inexperienceable' in the particular given, concrete, context. Thus, for example, the nature of the Christian mystic's pre-mystical consciousness informs the mystical consciousness such that he experiences the mystic reality in terms of Jesus, the Trinity, or a personal God, etc., rather than in terms of the non-personal, non-everything, to be precise, Buddhist doctrine of nirvana.[14] Care must also be taken to note that even the plurality of experience found in Hindu, Christian, Muslim, Jewish, Buddhist mystical traditions, etc., have to be broken down into smaller units. Thus we find, for example, in Hinduism[15] monistic, pantheistic, and theistic trends, while Christianity knows both absorptive and non-absorptive forms of mysticism. And again close attention has to be paid to the organic changes in ideology and historical development which specific traditions undergo internally, and how these changes affect the mystical experiences of mystics respectively in each tradition. For example, absorptive mysticism is not found in the earliest strata of Christian mysticism, while again the Jewish mystical experience of Talmudic times known as *merkabah* mysticism based on the chariot vision of Ezekiel is different from the Zoharic (late thirteenth century) and Lurianic (sixteenth century on) mysticism of the later Middle Ages more thoroughly suffused as it is by gnostic elements. And, I repeat, the remainder of this paper will attempt to provide the full supporting evidence and argumentation that this process of differentiation of mystical experience into the patterns and symbols of established religious communities is experiential and does not only take place in the postexperiential process of reporting and interpreting the experience itself: it is at work before, during, and after the experience.

We can see the significance, as well as the failure to recognize the significance, of the issue being raised if we look at W. T. Stace's[16] extremely influential discussion of mysticism and philosophy. Stace begins with an opening chapter entitled 'Presuppositions of the Inquiry' as part of which he takes up the familiar distinction between experience and interpretation and argues that this is a distinction which must be respected, though he holds that it generally is not, even by the best investigators into the subject. In the course of this discussion he gives the following opening example which seems most promising.

> It is probably impossible. . . to isolate 'pure' experience. Yet, although we may never be able to find sense experience completely free of any interpretation, it can hardly be doubted that a sensation is one thing and its conceptual interpretation is another thing. That is to say, they are distinguishable though not completely separable. There is a doubtless apocryphal but well-known anecdote about the American visitor in London who tried to shake hands with a waxwork policeman in the entrance of Madame Tussaud's. If such an incident ever occurred, it must have been because the visitor had a sense experience which he first wrongly interpreted as a live policeman and later interpreted

correctly as a wax figure. If the sentence which I have just written is intelligible, it proves that an interpretation is distinguishable from an experience; for there could not otherwise be two interpretations of one experience.[17]

Stace goes on to add the further correct observation regarding the event at Madame Tussaud's.

> There were two successive interpretations, although it may be true that at no time was the experience free of interpretation and even that such a pure experience is psychologically impossible. No doubt the original something seen at the entrance was immediately recognized as a material object, as having some sort of colour, and as having the general shape of a human being. And since this involved the application of classificatory concepts to the sensations, there was from the first some degree of interpretation. It seems a safe position to say that there is an intelligible distinction between experience and interpretation, even if it be true that we can never come upon a quite uninterpreted experience.[18]

Yet after this most auspicious beginning to his inquiry, indeed in the very argument which Stace generates from it, it is clear that Stace fails to grasp clearly the force of this concern about the impossibility of 'pure' experience and what this entails. For Stace turns this discussion into a discussion of the post-experience interpretation placed on the experience rather than pursuing *in any sense at all* the primary epistemological issues which the original recognition requires. He immediately turns to 'the difficulty of deciding what part of a mystic's descriptive account of his experience ought to be regarded as actually experienced and what part should be taken as his interpretation'. Then he again simple-mindedly turns to the issue of whether all mystical experiences are the same or not based on the discussion of their post-experiential reports.

> Now the first question—how far the mystical experiences *reported* by Christians, Muslims, Jews, Hindus, and Buddhists, and also by mystics who have not been adherents of any specific religious creed, are similar or different—is one of extreme difficulty. We shall have to struggle with it, but we cannot hope to get anywhere near a true answer unless we make the distinction between experience and interpretation and endeavour to apply it to our material. The reason for this may be made clear by the following example.

> The Christian mystic *usually* says that what he experiences is 'union with God'. The Hindu mystic *says* that his experience is one in which his individual self is identical with Brahman or the Universal Self. The Christian *says* that his experience supports theism and is not an experience of actual identity with God, and *he understands* 'union' as not involving identity but some other relation such as resemblance. The Hindu insists on identity, and says that his experience establishes what writers on mysticism usually call 'pantheism'—though Hindus usually do not use that western word. The Buddhist mystic—at least according to some versions of Buddhism—does not speak of God or Brahman or a Universal Self, but interprets his experience in terms which do not include the concept of a Supreme Being at all.

> There are thus great differences of belief here, although the beliefs are all equally said to be founded on mystical experiences.[19]

Stace's failure to appreciate the complexity of the nature of 'experience' with its linguistic, social, historical, and conceptual contextuality, and the severe limitations of his concentration on a naively conceived distinction between experience and interpretation become clear when he takes up what he considers to be Zaehner's position as argued in *Mysticism Sacred and Profane*. Zaehner argues that the original mystical reports reveal *different* experiences, not only different reports of the same experience; that is, it is not just a case of recognizing the distinction of experience and interpretation and then simply comparing alternative interpretations of the same given. Stace tries to reply to Zaehner's thesis by suggesting that:

> Professor Zaehner, who is a Roman Catholic, insists that their experiences [of Christian and Hindu mystics] must have been different because Eckhart and Ruysbroeck *built their accounts of the experience into the orthodox Trinitarian theology which they accepted from the Church, whereas the Hindus understood it pantheistically*—pantheism being, according to Catholic theologians, a serious 'heresy' . . . the point is that Professor Zaehner's conclusion simply does not follow from the mere fact that the *beliefs* which Christian mystics *based upon their experiences* are different from the *beliefs* which the Indians *based on theirs*. And the difference of beliefs is really the only evidence which he offers for his view. A genuine grasp of the distinction between experience and interpretation, and especially of the difficulties involved in applying it, might have resulted in a fuller, fairer, and more impartial examination and treatment of the two possible hypotheses.[20]

It is highly instructive to note that Stace tries to reject Zaehner's charge on the basis of the distinction between experience and interpretation without at all recognizing the need to ask the fundamental question: what does the Christian bring to his experience and how does it affect that experience, and what does the Hindu bring to his experience and how does it affect that experience? The focus of Stace's remarks is on the relation between the mystics' experience and 'the beliefs which the mystics based upon their experiences'. Here the symmetry is always one-directional: from 'experience' to 'beliefs'. There is no recognition that this relationship contains a two-directional symmetry: beliefs shape experience, just as experience shapes belief. To take, for the moment, a non-controversial example of this, consider Manet's paintings of Notre Dame. Manet 'knew' Notre Dame was a Gothic cathedral, and so 'saw' it as a Gothic cathedral as testified to by his paintings which present Notre Dame with Gothic archways. Yet close examination will reveal that certain of the archways of Notre Dame which Manet painted as Gothic are in fact Romanesque.[21] As Coleridge reminded us: 'the mind half-sees and half-creates'. Reflection now also reminds us that Stace failed in a similar fashion to appreciate the need to investigate the deep issues involved in what the American visitor at Madame Tussaud's brought to his experience. In order to treat adequately the rich evidence presented by mystics, concentration solely on post-experiential reports and the use of a naive distinction—almost universally held by scholars—between claimed 'raw experience' and interpretation, will not do.

As Stace has mentioned Zaehner, the other leading modern investigator of the subject, let us briefly look at his account. Zaehner, in contradistinction to Stace, is aware both by virtue of training, being a most eminent Orientalist and holder of the Spalding Chair in Eastern Religions at Oxford University from 1953 to 1967, as well as in respect of personal experience,[22] that it is not so easy to draw all mystical experience together in one basically undifferentiated category.[23] Indeed, in his Gifford lectures he writes with especial regard to Hinduism, but in order to make a more general point, that Hinduism 'gives the lie . . . to the facile assumption that "mysticism is essentially one and the same whatever may be the religion professed by the individual mystic" '.[24] Zaehner, in addition, goes on to note correctly that the view that mysticism is 'a constant and unwavering phenomenon of the universal longing of the human spirit for personal communion with God'[25] while true of western mysticism and thus pardonable as a description of western mysticism, is inappropriate, nay even inaccurate when applied to 'the kind of mysticism with which we became acquainted in the Upanishads, let alone with the experience of nirvana as described in early Buddhist texts'.[26] Yet, despite Zaehner's insight into the need to acknowledge the diversity of the mystical evidences, there are severe weaknesses in his position which prevent it from making the contribution to the subject it promised. These weaknesses are of three kinds: first, there is the correct objection that Zaehner's evidence is made up exclusively of post-experiential testimony which, on the one hand, neither respects the experience-interpretation distinction in a fashion which is sufficiently rigorous to satisfy Stace, nor on the other—and this is the crucial point for our concern of which Stace is oblivious—makes the necessary inquiry into the logical and social-contextual conditions of mystical experience which would justify rejecting Stace's simplistic distinction. Secondly, Zaehner's own strong Catholic biases colour his entire investigation and make much of his work appear to be special pleading for Catholic Christianity, or at least for western monotheism over against eastern monism. For example, in his *Hindu and Muslim Mysticism* Zaehner injudiciously, not to say dogmatically, writes: 'Both Najm al-Din Razi, defending Islamic orthodoxy, and Ibn Tufayl, defending sanity, expose the monist's pretension to be God as the "misgrounded conceit" it so manifestly is.'[27] While again in his *Mysticism Sacred and Profane* he attempts to relate the different types of mysticism, especially that between what he calls monistic and theistic mysticism to his own christological understanding of Adam's fall.[28]

Lastly, Zaehner's phenomenology is not adequate. It *is* more sophisticated than Stace's and that of almost all earlier investigators, and its real achievements should be acknowledged. Yet Zaehner's views will not do as a final statement of the problem, or indeed even of an interim one, because it stops too short in its search for the full and diverse meaning(s), leading to a recognition of the relevant diversity, of the nature of mystical experience, especially in terms of its contexts, conditions, and relation to language, beliefs, and cultural configurations. As a consequence his threefold typological distinction for handling cross-cultural mystical experiences—the theistic, the monistic, and the naturalistic ('panenhenic' in Zaehner's vocabulary)—turns out to be an advance over most alternative accounts, as we have said, though overly simplistic and reductionistic. For example, both Jewish and Christian mystics are for the most part theistic in the broad sense, yet the experience of Jewish mystics is radically different from that met in Christian circles. And again the 'theism' of the Bhagavad Gita or of Ramanuja is markedly different from the theism of Teresa of Avila, Isaac Luria, or Al Hallaj. Alternatively, the monism of Shankara is not the monism of Spinoza or Eckhart. And again Buddhism, for example, though classified according to Zaehner's phenomenology as monistic, is really not to be so pigeon-holed.[29] Zaehner achieves this 'monistict identification of Buddhism only by misusing the texts, and attributing to Buddhism doctrines it does not hold, especially surprising in this respect being his attribution of the doctrine of *Atman*, the doctrine of a substantial self, to the Buddha. Zaehner notwithstanding, the Buddha seems to have made the denial of the *atman* doctrine which was central to Hinduism, a central, if not *the* central basis for his own revolutionary position. Thus, the supposed 'monism' of the Buddhists who deny the existence of a substantial self or soul can hardly be equated, except by manipulation of evidence and ignoring of facts, with, say the Advaitan monistic experience which claims that there is one universal Self, Brahman. which is the ground of all being and in which each particular individual participates and finds his ultimate salvation. Zaehner's well-known investigations flounder because his methodological, hermeneutical, and especially epistemological resources are weak. Indeed, his researches reinforce the felt pressing need to pursue such inquiries in more sophisticated conceptual terms.

This failure to investigate or to consider in one's investigation of mystical experience the *conditions of experience* in general and the specific conditions of religious/mystical experience in particular is a deficiency which skews the entire discussion in ways which distort any and all conclusions or suggestions made. Let us return, therefore, to this topic. We recall, at the outset, the wisdom of the remark, 'the child is father to the man'. This holds for epistemic inquiry also, in regard both to the logical-conceptual aspect of the inquiry and to the cultural-social aspect, though, of course, the logical-conceptual aspect involves ideas and conditions which are, on another level, to be strictly divorced from this sort of approach, as we shall see. Let us investigate the methodological significance of this phrase as it applies in the case of a Jewish mystic, as an opening gambit.

In the cultural-social sphere the Jewish mystic will have learnt and been conditioned in all kinds of ways from childhood up that: (1) there is more to reality than this physical world; (2) that this 'more' than physical reality is an ultimate Reality which is a personal God; (3) that this God created the world and men; (4) that men have spiritual souls that commune with God; (5) that God enters into covenants with men; (6) that even in covenants He remains distinct; (7) that God's Being and man's being are ontologically distinct;

(8) that God entered into special covenants with Abraham and his heirs, Israel; (9) that these covenants are expressed in the acts of circumcision and the giving of the Torah; (10) that the Torah and its commandments (*mitzvot*) are the most perfect expression of God's Will as well as the most perfect means of relation between man and God, and so on. Moreover, the Jewish mystic will have learnt to fit all these items into a special 'mystical theology' known by the broad term of Kabbalah, in which the visible and perceivable is the unreal and the unperceived and nonsensual is the real. One could extend this comparatively small list at great length. All these cultural-social beliefs and their attendant practices, especially in the myriad practice of the *mitzvot*, clearly affect the way in which the Jewish mystic views the world, the God who created it, the way to approach this God, and what to expect when one does finally come to approach this God. That is to say, the entire life of the Jewish mystic is permeated from childhood up by images, concepts, symbols, ideological values, and ritual behaviour which there is no reason to believe he leaves behind in his experience. Rather, these images, beliefs, symbols, and rituals define, *in advance*, what the experience *he wants to have*, and which he then does have, will be like. Without making the discussion too complex in its detail of Jewish mystical theory and practice (traditionally called theoretical Kabbalah and practical Kabbalah, though there is much overlap and the latter is predicated on the theology of the former), let us consider the most essential feature of Jewish mystical thinking and its related behaviour, unique to Jewish mystics, namely, the centrality of the performance of the *mitzvot* (commandments) for reaching the mystic goal and how this interpenetration of ritual and ethical actions (*mitzvot*) with the goal of relation to God affects the kind of experience one *anticipates* having and then, *in fact*, does have.[30]

The Jewish mystic performs the *mitzvot* as a necessity on the mystic's way because he conceives of himself, the world (or cosmos), and God in a very special light. Foremost, perhaps, among the elements of his self-consciousness is his conception of God as the sort of Being who is in some sense personal and, even more, who is ethically and evaluatively personal, i.e. a God who is affected by good deeds and acts of obedience, and the relation to Whom is affected by the proper performance of prescribed actions. Thus, the Jewish mystic's experience is a preconditioned experience of a (moral-personal) God. We see this pre-experiential configurative element, for example, in the details of the central Kabbalistic doctrine of the relation of human action and the *Sefiroth* (Divine Emanations which comprise the highest levels of the upper worlds) in which every *Sefirah* is related to a human ethical counterpart, so that the perfect performance of ethical behaviour becomes, above all, the way towards relation with these Divine Emanations. More generally the level of one's experience with the different rungs of the *Sefiroth* (of which there are ten) is dependent on one's ethical and ritual behaviour (*mitzvot*), and especially on prayer done with the right commitment and concentration (known as *kavvanah*). The Jewish mystics believe that such mystical prayer leads the soul on its upward ascent because mystical prayer leads to a recognition of, and contact with, the true meaning of God's 'Names' which are the real ontological structure of the upper worlds.[31]

That this complex pre-experiential pattern affects the actual experience of the Jewish mystic is an unavoidable conclusion. It can be ascertained clearly in the Jewish mystic's experience or perhaps a better way to describe it might be to refer to the Jewish mystic's 'non-experience'. That is to say, the Jewish conditioning pattern so strongly impresses that tradition's mystics (as all Jews) with the fact that one does *not* have mystical experiences of God in which one loses one's identity in ecstatic moments of unity, that the Jewish mystic rarely, if ever, has such experiences. What the Jewish mystic experiences is, perhaps, the Divine Throne, or the angel Metatron, or aspects of the *Sefiroth*, or the heavenly court and palaces, or the Hidden Torah, or God's secret Names, but not loss of self in unity with God. The absence of the kinds of experience of unity one often, but mistakenly, associates with mysticism, even as the 'essence of mysticism', in the Jewish mystical context, is *very* strong evidence that pre-experiential conditioning affects the nature of the experience one actually has. Because the Jew is taught that such experiences of unity do not happen for reasons flowing out of the Jewish theological tradition, he does not, in fact, have such experiences.[31A] This is a formative pre-experiential element rather than only a post-experiential fact necessitated by Jewish orthodox requirements, as Stace might suggest, being of the essential character of the experience itself. The logic of experience requires the adoption of this account and the evidence supports it. [32]

There is no evidence but *a priori* theorizing in the face of the actual evidence to the contrary, that this non-unitive characterization of the experience of the Jewish mystic is *merely* the product of the post-experiential report, whose form is necessitated by social or religious orthodoxies and imposed on what, in fact, was basically an experience of an altogether different (unitive) sort. Rather, these orthodox concerns, which are indeed very real, are much more deeply rooted and much more powerful, shaping the imaginative and experiential capacities of the Jewish mystic from childhood up and pre-forming his organizing perceptual schema. However, Stace, for example, only sees this constructive aspect of the external factors as they work on one's internal consciousness in terms of the post-experiential report rather than in terms of both their before and after character—a curious blindness in support of a passionately held theory.

Let us stay with this example a little longer and develop its deepest implication. In the Jewish mystical tradition the ultimate state of mystical experience is called *devekuth*, which literally means 'adhesion to' or 'clinging to' God. That is to say, in the Jewish tradition the strong monotheistic emphasis on God's uniqueness is understood to entail not only his numerical unity and perfection but also his qualitative, ontological, distinction from his creations. And even though this distinction is blurred somewhat in the Zoharic and later Lurianic Kabbalah, with their theories of emanation rather than creation, even there God's transcendental majesty and distinctiveness is essential and is retained by the reference to God in himself as *Eyn Sof*, literally 'without end', but used more broadly to refer to God's ultimate and radical Otherness and unknowability, both epistemologically and ontologically. As a consequence, Jewish mystics envisioned the ultimate goal of mystical relation, *devekuth*, not as absorption into God, or as unity with the divine but rather as a loving intimacy, a 'clinging to' God, a relation which all the time is aware of the duality of God and mystic, i.e. which *experiences* God as Other rather than Self. All Jewish mystical literature reflects this teaching of *devekuth* as the goal to be sought and, even more importantly, all Jewish mystical testimonies conform to this pattern. Now one could say: 'but this is because of social pressure'—but what evidence is there for saying this? Moreover, is it not more reasonable to relate the formative milieu to the experience itself and then read the available evidences as confirmation of the milieu-affecting character of the totality of the experience, rather than accounting for the material in more artificial ways?

To bring our point into still sharper focus let us shift our concern and compare the Jewish experience of *devekuth* to a radically different mystical experience found in a mystical tradition near the other end of the mystical spectrum, that of the Buddhist. The preconditioning of the Buddhist consciousness is very different from that of the Jewish and this difference generates the radically different mystical experience which the Buddhist aims at and reaches. Consider, for example, the following concrete elements which the Buddhist *learns* from his tradition starting with the 'four noble truths' which are the foundation of his tradition. These Truths are:

(a) 'Birth is suffering, old age is suffering, disease is suffering, death is suffering, association is suffering, separation from what is pleasant is suffering, not obtaining what one desires is suffering . . .;

(b) The cause of suffering is 'craving' or 'desire', 'craving for sensual desires, and craving for becoming, and craving for nonexistence';

(c) Suffering can be overcome by the proper discipline and understanding;

(d) There is an eightfold path which leads to the cessation of suffering (i.e. *nirvana*).

These eight ways are: (1) Right understanding, i.e. understanding the four noble truths; (2) Right thought, i.e. thought free from desire and craving and cruelty. It is referred to as *samkalpa* (the proper 'shaping together' of one's consciousness); (3) Right speech, i.e. refraining from lying, slander, malicious gossip, frivolous speech; (4) Right action, i.e. the avoidance especially of killing, stealing, and general misconduct; (5) Right livelihood, i.e. not earning a living by inappropriate means, for example, as an astrologer; (6) Right effort, i.e. striving to purify oneself of evil thoughts; (7) Right mindfulness, i.e. being properly mindful of the nature of one's body and mind; (8) Right concentration, i.e. practicing the proper meditation patterns especially the four *dhyanas* or trance states. Thus we see that the Buddhist is conditioned to reach *nirvana* by *sila* or moral behaviour, *samadhi* or concentration and *prajna* or wisdom.[33]

These elements of the four noble truths were then further elaborated upon in the Buddha's second great sermon, the 'Discourse on the Marks of Not-Self' in which he taught the essential doctrines of 'no-self', i.e. that there is no simple, pure substance which is permanent and which has its own independent substantial existence analogous to the doctrine of the soul in the western traditions or to *atman* in Hinduism. Indeed, the no-self *anatman* doctrine is a reaction to the Hindu emphasis. Related to this no-self doctrine is also the important doctrine of *pratityasamutpata* 'dependent origination'. We are also taught the doctrine of the impermanence of all things. The only 'something'—or is it a nothing?—which avoids *anitya* (impermanence) and which we have as our goal is nirvana wherein we avoid the wheel of suffering which is the condition of all existing realities. The stages of sanctification that carry a man upwards towards *nirvana* have been summarized as follows:

> In passing from existence as a common person (*prthagjana* to experiencing nirvana, several stages can be delineated. The first task is to become a member of the family of spiritually elect noble personages (*arya pudgalas*). To do this one must first make himself fit to commence the practices that will make him an *arya pudgala*. Even to begin this quest is significant, resulting in the stage of *gotrabhu* or member of the family (of *aryas*). From here, depending on temperament and capability, one of two courses is open: either the follower in faith (*skaddhan-usarin*) for those with mild faculties, or the follower of Dharma (*Dharmanusarin*), for those of keen intellect. By progressively gaining insight into each of the four noble truths, one becomes, at the culmination of the process, a *srotapanna* or 'streamwinner', the first class of the *arya pudgalas*. Having abandoned totally belief in the self, doubts about the Three Jewels (i.e. Buddha, Dharma, Samgha), and belief in the efficacy of rituals, the streamwinner is assured of enlightenment within one more lifetime. Progressing further still, the adept becomes an *anagamin* or 'non-returner', assured of enlightenment during his current lifetime. When all negative qualities have been eradicated and the adept is pure in all respects, he is able experientially to realize nirvana, thus becoming an *arhant*, and establishing himself as a true saint in Buddhism.[34]

This brings us directly to *nirvana*, the goal of the entire Buddhist enterprise in all its elaborate detail. While it is a subject of fiercely debated divergent opinion among Buddhologists, for our purposes it seems fair to say that *nirvana*: (1) is the recognition that belief in the phenomenal 'self' of mundane existence is an illusion; (2) is most especially characterized by the extinction of 'suffering' which is the predominant feature of ordinary reality; (3) is not a conditional or conditioned reality; (4) is in some positive way the attainment of unique wisdom or insight into the impermanence (*anitya*) of all existing things; (5) is not a Being; (6) is a state or condition, i.e. in the sense of being 'Nirvanaized'; (7) is not a relational state of being.[35]

From this complex structure let us concentrate especially on two cardinal features of the Buddhist account. First, the basis of the entire system is the awareness of suffering in the world and the goal of the system is the extinction of suffering; secondly, the goal, *nirvana*, is not a relational state in which the finite self encounters a saving or loving transcendental Being—God—but rather is a new ontological (if this term is not inappropriate) state of being (if these terms are not inappropriate). That there is no encounter of any sort results from the fact that there is no real self and no transcendental other self. Again, it should also be noted that in the Buddhist doctrine there is no divine will which plays any role as there is no divinity. Rather one has in place of the divine will the strict law of ethical causality, *Karma*, which is at the root of the causal chain of existence, re-existence or reincarnation, and release.[36]

Just setting this Buddhist understanding of the nature of things over against the Jewish should, in itself, already be strong evidence for the thesis that what the Buddhist experiences as *nirvana* is different from what the Jew experiences as *devekuth*. However, let us draw this out more clearly. To begin, when the Jewish mystic performs his special mystical devotions and meditations, *kavvanot*, he does so in order to *purify his soul*, i.e. to remove the soul from its entrapment in the material world in order to liberate it for its upward spiritual ascent culminating in *devekuth*, adhesion to God's emanations, the *Sefiroth*. The Buddhist mystic, on the other hand, performs his meditative practices as an integral part of the Buddhist mystical quest, not in order to free the soul from the body and purify it, but rather in order to annihilate suffering by overcoming any notion of 'self', holding that the very notion of a substantial 'self' or 'soul' is the essential illusion which generates the entire process of suffering. Buddhist literature specifically represents the Buddha as criticizing the belief in a permanent or substantial self (the Hindu doctrine of *atman*) as a false, even pernicious, doctrine which, paradoxically, in so far as it encourages egoism in one's pursuit of one's own eternal happiness, makes the fulfilment of one's happiness an impossibility.

In addition to its insistence on the extinction of suffering through the elimination of the 'self' *nirvana* is also not a relational state, i.e. it is no' the meeting of two distinct selves or realities who come together in loving embrace. *Nirvana* is the absence of all relation, all personality, all love, all feeling, all individuality, all identity. *Nirvana* is the achievement (if we can use this term, but we have no better one) of calm, of peace, of tranquillity. While it is the banishment of care or anxiety, of concern or striving, it is not the creation of a new condition of meeting. *Nirvana* is no 'something', nor does it contain or permit the continued existence of either individual beings or one grand Being. Its ontology can not even be easily classed as theistic, monistic, or naturalistic. In the world of religious ideas it comes the closest to reminding one of Wittgenstein's remark made in another connection about 'not being a something nor a nothing either'.[37] Moreover, and this cannot be emphasized too strongly, it is this theoretical structure of the impermanence of all existence, the resultant suffering of all beings, and the doctrines of no-self, meditation, etc., upon which the whole of Buddhist life and its goal, *nirvana* is built. The Buddhist understanding of reality generates the entire elaborate regimen of Buddhist practice, and it is this understanding of reality which defines in advance what the Buddhist mystic is seeking and what we can tell, from the evidence, he finds. To think that his pre-conditioned consciousness of how things are and how to find release from suffering in *nirvana* is extraneous to the actual Buddhist mystical experience is bizarre.

Whatever *nirvana* is, and indeed whatever *devekuth* is, in so far as words mean anything and philosophical inquiry has any significance, there is no way one can describe, let alone equate, the experience of *nirvana* and *devekuth* on the basis of the evidence. There is no intelligible way that anyone can legitimately argue that a 'no-self' experience of 'empty' calm is the same experience as the experience of intense, loving, intimate relationship between two substantial selves, one of whom is conceived of as the personal God of western religion and all that this entails. The losing of self is not equivalent to the finding of another, especially when this other is conceived of as the God of Jewish tradition. To emphasize one key issue: one is especially struck in Jewish mysticism by the imagery of love, even including very pronounced sexual imagery, which is used to express all sorts of 'relations' relevant to the kabbalistic mind. This aspect is totally absent from early Indian Buddhism which equates sexuality with desire and sees desire as the basic element which causes suffering and which is to be overcome in *nirvana*. Now, this is not to *evaluate* either the truth-claims of the sought and reported experiences in Judaism and Buddhism, etc, or to presume to rank them in terms of better or worse as Otto and Zaehner, for example, quite arbitrarily do, or again, as D. T. Suzuki does, but now reversing the dogmatism and opting for the superiority of Zen Buddhism. What I wish to show is only that there is a clear causal connection between the religious and social structure one brings to experience and the nature of one's actual religious experience.

A further logical point needs to be made, This deals with my opening remark in the previous paragraph that if words mean anything my position seems to be the only reasonable one to adopt. Many students of mysticism might see this remark as their 'escape hatch' for avoiding my conclusion. After all, they might argue, all mystics are wary about using language to describe their experience, and many are absolutely opposed to its employment, arguing a form of 'I don't mean what I say and I don't say what I mean'. Also, we are sure to be reminded of the well-known mystical penchant for paradox and ineffability as relevant at this point. However, this 'escape' is no escape at all. It fails to provide the desired way out because it fails to realize that, if the mystic does not mean what he says and his words have *no* literal meaning whatsoever, then not only is it impossible to establish my pluralistic view, but it is also logically impossible to establish any view whatsoever. If none of the mystics" utterances carry any literal meaning then they cannot serve as the *data* for any position, not mine, and certainly not the view that all mystical experiences are the same, or reducible to a small class of phenomenological categories.

We can shed further light on this issue by moving only a short sideways step in the study of mysticism and introducing one further tradition, Christianity, that seems close to the Jewish but which, in fact, introduces new elements which are clearly reflective of a larger theoretical pattern moulding the mystical consciousness of the Christian mystic. Space prevents us from spelling out the forces at work in Christian traditions in the same detail as we have for Judaism and Buddhism, but let us consider this one essential element. In Christian mysticism we have two types of mystical experience, the non-absorptive type which is reminiscent of Jewish mysticism and its doctrine of *devekuth*, though still with a difference, and the absorptive (or unitive) type in which the goal sought and experience reached is a transcendence of the distinction between self and God and the absorption of the self into God in an allembracing unity. This absorptive type is certainly a common type of Christian mystical experience and is what students of mysticism often, though perhaps mistakenly, consider the paradigm of Christian mysticism. The great Flemish mystic, John Ruysbroeck (1293-1381), is thus able to express his experience in the fascinating expression 'To eat and to be eaten! This is union!. . . Since his desire is without measure, to be devoured of him does not greatly amaze me.'[38] That is to say, in more extreme form, what others have referred to as the loss of self in the 'ocean pacific' of God, or what Eckhart refers to when he writes: 'If I am to know God directly, I must become completely he and he I: so that this he and this I become and are one I.'[39] What permits, perhaps even encourages, this unitive, absorptive mysticism of the divine he and the finite I found in Christian mysticism, though absent from its Jewish counterpart, is, I believe, the formative influence of the essential incarnational theology of Christianity which is predicated upon an admixing of human and divine elements in the person of Jesus which is outside the limits of the Judaic consciousness. Thus, an essential element of the model of Christian spirituality is one of divine-human interpenetration on the ontological level which allows for a unity of divine and human which Judaism rules out. Essential here too is the Neoplatonic influence on Christian thought, especially for Christian mysticism as represented by the greatest of all Neoplatonic mystics, Plotinus.[40] Moreover, to classify this *unio mystica* of the Christian mystic, or rather of some Christian mystics, is not as easy a task as it has appeared to most investigators. The difficulty emerges because union with the divine, when the divinity is understood in christological and incarnational terms is not equatable with either (a) the dualistic experience of *devekuth* (b) the no-self, no-God, no-relation experience of *nirvana* (c) the naturalistic mysticism of those like Richard Jefferies; (d) the non-absorptive mysticism of non-Jewish mystics whose experiences differ from that of *devekuth*; or even (e) the absorptive mystics who superficially seem closest, such as the Advaitans.

It should also be noted that even the absorptive, non-absorptive dichotomy at work in Christian mysticism which might appear to contradict the contextual rootedness of mystical experience in fact supports it. The unitive Christian mystics are invariably those such as Eckhart, Tauler, and Suso, who have been schooled on Plotinus, Dionysius the Areopagite, and Augustine, i.e. the strong Neoplatonic current in Christian intellectual history. Book VI of Plotinus's *Enneads* provides the inspiration for this conceptualization of the final ascension of the soul into unity with the Good. Plotinus describes it as a final ineffable absorption of the self back into the perfect absolute One which transcends; back into the One which alone exists.[41] The study of Plotinus and the Neoplatonic mystical tradition shaped the mystic's 'mind's eye' so that his experience conformed to it. To think that the 'unitive' mystic merely describes his experience in this way is to distort the situation which gave rise to the experience, the experience itself, and the report of the experience. Thus, for example, seriously to credit that Augustine did not have the unitive experience described in his *Confessions* (Bk. 9) but only used this language is unwarranted for two strong reasons at least: (1) surely an Augustine would not consciously *mis*describe his experience; (2) the theory of misdescription due to orthodox pressures is untenable in Augustine's case because, in fact, the unitive account he gives is more in conflict, though little did he seem to know it, with Christian orthodoxy than a relational description would have been. The evidence for this second contention is the sad fate which some of Augustine's 'absorptive' heirs met at the hands of the Church. Dogmatic reasons aside, be they philosophical dogmas or theological ones, there is no good evidence for denying that Augustine's experience was of the *unitive* character he describes it as possessing. On the contrary, his entire life was a long preparation for just such an experience: 'Thou hast made us for thyself and our hearts are restless until they rest in thee.'

If we stay with the theme of theological and social contextualism a little longer, we shall also notice one further feature of importance deserving of note, as well as of further study. In almost all mystical traditions, we find the importance of a teacher or *guru* who leads the novice along 'the way'. In the Jewish tradition, there is a strong aversion to auto-didacticism both in traditional rabbinic and even more in mystical matters. Indeed, in the Jewish tradition, until the historic calamity of the expulsion from Spain in 1492 called for a radical new approach to mysticism, mystical wisdom was always held very close by its devotees and was only taught in small circles to a select few. The constant fear was expressed that this knowledge, if obtained by the unlettered without the guidance of a teacher, could lead to antinomianism and heresy, as indeed happened in the seventeenth-century pseudo-messianic movement known as Sabbatianism[42] and the eighteenth-century pseudomessianic movement known as Frankism.[43] As a consequence, Jewish mystics show a close conformity of ideological background, shared experience, and theological reflection. This feature is pronounced in Jewish mysticism, moreover, because of the believed ability of Jewish mystics to escape from a mystical solipsism through the 'public' language of the Torah which served as a mystical lexicon in Jewish mystical circles and which also accounts for its eventual, highly structured, systemic nature, paradigmatically represented in the Zoharic[44] and Lurianic[45] schools. Mention of the Lurianic 'school' is especially noteworthy because it demonstrably reinforces the shared, taught, communal nature of this mystical theory which emerged in the town of Safed[46] in northern Israel in the sixteenth century. The development of Lurianic mysticism into the mass mystical movement surrounding the pseudo-messiah Sabbatai Zevi in the seventeenth century is also further weighty evidence to be considered.

In the Buddhist tradition, one also finds the same emphasis on being guided along the path towards *nirvana* by a qualified teacher. Only *a* Buddha reaches self-enlightenment, all others must be helped towards this end. No less an authority than the late Richard Robinson has argued: 'Every form of Buddhism has held that guides are necessary.'[47] Here too, one sees not only the importance of a qualified teacher or *bhiksu*, but also how this insistence on proper instruction grew into the widespread institution of Buddhist monasticism,[48] with all its strict discipline and ideological commitments. And these emphases, of course, are not unique to Buddhism, the institution of the *guru*-like master being found in all eastern traditions, as for example, Hinduism especially in its Trantric variety, and Zen. The Zen tradition is highly instructive here, for though it made spontaneity the great virtue in achieving *satori*, this spontaneity was achieved through the mediating role which the Zen master played in the 'enlightenment' of his disciples. Not only were the Zen masters considered the paradigms of Zen practice to be emulated by their disciples, but they even became the objects of Zen meditation for their disciples. Even more importantly, it is the Zen master, through the seemingly meaningless *koans* which he sets his students to meditate upon as well as in the purposeful physical and mental abuse he subjects his students to, who destroys the illusions in which the disciple is imprisoned and which prevent him from reaching *satori*. The master induces in the disciple the condition of 'Zen sickness' which allows the disciple to break the bonds of conditional experience and to encounter reality as it really is, in its 'suchness'.[49]

Again, this aspect of the mystical situation is highly focused in the history of Sufism which developed a widespread, highly refined, tradition of Sufi-schools which aided the believer *salak at-tariq* ('travelling the Path'). The essence of these mystical Orders, often centred in special Sufi monasteries known as *khanaqahs*, was the formal relation of master and disciple, of *murshid* and *murid*, based upon the ideology that, though each man, potentially, latently, possessed the ability to merge with Allah in ecstatic union (*fana*), this potency could be actualized only with the assistance of a qualified master (except in the case of a small spiritual elite or elect known as *khawass* or *Suf'ya* on whom Allah has bestowed special favour). The disciple followed the *tariqa* ('the way') which was a *practical* method for moving upward through a succession of stages (*maqamat*) culminating in the experience of *fana*—unity in Allah. The *tariqa* consisted of set prayers, supererogatory exercises, other varied liturgical and penitential acts, fasts, retreats, vigils and the like. This highly structured procedure prepared the disciple for his experience, i.e. it 'prepared' him in the sense of putting him in the specifically Sufi frame of consciousness both ideologically and existentially, for his ecstatic experience, the form of which was also anticipated in advance.[50] Likewise, the overwhelming preponderance of Christian mystics are found in monasteries and holy orders with their lives centred around chastity, 'good works', and an extremely rigorous regimen of prayer. Fritz Staal has also recently reminded us that the Mexican Indian teacher, Don Juan, is essential for Castaneda's remarkable experiences, whatever one thinks of Castaneda's experiences.[51]

In all these instances, one must ask 'what does the *guru* teach?' The answer is that he teaches a *specific* way and a *specific* goal; his students follow him along the former because they want to reach the latter. Thus, to take one example, the Buddhist 'seeker' comes to his master (and the *Sangha*) and follows his prescribed meditations and yoga practices to reach that state in which suffering is annihilated and the erroneous notion of self, known as the doctrine of *anatmavada*, is completely overcome. Alternatively the Hindu 'seeker' loyally adheres to his *guru's* instructions because he desires to affirm the ultimacy of his self and its relation to the universal self, known as *atmavada*. Again, the *Murid* is loyal to the rigorous discipline of his *Murshid* because he seeks to merge his soul with the personal God of Islam; while the Jewish Kabbalist practices his regimen of prayer and asceticism to find *devekuth* with God's extended-emanated being manifest in the *Sefiroth*. The Buddhist *guru* does *not* teach what the Hindu *guru* teaches, though superficial association of the term confuses the unwary. The *Murshid* does not teach what the Kabbalist teaches, nor again does Teresa of Avila teach St John of the Cross the same 'way' as Don Juan [52] or the Taoist Master. Decisive proof of this is found not only in a close examination of the respective 'teachings' of the various teachers but also in the polemical spirit manifest by many, if not most, mystical masters. Shankara does not shrink from entering into heated polemics with his Buddhist opponents about the meaning of the ultimate experience, understood by him in a non-personal monistic way, or again with his more theistically-minded Hindu colleagues—and of saying that they are wrong! They do not understand! They do not have the ultimate experience!—only he and *his* students find the ultimate experience because only they are properly equipped to find it. Alternatively, in the Christian tradition we find, for example, Ruysbroeck prepared to criticize those mystics for whom mystic experience does not involve moral imperatives as inferior, while Zen Buddhists have tests and rules for investigating whether a person really has achieved *satori* or *nirvana*.[53] For example, the great Zen master Hakuin records in his autobiography, the *Itsumade-gusa*, that after an early experience he was convined that he had reached the condition of enlightenment and set off to report this good news to Etan, the aged hermit of Shojuan. Upon interrogation by the Master, Hakuin was found to be still wanting and was rebuked with the epithet, 'You poor child of the devil in a dark dungeon'. After further study Hakuin reports that 'the enlightenment flashed upon my mind', and when he was tested anew by Etan 'the master now stroked my back with his fan' (i.e. a sign of approval).[54] It should also be noted that classical mystics do not talk about the abstraction 'mysticism'; they talk only about their tradition, their 'way', their 'goal': they do not recognize the legitimacy of any other. The ecumenical overtones associated with mysticism have come primarily from non-mystics of recent vintage for their purposes.

The experience that the mystic or yoga has is the experience he seeks as a consequence of the shared beliefs he holds through his metaphysical doctrinal commitments.

Closely allied to the erroneous contention that we can achieve a state of pure consciousness is the oft used notion of the 'given' or the 'suchness' or the 'real' to describe the pure state of mystical experience which transcends all contextual epistemological colouring. But what sense do these terms have? What is the 'given' or the 'suchness' or even the 'real'?[55] Analysis of these terms indicates their relativity; they are applied to a variety of alternative and even mutually exclusive 'states of affairs' and 'states of no-affairs'. This variety itself should alert us to the real danger and arbitrariness involved in this gambit. Phenomenologists seem especially prone to this fruitless naively—all intuit the 'given' but their intuitions differ significantly. It can fairly be said that no attempt to state clearly or individuate the 'given' has succeeded. Indeed, talk of the 'given' seems to be a move made to short-circuit the very sort of epistemological inquiry here being engaged in, but such a move fails because there is no evidence that there is any 'given' which can be disclosed without the imposition of the mediating conditions of the knower. All 'givers' are also the product of the processes of 'choosing', 'shaping', and 'receiving'. That is, the 'given' is appropriated through acts which shape it into forms which we can make intelligible to ourselves given our conceptual constitution, and which structure it in order to respond to the specific contextual needs and mechanisms of consciousness of the receiver. This description of the epistemic activity, even the epistemic activity involved in mystical experience, of course requires what in the Kantian idiom, though not in Kant's own manner, would be called a 'transcendental deduction',[56] i.e. an argument which reveals *both* conditions of knowing in general as well as the grounds of its own operation and which is thematized according to specific possibilities—and this seems both appropriate and necessary, though its structure cannot even be outlined here. There seems no other way to get at the issue that would be philosophically satisfactory and which would satisfy our interest in the legitimation of the conditions of our knowledge, mystical knowledge included. This means that the mystic *even* in his state of reconditioned consciousness is also a shaper of his experience; that he is not a *tabula rasa* on which the 'ultimate' or the 'given' simply impinges itself—whatever ultimate he happens to be seeking and happens to find. This much is certain: the mystical experience must be mediated by the kind of beings we are. And the kind of beings we are require that experience be not only instantaneous and discontinuous, but that it also involve memory, apprehension, expectation, language, accumulation of prior experience, concepts, and expectations, with each experience being built on the back of all these elements and being shaped anew by each fresh experience. Thus experience of x—be x God or *nirvana*—is conditioned both linguistically and cognitively by a variety of factors *including the expectation of what will be experienced*. Related to these expectations are also future directed activities such as meditation, fasting, ritual ablutions, self-mortification, and so on, which create further expectations about what the future and future states of consciousness will be like. There is obviously a self-fulfilling prophetic aspect to this sort of activity.

TWO EPISTEMOLOGICAL MODELS FOR THE INTERPRETATION OF MYSTICISM

by Sallie B. King

This essay is composed of two parts. The first offers a criticism of the pluralist conception of mysticism and the epistemological model on which it is based. I argue that this model is inadequate and improperly reduces mystical experiences to doctrine. The second part of the article proposes an alternative epistemological model and examines its implications for the study of mysticism.[57]

To determine which phenomena to include in, and which to exclude from our analysis requires a definition of mysticism. But there is no generally accepted definition for this term. Recent studies which display the variety of phenomena normally included in the category of the mystical make it doubtful that any single essence pervades the various phenomena and furnishes the necessary unifying element for the construction of a definition. In practice scholars have employed Wittgenstein's notion of "family resemblances" and applied it to a definition of "mysticism."[58] The basic idea of this approach is that some words, such as "religion," are instanced by members that share a whole set of characteristics, no one of which must be possessed by all or by any individual in order to justify its inclusion in the class. The set of characteristics is shared by the group of members in such a way that a whole list of characteristics might overlap among the group in endlessly varying ways. By applying this sort of understanding to "mysticism," we can speak about it without forcing ourselves to search for some common "essence" or necessary characteristic.[59]

The "family resemblance" model, however, should not obscure the experiential character of mysticism. While no particular form of experience can be singled out as essential, it is critical to acknowledge that mysticism is based upon mystical experience in whatever particular form or forms that experience may take. It must be recognized that "mysticism" refers to that group of phenomena comprised of mystical experience, practices and lifestyles conducive to mystical experience, speeches and writing composed on the basis of mystical experience and lives transformed by mystical experience. While it is necessary, in connection with mysticism, to discuss literature, institutions and persons, it must be remembered at all times that insofar as the subject of discussion is a mystical phenomenon, it always points beyond itself to mystical experience as such. The experiential element is not to be eliminated since it is the basis of all the other and related factors. Ninian Smart uses the term "mysticism" in reference to "the contemplative life and experience," (76) and this indeed is the heart of the matter: "mysticism" primarily has to do with a life and an experience, and only secondarily with a body of literature, or a philosophy based on the experience. Of course, the scholar's primary access to mystical phenomena is through the literature of mysticism. The point is, however, that it is not useful, and in fact seriously obscures the matter, to forget that there are experiences and lives on which that literature is based. Part One of this paper justifies this perspective.

I.

"The pluralist understanding of mysticism" holds that there is no such thing as mysticism as such; there are only mysticisms: Jewish mysticism, Christian mysticism, and Buddhist mysticism, nature mysticism, theistic mysticism, monistic mysticism, etc. It is claimed that these experiences are sufficiently dissimilar to one another to make it impossible to speak of "mysticism" as if there were a single phenomenon to which the word referred. Perhaps the classic formulation of this view is found in the work of Gershom Scholem:

> there is no such thing as mysticism in the abstract, that is to say, a phenomenon or experience which has no particular relation to other religious phenomena. There is no mysticism as such, there is only the mysticism of a particular religious system, Christian, Islamic, Jewish mysticism and so on. (5-6)

Steven Katz's work offers the clearest statement of the epistemological model that forms the foundation of the pluralist understanding of mysticism. Katz makes the "single epistemological assumption that . . . there are NO pure (i.e., unmediated) experiences." (26) On this basis, he argues that mystical experience is conditioned by tradition and that therefore mysticism is irreducibly pluralistic.[60]

Katz's straightforward statement of this presupposition is a key to the evaluation of the pluralist position it represents. This assumption ultimately derives from a post-Wittgensteinian epistemological model that holds that there are no "private languages," no purely private experiences, and no purely "private" realm at all because all of our experience derives its meaningfulness from the public realm of culture and language. A moment of sadness, for example, though apparently a private experience, is for Wittgenstein only meaningfully a moment of sadness because of the larger context within which that moment occurs. The larger context is the public world of language. In other words, the meaning of the "private" moment derives from the public world and as such, the "private" moment is not in fact private at all. Wittgenstein himself, in *Philosophical Investigations*, is ambiguous, but the book as a whole has been received as an attack on the concept of private experience.

In the philosophy of language, and in Katz's interpretation in particular, this thesis means that no experiences are free of the conditioning power of the public world of language and culture. This is what it means to say that there are no unmediated experiences.

An example or two may suffice to establish Katz's position. Having summarized the Jewish doctrine of *devekuth* and the Buddhist doctrine of *nirvana*, Katz goes on to say, "Just setting this Buddhist understanding of the nature of things [i.e., doctrine] over against the Jewish should, in itself, already be strong evidence for the thesis that what the Buddhist experiences as *nirvana* is different from what the Jew experiences as *devekuth*" (38). Here Katz claims that the doctrinal difference between Buddhism and Judaism is "strong evidence" that the experiences of the Jew and the Buddhist are also, and in a parallel fashion, different. Note that there is no discussion of experience as such. Rather, Katz uses doctrinal evidence to draw conclusions about experience. Consequently, he reduces experience to doctrine. For Katz, the experience is so utterly conditioned by the training that precedes it that it becomes a mere reproduction of that training. Katz continues his argument as follows:

> Let us draw this out more clearly. To begin, when the Jewish mystic performs his special mystical devotions and meditations . . . he does so in order to *purify his soul* . . . in order to liberate it for its upward spiritual ascent culminating in *devekuth*, adhesion to God's emanations, the *Sefiroth*. The Buddhist mystic, on the other hand, performs his meditative practices . . . not in order to free the soul from the body and purify it, but rather in order to annihilate suffering by overcoming any notion of 'self'. . . . (38-9)

But this is a comparison of doctrine and does not clarify for us anything about the experiences themselves. Surely this is a case of reducing mystical experience to doctrine. Katz explains that "*nirvana* is also not a relational state, i.e., it is *not* the meeting of two distinct selves or realities who come together in loving embrace. *Nirvana* is the absence of all relation, all personality, all love, all feeling, all individuality, all identity" (39). This is a statement of early Buddhist doctrine; Katz misleads us to the extent that he conflates the doctrinal usage of the term *nirvana* with the problematic usage of the term in connection with Buddhist mystical experience. *Nirvana*, doctrinally, may be the "absence of all relation," etc., but what is it experientially? This is another matter indeed, though of course there is an important relation between the two. Katz's position is a virtual mirror image of Stace's, which he rejects (Katz: 27ff; Smith: 556). Both Stace and Katz recognize the similarity or "fit" between the report a mystic gives of his/her mystical experience and the doctrinal language of the religious tradition to which s/he belongs. Whereas Stace points to this fit and declares that the report is an interpretation of the experience in the language culturally available to the mystic, Katz points to the same fit and declares the experience an interpretation of the culturally available tradition. Katz thereby negates the validity of mystical experience as a *sui generis* phenomenon. We have made no progress beyond Stace with Katz; we remain mired in the problem of the nature of the phenomenon—mystical experience—itself. But neither Stace nor Katz can justify his claim as to the primacy of experience or tradition.

Carl Keller makes the reduction of mystical experience to doctrine explicit. After pointing out, as I would agree, that "texts do not necessarily reflect experience" and emphasizing that the scholar "must be conscious of the gap which separates linguistic expression from experience," he goes on to emphasize that the terminology and ideology of one mystical system (e.g., Hindu) are utterly different from the next (e.g., Muslim or Christian). "In the light of all this," he writes, "we cannot help feeling how far R.C. Zaehner was from the target when he pretended that 'comparisons between mystical writing of quite divergent religions are at least comparisons between like and like.' In reality," continues Keller, "when we compare mystical texts, we are comparing doctrinal systems (95)."[61]

The comparative study of doctrinal systems can and does proceed without reference to mysticism. If the comparative study of mysticism is to be a study solely of doctrinal systems, it is not a study of mysticism at all. I am troubled by the suggestion that Zaehner was so utterly misguided in his statement that to compare mysticisms is to compare like and like. If we reduce the comparative study of mysticism to the comparison of doctrine, of course similarity becomes more difficult to identify. Keller acknowledges the gap between linguistic expression and experience but then bypasses experience entirely with his focus on doctrine. This reduction overlooks the critical, and problematic, qualities of mystical experience.

The reduction of experience to doctrine leaves unexplained, for example, the affinity that some mystics of different traditions appear to feel for each other. Practicing mystics, as opposed to scholars of mysticism, often feel drawn to each other and express a sense of mutual understanding across cultural and doctrinal lines. A good example of this phenomenon can be found in *The Asian Journal of Thomas Merton*. While traveling in the Himalayas, Merton met a Tibetan Buddhist monk with whom he talked for two hours about religious doctrine, practice, and experience. "We started talking about dzogchen and Nyingmapa meditation and direct realization and soon saw that we agreed very well." Merton comments,

> The unspoken or half-spoken message of the talk was our complete understanding of each other as people who were somehow *on the edge* of great realization and knew it and were trying, somehow or other, to go out and get lost in it—and that it was a grace for us to meet one another . . . . [The Rimpoche] was surprised at getting on so well with a Christian and at one point laughed and said, "There must be something wrong here!" (143-4)

Perhaps on the basis of such experience Merton called for dialogue or communication "in depth, at the very ground of monastic and of human experience (Burton: 314)." With the mystics he met in Asia Merton felt an affinity of the experiential spiritual life to which differences of doctrine were irrelevant. This is a phenomenon which we as scholars should take as seriously as the obvious divergences in the literature of the various mystical traditions. Unlike most mystical writing, this statement is made in a pluralistic setting and directly demonstrates the dismissal by an important mystic of any supposed insuperability of doctrinal and cultural barriers. This should make us as scholars hesitate to dismiss the possibility of cross-cultural affinity or dialogue "in depth." With the pluralists' view, however, the possibility of exploring such dialogue is completely negated.

Katz offers both a strong and a weak thesis. The weak thesis is destructive and argues against "the preconceived notion that all mystical experience is the same or similar" (65). The strong thesis is constructive and attempts to establish the pluralistic claim that mystical experience is dependent upon and shaped by the culture of which it is a part; therefore, mystical experience is irreducibly pluralistic, just as are religious traditions, and cannot be reduced to any fundamental, cross-culturally valid core.

To illustrate Katz's use of his strong and weak thesis, and to illustrate the difference between the two, we may return to the example cited above. Speaking about the Buddhist *nirvana* and the Jewish *devekuth* he says,

> Whatever *nirvana* is, and indeed whatever *devekuth* is, in so far as words mean anything and philosophical inquiry has any significance, there is no way one can describe, let alone equate, the experience of *nirvana* and *devekuth* on the basis of the evidence. There is no intelligible way that anyone can legitimately argue that a "no-self" experience of "empty" calm is the same experience as the experience of intense, loving, intimate relationship between two substantial selves, one of whom is conceived of as the personal God of western religion. . . . (39-40)

This much is the weak thesis, the attack on the belief that the experiences are the "same." And thus far I am in general agreement with Katz, though I would prefer to say that we cannot be confident that the experiences *are* the "same" insofar as we have no evidence to establish that they are the same.[62]

On the other hand, the strong thesis requires a great deal more in the way of intellectual assent. Katz continues, "The losing of self is not equivalent to the finding of another . . . ."(40) Elsewhere he writes, ". . . the Hindu experience of Brahman and the Christian experience of God are not the same" (26). Here we are required to agree not only that we do not have evidence to establish that the experiences in question are the same, but also that we *do* have evidence to establish that they are different. This is a much broader thesis, which cannot be supported.

More is at issue here than the status of mysticism as a category with cross-cultural validity. The assumption that there are no unmediated experiences also negates the very foundation of yoga, most of Buddhism, large segments of Hinduism, and philosophical Taoism. The issue is not just one of cross-cultural analysis and understanding, but of the status of most of the great Asian religious traditions in and of themselves. At stake is not only what scholars such as Stace and Zaehner say about mystical experience, but what many great traditions say about themselves.

The pluralist account states variously that tradition conditions, shapes, and/or determines the form and content of mystical experience. So, for example, Katz asserts, "the forms of consciousness which the mystic brings to experience set structured and limiting parameters on what the experience will be"(26). And again: "This much is certain: the mystical experience must be mediated by the kind of beings we are. . . . Thus experience of *x*—be *x* God or *nirvana*—is conditioned both linguistically and cognitively by a variety of factors *including the expectation of what will be experienced* (59)." Though there are occasional exceptions (such as when Katz states "beliefs shape experience, just as experience shapes belief" (30)) the overall impression Katz leaves is that mysticism is a matter of a one-way street; a given religious tradition produces the experience of the mystic, and the mystical experience contains no elements that are unconditioned but is entirely the product of the teaching and training that the mystic has received prior to the mystical experience. The strongest language speaks of causality and indicates a cause and effect relationship between religious tradition and mystical experience. Thus Katz asserts, "What I wish to show is only that there is a clear causal connection between the religious and social structure one brings to experience and the nature of one's actual religious experience" (40).

But consider some other forms of experience that are in some sense said to be ineffable. In particular, let us analyze the relationship between these experiences and the contexts in which they occur. Take for example, the experience of drinking and tasting coffee. One who drinks coffee knows exactly what coffee tastes like but will be incapable of describing that taste. (This knowledge is, moreover, verifiable insofar as we can give the subject coffee, tea, and other drinks to taste and test the subject's ability to identify the correct drink as coffee.) What is the relationship between the first taste of coffee one acquires and the context of that experience—the "tradition" of coffee drinkers whom one has heard exclaiming that coffee is delicious, invigorating, relaxing, bitter, etc.; the advertisements for coffee with their visual images, jingles, slogans; the countless childhood experiences of watching one's parents drink their morning coffee and perhaps undergoing noticeable personality changes in the process—what is the relationship between all this and one's own first direct taste? Is it possible to say—as the pluralists do with respect to mystical experience—that this experience is produced, brought into being, caused by that pre-existing context of tradition?

Think about one's own experience of tasting coffee, or anything else for that matter. Certainly one may be predisposed to like or dislike coffee depending upon what one has heard and witnessed with respect to coffee. One may eagerly seek out an opportunity to acquire such experience or try to avoid it. Being told that coffee is bitter would certainly predispose one to find bitterness in the taste. But there, I claim, is where the conditioning power of the "coffee tradition" ends. It cannot cause the subject to have the total experience s/he has upon drinking coffee. Why? The main reason is that the taste of coffee is ineffable: in all the words, lifestyles, and art forms associated with the cult of coffee, there is nowhere even an approximation of an adequate description of the taste of coffee. The power of the coffee tradition to convey information about the taste of coffee is limited to the point of insignificance compared to the power of the sensation of tasting coffee in experience.

The same point is made, of course, with respect to the content of mystical experience: it cannot be adequately described. This is not to say that nothing is said about it or that the things that are said about it do not convey certain amounts of information. It is simply to emphasize that what is said is radically inadequate. For this reason, it is impossible for the tradition (religious or coffee) to produce or cause the experience in its fullness—its resources are radically inadequate. I emphasize this point: the coffee tradition in this country overwhelmingly invades our minds. The act of drinking coffee in its totality can by no means be said to be an unmediated experience. Nonetheless, before one drinks coffee one really has no idea what it tastes like; after one cup, one knows exactly. How far does the conditioning power of the coffee tradition extend? In the end, though drinking coffee is a mediated experience, that mediation is a relatively insignificant element of the experience itself.

Granted, coffee is an empirical object with relatively constant physical and censorial traits, while the content of a mystical experience is none of these. I do not intend to directly equate the former kind of experience with the latter. The point of speaking of coffee is to enable us to see the inadequacy of the Wittgensteinian model. We cannot as easily see the inadequacy of this model in its application to mystical experience because we don't all share common knowledge of this kind of experience. When we turn to experience we share, such as drinking coffee, and show the inadequacy of the model with respect to such experience, we "demystify" the model itself. If the epistemological model with which a pluralist such as Katz works is this inadequate in helping us to properly understand a mundane experience like drinking coffee, how could it possibly help us to understand a family of experiences we scarcely understand at all, the mystical?

Let us take another example: the experience of listening to music. I would argue that, like the experience of drinking and tasting coffee, the experience of listening to and hearing music is an experience that occurs within a context, a musical tradition in this case, but that this context by no means can be said to determine, cause, or exhaust the experience of hearing music itself. To be sure, listening to music is an experience which is shaped by one's musical training (van Buren:63). Clearly, a trained and experienced Japanese hears things in classical koto music that an untrained American does not. The experience is different for the two persons, moreover, in the very sense that the meaning and value of the experience is different for them. Does this mean that the training of the Japanese caused that experience with its accompanying sense of meaning and value, or that the experience of listening to that music can be *reduced* to that training? Certainly not. Despite the fact that a complex and extensive technical vocabulary has been developed within a given musical tradition, there is always more to the experience of hearing music than can be conveyed in words—sounds, rhythms and tones are not concepts. Wittgenstein himself recognized the reality of nonverbal cognition when he wrote,

> Compare *knowing* and *saying*:
>   how many feet high Mont Blanc is—
>   how the word "game is used—
>   how a clarinet sounds.
> If you are surprised that one can know something and not be able to say
> it, you are perhaps chinking of a case like the first. Certainly not of one
> like the third. (36, remark No. 78)

Moreover, a musically talented person could educate herself in music through her own efforts without recourse to the shared historical and verbal musical tradition simply by listening again and again to music. True, this sort of training would not enable that person to discuss music with others inside or outside of the musical tradition, but that person herself would have knowledge. She would become capable of distinguishing between different forms of music, different themes within a given piece, characteristic styles of various composers, etc. If she wished, she could then invent terms for these various distinctions and proceed to establish her own tradition of musical appreciation and interpretation.

What is the parallel between music and mystical experience? Both occur within a cultural context. Both contain moments of non-verbal cognition. In music neither the technical vocabulary of the music critic nor the evocative language of the music enthusiast can come close, as Wittgenstein remarks, to saying how a clarinet sounds. The censorial experience of listening to music, as of drinking coffee, illustrates that there is something even in mundane experience that eludes the grasp of language: our ordinary lives are full of qualities beyond the denotative reach of our words. Our experiences of coffee, music, etc. are rich with these non-verbal qualities. This being the case, the resources of the coffee and music traditions are inadequate to produce those experiences. Likewise mysticism: the experience itself occurs within a context, a religious tradition, an individual's own personal history and concerns, etc. But as with music, these things do not exhaust the content of experiences which occur within such contexts. Mysticism is not a censorial experience, but it is (or can be) like the others in being a non-verbal experience occurring in the context of a verbal tradition. In coffee and music we have seen the reality of non-verbal cognition; we have seen the impossibility of the verbal-cultural tradition producing the experience. These things clearly demonstrate the inadequacy of the Wittgensteinian model, as applied to mysticism by Katz, in its insistence upon: (1) the notion of the tradition as the cause of the experience; and (2) the view that experience can reduce to doctrine, as if it contained nothing more.

Likewise, we have no justification to assume that the experience itself cannot be instructive. Like the woman listening to music who can invent her own musical tradition, the mystic attending to mystical experience(s) can invent a new religious tradition. Mystics clearly learn from their experiences. There are, after all, mystical innovators and founders of traditions (though this of course does not mean that these new traditions or innovations within established traditions are developed entirely without reference to the verbal tradition). For this to be possible something more, something new must come to the mystic above and beyond that for which the tradition with its teaching and training prepares him or her. In sum, the pluralists have a valid and important point in indicating that mystical experience occurs within a context. But it is critical that we not *reduce* mysticism to that context. Our acknowledgment of the contextuality of mystical experience does not require our acquiescence to the reduction of mystical experience to that context, namely, doctrine.

Katz and Penner argue with respect to the interpretation of mystical experience that language is all we have; as Penner puts it, experience can't explain language, language explains experience (91). This statement, which may appear to be inarguable, overlooks two things: (1) the existence of non-linguistic expressions of mystical experience in painting, music, gestures (think of Zen), etc. and (2) the issue of the *adequacy* of language to explain experience: language doesn't necessarily explain experience well. Katz, for his part, states, if the mystic does not mean what he says and his words have *no* literal meaning whatsoever, then . . . it is . . . logically impossible to establish any view whatsoever. If none of the mystics' utterances carry any literal meaning then they cannot serve as the *data* for any position . . . . (40)

This quotation reveals Katz's excessive reliance upon the literal, referential function of language and ignores the demonstrations by such scholars as van Buren and Streng of the other important ways, such as the poetic or transformative modes, in which religious language functions. This is not accidental. Pluralists must believe that the fit between language and experience is quite good in order to be in a position to claim that language plays the powerful causative role they assign to it in the formation of experience. Thus Katz is led by this belief to state that " 'God' can be 'God', 'Brahman' can be 'Brahman' and *nirvana* can be *nirvana* without any reductionist attempt to equate the concept 'God' with that of 'Brahman', or 'Brahman' with *nirvana*" (66). This statement ignores the problems of assuming that these terms function as simple concepts (Streng 1967, 1968; King). For the mystic, 'God' need not necessarily be 'God,' 'Brahman' cannot be 'Brahman,' and *nirvana* is certainly not *nirvana*.[63] Granted, such beliefs about language as these are part of the doctrinal context in which religious experience occurs. The purpose of such doctrinal statements, though, is to alert us to problems at the interface of religious experience and language.[64]

The danger of Katz's and Penner's approach is that it reduces mystical experience to mystical language for reasons of methodological convenience. There is a parallel situation in psychology with respect to methodological and theoretical behaviorism. Starting from the observation that the so-called "inner world" is inaccessible to scientific observation, behaviorists limited themselves to what their scientific methodology could adequately study: human behavior. What began as a concern with methodological propriety, however, resulted in theoretical reductionism such that many behaviorists explained away mental and emotional phenomena altogether, "mind" became a four-letter word, and human beings were reduced to a set of material functions and processes. The ultimate result was the impoverishment of a great discipline.

We run a similar risk with the question of mystical experience and the language associated with it. Insofar as language is our primary given, there is a natural and justifiable tendency to call for the limitation of our study to the phenomena our methods can handle—here, language (i.e., mystical texts). But this step obligates us to remain keenly sensitive to the problematic interface of language and experience—to the poetic and transformative functions of language, for example, to questions of the adequacy of language, to the use of silence and art in mysticism. Mystical language points beyond itself to mystical experience. Comparison of doctrine is not comparison of mystical experience. I would very much regret seeing the kind of reductionism which has plagued psychology become normative in religious studies. It would be better, if necessary, to frankly acknowledge that the phenomena of mystical experience are beyond our reach and live with the consequences of that admission than to reduce mysticism to less than it is for the sake of method.

Moreover, it is important to note that mystics themselves are often suspicious of such phenomena as visions and auditions, which clearly must be conditioned by a religious tradition. For example, St. John of the Cross said of visions and auditions, "inasmuch as they are exterior and physical, the less is the likelihood of their being from God. That which properly and generally comes from God is a purely spiritual communication; wherein there is greater security and profit for the soul than through the senses, wherein there is usually much danger and delusion. . . ." (Underhill:280-1) Such examples could be multiplied many times. As Evelyn Underhill says, "the mystics are all but unanimous in their refusal to attribute importance to any kind of visionary experience. The natural timidity and stern self-criticism with which they approach auditions is here greatly increased: and this, if taken to heart, might well give pause to their more extreme enemies and defenders" (279-80).

To make the case against the assumption that all aspects of all experiences are mediated or conditioned and the application of that assumption to mysticism, it is not necessary to show that all mystical phenomena are unconditioned. It suffices to demonstrate that some aspects of some mystical experiences may be free of the conditioning power of tradition. This I believe I have done. It is quite right to see mystical experiences as contextualized within religious traditions and to indicate the influence of tradition on shaping some mystical phenomena, especially such phenomena as visions and auditions. What is not right is to insist on the all-encompassing and universal nature of such conditioning power.

In this first part of the essay I have: (1) argued against the assumption that there are no unmediated experiences; (2) demonstrated the way in which the epistemological model underpinning the pluralist position results in an approach which is reductive; and (3) shown that the conclusions reached by way of this method are invalidated by this reductive quality. My analysis of Katz's work has demonstrated that in practice the use of the Wittgensteinian epistemology results in a method in which the mystical experience as such cancels out and we are left only with a discussion of doctrine or philosophy. I conclude that we must not accept the strong thesis that mysticism is irreducibly pluralistic insofar as the evidence supporting this thesis is derived from a radically inadequate epistemological stance. I suggest that at present the crosscultural affinity of mystical experiences is very much an open question as is the possibility of unmediated experience.[65]

II.

To carry on the discussion of mysticism across cross-cultural lines we may focus upon two problems: language and method. The latter will detain us longer, but we should briefly consider the former. To promote dialogue across the lines of religious traditions scholars must be willing to give up exclusive adherence to intra-faith terms as the only terms that adequately express mystical experience within a tradition. Some may not be willing to take this step. A pluralist like Scholem, who believes that there is only, e.g., Hindu mysticism and Jewish mysticism, will find Hindu and Jewish terms, respectively, quite adequate to convey those experiences. But as we have seen, this approach eliminates the distinction between doctrine and experience in such a way that the distinctively experiential elements of mysticism become lost. It also eliminates the possibility of genuine dialogue.

Language that may possibly, however problematically, hold out some degree of hope for cross-cultural communication falls into two overlapping categories: psychological and phenomenological-descriptive. Such terms, especially the psychological, may already be excessively culture- and ideology-bound, but they are a clear improvement over religiously doctrinal terms for our purposes and can be used with an appropriately critical and skeptical attitude.

As for method, the first need is an adequate epistemological model. If, as I have argued, the Wittgensteinian model is not adequate for the purpose of understanding mysticism and excessively predetermines the result of our inquiry by eliminating the possibility of considering an element of unconditioned experience in mysticism, we need to begin with another epistemological model. I propose a Buddhist/phenomenological model.[66] Some will no doubt believe that this model also predetermines too much. While cognizant of this problem, I advocate this model nonetheless, in the belief that it fits the phenomena better than the Wittgensteinian model does.

The view which I call the "Buddhist-phenomenological epistemological model" is elaborated in the Buddhist Yogacara school of India in the works of Asariga and Vasubandhu and in Paramartha's Chinese works related to this sect.[67] It is also expressed in Nishida's concept of "pure experience" (Waldenfels:40). The phenomenologists to whom I refer are the philosophical phenomenologists, primarily Husserl. I do not argue here for the similarity of the two philosophies; I limit my assertion to the single point of agreement between the two—the given of "primitive" experience prior to a division into subjective and objective components of experience. Though I employ primarily the terminology of Yogacara Buddhism, the general outline of this epistemological model is shared by the philosophical phenomenological tradition.

According to the Buddhist-phenomenological epistemological model, "primitive" experience, experience as it is "given" to us before reflective interpretation upon that experience, is understood as a state in which there is no dichotomy between subject and object. In this model, experience is "given" to us first and fundamentally in a pre-reflective form as "consciousness-of"; all experience possesses this structure. All experience incorporates awareness or consciousness (later, reflectively, separated out from the rest of experience and labeled the subjective element in experience) and content (later, reflectively, separated out from the rest of experience and labeled the objective element in experience, the content "of" consciousness in a given moment of experience). Phenomenology and Yogacara Buddhism, both of which take as one of their primary tasks the study of the structure of the consciousness-process, both observe that experience is primitively given as a unitary whole whose structure is "consciousness-of." Within experience as such, this structure is an indivisible unit; insofar as it remains present experience, it cannot be broken into component parts. Only with subsequent reflection that makes experience into an "object" of study is it possible for us to divide experience into two component parts. This division is a product of reflective analysis and is in no way part of experience as immediately, or "primitively" given in the present.

Because, though, (and here the more properly Buddhist analysis begins) we are reflective beings and do look back on our experience in order to understand it, we are deeply in the habit of construing our experience as an experience of a subject perceiving or conceiving an object. In the moment in which we "have" our experience (or as a Buddhist might say, we "are" our experience), there is, experientially, no subject experiencing an object. There is just experiencing. But the next moment, we look back and see ourselves as subjects, experiencing particular objects. Again, because our self-knowledge and our understanding of the world tend to derive largely from reflection, we for the most part tend to believe that what we see in reflection is the true nature of ourselves, experience, and the world. We ordinarily live our lives as spectators of our experience, rather than in the immediately given presence of primitive experience. Yogacara Buddhists, on the other hand, believe the true nature of ourselves, experience, and the world is not found in reflective experience, but in a state in which the bifurcation of experience into the categories of subject and object is overcome. The practice of Yogacara Buddhism (and Zen follows it in this) is intended to help us to overcome the subject-object split, which we feel and in which we believe, in order to discover the primitive unity of experience as it is directly given to us. Such a change would naturally also entail a radically altered sense of self.

There is no need for us to accept the Yogacara claim that what I am calling primitive consciousness reveals "true reality." We may, in phenomenological fashion, bracket this metaphysical claim and consider only the phenomenological claim that the account given above is an accurate description of a kind of experience that is available to us and is experienced on some occasions by some persons. This much I do suggest that we accept and, indeed, it seems to be unobjectionable.

Meditation, both Buddhist and other varieties, is frequently described as a state in which the experiential sense of a division between subject and object is eliminated. This, indeed, is one aspect of concentration. If one concentrates, for example, on a candle flame to the exclusion of all else, sooner or later there will be only "consciousness-of" candle flame, with no sense of a separate self perceiving a separate candle flame attendant upon this awareness. When one looks back retrospectively upon such meditative experiences, if one attends carefully to what was in the experience itself, one will even later not want to speak of such experience in the language of subject and object. Such subject-object language does not fit the case. (Though one may, of course, finally accede to the demands of, for example, the English language, and use such terms despite their unsuitable nature.)

I propose that we understand mysticism by means of this epistemological model. In this view, mystical experience is a form of awareness in which the experiential sense of a separate subject and object is not present. It is pure "consciousness-of" something so powerfully meaningful and valuable to the person involved that that person is radically transformed by that experience. This way of understanding mystical experience sheds light on certain structural elements of mystical experience that are commonly reported. For example, the immediacy, directness, or vividness of mystical experience can be seen as a function of the removal of subject-object separation. Insofar as the very nature of primitive experience is no separation of the individual from what is experienced, a sense of immediacy is inevitable. Again, talk of a sense of experiential unity in reports of mystical experience would be expected in cases in which there is no separation between subject and object, or experiencer and experienced.

What does this entail? If the above epistemological model is appropriate for the interpretation of mystical experience, there is no way to speak of any "objects" as such encountered in that experience. Wittgenstein is right to the extent that it is necessary to have communal or group confirmation—shared experience in other words—in order to affirm with confidence the existence of a given object. Errors, projections, and hallucinations can create pseudo-objects indistinguishable for an individual from real objects, whether one is in ordinary consciousness or meditative consciousness. The nature of consciousness, based as it is in primitive "consciousness-of," makes it strictly impossible for an individual to determine where precisely she or he stops and the object of consciousness begins. Only group communication about shared experience can confirm the reality of an object. If this be the case, then the great line of demarcation in the mystical world between monistic and theistic experience is meaningless insofar as it applies to the experiences themselves. Within mystical experience or looking back upon mystical experience, one has no resources whatsoever to draw a line between self and other. On these grounds, I agree with Ninian Smart that monistic and theistic experiences are essentially similar (85), but I would want to stress that they are similar in the sense that the experiencer cannot determine which description is to be preferred because of the nature of mystical experience as primitive "consciousness-of."

A second facet that complicates this problem is that in mystical experience the self is undergoing transformation. By "self" I mean experiential self-sense, which is what remains if we bracket, in phenomenological fashion, the question of the existence of a metaphysical, entitative self. Evidence of the claim that mystical experience entails radical transformation of the self-sense is found in St. Paul's "Not I, but Christ in me," al-Hallaj's impassioned declarations that he was God, widespread talk of dying to the self, Zen master Hakuin's Great Death and talk in Hinduism and Buddhism of realizing the true self (Atman, Buddha nature, original mind). I do not mean to imply that these terms all reduce to the same meaning; far from it! But they are all evidence that the mystic path entails radical self-transformation, precisely in that one's sense of who and what one is is overturned at its foundation. This being the case, how could a mystic be expected to determine what is self and what is other in a mystical experience? The self is in fact becoming other-than-what- it-was .

None of this is to say that mystical experiences are all of the unitive, monistic type, variously interpreted. There are no grounds for such an interpretation. Given the primitive nature of the experience as that which exists before subject and object are distinguished by reflective consciousness, it could be that an object is there and that theistic language is more appropriate, either in all cases or in a given case. In the last analysis, however, neither unitive nor theistic language seems fully satisfactory for a first-person phenomenological account.

I said above that mystical experience is pure "consciousness-of" something so powerfully meaningful and valuable to the individual involved that that person is radically transformed by the experience. I need to clarify and narrow this statement. A mystical experience is an encounter with that which grounds one's existence, one's phenomenal selfhood, one's values; it is an encounter, in other words, with that which, while it may or may not be an entity of any kind, constitutes the ground for the possibility and meaning of my finite experience. I purposely speak of a "ground" here in order to leave as open as possible the question of the extent to which this ground is self or other. One can insert into this formula language of creation by the Wholly Other or manifestation of finite form out of Absolute Being. Even radically apophatic (via *negativa*) language can be appropriate here, though this is more difficult. Tao as Nonbeing could be such a ground. The most difficult cases are the Buddhist. But since in Mahayana Buddhism *samsara* is *nirvana,* or in other words, supreme value is present in the particulars of mundane experience, seeing the "Thusness" of "what is" fits this description, as does Zen's pure awareness of this moment. The more negative language of Nagarjuna or of Theravada accounts of *nirvana* reveal an absolute commitment to the apophatic path. But even these fit the present analysis, for all that my characterization of mystical experience requires is an existential grounding—a vivid experiential realization of that into which one fits as a cognizing, valuing, existing individual. Does not realization of the *Heart Sutra's* "form is emptiness and emptiness is form" entail grounding in such an existential sense? And when the Buddha, in speaking of *nirvana*, says:

> O bhikkhus, there is the unborn, ungrown, and unconditioned. Were there not the unborn, ungrown, and unconditioned, there would be no escape for the born, grown, and conditioned. Since there is the unborn, ungrown, and unconditioned, so there is escape for the born, grown, and conditioned. (*Udana*, cited in Rahula: 37)

are we not talking about existential grounding? Thus, even though a given tradition may deny, as Indian Buddhism does, that there is anything in any sense whatsoever that is either the basis or the source of the individual's being, that tradition in its mystical dimension still points towards an existential grounding of the individual. This, then, can serve as a cross-culturally valid component of mystical experience: an experience that leaves one existentially grounded.

There is also an element of axiological grounding: an encounter with absolute value. This is partly related to the factor of existential grounding and partly separable from it. As related to the above, it is clear that what grounds one existentially will possess superlative value for one. One may also, separately, speak of the non-existential qualities that emerge in mystical experience. Mystics frequently report feelings of bliss, ecstasy, or of serene joy, deep peace; Otto speaks of the fascination of the numinous. Such reports are evidence of a grounding in values produced by mystical experience, an experiential encounter with a source of superlative, intrinsic value. Again, such language fits the Tao even inasmuch as it is Non-being. It even fits emptiness—not in the sense that emptiness as such possesses value, which is impossible since it is only a tool, but in the sense that the transformation engendered by the discipline of emptiness possesses value.

This leaves us with a provisional definition of mystical experience: mystical experience is a form of primitive experience (a form of experience prior to the division of experience into subject and object components) in which there is radical transformation of the experiential self sense, and radical axiological and existential grounding. This definition, though, is inadequate insofar as it fails to include stages on the path (in some cases and traditions) towards such experience: the dropping of body and mind, the Great Death, the desert, etc.

What does our proposed epistemological model indicate about the possibility of unmediated experience? We first need to examine the concept "unmediated" as it is used in this context. I have argued that "primitive" and mystical experience is constituted by experiential unity prior to a subject-object split. The structure of such experience is "consciousness-of." In the language of phenomenology, this means we bring a "noetic correlate" with us to each moment of experience; we bring ourselves to experience *in some fashion*. But all of our sensory, perceptual, cognitive, emotive, and other faculties are not engaged in every momentary experience. If the primitive experience is a *concentrated* looking at a flower, then we bring ourselves as visual beings to the experience. If the primitive experience is a *concentrated* smelling of a flower, we bring ourselves as olfactory beings to the experience. By "concentrated" I mean the one-pointed mind spoken of in Buddhism; as mentioned above, concentration such as that cultivated in meditation entails the focusing of awareness on a single point. There is no need to posit the presence of ourselves as tactile, auditory, tasting, emotive, linguistic beings in these moments of concentrated use of other senses. These other functions are not engaged at this moment.

So the question becomes: What is engaged, what is "turned on" in a *given* mystical experience? Buddhists, who believe in psychophysical unity, sometimes make much of the fact that meditation is an embodied experience-process. In mysticism generally, there are auditions, visions, automatic speech, stigmata, etc.—obviously the mystic brings the corresponding noetic correlate along in these cases. (And, as mentioned above, we should recall that many mystics are negatively impressed with such sense-based experiences.) Moreover, our discussion above of the experiences of drinking coffee and listening to music established, I believe, that there can be non-verbal knowledge gained from non-verbal experience.

Do we then want to call this kind of thing "mediation"? Let us examine the term. The concept of mediation indicates the presence of something coming in between the subject experiencer and the object experienced, as in: the concepts of the tradition come between the mystic and the contents of the mystical experience. (Note that this model could correlate with either Stace's or Katz's view.) But on our epistemological model there is no division between subject and object; hence, it is misleading to think in terms of mediation. *However*, there is a noetic correlate in experience, whether censorial, non-verbal cognitive, or whatever.[68] Perhaps a better term than mediation is embodiment: all experience is embodied, in the sense that a noetic correlate is present.

In sum, this means that if we ask "can there be unmediated experience?" we must reply that there cannot be unembodied experience. But why should we suppose that there cannot be moments of experience free of the influence of ideas, concepts, words, philosophies and religious traditions? We do not constantly have our linguistic functions turned on in every moment. Not only is the turning off of this function the very purpose of many forms of meditation, but we can think of many examples of secular experience in which the individual experiences in the "primitive" mode without the presence of verbal functions in the noetic correlate. When one gives oneself up completely to the present moment of physical exertion in sports, or the present moment of sound in listening to music, or the present moment of singing, there is no experiential sense of a separate self. There is just the event, in which one is "lost." We can all think of moments in which the sense of a separate self was absent and the events of the moment—musical, physical, or whatever—simply played themselves. If the event itself is not linguistic in nature, there is no need to assume a linguistic element in the noetic correlate. But one can look back on these experiences and say something about them, however inadequately in some cases; there was "consciousness-of" in these experiences. Here again, then, is evidence for non-verbal cognition. One learns from these experiences; the body and non-verbal components of awareness have knowledge that reflective consciousness can later examine and process in its own way.

In conclusion, from the vantage point of this proposed epistemological model, the very question of unmediated experience is misconceived. We need to examine more carefully what, in each *particular* case, the mystic brings to the experience as the noetic correlate of that experience. We do not need to assume in every case that the mystic brings along the baggage of her or his religious tradition and culture to each experience, though in some cases it is no doubt true. We do need to further examine the manner in which reflective consciousness inspects non-verbal knowledge and issues its report: this, it seems to me, is one of the key nuts to crack in understanding the phenomena of mystical experience. If I am right in suggesting that phenomenological data for such an inquiry can be found in both mystical experiences and the kinds of secular experiences discussed above, a resolution to this puzzle may not elude us indefinitely.

References

Burton, Naomi, et al. 1973. *The Asian Journal of Thomas Merton*. New York: New Directions.

Cousins, Ewert. 1986. "Transcultural Phenomenology and Meister Eckhart." In *Mysticism: Medieval and Modern*, pp. 101-108. Ed. by Valerie MI Lagorio. Salzburg, Austria: Institut for Anglistik and Amerikanistik, Universitat Salzburg.

Edwards, Rem. 1972. *Reason and Religion: An Introduction to the Philosophy of Religion*. New York: Harcourt Brace.

Griffiths, Paul J. 1986. *On Being Mindless: Buddhist Meditation and the Mind-Body Problem*. La Salle, IL: Open Court.

Hakeda, Yoshito S., trans. 1967. *The Awakening of Faith*. New York: Columbia.

Katz, Steven T. 1978. "Language, Epistemology, and Mysticism." In *Mysticism and Philosophical Analysis*, pp. 22-74. Ed. by Steven T. Katz. New York: Oxford University Press.

Keller, Carl. A. 1978. "Mystical Literature." In *Mysticism and Philosophical Analysis*, pp. 75-100. Ed. by Steven T. Katz. New York: Oxford University Press.

King, Sallie B. 1978. "Concepts, Anti-Concepts and Religious Experience." *Religious Studies* 14: 445-458.

Penner, Hans H. 1983. "The Mystical Illusion." In *Mysticism and Religious Traditions*, pp. 89-116. Ed. by Steven T. Katz. New York: Oxford University Press.

Poole, Fitz John. 1986. "Metaphors and Maps: Towards Comparison in the Anthropology of Religion." *Journal of the American Academy of Religion* 54: 411-457.

Rahula, Walpola. 1974. *What the Buddha Taught.* Rev. ed. New York: Grove Press.

Scholem, Gershom. 1941. *Major Trends in Jewish Mysticism.* 3rd edition. New York: Schocken Books.

Smart, Ninian. 1965. "Interpretation and Mystical Experience." *Religious Studies* 1: 75-87.

Smith, Huston. 1987. "Is There a Perennial Philosophy?" *Journal of the American Academy of Religion* 55: 553-566.

Streng, Frederick J. 1967. *Emptiness: A Study in Religious Meaning.* Nashville: Abingdon Press.

_____. 1978. "Language and Mystical Awareness" in *Mysticism and Philosophical Analysis*, pp. 141-169. Ed. by Steven T. Katz. New York: Oxford University Press.

Ueda, Yoshifumi. 1967. "Two Main Streams of Thought in Yogacara Philosophy." *Philosophy East and West* 17: 155-165.

Underhill, Evelyn. 1961. *Mysticism.* New York: E.P.Dutton.

van Buren, Paul. 1972. *The Edges of Language: An Essay in the Logic of a Religion.* New York: Macmillan.

Waldenfels, Hans. 1980. *Absolute Nothingness: Foundations for a Buddhist-Christian Dialogue.* Trans. by J.W. Heisig. New York: Paulist Press.

Willis, Janice Dean. 1979. *On Knowing Reality: The Tattvartha Chapter of Asariga's Bodhisattvabhumi.* New York: Columbia.

Wittgenstein, L. 1968. *Philosophical Investigations.* 3rd edition. Trans. by G.E.M. Anscombe. New York: Macmillan.

Notes

1. For a complete defence of this position, see my forthcoming paper on 'Mystical Experience and Theological Truth'.

2. See Ninian Smart's essay 'Interpretation and Mystical Experience in *Religious Studies*, vol. 1, no. I (1965).

3. See, for example, R. Panikkar's *The Unknown Christ of Hinduism* (London, 1964) and *Kultmysterium in Hinduismus und Christentum* (Munich, 1964).

4. See Aldous Huxley, *The Perennial Philosophy* (London, 1946) and Fritjof Schuuon, *The Transcendental Unity of Religions* (New York, 1953).

5. See, for example, A. Leonard, 'Studies on the Phenomena of Mystical Experience' in *Mystery and Mysticism* (London, 1956); R. Otto's *Mysticism East and West* (New York, 1957), and D. T. Suzuki's, *Mysticism Christian and Buddhist* (London, 1957). See also F. Heiler, *Prayer* (London, 1933); J. Maréchal, *Studies in the Psychology of the Mystics* (London, 1927); William Johnston, *The Still Point* (New York, 1970); James Pratt, *The Religious Consciousness* (New York, 1930); E. Underhill, *Mysticism* (London, 1911).

6. R. C. Zaehner's three major studies of mysticism are *Hindu and Muslim Mysticism* (London. 1960); *Mysticism, Sacred and Profane* (London, 1957; New York, 1961); and *Concordant Discord* (London, 1970). See also his *Our Savage God* (London, 1974).

7. W. T. Stace's two major contributions to the study of mysticism are *The Teachings of the Mystics* (New York, 1960); and *Mysticism and Philosophy* (Philadelphia, 1960; London, 1961).

8. Ninian Smart's major contributions to the study of mysticism are *Reasons and Faiths* (London, 1958); *The Philosophy of Religion* (New York, 1970); 'Interpretation and Mystical Experience' in *Religious Studies*, vol. 1, no. I (1965); 'Mystical Experience' in W. H. Capitan and D. Merrill (eds.) *Art, Mind and Religion* (Pittsburgh, 1967), pp. 133 58; 'Mystical Experience' in *Sophia*, I (1962), pp. 19-25;'History of Mysticism' in P. Edwards (ed.), *Encyclopedia of Philosophy* (New York), Vol. 5. See also the essay by Prof. Smart in the present volume.

9. For criticism of Zaehner see below pages 30-32.

10. For criticism of Stace see below pages 27-30. It is also important to recognize Stace's fundamental bias in favour of a monistic account of mysticism which sees the monistic as the most authentic form of mysticism. This bias corrupts much of his handling

of evidence and the nature of his arguments and judgements. See also W. J. Wainwright, 'Stace and Mysticism', in *Journal of Religion*, 50 (1970), pp. 139-54.

11. Smart's studies are problematic on this crucial point and at times he even lapses into holding what we have called Thesis II. Thus, for example, in summarizing the results of his critique of Zaehner in his paper on 'Interpretation and Mystical Experience' in *Religious Studies*, vol. 1, No. I (1965) he writes: 'To put the possibility which I am canvassing in a simple form, it can be reduced to the following theses:
    1. Phenomenologically, mysticism is everywhere the same.
    2. Different flavours, however, accrue to the experiences of mystics because of their different ways of life and modes of autointerpretation.
    3. The truth of interpretation depends in large measure on factors extrinsic to the mystical experience itself.'

12. We shall critically consider these phenomenological typologies, however, later in this paper in light of our more general thesis about the nature of mystical experience.

13. I have read every major study of this subject known to me and in my reading the only two students of the subject who seem *sufficiently* to recognize the full meaning and implications of this issue in a systematic way for the study of mysticism are R. C. Zaehner and Ninian Smart. Yet even they do very little with it. The point is also recognized in a narrow context by H. P. Owen in his article on 'Christian Mysticism' in *Religious Studies* 7 (1971), pp. 31-42.

14. For a technical discussion of the Buddhist doctrine of *nirvana* see D. Kalupahana, *Buddhist Philosophy* (Hawaii, 1976), pp. 69-90; C. Prebish (ed.), *Buddhism: A Modern Perspective* (Pennsylvania, 1975); L. de la Vallée Poussin, *Nirvana* (Paris, 1923); L. B. Homer, *The Early Buddhist Theory of Man Perfected* (London, 1936); R. Johansson, *The Psychology of Nirvana* (New York, 1970); T. Stcherbatsky, *The Buddhist Conception of Nirvana* (Leningrad, 1927); G. R. Welbon, *The Buddhist Nirvana and Its Western Interpreters* (Chicago, 1968).

15. R. C. Zaehner, for example, claims to identify four distinct types of mysticism in Hinduism. See his *Concordant Discord* (London, 1970;, p. 204 ff.

16. W. T. Stace, *Mysticism and Philosophy*, pp. 31-8.

17. W. T. Stace, *Mysticism and Philosophy*, p. 31.

18. W. T. Stace, *Mysticism and Philosophy*, p. 31 f

19. W. T. Stace, *Mysticism and Philosophy*, p. 34.

20. W. T. Stace, *Mysticism and Philosophy*, p. 36.

21. For more details of this sort of phenomenon in artistic perception, see E. H. Gombrich, *Art and Illusion* (London, 1960). See also Gombrich's essay 'The Evidence of Images' in C. S. Singleton (ed.), *Interpretation* (Baltimore, 1969), pp. 35-104.

22. See the Introduction to Zaehner's *Mysticism, Sacred and Profane* where he refers to his own youthful,. natural, mystical experience undergone at age 20 (pp. xii f). See also his *Our Savage God* (London, 1974), pp. 209-10.

23. Though Stace divides mystical experience into two types, 'introversive' and 'extrovertive', he holds that both are really forms of a more ultimate absorptive pattern of a monistic sort. Thus this division is really only heuristic and preliminary.

24. R. C. Zaehner, *Concordant Discord*, p. 194.

25. R. C. Zaehner, *Concordant Discord*, p. 194.

26. R. C. Zaehner, *Concordant Discord*, p. 194.

27. See R. C. Zaehner, *Hindu and Muslim Mysticism* (London, 1960), p. 188.

28. See for this quite bizarre discussion R. C. Zaehner, *Mysticism, Sacred and Profane* (London, 1957; New York, 1961), pp. 191-2. For a critical discussion of Zaehner's position see N. Smart, 'Interpretation and Mystical Experience', *Religious Studies*, vol. 1, No. I (1965); F. Staal, *Exploring Mysticism* (London, 1975). See also N. Pike's criticism of Smart, 'Comments', in W. H. Capitan and D. D. Merrill (eds.), *Art, Mind and Religion* (Pittsburgh, 1967), pp. 144 50.

29. See for an extended discussion of this point to which I am indebted, N. Smart, 'Interpretation and Mystical Experience' in *Religious Studies*, vol. 1, No. I (1965), pp. 81-4.

30. For further material on the Jewish tradition see S. Katz, *Jewish Concepts* (New York, 1977); E. Urbach, *The Sages* (Jerusalem, 1975); S. Schecter, *Some Aspects of Rabbinic Theology* (New York, 1961); H. Donin, *To Be a Jew* (New York, 1972); G. F. Moore, *Judaism* (New York, 1973); M. Steinberg, *Basic Judaism* (New York, 1947).

31. See G. Scholem's *Kabbalah* (New York, 1974) and his *On the Kabbalah and its Symbolism* (New York, 1965).

31A. For more on 'Devekuth' see G. Scholem's *Kabbalah* (New York, 1974); *Major Trends in Jewish Mysticism* (New York, 1954); and his essay 'Devekuth' in his *The Messianic Idea in Judaism* (New York, 1972). pp. 203-26. For additional material of importance, and a disagreement with Scholem's view see I. Tishby's *Mishnal Ha-Zohar* [in Hebrew] (Jerusalem, 1961), Vol. 2, pp. 287ff. Scholem's position, however, appears to me to be the substantially correct one.

32.   Ninian Smart's view as stated in his article 'Interpretation and Mystical Experience', in *Religious Studies*, vol. 1, No. I (1965), seems to me also to be mistaken on this issue. His position is too close to that of Stace's in stressing the distinction between 'experience' and its 'interpretation' and fails, I believe. to see the essential importance of the pre-conditioning of the mystic's experience. He writes: 'This seems to me a clear indication that the monistic and theistic experiences are essentially similar; and that it is the correct interpretation of them which is at issue' (p. 85).

33.   This account generally follows the excellent summary of the Buddhist position in C. Prebish (ed.), *Buddhism: A Modern Perspective* (Pennsylvania, 1975), pp. 29-35. See also E. Conze, *Buddhism: Its Essence and Development* (London, 1974; New York, 1965); R. Robinson, *The Buddhist Religion* (California, 1970):W. Rahula. *What the Buddha Taught* (New York, 1962): D. Rhys, *Buddhism* (London, 1914).

34.   Perspective C. Prebish (ed.), *Buddhism: A Modern Perspective*, p. 34.

35.   On *nirvana*, see sources cited in note 14 above.

36.   In addition to the sources cited above in note 33, see N. Smart, *Doctrine and Argument in Indian Philosophy0* (London, 1964); S. Radhakrishnan, *Indian Philosophy* (London, 1941); K. N. Jayatilleka, *Early Buddhist Theory of Knowledge* (London, 1963); D. Kalupahana, *Causality The Central Philosophy of Buddhism* (Hawaii, 1975); E. Conze, *Buddhist Thought in India* (Michigan, 1967); K. N. Jayatilleka, *Survival and Karma in Buddhist Perspective* (Kandy, 1969).

37.   L. Wittgenstein, *Philosophical Investigations* (Oxford, 1958), section 304.

38.   John Ruysbroeck, 'Regnum Deum Amantium', ch. 22, cited by E. Underhill, *Mysticism* (London, 1911), p. 425.

39.   Meister Eckhart, *Mystische Schriften* (Berlin, 1903), p. 122.

40.   For more on Plotinus, see A. H. Armstrong, *Plotinus* (London, 1953); W. R. Inge, *The Philosophy of Plotinus,* 2 vols. (London, 1918); E. Underhill, *Mysticism* (London, 1911); A. H. Armstrong, 'Plotinus', in A. H. Armstrong (ed.), *Cambridge History of Later Greek and Early Medieval Philosophy* (Cambridge, 1967). pp. 195-271; E. Brehier, *La Philosophie de Plotin* (Paris, 1961); J. M. Rist, *Plotinus: The Road to Reality* (Cambridge, 1967). This work also includes a full Bibliography for further research.

41.   Plotinus, *Enneads*, VI, 7:34 in Creuzer (ed.), *Plotini Opera Omnia* (Oxford, 1835).

42.   On the fascinating history of Sabbatianism see G. Scholem, *Sabbatai Sevi* (Princeton, 1973). For a shorter resume of Scholem's research, see ch. 8 of his *Major Trends in Jewish Mysticism* (New York, 1954) and his *Kabbalah* (New York, 1974).

43.   On the Frankist movement, see G. Scholem, *Major Trends*, ch. 8.

44.   For more details of the Zoharic system, see G. Scholem's *Kabbalah* (includes a complete Bibliography for further research); and his *On The Kabbalah and Its Symbolism* (New York, 1965). There is also a translation of the major part of the Zohar in English by H. Sperling and M. Simon (London, 1931-4), 5 vols.

45.   On Lurianic Kabbalah, see G. Scholem, *Major Trends*, ch. 7; see also the relevant sections of Scholem's *Kabbalah*.

46.   On the mystical school of Safed, which included Isaac Luria, Moses Cordovero, and Joseph Karo, among others, see S. Schechter, 'Safed in the Sixteenth Century' in his *Studies in Judaism*, 2nd Series (Philadelphia, 1908), pp. 202-306. See also R. J. Z. Werblowsky, *Joseph Karo* (Oxford, 1962).

47.   R. Robinson, *The Buddhist Religion* (California, 1970), p. 33.

48.   On Buddhist monasticism see C. Prebish, *Buddhist Monastic Orders* (Pennsylvania, 1975). See also N. Dutt, *Early Monastic Buddhism* (Calcutta, 1960); S. Dutt, *Buddhist Monks and Monasteries of India* (London, 1962); 1. B. Homer, trans., *The Book of Discipline,* 6 vols. (London, 1938 66); G. De, *Democracy in Early Buddhist Sangha* (Calcutta, 1955).

49.   For more on Zen Buddhism, see Shoku Watanabe, *Japanese Buddhism* (Tokyo, 1968); H. Dumoulin, A *History of Zen Buddhism* (London and. New York, 1963); D. T. Suzuki, *Introduction to Zen Buddhism* (New York, 1964; London, 1969); J. Kitagawa, *Religion in Japanese History* (New York, 1966); D. T. Suzuki, *Essays in Zen Buddhism*, 3 vols. (London, 1949-53).

50.   See on Sufi monasticism and the Sufi orders, the excellent work by J. Spencer Trimingham entitled *Sufi Orders* (Oxford, 1971). See also A. Schimmel, *Mystical Dimensions of Islam* (North Carolina, 1975); R. Gramlich, *Die schutischen Derwischorden Persiens* (Wiesbaden, 1965).

51.   See F. Staal, *Exploring Mysticism* (London, 1975).

52.   This is the name of Carlos Castaneda's Mexican Indian teacher. See Castaneda's trilogy *Teachings of Don Juan: A Yaqui Way of Knowledge* (Berkeley, 1970); *A Separate Reality: Further Conversations with Don Juan* (New York, 1971); and *Journey to Ixtlan* (New York, 1972).

53.   For Zen sources on 'testing' *nirvana* or *satori* see the discussion of the Zen koan and other procedures which take place between a Zen Master and his disciples. Some discussion of this matter can be found in, for example, H Dumoulin, *A History of Zen Buddhism* (London and New York, 1963); P. Kapleau, *The Three Pillars of Zen* (Boston, 1967); Guy Welbon, *The*

Buddhist Nirvana and its Western Interpreters (Chicago, 1968); E. Lamotte, *Histoire du Buddhisme indien* (Paris, 1967); D. T. Suzuki, Introduction to Zen Buddhism (Kyoto, 1934); *Zen Comments on the Mumonkan* (New York, 1974).

54. For details see Hakuin's autobiography, 'The Itsu-made-gusa' in *Hakuin Osho Zenshu*, I, pp. 149-230 (Tokyo, 1935). See also his more extended treatment of this topic in his 'Orategama' in *Hakuin Osho Zenshui*, V, pp. 105-246. See also the chronicle of Hakuin's life prepared by his disciple Enji Torei entitled 'Shinki - dokumyo Zenzi nempuingyokaku' (Chronicle of Hakuin) in *Hakuin Osho Zenshui*, I, pp. 1-78. For a brief, helpful discussion of these events see H. Dumoulin, A *History of Zen Buddhism* (London and New York, 1963), pp. 247-55.

55. For an interesting discussion of several senses of the term 'real', see J. Bennett, 'Real' in K. T. Fann (ed.), *Symposium on J. L. Austin* (London, 1969), pp. 267-83.

56. Kant defined transcendental knowledge as follows: 'I call *transcendental* all knowledge which is occupied not so much with objects as with the mode of our knowledge of objects in general in so far as this mode of knowledge is to be possible *a priori*', *Critique of Pure Reason*, B25. See also Kant's *Critique of Judgement*, 'Introduction'. On the contemporary discussion of what is involved in trying to frame such a 'transcendental deduction', see W. van O. Quine's *Word and Object* (Cambridge, Mass., 1960) as well as his *Ontological Relativity and Other Essays* (New York, 1969). See also P. F. Strawson, *Individuals* (London, 1959) and his *Bounds of Sense* (London, 1966). Of the recent journal literature see M. S. Gram, 'Transcendental Arguments', *Nous* 5 (1971), pp. 5-26; and Gram again in: 'Hintikka and Spurious Transcendentalism' in *Nous* 8 (1974); 'Categories and Transcendental Arguments', in *Man and World* 6 (1973); 'Must Transcendental Arguments be Spurious?' in *Kant-Studien* 65 (1974). See also J. Hintikka 'Transcendental Arguments' in *Nous* 6 (1972), pp. 274-81. The back issues of *Kant-Studien* have many other papers of interest and relevance on this theme too numerous to list separately here.

57. Part One of this paper was first presented at the national AAR meeting in 1986. At that time I received the valuable responses of Steven Katz and Robert Gimello, for which I thank them. I also wish to thank Mark Johnson, Tom Dean, and Shigenon Nagatomo for reading this paper at venous stages of its development and responding with helpful suggestions, some of which I have incorporated

58. This has been done elsewhere with respect to a definition of "religion" to considerable profit (Edwards:14ff).

59. This is a serious problem for the present discussion. I would argue that a number of the passages discussed as examples of mystical literature by some of the pluralist interpreters of mysticism in fact are not clearly mystical and hence were inappropriately used as data for the discussion of the nature of mysticism. For example, several of the texts cited by Carl A. Keller (1978), such as some of the dialogues and commentaries, are not mystical but philosophical or pedagogical in nature. It is a real question how far we can proceed with the analysis of mysticism without criteria determining what is to be included and what excluded in the class of mystical phenomena and texts.

60. In his critical response to Katz, Huston Smith begins by focusing on the same epistemological assumption (553).

61. The imbedded quotation is from R.C. Zaehner, *Hindu and Muslim Mysticism* (London, 1960), p. 2.

62. Similarity is another matter. "Similar" is a vague term; in fact, to speak of mysticism at all (which, of course, some would prefer we did not), we must be willing to grant some degree of similarity. What degree of similarity we are willing to recognize remains precisely the question at issue.

63. Smith also makes this point (564).

64. Moreover, it seems likely that such doctrines about language in fact originally derive from religious experience.

65. While I agree with Huston Smith on several points of criticism of Katz, I do nor agree with the. perennialist position which Smith champions. Smith, as a perennialist, believes in the "transcendent unity of religions" (Smith:563). I make no claim for such unity—on this point I am anagnostic; I claim only that pluralism is unproven, not that unity is demonstrated. Moreover, I question whether the position presented in Smith's paper is as inclusive as he claims. It stokes me as distinctively Hindu in outlook and incompatible, despite his claims to the contrary, with Buddhism. A Buddhist would not speak of "another, more fundamental world underlying our familiar, quotidian one" (Smith:565). The position I construct in Pan Two of this paper is shaped by Buddhist philosophy and thus sharply differs from Smith's perennialism.

66. In a very thought-provoking article, Ewert Cousins (see references) uses phenomenological method in a different way and to different ends than I suggest.

67.   Until recently, the usual understanding of Asariga and Vasubandhu presented in western scholarship has been that they and
      their school represent monistic Idealism. In my interpretation of these thinkers, I agree with those who argue that they are not
      monistic Idealists. Instead, they should be seen as theorists with a new interpretation of *sunyata* in which both subject and
      object are empty and in which the cessation of the act of projecting mental constructions onto reality is called "Mind-only"
      (Willis, Ueda). Paramartha's similar views can be discerned by a close reading of the Awakening of Faith (Hakeda). I am
      presently working on a study of Paramartha's *Fo Hsing Lun* (*Buddha Nature Treatise*), which will bring this point into greater
      relief.

68.   The only exception would be in moments of complete unconsciousness—in which cas it becomes problematic to speak of
      experience at all. For an interesting discussion of such "unconscious experience" from the Buddhist perspective, see Griffiths,
      On Being Mindless.

DEAUTOMATIZATION AND THE MYSTIC EXPERIENCE

by Arthur J. Deikman, M.D.

To study the mystic experience one must turn initially to material that appears unscientific, is couched in religious terms, and seems completely subjective. Yet these religious writings are data and not to be dismissed as something divorced from the reality with which psychological science is concerned. The following passage from *The Cloud of Unknowing*, a fourteenth-century religious treatise, describes a procedure to be followed in order to attain an intuitive knowledge of God. Such an intuitive experience is called mystical because it is considered beyond the scope of language to convey. However, a careful reading will show that these instructions contain within their religious idiom psychological ideas pertinent to the study and understanding of a wide range of phenomena not necessarily connected with theological issues:

> . . . forget all the creatures that ever God made and the works of them, so that thy thought or thy desire
> be not directed or stretched to any of them, neither in general nor in special. . . . At the first time when
> thou dost it, thou findst but a darkness and as it were a kind of unknowing, thou knowest not what,
> saving that thou feelest in thy will a naked intent unto God . . . thou mayest neither see him clearly by
> light of understanding in thy reason, nor feel him in sweetness of love in thy affection . . . if ever thou
> shalt see him or feel him as it may be here, it must always be in this cloud and in this darkness. . . .
> Smite upon that thick cloud of unknowing with a sharp dart of longing love (Knowles, 1961, p. 77).

Specific questions are raised by this subjective account: What constitutes a state of consciousness whose content is not rational thought ("understanding in thy reason"), affective ("sweetness of love"), or sensate ("darkness," "cloud of unknowing")? By what means do both an active "forgetting" and an objectless "longing" bring about such a state? A comparison of this passage with others in the classical mystic literature indicates that the author is referring to the activities of renunciation and contemplative meditation. This paper will present a psychological model of the mystic experience based on the assumptions that meditation and renunciation are primary techniques for producing it, and that the process can be conceptualized as one of deautomatization.

Phenomena of the Mystic Experience

Accounts of mystic experiences can be categorized as (a) untrained-sensate, (b) trained-sensate, and (c) trained-transcendent. "Untrained-sensate" refers to phenomena occurring in persons not regularly engaged in meditation, prayer, or other exercises aimed at achieving a religious experience. These persons come from all occupations and classes. The mystic state they report is one of intense affective, perceptual, and cognitive phenomena that appear to be extensions of familiar psychological processes. Nature and drugs are the most frequent precipitating factors. James cites the account of Trevor to illustrate a nature experience:

> For nearly an hour I walked along the road to the "Cat and Fiddle," and then returned. On the way back, suddenly, without warning, I felt that I was in heaven—an inward state of peace and joy and assurance indescribably intense, accompanied with a sense of being bathed in a warm glow of light, as though the external condition had brought about the internal effect—a feeling of having passed, beyond the body, though the scene around me stood out more clearly and as if nearer to me than before, by reason of the illumination in the midst of which I seemed to be placed. This deep emotion lasted, though with decreasing strength, until I reached home, and for some time after only gradually passing away (James, *The Varieties of Religious Experience,* 1929 ea., p. 388).

More recent accounts of experiences with LSD-25 and related drugs fall into the same group (Watts, 1962).

The "trained-sensate" category refers to essentially the same phenomena occurring in religious persons in the West and in the East who have deliberately sought "grace," "enlightenment," or "union" by means of long practice in concentration and renunciation (contemplative meditation, Yoga, and so forth). One example of this group is Richard Rolle, who wrote:

> . . . I was sitting in a certain chapel, and while I was taking pleasure in the delight of some prayer or meditation, I suddenly felt within me an unwonted and pleasant fire. When I had for long doubted from whence it came, I learned by experience that it came from the Creator and not from creature, since I found it ever more pleasing and full of heat . . . (Knowles, 1961, p. 57).

A more elaborate experience is recorded by Julian of Norwich:

> In this (moment) suddenly I saw the red blood trickle down from under the garland hot and freshly and right plenteously. . . . And in the same strewing suddenly the Trinity fulfilled my heart most of joy. And so I understood it shall be in heaven without end to all that shall come there (Warrack, 1952, p. 8).

Visions, feelings of "fire," "sweetness," "song," and joy are various accompaniments of this type of experience.

The untrained-sensate and the trained-sensate states are phenomenologically indistinguishable, with the qualification that the trained mystics report experiences conforming more closely to the specific religious cosmology to which they are accustomed. As one might expect, an experience occurring as the result of training, with the support of a formal social structure, and capable of being repeated, tends to have a more significant and persisting psychological effect. However, spontaneous conversion experiences are also noteworthy for their influence on a person's life. Typical of all mystic experience is a more or less gradual fading away of the state, leaving only a memory and a longing for that which was experienced.

Mystics such as St. John of the Cross and St. Teresa of Avila, commentators such as Poulain, and Eastern mystic literature in general, divide the effects and stages through which mystics progress into a lesser experience of strong emotion and ideation (sensate) and a higher, ultimate experience that goes beyond affect or ideation. It is the latter experience, occurring almost always in association with long training, that characterizes the "trained-transcendent" group. The trans-sensate aspect is stated specifically by a number of authors, such as Walter Hilton and St. John of the Cross:

> From what I have said you may understand that visions of revelations by spirits, whether seen in bodily form or in the imagination, and whether in sleeping or waking, do not constitute true contemplation. This applies equally to any other sensible experiences of seemingly spiritual origin,

whether of sound, taste, smell or of warmth felt like a glowing fire m the breast or in other parts of the body, anything, indeed, that can be experienced by the physical senses (Hilton, 1953, pp. 14-15).

. . . that inward wisdom is so simple, so general and so spiritual that it has not entered into the umderstanding enwrapped or clad in any form or image subject to sense, it follows that sense and imagination (as it has not entered through them nor has taken their form and color) cannot account for it or imagine it, so as to say anything concerning it, although the soul be clearly aware that it is experiencing and partaking of that rare and delectable wisdom (St. John of the Cross, 1953, Vol. I, p. 457).

A similar distinction between lower (sensate) and higher (transcendent) contemplative states may be found in Yoga texts. "Conscious concentration" is a preliminary step to "concentration which is not conscious (of objects)."

For practice when directed towards any supporting-object is not capable of serving as an instrument to this [concentration not conscious of an object]. . . . Mind-stuff, when engaged in the practice of this [imperceptible object], seems as if it were itself non-existent and without any supporting-object. Thus [arises] that concentration [called] seedless, [without sensational stimulus], which is not conscious of objects (Woods, 1914, p. 42).

In the transcendent state, multiplicity disappears and a sense of union with the One or with All occurs. "When all lesser things and ideas are transcended and forgotten, and there remains only a perfect state of imagelessness where Tathagata and Tathata are merged into perfect Oneness . . ." (Goddard, 1938, p. 322).

Then the spirit is transported high above all the faculties into a void of immense solitude whereof no mortal can adequately speak. It is the mysterious darkness wherein is concealed the limitless Good. To such an extent are we admitted and absorbed into something that is one, simple, divine, and illimitable, that we seem no longer distinguishable from it. . . . In this unity, the feeling of multiplicity disappears. When, afterwards, these persons come to themselves again, they find themselves possessed of a distinct knowledge of things, more luminous and more perfect than that of others. . . . This obscurity is a light to which no created intelligence can arrive by its own nature (Poulain, 1950, p. 272)

This state is described in all the literatures as one in which the mystic is passive in that he has abandoned striving. He sees "grace" to be the action of God on himself and feels himself to be receptive. In addition some descriptions indicate that the senses and faculties of thought feel suspended, a state described in Catholic literature as the "ligature."

Human variety is reflected in the superficial differences between the various mystic records. However, perusal of these accounts leads one to agree with Maréchal when he writes,

A very delicate psychological problem is thus raised: the consensus of the testimonies we have educed is too unanimous to be rejected. It compels us to recognize the existence in certain subjects of a special psychological state, which generally results from a very close interior concentration, sustained by an intense affective movement, but which, on the other hand, no longer presents any trace of "discursiveness," spatial imagination, or reflex consciousness. And the disconcerting question arises: after images and concepts and the conscious Ego have been abolished, what subsists of the intellectual life? Multiplicity will have disappeared, true, but to the advantage of what kind of unity? (Maréchal, 1964, p. 185.)

In summary, mystic literature suggests that various kinds of people have attained what they considered to be exalted states of mind and feeling, states that may be grouped in three divisions:

untrained-sensate, trained-sensate, and trained-transcendent. The most important distinction would appear to be between an experience grounded in customary affect, sensations, and ideations, and an experience that is said to transcend such modalities.

Basic Mystic Techniques

How is the mystic experience produced? To answer this question I will examine the two basic techniques involved in mystical exercises: contemplation and renunciation.

Contemplation is, ideally, a nonanalytic apprehension of an object or idea—nonanalytic because discursive thought is banished and the attempt is made to empty the mind of everything except the percept of the object in question. Thought is conceived of as an interference with the direct contact that yields essential knowledge through perception alone. The renunciation of worldly goals and pleasures, both physical and psychological, is an extension of the same principle of freeing oneself from distractions that interfere with the perception of higher realisms or more beautiful aspects of existence. The renunciation prescribed is most thorough and quite explicit in all texts. The passage that begins this paper instructs, "Forget all the creatures that ever God made . . . so that thy thought . . . be not directed . . . to any of them. . . ." In the Lankavatra Scripture one reads. ". . . he must seek to annihilate all vagrant thoughts and notions belonging to the externality of things, and all ideas of individuality and generality, of suffering and impermanence, and cultivate the noblest ideas of egolessness and emptiness and imagelessness . . ." (Goddard, 1938, p. 323). Meister Eckhart promises: "If we keep ourselves free from the things that are outside us, God will give us in exchange everything that is in heaven, . . . itself with all its powers . . ." (Clark and Skinner, 1958, p. 104). In Hilton one reads, "Therefore if you desire to discover your soul, withdraw your thoughts from outward and material things, forgetting if possible your own body and its five senses . . ." (Hilton, 1953, p. 205). St. John calls for the explicit banishment of memory:

> Of all these forms and manners of knowledge the soul must strip and void itself, and it must strive to lose the imaginary apprehension of them, so that there may be left in it no kind of impression of knowledge, nor trace of aught soever, but rather the soul must remain barren and bare, as if these forms had never passed through it and in total oblivion and suspension. And this cannot happen unless the memory be annihilated as to all its forms, if it is to be united with God (St. John of the Cross, 1953, p. 227).

In most Western and Eastern mystic practice, renunciation also extends to the actual life situation of the mystic. Poverty, chastity, and the solitary way are regarded as essential to the attainment of mystic union. Zen Buddhism, however, sees the ordinary life as a proper vehicle for "satori" as long as the "worldly" passions and desires are given up, and with them the intellectual approach to experience. "When I am in my isness, thoroughly purged of all intellectual sediments, I have my freedom in its primary sense . . . free from intellectual complexities and moralistic attachments . . ." (Suzuki, 1959, p. 19).

Instructions for performing contemplative meditation indicate that a very active effort is made to exclude outer and inner stimuli, to devalue and banish them, and at the same time to focus attention on the meditative object. In this active phase of contemplation the concentration of attention upon particular objects, ideas, physical movements, or breathing exercises is advised as an aid to diverting attention from its usual channels and restricting it to a monotonous focus.[1] Patanjali comments,

> Binding the mind-stuff to a place is fixed-attention. . . . Focusedness of the presented idea on that place is contemplation. . . . This same [contemplation] shining forth [in consciousness] as the intended object and nothing more, and, as it were, emptied of itself, is concentration. . . . The three in

one are constraint. . . . Even these [three] are indirect aids to seedless [concentration] (Woods, 1914, pp. 203-8)

Elaborate instructions are found in Yoga for the selection of objects for contemplation and for the proper utilization of posture and breathing to create optimal conditions for concentration. Such techniques are not usually found in the Western religious literature except in the form of the injunction to keep the self oriented toward God and to fight the distractions which are seen as coming from the devil. (*The Spiritual Exercises of St. Ignatius* [Puhl, 1962] is a possible exception.)

The active phase of contemplative meditation is a preliminary to the stage of full contemplation, in which the subject is caught up and absorbed in a process he initiated but which now seems autonomous, requiring no effort. Instead, passivity—self-surrender—is called for, an open receptivity amidst the "darkness" resulting from the banishment of thoughts and sensations and the renunciation of goals and desires directed toward the world.

> When this active effort of mental concentration is successful, it is followed by a more passive, receptive state of *samadhi* in which the earnest disciple will enter into the blissful abode of noble wisdom . . . (Goddard, 1938, p. 323).

> For if such a soul should desire to make any effort of its own with its interior faculties, this means that it will hinder and love the blessings which . . . God is instilling into it and impressing upon it (Hilton, 1953, p. 380).

It should not be forgotten that the techniques of contemplation and renunciation are exercised within the structure of some sort of theological schema. This schema is used to interpret and organize the experiences that occur. However, mere doctrine is usually not enough. The Eastern texts insist on the necessity for being guided by a guru (an experienced teacher), for safety's sake as well as in order to attain the spiritual goal. In Western religion, a "spiritual advisor" serves as guide and teacher. The presence of a motivating and organizing conceptual structure and the support and encouragement of a teacher are undoubtedly important in helping a person to persist in the meditation exercises and to achieve the marked personality changes that can occur through success in this endeavor. Enduring personality change is made more likely by the emphasis on adapting behavior to the values and insights associated both with the doctrinal structure and with the stages of mystical experience.

How can one explain the phenomena and their relation to these techniques? Most explanations in the psychological and psychoanalytic literature have been general statements emphasizing a regression to the early infant-mother symbiotic relationship. These statements range from an extreme position, such as Alexander's (1931), where Buddhist training is described as a withdrawal of libido from the world to be reinvested in the ego until an intrauterine narcissism is achieved—"the pure narcissism of the sperm"—to the basic statement of Freud's (1961, vol. 21, pp. 64-73) that "oceanic feeling" is a memory of a relatively undifferentiated infantile ego state. Lewin (1950, pp. 149-55) in particular has developed this concept. In recent years hypotheses have been advanced uniting the concepts of regression and of active adaptation. The works of Kris (1952, p. 302), Fingarette (1963), and Prince and Savage (1965) illustrate this approach to the mystic experience. This paper will attempt an explanation of mystic phenomena from a different point of view, that of attentional mechanisms in perception and cognition.

Deautomatization

In earlier studies of experimental meditation, I hypothesized that mystic phenomena were a consequence of a *deautomatization* of the psychological structures that organize, limit, select, and interpret perceptual stimuli.

I suggested the hypotheses of sensory translation, reality transfer, and perceptual expansion to explain certain unusual perceptions of the meditation subjects (Deikman, 1966b). At this point I will try to present an integrated formulation that relates these concepts to the classical mystic techniques of renunciation and contemplation.

Deautomatization is a concept stemming from Hartmann's (1958, pp. 88-91) discussion of the automatization of motor behavior:

> In well-established achievements they [motor apparatuses] function automatically: the integration of the somatic systems involved in the action is automatized, and so is the integration of the individual mental acts involved in it. With increasing exercise of the action its intermediate steps disappear from consciousness . . . not only motor behavior but perception and thinking, too, show automatization. . . .
>
> It is obvious that automatization may have economic advantages, in saving attention cathexis in particular and simple cathexis of consciousness in general . . . . Here, as in most adaptation processes, we have a purposive provision for the average expectable range of tasks.

Gill and Brenman (1959, p. 178) developed the concept of deautomatization:

> Deautomatization is an undoing of the automatizations of apparatuses—both means and goal structures—directed toward the environment. Deautomatization is, as it were, a shake-up which can be followed by an advance or a retreat in the level of organization . . . . Some manipulation of the attention directed toward the functioning of an apparatus is necessary if it is to be deautomatized.

Thus, deautomatization may be conceptualized as the undoing of automatization, presumably by *reinvesting actions and percepts with attention*.

The concept of *psychological structures* follows the definition by Rapaport and Gill (1959, pp. 157-58):

> *Structures are configurations of a slow rate of change . . . within which, between which, and by means of which mental processes take place. . . . Structures are hierarchically ordered . . . .* This assumption . . . is significant because it is the foundation for the psychoanalytic propositions concerning differentiation (whether resulting in discrete structures which are then co-ordinated, or in the increased internal articulation of structures), and because it implies that the quality of a process depends upon the level of the structural hierarchy on which it takes place.

The deautomatization of a structure may result in a shift to a structure lower in the hierarchy, rather than a complete cessation of the particular function involved.

Contemplative Meditation

In reflecting on the technique of contemplative meditation, one can see that it seems to constitute just such a manipulation of attention as is required to produce deautomatization. The percept receives intense attention while the use of attention for abstract categorization and thought is explicitly prohibited. Since automatization normally accomplishes the transfer of attention *from* a percept or action to abstract thought activity, the meditation procedure exerts a force in the reverse direction. Cognition is inhibited in favor of perception; the active intellectual style is replaced by a receptive perceptual mode.

Automatization is a hierarchically organized developmental process, so one would expect deautomatization to result in a shift toward a perceptual and cognitive organization characterized as "primitive," that is, an organization preceding the analytic, abstract, intellectual mode typical of present-day adult thought. The perceptual and cognitive functioning of children and of people of primitive cultures have been studied by Werner, who described primitive imagery and thought as (a) relatively more vivid and sensuous, (b) syncretic, (c) physiognomie and animated, (d) dedifferentiated with respect to the distinctions between self and object and between objects, and (e) characterized by a dedifferentiation and fusion of sense modalities. In a statement based on studies of eidetic imagery in children as well as on broader studies of perceptual development, Werner (1957, p. 152) states:

> . . . The image . . . gradually changed in functional character. It becomes essentially subject to the exigencies of abstract thought. Once the image changes in function and becomes an instrument in reflective thought, its structure will also change. It is only through such structural change that the image can serve as an instrument of expression in abstract mental activity. This is why, of necessity the sensuousness, fullness of detail, the color and vivacity of the image must fade.

Theoretically, deautomatization should reverse this development in the direction of primitive thought, and it is striking to note that classical accounts of mystic experience emphasize the phenomenon of Unity. Unity can be viewed as a dedifferentiation that merges all boundaries until the self is no longer experienced as a separate object and customary perceptual and cognitive distinctions are no longer applicable. In this respect, the mystic literature is consistent with the deautomatization hypothesis. If one searches for evidence of changes in the mystic's experience of the external world, the classical literature is of less help, because the mystic's orientation is inward rather than outward and he tends to write about God rather than nature. However, in certain accounts of untrained-sensate experience there is evidence of a gain in sensory richness and vividness. James (1929, pp. 243-44), in describing the conversion experience, states: "A third peculiarity of the assurance state is the objective change which the world often appears to undergo, 'An appearance of newness beautifies every object.' . . ." He quotes Billy Bray: ". . . I shouted for joy, I praised God with my whole heart. . . . I remember this, that everything looked new to me, the people, the fields, the cattle, the trees. I was like a new man in a new world." Another example, this one from a woman, "I pled for mercy and had a vivid realization of forgiveness and renewal of my nature. When rising from my knees I exclaimed, 'Old things have passed away, all things have become new.' It was like entering another world, a new state of existence. Natural objects were glorified. My spiritual vision was so clarified that I saw beauty in every material object in the universe. . . ." Again, "The appearance of everything was altered, there seemed to be as it were a calm, a sweet cast or appearance of divine glory in almost everything."

Such a change in a person's perception of the world has been called by Underhill (1955, p. 235), "clarity of vision, a heightening of physical perception," and she quotes Blake's phrase, "cleanse the doors of perception." It is hard to document this perceptual alteration because the autobiographical accounts that Underhill, James, and others cite are a blend of the mystic's spiritual feeling and his actual perception, with the result that the spiritual content dominates the description the mystic gives of the physical world. However, these accounts do suggest that a "new vision" takes place, colored by an inner exaltation. Their authors report perceiving a new brilliance to the world, of seeing everything as if for the first time, of noticing beauty which for the most part they may have previously passed by without seeing. Although such descriptions do not prove a change in sensory perception, they strongly imply it. These particular phenomena appear quite variable and are not mentioned in many mystic accounts. However, direct evidence was obtained on this point in the meditation experiments already cited (Deikman, 1963, 1966b). There it was possible to ask questions and to analyze the subjects' reports to obtain information on their perceptual experiences. The phenomena the subjects reported fulfilled Werner's criteria completely, although the extent of change varied from one subject to the next. They described their reactions to the percept, a blue vase, as follows: (a) an increased vividness and richness of the percept—"more vivid," "luminous"; (b) animation in the vase, which seemed to move with a life of its own; (c) a marked decrease in self-object distinction, occurring in those subjects who continued longest in the experiments: ". . . I really began to feel, you know, almost as though the blue and I were perhaps merging, or that vase and I were. . . . It was as though everything was sort of merging . . ."; (d) syncretic thought and a fusing and alteration of normal perceptual modes: "I began to feel this light going back and forth," "When the vase changes shape I feel this in my body," "I'm still not sure, though, whether it's the motion in the rings or if it's the rings [concentric rings of light between the subject and the vase]. But in a certain way it is real . . . it's not real in the sense that you can see it, touch it, smell it or anything but it certainly is real in the sense that you can experience it happening." The perceptual and cognitive changes that did occur in the subjects were consistently in the direction of a more "primitive" organiztion.[2]

Thus, the available evidence supports the hypothesis that a deautomazation is produced by contemplative meditation. One might be tempted to call this deautomazation a regression to the perceptual and cognitive state of the child or infant. However, such a concept rests on assumptions as to the child's experience of the world that cannot yet be verified. In an oft-quoted passage, Wordsworth (1904, p. 353) writes:

> There was a time when meadow, grove, and stream,
> The earth, and every common sight,
> To me did seem
> Apparelled in celestial light,
> The glory and the freshness of a dream.

However, he may be confusing childhood with what is actually a reconstruction based on an interaction of adult associative capacities with the *memory* of the more direct sensory contact of the child. "Glory" is probably an adult product. Rather than speaking of a return to childhood, it is more accurate to say that the undoing of automatic perceptual and cognitive structures permits a gain in sensory intensity and richness at the expense of abstract categorization and differentiation. One might call the direction regressive in a developmental sense, but the actual experience is probably not within the psychological scope of any child. It is a deautomatization occurring in an adult mind, and the experience gains its richness from adult memories and functions now subject to a different mode of consciousness.

Renunciation

The deautomatization produced by contemplative meditation is enhanced and aided by the adoption of renunciation as a goal and a life style, a renunciation not confined to the brief meditative period alone. Poverty, chastity, isolation, and silence are traditional techniques prescribed for pursuing the mystic path: To experience God, keep your thoughts turned to God and away from the world and the body that binds one to the world. The meditative strategy is carried over into all segments of the subject's life. The mystic strives to banish from awareness the objects of the world and the desires directed toward them. To the extent that perceptual and cognitive structures require the "nutriment" of their accustomed stimuli for adequate functioning, renunciation would be expected to weaken and even disrupt these structures, thus tending to produce an unusual experience (Rapaport, 1951). Such an isolation from nutritive stimuli probably occurs internally as well. The subjects of the meditation experiment quoted earlier reported that a decrease in responsiveness to distracting stimuli took place as they became more practiced. They became more effective, with less effort, in barring unwanted stimuli from awareness. These reports suggest that psychological barrier structures were established as the subjects became more adept (Deikman, 1963, p. 338). EEG studies of Zen monks yielded similar results. The effect of a distracting stimulus, as measured by the disappearance of alpha rhythm, was most prominent in the novices, less prominent in those of intermediate training, and almost absent in the master (Kasamatsu & Hirai, 1963). It may be that the intensive, long-term practice of meditation creates temporary stimulus barriers producing a functional state of sensory isolation.[3] On the basis of sensory isolation experiments it would be expected that long-term deprivation (or decreased variability) of a particular class of stimulus "nutriment" would cause an alteration in those functions previously established to deal with that class of stimuli (Schultz, 1965, pp. 95-97; Solomon et al., 1961, pp. 226-37). These alterations seem to be a type of deautomatization, as defined earlier—for example, the reported increased brightness of colors and the impairment of perceptual skills such as color discrimination (Zubek et al., 1961). Thus, renunciation alone can be viewed as producing deautomatization. When combined with contemplative meditation, it produces a very powerful effect.

Finally, the more renunciation is achieved, the more the mystic is committed to his goal of Union or Enlightenment. His motivation necessarily increases, for having abandoned the world, he has no other hope of sustenance.

Principal Features of the Mystic Experience

Granted that deautomatization takes place, it is necessary to explain five principal features of the mystic experience: (a) intense realness, (b) unusual sensations, (c) unity, (d) ineffability, and (e) trans-sensate phenomena.

Realness

It is assumed by those who have had a mystic experience, whether induced by years of meditation or by a single dose of LSD, that the truthfulness of the experience is attested to by its sense of realness. The criticism of skeptics is often met with the statement, "You have to experience it yourself and then you will understand." This means that if one has the actual experience he will be convinced by its intense *feeling of reality*. "I know it was real because it was more real than my talking to you now." But "realness" is not evidence. Indeed, there are many clinical examples of variability in the intensity of the feeling of realness that is not correlated with corresponding variability in the reality. A dream may be so "real" as to carry conviction into the waking state, although its content may be bizarre beyond correspondence to this world or to any other. Psychosis is often preceded or accompanied by a sense that the world is *less real* than nominally, sometimes that it is more real, or has a different reality. The phenomenon of depersonalization demonstrates the potential for an alteration in the sense of the realness of one's own person, although one's evidential self undergoes no change whatsoever. However, in the case of depersonalization, or of derealization, the distinction between what is external and what is internal is still clear. What changes is the quality of realness attached to those object representations. Thus it appears that (a) the *feeling* of realness represents a function distinct from that of reality *judgment*, although they usually operate in synchrony; (b) the feeling of realness is not inherent in sensations, per se; and (c) realness can be considered a quantity function capable of displacement and therefore, of intensification, reduction, and transfer, affecting all varieties of ideational and censorial contents.[4]

From a developmental point of view, it is clear that biological survival depends on a clear sense of what is palpable and what is not. The sense of reality necessarily becomes fused with the object world. When one considers that meditation combined with renunciation brings about a profound disruption of the subject's normal psychological relationship to the world, it becomes plausible that the practice of such mystic techniques would be associated with a significant alteration of the feeling of reality. The quality of reality formerly attached to objects becomes attached to the particular sensations and ideas that enter awareness during periods of perceptual and cognitive deautomatization. Stimuli of the inner world become invested with the feeling of reality ordinarily bestowed on objects. Through what might be termed "reality transfer," *thoughts and images become real* (Deikman, 1966b, pp. 109-11).

Unusual Percepts

The sensations and ideation occurring during mystic deautomatization are often very unusual; they do not seem part of the continuum of everyday consciousness. "All at once, without warning of any kind, he found himself wrapped around as it were by a flame colored cloud" (Bucke, 1961, p. 8). Perceptions of encompassing light, infinite energy, ineffable visions, and incommunicable knowledge are remarkable in their seeming distinction from perceptions of the phenomena of the "natural world." According to mystics, these experiences are different because they pertain to a higher transcendent reality. What is perceived is said to come from another world, or at least another dimension. Although such a possibility cannot be ruled out, many of the phenomena can be understood as representing an *unusual mode of perception*, rather than an unusual external stimulus.

In the studies of experimental meditation already mentioned, two long-term subjects reported vivid experiences of light and force. For example:

> . . . shortly I began to sense motion and shifting of light and dark as this became stronger and stronger. Now when this happens it's happening not only in my vision but it's happening or it feels like a physical kind of thing. It's connected with feelings of attraction, expansion, absorption and suddenly my vision pinpointed on a particular place and . . . I was in the grip of a very powerful sensation and this became the center (Deikman, 1966b, p. 109).

This report suggests that the perception of motion and shifting light and darkness may have been the perception of the *movement* of attention among various psychic contents (whatever such "movement" might actually be). "Attraction," "expansion," "absorption," would thus reflect the dynamics of the effort to focus attention—successful focusing is experienced as being "in the grip of" a powerful force. Another example: ". . . when the vase changes shape . . . I feel this in my body and particularly in my eyes . . . there is an actual kind of physical sensation as though something is moving there which recreates the shape of the vase" (Deikman, 1966b, p. 109). In this instance, the subject might have experienced the perception of a resynthesis taking place following deautomatization of the normal percept; that is, the percept of the vase was being reconstructed outside of normal awareness and the *process* of reconstruction was perceived as a physical sensation. I have termed this hypothetical perceptual mode "*sensory translation*," defining it as the perception of psychic *action* (conflict, repression, problem solving, attentiveness, and so forth) via the relatively unstructured sensations of light, color, movement, force, sound, smell, or taste (Kris, 1952; Deikman, 1966b, pp. 108-9). This concept is related to Silberer's (1951) concept of hypnagogic phenomena but differs in its referents and genesis. In the hypnagogic state and in dreaming, a *symbolic* translation of psychic activity and ideas occurs. Although light, force, and movement may play a part in hypnagogic and dream constructions, the predominant percepts are complex visual, verbal, conceptual, and activity images. "Sensory translation" refers to the experience of nonverbal, simple, concrete perceptual equivalents of psychic action.[5]

The concept of sensory translation offers an intriguing explanation for the ubiquitous use of light as a metaphor for mystic experience. It may not be just a metaphor. "Illumination" may be derived from an actual sensory experience occurring when in the cognitive act of unification, a liberation of energy takes place, or when a resolution of unconscious conflict occurs, permitting the experience of "peace," "presence," and the like. Liberated energy experience as light may be the core sensory experience of mysticism.

If the hypothesis of sensory translation is correct, it presents the problem of why sensory translation comes into operation in any particular instance.

In general, it appears that sensory translation may occur when (a) heightened attention is directed to the sensory pathways, (b) controlled analytic thought is absent, and (c) the subject's attitude is one of receptivity to stimuli (openness instead of defensiveness or suspiciousness). Training in contemplative meditation is specifically directed toward attaining a state with those characteristics. Laski (1961) reports that spontaneous mystic experiences may occur during such diverse activities as childbirth, viewing landscapes, listening to music, or having sexual intercourse. Although her subjects gave little description of their thought processes preceding the ecstasies, they were all involved at the time in intense sensory activities in which the three conditions listed above would tend to prevail. Those conditions seem also to apply to the mystical experiences associated with LSD. The state of mind induced by hallucinogenic drugs is reported to be one of increased sensory attention accompanied by an impairment or loss of different intellectual functions (Crocket et al., 1963; Watts, 1962; Michaux, 1963) With regard to the criterion of receptivity, if paranoid reactions occur during the drug state they are inimical to an ecstatic experience. On the other hand, when drug subjects lose their defensiveness and suspiciousness so that they "accept" rather than fight their situation, the "transcendent" experience often ensues (Sherwood et al., 1962) Thus, the general psychological context may be described as *perceptual concentration*. In this special state of consciousness the subject becomes aware of certain intra-psychic processes ordinarily excluded from or beyond the scope of awareness. The vehicle for this perception appears to be amorphous sensation, made real by a displacement of reality feeling ("reality transfer") and thus misinterpreted as being of external origin.

Unity

Experiencing one's self as one with the universe or with God is the hallmark of the mystic experience, regardless of its cultural context. As James (1929, p. 410) puts it,

> This overcoming of all the usual barriers between the individual and the Absolute is the great mystic achievement. In mystic states we both become one with the Absolute and we become aware of our oneness. This is the everlasting and triumphant mystical tradition hardly altered by differences of clime or creed. In Hinduism, in Neoplatonism, in Sufism, in Christian mysticism, in Whitmanism, we find the same recurring note, so that there is about mystical utterance an eternal unanimity which ought to make a critic stop and think, and which brings it about that the mystical classics have, as has been said neither birthday nor native land. Perpetually telling of the unity of man with God, their speech antedates languages, and they do not grow old.

I have already referred to explanations of this phenomenon in terms of regression. Two additional hypotheses should be considered: On the one hand, the perception of unity may be the perception of one's own psychic structure; on the other hand, the experience may be a perception of the real structure of the world.

It is a commonplace chat we do not experience the world directly. Instead, we have an experience of sensation and associated memories from which we infer the nature of the stimulating object As far as anyone can tell, the actual *substance* of the perception is the electrochemical activity chat constitutes perception and thinking. From this point of view, the contents of awareness are homogeneous. They are variations of the same substance. If awareness were turned back upon itself, as postulated for sensory translation, this fundamental homogeneity (unity) of perceived reality—the electrochemical activity—might itself be experienced as a truth about the outer world, rather than the inner one. Unity, the idea and the experience that we are one with the world and with God, would thus constitute a valid perception insofar as it pertained to the nature of the thought process, but need not in itself be a correct perception of the external world.

Logically, there is also the possibility that the perception of unity does correctly evaluate the external world. As described earlier, deautomatization is an undoing of a psychic structure permitting the experience of increased detail and sensation at the price of requiring more attention. With such attention, it is possible that deautomatization may permit the awareness of new dimensions of the total stimulus array—a process of "*perceptual expansion.*" The studies of Werner (1957), Von Senden (1960), and Shapiro (1960) suggest that development from infancy to adulthood is accompanied by an organization of the perceptual and cognitive world that has as its price the selection of some stimuli and stimulus qualities to the exclusion of others. If the automatization underlying that organization is reversed, or temporarily suspended, aspects of reality that were formerly unavailable might then enter awareness. Unity may in fact be a property of the real world that becomes perceptible via the techniques of meditation and renunciation, or under the special conditions, as yet unknown, that create the spontaneous, brief mystic experience of untrained persons.

Ineffability

Mystic experiences are ineffable, incapable of being expressed to another person. Although mystics sometimes write long accounts, they maintain that the experience cannot be communicated by words or by reference to similar experiences from ordinary life. They feel at a loss for appropriate words to communicate the intense realness, the unusual sensations, and the unity cognition already mentioned. However, a careful examination of mystic phenomena indicates chat there are at least several types of experiences, all of which are "indescribable" but each of which differs substantially in content and formal characteristics. Error and confusion result when these several states of consciousness are lumped together as "the mystic experience" on the basis of their common characteristic of ineffability.

To begin with, one type of mystic experience cannot be communicated in words because it is probably based on primitive memories and related to fantasies of a preverbal (infantile) or nonverbal sensory experience.[6] Certain mystical reports that speak of being blissfully enfolded, comforted and bathed in the love of God are very suggestive of the prototypical "undifferentiated state," the union of infant and breast, emphasized by psychoanalytic explanations of mystical phenomena. Indeed, it seems highly plausible that such early memories and fantasies might be reexperienced as a consequence of (a) the regression in thought processes brought about by renunciation and contemplative meditation, and (b) the activation of infantile longings by the guiding religious promise—that is, "that a benign deity would reward childlike surrender with permanent euphoria" (Moller, 1965, p. 127). In addition, the conditions of functional sensory isolation associated with mystic training may contribute to an increase in recall and vividness of such memories (Suraci, 1964).

A second type of mystical experience is equally ineffable but strikingly different—namely, a revelation too complex to be verbalized. Such experiences are reported frequently by those who have drug-induced mystical experiences. In such states the subject has a revelation of the significance and interrelationships of many dimensions of life; he becomes aware of many levels of meaning simultaneously and "understands" the totality of existence. The question of whether such knowledge is actual or an illusion remains unanswered; however if such a multileveled comprehension were to occur, it would be difficult—perhaps impossible—to express verbally. Ordinary language is structured to follow the logical development of one idea at a time and it might be quite inadequate to express an experience encompassing a large number of concepts simultaneously. William James suggested that "states of mystical intuition may be only very sudden and great extensions of the ordinary 'field of consciousness.' " He used the image of the vast reaches of a tidal flat exposed by the lowering of the water level (James, 1920, pp. 500-13). However, mystic revelation may be ineffable, not only because of the sudden broadening of consciousness that James suggests, but also because of a new "vertical" organization of the concepts.[7] For example, for a short while after reading *The Decline and Fall of the Roman Empire*, one may be aware of the immense vista of a civilization's history as Gibbon recreated it. That experience can hardly be conveyed except through the medium of the book itself, and to that extent it is ineffable, and a minor version of James's widened consciousness. Suppose one then read *War and Peace* and acquired Tolstoy's perspective of historical events and their determination by chance factors. Again, this is an experience hard to express without returning to the novel. Now suppose one could "see" not only each of these world views individually but also their parallel relationships to each other, and the cross connections between the individual conceptual structures. And then suppose one added to these conceptual strata the biochemical perspective expressed by *The Fitness of the Environment* (Henderson, 1958), a work which deals, among other things, with the unique and vital properties of the water molecule. Then the vertical interrelationships of all these extensive schemata might, indeed, be beyond verbal expression, beyond ordinary conceptual capacities—in other words, they would approach the ineffable.

Trans-Sensate Phenomena

A third type of ineffable experience is that which I have described earlier as the "trained-transcendent" mystical experience. The author of *The Cloud of Unknowing*, St. John of the Cross, Walter Hilton, and others are very specific in describing a new perceptual experience that does not include feelings of warmth, sweetness, visions, or any other elements of familiar sensory or intellectual experience. They emphasize that the experience *goes beyond* the customary sensory pathways, ideas, and memories. As I have shown, they describe the state as definitely not blank or empty but as filled with intense, profound, vivid perception which they regard as the ultimate goal of the mystic path.[8] If one accepts their descriptions as phenomenologically accurate, one is presented with the problem of explaining the nature of such a state and the process by which it occurs. Following the hypotheses presented earlier in this paper, I would like to suggest that such experiences are the result of the operation of a new perceptual capacity responsive to dimensions of the stimulus array previously ignored or blocked from awareness. For such mystics, renunciation has weakened and temporarily removed the ordinary objects of consciousness as a focus of awareness. Contemplative meditation has undone the logical organization of consciousness. At the same time, the mystic is intensely *motivated* to perceive something. If undeveloped or unutilized perceptual capacities do exist, it seems likely that they would be mobilized and come into operation under such conditions. The perceptual experience that would then take place would be one outside of customary verbal or sensory reference. It would be *unidentifiable*, hence indescribable. The high value, the meaningfulness, and the intensity reported of such experiences suggest that the perception has a different scope from that of normal consciousness. The loss of "self" characteristic of the trans-sensate experience indicates that the new perceptual mode is not associated with reflective awareness—the "I" of normal consciousness is in abeyance.

Conclusion

A mystic experience is the production of an unusual state of consciousness. This state is brought about by a deautomatization of hierarchically ordered structures that ordinarily conserve attentional energy for maximum efficiency in achieving the basic goals of the individual: biological survival as an organism and psychological survival as a personality. Perceptual selection and cognitive patterning are in the service of these goals. Under special conditions of dysfunction, such as in acute psychosis or in LSD states, or under special goal conditions such as exist in religious mystics, the pragmatic systems of automatic selection are set aside or break down, in favor of alternate modes of consciousness whose stimulus processing may be less efficient from a biological point of view but whose very inefficiency may permit the experience of aspects of the real world formerly excluded or ignored. The extent to which such a shift takes place is a function of the motivation of the individual, his particular neurophysiological state, and the environmental conditions encouraging or discouraging such a change.

A final comment should be made. The content of the mystic experience reflects not only its unusual mode of consciousness but also the particular stimuli being processed through that mode. The mystic experience can be beatific, satanic, revelatory, or psychotic, depending on the stimuli predominant in each case. Such an explanation says nothing conclusive about the source of "transcendent" stimuli. God or the

Unconscious share equal possibilities here and one's interpretation will reflect one's presuppositions and beliefs. The mystic vision is one of unity, and modern physics lends some support to this perception when it asserts that the world and its living forms are variations of the same elements. However, there is no evidence that separateness and differences are illusions (as affirmed by Vedanta) or that God or a transcendent reality exists (as affirmed by Western religions). The available scientific evidence tends to support the view that the mystic experience is one of internal perception, an experience that can be ecstatic, profound, or therapeutic for purely internal reasons. Yet for psychological science, the problem of understanding such internal processes is hardly less complex than the theological problem of understanding God. Indeed, regardless of one's direction in the search to know what reality is, a feeling of awe, beauty, reverence, and humility seems to be the product of one's efforts. Since these emotions are characteristic of the mystic experience itself, the question of the epistemological validity of that experience may have less importance than was initially supposed.

Notes

1. Breathing exercises can also affect the carbon dioxide content of the blood and thus alter the state of consciousness chemically.

2. As dedifferentiation of the vase progressed, however, a fusion of background and object tended to occur with a concomitant loss of color and vividness.

3. It has been postulated by McReynolds (1960, p. 269) that a related stimulus barrier system may be operative in schizophrenia.

4. Paul Federn's (1955, pp. 241-60) idea that the normal feeling of reality requires an adequate investment of energy (libido) in the ego boundary, points toward the notion of a quantity of "realness." Avery Weisman (1958) has developed and extended this idea, but prefers the more encompassing concept of "libidinal fields" to that of ego boundaries.

5. Somewhat related concepts, although extreme in scope, are those advanced by Michaux (1962, pp.7-9), who suggests that the frequent experience of waves or vibrations in hallucinogenic drug states is the result of direct perception of the "brain waves" measured by the EEG; and by Leary (1964, pp. 330-39), who suggests that hallucinogenic drugs permit a "direct awareness of the processes which physicists and biochemists and neurologists measure," for example, electrons in orbit or the interaction of cells.

6. Schachtel (1959, p. 284) regards early childhood, beyond infancy, as unrememberable for structural reasons: "It is not merely the repression of a specific content, such as early sexual experience, that accounts for the general childhood amnesia; the biologically, culturally, and socially influenced process of memory organization results in the formation of categories (schemata) of memory which are not suitable vehicles to receive and reproduce experiences of the quality and intensity typical of early childhood." It would follow that verbal structures would likewise be "unsuitable."

7. A similar description concerning "vertical" listening to music is made by Ehrenzweig (1964, pp. 385-87).

8. Ehrenzweig (1964, p. 382) proposes that mystic "blankness" is due to a structural limitation: ". . . the true mystic orison becomes empty yet filled with intense experience. . . . This full emptiness. . . . It is the direct result of our conscious failure to grasp imagery formed on more primitive levels of differentiation . . . . Owing to their incompatible shapes, these images cancelled each other out on the way up to consciousness and so produce in our surface experience a blank 'abstract' image still replete with unconscious fantasy."

THE NOBLE LIE

THE NOBLE LIE: THE FUTURE OF RELIGION

by James W. Ward

> How then may we devise one of those needful falsehoods of which we lately spoke — just one royal lie which may deceive the rulers, if that be possible, and at any rate the rest of the city?[1]

> Plato, *The Republic*, Book III

Introduction

In the *Republic*, Plato referred to the necessity of creating a public religion as a "needful falsehood" and a royal, or noble, lie. For much of the history of the West, religion has been understood as necessary for social cohesion. Nonetheless, for approximately three hundred years, intellectuals in the West have been predicting that religion, Christianity in particular, but often religion in general, is a doomed worldview that would not, and could not, survive as a socially or personally significant force. These intellectuals have included theologians. For example, the German theologian Dietrich Bonhoeffer (1906-1945) believed that the world was moving toward "no religion at all" and that Christianity itself would have to remove "the outer garb of religion."[2]

In what follows, I will provide some historical context for understanding why so many, for so long, have been predicting the decline of religion, particularly Christianity. In exploring this history, I will consider the relationship of religion to understandings of the meaning of life and of the moral life. As this is a complex relationship, more complex than can be fully developed here, this is only a partial history.

In considering the relationship of religion, morality, and the meaning of life, I will first consider the contemplative and ascetic life. Ascetic practices range from fairly mild practices such as the denial of certain pleasures, meditation, disciplined prayer, and short periods of fasting to potentially harsh and dangerous

269

practices such as extreme fasting, self infliction of pain, self-mutilation, and social isolation.[3] Contemplative lives, or ones in which detachment from the world allows for activities such as study, meditation, and prayer, typically require a certain level of asceticism, and often require certain vows, such as poverty, chastity, and obedience.

To provide some context for an understanding of the desire for an ascetic and contemplative life, I will discuss the understandings of the superiority of the contemplative life held by Plato and Aristotle, the transformation of this by two of perhaps the most influential Christian thinkers, Augustine and Aquinas, and the finally the way this was rejected by Reformation thought. The rejection of the ascetic and the monastic life by the Reformers made space for the relatively modern affirmation of ordinary life. The fracturing of the medieval synthesis, and the rise of science, paved the way for modern Western liberal secular societies. I will conclude by considering the implications of the decline of religion, as understood by philosophers, psychologists, and sociologists and the question of whether religion really is in a state of decline.

The Active versus the Contemplative Life

> Just as there are three things that are assigned to a happy conduct of life—the goods that we have in fact already mentioned as the greatest available for human beings, virtue, wisdom, and pleasure—so too we see three lives which all who have the opportunity choose to live, the political, the philosophical, and the pleasure-loving.[4]

> Aristotle

What is the meaning of life, more specifically of human life? Today many might consider this question to be meaningless or unanswerable. Many of those who grant that there is, or could be, an answer to this question also might grant that it is relative or subjective. This was not the perspective of Plato or Aristotle.

Plato and Aristotle

Plato and Aristotle understood the world as a cosmos, as exhibiting a kind of order. They also understood the world teleologically, as the realization of an end or purpose. Everything participated in this order and served some purpose or end, including human life. When Plato and Aristotle consider the nature of the good life, of human happiness, they assume that this is a question about the purpose of human life. Both Plato and Aristotle understood this to be a question about human excellence or perfection.

Both Plato and Aristotle rejected the life of pleasure pursued for its own sake as representative of the good life. From Plato and Aristotle, we inherit an understanding of rationality as the highest end of human life and of philosophical contemplation as the highest form of rationality. Though much has been made of the break between Plato and Aristotle, both emphasize that contemplation of the eternal and unchanging is the highest exercise of human rationality. For Plato, such contemplation should be focused on the form of the good. Aristotle understood the highest object of contemplation to be the prime or unmoved mover. Philosophical contemplation is the end or meaning of human life.

Such contemplation is also essential to the moral life. For Plato this was so because contemplation of the form of the good was necessary for wisdom, the virtue, or perfection, Plato associated with reason or understanding. For Plato, the moral life required an orientation toward the good. Such an orientation requires that we not be ruled by our appetites or desires. This would lead to discord and conflict. We also cannot be ruled by our emotions. Though the moral life may require that our emotions come to the aid of reason, the moral life and the good life is a rational life.[5] Though Aristotle would modify and elaborate on this view, he would not substantially depart from it.

Let us revisit then the question posed at the beginning of this essay—what is the relationship between religion and the meaning of life and the moral life? In the thought of Plato and Aristotle, thought influential for much of the history of the Western world, we find a certain kind of answer. The goal of life should be philosophical contemplation. This contemplation serves an essentially religious purpose and is fundamental to the moral life.

Some might object that I have overlooked the importance of political life, particularly for Aristotle. It is true that Aristotle defined human beings as political animals. Both Plato and Aristotle, it could be argued, believed that the virtues could not be realized apart from the polis, or city-state. We should ask, however, whether Aristotle believed contemplation or political participation to be the ultimate good of human life. Aristotle's answer can be seen in the following.

> For this activity [contemplation] is the best (since not only is intellect the best thing in us, but the objects of intellect are the best of knowable objects); and, secondly, it is the most continuous, since we can contemplate truth more continuously than we can *do* anything. ....So if among excellent actions political and military actions are distinguished by nobility and greatness, and these are unleisurely and aim at an end and are not desirable for their own sake, but the activity of intellect, which is contemplative, seems both to be superior in worth and to aim at no end beyond itself, and to have its pleasure proper to itself (and this augments the activity), and the self-sufficiency, leisureness, unweariedness (so far as this is possible for man), and all the other attributes ascribed to the blessed man are evidently those connected with this activity, it follows that this will be the complete happiness of man...

Aristotle characterizes the intellect as "divine." He encourages us not to follow the advice of those who urge us to consider "human things", but to "as far as we can, make ourselves immortal, and strain every nerve to live in accordance with the best thing in us..."[6]

For Aristotle, as for Plato, the good life requires us to perfect each aspect of ourselves and to find the proper balance between these aspects. Philosophical contemplation is an exercise of that which is best in us, our rationality. In order to exercise this capacity as individuals, we must be moral, because we are also social creatures, the goal of life, philosophical contemplation, also requires social and political organization.[7]

The Christian Transformation of the Greek Ideal

This understanding of the good, the moral life, and the good life was to have a profound effect on Judaism, Christianity, and Islam. All of the monotheistic religions assert in various ways that human beings, more than the other creatures of creation, have been made in the image of God. This *imago dei* has often been understood as our rationality. With Christian understandings of sin came understandings that this *imago dei* had been obscured or even obliterated. In order to realize our perfection as *imago dei*, the proper order to our nature had to be restored. There were certainly other sources for an understanding of what our nature should be other than Greek, but Greek thought provided a strong vision of the necessary interrelationship of an orientation toward the good, morality, and the meaning of life.

From Plato and Aristotle, Jewish, Christian, and Islamic theologians also inherited a notion of perfection as eternal, self-sufficient, and unchanging. All of the monotheistic religions would struggle to reconcile their understanding of God as a God active in history and of their scripture as revealed truth with the eternal, unchanging prime mover of Greek philosophy and with the truth of classical Greek wisdom.

In most of what follows, I will focus on Christianity. From Greek thought, Christian thought also inherited certain hierarchical dichotomies of spirit/body, immaterial/material, and eternal/temporal, with the first in each pair of dichotomies considered to be superior to the second. Though Christian thought would wrestle with the dualism of Platonism and Neoplatonism, within this framework, we can construct something of an argument for the necessity of an ascetic and contemplative life for the religious life. By denying the body and directing one's attention away from the temptations of the body and the world, we can more easily focus on the spiritual. The extent to which one could live such a life could be seen as evidence of the power of one's spirit and/or evidence of one's blessedness.

Christian thought would also inherit an understanding of gradations of perfection. The thought of Plato and Aristotle was clearly elitist. Some lives were not only more moral but also more human. Both Plato and Aristotle restrict the number of those who can participate in philosophic contemplation and in government of the state. This can be seen in Plato's discussion of the role of the different classes in his ideal state, and in Aristotle's distinction between those activities which are necessary for the maintenance of life and those activities which are necessary for the good life.[8] The philosopher Charles Taylor describes this in the following way: "You can't pursue the good life without pursuing life. But an existence dedicated to this latter goal alone is not a fully human one."[9] The influence of these hierarchical and elitist understandings would impact not only understandings of religious life but also of civic life. Not only was participation in the monastic life restricted, participation in the government of the state was also restricted. The idea that not everyone was capable, or worthy, of participating in civic life was a basis for many of the reservations against democracy as a form of government.[10]

Though Greek thought influenced Christian thought, it is also the case that Christian thinkers did not uncritically adopt Greek philosophical positions. Tertullian, a Christian thinker from around 200 C.E., summarized Christian opposition to classical culture: "What does Athens have to do with Jerusalem? What does the Academy have to do with the church?"[11]

To be fair, it must be recognized that various internal and external sources influenced Christian understandings of the monastic life. In Paul's discussion of marriage in I Corinthians 7, for example, Paul argues that marriage is not a sin, and is the appropriate course of action for those who cannot control their desires, but those who can control their desires and not marry are spared anxiety and can better serve the Lord. Paul's justification for this is that the return of the Lord is immanent, and we are better served by focusing on service to God than service to the world. Stoic doctrine also held that wisdom required control of the passions. Various religions in the area of the Mediterranean basin included some form of the monastic life including "sacred virgins, celibate priests, eunuchs, and others whose lifestyle set them apart for the service of the gods."[12] Scripture, classical philosophy, and other religious practices of the world of the early church influenced early Christian monasticism.

Two of the most famous early Christian monastics, Paul and Anthony, retreated to the desert of Egypt. Paul fled persecution. When his parents died when he was young, Anthony received an inheritance sufficient to insure a comfortable life both for himself and his sister. If we believe the report of Athanasius, Anthony based on his understanding of Matthew 19:21, in which Jesus instructs the rich young ruler to sell his possessions and give to the poor, decided to sell all of his inheritance. Anthony reserved a portion for the care of his sister and gave his possessions to the poor. Later he relinquished even this, placed his sister "under the care of the virgins of the church" and retreated to the desert.[13] Anthony eventually acquired a reputation as a saint and would play a role in one of the early controversies in the Christian church, siding with Athanasius and his affirmation that Jesus was fully God against Arius's position that Jesus, as created by God, could not be God.

After the conversion of the Roman emperor Constantine, the church became increasingly powerful. Bishops could be prominent and prestigious. Many did not agree with the church's new position as an imperial church. The life of the desert monks became increasingly popular. Those seeking guidance often sought the counsel of Anthony. The numbers seeking the monastic life would lead to the development of a more communal monastic life.

Augustine

Augustine (354-430 C.E.), a Christian thinker of tremendous influence for Catholic and Protestant Christianity, was deeply influenced by Neoplatonic thought. Prior to his conversion, Augustine was a prominent professor of rhetoric in Milan. One of Augustine's difficulties in converting to Christianity was his difficulty in accepting the Bible, which from his perspective as a student of rhetoric often seemed lacking. Another problem Augustine had with Christianity was that of the problem of evil. Quickly stated, the problem can be stated in the following way: if God is all-powerful and all good, how can evil exist?

Augustine's Neoplatonism, a position he developed in Milan, helped him to overcome his intellectual reservations against Christianity. The goal of Neoplatonism was ecstatic union with the source of being itself. This source was considered to be one. All being was considered an emanation from this one source considered to be infinite and good. Neoplatonism understood evil as a movement away from the One. This provided a perspective for reconciling an all-good God with the existence of evil. In Milan, his mother encouraged him to hear the sermons of Ambrose. Ambrose's allegorical interpretations of much of the Bible that had troubled Augustine helped to reconcile him to the possibility that the Bible could contain truth. Allegorical interpretation was consistent with rhetoric and with a Neoplatonic perspective.

Augustine could not, however, take the step of converting to Christianity. Augustine was convinced that doing so would require him to surrender his ambition, his prominent career, and the pursuit of physical pleasure. It was at this time that Augustine reports that he prayed "Give me chastity and continence; but not too soon."[14]

His reading of *The Life of Saint Anthony* by Athanasius has been credited with contributing to his conversion to Christianity. After his conversion, Augustine was baptized, resigned his teaching position, and left for North Africa. There he hoped to live a life of simple, but not austere life of contemplation. Even after he was called from this life and appointed Bishop, Augustine attempted to maintain something of a monastic community. Though an argument could be made that Augustine preferred the contemplative life, in the passage below we can see that Augustine's understanding of the goals of life and of the contemplative life was not quite that of Plato and Aristotle.

> Or take the three modes of life: the contemplative, the active, the contemplative-active. A man can live the life of faith in any of the three and get to heaven. What is not indifferent is that he love truth and do what charity demands. No man must be so committed to contemplation as, in his contemplation, to give no thought to his neighbor's needs, not so absorbed in action as to dispense with the contemplation of God.[15]

Christianity introduces an emphasis on a life of faith and charity. One could also add that Christianity adds humility, a virtue not recognized by Plato or Aristotle. Augustine notes that a man can live by faith in any of the three modes of life. However, Augustine's preference for contemplation can be seen in the following quotation.

> Thus, it is the love of study that seeks a holy leisure; and only the compulsion of charity that shoulders necessary activity. If no such burden is placed on one's shoulders, time should be passed in study and contemplation. But, once the burden, it should be carried, since charity so demands. Even so, however, no one should give up entirely his delight in learning, for the sweetness he once knew may be lost and the burden he bears overwhelm him.[16]

Benedict

Though Augustine would influence the rule of monastic life, probably the most influential rule established for monastic life was that of Benedict's (480-543 C.E.). Eastern monasticism tended to focus more on solitude, renunciation of the world, disciple of the body, and struggled with the hierarchical developments in the church. Western monasticism, which Benedict helped to found, was more practical. The purpose of the monastic life was training for a life of mission in the world. Western monasticism tended to be more communal. It also, for the most part, did not live in tension with the hierarchy of the church, but rather became integral to the church.

Benedict's major contribution to the monastic life was his *Rule*. Benedict's *Rule* did not call for the kind of asceticism frequently practiced by the desert monks. Benedict required permanence and obedience. Monks would not be free to go as they pleased. Monks were to stay in the monastery they joined unless instructed to move. Benedict also required obedience to the *Rule* and to the direction of the abbot. Benedict also required that all monks participate in the physical labor required to sustain the community. This requirement was to consider the needs and capacities of monks, the old, the ill, and the very young, for example, were to be given appropriate tasks. Those from wealthy or prominent families were to receive no special status.

The life of the community was organized around eight communal hours of prayer.[17] These hours were kept by most of the medieval monastic communities. Most were devoted to the reciting of the Psalms and reading of Scripture.

The keeping of the hours would require books. The need to create these helped to establish the tradition of monastic scribes adept at the copying of the Bible and other books. Monastic centers would become centers for learning and medical care. They would also serve as hostels.

Different monastic orders would emerge such as the Dominican and the Jesuit. We turn now to Aquinas (1244-1274 C.E.), perhaps the most famous of the Dominicans, or the Order of Preachers. The focus of this order, not surprising for those of you with some familiarity with Aquinas, was that of study. It may come as a surprise to you to hear that Aquinas's family was not happy with his choice and actually locked him up in the family castle in an attempt to change his mind. Aquinas, however, would not yield, eventually escaped, and joined the order.

Aquinas

As we can see, Aquinas in his consideration of the merits of the active and the contemplative life draws on the Augustine's understanding. As had Augustine, Aquinas emphasizes faith and charity.

I answer that, As stated above (FS, Question [114], Article [4]), the root of merit is charity; and, while, as stated above (Question [25], Article [1]), charity consists in the love of God and our neighbor, the love of God is by itself more meritorious than the love of our neighbor, as stated above (Question [27], Article [8]). Wherefore that which pertains more directly to the love of God is generically more meritorious than that which pertains directly to the love of our neighbor for God's sake. Now the contemplative life pertains directly and immediately to the love of God; for Augustine says (De Civ. Dei xix, 19) that "the love of" the Divine "truth seeks a holy leisure," namely of the contemplative life, for it is that truth above all which the contemplative life seeks, as stated above (Question [181], Article [4], ad 2). On the other hand, the active life is more directly concerned with the love of our neighbor, because it is "busy about much serving" (Lk. 10:40). Wherefore the contemplative life is generically of greater merit than the active life. This is moreover asserted by Gregory (Hom. iii in Ezech.): "The contemplative life surpasses in merit the active life, because the latter labors under the stress of present work," by reason of the necessity of assisting our neighbor, "while the former with heartfelt relish has a foretaste of the coming rest," i.e. the contemplation of God.[18]

It is important to note the differences between Aquinas's understanding of the contemplative life and that of Aristotle's. Aquinas argued that the philosophical understanding of the end of human life considers the end, or perfection, of life that can be accomplished within the limits of human capability. The theological understanding of the end, or perfection of human life, considers the perfection of human life that transcends human capabilities, the vision of God which cannot be fully realized in this life, but only in the life to come. Whereas for Greek philosophy, philosophical contemplation had been the greatest good, Aquinas describes this as an incomplete or imperfect good. In the thought of Aquinas we can see a tendency characteristic of much of medieval thought, namely that of subsuming philosophy within theology. As the proper end of theology is God, and God is the ultimate end of human life and the most perfect being, knowledge of God is the highest, or most perfect knowledge attainable by human beings.

Before moving on, I would like to make a quick note about the history of the university. As Europe began to recover from the Dark Ages, and cities began to grow and prosper, students began to congregate in the urban centers of Europe. Initially they did so at the cathedral schools. Eventually schools united in what would come to be known as "general studies."[19] These would evolve into the universities of Europe. Though Western European universities can be found in the twelfth century, universities came to establish themselves as the main centers of study during the thirteenth century. Typically to be educated, one had to be from a prominent family, a member of an order, or both.

Aquinas, for example, came from an aristocratic family. His brothers and sisters assumed prominent roles in Italian society. His family's resistance to his choice came not from resistance to his choice of a career in the church, this was what they intended for their son, their resistance was to his choice of orders. The Dominican order was a younger, less prominent order, and they wanted him to join an order with higher social status.

This leads us to an important point. Though the beginnings of the Christian church had been humble, it had prospered after being adopted as the church of the Roman Empire by Constantine. Prominent families in Europe maneuvered to have children in certain religious orders as an indication of social status. The church had acquired power and wealth. Theology was the "queen of the sciences." The church also tried its best to regulate ideas, even after the Reformation. This can be seen for example in the condemnation of the thought of Copernicus (1473-1543) and Galileo (1564-1642). Corruption and abuses of power, long critiqued within the church, would help to set the stage for the Reformation.

The Reformation

What were the effects of the Reformation? As the contemporary Canadian philosopher Charles Taylor explains in *Sources of the Self,* prior to the Reformation, "the influential ideas of ethical hierarchy exalted the lives of contemplation and participation."[20] According to Taylor, the notion that the true task of philosophers was not a manipulation of, but a contemplative understanding of the world, was persistent enough that it encouraged resistance to the experimental science of Roger Bacon (1561-1626). Obviously something changed; Taylor describes this change as an affirmation of the ordinary life. Theoretical knowledge was no longer sufficient. Eventually, the prevailing opinion came to be that knowledge should have practical benefit; it should improve the quality of ordinary life. No longer was the good life thought to be accessible only to a privileged few.

When and why did this transition take place? Surprising perhaps, Taylor locates the origin of this transformation in two theologically/philosophically central notions of the Reformation. Taylor identifies these as rejection of the medieval notions of mediation and of the sacred.

The Reformers rejected the notion of priestly mediation and replaced it with the priesthood of all believers. According to Taylor, the Reformers understood the medieval church to be a body in which the efforts of some could work to effect the salvation both of themselves and others. This medieval salvation by works understanding was replaced by an understanding of salvation by faith alone. Personal commitment is required of every believer. This is not only a rejection of salvation by works; it is the rejection of the classical and medieval notions of hierarchy in the Christian life.

The Reformers also rejected medieval notions that the sacred reliably manifested itself in the sacraments and that the sacred might manifest itself in certain places, times, or actions in the world. Such an understanding was seen as a restriction of the omnipotence of God. According to Taylor, "therefore Protestant (particularly Calvinist) churches swept away pilgrimages, veneration of relics, visits to holy places, and a vast panorama of traditional Catholic rituals and pieties."[21]

This rejection of medieval notions of mediation and the sacred led not only to a rejection of celibate monastic life but to an affirmation of ordinary lay life. In Martin Luther's life (1483-1546 C.E.), this can be seen in his ceasing to be a monk and marrying a former nun. With the Reformation, we find another answer to the question of the relationship of religion, the meaning of life, and the moral life. The ideal life was no longer understood to be the monastic contemplative life. Christianity after the Reformation, as had Christianity prior to the Reformation, would struggle with the question of what sort of relationship Christians can have with the world. However, in Protestant Christianity, the Christian life can be fully lived in normal activities such as marriage, family, and work. The sociologist Max Weber would make much of this connection in his classic *The Protestant Ethic and the Spirit of Capitalism.*

Intertwined with this rejection of medieval notions of mediation and the sacred were rejections of the Greek metaphysical and teleological notions of perfection and the good life which themselves had been transformed by Christian understandings. This rejection could be understood as having an unanticipated consequence, a consequence that could be described as an increased secularization of the world. Over time, arenas such philosophy, science, politics, and economics established their autonomy from theology, and the God that once established kings, became a God "concerned exclusively with the inner quest or at most with frictions between individuals."[22]

Secularization and the Secularization Thesis

According to the sociologist Rodney Stark, the earliest pronouncement of the end of Christianity seems to have been made by Thomas Woolston. In about 1710, Woolston wrote that Christianity would disappear by 1900. Approximately fifty years later, Frederick the Great wrote to Voltaire that this prediction was too pessimistic and that the decline would happen much sooner. Voltaire's response was that he believed that it would end sometime in the next fifty years. In 1822, Thomas Jefferson predicted "there is not a young man now living in the United States who will not die a Unitarian."[23]

Secularization has been defined as the decline of the influence of religion in individual and social life. This means both a decline of the power of the church as a social organization and a decline in individual acceptance of, and participation in, religious beliefs and practices. Secularization and its implications have been explored both philosophically and by social sciences such as psychology and sociology. It is important to distinguish between secularization as an idea and secularization as sociological thesis, the secularization thesis.

As an idea and potential reality secularization has been of interest to philosophers because of the impact it could have on our understanding of the meaning of life and of morality. If the foundation for both has been established by religion, how can and should we respond when this foundation is undermined? Though this could be explored in many ways, I will focus on the responses of several philosophers to the philosophical dilemmas posed by secularization, namely Immanuel Kant, John Stuart Mill, Friedrich Nietzsche, Ludwig Feuerbach, and Karl Marx.

I will then move to considerations of early social scientific understandings of the process of secularization, and the subsequent formulations of a more formal secularization thesis. Social scientists have attempted to clarify the secularization thesis and to assess the extent to which it can be said to be occurring. For early social scientific understandings of religion, I will consider the work of Freud, the founder of psychoanalysis, and Emile Durkheim and Max Weber, sociologists whose work helped to establish the discipline of sociology of religion. I will then review the secularization thesis as understood by modern sociology of religion and consider recent work by Rodney Stark and Peter Berger, former prominent advocates of the position that secularization was indeed occurring who now argue that the secularization thesis does not appear to be supported.

I turn now to philosophical discussions of the decline of religion.

Social Consequences of the decline of religion

Until fairly recently, leaders in the west believed that a shared religion was necessary for the maintenance and governance of a state. A shared religion was considered to be necessary not only for public morality but also for social cohesion. We can see such a belief at work in Plato's Republic. Having made an argument for the three distinct classes in society, Plato's royal lie is the creation of a myth that would account for a class-based division of duties, responsibilities, and resources. These class divisions are now to be understood as a legacy from the earth itself. The people, created by their mother the earth, were endowed with the different metals that distinguish the three classes. Plato argued that though such a myth may not believed by the first or second generation, it could eventually be believed.

Post Reformation Europe was torn apart by religious wars. The Peace of Passau, signed in 1552 not long after the death of the reformer Martin Luther, granted a kind of religious freedom. With this, rulers who held to Catholicism or to the Augsburg Confession could choose their religion. In so doing, they also chose the religion of their subjects. Under the conditions of this peace, the emperor would no longer require that Protestant rulers return to Catholicism. However, this agreement was not sufficient to maintain peace. Tensions between Catholic and Protestant leaders would eventually lead to the Thirty Years' War. The Peace of Westphalia, signed in 1648, granted a new kind of religious freedom. Under this agreement, princes and subject were free to choose their own religion, as long as it was Catholic, Lutheran, or Reformed.

The "answer" to these religious wars was found in the gradual separation of church and state and an understanding of religion as a matter of private rather than public concern. Another eventual consequence, one could argue, was an understanding that the truth of religion, if it could be said to contain any truth at all, was subjective and relative. Science came to be understood as the arbiter of truth, not philosophy or theology. The modern scientific worldview came to displace the teleological and metaphysical worldview of the Greeks and, some would argue, religious, including the Christian, worldviews. Within this worldview, the question that made sense to Plato, Aristotle, Augustine, and Aquinas, the question of the ultimate end, or perfection, of human life, made no sense for we could no longer speak of ultimate ends. Some even began to predict that religion itself would disappear.

We seem to be, as the philosopher's might say, on the horn of a dilemma. If religion is necessary for social cohesion and public morality, and religion is eroded away by the acids of modernity, we face the choice of searching for truth or maintaining social order. Immanuel Kant, John Stuart Mill, Freiderich Nietzsche, Ludwig Feuerbach, and Karl Marx each responded to this perceived crisis in different ways. Kant and Mill formulated arguably the two most influential modern moral theories, deontological moral theory and utilitarian moral theory. Nietzsche is famous for having announced the "death of God" and for his exploration of the implications of this for our understanding of the value of life and of morality.

Kant

The German philosopher Immanuel Kant (1724-1804) was brought up in a culture of Lutheran pietism. This pietism emphasized the importance of the Bible, the priesthood of all believers, and a strict morality. Though Kant was not particularly religiously observant, he appreciated the qualities of devout pietists throughout his life. Nonetheless, because of his critiques of the traditional arguments for the existence of God, Kant became known as the "*Alleszermalmer* ('the man who crushes everything')."[24]

In fact, in one of his major philosophical works, *The Critique of Pure Reason*, Kant argues that the questions of human freedom, the immortality of the soul, and the existence of God are beyond the limits of human reason. Their truth can neither be established nor refuted by theoretical reason. Note here the difference between Kant and the philosophers and theologians we have considered to this point, all of whom would have argued that the truth of these questions, though perhaps not the full truth, could be determined by reason. In explaining the limits of reason, Kant is sometimes portrayed as protecting rational and scientific inquiry from irrational pursuits. However, it could be argued that in limiting the extent of scientific inquiry, Kant makes room for moral and religious belief. The following statement by Kant himself supports such an argument: "I have therefore found it necessary to deny knowledge, in order to make room for faith."[25]

One of the philosophical dilemmas Kant attempted to address was how to explain and preserve human freedom within the context of Newtonian physics. Newtonian physics was causal and deterministic. Human beings as bodies are a part of this deterministic universe. As such, they are governed by causal and deterministic laws. Understood in this way, human beings cannot be understood to be free.

Following a distinction made much earlier by Aristotle, Kant distinguishes theoretical reason, reason directed toward understanding, from practical reason, the reason which guides our behavior in the world. Though the existence of human freedom, the immortality of the soul, and God could not be established by theoretical reason, all of these must be postulated by practical reason to account for morality. Such postulates are teleological in nature; they assume an end of human life. As the contemporary moral philosopher Alisdair MacIntryre argues, "detach morality from that framework and you will no longer have morality; or, at the very least, you will have radically transformed its character."[26] MacIntrye argues that Kant's attempt to provide a foundation for morality fails because morality was eventually detached from such a framework.

Mill and the search for a common morality

It is perhaps not insignificant that John Stuart Mill's father, James, studied theology and obtained a license to preach. However, James Mill never exercised this right. He came to believe that it was not possible to believe that God, an all-good and all-powerful being, could exist given the amount of evil in the world. Instead, James Mill joined a group of philosophical radicals and become a friend and follower of Jeremy Bentham, considered to be the founder of modern utilitarianism. Bentham's thought would have significant influence on John Stuart Mill (1806-1873). When he was fifteen, Mill read one of Bentham's works and decided that he had found the one goal worthy enough to be a goal for his life- the reform of the world.[27]

Though Mill would devote his life to advocating utilitarianism, he did not uncritically accept Bentham's utilitarianism. Influenced by the thought of Saint-Simon and Coleridge, Mill came to understand history and social change in a way that Bentham had not. In the thought of Saint-Simon and Coleridge, Mill found an argument that societies occupied times of critical transition, or critical periods, and times of relative stability and social cohesion, or organic periods.

Mill came to agree with the French view that his age was a time of critical transition. During such times of critical transition, societies are in the process of evolving beyond ways of life that have become outdated. Mill understood shared moral agreement to be necessary for social cohesion. It could be argued that when religion was rejected a foundation for social cohesion and common morality, the task of social cohesion fell to morality. At any rate, the decline of Christianity and Christian morality, concerned Mill. Mill believed that it was necessary to construct a moral code that could be adopted both by those who had abandoned Christianity and those who continued to hold to a Christian moral code. Such a shared moral code was necessary if his society was to successfully transition from this time of critical transition to an organic period in which social cohesion was reestablished. Mill thought that utilitarianism could become such a shared moral code. In *After Virtue*, Alisdair MacIntyre argues that Mill's effort to establish a foundation for morality also failed, and that the philosopher who perhaps most vividly perceived the failure to find a secure foundation for morality and the consequences of this failure was Friedrich Nietzsche.

Nietzsche

Nietzsche (1844-1900) appears to have in mind the noble lie of Plato in the following: "That the lie is permitted as a means to pious ends is part of the theory of every priesthood . . . But philosophers, too, as soon as, with priestly ulterior motives, they form the intention of taking in hand the direction of humanity, at once also arrogate to themselves the right to tell lies: Plato before all..."[28] Nietzsche, it could be argued, followed the logic of the Enlightenment to its starkest conclusions.

> My demand upon the philosopher is known, that he take his stand *beyond* good and evil and leave the illusion of moral judgment beneath himself. This follows from an insight which I was the first to formulate: that *there are altogether no moral facts*. Moral judgments agree with religion ones in believing in realities which are no realities. Morality is merely an interpretation of certain phenomena- more precisely a misinterpretation.[29]

The passage above offers some indication of Nietzsche's blistering critiques not only of Christianity but also of utilitarianism and deontological moral theory. Some believed that Christian morality could be separated from a belief in God and other theological underpinnings. Nietzsche, however, argued that the death of God would lead inevitably to the rejection of Christian morality and values, indeed to the rejection all values.

Nietzsche was particularly concerned that this rejection of values could lead to nihilism, both in its active form in which it criticized all claims to truth, and in its passive form, in which it passively accepted the meaningless and absurdity of life.[30] Nietszsche argued that "morality was the greatest antidote (*Gegenmittel*) against practical and theoretical nihilism."

Nietzsche's description of the "death of God" and of nihilism is a complex one. He describes the death of God as an event that has already occurred, for which we are all responsible, and as an event that has yet to be fully realized and of which most of us are yet to be aware. This can be seen in the following excerpts from Nietzsche's *The Madman*.

> ..."Whither is God?" he cried. "I shall tell you. *We have killed him*—you and I. All of us are his murderers... There has never been a greater deed; and whoever will be born after us—for the sake of this deed he will be part of a higher history than all history hitherto."

> ...This tremendous event is still on its way, still wandering—has not yet reached the ears of man. Lightning and thunder requires time, the light of the stars requires time, deeds require time even after they are done, before they can be seen and heard. This deed is still more distant from them than the most distant stars—*and yet they have done it themselves*."[31]

In the thought of Nietzsche, we see yet another characterization of the ascetic contemplative life. Rather than see this life as an exercise of human perfection, Nietzsche sees it as a denial of life. In *Thus Spoke Zarathustra*, Nietzsche offers the following description of Christians: "They are despisers of life, atrophying and self-poisoned men, of whom the earth is weary; so let them be gone."[32] Nietzsche saw the "death of God" as an opportunity to create new, better more life affirming values. The destructive cycle of nihilism can be seen as positive in the sense that it clears the way for new and better values.

Feuerbach

The German philosopher Ludwig Feuerbach (1804-1873) described religion as our awareness of the infinite. However, for Feuerbach this awareness is not an awareness of some external reality, but an awareness of the infinity of human consciousness. Religion is ultimately our worship of our own human nature. God is a projection of human qualities such as wisdom, love, and mercy onto the universe. As we attribute these aspects to God, we divest them from our understanding of ourselves. In its denial of God, atheism allows us to reinvest these qualities into our understanding of ourselves. Feuerbach too believed that we were in a time of the decline of Christianity. Feurbach described his task in the following way: "The purpose of my writings, as also of my lectures, is to turn men from theologians into anthropologists, from theophiles into philanthropists, from candidates for the hereafter into students of the here and now, from religious and political lackeys of the heavenly and earthly monarchy and aristocracy into free, self-confident citizens of the world."[33]

Marx

Karl Marx (1818-1883) agreed with Feuerbach that religion was a kind of projection but argued that Feuerbach had not recognized the influence of our concrete social and economic conditions on this projection. Religion is not just an abstract projection of human nature. Religion is a reaction to and protest of real human distress. "Religion is the sigh of the oppressed creature, the heart of a heartless world, just as it is the spirit of spiritless conditions." However, the protest of religion is not as effective as it could be because of the religious emphasis on life after this one. Instead, religion becomes an "opium of the people."[34] It distracts people from addressing real social injustice.

Why predict a decline of religion?

Why have so many, for so long, predicted the decline of religion? Several explanations could be given for this. If religion is understood as belief, as an attempt to account for the world, then one argument for the rejection of religion would be that scientific accounts of the world are better accounts. Early Christian thought inherited, adopted, and modified a teleological understanding of the world. Within that framework, religious truth could be understood as consistent with reason. As that framework was modified or rejected, increasingly religious truth came to be seen as irrational. Questions about the meaning of life and morality also increasingly came be seen as meaningless in the sense that they could not be resolved through rational inquiry. MacIntyre argues that the attempts by Kant and Mill to find some secure foundation for morality ultimately could not succeed. Modern understandings of human freedom sever morality from any understanding of human nature and from teleological understandings. MacIntyre describes this as "a loss of traditional structures and content... seen by the most articulate of their philosophical spokesmen as the achievement by the self by the most articulate philosophical spokesmen as the achievement by the self of its proper autonomy." MacIntyre depicts this autonomy in the following way: "The self had been liberated from all those outmoded forms of social organization which had imprisoned it simultaneously within a belief in a theistic and teleological world order and within those hierarchical structures which attempted to legitimate themselves as part of such a world order."[35]

Psychological accounts that call for the decline of religion tend to describe religion as an attempt at compensation for some aspect of human nature, such as our relative powerlessness in the world. As we develop better ways of compensation, we will no longer require religion. If we understand religion sociologically, then one argument for the eventual decline of religion could be that as societies modernize, social structures inevitably change.

I will turn now to Freud's psychoanalytic understanding of religion.

Freud and *The Future of an Illusion*

Though Freud (1856-1939), the founder of psychoanalysis, tended to insist on its originality, many of his concepts seemed to have been anticipated by thinkers such as Nietzsche and Feuerbach. Like Nietzsche, Freud too believed that though religion had made important cultural contributions, our outgrowing of religion was both inevitable and necessary. Unlike Nietzsche, Freud thought that science offered us the means to outgrow our dependence on religion. Like Nietzsche, Freud too believed that this would not be without consequence. Unlike Nietzsche, Freud believed that for the educated, religious motives for civilized behavior will be replaced by other more secular ones. However, without religion "the great mass of the uneducated and oppressed" may pose a great danger to civilization. Freud describes the reason for this below.

> But it is another matter with the great mass of the uneducated and oppressed, who have every reason for being enemies of civilization. So long as they do not discover that people no longer believe in God, all is well. But they will discover it, infallibly, even if this piece of writing of mine is thinking, but without the change having taken place in them which scientific thinking brings about in people. Is there not a danger here that the hostility of these masses to civilization will throw itself against the weak spot that they have found in their task-mistress? If the sole reason why you must not kill your neighbor is because God has forbidden it and will severely punish you for it in this or the next life- then, when you learn that there is no God and that you need not fear His punishment, you will certainly kill your neighbor without hesitation, and you can only be prevented from doing so by mundane force. Thus either these dangerous masses must be held down most severely and kept most carefully away from any chance of intellectual awakening, or else the relationship between civilization and religion must undergo a fundamental revision.[36]

In his *The Future of an Illusion*, Freud described religion as a kind of individual and collective neurosis. Aware of our relative powerless and insignificance in the face of the world, we seek to calm and assure ourselves by constructing an all-powerful Father who loves us and will protect us. Freud considered the argument that even if religion is not true, perhaps we should live "as if" it were and roundly rejected it. Freud felt though that we would eventually outgrow the need for religion.

We have then, in the work of Nietzsche and Freud, another understanding of the relationship between religion, the meaning of life, and morality. Both accept that religion has provided us with both meaning and morality. However, both believe that religion is a kind of a lie we will eventually outgrow. This leads us to the question of whether we will eventually outgrow religion. I turn now to the secularization thesis.

Sociology of Religion and the Secularization Thesis

The most significant early voices in the sociology of religion were those of the French sociologist Emile Durkheim (1858-1917) and the German sociologist Max Weber (1864-1920). Durkheim's study of religion focused on the role of religion in the maintenance of social solidarity. According to the contemporary theologian Harvey Cox, the sociologist Talcott Parsons credited Emile Durkheim with teaching him that "it is not enough to say that religion is a social phenomenon." The truth is that "society is a religious phenomenon."[37] Weber rejected Marx's economic materialism and argued that an understanding of a culture's religion could provide us with important insights into the nature of that culture. Weber also argued that it is not enough to say that a society is driven, so to speak, by its economics, noting that the capitalism that Marx attempted to analyze had evolved in western Christian cultures in ways that it had not in other parts of the world. Weber focused on the relationship of religion, social control, and social change. The secularization thesis, in its more modern social scientific sense, was probably first articulated by Weber.

Succinctly stated, the secularization thesis is that the processes of modernization will lead to the inevitable decline of the significance of religion for societies and for individuals.[38] Three particular features of modernization have been focused on in studies of secularization: social differentiation, societalization, and rationalization.[39] Each of these impacts our understanding of the nature of the good life and of the moral life.

Social differentiation refers to the processes by which roles, which previously had been performed by a single institution, such as the church, gradually become specialized roles in other institutions (health care, education, and welfare for example). Though initially religious professionals may play a strong role in these new specialized roles and institutions, new specialists replace gradually religious professionals. Social differentiation, fueled in part by new occupations and the changes to occupations that accompany economic growth, often leads to a moral and religious fragmentation of society.

Societalization refers to the processes by which 'life is increasingly enmeshed and organized, not locally but societally (that society being most evidently, but not uniquely, the nation state)."[40] Large scale industry and commerce, the emergence of impersonal modern state bureaucracies, and the development of large urban centers lead to the decline of 'integrated, small scale communities' and to a growing sense of anonymity. This has two consequences for religious life. Religion has traditionally been used to "celebrate and legitimate" local community life.[41] As community life declines, these functions begin to lose their significance. Wallis and Bruce argue that the privatization of morality and religion is an inevitable consequence of the replacement of what Berger referred to as the sacred canopy, or an overarching religious and moral system, with competing moral and religious frameworks.

The third feature of modernization which has been linked to discussions of secularization is that of rationalization. Wallis and Bruce argue that the first two features, social differentiation and societalization, involve changes to the structure of society. Rationalization, however, concerns how people think and act. According to Bruce and Wallis, rationalization involves the pursuit of "this wordly" ends by means of technically efficient means. This rationalization, characterized by modern science and technology, has also led to the decline of the religious beliefs and practices.

The Decline of the Secularization Thesis

Today, once leading proponents of secularization theory, such as Berger and Stark have become publicly skeptical of the secularization thesis. Stark considers each feature of the secularization thesis and offers reasons for doubting each. Berger argues that the assumption that secularization and modernization track together has not been supported. He also argues that secularization has led to what he refers to as counter-secularization. I will try to quickly summarize their arguments.

Stark

In his article on secularization, Stark notes five general features of the secularization thesis. The first is that modernization is the cause of secularization. As industrialization, urbanization, rationalization increase, secularization will also increase. The second is that secularization theories predict the decline of not only organized religion but personal religious belief and practice. The third is that of all of the aspects of modernization, science poses the greatest challenge to religion. The fourth is that secularization is considered to be irreversible. The fifth is that though most secularization theorists focus on Christian cultures, the assumption is that it applies to all cultures.

In addressing modernization and the nature of secularization, Stark argues that it does not appear to be the case that modernization inevitably leads to secularization. Even the celebrated secularization of Europe does not seem to be supported historically. This is in part because of what could be referred to as the myth of Christian Europe. Historically it appears that there has never been much public participation in organized Christian religion in Northern and Western Europe. It also does not appear to be the case that personal Christian religious belief is in decline in Europe. Though most Europeans do not attend church, they do seem to hold to basic Christian beliefs and morals. With respect to the role of science in secularization, Stark offers the perhaps surprising report that the more scientific an American academic's discipline is, the higher the proportion who regard themselves to be religious. The irreversibility of secularization also does not appear to be supported. Stark points to the failure of the former Soviet Union to instill atheistic beliefs and the revival of organized religion in the former Soviet Union following its collapse. With respect to the applicability of the secularization thesis to other religions, Stark points to evidence that suggests that among Muslims, commitment to Islam seems to increase with modernization. In Japan, one of the world's most technologically advanced countries, Shinto, a traditional religion appears to be thriving. In Japan, new cars are often blessed at Shinto shrines. Exorcisms tend to be performed prior to the construction of homes, business offices, or factories. Children are often dedicated at Shinto shrines.[42]

Berger

According to Peter Berger, "a whole body of literature by historians and social scientists loosely labeled as 'secularization theory' is essentially mistaken."[43] Berger describes two basic stances religious movements can take toward modernity and secularization, rejection and adaption. The first response entails either religious revolution, an attempt to impose religious belief and practice, or the creation of religious sub-cultures, in which small cultures attempt to isolate themselves from the influences of modernity. Though both have been tried, neither has been, or likely could be, completely successful. However, adaption has also not been a successful strategy, indeed it could be argued that the religious movements that have succeeded have resisted adaption. Wallis and Bruce note that though religion can be seen to be diminishing, expect when it can be used to defend cultural identities or provide resources for cultural identity during times of cultural transition.

Berger argues that the relationship between religion and modernity is "a complicated one."(p. 3) Secularization of a society does not always correlate with secularization of the individuals within that society. Though the power and presence of some religious movements has declined, religious beliefs and practices, both old and new, remain. Berger also makes a point potentially very important for the question under consideration here. Namely that "religiously identified institutions can play social or political roles even when very few people believe or practice the religion that the institutions represent."(p. 3) Thus it would appear that secularization, even in places where it has had more influence than others, has not necessarily led to a situation in which the religious institutions are unable to play a social and political role.

The Noble Lie: Some Concluding Remarks

Though the debate over the truthfulness of the secularization thesis is not yet over, there is enough evidence at present to state that in spite of predictions to the contrary, religion is still with us, still providing meaning and informing the morality of many lives. It is fairly obvious that religion has changed and will continue to change; this, however, does not mean that religion will disappear.

How might we respond to the disagreement between positions such as Swenson's and Klemke's in this volume. Is there a way in which we can appreciate and explore the religion, ask serious questions about its relationship to the meaning of life and to the moral life, without having to choose Klemke's of Swenson's position. Perhaps there is. I will try to quickly describe it now.

We can distinguish between two basic approaches to the study of religion. One way seeks to define the essence of religion. We can refer to such an approach as substantive. Roger Schmidt in his *Exploring Religion* suggests the following substantive definition of religion as "a seeking ad responding to what is experienced as holy or ultimate."[44] Functional approaches tend to focus on a different set of questions, questions which address the roles religion plays in human life. What sorts of needs does religion address? How does it address them?

For example, from a psychological perspective, James W. Fowler attempts to address substantive and functional questions about the nature of faith in his *Stages of Faith: The Psychology of Human Development and the Quest for Meaning*. Fowler criticizes the modern tendency to equate faith with religious belief; instead Fowler describes faith as an "orientation of the total person."[45] Drawing on the developmental psychologies of Erikson, Piaget, Kohlberg, Fowler offers a depiction of the ways in which our cognitive, moral, and social development influences our own developing capacity for faith. From this perspective, positions such Klemke's and Swenson's could be evaluated developmentally.

In the introduction to his classic *The Elementary Forms of Religious Life,* the French sociologist Emile Durkheim makes the following functional argument for the truthfulness of all religions which could also apply to this debate.

> One must know how to go underneath the symbol to the reality which it represents and which gives it meaning. The most barbarous and the most fantastic rites and the strangest myths translate some human need, some aspect of life, either individual or social. The reasons with which the faithful justify them may be, and generally are, erroneous; but the true reasons do not cease to exist, and it is the duty of science to discover them. (p. 14-15)

In a continuation from a quote above, Nietszsche seems to make a similar point about moral judgments.

> Moral judgments are therefore never to be taken literally: so understood, they always contain mere absurdity. Semeiotically, however, they remain invaluable: they reveal, at least for those who know, the most valuable realities of cultures and inwardnesses which did not know enough to "understand" themselves.[46]

The American philosopher and psychologist William James in his classic *The Varieties of Religious Experience* offers us yet another perspective and potential test.

> What I then propose to do is, briefly stated, to test saintliness by common sense, to use human standards to help us decide how far the religious life commends itself as an ideal of human activity. If it commends itself, then any theological beliefs that may inspire it, in so far will stand accredited. If not, then they will be discredited, and all without reference to anything but human working principles.[47]

In a way that may seem reminiscent of Plato's search for truths beyond the truth of appearances, both Durkheim and Nietsche prompt us to seek a truth underneath the symbols we use, to seek the truth they reveal about us. James offers us a pragmatic criterion, that we test religious life by its fruits. I leave you then with a question rich enough for you to explore for the rest of your lives. What is the relationship between religion, the meaning of life, and morality?

Bibliography

Peter Berger. "The Desecularization of the World: A Global Overview", *The Desecularization of the World: Resurgent Religion and World Politics*. Oxford: Clarendon Press, 1992.

Harvey Cox. *Religion in the Secular City: Toward a Postmodern Theology*. New York: Simon & Schuster, 1984.

Emile Durkheim. *The Elementary Forms of Religious Life*. Joseph Ward Swain translator. New York: The Free Press, 1965.

James W. Fowler. *Stages of Faith: The Psychology of Human Development and the Quest for Meaning*. San Francisco: Harper & Row, 1981.

Justo L. Gonzalez. *The Story of Christianity: Volume One The Early Church to the Reformation*. Peabody, Massachusetts: Prince Press, 1999.

J.D. Kaplan, editor. *Dialogues of Plato*. Jowett translation. New York: Washington Square Press, 1950.

Hans Kung. *Does God Exist? An Answer for Today*. Edward Quinn translator. New York: Vintage Books, 1981.

William James. *The Varieties of Religious Experience*. Martin E. Marty, editor. New York: Penguin Books, 1982.

Walter Kaufmann editor and translator. *The Portable Nietzsche*. New York: Penguin Books, 1982.

Alisdair MacIntyre. *After Virtue: A Study in Moral Theory*. Second Edition. Notre Dame, Indiana: University of Notre Dame Press, 1984.

Alisdair MacIntyre. *Whose Justice? Which Rationality?* Notre Dame, Indiana: University of Notre Dame Press, 1988.

M.R. Miles. "Ascetic Practices", *Dictionary of Pastoral Care*, Rodney J. Hunter, General editor. Nashville: Abingdon Press, 1990.

Roger Schmidt. *Exploring Religion*. Belmont, California: Wadsworth, Inc., 1980.

Charles Taylor. *Sources of the Self: The Making of Modern Identity*. Cambridge, Massachussets: Harvard University Press, 1988.

Roy Wallace and Steve Bruce, "Secularization: The Orthodox Model", *Religion and Modernization: Sociologists and Historians Debate the Secularization Thesis*. Steve Bruce editor. Oxford: Clarendon Press, 1992.

Endnotes

[1] J.D. Kaplan editor, *Dialogues of Plato*. Jowett translation. New York: Pocket Books, New York, 1950, p. 268.

[2] Harvey Cox, *Religion in the Secular City: Toward a Postmodern Theology*. New York: Simon & Schuster, 1984, p. 202.

[3] See M.R. Miles, "Ascetic Practices", *Dictionary of Pastoral Care and Counseling*, Rodney J. Hunter, General editor, Abingdon Press, Nashville, 1990.

[4] Aristotle. *Eudemian Ethics, A New Aristotle Reader*. J.L. Ackrill editor. Princeton: Princeton University Press, 1987, Book 1, Chapter 4, p. 482.

[5] For a discussion of Plato's moral theory see Charles Taylor's, *Sources of the Self: The Making of Modern Identity*, Harvard University Press, Cambridge, Massachusetts, 1989. See also Alasdair MacIntyre's, *Whose Justice? Which Rationality?*, University of Notre Dame Press, Notre Dame, Indiana, 1988.

[6] Aristotle, *Nicomachean Ethics*, Book X, pp. 470-471.

[7] For a discussion of this see Alisdair MacIntyre's discussion of Aristotle on practical rationality in *Whose Justice? Whose Rationality?* Notre Dame, Indiana: University of Notre Dame Press, 1988.

[8] Taylor, p. 211.

[9] Ibid, p. 211.

[10] For examples of feminist analysis and critique of these ideas see Rosemary Radford Reuther's *Sexism and God-Talk: Toward a Feminist Theology*, Boston: Beacon Press, 1983. See also Catherine Keller's *From a Broken Web: Separation, Sexism, and the Self*, Boston: Beacon Press, 1986.

[11]Justo L. González, *The Story of Christianity: The Early Church to the Present Day Volume The Early Church to the Dawn of the Reformation*. Peabdy, Mass.: Prince Press, 1999.

[12]Ibid, p. 138.

[13]Ibid, pp. 139-140.

[14]Ibid, p. 211.

[15]Saint Augustine, *City of God*, ed. Vernon J. Bourke, Image Books, Garden City, New York, 1958, p. 467.

[16]Ibid, pp. 467-468.

[17]The eight hours were Matins, Lauds, Prime, Terce, Sext, None, Vespers, and Complines.

[18]Thomas Aquinas. *Summa Theologica*, q. 182 article 2.

[19]Gonzalez, p. 315.

[20]Taylor, p. 212.

[21]Ibid, p. 216.

[22]Cox, p. 200.

[23]Rodney Stark, "Secularization, R.I.P. (rest in peace)," *Sociology of Religion*, Fall, 1999. Accessed online at findarticles.com.

[24]Hans Küng, *Does God Exist? An Answer for Today*. Translated by Edward Quinn. New York: Vintage Books, 1981, p. 537.

[25]Ibid, p. 544.

[26]MacIntyre, *After Virtue*, p. 56.

[27]For a discussion of this, see Frederick Copleston, *A History of Philosophy, Book Three, Volume VIII*, New York: Doubleday, 1966.

[28]Friedrich Nietzsche, *The Will to Power*, Walter Kaufmann editor. New York: Vintage Books, 1968, p. 141.

[29]Friedrich Nietzsche, *Twilight of the Idols. The Portable Nietzsche*, edited and translated by Walter Kaufmann. New York: Penguin Group, 1976, p. 501.

[30]Copleston, Volume VII, p. 405.

[31]Nietzsche, *The Gay Science, The Portable Reader*, 95-96.

[32]Küng, p. 375.

[33]Ibid, p. 204.

[34]Ibid, p. 228.

[35]Ibid, p. 60.

[36]Sigmund Freud, *The Future of an Illusion. The Freud Reader*. Peter Gay editor. New York: W.W. Norton & Company, 1989.

[37]Cox, p. 204.

[38]Roy Wallace and Steve Bruce, "Secularization: The Orthodox Model," *Religion and Modernization: Sociologists and Historians Debate the Secularization Thesis*, ed. Steve Bruce. (Oxford: Clarendon Press, 1992).

[39]Ibid, p. 11.

[40]Ibid, p. 13.

[41]Ibid, p. 13.

[42]Rodney Stark, "Secularization, R.I.P. (rest in peace)," *Sociology of Religion*, Fall, 1999. Online. Findarticles.com. Accessed 11/29/2001.

[43]Peter Berger, "The Desecularization of the World: A Global Overview," *The Desecularization of the World: Resurgent Religion and World Politics*, p. 2.

[44]Roger Schmidt, *Exploring Religion*, Belmont, California: Wadsworth, Inc., 1980.

[45]James W. Fowler, *Stages of Faith, The Psychology of Human Development and the Quest for Meaning*. San Francisco: Harper & Row, 1981, p. 14.

[46]Nietzsche, *Twilight of the Idols*, p. 501.

[47]William James, *The Varieties of Religious Experience*, Martin E. Marty, editor. New York: Penguin Books, 1982, p. 331.

MORALITY AND CONTEMPORARY SOCIETY

LAID BARE: UNMASKING MADONNA

by Andrew Neil

Madonna's *Cherish* flowed from my Walkman as the jumbo jet banked south over Malibu and followed the Pacific Coast Highway towards Los Angeles International Airport. The next few months will determine whether the world will still cherish Madonna, probably the second most famous woman on the planet (after the Princess of Wales)

Her 128-page book of sexual fantasies, starkly titled *Sex*, has just gone on worldwide sale and its liberal lashings of whips, chains, knives, masks and studs—all the usual paraphernalia of sado-masochism—with words by Madonna and top-shelf pictures featuring Madonna, suggests it has been designed for the coffee table of a brothel

The book is accompanied by her latest album, called (no prizes for guessing) *Erotica*, the video of which has already been banned from daytime showing even by MTV (too much Madonna-in-bondage for its teeny-bopper viewers). Then, early next year—just to round off an S&M hat-trick—comes the release of her latest film, *Body of Evidence*, in which Madonna plays a sado-masochist (of course) accused of murdering her rich, old lover during sex.

I met Madonna in her stylish, understated house high in the Hollywood Hills above L.A. The simple white walls and traditional European art and furniture are light years from the flashy world of rock and the first thing that strikes you is that she looks barely big enough to hold a microphone, much less wield a whip. She was dressed in black pants, shirt and army-style boots.

I had been warned that Madonna could be brittle during interviews, especially if the line of questioning was not to her liking. Since I didn't think she was going to be amused by any of my questions, I began by revealing that, surprising as it may seem, we had something in common: we both started our musical careers as drummers, though hers has gone a little bit further than mine.

"Oh really! Well, I always had a fantasy about being a writer so we can envy each other," she replied. The bonding process over, I waded in.

Why have you done this book? Women in your business sometimes flaunt their bodies—or are forced to flaunt their bodies—to further the start of their career. When success comes, they usually regret they did so. But you . . .

"Why? why?" she interrupted, bridling at the thought of following a conventional career path.

"My career and the choices that I make are not based on what other people do. Where is the rule that you can't use your mind *and* your body from start to finish? This [the book] is essentially something that comes from my mind. My mind is, you know, a catalyst for the whole thing. I cast myself as an actress in this book. I play a role in this book. I take on the persona of a character named Dita Parlo, she's the narrator of the book."

I was puzzled by this distancing, since the public relations come on had been to bill the book as the enactment of Madonna's own private sexual fantasies. I needed to know more.

Tell me more about this woman.

"Dita Parlo?" she asks with a smile, which turns to a giggle. "She's the good-time girl. She's just a character, the narrator of the story."

Why did you have to assume another character to do this?

"Because I wanted to. Because it's not me." There was now a determined edge in her voice.

"It's Dita Parlo. It's like any other book you read. It's like anybody who writes stories; they choose to tell it in the first person or whatever. It's the way I chose to tell the story. Though I may be drawing from experiences, certainly not all of it is first-hand experience. A lot of it is my imagination, or stories that other people tell me, or things that I experience through other people. Like anybody who writes fiction, the line between fact and fiction is often practically non-existent.

"It's not me saying this is my life, here is me. There are erotic short stories and erotic imaginings, visual and literary, and I've cast myself in the role in terms of pictorials. I didn't see the point of saying Madonna because this is not Madonna *per se*, 100%; it's a character."

I wondered if she was already getting cold feet about the negative reaction to the book. Some who had seen it thought it disgustingly tacky. *The Sunday Times Magazine* editors who had considered buying the rights to it, turned it down, because only five out of the 128-odd illustrations were even on the margins of suitability for a broadsheet Sunday newspaper (the *Observer Magazine* belatedly bought the rights to help with its re-launch).

What's the difference between you and this character?

"Well, I couldn't even begin to tell."

She was a bit thrown by this, which made me all the more suspicious.

"She's just a character. That's like saying, if you go and see a movie and there is an actress in it and she plays a part and you say: well, what is the difference between you and the girl in the movie? It's not important. What is really important is what you get out of it when you look at it.

People will still see her as you.

"They see everything I do as me. When I did *Truth or Dare* [the documentary of her 1990 *Blonde Ambition* tour, released in Britain as *In bed with Madonna*] everyone said, 'Oh God, why do you want everybody to know you, what are you going to do after this, after everybody knows everything there is to know about you?' And I said: 'Please, if that's all there is to know about me I should just kill myself.'

"*Truth or Dare* is a documentary, but there is so much in it that was staged, or scenes that we improvised, like an Andy Warbol movie, or something. It's what I said before: some of it's real and some of it pretend and it's not necessary for the audience to know what's real and what isn't. I am basically offering myself up to play these parts and if people want to say that's me then that's fine, they can say it. I don't care, if it makes them feel better. It's not me in its entirety, though some of it is."

She finished with a certain contempt in her voice for anybody who could possible think differently. Later she remarked that "intelligent people" would see the "humour" of the book.

Do you see yourself as being some part of sexual revolutionary, and is this book part of it?

"Yes. I do. Absolutely."

With a messianic desire to spread this sexual revolution?

"It's, it's, it's . . . I don't see it so much as a sexual revolution as a human revolution. Sexual *repression* is responsible for a lot of bad behaviour." She laughs when she realises the irony of what she's just said.

"I think that for the last 10 years I have been trying to empower women, mostly. In all my work, my thing has always been not to be ashamed—of who you are, your body, your physicality, your desires, your sexual fantasies. The reason there is bigotry, and sexism and racism and homophobia and all those things, is fear. People are afraid of their own feelings, afraid of the unknown, afraid of what they don't know and I am saying: don't be afraid. It's OK to have this thought and this feeling.

"People who've seen and read my book have said: I have these feelings, too, but nobody wants to admit it. There is nothing wrong with it. That's what I'm saying. I think if people were comfortable with themselves and the way they felt—they didn't feel like they had to play all these different roles for society and people could just be honest about who they were—I think the world would be a better place. I know that would very idealistic, but I truly believe it."

Let's examine that. The key phrase you used was that sexual repression has been responsible for a lot of the world's ills (she nods agreement) **and individual unhappiness. But you could also argue that sexual liberation, or too much sexual liberation, has also been responsible for a lot of unhappiness.**

"Like what, for instance?"

There was a challenging edge to her voice.

Like the prevalence, for example, of too many poor, single-parent families.

She thought before answering.

"I don't think that has anything to do with the sexual revolution. I think has to do with [long pause] lack of education; I think that has to do with the fact that . . ." She stops as her thoughts change direction. "I mean, I don't think more people are having sex today than they were 100 years ago."

But they are. It's easier for an 18-year-old girl to have sex today than in Victorian times . . . she butts in before I could finish.

"I don't believe that. People just didn't talk about it. It's always been the same. It was just behind closed doors. I really don't believe that more people have sex now than they did 100 years ago."

Even allowing for Victorian hypocrisy on matters sexual, this showed a strange sense of historical reality, such as the liberating impact of the pill.

"I think maybe the single-parent family has a lot to do with women's liberation and the feminist movement and the fact that women have said: look, I don't have to choose this traditional lifestyle and get married and not work and raise children. I think that has something to do with it."

"I think that recession and poverty has a lot to do with it, because a lost of man can't raise their families and they leave their families and then the women are stuck with the children. In the ghettos there are no fathers around. But I am not going to blame that on the sexual revolution."

She then added a significant caveat: "Or if it is in some way a result of that it's . . . you know, revolution brings change and it's not always good; it's just a step that you have to go through."

It was a pretty high social price to pay, I thought, for the sake of some extra sexual liberation.

Surely that's the point. For a society to function successfully, there has to be some middle ground, some *modus vivendi*, between repression and sexual liberation.

"Well, we are so far this way on sexual repression [she points with both hands to the right] that if my contribution to society moves everybody a little bit over this way [swings both hands a little bit to the left] then that's good enough for me. I don't expect to change the world, to go all the way over there [points to far left].

"And my thing is not for everybody to have more sex; my thing is to be comfortable with who you are, whether you are gay or you are straight or whatever. To not feel repressed and to not feel afraid, to speak up and say: you know, I want to make love to you but I want you to wear a condom. You don't get what you want unless you say what you want so that is why we have all these unhappy people wandering around."

It all seemed a bit simplistic and we have been here before.

Didn't we go through that sexual revolution in the Sixties?

"Yes, but everybody was high and I am talking about doing it without the help of hallucinatory drugs, whatever . . ."

This seemed a comic-book view of the Sixties, but the Madonna was a teenager of the Seventies.

You think everybody was high in the Sixties?

"I think a lot of people were. I think if you were into the sexual revolution you were trying lots of other things."

But your argument still draws heavily on the Sixties "anything goes" approach. As you look back on the Sixties and its consequences . . .

"I am not saying anything goes." There was a hurt in her voice at the very suggestion. "I don't believe in irresponsible behavior. I don't believe in hurting other people."

You once said: "My idea of sexuality is very emotional and intellectual. What I am saying to the world is that feelings exist—gay, straight, dominant, submissive, masculine, feminine—and that they are all OK."

"Yeah, its OK to have those feelings is what I am saying. I don't think people should go round beating up on themselves and saying: oh God, I have this thought, I have this feeling, I am a bad person. Let me go beat up my child, my dog, because I hate myself for having these feelings, you know."

But there is a concentration in the book on what most of society would regard as sexual weirdness.

"Have you seen the book?" she shot back, in school ma'am tomes.

She already knew the answer to that, since no copies had been released. It was expected that she would show me the book during the interview, but she had tried that with another journalist and been uphappy with the written results. From what I had read and heard from my editors about the book , I wasn't too unhappy to miss the sneak preview.

"You shouldn't presume it to be anything until you've seen it yourself," she continued. "Most people that have elaborated on the book haven't seen it at all."

You showed it to a journalist from *Vanity Fair,* who's described its contents.

"And she paid attention to one photograph of me."

She wrote about spanking, whips, sado-masochism and so on. Is that unrepresentative of the book?

"No, there are some pictures like that. But the book is 128 pages and she'd written about maybe three of them. I was showing her an idea I had illustrated with photographs—an idea that existed in some of the passages that I had written. I think a lot of people's erotic fantasies are tying people up, spanking them . . . so that's what the picture was."

Should people act out these fantasies?

"If there is mutual consent, and I bring that up in the book. The definition of S & M is letting someone hurt you that you know would never hurt you. If it turns somebody on to be spanked before they have intercourse, so be it. Who cares, who are we to judge and say that is wrong? I know lots of people that are turned on by that.

"I am not saying that you should beat somebody up before you have sex with them or that you should force your way. That's not what I am talking about. But if you take a picture like that and you don't take the words to go with it, you take it out of context, and everyone is going to go: 'oh yes, she's condoning violence.' "

Surely there's a danger, for women in particular, of putting themselves in a position with somebody they think they can trust and it turns out they can't?

"Well, then she's a bad judge of character. I'm not talking about that, I'm talking about people that you do trust."

This seemed a bit harsh on some young girl who started with a bit of spanking, and ended up black and blue, or worse, at the hands of some brute.

It could be fatal couldn't it?

"Walking across the street can be fatal. That's not my responsibility. I am saying be smart. I am saying choose to do these things with somebody that you love, that you feel comfortable with, that you can trust. I am not talking about going out with perfect strangers and doing these things."

You say that sado-masochism is a mutual choice. But there is always the danger that you unleash a kind of evil, a dark side. Is there any discipline in your approach to sexuality?

"I don't understand the question.

I'm talking about the consequences of your sexual liberation . . .

"I'm dealing with sexual liberation of the mind. I believe people have a dark side . . ."

But you really believe that S&M is letting somebody hurt you that you know would never hurt you?

"That's what S&M means."

Or is that what it would mean in ideal circumstances?

"This book is based on fantasies in an ideal world—a world without abusive people, a world without Aids. It's a fantasy, a dream world, it's pretend, OK, so when I write this book I invite people to get lost in a dream world and to have a good time, to have fun with." Well, that's OK then.

One teenage girl I spoke to regarded you as a role model. She had read about this book and felt let down.

"That's the mistake right there. She mustn't read about the book. She must see it and judge for herself."

She's probably not old enough to buy it. You don't fear that a lot of young women are going to feel let down? Isn't there a responsibility to them?

"My responsibility is to myself as an artist, OK?" she stated curtly. "Second, I'm not a child and all the things I do may not necessarily be for a child's consumption. It may not be understood by a child, and I'm not claiming that it should. This book is for adults, OK, and when this child becomes an adult—she'll feel let down by me for a couple of years until she's old enough to see it—and once she can grasp it and understand it and see what I have to say, I will be restored, so to speak."

She laughs at the prospect, as if it were a foregone conclusion.

I want to talk to you about the effects that people like yourself have on popular culture. There is a debate developing in America about the effect of the entertainment industry on popular culture, on America's cultural attitudes, particularly the prevalence of violence.

Let me put a quote to you from Australian Writer, Richard Neville: *"Much of the world where dictators are dumped and walls crash down, the picture seems brighter. But in my local video store I see teenagers stockpiling at least 10 yours of horror, porn and pain for the weekend. Alone in a darkened space our moral sensibilities are no match for the Tinsel Town hype and the whizz-bung reviews, for sure as toxic residue kills the fish and the fowl, so the slaughter of our mean-spirited film makers and writers kills our spirit. It is renewal that is needed now, honour and optimism."*

What do you say to that?

"I think that's beautiful."

I think he would say your book and your new movie, Body of Evidence, fall into the category he's complaining about.

"He hasn't seen it. It's impossible to speak about until he has."

You don't think . . .

"Look," she interjected, her voice irritated. "There's violence everywhere. There's emotional violence. There's implied violence in just about everything a person does. You could cut somebody down and blow them apart with a word or you could shoot them apart with a gun. I think that what he says is very beautiful. I will address the issue of violence in movies if you'd like but I do not want to bring up my movie until people have seen it."

I'd rather be blown apart by a word than a gun any day and her reply dodged Neville's point. I persisted.

Is it a violent movie?

"There are violent things in it, because there is a violent relationship in it, a portrayal of a particular person. I don't think it's condoning it. It's presenting it."

So it is a part of Hollywood's violent output?

"I'm not gonna speak for Hollywood."

This was not a dialogue she relished, so I harked back to an earlier theme.

A lot of what you stand for (as I spoke she lay horizontal on a bench, left calf resting on right knee, her eyes studying the ceiling) **or lie for** (I thought the conversation needed a bit of humour at this stage) is **more liberation, more freedom, for a happier society.**

She thought for a moment.

"What are traditional values?"

Let me give you an example. So many social problems we face—the ghettos being the worst—are the result of the collapse of the nuclear family . . .

"Right, absolutely."

. . . that a lot what happened in the Sixties—and what you are doing is a continuation of that—helped to destroy the nuclear family. The result is a society with too many welfare mothers bringing up kids without a man in the house . . .

She became quite animated in her horizontal pose. "But you see, if people apply my ideals I don't think that it destroys the nuclear family. I think Bush is full of shit . . . he keeps saying all this shit about family values. Let's really take a look at this.

"To love your family means to accept them, OK. So if your kid comes home and says I'm gay, George Bush says that's wrong, there's something wrong with him. So he's not saying embrace your family and love them no matter what. Bullshit about family values.

"And if a women can't have an abortion in this country then she's going to have this kid and it's going to grow up and she's not going to be either economically able to take care of it, or emotionally she won't be able to take care of it and maybe it will be abused or neglected. That screws up the family even more."

She warned to her theme. "Those aren't family values, that's not embracing family values. Family values, to me it's like f*** the family in the house. It's the family of man, you know, and if we could all learn to accept our brothers and sisters and family of men as a whole, then the world would be a better place. This family values platform is like some kind of mumbo-jumbo Bush is thrwoing out for people to hold onto, becuase everyone is in such a sorry state right now because of the economy and the recession, and I am saying it's a bigger picture, it's the family of man and woman."

I wasn't talking about the agenda of the Republican party, I replied. I wasn't talking about espousing family values, then kicking your son out if he happens to be gay. I'm making the point that a society, which by your standards was sexually repressive, but in which the making, more kids finishing high school . . .

"OK. So do you think that what I have to say somehow negates the idea of having a family, and a mother and father present? I'm not against that. What I have to say is about tolerance and love. I am not saying f*** families, don't get married, don't believe in having families with mothers and fathers. I'm not against those things.

But you've got a better chance of being a tolerant person if you've been brought up in a stable home, finish high school, take a job. Then you're more likely to be tolerant, and tolerated , than a 16-year-old ghetto kid with a gun.

"Yes," she interrupts, but in a conciliatory tone. "Hey, I agree with that. Education is the key to everything. I totally agree with that. I'm not against that. I still don't understand how you are applying what I have to say and how it's against that."

Because your book, other things you've done and your attitudes in general are a continuation of the social liberalism of the Sixties.

"Well that's too bad." The tone was harsh again. "That's not what I am saying. My book is nothing to do with the social liberalism of the Sixties. It's one on one, it's human beings learning how to love their neighbour and tolerate each other, OK. I think that families are very important and having a mother and father is very important. I don't understand how the ideas that I present are against that. Why can't you have a family and still be open minded and accepting; why can't you? I don't get it. I don't see how what I have to say is opposed to that."

It's not exactly a family picture album.

"Because the idea of a family is not my idea of what is erotic, and I don't think it's erotic to anybody. Maybe it is, I don't know. This is my point of view, I'm not saying this is everybody's point of view and this is what you should have, I'm saying this is my point of view. That's it."

As I changed the tape, I asked her if she was happy to continue.

"Yes, it makes a change from being asked about my panties."

Don't worry, I said, I'll come to that.

ETHICS: THE GOLDEN RULE VS EGOISM

THE MORAL INSIGHT

by Josiah Royce

Josiah Royce (1855-1916), a professor of philosophy at Harvard University, was a colleague of William James and a teacher of George Santayana during what are known as the "golden years" of Harvard philosophy. Royce wrote in almost every area of philosophy, but is principally known as a proponent of idealism. His best known work in ethics is *The Philosophy of Loyalty* (1908).

For Royce the key to moral understanding lies in the realization that our neighbor is a center of experience and desire just as we are. Royce asks that we look upon that neighbor in much the same way we look upon our *future* selves—as a distant and somewhat unreal center of experience, but nevertheless of great concern. Sympathy and pity for another are not enough: Fellow feeling must also bring us to the point of what Royce calls the moral insight: "Such as that is for me, so is it for him, nothing less."

[The following] is our reflective account of the process that, in some form, must come to every one under the proper conditions. In this process we see the beginning of the real knowledge of duty to others. The process is one that any child can and does, under proper guidance, occasionally accomplish. It is the process by which we all are accustomed to try to teach humane behavior in concrete cases. We try to get people to realize what they are doing when they injure others. But to distinguish this process from the mere tender emotion of sympathy, with all its illusions, is what moralists have not carefully enough done. Our exposition [tries] to take this universally recognized process, to distinguish it from sympathy as such, and to set it up before the gates of ethical doctrine as the great producer of insight.

But when we say that to this insight common sense must come, under the given conditions, we do not mean to say: "So the man, once having attained insight, must act thenceforth." The realization of one's neighbor, in the full sense of the word realization, is indeed the resolution to treat him as if he were real, that is, to treat him unselfishly. But this resolution expresses and belongs to the moment of insight. Passion may cloud the insight in the very next moment. It always does cloud the insight after no very long time. It is as impossible for us to avoid the illusion of selfishness in our daily lives, as to escape seeing through the illusion at the moment of insight. We see the reality of our neighbor, that is, we determine to treat him as we do ourselves. But then we go back to daily action, and we feel the heat of hereditary passions, and we straightway forget what we have seen. Our neighbor becomes obscured. He is once more a foreign power. He is unreal. We are again deluded and selfish. This conflict goes on and will go on as long as we live after the manner of men. Moments of insight, with their accompanying resolutions; long stretches of delusion and selfishness: That is our life.

      To bring home this view . . . to the reader, we ask him to consider carefully just what experience he has when he tries to realize his neighbor in the full sense that we have insisted upon. Not pity as such is what we desire him to feel. For whether or not pity happens to work in him as selfishly and blindly as we have found that it often does work, still not the emotion, but its consequences, must in the most favorable case give us what we seek. All the forms of sympathy are mere impulses. It is the insight to which they bring us that has moral value. And again, the realization of our neighbor's existence is not at all the discovery that he is more or less useful to us personally. All that would contribute to selfishness. In an entirely different way we must realize his existence, if we are to be really altruistic. What then is our neighbor?

      We find that out by treating him in thought just as we do ourselves. What art thou? Thou art now just a present state, with its experiences, thoughts, and desires. But what is thy future Self? Simply future states, future experiences, future thoughts and desires, that, although not now existing for thee, are postulated by thee as certain to come, and as in some real relation to thy present Self. What then is thy neighbor? He too is a mass of states, of experiences, thoughts, and desires, just as real as thou art, no more but yet no less present to thy experience now than is thy future Self. He is not that face that frowns or smiles at thee, although often thou thinkest of him as only that. He is not the arm that strikes or defends thee, not the voice that speaks to thee, not that machine that gives thee what thou desirest when thou movest it with the offer of money. To be sure, thou dost often think of him as if he were that automaton yonder, that answers thee when thou speakest to it. But no, they neighbor is as actual, as concrete, as thou art. Just as thy future is real, though not now thine, so thy neighbor is real, though his thoughts never are thy thoughts. Dost thou believe this? Art thou sure what it means? This is for thee the turning-point of thy whole conduct towards him. What we now ask of thee is no sentiment, no gush of pity, no tremulous weakness of sympathy, but a calm, clear insight. . . .

      If he is real like thee, then is his life as bright a light, as warm a fire, to him, as thine to thee; his will is as full of struggling desires, of hard problems, of fateful decisions; his pains are as hateful, his joys as dear. Take whatever thou knowest of desire and of striving, of burning love and of fierce hatred, realize as fully as thou canst what that means, and then with clear certainty add: *Such as that is for me, so is it for him, nothing less.* If thou dost that, can he remain to thee what he has been, a picture, a plaything, a comedy, or a tragedy, in brief a mere Show? Behind all that show thou hast indeed dimly felt that there is something. Know that truth thoroughly. Thou hast regarded his thought, his feeling, as somehow different in sort from thine. Thou hast said: "A pain in him is not like a pain in me, but something far easier to bear." Thou hast made of him a ghost, as the imprudent man makes of his future self a ghost. Even when thou hast feared his scorn, his hate, his contempt, thou hast not fully made him for thee as real as thyself. His laughter at thee has made thy face feel hot, his frowns and clenched fists have cowed thee, his sneers have made thy throat feel choked. But that was only the social instinct in thee. It was not a full sense of his reality. Even so the little baby smiles back at one that smiles at it, but not because it realizes the approving joy of the other, only because it by instinct enjoys a smiling face; and even so the baby is frightened at harsh speech, but not because it realizes the other's anger. So, dimly and by instinct, thou hast lived with thy neighbor, and hast known him not, being blind. Thou hast even desired his pain, but thou hast not fully realized the pain that thou gavest. It has been to thee, not pain in itself, but the sight of his submission, of his tears, or of his pale terror. Of thy neighbor thou hast made a thing, no Self at all.

When thou hast loved, hast pitied, or hast reverenced thy neighbor, then thy feeling has possibly raised for a moment the veil of illusion. Then thou hast known what he truly is, a Self like thy present Self. But thy selfish feeling is too strong for thee. Thou hast forgotten soon again what thou hadst seen, and hast made even of thy beloved one only the instrument of thy own pleasure. Even out of thy power to pity thou hast made an object of thy vainglory. Thy reverence has turned again to pride. Thou hast accepted the illusion once more. No wonder that in his darkness thou findest selfishness the only rule of any meaning for thy conduct. Thou forgottest that without realization of thy future and as yet unreal self, even selfishness means nothing. Thou forgottest that if thou gavest thy present thought even so to the task of realizing thy neighbor's life, selfishness would seem no more plain to thee than the love of thy neighbor.

Have done then with this illusion that thy Self is all in all. Intuition tells thee no more about thy future Self than it tells thee about thy neighbors. Desire, bred in thee by generations of struggle for existence, emphasizes the expectation of thy own bodily future, the love for thy own bodily welfare, and makes thy body's life seem alone real. But simply try to know the truth. The truth is that all this world of life about thee is as real as thou art. All conscious life is conscious in its own measure. Pain is pain, joy is joy, everywhere even as in thee. The result of thy insight will be inevitable. The illusion vanishing, the glorious prospect opens before thy vision. Seeing the oneness of this life everywhere, the equal reality of all its moments, thou wilt be ready to treat it all with the reverence that prudence would have thee show to thy own little bit of future life. What prudence in its narrow respectability counseled, thou wilt be ready to do universally. As the prudent man, seeing the reality of his future self, inevitably works for it; so the enlightened man, seeing the reality of all conscious life, realizing that it is no shadow, but fact, at once and inevitably desires, if only for that one moment of insight, to enter into the service of the whole of it . . . . Lift up thy eyes, behold that life, and then turn away and forget it as thou canst; but if thou hast known that, thou hast begun to know thy duty.

THE DEEP BEAUTY OF THE GOLDEN RULE

by R. M. MacIver

R. M. MacIver (1882-1970) was a professor at Columbia University in sociology and political science. His works include *Academic Freedom in Our Time* (1967) and *Community: A Social Study* (1970).

R. M. MacIver finds in the Golden Rule—"Do unto others as you would have them do unto you"—the way out of the relativist impasse. It is a sensitive rule based on reason and common sense. It does not oppose itself to the norms of any given society because it does not tell anyone what to do. However, it does provide a policy to be followed which puts one on the alert: "If you would disapprove that another should treat you as you [are] treat[ing] him, is this not a sign that by the standards of your own values, you are mistreating him?" This procedural rule is universal precisely because it is compatible with the values of both parties, provided both respect the other's rights and liberties.

The subject that learned men call ethics is a wasteland on the philosophical map. Thousands of books have been written on this matter, learned books and popular books, books that argue and books that exhort. Most of them are empty and nearly all are vain. Some claim that pleasure is *the* good; some prefer the elusive and more enticing name of happiness; others reject such principles and speak of equally elusive goals such as self-fulfillment. Others claim that *the* good is to be found in looking away from the self in devotion to the whole—which whole? in the service of God—whose God?—even in the service of the State—who prescribes the service? Here indeed, if anywhere, after listening to the many words of many apostles, one goes out by the same door as one went in.

The reason is simple. You say: "This is the way you should behave." But I say: "No, that is not the way." You say: "This is right." But I say: "No, that is wrong, and this is right." You appeal to experience. I appeal to experience against you. You appeal to authority: it is not mine. What is left? If you are strong, you can punish me for behaving my way. But does that prove anything except that you are stronger than I? Does it prove the absurd dogma that might makes right? Is the slavemaster right because he owns the whip, or Torquemada because he can send his heretics to the flames?

From this impasse no system of ethical rules has been able to deliver itself. How can ethics lay down final principles of behavior that are not your values against mine, your group's values against my group's? . . . .

Does all this mean that a universal ethical principle, applicable alike to me and you, even where our values diverge, is impossible? That there is no rule to go by, based on reason itself, in this world of irreconcilable valuations?

There is no rule that can prescribe both my values and yours or decide between them. There is one universal rule, and one only, that can be laid down, on ethical grounds—that is, apart from the creeds of particular religions and apart from the ways of the tribe that falsely and arrogantly universalize themselves.

Do to others as you would have others do to you. This is the only rule that stands by itself in the light of its own reason, the only rule that can stand by itself in the naked, warring universe, in the face of the contending values of men and groups.

What makes it so? Let us first observe that the universal herein laid down is one of procedure. It prescribes a mode of behaving, not a goal of action. On the level of goals, of *final* values, there is irreconcilable conflict. One rule prescribes humility, another pride; one prescribes abstinence, another commends the flesh-pots; and so forth through endless variations. All of us wish that *our* principle could be universal; most of us believe that it *should* be, that our *ought* ought to be all men's *ought*, but since we differ there can be on this level, no possible agreement.

When we want to make our ethical principle prevail we try to persuade others, to "convert" them. Some may freely respond, if their deeper values are near enough to ours. Others will certainly resist and some will seek to persuade us in turn—why shouldn't they? Then we can go no further except by resort to force and fraud. We can, if we are strong, dominate some and we can bribe others. We compromise our own values in doing so and we do not in the end succeed; even if we were masters of the whole world we could never succeed in making our principle universal. We could only make it falsely tyrannous.

So if we look for a principle in the name of which we can appeal to all men, one to which their reason can respond in spite of their differences, we must follow another road. When we try to make our values prevail over those cherished by others, we attack their values, their dynamic of behavior, their living will. If we go far enough we assault their very being. For the will is simply valuation in action. Now the deep beauty of the golden rule is that instead of attacking the will that is in other men, it offers their will a new dimension. "Do as you *would* have others . . ." As *you* would will others to do. It bids you expand your vision, see yourself in new relationships. It bids you transcend your insulation, see yourself in the place of others, see others in your place. It bids you test your values or at least your way of pursuing them. If you would disapprove that another should treat you as you treat him, the situations being reversed is not that a sign that, by the standard of your own values, you are mistreating him?

This principle obviously makes for a vastly greater harmony in the social scheme. At the same time it is the only universal of ethics that does not take sides with or contend with contending values. It contains no dogma. It bids everyone follow his own rule, as it would apply *apart* from the accident of his particular fortunes. It bids him enlarge his own rule, as it would apply whether he is up or whether he is down. It is an accident that you are up and I am down. In another situation you would be down and I would be up. That accident has nothing to do with my *final* values or with yours . . . .

It follows that while this first principle attacks no intrinsic values, no primary attachments of men to goods that reach beyond themselves, it nevertheless purifies every attachment, every creed, of its accidents, its irrelevancies, its excesses, its false reliance on power. It saves every human value from the corruption that comes from the arrogance of detachment and exclusiveness, from the shell of the kind of absolutism that imprisons its vitality.

At this point a word of caution is in order. The golden rule does not solve for us our ethical problems but offers only a way of approach. It does not prescribe our treatment of others but only the spirit in which we should treat them. It has no simple mechanical application and often enough is hard to apply—what general principle is not? It certainly does not bid us treat others as others *want* us to treat them—that would be an absurdity. The convicted criminal wants the judge to set him free. If the judge acts in the spirit of the golden rule, within the limits of the discretion permitted him as judge, he might instead reason somewhat as follows: "How would I feel the judge ought to treat *me* were I in this man's place? What could I—the man I am and yet somehow standing where this criminal stands—properly ask the judge to do for me, to me? In this spirit I shall assess his guilt and his punishment. In this spirit I shall give full consideration to the conditions under which he acted. I shall try to understand *him*, to do what I properly can for him, while at the same time I fulfill my judicial duty in protecting society against the dangers that arise if criminals such as he go free."

"Do to others as you would have others do to you." The disease to which all values are subject is the growth of a hard insulation. "I am right: I have the truth. If you differ from me, you are a heretic, you are in error. *Therefore* while you must allow me every liberty when you are in power I need not, in truth I ought not to, show any similar consideration for you." The barb of falsehood has already begun to vitiate the cherished value. While *you* are in power I advocate the equal rights of all creeds: when *I* am in power, I reject any such claim as ridiculous. This is the position taken by various brands of totalitarianism, and the communists in particular have made it a favorite technique in the process of gaining power, clamoring for rights they will use to destroy the rights of those who grant them. Religious groups have followed the same line. Roman Catholics, Calvinists, Lutherans, Presbyterians, and others have on occasion vociferously advocated religious liberty where they were in the minority, often to curb it where in turn they became dominant.

This gross inconsistency on the part of religious groups was flagrantly displayed in earlier centuries, but examples are still not infrequent. Here is one. *La Civilita Catholicá*, a Jesuit organ published in Rome, has come out as follows:

> The Roman Catholic Church, convinced, through its divine prerogatives, of being the only true church, must demand the right to freedom for herself alone, because such a right can only be possessed by truth, never by error. As to other religions, the church will certainly never draw the sword, but she will require that by legitimate means they shall not be allowed to propagate false doctrine. Consequently, in a state where the majority of the people are Catholic, the Church will require that legal existence be denied to error . . . . In some countries, Catholics will be obliged to ask full religious freedom for all, resigned at being forced to cohabitate where they alone should rightly be allowed to live . . . . The Church cannot blush for her own want of tolerance, as she asserts it in principle and applies it in practice.)[1]

Since this statement has the merit of honesty it well illustrates the fundamental lack of rationality that lies behind all such violations of the golden rule. The argument runs: "Roman Catholics know they possess the truth; *therefore* they should not permit others to propagate error." By parity of reasoning why should not Protestants say—and indeed they have often said it—"We know we possess the truth; therefore we should not tolerate the errors of Roman Catholics." Why then should not atheists say: "We know we possess the truth; therefore we should not tolerate the errors of dogmatic religion."

No matter what we believe, we are equally convinced that *we* are right. We have to be. That is what belief means, and we must all believe something. The Roman Catholic Church is entitled to declare that all other religious groups are sunk in error. But what follows? That other groups have not the right to believe they are right? That you have the right to repress them while they have no right to repress you? That they should concede to you what you should not concede to them? Such reasoning is mere childishness. Beyond it lies the greater foolishness that truth is advanced by the forceful suppression of those who believe differently from you. Beyond that lies the pernicious distortion of meanings which claims that liberty is only "the liberty to do right"—the "liberty" for me to do what *you* think is right. This perversion of the meaning of liberty has been the delight of all totalitarians. And it might be well to reflect that it was the radical Rousseau who first introduced the doctrine that men could be "forced to be free."

How much do they have truth who think they must guard it within the fortress of their own might? How little that guarding has availed in the past! How often it has kept truth outside while superstition grew moldy within! How often has the false alliance of belief and force led to civil dissension and the futile ruin of war! But if history means nothing to those who call themselves "Christian" and still claim exclusive civil rights for their particular faith, at least they might blush before this word of one they call their Master: "All things therefore whatsoever ye would that men should do unto you, even so do ye also unto them; for this is the law and the prophets."

OF THE MORALS OF THE CATHOLIC CHURCH

by Saint Augustine

> Saint Augustine (A.D. 354-420), born in North Africa, is recognized as one of the very greatest Christian philosophers. His best known works are his *Confessions* (A.D. 400) and *The City of God* (A.D. 427).

> Augustine defines happiness as the enjoyment of the highest good. The highest good is not something that can be lost by accident or misfortune, for then we cannot enjoy it confidently Such a good must therefore be of the soul and not the body. Augustine concludes that the chief good is the possession of virtue. The virtuous Christian follows God, avoiding sin and obeying His will.

Happiness is in the enjoyment of man's chief good. Two conditions of the chief good: 1st, Nothing is better than it; 2nd, it cannot be lost against the will.

How then, according to reason, ought man to live? We all certainly desire to live happily; and there is no human being but assents to this statement almost before it is made. But the title happy cannot, in my opinion, belong either to him who has not what he loves, whatever it may be, or to him who has what he loves if it is hurtful, or to him who does not love what he has, although it is good in perfection. For one who seeks what he cannot obtain suffers torture, and one who has got what is not desirable is cheated, and one who does not seek for what is worth seeking for is diseased. Now in all these cases the mind cannot but be unhappy, and happiness and unhappiness cannot reside at the same time in one man; so in none of these cases can the man be happy. I find, then, a fourth case, where the happy life exists,—when that which is man's chief good is both loved and possessed. For what do we call enjoyment but having at hand the object of love? And no one can be happy who does not enjoy what is man's chief good, nor is there any one who enjoys this who is not happy. We must then have at hand our chief good, if we think of living happily.

We must now inquire what is man's chief good, which of course cannot be anything inferior to man himself. For whoever follows after what is inferior to himself, becomes himself inferior. But every man is bound to follow what is best. Wherefore man's chief good is not inferior to man. Is it then something similar to man himself? It must be so, if there is nothing above man which he is capable of enjoying. But if we find something which is both superior to man, and can be possessed by the man who loves it, who can doubt that in seeking for happiness man should endeavour to reach that which is more excellent than the being who makes the endeavour? For if happiness consists in the enjoyment of a good than which there is nothing better, which we call the chief good, how can a man be properly called happy who has not yet attained to his chief good? or how can that be the chief good beyond which something better remains for us to arrive at? Such, then, being the chief good, it must be something which cannot be lost against the will. For no one can feel confident regarding a good which he knows can be taken from him, although he wishes to keep and cherish it. But if a man feels no confidence regarding the good which he enjoys, how can he be happy while in such fear of losing it?

Man—what?

Let us then see what is better than man. This must necessarily be hard to find, unless we first ask and examine what man is. I am not now called upon to give a definition of man. The question here seems to me to be,—since almost all agree, or at least, which is enough, those I have now to do with are of the same opinion with me, that we are made up of soul and body,—What is man? Is he both of these? or is he the body only, or the soul only? For although the things are two, soul and body, and although neither without the other could be called man (for the body would not be man without the soul, nor again would the soul be man if there were not a body animated by it), still it is possible that one of these may be held to be man, and may be called so. What then do we call man? Is he soul and body, as in a double harness, or like a centaur? Or do we mean the body only, as being in the service of the soul which rules it, as the word lamp denotes not the light and the case together, but only the case, though on account of the light? Or do we mean only mind, and that on account of the body which it rules, as horseman means not the man and the horse, but the man only, and that as employed in ruling the horse? This dispute is not easy to settle; or, if the proof is plain, the statement requires time. This is an expenditure of time and strength which we need not incur. For whether the name man belongs to both, or only to the soul, the chief good of man is not the chief good of the body; but what is the chief good either of both soul and body, or of the soul only, that is man's chief good.

Man's chief good is not the chief good of the body only, but the chief good of the soul.

Now if we ask what is the chief good of the body, reason obliges us to admit that it is that by means of which the body comes to be in its best state. But of all the things which invigorate the body, there is nothing better or greater than the soul. The chief good of the body, then, is not bodily pleasure, not absence of pain, not strength, not beauty, not swiftness, or whatever else is usually reckoned among the goods of the body, but simply the soul. For all the things mentioned the soul supplies to the body by its presence, and, what is above them all, life. Hence I conclude that the soul is not the chief good of man, whether we give the name of man to soul and body together, or to the soul alone. For as, according to reason, the chief good of the body is that which is better than the body, and from which the body receives vigour and life, so whether the soul itself is man, or soul and body both, we must discover whether there is anything which goes before the soul itself, in following which the soul comes to the perfection of good of which it is capable in its own kind. If such a thing can be found, all uncertainty must be at an end, and we must pronounce this to be really and truly the chief good of man.

If, again, the body is man, it must be admitted that the soul is the chief good of man. But clearly, when we treat of morals—when we inquire what manner of life must be held in order to obtain happiness—it is not the body to which the precepts are addressed, it is not bodily discipline which we discuss. In short, the observance of good customs belongs to that part of us which inquires and learns, which are the prerogatives of the soul; so, when we speak of attaining to virtue, the question does not regard the body. But if it follows, as it does, that the body which is ruled over by a soul possessed of virtue is ruled both better and more honourably, and is in its greatest perfection in consequence of the perfection of the soul which rightfully governs it, that which gives perfection to the soul will be man's chief good, though we call the body man. For if my coachman, in obedience to me, feeds and drives the horses he has charge of in the most satisfactory manner, himself enjoying the more of my bounty in proportion to his good conduct, can any one deny that the good condition of the horses, as well as that of the coachman, is due to me? So the question seems to me to be not, whether soul and body is man, or the soul only, or body only, but what gives perfection to the soul; for when this is obtained, a man cannot but be either perfect, or at least much better than in the absence of this one thing.

Virtue gives perfection to the soul; the soul obtains virtue by following God; following God is the happy life.

No one will question that virtue gives perfection to the soul. But it is a very proper subject of inquiry whether this virtue can exist by itself or only in the soul. Here again arises a profound discussion, needing lengthy treatment; but perhaps my summary will serve the purpose. God will, I trust, assist me, so that, notwithstanding our feebleness, we may give instruction on these great matters briefly as well as intelligibly. In either case, whether virtue can exist by itself without the soul, or can exist only in the soul, undoubtedly in the pursuit of virtue the soul follows after something, and this must be either the soul itself, or virtue, or something else. But if the soul follows after itself in the pursuit of virtue, it follows after a foolish thing; for before obtaining virtue it is foolish. Now the height of a follower's desire is to reach that which he follows after. So the soul must either not wish to reach what it follows after, which is utterly absurd and unreasonable, or, in following after itself while foolish, it reaches the folly which it flees from. But if it follows after virtue in the desire to reach it, how can it follow what does not exist? or how can it desire to reach what it already possesses? Either, therefore, virtue exists beyond the soul, or if we are not allowed to give the name of virtue except to the habit and disposition of the wise soul, which can exist only in the soul, we must allow that the soul follows after something else in order that virtue may be produced in itself; for neither by following after nothing, nor by following after folly, can the soul, according to my reasoning, attain to wisdom.

This something else, then, by following after which the soul becomes possessed of virtue and wisdom, is either a wise man or God. But we have said already that it must be something that we cannot lose against our will. No one can think it necessary to ask whether a wise man, supposing we are content to follow after him, can be taken from us in spite of our unwillingness or our persistence. God then remains, in following after whom we live well, and in reaching whom we live both well and happily.

THE OBJECTIVE BASIS OF MORALITY

by Thomas Nagel

Thomas Nagel (b. 1937) is a professor of philosophy at New York University. He is the author of numerous articles and books including *Mortal Questions* (1990), *The View from Nowhere* (1986), and *Equality and Partiality* (1991)

The biblical injunction to love thy neighbor as thyself is often interpreted negatively as the injunction *not* to do unto your neighbor what you would *not* have your neighbor do unto you. Thomas Nagel argues that this principle is universally valid apart from any religious beliefs one might have. He notes that we all feel resentful when someone whom we have not provoked harms us: since he had no reason to harm us he shouldn't have. Nagel points out that such resentment is reasonable and is the basis of a universal and objective principle that all such harm is morally wrong.

Suppose you work in a library, checking people's books as they leave, and a friend asks you to let him smuggle out a hard-to-find reference work that he wants to own.

You might hesitate to agree for various reasons. You might be afraid that he'll be caught, and that both you and he will then get into trouble. You might want the book to stay in the library so that you can consult it yourself.

But you may also think that what he proposes is wrong—that he shouldn't do it and you shouldn't help him. If you think that, what does it mean, and what, if anything, makes it true?

To say it's wrong is not just to say it's against the rules. There can be bad rules which prohibit what isn't wrong—like a law against criticizing the government. A rule can also be bad because it requires something that *is* wrong—like a law that requires racial segregation in hotels and restaurants. The ideas of wrong and right are different from the ideas of what is and is not against the rules. Otherwise they couldn't be used in the evaluation of rules as well as of actions.

If you think it would be wrong to help your friend steal the book, then you will feel uncomfortable about doing it: in some way you won't want to do it, even if you are also reluctant to refuse help to a friend. Where does the desire not to do it come from; what is its motive, the reason behind it?

There are various ways in which something can be wrong, but in this case, if you had to explain it, you'd probably say that it would be unfair to other users of the library who may be just as interested in the book as your friend is, but who consult it in the reference room, where anyone who needs it can find it. You may also feel that to let him take it would betray your employers, who are paying you precisely to keep this sort of thing from happening.

These thoughts have to do with effects on others—not necessarily effects on their feelings, since they may never find out about it, but some kind of damage nevertheless. In general, the thought that something is wrong depends on its impact not just on the person who does it but on other people. They wouldn't like it, and they'd object if they found out.

But suppose you try to explain all this to your friend, and he says, "I know the head librarian wouldn't like it if he found out, and probably some of the other users of the library would be unhappy to find the book gone, but who cares? I want the book; why should I care about them?"

The argument that it would be wrong is supposed to give him a reason not to do it. But if someone just doesn't care about other people, what reason does he have to refrain from doing any of the things usually thought to be wrong, if he can get away with it: what reason does he have not to kill, steal, lie, or hurt others? If he can get what he wants by doing such things, why shouldn't he? And if there's no reason why he shouldn't, in what sense is it wrong?

chapter 13

Of course most people do care about others to some extent. But if someone doesn't care, most of us wouldn't conclude that he's exempt from morality. A person who kills someone just to steal his wallet, without caring about the victim, is not automatically excused. The fact that he doesn't care doesn't make it all right: he *should* care. But *why* should he care?

There have been many attempts to answer this question. One type of answer tries to identify something else that the person already cares about, and then connect morality to it.

For example, some people believe that even if you can get away with awful crimes on this earth, and are not punished by the law or your fellow men, such acts are forbidden by God, who will punish you after death (and reward you if you didn't do wrong when you were tempted to). So even when it seems to be in your interest to do such a thing, it really isn't. Some people have even believed that if there is no God to back up moral requirements with the threat of punishment and the promise of reward, morality is an illusion: "If God does not exist, everything is permitted."

This is a rather crude version of the religious foundation for morality. A more appealing version might be that the motive for obeying God's commands is not fear but love. He loves you, and you should love Him, and should wish to obey His commands in order not to offend Him.

But however we interpret the religious motivation, there are three objections to this type of answer. First, plenty of people who don't believe in God still make judgments of right and wrong, and think no one should kill another for his wallet even if he can be sure to get away with it. Second, if God exists, and forbids what's wrong, that still isn't what *makes* it wrong. Murder is wrong in itself, and that's *why* God forbids it (if He does). God couldn't make just any old thing wrong—like putting on your left sock before your right—simply by prohibiting it. If God would punish you for doing that it would be inadvisable to do it, but it wouldn't be wrong. Third, fear of punishment and hope of reward, and even love of God, seem not to be the right motives for morality. If you think it's wrong to kill, cheat, or steal, you should want to avoid doing such things because they are bad things to do to the victims, not just because you fear the consequences for yourself, or because you don't want to offend your Creator.

This third objection also applies to other explanations of the force of morality which appeal to the interests of the person who must act. For example, it may be said that you should treat others with consideration so that they'll do the same for you. This may be sound advice, but it is valid only so far as you think what you do will affect how others treat you. It's not a reason for doing the right thing if others won't find out about it, or against doing the wrong thing if you can get away with it (like being a hit and run driver).

There is no substitute for a direct concern for other people as the basis of morality. But morality is supposed to apply to everyone: and can we assume that everyone has such a concern for others? Obviously not: some people are very selfish, and even those who are not selfish may care only about the people they know, and not about everyone. So where will we find a reason that everyone has not to hurt other people, even those they don't know?

Well, there's one general argument against hurting other people which can be given to anybody who understands English (or any other language), and which seems to show that he has *some* reason to care about others, even if in the end his selfish motives are so strong that he persists in treating other people badly anyway. It's an argument that I'm sure you've heard, and it goes like this: "How would you like it if someone did that to you?"

It's not easy to explain how this argument is supposed to work. Suppose you're about to steal someone else's umbrella as you leave a restaurant in a rainstorm, and a bystander says, "How would you like it if someone did that to you?" Why is it supposed to make you hesitate, or feel guilty?

Obviously the direct answer to the question is supposed to be, "I wouldn't like it at all!" But what's the next step? Suppose you were to say, "I wouldn't like it if someone did that to me. But luckily no one *is* doing it to me. I'm doing it to someone else, and I don't mind that at all!"

This answer misses the point of the question. When you are asked how you would like it if someone did that to you, you are supposed to think about all the feelings you would have if someone stole your umbrella. And that includes more than just "not liking it"—as you wouldn't "like it" if you stubbed your toe on a rock. If someone stole your umbrella you'd *resent* it. You'd have feelings about the umbrella thief, not just about the loss of the umbrella. You'd think, "Where does he get off, taking my umbrella that I bought with my hard-earned money and that I had the foresight to bring after reading the weather report? Why didn't he bring his own umbrella?" and so forth.

When our own interests are threatened by the inconsiderate behavior of others, most of us find it easy to appreciate that those others have a reason to be more considerate. When you are hurt, you probably feel that other people should care about it: you don't think it's no concern of theirs, and that they have no reason to avoid hurting you. That is the feeling that the "How would you like it?" argument is supposed to arouse.

Because if you admit that you would *resent* it if someone else did to you what you are now doing to him, you are admitting that you think he would have a reason not to do it to you. And if you admit that, you have to consider what that reason is. It couldn't be just that it's *you* that he's hurting, of all the people in the world. There's no special reason for him not to steal *your* umbrella, as opposed to anyone else's. There's nothing so special about you. Whatever the reason is, it's a reason he would have against hurting anyone else in the same way. And it's a reason anyone else would have too, in a similar situation, against hurting you or anyone else.

But if it's a reason anyone would have not to hurt anyone else in this way, then it's a reason *you* have not to hurt someone else in this way (since *anyone* means *everyone*). Therefore it's a reason not to steal the other person's umbrella now.

This is a matter of simple consistency. Once you admit that another person would have a reason not to harm you in similar circumstances, and once you admit that the reason he would have is very general and doesn't apply only to you, or to him, then to be consistent you have to admit that the same reason applies to you now. You shouldn't steal the umbrella, and you ought to feel guilty if you do.

Someone could escape from this argument if, when he was asked, "How would you like it if someone did that to you?" he answered, "I wouldn't resent it at all. I wouldn't *like* it if someone stole my umbrella in a rainstorm, but I wouldn't think there was any reason for him to consider my feelings about it." But how many people could honestly give that answer? I think most people, unless they're crazy, would think that their own interests and harms matter, not only to themselves, but in a way that gives other people a reason to care about them too. We all think that when we suffer it is not just bad *for us*, but *bad, period*.

The basis of morality is a belief that good and harm to particular people (or animals) is good or bad not just from their point of view, but from a more general point of view, which every thinking person can understand. That means that each person has a reason to consider not only his own interests but the interests of others in deciding what to do. And it isn't enough if he is considerate only of some others— his family and friends, those he specially cares about. Of course he will care more about certain people, and also about himself. But he has some reason to consider the effect of what he does on the good or harm of everyone. If he's like most of us, that is what he thinks others should do with regard to him, even if they aren't friends of his.

THE RING OF GYGES

by Plato

Plato [*ca* 428-348 (or 347) B.C.], considered by many to be the greatest philosopher who ever lived, is the author of *The Republic* and other great dialogues. Plato's influence on Western culture is incalculable.

In *The Republic*, Plato describes the ideal society where justice reigns supreme. It opens with a scene in which Socrates confronts powerful arguments that disparage justice. We find Glaucon summarizing the views of those who think that justice is merely a compromise between the freedom to do wrong with impunity and to suffer wrong without redress. Because we would risk punitive action by doing wrong, we accept a limitation on our freedom. So justice is a kind of arrangement (like a system of traffic lights) that is not in itself valuable or desirable, but is put in place (to prevent accidents) to prevent our suffering wrong from others.

The Ring of Gyges rendered the wearer invisible, enabling the shepherd Gyges to do as he pleased without fear of reprisal—and he used it to murder the King of Lydia. But did Gyges behave unnaturally? Glaucon argues that anyone in Gyges' situation would be a fool not to take full advantage of the power to do wrong with impunity. This suggests that justice is nothing more than a preventive device—only we lack the power that Gyges possessed.

In the remainder of *The Republic*, Socrates argues that the citizens of an ideal society would be just because they loved justice and not (merely) because they feared the consequences of suffering injustice.

GLAUCON (TO SOCRATES): I have never heard from anyone the sort of defence of justice that I want to hear, proving that it is better than injustice. I want to hear it praised for itself, and I think I am most likely to hear this from you. Therefore I am going to speak at length in praise of the unjust life and in doing so I will show you the way I want to hear you denouncing injustice and praising justice. See whether you want to hear what I suggest.

SOCRATES: I want it more than anything else. Indeed, what subject would a man of sense talk and hear about more often with enjoyment?

GLAUCON: Splendid, then listen while I deal with the first subject I mentioned: the nature and origin of justice.

They say that to do wrong is naturally good, to be wronged is bad, but the suffering of injury so far exceeds in badness the good of inflicting it that when men have done wrong to each other and suffered it, and have had a taste of both, those who are unable to avoid the latter and practise the former decide that it is profitable to come to an agreement with each other neither to inflict injury nor to suffer it. As a result they begin to make laws and covenants, and the law's command they call lawful and just. This, they say, is the origin and essence of justice; it stands between the best and the worst, the best being to do wrong without paying the penalty and the worst to be wronged without the power of revenge. The just then is a mean between two extremes; it is welcomed and honoured because of men's lack of the power to do wrong. The man who has that power, the real man, would not make a compact with anyone not to inflict injury or suffer it. For him that would be madness. This then, Socrates, is, according to their argument, the nature and origin of justice.

Even those who practice justice do so against their will because they lack the power to do wrong. This we could realize very clearly if we imagined ourselves granting to both the just and the unjust the freedom to do whatever they liked. We could then follow both of them and observe where their desires led them, and we would catch the just man redhanded travelling the same road as the unjust. The reason is the desire for undue gain which every organism by nature pursues as a good, but the law forcibly sidetracks him to honour equality. The freedom I just mentioned would most easily occur if these men had the power which they say the ancestor of the Lydian Gyges possessed. The story is that he was a shepherd in the service of the ruler of Lydia. There was a violent rainstorm and an earthquake which broke open the ground and created a chasm at the place where he was tending sheep. Seeing this and marvelling, he went down into it. He saw, besides many other wonders of which we are told, a hollow bronze horse. There were windowlike openings in it; he climbed through them and caught sight of a corpse which seemed of more than human stature, wearing nothing but a ring of gold on its finger. This ring the shepherd put on and came out. He arrived at the usual monthly meeting which reported to the king on the state of the flocks, wearing the ring. As he was sitting among the others he happened to twist the hoop of the ring towards himself, to the inside of his hand, and as he did this he became invisible to those sitting near him and they went on talking as if he had gone. He marvelled at this and, fingering the ring, he turned the hoop outward again and became visible. Perceiving this he tested whether the ring had this power and so it happened: if he turned the hoop inwards he became invisible, but was visible when he turned it outwards. When he realized this, he at once arranged to become one of the messengers to the king. He went, committed adultery with the king's wife, attacked the king with her help, killed him, and took over the kingdom.

Now if there were two such rings, one worn by the just man, the other by the unjust, no one, as these people think, would be so incorruptible that he would stay on the path of justice or bring himself to keep away from other people's property and not touch it, when he could with impunity take whatever he wanted from the market, go into houses and have sexual relations with anyone he wanted, kill anyone, free all those he wished from prison, and do the other things which would make him like a god among men. His actions would be in no way different from those of the other and they would both follow the same path. This, some would say, is a great proof that no one is just willingly but under compulsion, so that justice is not one's private good, since wherever either thought he could do wrong with impunity he would do so.[2] Every man believes that injustice is much more profitable to himself than justice, and any exponent of this argument will say that he is right. The man who did not wish to do wrong with that opportunity, and did not touch other people's property, would be thought by those who knew it to be very foolish and miserable. They would praise him in public, thus deceiving one another, for fear of being wronged. So much for my second topic.

As for the choice between the lives we are discussing, we shall be able to make a correct judgment about it only if we put the most just man and the most unjust man face to face; otherwise we cannot do so. By face to face I mean this: let us grant to the unjust the fullest degree of injustice and to the just the fullest justice, each being perfect in his own pursuit.

First, the unjust man will act as clever craftsmen do—a top navigator for example or physician distinguishes what his craft can do and what it cannot; the former he will undertake, the latter he will pass by, and when he slips he can put things right. So the unjust man's correct attempts at wrongdoing must remain secret; the one who is caught must be considered a poor performer, for the extreme of injustice is to have a reputation for justice, and our perfectly unjust man must be granted perfection in injustice. We must not take this from him, but we must allow that, while committing the greatest crimes, he has provided himself with the greatest reputation for justice; if he makes a slip he must be able to put it right; he must be a sufficiently persuasive speaker if some wrongdoing of his is made public; he must be able to use force, where force is needed, with the help of his courage, his strength, and the friends and wealth with which he has provided himself.

Having described such a man, let us now in our argument put beside him the just man, simple as he is and noble, who, as Aeschylus put it, does not wish to appear just but to be so. We must take away his reputation, for a reputation for justice would bring him honour and rewards, and it would then not be clear whether he is what he is for justice's sake or for the sake of rewards and honour. We must strip him of everything except justice and make him the complete opposite of the other. Though he does no wrong, he must have the greatest reputation for wrongdoing so that he may be tested for justice by not weakening under ill repute and its consequences. Let him go his incorruptible way until death with a reputation for injustice throughout his life, just though he is, so that our two men may reach the extremes, one of justice, the other of injustice, and let them be judged as to which of the two is the happier.

SOCRATES: Whew! My dear Glaucon, what a mighty scouring you have given those two characters, as if they were statues in a competition.

THE VIRTUE OF SELFISHNESS

by Ayn Rand

Ayn Rand (1905-1982) is a well-known novelist and social thinker whose individualist philosophy, "objectivism," continues to be highly influential. Her major works include *The Fountainhead* (1943) and *Atlas Shrugged* (1957).

Rand defines selfishness as "concern with one's own interests," and she asks why this should be considered a vice. Altruism, the selfless pursuit of the good of others, is a dangerous ideal that engenders guilt and cynicism in those who seek to practice it and impose it on others: "Cynicism, because they neither practice nor accept the altruist morality—guilt, because they dare not reject it." Rand believes that a responsible concern for one's own interests is the essence of a moral existence.

The title of this [essay] may evoke the kind of question that I hear once in a while: "Why do you use the word 'selfishness' to denote virtuous qualities of character, when that word antagonizes so many people to whom it does not mean the things you mean?"

To those who ask it, my answer is: "For the reason that makes you afraid of it."

But there are others, who would not ask that question, sensing the moral cowardice it implies, yet who are unable to formulate my actual reason or to identify the profound moral issue involved. It is to them that I will give a more explicit answer.

It is not a mere semantic issue nor a matter of arbitrary choice. The meaning ascribed in popular usage to the word "selfishness" is not merely wrong: it represents a devastating intellectual "package-deal," which is responsible, more than any other single factor, for the arrested moral development of mankind.

In popular usage, the word "selfishness" is a synonym of evil; the image it conjures is of a murderous brute who tramples over piles of corpses to achieve his own ends, who cares for no living being and pursues nothing but the gratification of the mindless whims of any immediate moment.

Yes the exact meaning and dictionary definition of the word "selfishness" is: *concern with one's own interests.*

This concept does not include a moral evaluation; it does not tell us whether concern with one's own interests is good or evil; nor does it tell us what constitutes man's actual interests. It is the task of ethics to answer such questions.

The ethics of altruism has created the image of the brute, as its answer, in order to make men accept two inhuman tenets: (a) that any concern with one's own interests is evil, regardless of what these interests might be, and (b) that the brute's activities are *in fact* to one's own interest (which altruism enjoins man to renounce for the sake of his neighbors).

For a view of the nature of altruism, its consequences and the enormity of the moral corruption it perpetrates, I shall refer you to *Atlas Shrugged*—or to any of today's newspaper headlines. What concerns us here is altruism's *default* in the field of ethical theory.

There are two moral questions which altruism lumps together into one "package-deal": (1) What are values? (2) Who should be the beneficiary of values? Altruism substitutes the second for the first; it evades the task of defining a code of moral values, thus leaving man, in fact, without moral guidance.

Altruism declares that any action taken for the benefit of others is good, and any action taken for one's own benefit is evil. Thus the *beneficiary* of an action is the only criterion of moral value—and so long as the beneficiary is anybody other than oneself, anything goes.

Hence the appalling immorality, the chronic injustice, the grotesque double standards, the insoluble conflicts and contradictions that have characterized human relationships and human societies throughout history, under all the variants of the altruist ethics.

Observe the indecency of what passes for moral judgments today. An industrialist who produces a fortune, and a gangster who robs a bank are regarded as equally immoral, since they both sought wealth for their own "selfish" benefit. A young man who gives up his career in order to support his parents and never rises beyond the rank of grocery clerk is regarded as morally superior to the young man who endures an excruciating struggle and achieves his personal ambition. A dictator is regarded as moral, since the unspeakable atrocities he committed were intended to benefit "the people," not himself.

Observe what this beneficiary-criterion of morality does to a man's life. The first thing he learns is that morality is his enemy: he has nothing to gain from it, he can only lose; self-inflicted loss, self-inflicted pain and the gray, debilitating pall of an incomprehensible duty is all that he can expect. He may hope that others might occasionally sacrifice themselves for his benefit, as he grudgingly sacrifices himself for theirs, but he knows that the relationship will bring mutual resentment, not pleasure—and that, morally, their pursuit of values will be like an exchange of unwanted, unchosen Christmas presents, which neither is morally permitted to buy for himself. Apart from such times as he manages to perform some act of self-sacrifice, he possesses no moral significance: morality takes no cognizance of him and has nothing to say to him for guidance in the crucial issues of his life; it is only his own personal, private, "selfish" life and, as such, it is regarded either as evil or, at best, *amoral.*

Since nature does not provide man with an automatic form of survival, since he has to support his life by his own effort, the doctrine that concern with one's own interests is evil means that man's desire to live is evil—that man's life, as such, is evil. No doctrine could be more evil than that.

Yet that is the meaning of altruism, implicit in such examples as the equation of an industrialist with a robber. There is a fundamental moral difference between a man who sees his self-interest in production and a man who sees it in robbery. The evil of a robber does *not* lie in the fact that he pursues his own interests, but in *what* he regards as to his own interest; *not* in the fact that he pursues his values, but in *what* he chose to value; *not* in the fact that he wants to live, but in the fact that he wants to live on a subhuman level . . . .

If it is true that what I mean by "selfishness" is not what is meant conventionally, then *this* is one of the worst indictments of altruism: it means that altruism *permits no concept* of a self-respecting, self-supporting man—a man who supports his life by his own effort and neither sacrifices himself nor others. It means that altruism permits no view of men except as sacrificial animals and profiteers-on-sacrifice, as victims and parasites—that it permits no concept of a benevolent coexistence among men—that it permits no concept of *justice*.

If you wonder about the reasons behind the ugly mixture of cynicism and guilt in which most men spend their lives, these are the reasons: cynicism, because they neither practice nor accept the altruist morality—guilt, because they dare not reject it.

To rebel against so devastating an evil, one has to rebel against its basic premise. To redeem both man and morality, it is the concept of "*selfishness*" that one has to redeem.

chapter 14

DEONTOLOGICAL OR NONCONSEQUENTIAL ETHICS

GOOD WILL, DUTY, AND THE CATEGORICAL IMPERATIVE

by Immanuel Kant
Translated by T. K. *Abbott*

Immanuel Kant (1724-1804) is considered to be one of the greatest philosophers of all time. He lived in Königsberg, in East Prussia, and was a professor at the University there. Kant made significant and highly original contributions to esthetics, jurisprudence, and the philosophy of religion as well as to ethics and epistemology. His best known works are the *Critique of Pure Reason* (1781) and the *Foundations of the Metaphysics of Morals* (1785).

Human beings have desires and appetites. They are also rational, capable of knowing what is right, and capable of willing to do it. They can therefore exercise their wills in the rational control of desire for the purpose of right action. This is what persons of moral worth do. According to Kant, to possess moral worth is more important than to possess intelligence, humor, strength, or any other talent of the mind or body These talents are valuable but moral worth has *absolute* value, commanding not mere admiration but reverence and respect. Human beings who do right merely because it pleases them are not yet intrinsically moral. For had it pleased them they would have done wrong. To act morally is to act from no other motive than the motive of doing what is right. This kind of motive has nothing to do with anything as subjective as pleasure. To do right out of principle is to recognize an objective right that imposes an obligation on any rational being. Moral persons act in such a way that they could will that the principles of their actions should be universal laws for everyone else as well. This is one test of a moral act: Is it the kind of act that everyone should perform? Kant illustrates how this test can be applied to determine whether a given principle is moral and objective or merely subjective. For example, I may wish to break a promise, but that cannot be moral since I cannot will that promise-breaking be a universal practice.

Universal principles impose *categorical* imperatives. An imperative is a demand that I act in a certain fashion. For example, if I want to buy a house, it is imperative that I learn something about houses. But "Learn about houses!" is a *hypothetical* imperative since it is *conditional* on my wanting to buy a house. A *categorical* imperative is unconditional. An example is "Keep your promises." Thus an imperative is not preceded by any condition such as "if you want a good reputation." Hypothetical imperatives are "prudential": "If you want security, buy theft insurance." Categorical imperatives are moral: "Do not lie!" Kant argues that the categorical imperative presupposes the absolute worth of all rational beings as ends in themselves. Thus another formulation of the categorical imperative is, "So act as to treat humanity . . . as an end withal, never as a means only." Kant calls the domain of beings that are to be treated in this way the "kingdom of ends."

Moral Doctrines and Moral Theories

Nothing can possibly be conceived in the world, or even out of it, which can be called good, without qualification, except a Good Will. Intelligence, wit, judgment, and the other *talents* of the mind, however they may be named, or courage, resolution, perseverance, as qualities of temperament, are undoubtedly good and desirable in many respects; but these gifts of nature may also become extremely bad and mischievous if the will which is to make use of them, and which, therefore, constitutes what is called *character*, is not good. It is the same with the *gifts of fortune*. Power, riches, honour, even health, and the general well-being and contentment with one's condition which is called *happiness*, inspire pride, and often presumption, if there is not a good will to correct the influence of these on the mind, and with this also to rectify the whole principle of acting, and adapt it to its end. The sight of a being who is not adorned with a single feature of a pure and good will, enjoying unbroken prosperity, can never give pleasure to an impartial rational spectator. Thus a good will appears to constitute the indispensable condition even of being worthy of happiness.

There are even some qualities which are of service to this good will itself, and may facilitate its action, yet which have no intrinsic unconditional value, but always presuppose a good will, and this qualifies the esteem that we justly have for them, and does not permit us to regard them as absolutely good. Moderation in the affections and passions, self-control, and calm deliberation are not only good in many respects, but even seem to constitute part of the intrinsic worth of the person; but they are far from deserving to be called good without qualification, although they have been so unconditionally praised by the ancients. For without the principles of a good will, they may become extremely bad; and the coolness of a villain not only makes him far more dangerous, but also directly makes him more abominable in our eyes than he would have been without it.

A good will is good not because of what it performs or effects, not by its aptness for the attainment of some proposed end, but simply by virtue of the volition, that is, it is good in itself, and considered by itself is to be esteemed much higher than all that can be brought about by it in favour of any inclination, nay, even of the sum-total of all inclinations. Even if it should happen that, owing to special disfavour of fortune, or the niggardly provision of a step-motherly nature, this will should wholly lack power to accomplish its purpose, if with its greatest efforts it should yet achieve nothing, and there should remain only the good will (not, to be sure, a mere wish, but the summoning of all means in our power), then, like a jewel, it would still shine by its own light, as a thing which has its whole value in itself. Its usefulness or fruitlessness can neither add to nor take away anything from this value.

Thus the moral worth of an action does not lie in the effect expected from it, nor in any principle of action which requires to borrow its motive from this expected effect. For all these effects—agreeableness of one's condition, and even the promotion of the happiness of others—could have been also brought about by other causes, so that for this there would have been no need of the will of a rational being; whereas it is in this alone that the supreme and unconditional good can be found. The pre-eminent good which we call moral can therefore consist in nothing else than *the conception of law* in itself, *which certainly is only possible in a rational being*, in so far as this conception, and not the expected effect, determines the will. This is a good which is already present in the person who acts accordingly, and we have not to wait for it to appear first in the result.

But what sort of law can that be, the conception of which must determine the will, even without paying any regard to the effect expected from it, in order that this will may be called good absolutely and without qualification? As I have deprived the will of every impulse which could arise to it from obedience to any law, there remains nothing but the universal conformity of its actions to law in general, which alone is to serve the will as a principle, *i.e.* I am never to act otherwise than *so that I could also will that my maxim should become a universal law*. Here, now, it is the simple conformity to law in general, without assuming any particular law applicable to certain actions, that serves the will as its principle, and must so serve it, if duty is not to be a vain delusion and a chimerical notion. The common reason of men in its practical judgments perfectly coincides with this and always has in view of the principle here suggested. Let the question be, for example: May I when in distress make a promise with the intention not to keep it? I readily distinguish here between the two significations which the question may have: Whether it is prudent, or whether it is right, to make a false promise? The former may undoubtedly often be the case. I see clearly indeed that it is not enough to extricate myself from a present difficulty by means of this subterfuge, but it must be well considered whether there may not hereafter spring from this lie much greater inconvenience than that from which I now free myself, and as, with all my supposed *cunning*, the consequences cannot be so easily foreseen but that credit once lost may be much more injurious to me than any mischief which I seek to avoid at present, it should be considered whether it would not be more *prudent* to act herein according to a universal maxim, and to make it a habit to promise nothing except with the intention of keeping it. But it is soon clear to me that such a maxim will still only be based on the fear of consequences. Now it is a wholly different thing to be truthful from duty, and to be so from apprehension of injurious consequences. In the first case, the very notion of the action already implies a law for me; in the second case, I must first look about elsewhere to see what results may be combined with it which would affect myself. For to deviate from the principle of duty is beyond all doubt wicked; but to be unfaithful to my maxim of prudence may often be very advantageous to me, although to abide by it is certainly safer. The shortest way, however, and an unerring one, to discover the answer to this question whether a lying promise is consistent with duty, is to ask myself, Should I be content that my maxim (to extricate myself from difficulty by a false promise) should hold good as a universal law, for myself as well as for others? And should I be able to say to myself, "Everyone may make a deceitful promise when he finds himself in a difficulty from which he cannot otherwise extricate himself"? Then I presently become aware that while I can will the lie, I can by no means will that lying should be a universal law. For with such a law there would be no promises at all, since it would be in vain to allege my intention in regard to my future actions to those who would not believe this allegation, or if they over-hastily did so, would pay me back in my own coin. Hence my maxim, as soon as it should be made a universal law, would necessarily destroy itself.

I do not, therefore, need any far-reaching penetration to discern what I have to do in order that my will be morally good. Inexperienced in the course of the world, incapable of being prepared for all its contingencies, I only ask myself: Canst thou also will that thy maxim should be a universal law? If not, then it must be rejected, and that not because of a disadvantage accruing from it to myself or even to others, but because it cannot enter as a principle into a possible universal legislation, and reason extorts from me immediate respect for such legislation. I do not indeed as yet *discern* on what this respect is based (this the philosopher may inquire), but at least I understand this, that it is an estimation of the worth which far outweighs all worth of what is recommended by inclination, and that the necessity of acting from *pure* respect for the practical law is what constitutes duty, to which every other motive must give place, because it is the condition of a will being good *in itself* and the worth of such a will is above everything. . . .

. . . Everything in nature works according to laws. Rational beings alone have the faculty of acting according *to the conception* of laws, that is according to principles, *i.e.* have a *will*. Since the deduction of actions from principles requires *reason*, the will is nothing but practical reason. If reason infallibly determines the will, then the actions of such a being which are recognized as objectively necessary are subjectively necessary also, *i.e.* the will is a faculty to choose *that only* which reason independent on inclination recognizes as practically necessary, *i.e.* as good. But if reason of itself does not sufficiently determine the will, if the latter is subject also to subjective conditions (particular impulses) which do not always coincide with the objective conditions; in a word, if the will does not *in itself* completely accord with reason (which is actually the case with men), then the actions which objectively are recognized as necessary are subjectively contingent, and the determination of such a will according to objective laws is *obligation*, that is to say, the relation of the objective laws to a will that is not thoroughly good is conceived as the determination of the will of a rational being by principles of reason, but which the will from its nature does not of necessity follow.

The conception of an objective principle, in so far as it is obligatory for a will, is called a command (of reason), and the formula of the command is called an Imperative . . . .

Now all *imperatives* command either *hypothetically* or *categorically*. The former represent the practical necessity of a possible action as means to something else that is willed (or at least which one might possibly will). The categorical imperative would be that which represented an action as necessary of itself without reference to another end, *i.e.* as objectively necessary.

Since every practical law represents a possible action as good, and on this account, for a subject who is practically determinable by reason, necessary, all imperatives are formulae determining an action which is necessary according to the principle of a will good in some respects. If now the action is good only as a means *to something else,* then the imperative is *hypothetical*; if it is conceived as good *in itself* and consequently as being necessarily the principle of a will which of itself conforms to reason, then it is *categorical.* . . .

When I conceive a hypothetical imperative, in general I do not know beforehand what it will contain until I am given the condition. But when I conceive a categorical imperative, I know at once what it contains. For as the imperative contains besides the law only the necessity that the maxims shall conform to this law, while the law contains no conditions restricting it, there remains nothing but the general statement that the maxim of the action should conform to a universal law, and it is this conformity alone that the imperative properly represents as necessary.

There is . . . but one categorical imperative, namely, this: *Act only on that maxim whereby thou canst at the same time will that it should become a universal law.*

Now if all imperatives of duty can be deduced from this one imperative as from their principle, then, although it should remain undecided whether what is called duty is not merely a vain notion, yet at least we shall be able to show what we understand by it and what this notion means.

Since the universality of the law according to which effects are produced constitutes what is properly called *nature* in the most general sense (as to form), that is the existence of things so far as it is determined by general laws, the imperative of duty may be expressed thus: *Act as if the maxim of thy action were to become by thy will a universal law of nature.*

We will now enumerate a few duties, adopting the usual division of them into duties to ourselves and to others, and into perfect and imperfect duties.

1. A man reduced to despair by a series of misfortunes feels wearied of life, but is still so far in possession of his reason that he can ask himself whether it would not be contrary to his duty to himself to take his own life. Now he inquires whether the maxim of his action could become a

universal law of nature. His maxim is: From self-love I adopt it as a principle to shorten my life when its longer duration is likely to bring more evil than satisfaction. It is asked then simply whether this principle founded on self-love can become a universal law of nature. Now we see at once that a system of nature of which it should be a law to destroy life by means of the very feeling whose special nature it is to impel to the improvement of life would contradict itself, and therefore could not exist as a system of nature; hence that maxim cannot possibly exist as a universal law of nature, and consequently would be wholly inconsistent with the supreme principle of all duty.

2. Another finds himself forced by necessity to borrow money. He knows that he will not be able to repay it, but sees also that nothing will be lent to him, unless he promises stoutly to repay it in a definite time. He desires to make this promise, but he has still so much conscience as to ask himself: Is it not unlawful and inconsistent with duty to get out of a difficulty in this way? Suppose, however, that he resolves to do so, then the maxim of his action would be expressed thus: When I think myself in want of money, I will borrow money and promise to repay it, although I know that I never can do so. Now this principle of self-love or of one's own advantage may perhaps be consistent with my whole future welfare; but the question now is, Is it right? I change then the suggestion of self-love into a universal law, and state the question thus: How would it be if my maxim were a universal law? Then I see at once that it could never hold as a universal law of nature, but would necessarily contradict itself. For supposing it to be a universal law that everyone when he thinks himself in a difficulty should be able to promise whatever he pleases, with the purpose of not keeping his promise, the promise itself would become impossible, as well as the end that one might have in view in it, since no one would consider that anything was promised to him, but would ridicule all such statements as vain pretences.

3. A third finds in himself a talent which with the help of some culture might make him a useful man in many respects. But he finds himself in comfortable circumstances, and prefers to indulge in pleasure rather than to take pains in enlarging and improving his happy natural capacities. He asks, however, whether his maxim of neglect of his natural gifts, besides agreeing with his inclination to indulgence, agrees also with what is called duty. He sees then that a system of nature could indeed subsist with such a universal law although men (like the South Sea islanders) should let their talents rest, and resolve to devote their lives merely to idleness, amusement, and propagation of their species—in a word, to enjoyment; but he cannot possibly *will* that this should be a universal law of nature, or be implanted in us as such by a natural instinct. For, as a rational being, he necessarily wills that his faculties be developed, since they serve him, and have been given him, for all sorts of possible purposes.

4. A fourth, who is in prosperity, while he sees that others have to contend with great wretchedness and that he could help them, thinks: What concern is it of mine? Let everyone be as happy as Heaven pleases, or as he can make himself; I will take nothing from him nor even envy him, only I do not wish to contribute anything to his welfare or to his assistance in distress! Now no doubt if such a mode of thinking were a universal law, the human race might very well subsist, and doubtless even better than in a state in which everyone talks of sympathy and good-will, or even takes care occasionally to put it into practice, but, on the other side, also cheats when he can, betrays the rights of men, or otherwise violates them. But although it is possible that a universal law of nature might exist in accordance with that maxim, it is impossible to *will* that such a principle should have the universal validity of a law of nature. For a will which resolved this would contradict itself, inasmuch as many cases might occur in

which one would have need of the love and sympathy of others, and in which, by such a law of nature, sprung from his own will, he would deprive himself of all hope of the aid he desires. . . .

We have thus established at least this much, that if duty is a conception which is to have any import and real legislative authority for our actions, it can only be expressed in categorical, and not at all in hypothetical imperatives. We have also, which is of great importance, exhibited clearly and definitely for every practical application the content of the categorical imperative, which must contain the principle of all duty if there is such a thing at all. We have not yet, however, advanced so far as to prove *à priori* that there actually is such an imperative, that there is a practical law which commands absolutely of itself, and without any other impulse, and that the following of this law is duty . . . .

Now I say: man and generally any rational being *exists* as an end in himself, *not merely as a means* to be arbitrarily used by this or that will, but in all his actions, whether they concern himself or other rational beings, must be always regarded at the same time as an end. All objects of the inclinations have only a conditional worth; for if the inclinations and the wants founded on them did not exist, then their object would be without value. But the inclinations themselves being sources of want are so far from having an absolute worth for which they should be desired, that, on the contrary, it must be the universal wish of every rational being to be wholly free from them. Thus the worth of any object which is *to be acquired* by our action is always conditional. Beings whose existence depends not on our will but on nature's, have nevertheless, if they are non-rational beings, only a relative value as means, and are therefore called *things*; rational beings, on the contrary, are called *persons*, because their very nature points them out as ends in themselves, that is as something which must not be used merely as means, and so far therefore restricts freedom of action (and is an object of respect). These, therefore, are not merely subjective ends whose existence has a worth *for us* as an effort of our action, but *objective ends,* that is things whose existence is an end in itself: an end moreover for which no other can be substituted, which they should subserve *merely* as means, for otherwise nothing whatever would possess *absolute worth*; but if all worth were conditioned and therefore contingent, then there would be no supreme practical principle of reason whatever.

If then there is a supreme practical principle or, in respect of the human will, a categorical imperative, it must be one which, being drawn from the conception of that which is necessarily an end for everyone because it is an *an end in itself,* constitutes an *objective* principle of will, and can therefore serve as a universal practical law. The foundation of this principle is: *rational nature exists as an end in itself*. Man necessarily conceives his own existence as being so: so far then this is a *subjective* principle of human actions. But every other rational being regards its existence similarly, just on the same rational principle, that holds for me: so that it is at the same time an objective principle, from which as a supreme practical law all laws of the will must be capable of being deduced. Accordingly the practical imperative will be as follows: *So act as to treat humanity, whether in thine own person or in that of any other, in every case as an end withal, never as means only* . . . .

The conception of every rational being as one which must consider itself as giving all the maxims of its will universal laws, so as to judge itself and its actions from this point of view—this conception leads to another which depends on it and is very fruitful, namely, that of a *kingdom of ends*.

By a *kingdom* I understand the union of different rational beings in a system by common laws. Now since it is by laws that ends are determined as regards their universal validity, hence, if we abstract from the personal differences of rational beings, and likewise from all the content of their private ends, we shall be able to conceive all ends combined in a systematic whole (including both rational beings as ends in themselves, and also the special ends which each may propose of himself), that is to say, we can conceive a kingdom of ends, which on the preceding principles is possible.

For all rational beings come under the *law* that each of them must treat itself and all others *never merely as means*, but in every case *at the same time as ends in themselves*. Hence results a systematic union of rational beings by common objective laws, *i.e.* a kingdom which may be called a kingdom of ends. . . .

THE WORLD OF EPICTETUS

by Vice Admiral James Stockdale, USN

James Stockdale (b. 1923) spent ten years in Vietnam, two as a combat naval aviator and eight as a prisoner of war (four years in solitary confinement). He received the Congressional Medal of Honor and, since retiring from the Navy as president of the War College, has pursued the scholarly life. Stockdale has ten honorary degrees and is currently a Senior Fellow at the Hoover Institution on War, Revolution and Peace. His books include *In Love and War* (1984), *A Vietnam Experience: Ten Years of Reflection* (1985), and *Courage Under Fire: Testing Epictetus' Doctrines in a Lab of Human Behavior* (1993).

James Stockdale was a senior naval wing commander when he was shot down over North Vietnam in 1965. The article tells of the resources Stockdale found in himself in order to survive the ordeal with his sense of self-respect intact. Not all his fellow prisoners were as internally resourceful. Stockdale reports that he owed a great deal to a classical education that gave him an invaluable perspective on his situation. He learned from literature and from the Bible (Job especially) that life is not fair. The *Enchiridion* of Epictetus taught him to concern himself only with what was within his power. As a prisoner, he was physically powerless and had to learn to control and strengthen his will. He learned that integrity was far more valuable than sleep or food if the latter were obtained from his captors at the price of loss of self-respect. He learned that persons of little learning or philosophy were more vulnerable to brainwashing and the weakness that leads to treasonable betrayal of fellow prisoners. As a result, Stockdale recommends training in history and philosophy for professional soldiers. "In stress situations, the fundamental, the hardcore classical subjects, are what serve best."

In 1965 I was a forty-one-year-old commander, the senior pilot of Air Wing 16, flying combat missions in the area just south of Hanoi from the aircraft carrier *Oriskany*. By September of that year I had grown quite accustomed to briefing dozens of pilots and leading them on daily air strikes; I had flown nearly 200 missions myself and knew the countryside of North Vietnam like the back of my hand. On the ninth of that month I led about thirty-five airplanes to the Thanh Hoa Bridge, just west of that city. That bridge was tough; we had been bouncing 500-pounders off it for weeks.

The September 9 raid held special meaning for *Oriskany* pilots because of a special bomb load we had improvised; we were going in with our biggest, the 2000-pounders, hung not only on our attack planes but on our F-8 fighter-bombers as well. This increase in bridge-busting capability came from the innovative brain of a major flying with my Marine fighter squadron. He had figured out how we could jury-rig some switches, hang the big bombs, pump out some of the fuel to stay within takeoff weight limits, and then top off our tanks from our airborne refuelers while en route to the target. Although the pilot had to throw several switches in sequence to get rid of his bombs, a procedure requiring above-average cockpit agility, we routinely operated on the premise that all pilots of Air Wing 16 were above average. I test-flew the new load on a mission, thought it over, and approved it; that's the way we did business.

Our spirit was up. That morning, the *Oriskany* Air Wing was finally going to drop the bridge that was becoming a North Vietnamese symbol of resistance. You can imagine our dismay when we crossed the coast and the weather scout I had sent on ahead radioed back that ceiling and visibility were zero-zero in the bridge area. In the tiny cockpit of my A-4 at the front of the pack, I pushed the button on the throttle, spoke into the radio mike in my oxygen mask, and told the formation to split up and proceed in pairs to the secondary targets I had specified in my contingency briefing. What a letdown.

The adrenaline stopped flowing as my wingman and I broke left and down and started sauntering along toward our "milk run" target: boxcars on a railroad siding between Vinh and Thanh Hoa, where the flak was light. Descending through 10,000 feet, I unsnapped my oxygen mask and let it dangle, giving my pinched face a rest—no reason to stay uncomfortable on this run.

As I glided toward that easy target, I'm sure I felt totally self-satisfied. I had the top combat job that a Navy commander can hold and I was in tune with my environment. I was confident—I knew airplanes and flying inside out. I was comfortable with the people I worked with and I knew the trade so well that I often improvised variations in accepted procedures and encouraged others to do so under my watchful eye. I was on top. I thought I had found every key to success and had no doubt that my Academy and test-pilot schooling had provided me with everything I needed in life.

I passed down the middle of those boxcars and smiled as I saw the results of my instinctive timing. A neat pattern—perfection. I was just pulling out of my dive low to the ground when I heard a noise I hadn't expected—the *boom boom boom* of a 57-millimeter gun—and then I saw it just behind my wingtip. I was hit—all the red lights came on, my control system was going out—and I could barely keep that plane from flying into the ground while I got that damned oxygen mask up to my mouth so I could tell my wingman that I was about to eject. What rotten luck. And on a "milk run"!

The descent in the chute was quiet except for occasional rifle shots from the streets below. My mind was clear, and I said to myself, "five years." I knew we were making a mess of the war in Southeast Asia, but I didn't think it would last longer than that; I was also naive about the resources I would need in order to survive a lengthy period of captivity.

The Durants have said that culture is a thin and fragile veneer that superimposes itself on mankind. For the first time I was on my own, without the veneer. I was to spend years searching through and refining my bag of memories, looking for useful tools, things of value. The values were there, but they were all mixed up with technology, bureaucracy, and expediency, and had to be brought up into the open.

Education should take care to illuminate values, not bury them amongst the trivia. Are our students getting the message that without personal integrity intellectual skills are worthless?

Integrity is one of those words which many people keep in that desk drawer labeled "too hard." It's not a topic for the dinner table or the cocktail party. You can't buy or sell it. When supported with education, a person's integrity can give him something to rely on when his perspective seems to blur, when rules and principles seem to waver, and when he's faced with hard choices of right or wrong. It's something to keep him on the right track, something to keep him afloat when he's drowning; if only for practical reasons, it is an attribute that should be kept at the very top of a young person's consciousness.

The importance of the latter point is highlighted in prison camps, where everyday human nature, stripped bare, can be studied under a magnifying glass in accelerated time. Lessons spotlighted and absorbed in that laboratory sharpen one's eye for their abstruse but highly relevant applications in the "real time" world of now.

In the five years since I've been out of prison, I've participated several times in the process of selecting senior naval officers for promotion or important command assignments. I doubt that the experience is significantly different from that of executives who sit on "selection boards" in any large hierarchy. The system must be formal, objective, and fair; if you've seen one, you've probably seen them all. Navy selection board proceedings go something like this.

The first time you know the identity of the other members of the board is when you walk into a boardroom at eight o'clock on an appointed morning. The first order of business is to stand, raise your right hand, put your left hand on the Bible, and swear to make the best judgment you can, on the basis of merit, without prejudice. You're sworn to confidentiality regarding all board members' remarks during the proceedings. Board members are chosen for their experience and understanding; they often have knowledge of the particular individuals under consideration. They must feel free to speak their minds. They read and grade dozens of dossiers, and each candidate is discussed extensively. At voting time, a member casts his vote by selecting and pushing a "percent confidence" button, visible only to himself, on a console attached to his chair. When the last member pushes his button, a totalizer displays the numerical average "confidence" of the board. No one knows who voted what.

I'm always impressed by the fact that every effort is made to be fair to the candidate. Some are clearly out, some are clearly in; the borderline cases are the tough ones. You go over and over those in the "middle pile" and usually you vote and revote until late at night. In all the boards I've sat on, no inference or statement in a "jacket" is as sure to portend a low confidence score on the vote as evidence of a lack of directness or rectitude of a candidate in his dealings with others. Any hint of moral turpitude really turns people off. When the crunch comes, they prefer to work with forthright plodders rather than with devious geniuses. I don't believe that this preference is unique to the military. In any hierarchy where people's fates are decided by committees or boards, those who lose credibility with their peers and who cause their superiors to doubt their directness, honesty, or integrity are dead. Recovery isn't possible.

The linkage of men's ethics, reputations, and fates can be studied in even more vivid detail in prison camp. In that brutally controlled environment a perceptive enemy can get his hooks into the slightest chink in a man's ethical armor and accelerate his downfall. Given the right opening, the right moral weakness, a certain susceptibility on the part of the prisoner, a clever extortionist can drive his victim into a downhill slide that will ruin his image, self-respect, and life in a very short time.

There are some uncharted aspects to this, some traits of susceptibility which I don't think psychologists yet have words for. I am thinking of the tragedy that can befall a person who has such a need for love or attention that he will sell his soul for it. I use tragedy with the rigorous definition Aristotle applied to it: the story of a good man with a flaw who comes to an unjustified bad end. This is a rather delicate point and one that I want to emphasize. We had very very few collaborators in prison, and comparatively few Aristotelian tragedies, but the story and fate of one of these good men with a flaw might be instructive.

He was handsome, smart, articulate, and smooth. He was almost sincere. He was obsessed with success. When the going got tough, he decided expediency was preferable to principle.

This man was a classical opportunist. He befriended and worked for the enemy to the detriment of his fellow Americans. He made a tacit deal; moreover, he accepted favors (a violation of the code of conduct). In time, out of fear and shame, he withdrew; we could not get him to communicate with the American prisoner organization.

I couldn't learn what made the man tick. One of my best friends in prison, one of the wisest persons I have ever known, had once been in a squadron with this fellow. In prisoners' code I tapped a question to my philosophical friend: "What in the world is going on with that fink?"

"You're going to be surprised at what I have to say," he meticulously tapped back. "In a squadron he pushes himself forward and dominates the scene. He's a continual fountain of information. He's the person everybody relies on for inside dope. He works like mad; often flies more hops than others. It drives him crazy if he's not liked. He tends to grovel and ingratiate himself before others. I didn't realize he was really pathetic until I was sitting around with him and his wife one night when he was spinning his yarns of delusions of grandeur, telling of his great successes and his pending ascension to the top. His wife knew him better than anybody else; she shook her head with genuine sympathy and said to him: 'Gee, you're just a phony.'"

In prison, this man had somehow reached the point where he was willing to sell his soul just to satisfy this need, this immaturity. The only way he could get the attention that he demanded from authority was to grovel and ingratiate himself before the enemy. As a soldier he was a miserable failure, but he had not crossed the boundary of willful treason; he was not written off as an irrevocable loss, as were the two patent collaborators with whom the Vietnamese soon arranged that he live.

As we American POWs built our civilization, and wrote our own laws (which we leaders obliged all to memorize), we also codified certain principles which formed the backbone of our policies and attitudes. I codified the principles of compassion, rehabilitation, and forgiveness with the slogan: "It is neither American nor Christian to nag a repentant sinner to his grave." (Some didn't like it, thought it seemed soft on finks.) And so, we really gave this man a chance. Over time, our efforts worked. After five years of self-indulgence he got himself together and started to communicate with the prisoner organization. I sent the message "Are you on the team or not?"; he replied, "Yes," and came back. He told the Vietnamese that he didn't want to play their dirty games anymore. He wanted to get away from those willful collaborators and he came back and he was accepted, after a fashion.

I wish that were the end of the story. Although he came back, joined us, and even became a leader of sorts, he never totally won himself back. No matter how forgiving we were, he was conscious that many resented him—not so much because he was weak but because he had broken what we might call a gentleman's code. In all of those years when he, a senior officer, had willingly participated in making tape recordings of anti-American material, he had deeply offended the sensibilities of the American prisoners who were forced to listen to him. To most of us it wasn't the rhetoric of the war or the goodness or the badness of this or that issue that counted. The object of our highest value was the well-being of our fellow prisoners. He had broken that code and hurt some of those people. Some thought that as an informer he had indirectly hurt them physically. I don't believe that. What indisputably hurt them was his not having the sensitivity to realize the damage his opportunistic conduct would do to the morale of a bunch of Middle American guys with Middle American attitudes which they naturally cherished. He should have known that in those solitary cells where his tapes were piped were idealistic, direct, patriotic fellows who would be crushed and embarrassed to have him, a senior man in excellent physical shape, so obviously not under torture, telling the world that the war was wrong. Even if he believed what he said, which he did not, he should have had the common decency to keep his mouth shut. You can sit and think anything you want, but when you insensitively cut down those who want to love and help you, you cross a line. He seemed to sense that he could never truly be one of us.

And yet he was likable—particularly back in civilization after release—when tension was off, and making a deal did not seem so important. He exuded charm and "hail fellow" sophistication. He wanted so to be liked by all those men he had once discarded in his search for new friends, new deals, new fields to conquer in Hanoi. The tragedy of his life was obvious to us all. Tears were shed by some of his old prison mates when he was killed in an accident that strongly resembled suicide some months later. The Greek drama had run its course. He was right out of Aristotle's book, a good man with a flaw who had come to an unjustified bad end. The flaw was insecurity: the need to ingratiate himself, the need for love and adulation at any price.

He reminded me of Paul Newman in *The Hustler*. Newman couldn't stand success. He knew how to make a deal. He was handsome, he was smart, he was attractive to everybody; but he had to have adulation, and therein lay the seed of tragedy. Playing high-stakes pool against old Minnesota Fats (Jackie Gleason), Newman was well in the lead, and getting more full of himself by the hour. George C. Scott, the pool bettor, whispered to his partner: "I'm going to keep betting on Minnesota Fats; this other guy [Newman] is a born loser—he's all skill and no character." And he was right, a born loser—I think that's the message.

How can we educate to avoid these casualties? Can we by means of education prevent this kind of tragedy? What we prisoners were in was a one-way leverage game in which the other side had all the mechanical advantage. I suppose you could say that we all live in a leverage world to some degree; we all experience people trying to use us in one way or another. The difference in Hanoi was the degradation of the ends (to be used as propaganda agents of an enemy, or as informers on your fellow Americans), and the power of the means (total environmental control including solitary confinement, restraint by means of leg-irons and handcuffs, and torture). Extortionists always go down the same track: the imposition of guilt and fear for having disobeyed their rules, followed in turn by punishment, apology, confession, and atonement (their payoff). Our captors would go to great lengths to get a man to compromise his own code, even if only slightly, and then they would hold that in their bag, and the next time get him to go a little further.

Some people are psychologically, if not physically, at home in extortion environments. They are tough people who instinctively avoid getting sucked into the undertows. They never kid themselves or their friends; if they miss the mark they admit it. But there's another category of person who gets tripped up. He makes a small compromise, perhaps rationalizes it, and then makes another one; and then he gets depressed, full of shame, lonesome, loses his willpower and self-respect, and comes to a tragic end. Somewhere along the line he realizes that he has turned a corner that he didn't mean to turn. All too late he realizes that he has been worshiping the wrong gods and discovers the wisdom of the ages: life is not fair.

In sorting out the story after our release, we found that most of us had come to combat constant mental and physical pressure in much the same way. We discovered that when a person is alone in a cell and sees the door open only once or twice a day for a bowl of soup, he realizes after a period of weeks in isolation and darkness that he has to build some sort of ritual into his life if he wants to avoid becoming an animal. Ritual fills a need in a hard life and it's easy to see how formal church ritual grew. For almost all of us, this ritual was built around prayer, exercise, and clandestine communication. The prayers I said during those days were prayers of quality with ideas of substance. We found that over the course of time our minds had a tremendous capacity for invention and introspection, but had the weakness of being an integral part of our bodies. I remembered Descartes and how in his philosophy he separated mind and body. One time I cursed my body for the way it decayed my mind. I had decided that I would become a Gandhi. I would have to be carried around on a pallet and in that state I could not be used by my captors for propaganda purposes. After about ten days of fasting, I found that I had become so depressed that soon I would risk going into interrogation ready to spill my guts just looking for a friend. I tapped to the guy next door and I said, "Gosh, how I wish Descartes could have been right, but he's wrong." He was a little slow to reply; I reviewed Descartes's deduction with him and explained how I had discovered that body and mind are inseparable.

On the positive side, I discovered the tremendous file-cabinet volume of the human mind. You can memorize an incredible amount of material and you can draw the past out of your memory with remarkable recall by easing slowly toward the event you seek and not crowding the mind too closely. You'll try to remember who was at your birthday party when you were five years old, and you can get it, but only after months of effort. You can break the locks and find the answers, but you need time and solitude to learn how to use this marvelous device in your head which is the greatest computer on earth.

Of course many of the things we recalled from the past were utterly useless as sources of strength or practicality. For instance, events brought back from cocktail parties or insincere social contacts were almost repugnant because of their emptiness, their utter lack of value. More often than not, the locks worth picking had been on old schoolroom doors. School days can be thought of as a time when one is filling the important stacks of one's memory library. For me, the golden doors were labeled history and the classics. The historical perspective which enabled a man to take himself away from all the agitation, not necessarily to see a rosy lining, but to see the real nature of the situation he faced, was truly a thing of value.

Here's how this historical perspective helped me see the reality of my own situation and thus cope better with it. I learned from a Vietnamese prisoner that the same cells we occupied had in years before been lived in by many of the leaders of the Hanoi government. From my history lessons I recalled that when metropolitan France permitted communists in the government in 1936, the communists who occupied cells in Vietnam were set free. I marveled at the cycle of history, all within my memory, which prompted Hitler's rise in Germany, then led to the rise of the Popular Front in France, and finally vacated this cell of mine halfway around the world ("Perhaps Pham Van Dong lived here"). I came to understand what tough people these were. I was willing to fight them to the death, but I grew to realize that hatred was an indulgence, a very inefficient emotion. I remember thinking, "If you were committed to beating the dealer in a gambling casino, would *hating* him help your game?" In a pidgin English propaganda book the guard gave me, speeches by these old communists about their prison experiences stressed how they learned to beat down the enemy by being united. It seemed comforting to know that we were united against the communist administration of Hoa Lo prison just as the Vietnamese communists had united against the French administration of Hoa Lo in the thirties. Prisoners are prisoners, and there's only one way to beat administrations. We resolved to do it better in the sixties than they had in the thirties. You don't base system-beating on any thought of political idealism; you do it as a competitive thing, as an expression of self-respect.

Education in the classics teaches you that all organizations since the beginning of time have used the power of guilt; that cycles are repetitive; and that this is the way of the world. It's a naive person who comes in and says, "Let's see, what's good and what's bad?" That's a quagmire. You can get out of that quagmire only by recalling how wise men before you accommodated the same dilemmas. And I believe a good classical education and an understanding of history can best determine the rules you should live by. They also give you the power to analyze reasons for these rules and guide you as to how to apply them to your own situation. In a broader sense, all my education helped me. Naval Academy discipline and body contact sports helped me. But the education which I found myself using most was what I got in graduate school. The messages of history and philosophy I used were simple.

The first one is this business about life not being fair. That is a very important lesson and I learned it from a wonderful man named Philip Rhinelander. As a lieutenant commander in the Navy studying political science at Stanford University in 1961, I went over to philosophy corner one day and an older gentleman said, "Can I help you?" I said, "Yes, I'd like to take some courses in philosophy." I told him I'd been in college for six years and had never had a course in philosophy. He couldn't believe it. I told him that I was a naval officer and he said, "Well, I used to be in the Navy. Sit down." Philip Rhinelander became a great influence in my life.

He had been a Harvard lawyer and had pleaded cases before the Supreme Court and then gone to war as a reserve officer. When he came back he took his doctorate at Harvard. He was also a music composer, had been director of general education at Harvard, dean of the School of Humanities and Sciences at Stanford, and by the time I met him had by choice returned to teaching in the classroom. He said, "The course I'm teaching is my personal two-term favorite—The Problem of Good and Evil—and we're starting our second term." He said the message of his course was from the Book of Job. The number one problem in this world is that people are not able to accommodate the lesson in the book.

He recounted the story of Job. It starts out by establishing that Job was the most honorable of men. Then he lost all his goods. He also lost his reputation, which is what really hurt. His wife was badgering him to admit his sins, but he knew he had made no errors. He was not a patient man and demanded to speak to the Lord. When the Lord appeared in the whirlwind, he said, "Now, Job, you have to shape up! Life is not fair." That's my interpretation and that's the way the book ended for hundreds of years. I agree with those of the opinion that the happy ending was spliced on many years later. If you read it, you'll note that the meter changes. People couldn't live with the original message. Here was a good man who came to unexplained grief, and the Lord told him: "That's the way it is. Don't challenge me. This is my world and you either live in it as I designed it or get out."

This was a great comfort to me in prison. It answered the question "Why me?" I cast aside any thoughts of being punished for past actions. Sometimes I shared the message with fellow prisoners as I tapped through the walls to them, but I learned to be selective. It's a strong message which upsets some people.

Rhinelander also passed on to me another piece of classical information which I found of great value. On the day of our last session together he said, "You're a military man, let me give you a book to remember me by. It's a book of military ethics." He handed it to me, and I bade him goodbye with great emotion. I took the book home and that night started to read it. It was the *Enchiridion* of the philosopher Epictetus, his "manual" for the Roman field soldier.

As I began to read, I thought to myself in disbelief, "Does Rhinelander think I'm going to draw lessons for my life from this thing? I'm a fighter pilot. I'm a technical man. I'm a test pilot. I know how to get people to do technical work. I play golf; I drink martinis. I know how to get ahead in my profession. And what does he hand me? A book that says in part, 'It's better to die in hunger, exempt from guilt and fear, than to live in affluence and with perturbation.' " I remembered this later in prison because perturbation was what I was living with. When I ejected from the airplane on that September morn in 1965, I had left the land of technology. I had entered the world of Epictetus, and it's a world that few of us, whether we know it or not, are ever far away from.

In Palo Alto, I had read this book, not with contentment, but with annoyance. Statement after statement: "Men are disturbed not by things, but by the view that they take of them." "Do not be concerned with things which are beyond your power." "Demand not that events should happen as you wish, but wish them to happen as they do happen and you will go on well." This is stoicism. It's not the last word, but it's a viewpoint that comes in handy in many circumstances, and it surely did for me. Particularly this line: "Lameness is an impediment to the body but not to the will." That was significant for me because I wasn't able to stand up and support myself on my badly broken leg for the first couple of years I was in solitary confinement.

Other statements of Epictetus took on added meaning in the light of extortions which often began with our captors' callous pleas: "If you are just reasonable with us we will compensate you. You get your meals, you get to sleep, you won't be pestered, you might even get a cellmate." The catch was that by being "reasonable with us" our enemies meant being their informers, their propagandists. The old stoic had said, "If I can get the things I need with the preservation of my honor and fidelity and self-respect, show me the way and I will get them. But, if you require me to lose my own proper good, that you may gain what is no good, consider how unreasonable and foolish you are." To love our fellow prisoners was within our power. To betray, to propagandize, to disillusion conscientious and patriotic shipmates and destroy their morale so that they in turn would be destroyed was to lose one's proper good.

What attributes serve you well in the extortion environment? We learned there, above all else, that the best defense is to keep your conscience clean. When we did something we were ashamed of, and our captors realized we were ashamed of it, we were in trouble. A little white lie is where extortion and ultimately blackmail start. In 1965, I was crippled and I was alone. I realized that they had all the power. I couldn't see how I was ever going to get out with my honor and self-respect. The one thing I came to realize was that if you don't lose integrity you can't be had and you can't be hurt. Compromises multiply and build up when you're working against a skilled extortionist or a good manipulator. You can't be had if you don't take that first shortcut, or "meet them halfway," as they say, or look for that tacit "deal," or make that first compromise.

Bob North, a political science professor at Stanford, taught me a course called Comparative Marxist Thought. This was not an anticommunist course. It was the study of dogma and thought patterns. We read no criticism of Marxism, only primary sources. All year we read the works of Marx and Lenin. In Hanoi, I understood more about Marxist theory than my interrogator did. I was able to say to that interrogator, "That's not what Lenin said; you're a deviationist."

One of the things North talked about was brainwashing. A psychologist who studied the Korean prisoner situation, which somewhat paralleled ours, concluded that three categories of prisoners were involved there. The first was the redneck Marine sergeant from Tennessee who had an eighth-grade education. He would get in that interrogation room and they would say that the Spanish-American War was started by the bomb within the *Maine*, which might be true, and he would answer, "B.S." They would show him something about racial unrest in Detroit. "B.S." There was no way they could get to him; his mind was made up. He was a straight guy, red, white, and blue, and everything else was B.S.! He didn't give it a second thought. Not much of a historian, perhaps, but a good security risk.

In the next category were the sophisticates. They were the fellows who could be told these same things about the horrors of American history and our social problems, but had heard it all before, knew both sides of every story, and thought we were on the right track. They weren't ashamed that we had robber barons at a certain time in our history; they were aware of the skeletons in most civilizations' closets. They could not be emotionally involved and so they were good security risks.

The ones who were in trouble were the high school graduates who had enough sense to pick up the innuendo, and yet not enough education to accommodate it properly. Not many of them fell, but most of the men that got entangled started from that background.

The psychologist's point is possibly oversimplistic, but I think his message has some validity. A little knowledge is a dangerous thing.

Generally speaking, I think education is a tremendous defense; the broader, the better. After I was shot down my wife, Sybil, found a clipping glued in the front of my collegiate dictionary: "Education is an ornament in prosperity and a refuge in adversity." She certainly agrees with me on that. Most of us prisoners found that the so-called practical academic exercises in how to do things, which I'm told are proliferating, were useless. I'm not saying that we should base education on training people to be in prison, but I am saying that in stress situations, the fundamentals, the hardcore classical subjects, are what serve best.

Theatrics also helped sustain me. My mother had been a drama coach when I was young and I was in many of her plays. In prison I learned how to manufacture a personality and live it, crawl into it, and hold that role without deviation. During interrogations, I'd check the responses I got to different kinds of behavior. They'd get worried when I did things irrationally. And so, every so often, I would play that "irrational" role and come completely unglued. When I could tell that pressure to make a public exhibition of me was building, I'd stand up, tip the table over, attempt to throw the chair through the window, and say, "No way, Goddammit! I'm not doing that! Now, come over here and fight!" This was a risky ploy, because if they thought you were acting, they would slam you into the ropes and make you scream in pain like a baby. You could watch their faces and read their minds. They had expected me to behave like a stoic. But a man would be a fool to make their job easy by being conventional and predictable. I could feel the tide turn in my favor at that magic moment when their anger turned to pleading: "Calm down, now calm down." The payoff would come when they decided that the risk of my going haywire in front of some touring American professor on a "fact-finding" mission was too great. More important, they had reason to believe that I would tell the truth—namely, that I had been in solitary confinement for four years and tortured fifteen times— without fear of future consequences. So theatrical training proved helpful to me.

Can you educate for leadership? I think you can, but the communists would probably say no. One day in an argument with an interrogator, I said, "You are so proud of being a party member, what are the criteria?" He said in a flurry of anger, "There are only four: you have to be seventeen years old, you have to be selfless, you have to be smart enough to understand the theory, and you've got to be a person who innately influences others." He stressed that fourth one. I think psychologists would say that leadership is innate, and there is truth in that. But, I also think you can learn some leadership traits that naturally accrue from a good education: compassion is a necessity for leaders, as are spontaneity, bravery, self-discipline, honesty, and above all, integrity.

I remember being disappointed about a month after I was back when one of my young friends, a prison mate, came running up after a reunion at the Naval Academy. He said with glee, "This is really great, you won't believe how this country has advanced. They've practically done away with plebe year at the Academy, and they've got computers in the basement of Bancroft Hall." I thought, "My God, if there was anything that helped us get through those eight years, it was plebe year, and if anything screwed up that war, it was computers!"

A CRITIQUE OF KANTIASM

by Richard Taylor

Richard Taylor (b. 1919) is Professor Emeritus at the University of Rochester. Among his many books are *Good and Evil* (1971), *With Heart and Mind* (1973), and *Ethics, Faith and Reason* (1985).

Taylor criticizes Kant's moral philosophy for being too abstract and intellectual. We ordinarily think of a person of good will as someone with a kindly and sympathetic nature. Not so for Kant. His person of good will acts from respect for the moral law. To Kant, acts done solely out of kindness and sympathy have no moral worth. Taylor recommends a moral system less abstract and metaphysical and more compatible with human nature.

It is not my intention to give any detailed exposition of Kant's ethical system. I propose instead to discuss certain of Kant's basic ideas in order to illustrate a certain approach to ethics that I think is essentially wrong. For this I could have chosen the ideas of some other modern moralist, but I prefer to illustrate my points by Kant's thought. I am doing this first because of his great fame and the reverence with which many philosophers still regard him, and secondly because it would be difficult to find any modern thinker who has carried to such an extreme the philosophical presuppositions that I am eager to repudiate. I shall, thus, use some of Kant's ideas to show how the basic ideas of morality, born originally of men's practical needs as social beings and having to do originally with men's practical relations with each other, can, under the influence of philosophy, become so detached from the world that they become pure abstractions, having no longer anything to do with morality insofar as this is a practical concern of men. Philosophical or metaphysical morals thereby ceases to have much connection with the morality that is the abiding practical concern of men and becomes, instead, a purely intellectual thing, something to contemplate and appreciate, much as one would appreciate a geometrical demonstration. Its vocabulary, which is the very vocabulary of everyday morals, no longer has the same meaning, but instead represents a realm of pure abstractions. Intellectually satisfying as this might be, it is nevertheless highly dangerous, for it leads men to suppose that the problems of ethics are essentially intellectual problems, that they are simply philosophical questions in need of philosophical answers. The result is that the eyes of the moralist are directed away from the world, in which moral problems are the most important problems there are, and toward a really nonexistent realm, a realm of ideas rather than things. The image of the philosophical and metaphysical moralist, who is quite lacking in any knowledge of the world and whose ideas about it are of the childish sort learned in a Sunday school, is a familiar one. He is a moralist whose dialectic is penetrating and whose reasoning is clear—he grapples with many philosophical problems of morality and has many subtle answers to philosophical difficulties—but who has little appreciation of the pain and sorrow of the world beyond the knowledge that it is there.

Duty and Law

Laws, as practical rules of human invention, find no place in Kant's metaphysical morals. The Moral Law that replaces them is sundered from any practical human concerns, for it seemed to Kant that men's practical ends and their moral obligations were not only quite different things but, more often than not, were actually opposed to each other. Obligations, which were originally only relations between men arising from mutual undertakings for mutual advantage, similarly disappear from the Kantian morality, to be replaced by an abstract sort of moral obligation that has no connection whatsoever with any earthly good. Duties—which were originally and are still imposed by rulers on subjects, masters on servants, employers on workmen, and so on, in return for certain compensations, privileges, and rights—are replaced by Kant with Duty in the abstract. This abstract Duty is deemed by him to be the sole proper motive of moral conduct; yet, it is not a duty *to* anyone, or a duty to do any particular thing. Men have always understood the notion of one's duty to sovereign or master, and Christians well understood the idea of duty toward God. In such cases, one's duty consisted simply of compliance with commands. But in Kant's system, duties are sundered from particular commands, and Duty becomes something singular and metaphysical. We are, according to this system, to do always what Duty requires, for no other reason than that Duty does require it. Beyond a few heterogeneous examples for illustration, we never learn from Kant just what this is, save only that it is the obligation to act from respect for the Moral Law. A man must cling to life, for example, and give no thought to suicide—not because any lawgiver or God has commanded it, not because things might work out all right for him if he sticks it out a little longer, but just because Duty requires it. A man must also help others in distress; not, again, because any man or God has admonished him to, not just because they need him, or because he cares for them, or because he wants to see their baneful condition improved—indeed, it is best that he have no such feelings at all—but just because it is his Duty.

The Good Will

It is in such terms that Kant defined the *good will*, declaring it to be the only thing in the universe that is unqualifiedly good. Now we normally think of a man of good will as one who loves his fellow men, as one whose happiness is sympathetically bound up with that of others, and as one who has a keen and constant desire to abolish the suffering around him and make the lot of his neighbor more tolerable than it might be without his helping hand. Not so for Kant. Indeed, he dismisses the actions of such persons, "so sympathetically constituted that . . . they find an inner satisfaction in spreading joy, and rejoice in the contentment of others which they have made possible," as devoid of any moral worth. Human conduct, to have any genuine moral worth, must not spring from any such amiable feelings as these; these are, after all, nothing but human feelings; they are not *moral* incentives. To have genuine moral worth, according to this moralist, our actions must spring from the sense of Duty and nothing else. And one acts dutifully if he acts, not from love or concern for his fellows, but from respect for the Moral Law.

The Categorical Imperative

The Moral Law assumed, in Kant's thought, the form of an imperative, or command But unlike any command that was ever before heard by any man, this one issues from no commander! Like a question that no one ever asks, or an assertion that no one ever affirms, it is a command that no God or man ever promulgates. It is promulgated by Reason. Nor is this the humble rationality of living, mortal men; it is Reason itself, again in the abstract. And unlike what one would ordinarily think of as a command, this one has no definite content. It is simply the form, Kant says, not of any actual laws, but of The Law, which is again, of course, something abstract. It has, unlike any other imperative of which one has ever heard, no purpose or end. It is not the means to the achievement of anything; and it has no relation to what anyone wants. For this reason Kant called it the Categorical Imperative, a command that is supposed to command absolutely and for its own sake. The Categorical Imperative does not bid us to act in a manner calculated to advance human well-being, for the weal and woe of men has for Kant no necessary connection with morality. It does not bid us to act as we would want others to act, for what any men want has no more bearing on morals than what they happen to feel. This Imperative does not, in fact, bid us to do anything at all, nor, indeed, even to have any generous or sympathetic motive, but only to honor some maxim or rational principle of conduct. We are, whatever we do, to act in such a manner that we could, consistently with reason, will this maxim to be a universal Law, even a Law of Nature, binding on all rational beings. Kant does not ask us to consider how other rational beings, thus bound, might feel about our maxims, for again, how anyone happens to feel about anything has no bearing on morality anyway. It is Reason that counts. It is not the living and suffering human beings who manage sometimes to be reasonable but most of the time are not. It is not men's needs and wants, or any human desires, or any practical human goods. To act immorally is to act contrary to Reason; it is to commit a sort of metaphysical blunder in the relationship between one's behavior and his generalized motive. Human needs and feelings have so little to do with this that they are not even allowed into the picture. If a man reaches forth to help the sick, the troubled, or the dying, this must not be done from any motive of compassion or sentiment of love. Such love, as a feeling, is dismissed by Kant as "pathological," because it is not prompted by that rational respect for Duty that filled Kant with such awe. Indeed, Kant thought that such human feelings as love and compassion should not even be allowed to cooperate in the performance of Duty, for we must act solely *from* Duty, and not merely in *accordance* with it. Such feelings as love, sympathy, and friendship are therefore regarded by Kant as positively dangerous. They incline men to do from sheer goodness of heart what should be done only from Reason and respect for the Moral Law. To be genuinely moral, a man must tear himself away from his inclinations as a loving human being, drown the sympathetic promptings of his heart, scorn any fruits of his efforts, think last of all of the feelings, needs, desires, and inclinations either of himself or of his fellows and, perhaps detesting what he has to do, do it anyway—solely from respect for the Law.

Rational Nature as an End

This Moral Law is otherwise represented by Kant as respect for Rational Nature, something that again, of course, exists only in the abstract but is, presumably, somehow exemplified in men and, Kant thought, in God. Indeed, it is the only thing in men that Kant considered worthy of a philosopher's attention. Because men are deemed to embody this Rational Nature, human nature is declared to be an End in Itself, to possess an absolute Worth, or Dignity. This kind of absolute End is not like ordinary ends or goals, something relative to the aims or purposes of any creature. It is not anything anyone wants or would be moved to try to achieve. It is, like so many of Kant's abstractions, an absolute end. And the Worth that he supposes Rational Nature to possess is no worth *for* or *to* anything; it, too, is an abstract or absolute Worth. Kant peoples a veritable utopia, which he of course does not imagine as existing, with these Ends in Themselves, and calls it the Kingdom of Ends. Ends in Themselves are, thus, not to be thought of as those men that live and toil on earth; they are not suffering, rejoicing, fumbling, living, and dying human beings; they are not men that anyone has ever seen, or would be apt to recognize as men if he did see them, or apt to like very much if he did recognize them. They are abstract things, reifications of Rational Nature, fabricated by Kant and now called Rational Beings or Ends in Themselves. Their purpose, unlike that of any creature under the sun, is not to sorrow and rejoice, not to love and hate, not to beget offspring, not to grow old and die, and not to get on as best they can to such destinies as the world has allotted them. Their purpose is just to *legislate*—to legislate morally and rationally for this rational Kingdom of Ends.

The Significance of Kant

Kant's system thus represents the rational, logical conclusion of the natural or true morality that was begotten by the Greeks, of the absolute distinction that they drew, and that men still want to draw. This is the distinction between what *is*, or the realm of observation and science, and what *ought* to be, or the realm of obligation and morals. No one has ever suggested that Kant was irrational, and although it is doubtful that his ideas have ever had much impact on human behavior, they have had a profound impact on philosophy, which has always prized reason and abstraction and tended to scorn fact. Kant's metaphysical system of morals rests on notions that are still a part of the fabric of our intellectual culture and inheritance. His greatest merit is that he was consistent. He showed men what sort of metaphysic of morals they must have—if they suppose that morality has any metaphysic, or any logic and method of its own. He showed what morality must be if we suppose it to be something rational and at the same time nonempirical or divorced from psychology, anthropology, or any science of man. That general conception of morals is, of course, still common in philosophy, and still permeates judicial thought, where it expresses itself in the ideas of guilt and desert. A man is thought to be "deserving" of punishment if he did, and could have avoided doing, something "wrong." Our basic moral presuppositions, in short, are still very much the same as Kant's, and Kant shows where they lead. We still assume, as he did, a basic dichotomy between what in fact *is* and what morally *ought* to be, between what the Greeks called convention and nature. Like the Greeks, and like Kant, we still feel a desperate need to *know* what, by nature or by some natural or rational moral principle, *ought* to be. Kant was entirely right in insisting that no knowledge of what in fact is—no knowledge of human nature, of history, of anthropology, or psychology—can yield this knowledge. But Kant did not consider, and many philosophical minds still think it somehow perverse to consider, that there may be no such knowledge—and not merely because no man has managed to attain it, but because there may really be nothing there to know in the first place. There may be no such thing as a true morality. Perhaps the basic facts of morality are, as Protagoras thought, conventions; that is, the practical formulas, some workable and some not, for enabling men to achieve whatever ideals and aspirations happen to move them. In the Kantian scheme, such considerations have nothing to do with morality which is concerned, not with what is, but with what morally ought to be, with what is in his strange sense commanded. According to the Protagorean scheme, on the other hand, such considerations exhaust the whole subject of morals. Here we are, human beings, possessed of needs, feelings, capacities, and aims that are for the most part not of our creation but are simply part of our endowment as human beings. These are the grist, the data, and the subject matter of morals. The problem is how we get from where we are to where we want to go. It is on our answer to this question that our whole happiness and our worth as human beings depends. Our problem is not whether our answers accord with nature or even with truth. Our problem is to find those answers that do in fact work, whose fruits are sunlight, warmth, and satisfaction in our lives as we live them.

chapter 15

UTILITARIAN OR CONSEQUENTIAL ETHICS

THE ONES WHO WALK AWAY FROM OMELAS

by Ursula Le Guin

Ursula Le Guin (b. 1929) is the author of numerous short stories and novels These include *The Word for World in Forest* (1976) and *Four Ways to Forgiveness* (1995).

Ursula Le Guin tells of a highly civilized place called Omelas. Its inhabitants are sophisticated and, by most standards, they are happy. Moreover, they are considerate and decent to one another—with one exception. That exception is a necessary condition for the general welfare. But some citizens cannot reconcile themselves to it. These walk away from Omelas never to return. Le Guin's parable bears on fundamental ethical dilemmas, but most particularly it raises serious questions about the adequacy of utilitarianism as an ethical philosophy.

With a clamor of bells that set the swallows soaring, the Festival of Summer came to the city. Omelas, bright-towered by the sea. The rigging of the boats in harbor sparkled with flags. In the streets between houses with red roofs and painted walls, between old moss-grown gardens and under avenues of trees, past great parks and public buildings, processions moved. Some were decorous: old people in long stiff robes of mauve and grey, grave master workmen, quiet, merry women carrying their babies and chatting as they walked. In other streets the music beat faster, a shimmering of gong and tambourine, and the people went dancing, the procession was a dance. Children dodged in and out, their high calls rising like the swallows' crossing flights over the music and the singing. All the processions wound towards the north side of the city, where on the great water-meadow called the Green Fields boys and girls, naked in the bright air, with mud-stained feet and ankles and long, lithe arms, exercised their restive horses before the race. The horses wore no gear at all but a halter without bit. Their manes were braided with streamers of silver, gold, and green. They flared their nostrils and pranced and boasted to one another; they were vastly excited, the horse being the only animal who has adopted our ceremonies as his own. Far off to the north and west the mountains stood up half encircling Omelas on her bay. The air of morning was so clear that the snow still crowning the Eighteen Peaks burned with white-gold fire across the miles of sunlit air, under the dark blue of the sky. There was just enough wind to make the banners that marked the racecourse snap and flutter now and then. In the silence of the broad green meadows one could hear the music winding through the city streets, farther and nearer and ever approaching, a cheerful faint sweetness of the air that from time to time trembled and gathered together and broke out into the great joyous clanging of the bells.

Joyous! How is one to tell about joy? How describe the citizens of Omelas?

They were not simple folk, you see, though they were happy. But we do not say the words of cheer much any more. All smiles have become archaic. Given a description such as this one tends to make certain assumptions. Given a description such as this one tends to look next for the King, mounted on a splendid stallion and surrounded by his noble knights, or perhaps in a golden litter borne by great-muscled slaves. But there was no king. They did not use swords, or keep slaves. They were not barbarians. I do not know the rules and laws of their society, but I suspect that they were singularly few. As they did without monarchy and slavery, so they also got on without the stock exchange, the advertisement, the secret police, and the bomb. Yet I repeat that these were not simple folk, not dulcet shepherds, noble savages, bland utopians. They were not less complex than us. The trouble is that we have a bad habit, encouraged by pedants and sophisticates, of considering happiness as something rather stupid. Only pain is intellectual, only evil interesting. This is the treason of the artist: a refusal to admit the banality of evil and the terrible boredom of pain. If you can't lick 'em, join 'em. If it hurts, repeat it. But to praise despair is to condemn delight, to embrace violence is to lose hold of everything else. We have almost lost hold; we can no longer describe a happy man, nor make any celebration of joy. How can I tell you about the people of Omelas? They were not naive and happy children—though their children were, in fact, happy. They were mature, intelligent, passionate adults whose lives were not wretched. O miracle! But I wish I could describe it better. I wish I could convince you. Omelas sounds in my words like a city in a fairy tale, long ago and far away, once upon a time. Perhaps it would be best if you imagined it as your own fancy bids, assuming it will rise to the occasion, for certainly I cannot suit you all. For instance, how about technology? I think that there would be no cars or helicopters in and above the streets; this follows from the fact that the people of Omelas are happy people. Happiness is based on a just discrimination of what is necessary, what is neither necessary nor destructive, and what is destructive. In the middle category, however—that of the unnecessary but undestructive, that of comfort, luxury, exuberance, etc.—they could perfectly well have central heating, subway trains, washing machines, and all kinds of marvelous devices not yet invented here, floating light-sources, fuelless power, a cure for the common cold. Or they could have none of that: it doesn't matter. As you like it. I incline to think that people from towns up and down the coast have been coming in to Omelas during the last days before the Festival on very fast little trains and double-decked trams and that the train station of Omelas is actually the handsomest building in town, though plainer than the magnificent Farmers' Market. But even granted trains, I fear that Omelas so far strikes some of you as goody-goody. Smiles, bells, parades, horses, bleh. If so, please add an orgy. If an orgy would help, don't hesitate. Let us not, however, have temples from which issue beautiful nude priests and priestesses already half in ecstasy and ready to copulate with any man or woman, lover or stranger, who desires union with the deep godhead of the blood, although that was my first idea. But really it would be better not to have any temples in Omelas—at least, not manned temples. Religion yes, clergy no. Surely the beautiful nudes can just wander about, offering themselves like divine souffles to the hunger of the needy and the rapture of the flesh. Let them join the processions. Let tambourines be struck above the copulations, and the glory of desire be proclaimed upon the gongs, and (a not unimportant point) let the offspring of these delightful rituals be beloved and looked after by all. One thing I know there is none of in Omelas is guilt. But what else should there be? I thought at first there were no drugs, but that is puritanical. For those who like it, the faint insistent sweetness of *drooz* may perfume the ways of the city, *drooz*, which first brings a great lightness and brilliance to the mind and limbs, and then after some hours a dreamy languor, and wonderful visions at last of the very arcane and inmost secrets of the Universe, as well as exciting the pleasure of sex beyond all belief; and it is not habit-forming. For more modest tastes I think there ought to be beer. What else, what else belongs in the joyous city? The sense of victory, surely, the celebration of courage. But as we did without clergy, let us do without soldiers. The joy built upon successful slaughter is not the right kind of joy; it will not do; it is fearful and it is trivial. A boundless and generous contentment, a magnanimous triumph felt not against some outer enemy but in communion with the finest and fairest in the souls of all men everywhere and the splendor of the world's summer: this is what swells the hearts of the people of Omelas, and the victory they celebrate is that of life. I really don't think many of them need to take *drooz*.

Most of the processions have reached the Green Fields by now. A marvelous smell of cooking goes forth from the red and blue tents of the provisioners. The faces of small children are amiably sticky; in the benign grey beard of a man a couple of crumbs of rich pastry are entangled. The youths and girls have mounted their horses and are beginning to group around the starting line of the course. An old woman, small, fat, and laughing, is passing out flowers from a basket, and tall young men wear her flowers in their shining hair. A child of nine or ten sits at the edge of the crowd, alone, playing on a wooden flute. People pause to listen, and they smile, but they do not speak to him, for he never ceases playing and never sees them, his dark eyes wholly rapt in the sweet, thin magic of the tune.

He finishes, and slowly lowers his hands holding the wooden flute.

As if that little private silence were the signal, all at once a trumpet sounds from the pavilion near the starting line: imperious, melancholy, piercing. The horses rear on their slender legs, and some of them neigh in answer. Sober-faced, the young riders stroke the horses' necks and soothe them, whispering, "Quiet, quiet, there my beauty, my hope. . . ." They begin to form in rank along the starting line. The crowds along the racecourse are like a field of grass and flowers in the wind. The Festival of Summer has begun.

Do you believe? Do you accept the festival, the city, the joy? No? Then let me describe one more thing.

In a basement under one of the beautiful public buildings of Omelas, or perhaps in the cellar of one of its spacious private homes, there is a room. It has one locked door, and no window. A little light seeps in dustily between cracks in the boards, secondhand from a cobwebbed window somewhere across the cellar. In one corner of the little room a couple of mops, with stiff, clotted, foul-smelling heads, stand near a rusty bucket. The floor is dirt, a little damp to the touch, as cellar dirt usually is. The room is about three paces long and two wide: a mere broom closet or disused tool room. In the room a child is sitting. It could be a boy or a girl. It looks about six, but actually is nearly ten. It is feeble-minded. Perhaps it was born defective, or perhaps it has become imbecile through fear, malnutrition, and neglect. It picks its nose and occasionally fumbles vaguely with its toes or genitals, as it sits hunched in the corner farthest from the bucket and the two mops. It is afraid of the mops. It finds them horrible. It shuts its eyes, but it knows the mops are still standing there; and the door is locked; and nobody will come. The door is always locked; and nobody ever comes, except that sometimes—the child has no understanding of time or interval—sometimes the door rattles terribly and opens, and a person, or several people, are there. One of them may come in and kick the child to make it stand up. The others never come close, but peer in at it with frightened, disgusted eyes. The food bowl and the water jug are hastily filled, the door is locked, the eyes disappear. The people at the door never say anything, but the child, who has not always lived in the tool room, and can remember sunlight and its mother's voice, sometimes speaks. "I will be good," it says. "Please let me out. I will be good!" They never answer. The child used to scream for help at night, and cry a good deal, but now it only makes a kind of whining, "eh-haa, eh-haa," and it speaks less and less often. It is so thin there are no calves to its legs; its belly protrudes; it lives on a half-bowl of corn meal and grease a day. It is naked. Its buttocks and thighs are a mass of festered sores, as it sits in its own excrement continually.

They all know it is there, all the people of Omelas. Some of them have come to see it, others are content merely to know it is there. They all know that it has to be there. Some of them understand why, and some do not, but they all understand that their happiness, the beauty of their city, the tenderness of their friendships, the health of their children, the wisdom of their scholars, the skill of their makers, even the abundance of their harvest and the kindly weathers of their skies, depend wholly on this child's abominable misery.

This is usually explained when they are between eight and twelve, whenever they seem capable of understanding; and most of those who come to see the child are young people, though often enough an adult comes, or comes back, to see the child. No matter how well the matter has been explained to them, these young spectators are always shocked and sickened at the sight. They feel disgust, which they had thought themselves superior to. They feel anger, outrage, impotence, despite all the explanations. They would like to do something for the child. But there is nothing they can do. If the child were brought up into the sunlight out of that vile place, if it were cleaned and fed and comforted, that would be a good thing, indeed; but if it were done, in that day and hour all the prosperity and beauty and delight of Omelas would wither and be destroyed. Those are the terms. To exchange all the goodness and grace of every life in Omelas for that single, small improvement: to throw away the happiness of thousands for the chance of the happiness of one: that would be to let guilt within the walls indeed.

The terms are strict and absolute; there may not even be a kind word spoken to the child.

Often the young people go home in tears, or in a tearless rage, when they have seen the child and faced this terrible paradox. They may brood over it for weeks or years. But as time goes on they begin to realize that even if the child could be released, it would not get much good of its freedom: a little vague pleasure of warmth and food, no doubt, but little more. It is too degraded and imbecile to know any real joy. It has been afraid too long ever to be free of fear. Its habits are too uncouth for it to respond to humane treatment. Indeed, after so long it would probably be wretched without walls about it to protect it, and darkness for its eyes, and its own excrement to sit in. Their tears at the bitter injustice dry when they begin to perceive the terrible justice of reality and to accept it. Yet it is their tears and anger, the trying of their generosity and the acceptance of their helplessness, which are perhaps the true source of the splendor of their lives. Theirs is no vapid, irresponsible happiness. They know that they, like the child, are not free. They know compassion. It is the existence of the child, and their knowledge of its existence, that makes possible the nobility of their architecture, the poignancy of their music, the profundity of their science. It is because of the child that they are so gentle with children. They know that if the wretched one were not there snivelling in the dark, the other one, the flute-player, could make no joyful music as the young riders line up in their beauty for the race in the sunlight of the first morning of summer.

Now do you believe in them? Are they not more credible? But there is one more thing to tell, and this is quite incredible.

At times one of the adolescent girls or boys who go to see the child does not go home to weep or rage, does not, in fact, go home at all. Sometimes also a man or woman much older falls silent for a day or two, and then leaves home. These people go out into the street, and walk down the street alone. They keep walking, and walk straight out of the city of Omelas, through the beautiful gates. They keep walking across the farmlands of Omelas. Each one goes alone, youth or girl, man or woman. Night falls; the traveler must pass down village streets, between the houses with yellow-lit windows, and on out into the darkness of the fields. Each alone, they go west or north, toward the mountains. They go on. They leave Omelas, they walk ahead into the darkness, and they do not come back. The place they go towards is a place even less imaginable to most of us than the city of happiness. I cannot describe it at all. It is possible that it does not exist. But they seem to know where they are going, the ones who walk away from Omelas.

THE PRINCIPLE OF UTILITY

by Jeremy Bentham

> Jeremy Bentham (1748-1832) is the father of modern Utilitarianism. He was one of the leading political philosophers of his time, and his book *The Principles of Morals and Legislation* is a classic of moral and political philosophy
>
> According to Bentham's "principle of utility," actions are right when they increase happiness and diminish misery, wrong when they have the opposite effect. By "utility" he means the property of producing pleasure or happiness in conscious beings. Thus we should always do those acts that tend to increase overall happiness. Bentham is known as a "hedonistic utilitarian": pleasure is to be pursued, pain to be avoided. A legislator, for example, should calculate the pleasure/pain ratio of each prospective law. Bentham proposes that we evaluate pleasures according to their intensity, duration, certainty, propinquity (nearness), fecundity (tendency to lead to other pleasures), purity (tendency *not* to be followed by pain), and, finally, extent (the number of persons to whom the pleasure extends). Bentham concedes that he cannot *prove* the truth of the principle of utility; but he claims that most of us implicitly accept it and act on it every day. And he suspects that any alternative principle will be "despotical, and hostile to all the rest of the human race."

Of the Principle of Utility

Nature has placed mankind under the governance of two sovereign masters, *pain* and *pleasure*. It is for them alone to point out what we ought to do, as well as to determine what we shall do. On the one hand the standard of right and wrong, on the other the chain of causes and effects, are fastened to their throne. They govern us in all we do, in all we say, in all we think: every effort we can make to throw off our subjection, will serve but to demonstrate and confirm it. In words a man may pretend to abjure their empire: but in reality he will remain subject to it all the while. The *principle of utility* recognises this subjection, and assumes it for the foundation of that system, the object of which is to rear the fabric of felicity by the hands of reason and of law. Systems which attempt to question it, deal in sounds instead of sense, in caprice instead of reason, in darkness instead of light.

But enough of metaphor and declamation: it is not by such means that moral science is to be improved.

The principle of utility is the foundation of the present work: it will be proper therefore at the outset to give an explicit and determinate account of what is meant by it. By the principle of utility is meant that principle which approves or disapproves of every action whatsoever, according to the tendency which it appears to have to augment or diminish the happiness of the party whose interest is in question: or, what is the same thing in other words, to promote or to oppose that happiness. I say of every action whatsoever; and therefore not only of every action of a private individual, but of every measure of government.

By utility is meant that property in any object, whereby it tends to produce benefit, advantage, pleasure, good, or happiness, (all this in the present case comes to the same thing) or (what comes again to the same thing) to prevent the happening of mischief, pain, evil, or unhappiness to the party whose interest is considered: if that party be the community in general, then the happiness of the community: if a particular individual, then the happiness of that individual.

The interest of the community is one of the most general expressions that can occur in the phraseology of morals: no wonder that the meaning of it is often lost. When it has a meaning, it is this. The community is a fictitious *body*, composed of the individual persons who are considered as constituting as it were its *members*. The interest of the community then is, what?—the sum of the interests of the several members who compose it.

It is in vain to talk of the interests of the community, without understanding what is the interest of the individual. A thing is said to promote the interest, or to be *for* the interest, of an individual, when it tends to add to the sum total of his pleasures: or, what comes to the same thing, to diminish the sum total of his pains.

An action then may be said to be conformable to the principle of utility, or, for shortness sake, to utility (meaning with respect to the community at large), when the tendency it has to augment the happiness of the community is greater than any it has to diminish it.

A measure of government (which is but a particular kind of action, performed by a particular person or persons) may be said to be conformable to or dictated by the principle of utility, when in like manner the tendency which it has to augment the happiness of the community is greater than any which it has to diminish it.

When an action, or in particular a measure of government, is supposed by a man to be conformable to the principle of utility, it may be convenient, for the purposes of discourse, to imagine a kind of law or dictate, called a law or dictate of utility: and to speak of the action in question, as being conformable to such law or dictate.

A man may be said to be a partisan of the principle of utility, when the approbation or disapprobation he annexes to any action, or to any measure, is determined by and proportioned to the tendency which he conceives it to have to augment or to diminish the happiness of the community: or in other words, to its conformity or unconformity to the laws or dictates of utility.

Of an action that is conformable to the principle of utility one may always say either that it is one that ought to be done, or at least that it is not one that ought not to be done. One may say also, that it is right it should be done; at least that it is not wrong it should be done: that it is a right action; at least that it is not a wrong action. When thus interpreted, the words *ought*, and *right* and *wrong*, and others of that stamp, have a meaning: when otherwise, they have none.

Has the rectitude of this principle been ever formally contested? It should seem that it had, by those who have not known what they have been meaning. Is it susceptible of any direct proof? it should seem not: for that which is used to prove every thing else, cannot itself be proved: a chain of proofs must have their commencement somewhere. To give such proof is as impossible as it is needless.

Not that there is or ever has been that human creature breathing, however stupid or perverse, who has not on many, perhaps on most occasions of his life, deferred to it. By the natural constitution of the human frame, on most occasions of their lives men in general embrace this principle, without thinking of it: if not for the ordering of their own actions, yet for the trying of their own actions, as well as of those of other men. There have been, at the same time, not many, perhaps, even of the most intelligent, who have been disposed to embrace it purely and without reserve. There are even few who have not taken some occasion or other to quarrel with it, either on account of their not understanding always how to apply it, or on account of some prejudice or other which they were afraid to examine into, or could not bear to part with. For such is the stuff that man is made of: in principle and in practice, in a right track and in a wrong one, the rarest of all human qualities is consistency.

When a man attempts to combat the principle of utility, it is with reasons drawn, without his being aware of it, from that very principle itself. His arguments, if they prove any thing, prove not that the principle is *wrong*, but that, according to the applications he supposes to be made of it, it is *misapplied*. Is it possible for a man to move the earth? Yes; but he must first find out another earth to stand upon.

To disprove the propriety of it by arguments is impossible; but, from the causes that have been mentioned, or from some confused or partial view of it, a man may happen to be disposed not to relish it. Where this is the case, if he thinks the settling of his opinions on such a subject worth the trouble, let him take the following steps, and at length, perhaps, he may come to reconcile himself to it.

Let him settle with himself, whether he would wish to discard this principle altogether; if so, let him consider what it is that all his reasonings (in matters of politics especially) can amount to?

If he would, let him settle with himself, whether he would judge and act without any principle, or whether there is any other he would judge and act by?

If there be, let him examine and satisfy himself whether the principle he thinks he has found is really any separate intelligible principle; or whether it be not a mere principle in words, a kind of phrase, which at bottom expresses neither more nor less than the mere averment of his own unfounded sentiments; that is, what in another person he might be apt to call caprice?

If he is inclined to think that his own approbation or disapprobation, annexed to the idea of an act, without any regard to its consequences, is a sufficient foundation for him to judge and act upon, let him ask himself whether his sentiment is to be a standard of right and wrong, with respect to every other man, or whether every man's sentiment has the same privilege of being a standard to itself?

In the first case, let him ask himself whether his principle is not despotical, and hostile to all the rest of human race?

In the second case, whether it is not anarchial, and whether at this rate there are not as many different standards of right and wrong as there are men? and whether even to the same man, the same thing, which is right to-day, may not (without the least change in its nature) be wrong to-morrow? and whether the same thing is not right and wrong in the same place at the same time? and in either case, whether all argument is not at an end? and whether, when two men have said, "I like this," and "I don't like it," they can (upon such a principle) have any thing more to say?

If he should have said to himself, No: for that the sentiment which he proposes as a standard must be grounded on reflection, let him say on what particulars the reflection is to turn? if on particulars having relation to the utility of the act, then let him say whether this is not deserting his own principle and borrowing assistance from that very one in opposition to which he sets it up: or if not on those particulars, on what other particulars?

If he should be for compounding the matter, and adopting his own principle in part, and the principle of utility in part, let him say how far he will adopt it?

When he has settled with himself where he will stop, then let him ask himself how he justifies to himself the adopting it so far? and why he will not adopt it any farther?

Admitting any other principle than the principle of utility to be a right principle, a principle that it is right for a man to pursue; admitting (what is not true) that the word *right* can have a meaning without reference to utility, let him say whether there is any such thing as a *motive* that a man can have to pursue the dictates of it: if there is, let him say what that motive is, and how it is to be distinguished from those which enforce the dictates of utility: if not, then lastly let him say what it is this other principle can be good for?

Pleasures then, and the avoidance of pains, are the *ends* which the legislator has in view: it behoves him therefore to understand their *value*. Pleasures and pains are the *instruments* he has to work with: it behoves him therefore to understand their force, which is again, in other words, their value.

To a person considered by *himself*, the value of a pleasure or pain considered by *itself*, will be greater or less, according to the four following circumstances:

1. Its *intensity*.
2. Its *duration*.
3. Its *certainty* or *uncertainty*.
4. Its *propinquity* or *remoteness*.

These are the circumstances which are to be considered in estimating a pleasure or a pain considered each of them by itself. But when the value of any pleasure or pain is considered for the purpose of estimating the tendency of any *act* by which it is produced, there are two other circumstances to be taken into the account; these are,

5. Its *fecundity*, or the chance it has of being followed by sensations of the *same* kind: that is, pleasures, if it be a pleasure: pains, if it be a pain.
6. Its *purity*, or the chance it has of *not* being followed by sensations of the *opposite* kind: that is, pains, if it be a pleasure: pleasures, if it be a pain.

These two last, however, are in strictness scarcely to be deemed properties of the pleasure or the pain itself; they are not, therefore, in strictness to be taken into the account of the value of that pleasure or that pain. They are in strictness to be deemed properties only of the act, or other event, by which such pleasure or pain has been produced; and accordingly are only to be taken into the account of the tendency of such act or such event.

To a *number* of persons, with reference to each of whom the value of a pleasure or a pain is considered, it will be greater or less, according to seven circumstances: to wit, the six preceding ones; *viz.*

1. Its *intensity*.
2. Its *duration*.
3. Its *certainty* or *uncertainty*.
4. Its *propinquity* or *remoteness*.
5. Its *fecundity*.
6. Its *purity*.

And one other; to wit:

7. Its *extent*; that is, the number of persons to whom it *extends*; or (in other words) who are affected by it.

To take an exact account then of the general tendency of any act, by which the interests of a community are affected, proceed as follows. Begin with any one person of those whose interest seem most immediately to be affected by it: and take an account,

1. Of the value of each distinguishable *pleasure* which appears to be produced by it in the *first* instance.
2. Of the value of each *pain* which appears to be produced by it in the *first* instance.
3. Of the value of each pleasure which appears to be produced by it after the first. This constitutes the *fecundity* of the first *pleasure* and the *impurity* of the first *pain*.
4. Of the value of each *pain* which appears to be produced by it *after* the first. This constitutes the *fecundity* of the first *pain*, and the *impurity* of the first pleasure.
5. Sum up all the values of all the *pleasures* on the one side, and those of all the pains on the other. The balance, if it be on the side of pleasure, will give the *good* tendency of the act upon the whole, with respect to the interests of that *individual* person; if on the side of pain, the *bad* tendency of it upon the whole.
6. Take an account of the *number* of persons whose interests appear to be concerned; and repeat the above process with respect to each. *Sum* up the numbers expressive of the degrees of *good* tendency, which the act has, with respect to each individual, in regard to whom the tendency of

it is *good* upon the whole: do this again with respect to each individual, in regard to whom the tendency of it is *bad* upon the whole. Take the *balance*; which, if on the side of *pleasure*, will give the general *good tendency* of the act, with respect to the total number or community of individuals concerned; if on the side of pain, the general *evil tendency*, with respect to the same community.

It is not to be expected that this process should be strictly pursued previously to every moral judgment, or to every legislative or judicial operation. It may, however, be always kept in view: and as near as the process actually pursued on these occasions approaches to it, so near will such process approach to the character of an exact one.

The same process is alike applicable to pleasure and pain, in whatever shape they appear: and by whatever denomination they are distinguished: to pleasure, whether it be called *good* (which is properly the cause or instrument of pleasure) or *profit* (which is distant pleasure, or the cause or instrument of distant pleasure), or *convenience*, or *advantage, benefit, emolument, happiness*, and so forth; to pain, whether it be called *evil* (which corresponds to *good*), or *mischief* or *inconvenience*, or *disadvantage*, or *loss*, or *unhappiness*, and so forth.

Nor is this a novel and unwarranted, any more than it is a useless theory. In all this there is nothing but what the practice of mankind, whatsoever they have a clear view of their own interest, is perfectly conformable to. An article of property, an estate in land, for instance, is valuable, on what account? On account of the pleasures of all kinds which it enables a man to produce, and what comes to the same thing the pains of all kinds which it enables him to avert. But the value of such an article of property is universally understood to rise or fall according to the length or shortness of the time which a man has in it: the certainty or uncertainty of its coming into possession: and the nearness or remoteness of the time at which, if at all, it is to come into possession. As to the *intensity* of the pleasures which a man may derive from it, this is never thought of, because it depends upon the use which each particular person may come to make of it; which cannot be estimated till the particular pleasures he may come to derive from it, or the particular pains he may come to exclude by means of it, are brought to view. For the same reason, neither does he think of the *fecundity* or *purity* of those pleasures.

A CRITIQUE OF UTILITARIANISM

by Bernard Williams

Bernard Williams (b. 1929) is Deutsch Professor of Philosophy at the University of California, Berkeley. His books include *Shame and Necessity* (1993), and *Making Sense of Humanity* (1995).

Bernard Williams's critique of consequentialism takes off from Smart's version of act-utilitarianism. If the consequences are decisive in determining the right/wrongness of an action, Williams says, then it will often be right to do what is *prima facie* wrong. He presents two cases in which, on utilitarian grounds, one would be forced to act in a way that violated one's intuitive moral feelings. In each case, "if the agent does not do a certain disagreeable thing, someone else will," and with much worse consequences. The utilitarian holds that the agent must then overcome his squeamishness and do the lesser evil. In one of Williams's examples, a soldier, Pedro, will shoot twenty innocent people unless a tourist, Jim, shoots one of them. If Jim agrees, the remaining nineteen will go free. So far as the utilitarian is concerned, it is quite obvious that for Jim to refrain from the murder is worse than letting Pedro kill nineteen more people. This position, Williams argues, shows that utilitarianism has a confused notion of responsibility and a totally inadequate notion of personal integrity. Williams argues that our deepest convictions, projects, and attitudes "do not compute" in the utilitarian calculus.

. . . [L]et us look . . . at two examples to see what utilitarianism might say about them, what we might say about utilitarianism and, most importantly of all, what would be implied by certain ways of thinking about the situations . . . .

(1) George, who has just taken his Ph.D. in chemistry, finds it extremely difficult to get a job. He is not very robust in health, which cuts down the number of jobs he might be able to do satisfactorily. His wife has to go out to work to keep them, which itself causes a great deal of strain, since they have small children and there are severe problems about looking after them. The results of all this, especially on the children, are damaging. An older chemist, who knows about this situation, says that he can get George a decently paid job in a certain laboratory, which pursues research into chemical and biological warfare. George says that he cannot accept this, since he is opposed to chemical and biological warfare. The older man replies that he is not too keen on it himself, come to that, but after all George's refusal is not going to make the job or the laboratory go away; what is more, he happens to know that if George refuses the job, it will certainly go to a contemporary of George's who is not inhibited by any such scruples and is likely if appointed to push along the research with greater zeal than George would. Indeed, it is not merely concern for George and his family, but (to speak frankly and in confidence) some alarm about this other man's excess of zeal, which has led the older man to offer to use his influence to get George the job. . . . George's wife, to whom he is deeply attached, has views (the details of which need not concern us) from which it follows that at least there is nothing particularly wrong with research into CBW. What should he do?

(2) Jim finds himself in the central square of a small South American town. Tied up against the wall are a row of twenty Indians, most terrified, a few defiant, in front of them several armed men in uniform. A heavy man in a sweat-stained khaki shirt turns out to be the captain in charge and, after a good deal of questioning of Jim which establishes that he got there by accident while on a botanical expedition, explains that the Indians are a random group of the inhabitants who, after recent acts of protest against the government, are just about to be killed to remind other possible protectors of the advantages of not protesting. However, since Jim is an honoured visitor from another land, the captain is happy to offer him a guest's privilege of killing one of the Indians himself. If Jim accepts, then as a special mark of the occasion, the other Indians will be let off. Of course, if Jim refuses, then there is no special occasion, and Pedro here will do what he was about to do when Jim arrived, and kill them all. Jim, with some desperate recollection of schoolboy fiction, wonders whether if he got hold of a gun, he could hold the captain, Pedro and the rest of the soldiers to threat, but it is quite clear from the set-up that nothing of that kind is going to work: any attempt at that sort of thing will mean that all the Indians will be killed, and himself. The men against the wall, and the other villagers, understand the situation, and are obviously begging him to accept. What should he do?

To these dilemmas, it seems to me that utilitarianism replies, in the first case, that George should accept the job, and in the second, that Jim should kill the Indian. Not only does utilitarianism give these answers but, if the situations are essentially as described and there are no further special factors, it regards them, it seems to me, as *obviously* the right answers. But many of us would certainly wonder whether, in (1), that could possibly be the right answer at all; and in the case of (2), even one who came to think that perhaps that was the answer, might well wonder whether it was obviously the answer. Nor is it just a question of the rightness or obviousness of these answers. It is also a question of what sort of considerations come into finding the answer. A feature of utilitarianism is that it cuts out a kind of consideration which for some others makes a difference to what they feel about such cases: a consideration involving the idea, as we might first and very simply put it, that each of us is specially responsible for what *he* does, rather than for what other people do. This is an idea closely connected with the value of integrity. It is often suspected that utilitarianism, at least in its direct forms makes integrity as a value more or less unintelligible. I shall try to show that this suspicion is correct . . . .

. . . I want to consider now two types of effect that are often invoked by utilitarians, and which might be invoked in connexion with these imaginary cases. The attitude or tone involved in invoking these effects may sometimes seem peculiar; but that sort of peculiarity soon becomes familiar in utilitarian discussions, and indeed it can be something of an achievement to retain a sense of it.

First, there is the psychological effect on the agent. Our descriptions of these situations have not so far taken account of how George or Jim will be after they have taken the one course or the other; and it might be said that if they take the course which seemed at first the utilitarian one, the effects on them will be in fact bad enough and extensive enough to cancel out the initial utilitarian advantages of that course. Now there is one version of this effect in which, for a utilitarian, some confusion must be involved, namely that in which the agent feels bad, his subsequent conduct and relations are crippled and so on, *because he thinks that he has done the wrong thing*—for if the balance of outcomes was as it appeared to be *before* invoking this effect, then he has not (from the utilitarian point of view) done the wrong thing. So that version of the effect, for a rational and utilitarian agent, could not possibly make any difference to the assessment of right and wrong. However, perhaps he is not a thoroughly rational agent, and is disposed to have bad feelings, whichever he decided to do. Now such feelings, which are from a strictly utilitarian point of view irrational—nothing, a utilitarian can point out, is advanced by having them—cannot, consistently, have any great weight in a utilitarian calculation. I shall consider in a moment an argument to suggest that they should have no weight at all in it. But short of that, the utilitarian could reasonably say that such feelings should not be encouraged, even if we accept their existence, and that to give them a lot of weight is to encourage them. Or, at the very best, even if they are straightforwardly and without any discount to be put into the calculation, their weight must be small: they are after all (and at best) one man's feelings.

That consideration might seem to have particular force in Jim's case. In George's case, his feelings represent a larger proportion of what is to be weighed, and are more commensurate in character with other items in the calculation. In Jim's case, however, his feelings might seem to be of very little weight compared with other things that are at stake. There is a powerful and recognizable appeal that can be made on this point: as that a refusal by Jim to do what he has been invited to do would be a kind of self-indulgent squeamishness. That is an appeal which can be made by other than utilitarians—indeed, there are some uses of it which cannot be consistently made by utilitarians, as when it essentially involves the idea that there is something dishonourable about such self-indulgence. But in some versions it is a familiar, and it must be said a powerful, weapon of utilitarianism. One must be clear, though, about what it can and cannot accomplish. The most it can do, so far as I can see, is to invite one to consider how seriously, and for what reasons, one feels that what one is invited to do is (in these circumstances) wrong, and in particular, to consider that question from the utilitarian point of view. When the agent is not seeing the situation from a utilitarian point of view, the appeal cannot force him to do so; and if he does come round to seeing it from a utilitarian point of view, there is virtually nothing left for the appeal to do. If he does not see it from a utilitarian point of view, he will not see his resistance to the invitation, and the unpleasant feelings he associates with accepting it, *just* as disagreeable experiences of his; they figure rather as emotional expressions of a thought that to accept would be wrong. He may be asked, as by the appeal, to consider whether he is right, and indeed whether he is fully serious, in thinking that. But the assertion of the appeal, that he is being self-indulgently squeamish, will not itself answer that question, or even help to answer it, since it essentially tells him to regard his feelings just as unpleasant experiences of his, and he cannot, by doing that, answer the question they pose when they are precisely not so regarded, but are regarded as indications of what he thinks is right and wrong. If he does come round fully to the utilitarian point of view then of course he will regard these feelings just as unpleasant experiences of his. And once Jim—at least—has come to see them in that light, there is nothing left for the appeal to do, since of *course* his feelings, so regarded, are of virtually no weight at all in relation to the other things at stake. The "squeamishness" appeal is not an argument which adds in a hitherto neglected consideration. Rather, it is an invitation to consider the situation, and one's own feelings, from a utilitarian point of view.

The reason why the squeamishness appeal can be very unsettling, and one can be unnerved by the suggestion of self-indulgence in going against utilitarian considerations, is not that we are utilitarians who are uncertain what utilitarian value to attach to our moral feelings, but that we are partially at least not utilitarians, and cannot regard our moral feelings merely as objects of utilitarian value. Because our moral relation to the world is partly given by such feelings, and by a sense of what we can or cannot "live with," to come to regard those feelings from a purely utilitarian point of view, that is to say, as happenings outside one's moral self, is to lose a sense of one's moral identity; to lose, in the most literal way, one's integrity. . . .

Integrity

The [two] situations have in common that if the agent does not do a certain disagreeable thing, someone else will, and in Jim's situation at least the result, the state of affairs after the other man has acted, if he does, will be worse than after Jim has acted, if Jim does. The same, on a smaller scale, is true of George's case. I have already suggested that it is inherent in consequentialism that it offers a strong doctrine of negative responsibility: if I know that if I do X, O_1 will eventuate, and if I refrain from doing X, O_2 will, and that O_2 is worse than O_1, then I am responsible for O_2 if I refrain voluntarily from doing X. "You could have prevented it," as will be said, and truly, to Jim, if he refuses, by the relatives of the other Indians . . . . [But] what occurs if Jim refrains from action is not solely twenty Indians dead, but *Pedro's killing twenty Indians* . . . . That may be enough for us to speak, in some sense, of Jim's responsibility for that outcome, if it occurs; but it is certainly not enough, it is worth noticing, for us to speak of Jim's *making those things happen*. For granted this way of their coming about, he could have made them happen only by making Pedro shoot, and there is no acceptable sense in which his refusal makes Pedro shoot. If the captain had said on Jim's refusal, "you leave me with no alternative," he would have been lying, like most who use that phrase. While the deaths, and the killing, may be the outcome of Jim's refusal, it is misleading to think, in such a case, of Jim having an *effect* on the world through the medium (as it happens) of Pedro's acts; for this is to leave Pedro out of the picture in his essential role of one who has intentions and projects, projects for realizing which Jim's refusal would leave an opportunity. Instead of thinking in terms of supposed effects of Jim's projects on Pedro, it is more revealing to think in terms of the effects of Pedro's projects on Jim's decision. . . .

Utilitarianism would do well . . . to acknowledge the evident fact that among the things that make people happy is not only making other people happy, but being taken up or involved in any of a vast range of projects, or—if we waive the evangelical and moralizing associations of the word—commitments. One can be committed to such things as a person, a cause, an institution, a career, one's own genius, or the pursuit of danger.

Now none of these is itself the *pursuit of happiness*: by an exceedingly ancient platitude, it is not at all clear that there could be anything which was just that, or at least anything that had the slightest chance of being successful. Happiness, rather, requires being involved in, or at least content with, something else. It is not impossible for utilitarianism to accept that point: it does not have to be saddled with a naïve and absurd philosophy of mind about the relation between desire and happiness. What it does have to say is that if such commitments are worth while, then pursuing the projects that flow from them, and realizing some of those projects, will make the person for whom they are worth while, happy. It may be that to claim that is still wrong: it may well be that a commitment can make sense to a man (can make sense of his life) without his supposing that it will make him *happy*. But that is not the present point; let us grant to utilitarianism that all worthwhile human projects must conduce, one way or another, to happiness. The point is that even if that is true, it does not follow, nor could it possibly be true, that those projects are themselves projects of pursuing happiness. One has to believe in, or at least want, or quite minimally, be content with, other things, for there to be anywhere that happiness can come from.

Utilitarianism, then, should be willing to agree that its general aim of maximizing happiness does not imply that what everyone is doing is just pursuing happiness. On the contrary, people have to be pursuing other things. What those other things may be, utilitarianism, sticking to its professed empirical stance, should be prepared just to find out. No doubt some possible projects it will want to discourage, on the grounds that their being pursued involves a negative balance of happiness to others: though even there, the unblinking accountant's eye of the strict utilitarian will have something to put in the positive column, the satisfactions of the destructive agent. Beyond that, there will be a vast variety of generally beneficent or at least harmless projects; and some no doubt, will take the form not just of tastes or fancies, but of what I have called "commitments." It may even be that the utilitarian researcher will find that many of those with commitments, who have really identified themselves with objects outside themselves, who are thoroughly involved with other persons, or institutions, or activities or causes, are actually happier than those whose projects and wants are not like that. If so, that is an important piece of utilitarian empirical lore.

When I say "happier" here, I have in mind the sort of consideration which any utilitarian would be committed to accepting: as for instance that such people are less likely to have a break-down or commit suicide. Of course that is not all that is actually involved, but the point in this argument is to use to the maximum degree utilitarian notions, in order to locate a breaking point in utilitarian thought. In appealing to this strictly utilitarian notion, I am being more consistent with utilitarianism than Smart is. In his struggles with the problem of the brain-electrode man, Smart . . . commends the idea that "happy" is a partly evaluative term, in the sense that we call "happiness" those kinds of satisfaction which, as things are, we approve of. But *by what standard* is this surplus element of approval supposed, from a utilitarian point of view, to be allocated? There is no source for it, on a strictly utilitarian view, except further degrees of satisfaction, but there are none of those available, or the problem would not arise. Nor does it help to appeal to the fact that we dislike in prospect things which we like when we get there, for from a utilitarian point of view it would seem that the original dislike was merely irrational or based on an error. Smart's argument at this point seems to be embarrassed by a well-known utilitarian uneasiness, which comes from a feeling that it is not respectable to ignore the "deep," while not having anywhere left in human life to locate it.

On a utilitarian view . . . [t]he determination to an indefinite degree of my decisions by other people's projects is just another aspect of my unlimited responsibility to act for the best in a causal framework formed to a considerable extent by their projects.

The decision so determined is, for utilitarianism, the right decision. But what if it conflicts with some project of mine? This, the utilitarian will say, has already been dealt with: the satisfaction to you of fulfilling your project, and any satisfaction to others of your so doing, have already been through the calculating device and have been found inadequate. Now in the case of many sorts of projects, that is a perfectly reasonable sort of answer. But in the case of projects of the sort I have called "commitments," those with which one is more deeply and extensively involved and identified, this cannot just by itself be an adequate answer, and there may be no adequate answer at all. For, to take the extreme sort of case, how can a man, as a utilitarian agent, come to regard as one satisfaction among others, and a dispensable one, a project or attitude round which he has built his life, just because someone else's projects have so structured the causal scene that that is how the utilitarian sum comes out?

The point here is not, as utilitarians may hasten to say, that if the project or attitude is that central to his life, then to abandon it will be very disagreeable to him and great loss of utility will be involved . . . . On the contrary, once he is prepared to look at it like that, the argument in any serious case is over anyway. The point is that he is identified with his actions as flowing from projects and attitudes which in some cases he takes seriously at the deepest level, as what his life is about (or, in some cases, this section of his life—seriousness is not necessarily the same as persistence). It is absurd to demand of such a man, when the sums come in from the utility network which the projects of others have in part determined, that he should just step aside from his own project and decision and acknowledge the decision which utilitarian calculation requires. It is to alienate him in a real sense from his actions and the source of his action in his own convictions. It is to make him into a channel between the input of everyone's projects, including his own, and an output of optimific decision; but this is to neglect the extent to which *his* actions and *his* decisions have to be seen as the actions and decisions which flow from the projects and attitudes with which he is most closely identified. It is thus, in the most literal sense, an attack on his integrity.

[T]he immediate point of all this is to draw one particular contrast with utilitarianism: that to reach a grounded decision . . . should not be regarded as a matter of just discontinuing one's reactions, impulses and deeply held projects in the face of the pattern of utilities, nor yet merely adding them in—but in the first instance of trying to understand them.

Of course, time and circumstances are unlikely to make a grounded decision, in Jim's case at least, possible. Very often, we just act, as a possibly confused result of the situation in which we are engaged. That, I suspect, is very often an exceedingly good thing.

ETHICS: THEORIES OF VIRTUE ETHICS

FROM CRUELTY TO GOODNESS

by Philip Hallie

Philip Hallie (b. 1922) was a professor of philosophy at Wesleyan University. His published works include *The Paradox of Cruelty* (1969) and *Lest Innocent Blood Be Shed* (1979).

Hallie considers institutionalized cruelty and finds that, besides physically assaulting its victims, it almost always assaults their dignity and self-respect. As an example of the opposite of institutionalized cruelty, Hallie cites the residents of the French village of Le Chambon who, at grave risk to their lives, saved 6,000 Jews from the Nazis. For him the contrary of being cruel is not merely ceasing to be cruel, nor is it fighting cruelty with violence and hatred (though this may be necessary). Rather, it is epitomized in the unambiguous and unpretentious goodness of the citizens of Le Chambon who followed the positive biblical injunctions "Defend the fatherless" and "Be your brother's keeper," as well as the negative injunctions "Thou shalt not murder or betray."

I am a student of ethics, of good and evil; but my approach to these two rather melodramatic terms is skeptical. I am in the tradition of the ancient Greek *skeptikoi*, whose name means "inquirers" or "investigators." And what we investigate is relationships among particular facts. What we put into doubt are the intricate webs of high-level abstractions that passed for philosophizing in the ancient world, and that still pass for philosophizing. My approach to good and evil emphasizes not abstract common nouns like "justice," but proper names and verbs. Names and verbs keep us close to the facts better than do our highfalutin common nouns. Names refer to particular people, and verbs connect subjects with predicates *in time,* while common nouns are above all this.

One of the words that is important to me is my own name. For me, philosophy is personal; it is closer to literature and history than it is to the exact sciences, closer to the passions, actions, and common sense of individual persons than to a dispassionate technical science. It has to do with the personal matter of wisdom. And so ethics for me is personal—my story, and not necessarily (though possibly) yours. It concerns particular people at particular times.

But ethics is more than such particulars. It involves abstractions, that is, rules, laws, ideals. When you look at the ethical magnates of history you see in their words and deeds two sorts of ethical rules: negative and positive. The negative rules are scattered throughout the Bible, but Moses brought down from Mount Sinai the main negative ethical rules of the West: Thou shalt not murder; thou shalt not betray. . . . The positive injunctions are similarly spread throughout the Bible. In the first chapter of the book of Isaiah we are told to ". . . defend the fatherless, plead for the widow." The negative ethic forbids certain actions; the positive ethic demands certain actions. To follow the negative ethic is to be decent, to have clean hands. But to follow the positive ethic, to be one's brother's keeper, is to be more than decent—it is to be active, even aggressive. If the negative ethic is one of decency, the positive one is the ethic of riskful, strenuous nobility.

In my early studies of particularized ethical terms, I found myself dwelling upon negative ethics, upon prohibitions. And among the most conspicuous prohibitions I found embodied in history was the prohibition against deliberate harmdoing, against cruelty. "Thou shalt not be cruel" had as much to do with the nightmare of history as did the prohibitions against murder and betrayal. In fact, many of the Ten Commandments—especially those against murder, adultery, stealing, and betrayal—were ways of prohibiting cruelty.

Early in my research it became clear that there are various approaches to cruelty, as the different commandments suggest. For instance, there is the way reflected in the origins of the word "cruel." The Latin *crudus* is related to still older words standing for bloodshed, or raw flesh. According to the etymology of the word, cruelty involves the spilling of blood.

But modern dictionaries give the word a different meaning. They define it as "disposed to giving pain." They emphasize awareness, not simply bloodshed. After all, they seem to say, you cannot be cruel to a dead body. There is no cruelty without consciousness.

And so I found myself studying the kinds of awareness associated with the hurting of human beings. It is certainly true that for millennia in history and literature people have been torturing each other not only with hard weapons but also with hard words.

Still, the word "pain" seemed to be a simplistic and superficial way of describing the many different sorts of cruelty. In Reska Weiss's *Journey Through Hell* (London, 1961) there is a brief passage of one of the deepest cruelties that Nazis perpetrated upon extermination camp inmates. On a march

> Urine and excrete poured down the prisoners' legs, and by nightfall the excrement, which had frozen to our limbs, gave off its stench.

And Weiss goes on to talk not in terms of "pain" or bloodshed, but in other terms:

> . . . We were really no longer human beings in the accepted sense. Not even animals, but putrefying corpses moving on two legs.

There is one factor that the idea of "pain" and the simpler idea of bloodshed do not touch: cruelty, not playful, quotidian teasing or ragging, but cruelty (what the anti-cruelty societies usually call "substantial cruelty") involves the maiming of a person's dignity, the crushing of a person's self-respect. Bloodshed, the idea of pain (which is usually something involving a localizable occurrence, localizable in a tooth, in a head, in short, in the body), these are superficial ideas of cruelty. A whip, bleeding flesh, these are what the journalists of cruelty emphasize, following the etymology and dictionary meaning of the word. But the depths of an understanding of cruelty lie in the depths of an understanding of human dignity and of how you can maim it without bloodshed, and often without localizable bodily pain.

In excremental assault, in the process of keeping camp inmates from wiping themselves or from going to the latrine, and in making them drink water from a toilet bowl full of excrete (and the excrete of the guards at that) localizable pain is nothing. Deep humiliation is everything. We human beings believe in hierarchies, whether we are skeptics or not about human value. There is a hierarchical gap between shit and me. We are even above using the word. We are "above" walking around besmirched with feces. Our dignity, whatever the origins of that dignity may be, does not permit it. In order to be able to want to live, in order to be able to walk erect, we must respect ourselves as beings "higher" than our feces. When we feel that we are not "higher" than dirt or filth, then our lives are maimed at the very center, in the very depths, not merely in some localizable portion of our bodies. And when our lives are so maimed we become things, slaves, instruments. From ancient times until this moment, and as long as there will be human beings on this planet, there are those who know this and will use it, just as the Roman slave owners and the Southern American slave owners knew it when—one time a year— they encouraged the slaves to drink all the alcohol they could drink so that they could get bestially drunk and then even more bestially sick afterwards, under the eyes of their generous owners. The self-hatred, the loss of self-respect that the Saturnalia created in ancient Rome, say, made it possible to continue using the slaves as things, since they themselves came to think of themselves as things, as subhuman tools of the owners and the overseers.

Institutionalized cruelty, I learned, is the subtlest kind of cruelty. In episodic cruelty the victim knows he is being hurt, and his victimizer knows it too. But in a persistent pattern of humiliation that endures for years in a community, both the victim and the victimizer find ways of obscuring the harm that is being done. Blacks come to think of themselves as inferior, even esthetically inferior (black is "dirty"); and Jews come to think of themselves as inferior, even esthetically (dark hair and aquiline noses are "ugly"), so that the way they are being treated is justified by their "actual" inferiority, by the inferiority they themselves feel.

A similar process happens in the minds of the victimizers in institutionalized cruelty. They feel that since they are superior, even esthetically ("to be blonde is to be beautiful"), they deserve to do what they wish, deserve to have these lower creatures under their control. The words of Heinrich Himmler, head of the Nazi SS, in Posen in the year 1943 in a speech to his SS subordinates in a closed session, show how institutionalized cruelty can obscure harmdoing:

> . . . the words come so easily. "The Jewish people will be exterminated," says every party member, "of course. It's in our program . . . extermination. We'll take care of it." And then they come, these nice 80 million Germans, and every one of them has his decent Jew. Sure the others are swine, but his one is a fine Jew . . . Most of you will know what it means to have seen 100 corpses together, or 500 to 1000. To have made one's way through that, and . . . to have remained a decent person throughout, that is what has made us hard. That is a page of glory in our history. . .

In this speech he was making a sharp distinction between the program of crushing the Jews and the personal sentiments of individual Germans. The program stretched over years; personal sentiments were momentary. He was pleading for the program, for institutionalized destruction.

But one of the most interesting parts of the speech occurs toward the end of it:

> . . . in sum, we can say that we fulfilled the heaviest of tasks [destroying the Jews] in love to our people. And we suffered no harm in our essence, in our soul, in our character . . . .

Commitment that overrides all sentimentality transforms cruelty and destruction into moral nobility, and commitment is the lifeblood of an institution.

Cruelty and the Power Relationships

But when I studied all these ways that we have used the word "cruelty," I was nagged by the feeling that I had not penetrated into its inner structure. I was classifying, sorting out symptoms; but symptoms are signals, and what were the symptoms signals *of*? I felt like a person who had been studying cancer by sorting out brief pains from persistent pains, pains in the belly from pains in the head. I was being superficial, and I was not asking the question, "What are the forces behind these kinds of cruelty?" I felt that there were such forces, but as yet I had not touched them.

Then one day I was reading in one of the great autobiographies of western civilization, Frederick Douglass's *Life and Times*. The passage I was reading was about Douglass's thoughts on the origins of slavery. He was asking himself: "How could these whites keep us enslaved?" And he suddenly realized:

> My faculties and powers of body and soul are not my own, but are the property of a fellow-mortal in no sense superior to me, except that he has the physical power to compel me to be owned and controlled by him. By the combined physical force of the community I am his slave—a slave for life.

 And then I saw that a disparity in power lay at the center of the dynamism of cruelty. If it was institutional cruelty it was in all likelihood a difference involving both verbal and physical power that kept the cruelty going. The power of the majority and the weakness of a minority were at the center of the institutional cruelty of slavery and of Nazi anti-Semitism. The whites not only outnumbered the blacks in America, but had economic and political ascendancy over them. But just as important as these "physical" powers was the power that words like "rigger" and "slave" gave the white majority. Their language sanctified if it did not create their power ascendancy over the blacks, and one of the most important projects of the slave-holders and their allies was that of seeing to it that the blacks themselves thought of themselves in just these powerless terms. They utilized the language to convince not only the whites but the blacks themselves that blacks were weak in mind, in will power, and in worth. These words were like the excremental assault in the killing camps of the Nazis: they diminished both the respect the victimizers might have for their victims and the respect the victims might have for themselves.

It occurred to me that if a power differential is crucial to the idea of cruelty, then when that power differential is maintained, cruelty will tend to be maintained, and when that power differential is eliminated, cruelty will tend to be eliminated. And this seemed to work. In all kinds of cruelty, violent and polite, episodic and institutional, when the victim arms himself with the appropriate strength, the cruelty diminishes or disappears. When Jews joined the Bush Warriors of France, the Maquis, and became powerful enough to strike at Vichy or the Nazis, they stopped being victims of French and Nazi cruelty. When Frederick Douglass learned to use the language with great skill and expressiveness, and when he learned to use his physical strength against his masters, the power differential between him and his masters diminished, and so did their cruelty to him. In his autobiography he wrote:

> A man without force is without the essential dignity of humanity. Human nature is so constituted that it cannot honor a helpless man, though it can pity him, and even this it cannot do long if signs of power do not arise.

When I looked back at my own childhood in Chicago, I remembered that the physical and mental cruelties that I suffered in the slums of the southwest side when I was about ten years old sharply diminished and finally disappeared when I learned how to defend myself physically and verbally. It is exactly this lesson that Douglass learned while growing up in the cruel institution of slavery.

Cruelty then, whatever else it is, is a kind of power relationship, an imbalance of power wherein the stronger party becomes the victimizer and the weaker becomes the victim. And since many general terms are most swiftly understood in relationship with their opposites (just as "heavy" can be understood most handily in relationship with what we mean by "light") the opposite of cruelty lay in a situation where there is no imbalance of power. The opposite of cruelty, I learned, was freedom from that unbalanced power relationship. Either the victim should get stronger and stand up to the victimizer, and thereby bring about a balance of their powers, or the victim should free himself from the whole relationship by flight.

In pursuing this line of thought, I came to believe that, again, dictionaries are misleading: many of them give "kindness" as the antonym for "cruelty." In studying slavery in America and the concentration camps of central Europe I found that kindness could be the ultimate cruelty, especially when it was given within that unbalanced power relationship. A kind overseer or a kind camp guard can exacerbate cruelty, can remind his victim that there are other relationships than the relationship of cruelty, and can make the victim deeply bitter, especially when he sees the self-satisfied smile of his victimizer. He is being cruelly treated when he is given a penny or a bun after having endured the crushing and grinding of his mental and bodily well-being. As Frederick Douglass put it:

> The kindness of the slave-master only gilded the chain. It detracted nothing from its weight or strength. The thought that men are for other and better uses than slavery throve best under the gentle treatment of a kind master.

No, I learned, the opposite of cruelty is not kindness. The opposite of the cruelty of the overseer in American slavery was not the kindness of that overseer for a moment or for a day. An episodic kindness is not the opposite of an institutionalized cruelty. The opposite of institutionalized cruelty is freedom from the cruel relationship.

It is important to see how perspectival the whole meaning of cruelty is. From the perspective of the SS guard or the southern overseer, a bit of bread, a smile is indeed a diminution of cruelty. But in the relationship of cruelty, the point of view of the victimizer is of only minor importance; it is the point of view of the victim that is authoritative. The victim feels the suffering in his own mind and body, whereas the victimizer, like Himmler's "hard" and "decent" Nazi, can be quite unaware of that suffering. The sword does not feel the pain that it inflicts. Do not ask it about suffering.

Goodness Personified in Le Chambon

All these considerations drove me to write my book *The Paradox of Cruelty*. But with the book behind me, I felt a deep discontent. I saw cruelty as an embodiment, a particular case of evil. But if cruelty is one of the main evils of human history, why is the opposite of cruelty not one of the key goods of human history? Freedom from the cruel relationship, either by escaping it or by redressing the imbalance of power, was not essential to what western philosophers and theologians have thought of as goodness. Escape is a negative affair. Goodness has something positive in it, something triumphantly affirmative.

Hoping for a hint of goodness in the very center of evil, I started looking closely at the so-called "medical experiments" of the Nazis upon children, usually Jewish and Gypsy children, in the death camps. Here were the weakest of the weak. Not only were they despised minorities, but they were, as individuals, still in their non-age. They were dependents. Here the power imbalance between the cruel experimenters and their victims was at its greatest. But instead of seeing light or finding insight by going down into this hell, into the deepest depth of cruelty, I found myself unwillingly becoming part of the world I was studying. I found myself either yearning to be viciously cruel to the victimizers of the children, or I found myself feeling compassion for the children, feeling their despair and pain as they looked up at the men and women in white coats cutting off their fingertips one at a time, or breaking their slender bones, or wounding their internal organs. Either I became a would-be victimizer or one more Jewish victim, and in either case I was not achieving insight, only misery, like so many other students of the Holocaust. And when I was trying to be "objective" about my studies, when I was succeeding at being indifferent to both the victimizers and the victims of these cruel relationships, I became cold; I became another monster who could look upon the maiming of a child with an indifferent eye.

To relieve this unending suffering, from time to time I would turn to the literature of the French resistance to the Nazis. I had been trained by the U.S. Army to understand it. The resistance was a way of trying to redress the power imbalance between Hitler's Fortress Europe and Hitler's victims, and so I saw it as an enemy of cruelty. Still, its methods were often cruel like the methods of most power struggles, and I had little hope of finding goodness here. We soldiers violated the negative ethic forbidding killing in order, we thought, to follow the positive ethic of being our brothers' keepers.

And then one gray April afternoon I found a brief article on the French village of Le Chambon-sur-Lignon. I shall not analyze here the tears of amazement and gladness and release from despair—in short, of joy—that I shed when I first read that story. Tears themselves interest me greatly—but not the tears of melancholy hindsight and existential despair; rather the tears of awe you experience when the realization of an ideal suddenly appears before your very eyes or thunders inside your mind; these tears interest me.

And one of the reasons I wept at first reading about Le Chambon in those brief, inaccurate pages was that at last I had discovered an embodiment of goodness in opposition to cruelty. I had discovered in the flesh and blood of history, in people with definite names in a definite place at a definite time in the nightmare of history, what no classical or religious ethicist could deny was goodness.

The French Protestant village of Le Chambon, located in the Cévennes Mountains of southeastern France, and with a population of about 3,500, saved the lives of about 6,000 people, most of them Jewish children whose parents had been murdered in the killing camps of central Europe. Under a national government which was not only collaborating with the Nazi conquerors of France but frequently trying to outdo the Germans in anti-Semitism in order to please their conquerors, and later under the day-to-day threat of destruction by the German Armed SS, they started to save children in the winter of 1940, the winter after the fall of France, and they continued to do so until the war in France was over. They sheltered the refugees in their own homes and in various houses they established especially for them; and they took many of them across the terrible mountains to neutral Geneva, Switzerland, in the teeth of French and German police and military power. The people of Le Chambon are poor, and the Huguenot faith to which they belong is a diminishing faith in Catholic and atheist France; but their spiritual power, their capacity to act in unison against the victimizers who surrounded them, was immense, and more than a match for the military power of those victimizers.

But for me as an ethicist the heart of the matter was not only their special power. What interested me was that they obeyed *both* the negative and the positive injunctions of ethics; they were good not only in the sense of trying to be their brothers' keepers, protecting the victim, "defending the fatherless," to use the language of Isaiah; they were also good in the sense that they obeyed the negative injunctions against killing and betraying. While those around them— including myself—were murdering in order presumably, to help mankind in some way or other, they murdered nobody, and betrayed not a single child in those long and dangerous four years. For me as an ethicist they were the embodiment of unambiguous goodness.

But for me as a student of cruelty they were something more: they were an embodiment of the opposite of cruelty. And so, somehow, at last, I had found goodness in opposition to cruelty. In studying their story, and in telling it in *Lest Innocent Blood Be Shed*, I learned that the opposite of cruelty is not simply freedom from the cruel relationship; it is *hospitality*. It lies not only in something negative, an absence of cruelty or of imbalance; it lies in unsentimental, efficacious love. The opposite of the cruelties of the camps was not the liberation of the camps, the cleaning out of the barracks and the cessation of the horrors. All of this was the *end* of the cruelty relationship, not the opposite of that relationship. And it was not even the end of it, because the victims would never forget and would remain in agony as long as they remembered their humiliation and suffering. No, the opposite of cruelty was not the liberation of the camps, not freedom; it was the hospitality of the people of Chambon, and of very few others during the Holocaust. The opposite of cruelty was the kind of goodness that happened in Chambon.

Let me explain the difference between liberation and hospitality by telling you about a letter I received a year ago from a woman who had been saved by the people of Le Chambon when she was a young girl. She wrote:

> Never was there a question that the Chambonnais would not share all they had with us, meager as it was. One Chambonnais once told me that even if there was less, they still would want more for us.

And she goes on:

> It was indeed a very different attitude from the one in Switzerland, which while saving us also resented us so much.
>
> If today we are not bitter people like most survivors it can only be due to the fact that we met people like the people of Le Chambon, who showed to us simply that life can be different, that there are people who care, that people can live together and even risk their own lives for their fellow man.

The Swiss liberated refugees and removed them from the cruel relationship; the people of Le Chambon did more. They taught them that goodness could conquer cruelty, that loving hospitality could remove them from the cruel relationship. And they taught me this, too.

It is important to emphasize that cruelty is not simply an episodic, momentary matter, especially institutional cruelty like that of Nazism or slavery. As we have seen throughout this essay, not only does it persist while it is being exerted upon the weak; *it can persist in the survivors* after they have escaped the power relationship. The survivors torture themselves, continue to suffer, continue to maim their own lives long after the actual torture is finished. The self-hatred and rage of the blacks and the despair of the native Americans and the Jews who have suffered under institutional crushing and maiming are continuations of original cruelties. And these continuations exist because only a superficial liberation from torture has occurred. The sword has stopped falling on their flesh in the old obvious ways, but the wounds still bleed. I am not saying that the village of Chambon healed these wounds—they go too deep. What I am saying is that the people I have talked to who were once children in Le Chambon have more hope for their species and more respect for themselves as human beings than most other survivors I have met. The enduring hospitality they met in Le Chambon helped them find realistic hope in a world of persisting cruelty.

What was the nature of this hospitality that saved and deeply changed so many lives? It is hard to summarize briefly what the Chambonnais did, and above all how they did it. The morning after a new refugee family came to town they would find on their front door a wreath with *"Bienvenue!"* "Welcome!" painted on a piece of cardboard attached to the wreath. Nobody knew who had brought the wreath; in effect, the whole town had brought it.

It was mainly the women of Chambon who gave so much more than shelter to these, the most hated enemies of the Nazis. There was Madame Barraud, a tiny Alsatian, who cared for the refugee boys in her house with all the love such a tiny body could hold, and who cared for the way they felt day and night. And there were others.

But there was one person without whom Le Chambon could not have become the safest place in Europe for Jews: the Huguenot minister of the village, André Trocmé. Trocmé was a passionately religious man. He was massive, more than six feet tall, blonde, with a quick temper. Once long after the war, while he was lecturing on the main project of his life, the promotion of the idea of nonviolence in international relations, one of the members of his audience started to whisper a few words to his neighbor. Trocmé let this go on for a few moments, then interrupted his speech, walked up to the astonished whisperer, raised his massive arm, pointed toward the door, and yelled, "Out! Out! Get out!" And the lecture was on nonviolence.

The center of his thought was the belief that God showed how important man was by becoming Himself a human being, and by becoming a particular sort of human being who was the embodiment of sacrificially generous love. For Trocmé, every human being was like Jesus, had God in him or her, and was just as precious as God Himself. And when Trocmé with the help of the Quakers and others organized his village into the most efficient rescue machine in Europe, he did so not only to save the Jews, but also to save the Nazis and their collaborators. He wanted to keep them from blackening their souls with more evil—he wanted to save them, the victimizers, from evil.

One of the reasons he was successful was that the Huguenots had been themselves persecuted for hundreds of years by the kings of France, and they knew what persecution was. In fact, when the people of Chambon took Jewish children and whole families across the mountains of southeastern France into neutral Switzerland, they often followed pathways that had been taken by Huguenots in their flight from the Dragoons of the French kings.

A particular incident from the story of Le Chambon during the Nazi occupation of France will explain succinctly why he was successful in making the village a village of refuge. But before I relate the story, I must point out that the people of the village did not think of themselves as "successful," let alone as "good." From their point of view, they did not do anything that required elaborate explanation. When I asked them why they helped these dangerous guests, they invariably answered, "What do you mean, 'Why'? Where else could they go? How could you turn them away? What is so special about being ready to help (*prête à servir*)? There was nothing else to do." And some of them laughed in amazement when I told them that I thought they were "good people." They saw no alternative to their actions and to the way they acted, and therefore they saw what they did as necessary, not something to be picked out for praise. Helping these guests was for them as natural as breathing or eating—one does not think of alternatives to these functions; they did not think of alternatives to sheltering people who were endangering not only the lives of their hosts but the lives of all the people of the village.

And now the story. One afternoon a refugee woman knocked on the door of a farmhouse outside the village. The farmers around the village proper were Protestants like most of the others in Chambon, but with one difference: they were mostly "Darbystes," followers of a strange Scot named Darby, who taught their ancestors in the nineteenth century to believe every word of the Bible, and indeed, who had them memorize the Bible. They were literal fundamentalists. The farm-woman opened the door to the refugee and invited her into the kitchen where it was warm. Standing in the middle of the floor the refugee, in heavily accented French, asked for eggs for her children. In those days of very short supplies, people with children often went to the farmers in the "gray market" (neither black nor exactly legal) to get necessary food. This was early in 1941, and the farmers were not yet accustomed to the refugees. The farm-woman looked into the eyes of the shawled refugee and asked, "Are you Jewish?" The woman started to tremble, but she could not lie, even though that question was usually the beginning of the end of life for Jews in Hitler's Fortress Europe. She answered, "Yes."

The woman ran from the kitchen to the staircase nearby, and while the refugee trembled with terror in the kitchen, she called up the stairs, "Husband, children, come down, come down! We have in our house at this very moment a representative of the Chosen People!"

Not all the Protestants in Chambon were Darbyste fundamentalists; but almost all were convinced that people are the children of God, and are as precious as God Himself. Their leaders were Huguenot preachers and their following of the negative and positive commandments of the Bible came in part from their personal generosity and courage, but also in part from the depths of their religious conviction that we are all children of God, and we must take care of each other lovingly. This combined with the ancient and deep historical ties between the Huguenots and the Jews of France and their own centuries of persecution by the Dragoons and Kings of France helped make them what they were, "always ready to help," as the Chambonnais saying goes.

A Choice of Perspectives

We have come a long way from cruelty to the people of Chambon, just as I have come a long way in my research from concrete evil to concrete goodness. Let me conclude with a point that has been alternately hinted at and stressed in the course of this essay.

A few months after *Lest Innocent Blood Be Shed* was published I received a letter from Massachusetts that opened as follows:

> I have read your book, and I believe that you mushy-minded moralists should be awakened to the facts. Nothing happened in Le Chambon, nothing of any importance whatsoever.
>
> The Holocaust, dear Professor, was like a geological event, like an earthquake. No person could start it; no person could change it; and no person could end it. And no small group of persons could do so either. It was the armies and the nations that performed actions that counted. Individuals did nothing. You sentimentalists have got to learn that the great masses and big political ideas make the difference. Your people and the people they saved simply do not exist.

Now between this position and mine there is an abyss that no amount of shouted arguments or facts can cross. And so I shall not answer this letter with a tightly organized reply. I shall answer it only by telling you that one of the reasons institutional cruelty exists and persists is that people believe that individuals can do nothing, that only vast ideologies and armies can act meaningfully. Every act of institutional cruelty—Nazism, slavery, and all the others—lives not with people in the concrete, but with abstractions that blind people to individuals. Himmler's speech to the SS leadership in 1943 is full of phrases like "exterminating a bacillus," and "The Jewish people will be exterminated." And in that speech he attacks any German who believes in "his decent Jew." Institutional cruelty, like other misleading approaches to ethics, blinds us to the victim's point of view; and when we are blind to that point of view we can countenance and perpetrate cruelty with impunity.

I have told you that I cannot and will not try to refute the letter from Massachusetts. I shall only summarize the point of view of this essay with another story.

I was lecturing a few months ago in Minneapolis, and when I finished talking about the Holocaust and the village of Le Chambon, a woman stood up and asked me if the village of Le Chambon was in the Department of Haute-Loire, the high sources of the Loire River. Obviously she was French, with her accent; and all French people know that there are many villages called "Le Chambon" in France, just as any American knows that there are many "Main Streets" in the United States. I said that Le Chambon was indeed in the Haute-Loire.

She said, "Then you have been speaking about the village that saved all three of my children. I want to thank you for writing this book, not only because the story will now be permanent, but also because I shall be able to talk about those terrible days with Americans now, for they will understand those days better than they have. You see, you Americans, though you sometimes cross the oceans, live on an island here as far as war is concerned . . ."

Then she asked to come up and say one sentence. There was not a sound, not even breathing, to be heard in the room. She came to the front of the room and said, "The Holocaust was storm, lightning, thunder, wind, rain, yes. And Le Chambon was the rainbow."

Only from her perspective can you understand the cruelty and the goodness I have been talking about, not from the point of view of the gentleman from Massachusetts. You must choose which perspective is best, and your choice will have much to do with your feelings about the preciousness of life, and not only the preciousness of other people's lives. If the lives of others are precious to you, your life will become more precious to you.

THE VIRTUE OF VIRTUE ETHICS

by Mark Liederbach

I. Introduction

Since the time of the Enlightenment, with its emphasis on rationality (evident in such influential figures as Immanuel Kant and John Stuart Mill), the determination of rules and/or principles as guides for determining moral obligation has been the focus of much modern ethical theory. Deontology and Utilitarianism (the subjects of the previous two chapters) are classic examples of such "action based" ethical theories.

The attempt of these ethical systems to enable a person "do the right thing" is certainly commendable, but they have not been without criticism. Chief among the claimed faults is the charge that while doing the right thing is important, such an approach pushes ethics into either an exacting form of legalism or a cold, calculating act of cost/benefit analysis. In either case, motivation to act morally tends to diminish into mere duty.

Virtue ethics avoids this fault by shifting focus away from act to person. That is, the focus is put on developing the character of a good person who will in turn display good moral behavior. Ethical theories, then, that place such emphasis on the development of personal character over and above the determination of particular acts are called *Virtue Theories*. Simply put, while deontological or utilitarian ethics focus on what a person does, virtue ethics emphasize *what kind of person someone is*.

For example, Greg, Kevin and Will are all seniors in college taking their last final exam in philosophy. As they sit down to take the test, each of them looks the exam over and realizes his worst fear has come true. Each realizes that he has studied the wrong material and is certain to "bomb the exam." In the panic of the moment each considers his options.

Greg, raised in a very religious home, never considers cheating as an option. He believes that not only would cheating be "against the rules," it is tantamount to stealing. Kevin, on the other hand, is considering his future. His father has told him that no more funds are available for further educational expenses. If Kevin fails the exam, he will be on his own to pay for another semester of courses. After weighing his options, he decides to "steal a look" at the exam of the person sitting next to him. Will is initially panicked and uncertain of what to do. The last thing he can do is fail. He is the father of two children, and failing this course would mean losing the job waiting for him upon graduation. However, as he considers his options, he comes to the conclusion that while cheating might "get him out of a jam," he's not "the kind of person who cheats," nor does he want to begin the journey toward becoming one.

In this case, both Greg and Kevin make their decisions about what to do based on act-oriented systems. For Greg, it is wrong to break the rules; for Kevin, the perceived benefits of cheating outweigh those of failing. For Will, the focus is character. This is the distinctive virtue of virtue ethics: instead of placing moral focus on the act, virtue theory focuses on the whole person as moral agent. By doing so virtue ethics closely links behavior with moral responsibility and personal character. Good action depends upon good character.

What is Virtue Ethic? A Snapshot View

The word "virtue" has its Latin roots in the word *virtus*, referring originally to the ancient Roman understanding of "manliness" often sought after in a good soldier (bravery, strength, etc.). With time, the term came to refer to qualities of excellence in any person. The classical Greek counterpart for this term is the word *arete*, meaning excellence of any variety. The modern understanding of the virtue, following these linguistic roots, is *a character trait or disposition in a person that enables an individual to live (at least that part of human existence) in an excellent manner*. Having a virtue implies an internal predisposition to act in a consistent manner in similar situations. "Virtue ethics," therefore, can be defined as a theory of ethics emphasizing excellence of character and the formation of virtues in a person so that when functioning together, these virtues enable a person to live a life of consistent excellence in the different contexts and circumstances of life.

Upon closer analysis, there are two implied ideas undergirding this definition that need further explication. First, virtue ethics emphasizes a *telos* (end or goal) for life that is specific. There is an emphasis on living a certain kind of life—a life of happiness. The term often translated as "happiness" in classic virtue theories is *eudaemonia*. The fullest meaning of *eudaemonia* implies a life distinguished from mere pursuit (or attainment) of pleasure. Instead, it consists of a life lived in light of the highest good toward which human beings should strive. When this "highest good," becomes the goal of human life, it offers hope of reaching true happiness or human flourishing. Secondly, there is an emphasis on the development of particular virtues or character traits that are necessary in order to attain to the highest end of human flourishing. It is the development and practice of these virtues (not rules or principles) that, in turn, leads to proper moral behavior in the varying contexts of life.

Two obvious questions arise from these points. First, what is this end, or *telos*, that will lead to a life of happiness and flourishing? And, which virtues must a person posses to be called "virtuous" and attain to a life of happiness?" Over the centuries these questions have been answered in various ways. Indeed, the differing answers have led to differing theories of virtue ethics. Plato, Augustine, Aristotle and Aquinas, men who have unmeasurably influenced philosophy and theology, will serve as examples.

II. Plato—Cardinal Virtues

Plato lived in Athens Greece between 428/7 and 348/7 B.C. He was co-founder of the famous Athenian school of philosophy known as the Academy. Alfred North Whitehead, renowned mathematician and process philosopher, once commented that the entire history of philosophy is a series of footnotes to Plato. While Plato authored many works, philosophical and moral thought is most clearly present in the *Republic*.

The End

Understanding Plato's moral theory and the importance of the virtues, requires one to first consider his metaphysics (assumptions about the nature of reality). For Plato, the universe has a dualistic nature composed of an imperfect physical world of perceived reality and an immaterial world of perfection that comprise actual reality. The former he calls the *world of perceptions or the world of becoming*, the latter he calls *the world of the Forms or the world of Being*.

While human beings live primarily in the world of perceptions, Plato argues that the higher reality, and the reality we should all attain to, is the world of the Forms. The world of the Forms is objective and unchanging, and the place in which the perfect Form of things actually exists. Thus, for example, when a human being looks at two colored pieces of cloth and says that one is "more red" than the other, the reason that he or she knows it is "more red" is through an intuitive comparison to the ideal or perfect redness that exists in the realm of the Forms. The Forms are immaterial realities that can only be known through the exercise of reason.

According to Plato, the highest end of human existence, then, is to know the Forms. This is what leads to human flourishing (*eudaemonia*). The journey to gain knowledge of the Forms is a long and arduous one. Ultimately it is only through the development and employment of certain virtues that one can reach this end. Those who wish to gain true knowledge of the forms must order their lives so as to subordinate their passions to reason and pursue excellence in intellectual and moral character or virtue.

Plato held a tripartate view of the soul. That is, the soul has three parts: the appetitive, the spirited, and the rational. The *appetitive* part of the soul refers primarily to the physical needs of a person (i.e., the desire for food, rest or sex). This part Plato considers the lowest, or most basic function of the person. The *spirited* part of the soul is higher than the appetitive. It relates to human drives like ambition or love. The *rational* part of the self is the one Plato considers the highest of all. He understands it to be akin to the divine in that it can attain to understanding of the Forms. Because it is the highest and most rational Plato maintains that it should rule or guide the appetive and spirited parts. It is when a person trains this highest functioning part of the soul to rule the other two, that he or she gains the ability to focus the energy of these parts of the self toward the highest end of human existence.

Virtues and the Forms

In this light, one can begin to see the importance that particular virtues might play. According to Plato, there are four particular character traits that should shape the virtuous person. The corporate functioning of these virtues will, in turn, enable a person to pursue understanding and knowledge of the Forms. Each of these four relate specifically to the differing parts and functions of the human soul. They are temperance, courage, wisdom and justice.

Plato identifies *temperance* as that virtue primarily linked to the appetitive part of the soul. A person is described as temperate when, instead of being ruled by basic desires and appetites, these desires are brought under control in light of a higher end. *Courage* is the virtue primarily related to the spirited part of the soul. A person is described as courageous when, in spite of feelings or desires to the contrary, a person puts into practice the most reasonable course of action. *Wisdom* (or *prudence*) is the virtue related to the rational part of the soul. It is tied closely with the knowledge of a person's ultimate good and the means of attaining it. Consequently, a person is said to be prudent when he or she allows the rational part of the soul to guide and harmonize the spirited and appetitive parts of the soul in the pursuit of true knowledge of the Forms. In addition to these three virtues Plato also describes a fourth—*justice*. Justice is the virtue that describes the harmonious operation of the tripartate soul toward its highest end. A person would be described as just, then, when all three parts of the soul are oriented and balanced in a manner that enables proper movement of the self toward true knowledge of the Forms.

When taken together, these four virtues (temperance, courage, prudence, justice) are sometimes described as *Cardinal Virtues*. The word *cardinal* comes from the Latin term *cardo*, meaning the *hinge* or *pivot* upon which a door turns. Therefore, the meaning of the word rightly implies that it is upon these four virtues that everything in Plato's ethics hinges. The corporate manifestation and employment of these virtues lead to a well-lived life of human flourishing. Through the development and practice of these virtues, a human can live a life guided by reason in pursuit of true knowledge of the Forms.

Clearly, then, Plato does not rely on legislated rules or predetermined principles in the determination of moral obligation. Rather, the primary concern is with the character of the agent acting in light of a particular end. Specific actions to be done in particular contexts should reflect the character traits necessary to gain true knowledge. Certainly there is a close link between good character and right action, but it is the former that is the point of emphasis.

III. Aristotle—The Golden Mean

Aristotle lived from 384-322 B.C. At the age of 17 he enrolled in Plato's Academy and proceeded to distinguish himself as a student and later as a teacher. After the death of Plato in 347 B.C. Aristotle became the boyhood tutor of Alexander the Great and later in life he founded his own school in Athens. His most influential discussions on ethics come from his *Nicomachean Ethics*.

The End

Like Plato, Aristotle also argues that the highest end of human existence is to attain to a state of *eudaemonia*—happiness, flourishing, or well-being. However, while they agree that all things by nature seek their own good, Aristotle argued that it is not by conforming to an external ideal (Forms) that one attains *eudaemonia*, but by discovering and fulfilling the highest purpose inherent in the nature of a thing. Behaving in a manner appropriate to that final or highest purpose is what leads to flourishing.

For example, while a knife can be used as a make-shift screwdriver, or a doorjam, its highest purpose is to cut. The knife, one might then say, fulfills its highest purpose when it is used to cut. Further, a knife is said to be an excellent knife when it cuts well. Therefore, when the highest purpose is discovered and the object functions according to this purpose, the object can be said to "be itself" in the highest sense.

In a similar manner Aristotle argues that humans have a particular end or purpose. Among all the qualities and abilities that humans have, Aristotle believes it is the ability to reason (both theoretically and deliberatively) that is particular to human beings. A human, then, fulfills her highest purpose when she reasons. Further, a person achieves a state of excellence when she reasons well. This is the highest end. *Eudaemonia* results from striving not only to fulfill the natural inclination to reason, but to have and develop the skills to do so in an excellent manner.

Virtues

The skills necessary for a human being to flourish are the virtues. Aristotle held that virtues are what enable excellence in both intellectual and deliberative (moral) pursuits. The moral virtues involve the rational control of passions or the habitual excellence of being able to deliberately choose an action in light of alternatives that are inappropriate for human flourishing. In order to be described as a virtue, this ability to control passions and avoid extreme alternatives must not be occasional in nature but an established part of a person's character transcending the impetus of momentary feelings or desires. In other words, virtues develop and are established through repeated practice of avoiding the extremes of excess or deficiency in any given context.

While Plato identified the cardinal virtues as being of central importance to living a *eudaemonistic* life, Aristotle did not attempt to give such a central list. Rather, he recognized and differentiated between many different virtues and their importance for fulfilling one's intellectual and moral capacity. Indeed, he listed many "intellectual virtues" that relate primarily to those excellences or habitual dispositions enabling scientific reasoning, and many "moral virtues" relating primarily to habitual dispositions or skills enabling proper moral deliberation. The development of these skills depends on the repeated choice of doing what a virtuous person would do in a given context. Thus, while the modern adage "practice makes perfect" may have some degree of truth to it, when it comes to Aristotle's view of ethics, a more appropriate understanding of his theory is "*perfect* practice makes perfect."

This begs the questions, "what constitutes perfect practice?" And, "how does one practice perfectly?" Aristotle's answer . . . one practices perfectly by aiming for the "golden mean" between the alternative extremes in any given situation.

Through this "doctrine of the mean," Aristotle holds that a virtuous person is one who strives to determine a point of behavior somewhere between the possible extremes by taking into consideration both the particular situation one finds oneself in and the personal tendencies to excess or deficiency one naturally displays. For example, a courageous army lieutenant will not simply order his platoon to attack an enemy position if they are outnumbered and obviously outgunned—to do so would be foolhardy. On the other hand, he would not simply avoid the fight because of fear. Instead, a truly courageous lieutenant would strive to find a solution in which the enemy can be engaged, but with a chance of success. By employing prudence the soldier may find that the best course of action might include waiting for reinforcements, or even retreating for a time until a better chance of success could be achieved. It all depends upon the situation at hand. The key is that the lieutenant must be aware of his personal tendencies toward one extreme or the other. Thus, the virtue of courage includes a prudential assessment of the situation. Are there 50 enemies soldiers to our 20, or are there 1000? Do they have only knives and spears against our machine guns, or do they have rockets, grenades, tanks and a fortified position? In addition, if the lieutenant knows himself to be prone to foolhardy risk-taking, the virtuous act for him would be to lean toward a decision limiting this tendency. If, on the other hand, he is prone toward fear, the virtuous decision might be to take greater risk than he would naturally be comfortable with. The virtuous behavior is that which is the mean between the two extremes in light of both the situation at hand the tendencies of the moral agent involved.

What becomes obvious at this point is that determining the mean in a given context, may not lead to the same behavior for each person in a similar situation. For this reason, the descriptive or evaluative language used in virtue ethics is often "good" or "bad" (as in *she made a good decision*) as opposed to normative assessments, such as "right" or "wrong" (*he did the right thing*). In pure virtue ethics, the proper or virtuous act is usually not predetermined as it would be in a deontological approach.

IV. Augustine

If Alfred North Whitehead's comments are true about the history of philosophy being a series of footnotes to Plato, it may well be argued that the history of western Christian theology is a series of footnotes to Saint Augustine. Augustine lived from 354 to 430 A.D. During his most influential years he served as the Bishop of a small North African village named Hippo. While Augustine was arguably not a pure virtue ethicist, there is no doubt that his ethical treatments flowed from a teleological understanding of reality and his view of proper moral behavior incorporated a heavy reliance on the virtue theory of Plato.

The End

Similar to Plato, Augustine argues that all humans attempt to reach a point of *eudaemonia* by striving for some form of happiness. He writes, "All men love happiness . . . Perverse folk not only want wickedness without unhappiness, which is an impossibility, but they want to be wicked on purpose to avoid being unhappy . . . In all the wickedness men commit, they always desire happiness . . . For the sake of driving away unhappiness and obtaining happiness, all men do whatever they do, good or bad."[1]

The problem, however, is that true happiness cannot be had by merely pursuing whatever one desires. In agreement with Plato he argues that true happiness must be understood, once again, in *eudaemonistic* terms—it is that which will lead to human flourishing. True happiness and human flourishing do not come from a hedonistic pursuit of personal desires, fleshly passions or pleasures. Happiness is not arbitrarily defined in terms of an individual's random wants or cravings. In both Plato and Augustine it is not the *pursuit* of happiness that legitimizes moral behavior, but it is in *that which a person pursues or seeks to find happiness* that moral action can take on its proper shape or form.

While clearly there are similarities with Plato, it is particularly in regard to the nature of the *telos* (end) that Augustine's thought turns in a different direction. While he agreed that there is a higher reality all strive for, he argued that Plato's conclusions about the nature of that higher reality were erroneous. Augustine believed that Plato's understanding of the realm of the Forms was a veiled and incomplete reference to the true end of human striving and longing—the Christian understanding of God. It is not in the attainment of knowledge and understanding of the realm of the Forms, as Plato concluded, that leads to human flourishing, rather, the human heart finds ultimate satisfaction only through enjoyment of God made known through Jesus Christ. The focus of moral living, then, primarily concerns a person's ability to distinguish between those ends or goals which are ultimately inferior in producing true happiness, from that which truly leads to human flourishing. The wise person does not settle for that which is inferior.

This does not imply that "the lower" or inferior ends for which persons strive are inherently bad; they are simply inferior. In fact, because he believed that all things are created by God, most pursuits have some level of value. The key for Augustine is that these things should never be sought after in such a way as to distract from the pursuit of that which is goodness in itself—God. To this end he writes of his own experience in his *Confessions*: "I was looking for Thee out there, and I threw myself, deformed as I was, upon those well formed things Thou has made."[2] By so doing he was in reality distracted from the highest proper end of human activity. Thus, for Augustine, the human moral problem is not pursuit of happiness, but the pursuit of happiness in a manner that deviates (or falls short) from the true object of human longing and the proper end of human flourishing. Only in love of God, according to Augustine, can humans "live well" and be truly happy.[3]

For this reason Augustine describes love as both an expression of internal longing and the means to the end of true happiness. Indeed, he begins his *Confessions* with the famous idea that the human heart is restless until it finds its rest in God. What makes Augustine so distinct from Plato on this point is his argument that the satisfaction of the human heart comes only through the selfless love of God displayed in the life, death, and resurrection of Jesus Christ. Love for God is not only the chief end of humankind, it is also the only means by which humans can experience true happiness and a flourishing life.

In light of this teleological and metaphysical understanding one can begin to see how Augustine's moral theory takes shape. All moral behavior, he argues, must be oriented toward a pursuit of happiness. As we have seen, however, the mere striving does not legitimize the actions taken. Desire for happiness does not lead to justification of "what ever it takes to make a person happy." Instead, Augustine argues that there is a higher reality to which all humans knowingly or unknowingly seek. Human flourishing is only attainable when the passions, desires, and affections of the person pursue that which alone is true source of true happiness—God.

Virtues: The Means to the End

> Let us hear, O Christ, what chief end Thou dost prescribe to us . . . 'Thou shalt love' He says 'the Lord the God' . . . What must be the measure of love . . . ? — 'with all thy heart . . . This we must strive after; to this we must refer all our plans. The perfection of all good things, our perfect good is God. We must neither come short of this, nor go beyond it; the one is dangerous, the other impossible.[4]

If, according to Augustine, the chief end of human existence is love of God, how does one pursue God in this manner? Augustine believed that a concentrated pursuit of the soul for God required not only the development of virtues, but their unification under the rubric of love for God. Plato's four cardinal virtues are subsumed under the one central virtue of love of God. It is only in light of a foundational love of God that the virtues can flow forth from proper motivation and conform to their proper end.

One could say, then, that the four cardinal virtues are for Augustine the material expressions of the one unifying virtue of Christian love. When appropriately formed and employed in a human life as an expression of love, these virtues become the means by which a person moves toward worship of, and intimacy with, God. Indeed, love not only unifies but transforms the virtues so as to provide ample motivation and proper guidance about moral behavior. He writes, "I hold virtue to be nothing else than perfect love of God . . . temperance is love keeping itself entire and incorrupt for God; fortitude is love bearing everything for the sake of God; Justice is love serving God only, and therefore ruling well all else; prudence is love making a right distinction between what helps it towards God and what might hinder it."[5]

In summary, then, the object of moral living, is to enhance and reflect the soul's love of God. When unified under the umbrella of love, Augustine understood the virtues as the characteristics that should define a person who truly loves God and desires to be like Jesus Christ. Ethical living is to be a practical manifestation of believing in and worshipping the Creator. Because the focus of the ethic is teleological, he believed that moral behavior should flow not from mere obedience to commands, but from a heart pursuing God—the source and enabler of human flourishing. When the heart is set in order then obedience to the commands of God become the appropriate expression of virtue.

Augustine, then, contributes two important elements to the development of virtue theory. First, he defines the highest end or *telos* of human existence as worshipful relationship with God through Jesus Christ. By so doing, he not only provides a specific goal towards which a person may strive (love of God culminating in the *beatific vision*, or final existence in the presence of God), but also opens the way for a virtue ethic to be guided by principles or rules as put forth by the Creator through Scripture. In essence, he developed a virtue ethic informed by deontological principles.

Second, he adopts the classical philosophical treatment of Plato and transforms it into a vehicle of the Christian faith and ethics by way of theological reinterpretation and adaptation. The four cardinal virtues remain vital to human flourishing but they only find proper expression and conform to an ideal form when brought under the rubric of Christian love.[6] If the virtues are pursued apart from this love, they may have some value in aiding moral activity, but ultimately, without true religion, such a pursuit would be a mere counterfeit of genuine virtue.[7]

V. Aquinas

While Plato's ideas and ethics where adapted to Christianity by Augustine, it was Aristotle's work that Thomas Aquinas adopted and adapted in the 13th century and which became, perhaps, the most dominant form of virtue ethics until recent times.

Thomas Aquinas (1225 to 1274) was a Dominican monk and scholar who taught theology at the University of Paris. Up to the 13th century, Platonic influences through the work of Augustine dominated ethical treatments. However, in the 12th century an important occurrence took place that would eventually change the face of Christian ethics. Parts of Aristotle's *Nichomachean Ethics* which had been lost to western philosophers and theologians once again became available in Latin. The result was a sort of Aristotelian revival amongst learned scholars. In fact, over time Aristotelian influences began to predominate in Christian ethical treatises. This was primarily a result of the work of Aquinas. It was chiefly in his *Summa Theologica* that Aquinas used many of the basic ideas of Aristotle to develop his own extensive contributions. Josef Kotva comments that "without sacrificing what is fundamental to the Christian tradition, Thomas ingeniously merged Christian theology and Scripture with Aristotle's ethics."[8]

The End

In a manner similar to Aristotle, Aquinas argued that an account of ethics must consider the natural end toward which all things tend. He argued (like Aristotle) that all things have a natural function. For example, the function of a knife is to cut. An excellent knife is one that cuts well. Like Aristotle, Aquinas argues that a proper understanding of virtue is an excellence in accord with a proper end or *telos*.

Also similar to Aristotle, Aquinas points out that humans alone have the capacity to reason and it is this ability that distinguishes humans from animals. Consequently, to reason is to function properly as a human being. To reason well is to live an excellent life. In this vein, Aquinas goes on to argue that when any person reasons well he or she can arrive at a basic conclusion (what Aquinas called the *first principle of practical reason*): all things act toward the Good. The first corollary of this basic principle is: do good and avoid evil. In other words, through basic reasoning one can reach the conclusion that for behavior to be considered fully human it must be done voluntarily and in light of a perceived good end. But of course, a *perceived* good is very different from an *actual* good end. Thus the question comes back to what does Aquinas believe to be the highest end toward which humans should strive?

Aquinas asserts that the good or highest end is the *eudaemonistic* life (of the life of human flourishing, happiness). Unlike Aristotle (and more like Augustine), however, Aquinas argued that while reasoning is an attribute unique to humans and which sets them apart from other created beings and objects, it is not the highest end. While he agreed with Aristotle that reasoned contemplation is vitally important, he argued (more like Augustine) that in order to reach its highest end, contemplation must be about the right thing. Reasoned contemplation is not an end in itself. The perfect or highest good (the *Summum bonum*) toward which humans must strive is the person of God and the ultimate end of life is the perfect contemplation or *vision* of God (*Beatific Vision*).

According to Aquinas, then, in order to evaluate a moral behavior as appropriate or good, it is must be properly ordered toward the highest end of human existence. This takes place as one develops virtues such as prudence (sometimes understood as right practical reason) to discern not only the final end but the steps to reach that end. The life of human flourishing or the good life "consists in the best possible use of one's rational powers (intellect and will) and of one's lower capacities (sense, cognition, sense appetites, and bodily activities) under the control of night reason."[9]

A hallmark element of Aquinas' ethical treatment emerges at this point. With the understanding that God is the ultimate end of human flourishing, Aquinas also posits that moral actions leading a person toward the vision of God must fall in line with the Divine Ordering of the universe or the "Eternal Law" of God. That is, appropriate moral behavior stems from right determination of God's Law and subsequent actions guided by that Law. While perfect understanding of God's eternal law is reserved for God alone, humans (according to Aquinas) have the ability to naturally perceive and cooperate in certain principles of the Eternal Law. The principles of Eternal Law which humans are able to perceive are called principles of "Natural Law." The most basic principle of natural law which Aquinas argues is self evident to all humans beings is "good is to be done and evil avoided" (the first principle of practical reason).

Moral action, then, is evaluated in light of its conformity to the Eternal law of God and the degree to which it is ordered toward the highest good of seeing God. Humans are given the task of working out in their everyday lives what moral actions are appropriate to that end. In addition to the guidance of natural law, Aquinas also argues that God provides humans with Scriptures ("divine Law"), for additional and corrective guidance toward the highest good.

One might ask at this point, "if humans have access to both natural law and divine law which they must obey in order to be moral, isn't Aquinas really offering an action based or deontological ethical theory?" The answer is that while certainly there are deontological or rule-based elements in Aquinas, it is best to understand these as "guides" which aid individuals move toward their proper end (*telos*). In other words, Aquinas sets the proper motivation and compliance with these rules and laws in the context of moving toward a goal of *eudaemonia*. In this light, natural laws serve as guideposts along the road to a life of true happiness and flourishing and the development of virtues. In addition, Aquinas understood that in order for someone to discern and then rightly apply the natural and divine laws in actual circumstances, he or she must develop life skills, or virtues, to properly direct his or her life.

Virtues—Natural and Theological

Aquinas maintained that God created human beings and then endowed them with a special gift known as "original justice." This gift provided humans with relational harmony with God as well as the ability to live morally perfect lives in line with the eternal law of God and toward the proper end. Due to sin, however, humans forfeited the gift of original justice, resulting in a weakened existence in a "fallen state" of being. In this fallen condition, humans maintain the ability to reason, but the human capacity to reason no longer is able to function with perfect integrity nor is it always oriented toward the ultimate goal.

The implication of this fallen or "sinful" state is that while humans can develop moral virtues and practice practical reason this does not necessarily mean they are doing so in perfect manner nor that the goal toward which behavior is oriented is the correct one. In order to discern the highest end and have appropriate moral behavior toward that end, humans are dependent upon more than the development of moral virtues. They need Divine help offered through the infusion of what Aquinas called the "theological virtues."

What results is a two-tiered virtue theory. The "natural virtues" Aquinas describes as qualities either inherent in a human being or acquirable through personal effort. Similar to Plato he emphasizes the cardinal virtues. Prudence—practical reasoning in judgment or right practical reason. Justice—the reasonable, willful determination of other regarding actions. Willing and doing good to other persons. Temperance—the reasonable ordering and control of passions that draw persons away from the final end of human kind specifically in regard to emotions and fleshly desires. And finally, fortitude—the reasonable ordering and control of passions or desires in order to courageously address particular circumstances and appropriately act toward the final end in spite of fears.[10]

A theological virtue, on the other hand, is one that is founded on the character of God and not acquirable through birth or human effort. Instead, the existence of a theological virtue in a person is dependent upon God who alone can bestow or *infuse* them into a person. Through God's grace when the theological virtues are infused into a believer there is a restoration of much of the *original justice* lost at the fall. Relational harmony with God is restored and humans are then able to once again act toward their right and ultimate end and the virtue of practical reason becomes right practical reason.

The theological virtues are of a higher order than the moral virtues in that they have God as their direct object and they are a special gift of divine love. The theological virtues are: Faith—the belief in, and loyalty to God. Hope—relating to the believer's response to the gift of God and his or her positive standing or position in light of the divine gift of salvation. It is stimulated by faith which in turn leads to an expectation that God will fulfill his promises of salvation regardless of circumstances. Love—that which transforms behavior by orienting it toward the proper end and giving the highest moral quality to all thoughts, intentions, and actions. Whereas Aquinas describes natural love as a passion that adapts itself toward the agent's perception of what is good, Christian love provides proper understanding of the highest good and true happiness and thereby ordering the passions in the right direction.

By developing this two-tiered virtue ethics Aquinas bridged Greek ideas of virtue ethics with Christian ideas of sin, redemption, sanctification (personal holiness) and law. While the cardinal virtues (justice, prudence, temperance, courage) remain important, the theological virtues (faith, hope, love) transform the natural virtues by orienting them toward their proper end. Hence, where Aristotle suggests virtues are developed predominantly by human effort, upbringing, and circumstances, Aquinas argues that possession of the virtues begins naturally but only reach their highest order through the divine gift of grace and with the aid of natural and divine law.

The development of the virtues, then, serves to enable the best evaluation and determination of how the self evident principles of natural law should be applied to a given situation in order to attain to the final end of human existence. The determination of moral action results from a syllogistic form of reasoning in which a self-evident principle of natural law is applied to a particular situation or circumstance an agent is facing, and a course of behavior is then chosen. The moral and theological virtues are the key ingredient enabling the proper application and ordering of the chosen behavior toward the final end.

VI. The Recovery of Virtue Theory Today

While some might prefer the non-theistic accounts of virtue theory (Plato and Aristotle) to the theistic versions (Augustine and Aquinas) the general approach of virtue ethics has been an enduring one. Even though the general tenor of modern ethics has moved away from virtue approaches, there seems to be a revival of sorts in regard to the important role virtue theory can play in today's morally uncertain climate. Indeed, many currently influential ethicists admit the need at least for a partial reintegration of virtue ethics[11] while others look to virtue theory once again as the basic form of ethical theory. In fact in recent years there has been some very influential work done attempting to pull from this rich tradition and bring application to today. Two examples are the works of Alasdair MacIntyre and Stanley Hauerwas.

Alasdair MacIntyre

Alasdair MacIntyre (1929—) is an American philosopher teaching at the University of Notre Dame. In 1981 he published his most well known work *After Virtue*, and followed that up with two other influential works *Whose Justice? Which Rationality?* and *Three Rival Versions of Moral Inquiry.*

According to MacIntyre, Enlightenment philosophy promised an ability to reason apart from personal perspectives and biases in hopes of reaching "the most rational conclusions" possible. In so doing it cast off traditional approaches to ethical theory in hopes of developing a moral basis founded on a rationality (pure reason) independent of history, context, human nature or human purpose. What resulted, however, was something far different.

MacIntyre suggests that instead of reaching a unifying consensus, Enlightenment philosophy led only to disagreements. He argues that the resulting condition of modern morality is a condition in which we possess only "fragments of a conceptual scheme, parts which now lack those contexts from which their significance was derived . . . We continue to use many of the key expressions . . . but we have—very largely, if not entirely—lost our comprehension, both theoretical and practical, of morality."[12] In particular MacIntyre argues that the adoption of Enlightenment morality and the rejection of Aristotelian teleology led to the denial that humans have any specific, identifiable purpose beyond individualized autonomous preference. The modern person, then, becomes simply a rational agent with no true purpose independent of his or her own will.

According to MacIntyre, then, the Enlightenment project was morally disastrous. To the contrary he points out that with Aristotle one could at least distinguish between the way we actually are and the way we should be. His conception of human beings as having a specific *telos* brought with it the possibility of moral accountability and the idea that we might fall short of the ideal. But with the rejection of Aristotelianism came the rejection of any such distinction. The practical result, he argues, is that our moral language is now deprived of content. Persons (and society) are now adrift in a sea of moral uncertainty. Therefore, in opposition to the modernistic trend MacIntyre believes that modern ethicists have the most to learn from a recovery of the Aristotelian tradition and the return to virtue based ethics.

Stanley Hauerwas

Stanley Hauerwas currently holds the Gilbert T. Rowe professorship of theological ethics at Duke Divinity School. Like MacIntyre, Hauerwas has a strong aversion to the ethical trajectory introduced by Enlightenment liberalism. His work emphasizes the need for ethical theories to recover the significance of virtues and virtuous living as fundamental to the nature of the good life. To this end he advocates a move away from claims to objective moral laws to guide ethical behavior and emphasizes instead the importance of developing virtues compliant with the particular community narrative (or tradition) to which one finds oneself loyal.

By appealing to the necessity of understanding the particular virtues of a given "narrative," Hauerwas advocates a community dependent version of virtue ethics. He argues that because humans are necessarily influenced by their context it is impossible to speak of ethics without recognizing the context of community from which ethics arise. Thus it is best to speak of ethics in terms of the "story" of a community or tradition. The use of language such as "story" should not imply that something that is not "true" or is somehow only a myth or fantasy, rather, "story" emphasizes the ongoing nature of the tradition and the progressive events and experiences a community shares as its basis and points of reference. Simply put, he believes "story" is the best way to talk of God and God's actions toward his people and it is in light of the end or *telos* inherent in that story that virtues become the key element in determining moral behavior.

In regard to the Christian story, which he advocates, Hauerwas asserts that the events that primarily shape the narrative, are the acts of creation and redemption. The Christian community develops around these events and forms its doctrines and morality in light of these events. For example, Hauerwas describes these Christian doctrines not as propositional truths but as products of the narrative which serve as "outlines" of the faith. Similarly, the rules and principles that are developed within the narrative serve as outer boundaries or limits of that narrative that alert individuals to the fact that a rejection of them essentially moves one outside of the narrative or story. In his *Community of Character* Hauerwas maintains that within the Christian narrative the doctrine of justification (salvation through the life, death, and resurrection of Christ) signifies the source of the Christian story and the doctrine of sanctification (moral growth in light of salvation) is the description of the journey we are to take in and through the narrative.

Christ, then, becomes the pattern for the Hauerwas' ethic. Christians are to strive to be like Christ. This striving is not patterned on "doing" but rather on "being." For this to occur, the emphasis is on the development of character traits like those modeled by Christ. Individuals within this community develop virtues through practice and the emulation of others within the narrative who exemplify Christian virtue. As individuals become more Christlike, they corporately form a community (the Church) that in turn exhibits a specific character that is distinct from the world. It becomes a community of character.

Two of the virtues emphasized as characteristic of the Christian community are "hope" and "patience." The hope of the Christian community lies in the claim that God is preeminently concerned with the outcome of human events and history. Therefore, humans should not place their hope in determining their own outcomes, but in following Christ. Christians place their hope in God to bring about what he wills in circumstances. Patience, then, is also an important virtue because followers of Christ must wait on God to bring about his desired ends as we attempt to follow him in spite of circumstances.

VII. Summary and Conclusion

Summarizing the basic characteristics of virtue ethics, it is important to keep central the idea that moral behavior is evaluated not in terms of whether or not an action is right or wrong, but whether the behavior is indicative of a good or bad person. That is, the ethical focus is on the person doing the act, not on the act itself.

The two necessary ingredients in the structure of a virtue ethic are an emphasis on the orientation of moral behavior toward the proper end and the development of personal character traits or virtues that enable a person to consistently act toward that end. Most theories of virtue ethics describe the end toward which persons should aim as *eudaemonia*—or human flourishing. Even though the understanding of what constitutes a *eudaemonistic* life may differ (as it does in the four classical theories discussed above), there is a clear understanding of an end or telos toward which an individual should guide moral behavior.

Similarly, virtue theories also emphasize the possession of enduring character qualities or traits known as virtues. Again, while the specific nature of those virtues may vary among differing theorists, the lack or possession of these qualities is the primary point of evaluation regarding morality. Integrating these elements one can say that if a person is oriented toward the proper end and they have the dispositional qualities in their character to move toward that end, then the action can be described as morally good, and the "rightness" of the particular action will usually follow. Indeed, the argument is that the moral behavior stemming from good persons will be both more consistent and qualitatively superior to those persons who act simply to follow rules.

If, then, virtue can be defined as the consistent character disposition moving toward a good end or goal, then it is possible to argue that the chief "virtue" of virtue ethics is the emphasis on the character of persons over and above specific acts in the evaluation of moral and ethical behavior. While many modern ethical theories focus on the determination of acts through the use of rules and principles, virtue ethics attempt to deal with the qualities and characteristic of the actor. While ethical theories focusing on rules or principles (such as deontology and consequentialism) run the risk of becoming empty forms of legalism or cold rationalistic self-maximizing, virtues ethics offers a different course. By emphasizing *being a good person* over and above *doing the right thing*, virtue ethics offers not only a whole person approach to ethics, but essentially links the action of a person to the character of a person. In a day and age that tends to separate the act from the person and divorce behavior from personal responsibility, that is a virtuous approach indeed.

Endnotes

[1] Augustine, *Psalm 32* sermon, 3.15.

[2] Augustine, *Confessions* 10. 27.39.

[3] Augustine, *Psalm 32* sermon 3.15,16.

[4] Augustine, *Moral Behavior* VIII.

[5] Augustine, *Moral Behavior* XV.

[6] Augustine, *On the morals of the Catholic Church* 15

[7] Augustine, *City of God* 19.25

[8] Joseph J. Kotva. *The Christian Case for Virtue Ethics* (Georgetown University Press: Wash, D.C., 1996), 1.

[9] Vernon J. Bourke "Thomistic Ethics," in *The Westminster Dictionary of Christian Ethics*, (Westminster Press, Philadelphia, 1967), 623.

[10] Thomas Aquinas *Summa Theologica* 1-11. 61.3c

[11] Beauchamp & Childress, for example, recognize the importance of virtues in the practice of medicine and medical ethics. See *Principles of Bioethics*, 4th ed. (New York: Oxford University Press, 1994).

[12] Alsdair MacIntyre, *After Virtue* (Notre Dame: Notre Dame, 1981), 2.

ETHICS: ETHICS AND MORAL DEVELOPMENT THEORIES

HABIT AND VIRTUE

by Aristotle

How does one become virtuous? According to Aristotle, although we are endowed by nature with the capacity to acquire virtue, we are not virtuous by nature. We become virtuous by performing virtuous acts repeatedly until such acts become "second nature." Legislators, too, seek to promote virtue in citizens by a moral education that habituates citizens to virtuous behavior. This goal is achieved by exposing young people to situations where they may exhibit courage or temperance and by reinforcing such behavior through repetition and reward for creditable performance. Right acts demonstrate moderation. For example, courageous acts avoid the extremes of cowardice on the one side and foolhardiness on the other.

Moral education is compared to training for strength. We become strong by *doing* things that require strength. Similarly, we become virtuous by behaving virtuously until such behavior "stands firm" in us. Pains and pleasures are used as incentives to virtuous behavior during moral training. Later, virtuous behavior becomes pleasurable to us as an end in itself.

Aristotle considers an objection to his view that we become virtuous by behaving virtuously: that it seems we must have been virtuous to begin with. Aristotle replies that our earliest virtuous activity may be somewhat random; the educator identifies the virtuous activity and reinforces it. After the right behavior is reinforced and the wrong behavior is rejected and rendered undesirable, the student has learned to be virtuous automatically. The virtue is internalized; it is no longer a virtue of deed, but of character. Virtuous behavior that stems from character is not random at all, but consists of acts done in the manner that a just or temperate person would do them.

Book II.

The moral virtues, then, are engendered in us neither *by* nor *contrary to* nature; we are constituted by nature to receive them, but their full development in us is due to habit.

Again, of all those faculties with which nature endows us we first acquire the potentialities, and only later effect their actualization. (This is evident in the case of the senses. It was not from repeated acts of seeing or hearing that we acquired the senses but the other way round: we had these senses before we used them; we did not acquire them as the result of using them.) But the virtues we do acquire by first exercising them, just as happens in the arts. Anything that we have to learn to do we learn by the actual doing of it: people become builders by building and instrumentalists by playing instruments. Similarly we become just by performing just acts, temperate by performing temperate ones, brave by performing brave ones. This view is supported by what happens in city-states. Legislators make their citizens good by habituation; this is the intention of every legislator, and those who do not carry it out fail of their object. This is what makes the difference between a good constitution and a bad one.

Again, the causes or means that bring about any form of excellence are the same as those that destroy it, and similarly with art; for it is as a result of playing the harp that people become good and bad harpists. The same principle applies to builders and all other craftsmen. Men will become good builders as a result of building well, and bad ones as a result of building badly. Otherwise there would be no need of anyone to teach them: they would all be *born* either good or bad. Now this holds good also of the virtues. It is the way that we behave in our dealings with other people that makes us just or unjust, and the way that we behave in the face of danger, accustoming ourselves to be timid or confident, that makes us brave or cowardly. Similarly with situations involving desires and angry feelings: some people become temperate and patient from one kind of conduct in such situations, others licentious and choleric from another. In a word, then, like activities produce like dispositions. Hence we must give our activities a certain quality, because it is their characteristics that determine the resulting dispositions. So it is a matter of no little importance what sort of habits we form from the earliest age—it makes a vast difference, or rather all the difference in the world.

In a practical science, so much depends on particular circumstances that only general rules can be given.

ii. Since the branch of philosophy on which we are at present engaged is not, like the others, theoretical in its aim—because we are studying not to know what goodness is, but how to become good men, since otherwise it would be useless—we must apply our minds to the problem of how our actions should be performed, because, as we have just said, it is these that actually determine our dispositions.

Now that we should act according to the right principle is common ground and may be assumed as a basis for discussion (the point will be discussed later, both what "the right principle" is, and how it is related to the other virtues). But we must first agree that any account of conduct must be stated in outline and not in precise detail, just as we said at the beginning that accounts are to be required only in such a form as befits their subject-matter. Now questions of conduct and expedience have as little fixity about them as questions of what is healthful; and if this is true of the general rule, it is still more true that its application to particular problems admits of no precision. For they do not fall under any art or professional tradition, but the agents are compelled at every step to think out for themselves what the circumstances demand, just as happens in the arts of medicine and navigation. However, although our present account is of this kind, we must try to support it.

A cardinal rule: right conduct is incompatible with excess or deficiency in feelings and actions.

First, then, we must consider this fact: that it is in the nature of moral qualities that they are destroyed by deficiency and excess, just as we can see (since we have to use the evidence of visible facts to throw light on those that are invisible) in the case of [bodily] health and strength. For both excessive and insufficient exercise destroy one's strength, and both eating and drinking too much or too little destroy health, whereas the right quantity produces, increases and preserves it. So it is the same with temperance, courage and the other virtues. The man who shuns and fears everything and stands up to nothing becomes a coward; the man who is afraid of nothing at all, but marches up to every danger, becomes foolhardy. Similarly the man who indulges in every pleasure and refrains from none becomes licentious; but if a man behaves like a boor and turns his back on every pleasure, he is a case of insensibility. Thus temperance and courage are destroyed by excess and deficiency and preserved by the mean.

Our virtues are exercised in the same kinds of action as gave rise to them.

But besides the fact that the virtues are induced and fostered as a result, and by the agency, of the same sort of actions as cause their destruction, the activities that flow from them will also consist in the same sort of actions. This is so in all the other more observable instances, e.g. in that of [bodily] strength. This results from taking plenty of nourishment and undergoing severe training, and it is the strong man that will be best able to carry out this programme. So with the virtues. It is by refraining from pleasures that we become temperate, and it is when we have become temperate that we are most able to abstain from pleasures. Similarly with courage; it is by habituating ourselves to make light of alarming situations and to face them that we become brave, and it is when we have become brave that we shall be most able to face an alarming situation.

The pleasure or pain that actions cause the agent may serve as an index of moral progress, since good conduct consists in a proper attitude towards pleasure and pain.

iii. The pleasure or pain that accompanies people's acts should be taken as a sign of their dispositions. A man who abstains from bodily pleasures and enjoys the very fact of so doing is temperate; if he finds it irksome he is licentious. Again, the man who faces danger gladly, or at least without distress, is brave; the one who feels distressed is a coward. For it is with pleasures and pains that moral goodness is concerned. Pleasure induces us to behave badly, and pain to shrink from fine actions. Hence the importance (as Plato says) of having been trained in some way from infancy to feel joy and grief at the right things: true education is precisely this. If the virtues are concerned with actions and feelings, and every feeling and every action is always accompanied by pleasure or pain, on this ground too virtue will be concerned with pleasures and pains. The fact that punishments are effected by their means is further evidence, because punishment is a kind of remedial treatment, and such treatment is naturally effected by contraries. Again, as we said above, every state of the soul attains its natural development in relation to, and in the sphere of, those conditions by which it is naturally made better or worse. Now when people become bad it is because of pleasures and pains, through seeking (or shunning) the wrong ones, or at the wrong time, or in the wrong way, or in any other manner in which such offences are distinguished by principle. This is why some thinkers actually define the virtues as forms of impassivity or tranquillity. But they are wrong in speaking absolutely instead of adding "in the right (or wrong) manner and at the right time" and any other due qualifications.

We have decided, then, that this kind of virtue disposes us to act in the best way with regard to pleasures and pains, and contrariwise with the corresponding vice. But we may obtain further light on the same point from the following considerations.

There are three factors that make for choice, and three that make for avoidance: the fine, the advantageous, and the pleasant, and their contraries, the base, the harmful, and the painful. Now with regard to all these the good man tends to go right and the bad man to go wrong, especially about pleasure. This is common to all animals, and accompanies all objects of choice, for clearly the fine and the advantageous are pleasant too. Consciousness of pleasure has grown up with all of us from our infancy, and therefore our life is so deeply imbued with this feeling that it is hard to remove all trace of it. Pleasure and pain are also the standards by which—to a greater or lesser extent— we regulate our actions. Since to feel pleasure and pain rightly or wrongly has no little effect upon conduct, it follows that our whole inquiry must be concerned with these sensations. Heraclitus says that it is hard to fight against emotion, but harder still to fight against pleasure; and the harder course is always the concern of both art and virtue, because success is better in the face of difficulty. Thus on this ground too the whole concern of both morality and political science must be with pleasures and pains, since the man who treats them rightly will be good and the one who treats them wrongly will be bad.

We may take this as a sufficient statement that virtue is concerned with pains and pleasures; that the actions that produce it also increase it, or if differently performed, destroy it; and that the actions that produce it also constitute the sphere of its activity.

Acts that are incidentally virtuous distinguished from those that are done knowingly, of choice, and from a virtuous disposition.

iv. A difficulty, however, may be raised as to how we can say that people must perform just actions if they are to become just, and temperate ones if they are to become temperate; because if they do what is just and temperate, they are just and temperate already, in the same way that if they use words or play music correctly they are already literate or musical. But surely this is not true even of the arts. It is possible to put a few words together correctly by accident, or at the prompting of another person; so the agent will only be literate if he does a literate act in a literate way, viz. in virtue of his own literacy. Nor, again, is there an analogy between the arts and the virtues. Works of art have their merit in themselves; so it is enough for them to be turned out with a certain quality of their own. But virtuous acts are not done in a just or temperate way merely because *they* have a certain quality, but only if the agent also acts in a certain state, viz. (1) if he knows what he is doing, (2) if he chooses it, and chooses it for its own sake, and (3) if he does it from a fixed and permanent disposition. Now these—knowledge excepted—are not reckoned as necessary qualifications for the arts as well. For the acquisition of virtues, on the other hand, knowledge has little or no force; but the other requirements are not of little but of supreme importance, granted that it is from the repeated performance of just and temperate acts that we acquire virtues. Acts, to be sure, are called just and temperate when they are such as a just or temperate man would do; but what makes the agent just or temperate is not merely the fact that he does such things, but the fact that he does them in the way that just and temperate men do. It is therefore right to say that a man becomes just by the performance of just, and temperate by the performance of temperate, acts; nor is there the smallest likelihood of any man's becoming good by not doing them. This is not, however, the course that most people follow: they have recourse to their principle, and imagine that they are being philosophical and that in this way they will become serious-minded—behaving rather like invalids who listen carefully to their doctor, but carry out none of his instructions. Just as the bodies of the latter will get no benefit from such treatment, so the souls of the former will get none from such philosophy . . . .

Book IX

So much for ethical theory. How can it be put into practice?

ix. Assuming, then, that we have given (in outline) a sufficient account of happiness and the several virtues, and also of friendship and pleasure, may we regard our undertaking as now completed? Or is the correct view that (as we have been saying) in the case of conduct the end consists not in gaining theoretical knowledge of the several points at issue, but rather in putting our knowledge into practice? In that case it is not enough to know about goodness; we must endeavour to possess and use it, or adopt any other means to become good ourselves. Now if discourses were enough in themselves to make people moral, to quote Theognis: "Many and fat would be the fees they earned," quite rightly; and to provide such discourses would be what is needed. But as it is we find that although they have the power to stimulate and encourage those of the young who are liberal-minded, and although they can render a generous and truly idealistic character susceptible of virtue, they are incapable of impelling the masses towards human perfection. For it is the nature of the many to be ruled by fear rather than by shame, and to refrain from evil not because of the disgrace but because of the punishments. Living under the sway of their feelings, they pursue their own pleasures and the means of obtaining them, and shun the pains that are their opposites; but of that which is fine and truly pleasurable they have not even a conception, since they have never had a taste of it. What discourse could ever reform people like that? To dislodge by argument habits long embedded in the character is a difficult if not impossible task. We should probably be content if the combination of all the means that are supposed to make us good enables us to attain some portion of goodness.

Goodness can only be induced in a suitably receptive character.

Some thinkers hold that it is by nature that people become good, others that it is by habit, and others that it is by instruction. The bounty of nature is clearly beyond our control; it is bestowed by some divine dispensation upon those who are truly fortunate. It is a regrettable fact that discussion and instruction are not effective in all cases: just as a piece of land has to be prepared beforehand if it is to nourish the seed, so the mind of the pupil has to be prepared in its habits if it is to enjoy and dislike the right things, because the man who lives in accordance with his feelings would not listen to an argument to dissuade him, or understand it if he did. And when a man is in that state, how is it possible to persuade him out of it? In general, feeling seems to yield not to argument but only to force. Therefore we must have a character to work on that has some affinity to virtue: one that appreciates what is noble and objects to what is base.

Education in goodness is best undertaken by the state.

But to obtain a right training for goodness from an early age is a hard thing, unless one has been brought up under right laws. For a temperate and hardy way of life is not a pleasant thing to most people, especially when they are young. For this reason upbringing and occupations should be regulated by law, because they will cease to be irksome when they have become habitual. But presumably it is not enough to have received the right upbringing and supervision in youth; they must keep on observing their regimen and accustoming themselves to it even after they are grown up; so we shall need laws to regulate these activities too, and indeed generally to cover the whole of life; for most people are readier to submit to compulsion and punishment than to argument and fine ideals. This is why some people think that although legislators ought to encourage people to goodness and appeal to their finer feelings, in the hope that those who have had a decent training in their habits will respond, they ought also to inflict chastisement and penalties on any who disobey through deficiency of character, and to deport the incorrigible altogether. For they hold that while the good man, whose life is related to a fine ideal, will listen to reason, the bad one whose object is pleasure must be controlled by pain, like a beast of burden. This is also why they say that the pains inflicted should be those that are most contrary to the favoured pleasures.

To resume, however: if (as we have said) in order to be a good man one must first have been brought up in the right way and trained in the right habits, and must thereafter spend one's life in reputable occupations, doing no wrong either with or against one's will: then this can be achieved by living under the guidance of some intelligence or right system that has effective force. Now the orders that a father gives have no forceful or compulsive power, nor indeed have those of any individual in general, unless he is a king or somebody of that sort; but law, being the pronouncement of a kind of practical wisdom or intelligence, does have the power of compulsion. And although people resent it when their impulses are opposed by human agents, even if the latter are in the right, the law causes no irritation by enjoining decent behaviour. Yet in Sparta alone, or almost alone, the lawgiver seems to have concerned himself with upbringing and daily life. In the great majority of states matters of this kind have been completely neglected, and every man lives his life as he likes, "laying down the law for wife and children," like the Cyclopes.

If neglected by the state, it can be supplied by the parent; but it calls for some knowledge of legislative science.

The best solution would be to introduce a proper system of public supervision of these matters. But if they continue to be completely neglected by the state, it would seem to be right for each individual to help his own children and friends on the way to goodness, and that he should have the power or at least the choice of doing this . . . . [P]roducing a right disposition in any person that is set before you is not a task for everybody: if anyone can do it, it is the man with knowledge—just as in the case of medicine and all the other professions that call for application and practical understanding.

THE CHILD AS A MORAL PHILOSOPHER

by Lawrence Kohlberg

Lawrence Kohlberg (1927-1987) was professor of education and social psychology at Harvard University. He wrote numerous articles on cognitive moral development and was director of the Harvard University Center for Moral Development and Education.

The psychologist Lawrence Kohlberg was interested in moral development. Like several other thinkers, he was concerned with the problems that arise in a relativistic approach to the teaching of values. In this essay Kohlberg says he will "demonstrate that moral education can be free from the charge of cultural relativity and arbitrary indoctrination." The problem of indoctrination cannot be dismissed by insisting that in teaching values the teacher need not indoctrinate students but merely "socialize" them. Nor can the problem of indoctrination be mitigated by confining teachers to the inculcation of "positive" values: for who is to say which values are to be called positive? Kohlberg also objects to values clarification, which avoids indoctrination by allowing the teacher to present a smorgasborg of values for the child to choose from. This only confuses the student and renders teachers ineffective as moral educators. (They cannot, for example, persuasively condemn cheating.)

With this background Kohlberg introduces his three-level (six-stage) theory of transcultural moral development. According to Kohlberg all children begin with a preconventional first level in which morality is determined largely by expected punishment and reward, move on to a conventional second level where social norms and need for approval dominate, and eventually proceed to a third level where the individual is self-motivated to adhere to universal moral principles. Good teachers do not indoctrinate; they merely assist students in moving from one stage to the next stage by helping them become conscious of where they currently are and by showing them where they might go next. Such forward movement is brought about by discussing problematic moral situations. For example, children are presented with the Heinz dilemma in which Heinz, who lacks the money to buy a lifesaving drug, obtains it by robbing the druggist. Children are asked whether Heinz did the right thing. Such discussion sharpens children's moral sensibility and also helps move children to a more sophisticated level of moral development.

Thus, Kohlberg's answer to relativism is to argue that in all societies individuals go through the very *same* stages of moral development—though in some cultures the majority of the population are fixed at a conventional level of moral development and have not reached the stage of universal justice. The ideal development goes beyond conventional morality to recognize universal principles of justice and equality.

Although *moral education* has a forbidding sound to teachers, they constantly practice it. They tell children what to do, make evaluations of children's behavior, and direct children's relations in the classrooms. Sometimes teachers do these things without being aware that they are engaging in moral education, but the children are aware of it. For example, my second-grade son told me that he did not want to be one of the bad boys. Asked "Who were the bad boys?" he replied, "The ones who don't put their books back where they belong and get yelled at." His teacher would have been surprised to know that her concerns with classroom management defined for her children what she and her school thought were basic moral values or that she was engaged in value indoctrination.

Most teachers are aware that they are teaching values, like it or not, and are very concerned as to whether this teaching is unjustified indoctrination. In particular, they are uncertain as to whether their own moral opinions should be presented as "moral truths," whether they should be expressed merely as personal opinion or should be omitted from classroom discussion entirely. As an example, an experienced junior high school teacher told us,

> My class deals with morality and right and wrong quite a bit. I don't expect all of them to agree with me; each has to satisfy himself according to his own convictions, as long as he is sincere and thinks he is pursuing what is right. I often discuss cheating this way but I always get *defeated*, because they still argue cheating is all right. After you accept the idea that kids have the right to build a position with logical arguments, you have to accept what they come out with, even though you drive at it ten times a year and they still come out with the same conclusion.

This teacher's confusion is apparent. She believes everyone should "have his own ideas," and yet she is most unhappy if this leads to a point where some of these ideas include the notion that "it's all right to cheat." In other words, she is smack up against the problem of relativity of values in moral education. Using this teacher as an example, I will attempt to demonstrate that moral education can be free from the charge of cultural relativity and arbitrary indoctrination that inhibits her when she talks about cheating.

Cop-Out Solutions to the Relativity Problem

To begin with, I want to reject a few cop-outs or false solutions sometimes suggested as solving the relativity problem. One is to call moral education *socialization*. Sociologists have sometimes claimed that moralization in the interests of classroom management and maintenance of the school as a social system is a hidden curriculum; that it performs hidden services in helping children adapt to society (Jackson, 1968). They have argued that, since praise and blame on the part of teachers is a necessary aspect of the socialization process, the teacher does not have to consider the psychological and philosophic issues of moral education. In learning to conform to the teacher's expectations and the school rules, children are becoming socialized, they are internalizing the norms and standards of society. In practice, it means that we call the teacher's yelling at her students for not putting their books away *socialization*. To label it *socialization* does not legitimate it as valid education, nor does it remove the charge of arbitrary indoctrination from it. Basically, this sociological argument implies that respect for social authority is a moral good in itself. Stated in different terms, the notion that it is valid for the teacher to have an unreflective hidden curriculum is based on the notion that the teacher is the agent of the state, the church, or the social system, rather than being a free moral agent dealing with children who are free moral agents. The notion that the teacher is the agent of the state is taken for granted in some educational systems, such as that of the Soviets. However, the moral curriculum is not hidden in Soviet education; it is done explicitly and well as straight indoctrination (Bronfenbrenner, 1968). For the moment, I will not argue what is wrong with indoctrination but will assume that it is incompatible with the conceptions of civil liberties that are central not only to American democracy but to any just social system.

Let us turn now to the second cop-out. This is to rely on vaguely positive and honorific-sounding terms such as "moral values" or "moral and spiritual values." We can see in the following statements how a program called "Teaching Children Values in the Upper Elementary School" (Carr and Wellenberg, 1966) relies on a vague usage of "moral and spiritual values":

> Many of our national leaders have expressed anxiety about an increasing lack of concern for personal moral and spiritual values. Throughout history, nations have sought value systems to help people live congenially. The Golden Rule and the Ten Commandments are examples of such value systems. Each pupil needs to acquire a foundation of sound values to help him act correctly and make proper choices between right and wrong, truth and untruth. The teacher can develop a sound value system in the following ways:
>
> 1. Be a good example.
> 2. Help young people to assess conflict situations and to gain insight into the development of constructive values and attitudes. Situations arise daily in which pupils can receive praise that will reinforce behavior that exemplified desired values.
> 3. Show young people how to make generalizations concerning experience through evaluation and expression of desirable values.
> 4. Help students acquire an understanding of the importance of values that society considers worthwhile.
> 5. Aid children to uphold and use positive values when confronted by adverse pressure from peers. [p. 11]

The problem, however, is to define these "positive values." We may agree that "positive values" are desirable, but the term conceals the fact that teachers, children, and societies have different ideas as to what constitutes "positive values." Although Carr and Wellenberg cite the Ten Commandments and the Golden Rule as "value systems sought by nations," they also could have used the code of Hitler or of the communist youth as examples of "value systems sought by nations."

I raise the issue of the "relativity of values" in this context because the words *moral, positive,* and *values* are interpreted by each teacher in a different way, depending on the teacher's own values and standards.

This becomes clear when we consider our third cop-out. This is the cop-out of defining moral values in terms of what I call a "bag of virtues." By a "bag of virtues," I mean a set of personality traits generally considered to be positive. Defining the aims of moral education in terms of a set of "virtues" is as old as Aristotle, who said, "Virtue . . . [is] of two kinds, intellectual and moral. . . . [The moral] virtues we get by first exercising them . . . we become just by doing just acts, temperate by doing temperate acts, brave by doing brave acts."

The attraction of such an approach is evident. Although it is true that people often cannot agree on details of right and wrong or even on fundamental moral principles, we all think such "traits" as honesty and responsibility are good things. By adding enough traits to the virtue bag, we eventually get a list that contains something to suit everyone.

This approach to moral education was widely prevalent in the public schools in the 1920s and 1930s and was called "character education." The educators and psychologists, such as Havighurst and Taba (1949), who developed these approaches defined character as the sum total of a set of "those traits of personality which are subject to the moral sanctions of society."

One difficulty with this approach to moral character is that everyone has his own bag. However, the problem runs deeper than the composition of a given list of virtues and vices. Although it may be true that the notion of teaching virtues, such as honesty or integrity, arouses little controversy, it is also true that a vague consensus on the goodness of these virtues conceals a great deal of actual disagreement over their definitions. What is one person's "integrity" is another person's "stubbornness," what is one person's honesty in "expressing your true feelings" is another person's insensitivity to the feelings of others. This is evident in controversial fields of adult behavior. Student protectors view their behavior as reflecting the virtues of altruism, idealism, awareness, and courage. Those in opposition regard the same behavior as reflecting the vices of irresponsibility and disrespect for "law and order." Although this difficulty can be recognized clearly in college education, it is easier for teachers of younger children to think that their judgments in terms of the bag of virtues are objective and independent of their own value biases. However, a parent will not agree that a child's specific failure to obey an "unreasonable" request by the teacher was wrong, even if the teacher calls the act "uncooperative," as some teachers are prone to do.

I have summarized three cop-outs from the relativity problem and rejected them. Socialization, teaching positive values, and developing a bag of virtues all leave the teacher where she was—stuck with her own personal value standards and biases to be imposed on her students. There is one last cop-out to the relativity problem. That is to lie back and enjoy it or encourage it. In the new social studies, this is called *value clarification*.

As summarized by Engel (in Simon, 1971, p. 902), this position holds that

> In the consideration of values, there is no single correct answer, but value clarification is supremely important. One must contrast value clarification and value inculcation. Inculcation suggests that the learner has limited control and hence limited responsibility in the development of his own values. He needs to be told what values are or what he should value.
>
> This is not to suggest, however, that nothing is ever inculcated. As a matter of fact, in order to clarify values, at least one principle needs to be adopted by all concerned. Perhaps the only way the principle can be adopted is through some procedure which might best be termed *inculcation*. That principle might be stated as follows: in the consideration of values there is no single correct answer. More specifically it might be said that the adequate posture both for students and teachers in clarifying values is openness.

Although the basic premise of this value clarification approach is that "everyone has his own values," it is further advocated that children can and should learn (1) to be more aware of their own values and how they relate to their decisions, (2) to make their values consistent and to order them in hierarchies for decisions, (3) to be more aware of the divergencies between their value hierarchies and those of others, and (4) to tolerate these divergencies. In other words, although values are regarded as arbitrary and relative, there may be universal, rational strategies for making decisions that maximize these values. Part of this rational strategy is to recognize that values are relative. Within this set of premises, it is quite logical to teach that values are relative as part of the overall program.

An elaboration of this approach can be found in *Decision Making: A Guide for Teachers Who Would Help Preadolescent Children Become Imaginative and Responsible Decision Makers* (Dodder and Dodder, 1968). In a portion of this book, modern social scientific perspectives are used to develop a curriculum unit entitled "Why Don't We All Make the Same Decisions?" A set of classroom materials and activities are then presented to demonstrate to children the following propositions: (1) we don't all make the same decisions because our values are different; (2) our values tend to originate outside ourselves; (3) our values are different because each of us has been influenced by different important others; and (4) our values are different because each of us has been influenced by a different cultural environment.

The teacher is told to have the children discuss moral dilemmas in such a way as to reveal those different values. As an example, one child might make a moral decision in terms of avoiding punishment, another in terms of the welfare of other people, another in terms of certain rules, another in terms of getting the most for himself. The children are then to be encouraged to discuss their values with each other and to recognize that everyone has different values. Whether or not "the welfare of others" is a more adequate value than "avoiding punishment" is not an issue to be raised by the teacher. Rather, the teacher is instructed to teach only that "our values are different."

Indeed, acceptance of the idea that *all* values are relative does, logically, lead to the conclusion that the teacher should not attempt to teach *any* particular moral values. This leaves the teacher in the quandary of our teacher who could not successfully argue against cheating. The students of a teacher who has been successful in communicating moral relativism will believe, like the teacher, that "everyone has his own bag" and that "everyone should keep doing his thing." If one of these students has learned his relativity lesson, when he is caught cheating he will argue that he did nothing wrong. The basis of his argument will be that his own hierarchy of values, which may be different from that of the teacher, made it right for him to cheat. Although recognizing that other people believe that cheating is wrong, he himself holds the "value" that one should cheat when the opportunity presents itself. If teachers want to be consistent and retain their relativistic beliefs, they would have to concede.

Now I am not criticizing the value clarification approach itself. It is a basic and valuable component of the new social studies curricula, as I have discussed (1973). My point is, rather, that value clarification is not a sufficient solution to the relativity problem. Furthermore, the actual teaching of relativism is itself an indoctrination or teaching of a fixed belief, a belief that we are going to show is not true scientifically or philosophically. . . .

A Typological Scheme on the Stages of Moral Thought

In other words, I am happy to report that I can propose a solution to the relativity problem that has plagued philosophers for three thousand years. I can say this with due modesty because it did not depend on being smart. It only happened that my colleagues and I were the first people in history to do detailed cross-cultural studies on the development of moral thinking.

The following dilemma should clarify the issue:

The Heinz Dilemma

In Europe, a woman was near death from a very bad disease, a special kind of cancer. There was one drug that the doctors thought might save her. It was a form of radium that a druggist in the same town had recently discovered. The drug was expensive to make, but the druggist was charging ten times what the drug cost him to make. He paid $200 for the radium and charged $2,000 for a small dose of the drug. The sick woman's husband, Heinz, went to everyone he knew to borrow the money, but he could get together only about $1,000, which was half of what it cost. He told the druggist that his wife was dying and asked him to sell it cheaper or let him pay later. But the druggist said, "No, I discovered the drug and I'm going to make money from it." Heinz got desperate and broke into the man's store to steal the drug for his wife.

Should the husband have done that? Was it right or wrong? Is your decision that it is right (or wrong) objectively right, is it morally universal, or is it your personal opinion? If you think it is morally right to steal the drug, you must face the fact that it is legally wrong. What is the basis of your view that it is morally right, then, more than your personal opinion? Is it anything that can be agreed on? If you think so, let me report the results of a National Opinion Research Survey on the question, asked of a representative sample of adult Americans. Seventy-five percent said it was wrong to steal, though most said they might do it.

Can one take anything but a relativist position on the question? By a relativist position, I mean a position like that of Bob, a high school senior. He said, "There's a million ways to look at it. Heinz had a moral decision to make. Was it worse to steal or let his wife die? In my mind, I can either condemn him or condone him. In this case, I think it was fine. But possibly the druggist was working on a capitalist morality of supply and demand."

I went on to ask Bob, "Would it be wrong if he didn't steal it?"

Bob replied, "It depends on how he is oriented morally. If he thinks it's worse to steal than to let his wife die, then it would be wrong what he did. It's all relative; what I would do is steal the drug. I can't say that's right or wrong or that it's what everyone should do."

But even if you agree with Bob's relativism you may not want to go as far as he did. He started the interview by wondering if he could answer because he "questioned the whole terminology, the whole moral bag." He continued, "But then I'm also an incredible moralist, a real puritan in some sense and moods. My moral judgment and the way I perceive things morally changes very much when my mood changes. When I'm in a cynical mood, I take a cynical view of morals, but still, whether I like it or not, I'm terribly moral in the way I look at things. But I'm not too comfortable with it." Bob's moral perspective was well expressed in the late Joe Gould's poem called "My Religion." Brief and to the point, the poem said, "In winter I'm a Buddhist, in the summer I'm a nudist."

Now, Bob's relativism rests on a confusion. The confusion is that between relativity as the social science fact that different people *do* have different moral values and relativity as the philosophic claim that people *ought* to have different moral values, that no moral values are justified for all people.

To illustrate, I quote a not atypical response of one of my graduate students to the same moral dilemma. She said, "I think he should steal it because if there is any such thing as a universal human value, it is the value of life, and that would justify it."

I then asked her, "Is there any such thing as a universal human value?" and she answered, "No, all values are relative to your culture."

She began by claiming that one ought to act in terms of the universal value of human life, implying that human life is a universal value in the sense that it is logical and desirable for all people to respect all human life, that one can demonstrate to other people that it is logical and desirable to act in this way. If she were clear in her thinking, she would see that the fact that all people do not always act in terms of this value does not contradict the claim that all people ought to always act in accordance with it. Because she made this confusion, she ended in total confusion.

What I am going to claim is that if we distinguish the issues of universality as fact and the possibility of universal moral ideals we get a positive answer to both questions. As far as facts go, I claim just the opposite of what Dodder and Dodder (1968) claimed to be basic social science truths. I claim that

1. We often make different decisions and yet have the same basic moral values.
2. Our values tend to originate inside ourselves as we process our social experience.
3. In every culture and subculture of the world, both the same basic moral values and the same steps toward moral maturity are found. Although social environments directly produce different specific beliefs (for example, smoking is wrong, eating pork is wrong), they do not engender different basic moral principles (for example, "consider the welfare of others," "treat other people equally," and so on).

4.   Basic values are different largely because we are at different levels of maturity in thinking about basic moral and social issues and concepts. Exposure to others more mature than ourselves helps stimulate maturity in our own value process.

All parents know that the basic values of their children do not come from the outside, from the parents, although many wish they did. For example, at the age of four my son joined the pacifist and vegetarian movement and refused to eat meat because, he said, it is bad to kill animals. In spite of his parents' attempts to dissuade him by arguing about the difference between justified and unjustified killing, he remained a vegetarian for six months. However, he did recognize that some forms of killing were "legitimate." One night I read to him from a book about Eskimo life that included a description of a seal-killing expedition. While listening to the story, he became very angry and said, "You know, there is one kind of meat I would eat, Eskimo meat. It's bad to kill animals so it's all right to eat Eskimos."

This episode illustrates (1) that children often generate their own moral values and maintain them in the face of cultural training, and (2) that these values have universal roots. Every child believes it is bad to kill because regard for the lives of others or pain at death is a natural empathic response, although it is not necessarily universally and consistently maintained. In this example, the value of life led both to vegetarianism and to the desire to kill Eskimos. This latter desire comes also from a universal value tendency: a belief in justice or reciprocity here expressed in terms of revenge or punishment (at higher levels, the belief that those who infringe on the rights of others cannot expect their own rights to be respected).

I quoted my son's response because it is shockingly different from the way you think and yet it has universal elements you will recognize. What is the shocking difference between my son's way of thinking and your own? If you are a psychoanalyst, you will start thinking about oral cannibalistic fantasies and defenses against them and all that. However, that is not really what the difference is at all. You do not have to be cannibalistic to wonder why it is right for humans to kill and eat animals but it is not right for animals or humans to kill and eat humans. The response really shows that my son was a philosopher, like every young child: he wondered about things that most grownups take for granted. If you want to study children, however, you have to be a bit of a philosopher yourself and ask the moral philosopher's question: "Why is it all right to kill and eat animals but not humans?" I wonder how many of you can give a good answer. In any case, Piaget started the modern study of child development by recognizing that the child, like the adult philosopher, was puzzled by the basic questions of life: by the meaning of space, time, causality, life, death, right and wrong, and so on. What he found was that the child asked all the great philosophic questions but answered them in a very different way from the adults. This way was so different that Piaget called the difference a difference in stage or quality of thinking, rather than a difference in amount of knowledge or accuracy of thinking. The difference in thinking between you and my son, then, is basically a difference in stage.

My own work on morality started from Piaget's notions of stages and Piaget's notion that the child was a philosopher. Inspired by Jean Piaget's (1948) pioneering effort to apply a structural approach to moral development, I have gradually elaborated over the years a typological scheme describing general stages of moral thought that can be defined independently of the specific content of particular moral decisions or actions. We studied seventy-five American boys from early adolescence on. These youths were continually presented with hypothetical moral dilemmas, all deliberately philosophical, some found in medieval works of casuistry. On the basis of their reasoning about these dilemmas at a given age, we constructed the typology of definite and universal levels of development in moral thought.

The typology contains three distinct levels of moral thinking, and within each of these levels are two related stages. These levels and stages may be considered separate moral philosophies, distinct views of the social-moral world.

We can speak of the children as having their own morality or series of moralities. Adults seldom listen to children's moralizing. If children throw back a few adult clichés and behave themselves, most parents—and many anthropologists and psychologists as well—think that the children have adopted or internalized the appropriate parental standards.

Actually, as soon as we talk with children about morality we find that they have many ways of making judgments that are not "internalized" from the outside and that do not come in any direct and obvious way from parents, teachers, or even peers.

The preconventional level is the first of three levels of moral thinking; the second level is conventional; and the third is postconventional or autonomous. Although preconventional children are often "well behaved" and responsive to cultural labels of good and bad, they interpret these labels in terms of their physical consequences (punishment, reward, exchange of favors) or in terms of the physical power of those who enunciate the rules and labels of good and bad.

This level is usually occupied by children aged four to ten, a fact well known to sensitive observers of children. The capacity of "properly behaved" children of this age to engage in cruel behavior when there are holes in the power structure is sometimes noted as tragic (*Lord of the Flies* and *High Wind in Jamaica*), sometimes as comic (Lucy in *Peanuts*).

The second or conventional level also can be described as *conformist*—but that is perhaps too smug a term. Maintaining the expectations and rules of the individual's family, group, or nation is perceived as valuable in its own right. There is a concern not only with conforming to the individual's social order but in maintaining, supporting, and justifying this order.

The postconventional level is characterized by a major thrust toward autonomous moral principles that have validity and application apart from authority of the groups or people who hold them and apart from the individual's identification with those people or groups.

Within each of these three levels, there are two discernible stages. The following paragraphs explain the dual moral stages of each level just described.

Definition of Moral Stages

Preconventional Level

At this level, the child is responsive to cultural rules and labels of good and bad, right or wrong, but interprets these labels in terms of either the physical or the hedonistic consequences of action (punishment, reward, exchange of favors) or in terms of the physical power of those who enunciate the rules and labels. The level is divided into the following two stages:

Stage 1. The Punishment and Obedience Orientation

The physical consequences of action determine its goodness or badness regardless of the human meaning or value of these consequences. Avoidance of punishment and unquestioning deference to power are valued in their own right.

Stage 2. The Instrumental Relativist Orientation

Right action consists of that which instrumentally satisfies one's needs and occasionally the needs of others. Human relations are viewed in terms like those of the marketplace. Elements of fairness, reciprocity, and equal sharing are present, but they are always interpreted in a physical, pragmatic way. Reciprocity is a matter of "You scratch my back and I'll scratch yours."

Conventional Level

At this level, maintaining the expectations of the individual's family, group, or nation is perceived as valuable in its own right, regardless of immediate and obvious consequences. The attitude is not only one of conformity to personal expectations and social order, but of loyalty to it, of actively maintaining, supporting, and justifying the order and of identifying with the people or group involved in it. At this level, there are the following two stages:

Stage 3. The Interpersonal Concordance or "Good Boy—Nice Girl" Orientation

Good behavior is that which pleases or helps others and is approved by them. There is much conformity to stereotypical images of what is majority or "natural" behavior. Behavior is frequently judged by intention—the judgment "he means well" becomes important for the first time. One earns approval by being "nice."

Stage 4. Society Maintaining Orientation

There is an orientation toward authority, fixed rules, and the maintenance of the social order. Right behavior consists of doing one's duty, showing respect for authority, and maintaining the given social order for its own sake.

Postconventional, Autonomous, or Principled Level

At this level, there is a clear effort to define moral values and principles that have validity and application apart from the authority of the groups or people holding these principles and apart from the individual's own identification with these groups. This level again has two stages:

Stage 5. The Social Contract Orientation

Right action tends to be defined in terms of general individual rights and in terms of standards that have been critically examined and agreed on by the whole society. There is a clear awareness of the relativism of personal values and opinions and a corresponding emphasis on procedural rules for reaching consensus. Aside from what is constitutionally and democratically agreed on, the right is a matter of personal "values" and "opinion." The result is an emphasis on the "legal point of view," but with an emphasis on the possibility of changing law in terms of rational considerations of social utility (rather than freezing it in terms of Stage 4 "law and order"). Outside the legal realm, free agreement and contract are the binding elements of obligation. This is the ''official'' morality of the American government and Constitution.

Stage 6. The Universal Ethical Principle Orientation

Right is defined by the decision of conscience in accord with self-chosen ethical principles appealing to logical comprehensiveness, universality, and consistency. These principles are abstract and ethical (the Golden Rule, the categorical imperative); they are not concrete moral rules such as the Ten Commandments. At heart, these are universal principles of justice, of the reciprocity and equality of human rights, and of respect for the dignity of human beings as individuals.

To understand what these stages mean concretely, let us look at them with regard to two of twenty-five basic moral concepts or aspects used to form the dilemmas we used in our research. One such aspect, for instance, is "motive given for rule obedience or moral action." In this instance, the six stages look like this:

1. Obey rules to avoid punishment.
2. Conform to obtain rewards, have favors returned, and so on.
3. Conform to avoid disapproval and dislike by others.
4. Conform to avoid censure by legitimate authorities and resultant guilt.
5. Conform to maintain the respect of the impartial spectator judging in terms of community welfare.
6. Conform to avoid self-condemnation.

In another of these twenty-five moral aspects, the value of human life, the six stages can be defined thus:

1. The value of human life is confused with the value of physical objects and is based on the social status or physical attributes of the possessor.
2. The value of human life is seen as instrumental to the satisfaction of the needs of its possessor or of other people.
3. The value of human life is based on the empathy and affection of family members and others toward its possessor.
4. Life is conceived as sacred in terms of its place in a categorical moral or religious order of rights and duties.
5. Life is valued both in terms of its relation to community welfare and in terms of life being a universal human right.
6. Human life is sacred—a universal human value of respect for the individual.

I have called this scheme a *typology*. This is because about 67 percent of most people's thinking is at a single stage, regardless of the moral dilemma involved. We call our types *stages* because they seem to represent an invariant development sequence. "True" stages come one at a time and always in the same order.

In our stages, all movement is forward in sequence and does not skip steps. Children may move through these stages at varying speeds, of course, and may be found half in and half out of a particular stage. Individuals may stop at any given stage and at any age, but if they continue to move, they must move in accord with these steps. Moral reasoning of the conventional kind or Stages 3-4, never occurs before the preconventional Stage 1 and Stage 2 thought has taken place. No adult in Stage 4 has gone through Stage 5, but all Stage 5 adults have gone through Stage 4.

Although the evidence is not complete, my study strongly suggests that moral change fits the stage pattern just described.

As a single example of our findings of stage sequence, take the progress of two boys on the aspect "the value of human life." The first boy, Tommy, who had suggested that one should perhaps steal for an important person, is asked, "Is it better to save the life of one important person or a lot of unimportant people?" At age ten, he answers, "All the people that aren't important because one man just has one house, maybe a lot of furniture, but a whole bunch of people have an awful lot of furniture, and some of these poor people might have a lot of money and it doesn't look it."

Clearly Tommy is Stage 1: he confuses the value of a human being with the value of the property he possesses. Three years later (age thirteen), Tommy's conceptions of life's values are most clearly elicited by the question "Should the doctor 'mercy kill' a fatally ill woman requesting death because of her pain?" He answers, "Maybe it would be good to put her out of pain, she'd be better off that way. But the husband wouldn't want it, it's not like an animal. If a pet dies you can get along without it—it isn't something you really need. Well, you can get a new wife, but it's not really the same."

Here his answer is Stage 2: the value of the woman's life is partly contingent on its instrumental value to her husband, who cannot replace her as easily as he can a pet.

Three years later still (age sixteen), Tommy's conception of life's value is elicited by the same question, to which he replies, "It might be best for her, but her husband—it's human life—not like an animal; it just doesn't have the same relationship that a human being does to a family. You can become attached to a dog, but nothing like a human, you know."

Now Tommy has moved from a Stage 2 instrumental view of the woman's value to a Stage 3 view based on the husband's distinctively human empathy and love for someone in his family. Equally clearly, it lacks any basis for a universal human value of the woman's life, which would hold if she had no husband or if her husband did not love her. Tommy, then, has moved step by step through three stages during the age ten to sixteen. Although bright (IQ 120), he is a slow developer in moral judgment.

Let us take another boy, Richard, to show us sequential movement through the remaining three steps. At age thirteen, Richard said about the mercy killing, "If she requests it, it's really up to her. She is in such terrible pain, just the same as people are always putting animals out of their pain," and in general showed a mixture of Stage 2 and Stage 3 responses concerning the value of life. At sixteen, he said, "I don't know. In one way, it's murder, it's not right or privilege of man to decide who shall live and who should die. God put life into everybody on earth and you're taking away something from that person that came directly from God, and you're destroying something that is very sacred, it's in a way part of God and it's almost destroying a part of God when you kill a person. There's something of God in everyone."

Here Richard clearly displays a Stage 4 concept of life as sacred in terms of its place in a categorical moral or religious order. The value of human life is universal; it is true for all humans. It still, however, depends on something else—on respect for God and God's authority; it is not an autonomous human value. Presumably if God told Richard to murder, as God commanded Abraham to murder Isaac, he would do so.

At age twenty, Richard said to the same question, "There are more and more people in the medical profession who think it is a hardship on everyone, the person, the family, when you know they are going to die. When a person is kept alive by an artificial lung or kidney, it's more like being a vegetable than being a human. If it's her own choice, I think there are certain rights and privileges that go along with being a human being. I am a human being, and I have certain desires for life, and I think everybody else does too. You have a world of which you are the center, and everybody else does too, and in that sense we're all equal."

Richard's response is clearly Stage 5, in that the value of life is defined in terms of equal and universal human rights in a context of relativity ("You have a world of which you are the center, and in that sense we're all equal") and of concern for utility or welfare consequences.

At twenty-four, Richard says, "A human life, whoever it is, takes precedence over any other moral or legal value. A human life has inherent value whether or not it is valued by a particular individual. The worth of the individual human being is central where the principles of justice and love are normative for all human relationships."

This young man is at Stage 6 in seeing the value of human life as absolute in representing a universal and equal respect for the human as an individual. He has moved step by step through a sequence culminating in a definition of human life as centrally valuable rather than derived from or dependent on social or divine authority.

In a genuine and culturally universal sense, these steps lead toward an increased morality of value judgment, where morality is considered as a form of judging, as it has been in a philosophic tradition running from the analyses of Kant to those of the modern analytic or "ordinary language" philosophers. At Stage 6 people have disentangled judgments of—or language about—human life from status and property values (Stage 1); from its uses to others (Stage 2); from interpersonal affection (Stage 3); and so on; they have a means of moral judgment that is universal and impersonal. Stage 6 people answer in moral words such as *duty* or *morally right* and use them in a way implying universality, ideals and impersonality. They think and speak in phrases such as "regardless of who it was" or "I would do it in spite of punishment."

Universal Invariant Sequence of Moral Development

When I first decided to explore moral development in other cultures, I was told by anthropologist friends that I would have to throw away my culture-bound moral concepts and stories and start from scratch learning a whole new set of values for each new culture. My first try consisted of a brace of villages, one Atayal (Malaysian aboriginal) and the other Taiwanese.

My guide was a young Chinese ethnographer who had written an account of the moral and religious patterns of the Atayal and Taiwanese villages. Taiwanese boys in the ten to thirteen age group were asked about a story involving theft of food: A man's wife is starving to death but the store owner would not give the man any food unless he could pay, and he cannot. Should he break in and steal some food? Why? Many of the boys said, "He should steal the food for his wife because if she dies he'll have to pay for her funeral, and that costs a lot."

My guide was amused by these responses, but I was relieved: they were, of course, "classic" Stage 2 responses. In the Atayal village, funerals were not such a big thing, so the Stage 2 boys said, "He should steal the food because he needs his wife to cook for him."

This means that we have to consult our anthropologists to know what content Stage 2 children will include in instrumental exchange calculations, or what Stage 4 adults will identify as the proper social order. But one certainly does not have to start from scratch. What made my guide laugh was the difference in form between the children's Stage 2 thought and his own, a difference definable independently of particular cultures.

Figures 1 and 2 indicate the cultural universality of the sequence of stages we have found. Figure 1 presents the age trends for middle-class urban boys in the United States, Taiwan, and Mexico. At age ten in each country, the order of use of each stage is the same as the order of its difficulty or maturity.

In the United States, by age sixteen the order is the reverse, from the highest to the lowest, except that Stage 6 is still little used. At age thirteen, the good-boy middle stage (Stage 3) is most used.

The results in Mexico and Taiwan are the same, except that development is a little slower. The most conspicuous feature is that, at the age of sixteen, Stage 5 thinking is much more salient in the United States than in Mexico or Taiwan. Nevertheless, it is present in the other countries, so we know that this is not purely an American democratic construct.

Figure 2 shows strikingly similar results from two isolated villages, one in Yucatan, one in Turkey. Although conventional moral thought increases steadily from ages ten to sixteen, it still has not achieved a clear ascendancy over preconventional thought.

Trends for lower-class urban groups are intermediate in the rate of development between those for the middle-class and for the village boys. In the three divergent cultures that I studied, middle-class children were found to be more advanced in moral judgment than matched lower-class children. This was not due to the fact that the middle-class children heavily favored some one type of thought that could be seen as corresponding to the prevailing middle-class pattern. Instead, middle-class and working-class children move through the same sequences, but the middle-class children move faster and farther.

This sequence is not dependent on a particular religion or on any religion at all in the usual sense. I found no important differences in the development of moral thinking among Catholics, Protestants, Jews, Buddhists, Moslems, and atheists.

In summary, the nature of our sequence is not significantly affected by widely varying social, cultural, or religious conditions. The only thing that is affected is the rate at which individuals progress through this sequence.

FIGURE 1: Moral development of middle-class urban boys in the United States, Taiwan, and Mexico. At age ten, the stages are used according to difficulty. At age thirteen, Stage 3 is most used by all three groups. At age sixteen, U.S. boys have reversed the order of age ten stages (with the exception of 6). In Taiwan and Mexico, conventional (3-4) stages prevail at age sixteen, with Stage 5 also little used (Kohlberg, 1968a).

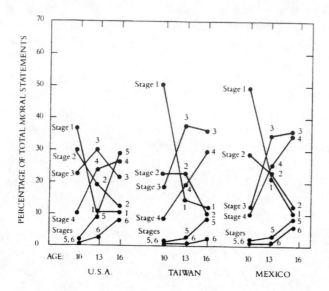

FIGURE 2: Two isolated villages, one in Turkey , the other in Yucatan, show similar patterns in moral thinking. There is no reversal of order, and conventional (stages 3—4) thought dose not gain in a clear ascendancy over prevonvential stages at age sixteen (Kohlberg, 1968a).

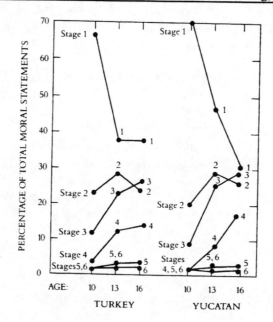

Why should there be such a universal invariant sequence of development? In answering this question, we need first to analyze these developing social concepts in terms of their internal logical structure. At each stage, the same basic moral concept or aspect is defined, but at each higher stage this definition is more differentiated, more integrated, and more general or universal. When one's concept of human life moves from Stage 1 to Stage 2, the value of life becomes more differentiated from the value of property, more integrated (the value of life enters an organizational hierarchy where it is "higher" than property so that one steals property in order to save life), and more universalized (the life of any sentient being is valuable regardless of status or property). The same advance is true at each stage in the hierarchy. Each step of development, then, is a better cognitive organization than the one before it, one that takes account of everything present in the previous stage but making new distinctions and organizes them into a more comprehensive or more equilibrated structure. The fact that this is the case has been demonstrated by a series of studies indicating that children and adolescents comprehend all stages up to their own, but not more than one stage beyond their own (Rest, 1973). And, importantly, they prefer this next stage.

Moral thought, then, seems to behave like all other kinds of thought. Progress through the moral levels and stages is characterized by increasing differentiation and increasing integration, and hence is the same kind of progress that scientific theory represents. Like acceptable scientific theory—or like any theory or structure of knowledge—moral thought may be considered partially to generate its own data as it goes along, or at least to expand so as to contain in a balanced, self-consistent way a wider and wider experiential field. The raw data in the case of our ethical philosophies may be considered as conflicts between roles, or values, or as the social order in which people live.

The social worlds of all people seem to contain the same basic structures. All the societies we have studied have the same basic institutions—family, economy, law, government. In addition, however, all societies are alike because they are societies—systems of defined complementary roles. In order to play a social role in the family, school, or society, children must implicitly take the role of others toward themselves and toward others in the group These roletaking tendencies form the basis of all social institutions. They represent various patternings of shared or complementary expectations.

In the preconventional and conventional levels (Stages 1-4), moral content or value is largely accidental or culture bound. Anything from "honesty" to "courage in battle" can be the central value. But in the higher postconventional levels, Socrates, Lincoln, Thoreau, and Martin Luther King tend to speak without confusion of tongues, as it were. This is because the ideal principles of any social structure are basically alike, if only because there simply are not that many principles that are articulate, comprehensive, and integrated enough to be satisfying to the human intellect. And most of these principles have gone by the name of justice.

I have discussed at some length the culturally universal sequences of stages of moral judgment. I have not entirely clarified how such a sequence helps to resolve relativistic questioning of moral principles, a task taken up in our Chapter 4, "From *Is* to *Ought*." It is easier to clarify how such a sequence helps resolve the dilemma of relativity versus indoctrination in values education. The sequence provides us with a concept of moral development that can be stimulated by education without indoctrination and yet that helps to move student judgment toward more adequate principles.

The way to stimulate stage growth is to pose real or hypothetical dilemmas to students in such a way as to arouse disagreement and uncertainty as to what is right. The teacher's primary role is to present such dilemmas and to ask Socratic questions that arouse student reasoning and focus student listening on one another's reasons.

I noted research by Rest (1973) showing that students prefer the highest stage of reasoning they comprehend but that they do not comprehend more than one stage above their own. As a result, assimilation of reasoning occurs primarily when it is the next stage up from the student's level. Developmental moral discussion thus arouses cognitive-moral conflict and exposes students to reasoning by other students at the next stage above their own.

Using this approach, Blatt and Kohlberg (1975) were able to stimulate one-third of experimental classes of students to advance one stage in a time period in which control classes remained unchanged in moral stage. One year later, the experimental classes retained their relative advance over the control classes.

The developmental approach, first experimentally elaborated by Blatt, is one that any thoughtful classroom teacher may practice. Unlike values clarification, its assumptions are not relativistic but, rather, are based on universal goals and principles. It asks the student for reasons, on the assumption that some reasons are more adequate than others.

The approach differs from indoctrinative approaches because it tries to move student's thinking in a direction that is natural for the student rather than moving the student in the direction of accepting the teacher's moral assumptions. It avoids preaching or didacticism linked to the teacher's authority . . . .

IN A DIFFERENT VOICE

by Carol Gilligan

Carol Gilligan (b. 1936) is professor of education in the Graduate School of Education at Harvard University. She has written numerous articles on moral psychology and is author of *In a Different Voice* (1982) and co-author of *Meeting at the Crossroads* (1992).

Carol Gilligan discusses "different ideas about human development, different ways of imagining the human condition, different notions of what is of value in life." She notes that developmental theories in psychology project an ideal that views individual development and maturation as moving away from emotional perspectives toward a stage of impersonal justice in dealing with others. According to Sigmund Freud, this moral ideal is more accessible to men than to women because women are "more often influenced in their judgments by feelings of affection and hostility." But Nancy Chodorow argues that women are *naturally* more attuned to others and that their moral ideals are defined through (emotional) attachment, rather than impersonal separation. Gilligan develops this theme by arguing that development itself should be redefined to give care and attachment an importance that is lacking in the standard (male) ideal of justice and autonomy.

The neglect of a woman's perspective has given a male bias to the findings of recent research in the psychology of moral education. Gilligan claims that Lawrence Kohlberg's six stages of moral development assume the impersonal male "justice perspective," thereby assuring the result that women are morally deficient because of their tendency to understand moral issues in emotional and personal ways. Kohlberg's research, which concentrates on male subjects, concludes that in the highest stages of moral development the individual uses universal impartial ethical principles to justify moral rights. Gilligan argues that this developmental ideal that emphasizes the "rights" perspective over the "care perspective" is biased against women. And indeed Kohlberg "finds" that women are fixed in the earlier stages of moral development as he defines them. A perspective that is sensitive to the ideal of responsibility and caring would do more justice to women and their particular life cycles. "Only when life cycle theorists divide their attention and begin to live with women as they have lived with men will their vision encompass both sexes and their theories become correspondingly more fertile."

In the second act of *The Cherry Orchard*, Lopahin, a young merchant, describes his life of hard work and success. Failing to convince Madame Ranevskaya to cut down the cherry orchard to save her estate, he will go on in the next act to buy it himself. He is the self-made man who, in purchasing the estate where his father and grandfather were slaves, seeks to eradicate the "awkward, unhappy life" of the past, replacing the cherry orchard with summer cottages where coming generations "will see a new life." In elaborating this developmental vision, he reveals the image of man that underlies and supports his activity: "At times when I can't go to sleep, I think: Lord, thou gavest us immense forests, unbounded fields and the widest horizons, and living in the midst of them we should indeed be giants"—at which point, Madame Ranevskaya interrupts him, saying, "You feel the need for giants—They are good only in fairy tales, anywhere else they only frighten us."

Conceptions of the human life cycle represent attempts to order and make coherent the unfolding experiences and perceptions, the changing wishes and realities of everyday life. But the nature of such conceptions depends in part on the position of the observer. The brief excerpt from Chekhov's play suggests that when the observer is a woman, the perspective may be of a different sort. Different judgments of the image of man as giant imply different ideas about human development, different ways of imagining the human condition, different notions of what is of value in life.

At a time when efforts are being made to eradicate discrimination between the sexes in the search for social equality and justice, the differences between the sexes are being rediscovered in the social sciences. This discovery occurs when theories formerly considered to be sexually neutral in their scientific objectivity are found instead to reflect a consistent observational and evaluative bias. Then the presumed neutrality of science, like that of language itself, gives way to the recognition that the categories of knowledge are human constructions. The fascination with point of view that has informed the fiction of the twentieth century and the corresponding recognition of the relativity of judgment infuse our scientific understanding as well when we begin to notice how accustomed we have become to seeing life through men's eyes.

A recent discovery of this sort pertains to the apparently innocent classic *The Elements of Style* by William Strunk and E. B. White. The Supreme Court ruling on the subject of discrimination in classroom texts led one teacher of English to notice that the elementary rules of English usage were being taught through examples which counterposed the birth of Napoleon, the writings of Coleridge, and statements such as "He was an interesting talker. A man who had traveled all over the world and lived in half a dozen countries," with "Well, Susan, this is a fine mess you are in" or, less drastically, "He saw a woman, accompanied by two children, walking slowly down the road."

Psychological theorists have fallen as innocently as Strunk and White into the same observational bias. Implicitly adopting the male life as the norm, they have tried to fashion women out of a masculine cloth. It all goes back, of course, to Adam and Eve—a story which shows, among other things, that if you make woman out of a man, you are bound to get into trouble. In the life cycle, as in the Garden of Eden, the woman has been the deviant.

The penchant of developmental theorists to project a masculine image, and one that appears frightening to women, goes back at least to Freud who built his theory of psychosexual development around the experiences of the male child that culminate in the Oedipus complex. In the 1920s, Freud struggled to resolve the contradictions posed for his theory by the differences in female anatomy and the different configuration of the young girl's early family relationships. After trying to fit women into his masculine conception, seeing them as envying that which they missed, he came instead to acknowledge, in the strength and persistence of women's pre-Oedipal attachments to their mothers, a developmental difference. He considered this difference in women's development to be responsible for what he saw as women's developmental failure.

Having tied the formation of the superego or conscience to castration anxiety, Freud considered women to be deprived by nature of the impetus for a clear-cut Oedipal resolution. Consequently, women's superego—the heir to the Oedipus complex—was compromised: it was never "so inexorable, so impersonal, so independent of its emotional origins as we require it to be in men." From this observation of difference, that "for women the level of what is ethically normal is different from what it is in men," Freud concluded that women "show less sense of justice than men, that they are less ready to submit to the great exigencies of life, that they are more often influenced in their judgements by feelings of affection or hostility."

Thus a problem in theory became cast as a problem in women's development, and the problem in women's development was located in their experience of relationships. Nancy Chodorow, attempting to account for "the reproduction within each generation of certain general and nearly universal differences that characterize masculine and feminine personality and roles," attributes these differences between the sexes not to anatomy but rather to "the fact that women, universally, are largely responsible for early child care." Because this early social environment differs for and is experienced differently by male and female children, basic sex differences recur in personality development. As a result, "in any given society, feminine personality comes to define itself in relation and connection to other people more than masculine personality does."

In her analysis, Chodorow relies primarily on Robert Stoller's studies which indicate that gender identity, the unchanging core of personality formation, is "with rare exception firmly and irreversibly established for both sexes by the time a child is around three." Given that for both sexes the primary caretaker in the first three years of life is typically female, the interpersonal dynamics of gender identity formation are different for boys and girls. Female identity formation takes place in a context of ongoing relationship since "mothers tend to experience their daughters as more like, and continuous with, themselves." Correspondingly, girls, in identifying themselves as female, experience themselves as like their mothers, thus fusing the experience of attachment with the process of identity formation. In contrast, "mothers experience their sons as a male opposite," and boys, in defining themselves as masculine, separate their mothers from themselves, thus curtailing "their primary love and sense of empathic tie." Consequently, male development entails a "more emphatic individuation and a more defensive firming of experienced ego boundaries." For boys, but not girls, "issues of differentiation have become intertwined with sexual issues."

Writing against the masculine bias of psychoanalytic theory, Chodorow argues that the existence of sex differences in the early experiences of individuation and relationship "does not mean that women have 'weaker' ego boundaries than men or are more prone to psychosis." It means instead that "girls emerge from this period with a basis for 'empathy' built into their primary definition of self in a way that boys do not." Chodorow thus replaces Freud's negative and derivative description of female psychology with a positive and direct account of her own: "Girls emerge with a stronger basis for experiencing another's needs or feelings as one's own (or of thinking that one is so experiencing another's needs and feelings). Furthermore, girls do not define themselves in terms of the denial of preoedipal relational modes to the same extent as do boys. Therefore, regression to these modes tends not to feel as much a basic threat to their ego. From very early, then, because they are parented by a person of the same gender . . . girls come to experience themselves as less differentiated than boys, as more continuous with and related to the external object-world, and as differently oriented to their inner object-world as well."

Consequently, relationships, and particularly issues of dependency, are experienced differently by women and men. For boys and men, separation and individuation are critically tied to gender identity since separation from the mother is essential for the development of masculinity. For girls and women, issues of femininity or feminine identity do not depend on the achievement of separation from the mother or on the progress of individuation. Since masculinity is defined through separation while feminity is defined through attachment, male gender identity is threatened by intimacy while female gender identity is threatened by separation. Thus males tend to have difficulty with relationships, while females tend to have problems with individuation. The quality of embeddedness in social interaction and personal relationships that characterizes women's lives in contrast to men's, however, becomes not only a descriptive difference but also a developmental liability when the milestones of childhood and adolescent development in the psychological literature are markers of increasing separation. Women's failure to separate then becomes by definition a failure to develop.

The sex differences in personality formation that Chodorow describes in early childhood appear during the middle childhood years in studies of children's games. Children's games are considered by George Herbert Mead and Jean Piaget as the crucible of social development during the school years. In games, children learn to take the role of the other and come to see themselves through another's eyes. In games, they learn respect for rules and come to understand the ways rules can be made and changed.

Janet Lever, considering the peer group to be the agent of socialization during the elementary school years and play to be a major activity of socialization at that time, set out to discover whether there are sex differences in the games that children play. Studying 181 fifth-grade, white, middle-class children, ages ten and eleven, she observed the organization and structure of their playtime activities. She watched the children as they played at school during recess and in physical education class, and in addition kept diaries of their accounts as to how they spent their out-of-school time. From this study, Lever reports sex differences: boys play out of doors more often than girls do; boys play more often in large and age-heterogeneous groups; they play competitive games more often, and their games last longer than girls' games. The last is in some ways the most interesting finding. Boys' games appeared to last longer not only because they required a higher level of skill and were thus less likely to become boring, but also because, when disputes arose in the course of a game, boys were able to resolve the disputes more effectively than girls: "During the course of this study, boys were seen quarrelling all the time, but not once was a game terminated because of a quarrel and no game was interrupted for more than seven minutes. In the gravest debates, the final word was always, to 'repeat the play,' generally followed by a chorus of 'cheater's proof.' " In fact, it seemed that the boys enjoyed the legal debates as much as they did the game itself, and even marginal players of lesser size or skill participated equally in these recurrent squabbles. In contrast, the eruption of disputes among girls tended to end the game.

Thus Lever extends and corroborates the observations of Piaget in his study of the rules of the game, where he finds boys becoming through childhood increasingly fascinated with the legal elaboration of rules and the development of fair procedures for adjudicating conflicts, a fascination that, he notes, does not hold for girls. Girls, Piaget observes, have a more "pragmatic" attitude toward rules, "regarding a rule as good as long as the game repaid it."

Girls are more tolerant in their attitudes toward rules, more willing to make exceptions, and more easily reconciled to innovations. As a result, the legal sense, which Piaget considers essential to moral development, "is far less developed in little girls than in boys."

The bias that leads Piaget to equate male development with child development also colors Lever's work. The assumption that shapes her discussion of results is that the male model is the better one since it fits the requirements for modern corporate success. In contrast, the sensitivity and care for the feelings of others that girls develop through their play have little market value and can even impede professional success. Lever implies that, given the realities of adult life, if a girl does not want to be left dependent on men, she will have to learn to play like a boy.

To Piaget's argument that children learn the respect for rules necessary for moral development by playing rule-bound games, Lawrence Kohlberg adds that these lessons are most effectively learned through the opportunities for role-taking that arise in the course of resolving disputes. Consequently, the moral lessons inherent in girls' play appear to be fewer than in boys'. Traditional girls' games like jump rope and hopscotch are turn-taking games, where competition is indirect since one person's success does not necessarily signify another's failure. Consequently, disputes requiring adjudication are less likely to occur. In fact, most of the girls whom Lever interviewed claimed that when a quarrel broke out, they ended the game. Rather than elaborating a system of rules for resolving disputes, girls subordinated the continuation of the game to the continuation of relationships.

Lever concludes that from the games they play, boys learn both the independence and the organizational skills necessary for coordinating the activities of large and diverse groups of people. By participating in controlled and socially approved competitive situations, they learn to deal with competition in a relatively forthright manner—to play with their enemies and to compete with their friends—all in accordance with the rules of the game. In contrast, girls' play tends to occur in smaller, more intimate groups, often the best-friend dyad, and in private places. This play replicates the social pattern of primary human relationships in that its organization is more cooperative. Thus, it points less, in Mead's terms, toward learning to take the role of "the generalized other," less toward the abstraction of human relationships. But it fosters the development of the empathy and sensitivity necessary for taking the role of "the particular other" and points more toward knowing the other as different from the self.

The sex differences in personality formation in early childhood that Chodorow derives from her analysis of the mother-child relationship are thus extended by Lever's observations of sex differences in the play activities of middle childhood. Together these accounts suggest that boys and girls arrive at puberty with a different interpersonal orientation and a different range of social experiences.

"It is obvious," Virginia Woolf says, "that the values of women differ very often from the values which have been made by the other sex." Yet, she adds, "it is the masculine values that prevail." As a result, women come to question the normality of their feelings and to alter their judgments in deference to the opinion of others. In the nineteenth-century novels written by women, Woolf sees at work "a mind which was slightly pulled from the straight and made to alter its clear vision in deference to external authority." The same deference to the values and opinions of others can be seen in the judgments of twentieth-century women. The difficulty women experience in finding or speaking publicly in their own voices emerges repeatedly in the form of qualification and self-doubt, but also in intimations of a divided judgment, a public assessment and private assessment which are fundamentally at odds.

Yet the deference and confusion that Woolf criticizes in women derive from the values she sees as their strength. Women's deference is rooted not only in their social subordination but also in the substance of their moral concern. Sensitivity to the needs of others and the assumption of responsibility for taking care lead women to attend to voices other than their own and to include in their judgment other points of view. Women's moral weakness, manifest in an apparent diffusion and confusion of judgment, is thus inseparable from women's moral strength, an overriding concern with relationships and responsibilities. The reluctance to judge may itself be indicative of the care and concern for others that infuse the psychology of women's development and are responsible for what is generally seen as problematic in its nature.

Thus women not only define themselves in a context of human relationship but also judge themselves in terms of their ability to care. Women's place in man's life cycle has been that of nurturer, caretaker, and helpmate, the weaver of those networks of relationships on which she in turn relies. But while women have thus taken care of men, men have, in their theories of psychological development, as in their economic arrangements, tended to assume or devalue that care. When the focus on individuation and individual achievement extends into adulthood and maturity is equated with personal autonomy, concern with relationships appears as a weakness of women rather than as a human strength.

The discrepancy between womanhood and adulthood is nowhere more evident than in the studies on sex-role stereotypes reported by Broverman, Vogel, Broverman, Clarkson, and Rosenkrantz. The repeated finding of these studies is that the qualities deemed necessary for adulthood—the capacity for autonomous thinking, clear decision-making, and responsible action—are those associated with masculinity and considered undesirable as attributes of the feminine self. The stereotypes suggest a splitting of love and work that relegates expressive capacities to women while placing instrumental abilities in the masculine domain. Yet looked at from a different perspective, these stereotypes reflect a conception of adulthood that is itself out of balance, favoring the separateness of the individual self over connection to others, and leaning more toward an autonomous life of work than toward the interdependence of love and care.

The discovery now being celebrated by men in mid-life of the importance of intimacy, relationships, and care is something that women have known from the beginning. However, because that knowledge in women has been considered "intuitive" or "instinctive," a function of anatomy coupled with destiny, psychologists have neglected to describe its development. In my research, I have found that women's moral development centers on the elaboration of that knowledge and thus delineates a critical line of psychological development in the lives of both of the sexes. The subject of moral development not only provides the final illustration of the reiterative pattern in the observation and assessment of sex differences in the literature on human development, but also indicates more particularly why the nature and significance of women's development has been for so long obscured and shrouded in mystery.

The criticism that Freud makes of women's sense of justice, seeing it as compromised in its refusal of blind impartiality, reappears not only in the work of Piaget but also in that of Kohlberg. While in Piaget's account of the moral judgment of the child, girls are an aside, a curiosity to whom he devotes four brief entries in an index that omits "boys" altogether because "the child" is assumed to be male, in the research from which Kohlberg derives his theory, females simply do not exist. Kohlberg's six stages that describe the development of moral judgment from childhood to adulthood are based empirically on a study of eighty-four boys whose development Kohlberg has followed for a period of over twenty years. Although Kohlberg claims universality for his stage sequence, those groups not included in his original sample rarely reach his higher stages.

Prominent among those who thus appear to be deficient in moral development when measured by Kohlberg's scale are women, whose judgments seem to exemplify the third stage of his six-stage sequence. At this stage morality is conceived in interpersonal terms and goodness is equated with helping and pleasing others. This conception of goodness is considered by Kohlberg and Kramer to be functional in the lives of mature women insofar as their lives take place in the home. Kohlberg and Kramer imply that only if women enter the traditional arena of male activity will they recognize the inadequacy of this moral perspective and progress like men toward higher stages where relationships are subordinated to rules (stage four) and rules to universal principles of justice (stages five and six).

Yet herein lies a paradox, for the very traits that traditionally have defined the "goodness" of women, their care for and sensitivity to the needs of others, are those that mark them as deficient in moral development. In this version of moral development, however, the conception of maturity is derived from the study of men's lives and reflects the importance of individuation in their development. Piaget, challenging the common impression that a developmental theory is built like a pyramid from its base in infancy, points out that a conception of development instead hangs from its vertex of maturity, the point toward which progress is traced. Thus, a change in the definition of maturity does not simply alter the description of the highest stage but recasts the understanding of development, changing the entire account.

When one begins with the study of women and derives developmental constructs from their lives, the outline of a moral conception different from that described by Freud, Piaget, or Kohlberg begins to emerge and informs a different description of development. In this conception, the moral problem arises from conflicting responsibilities rather than from competing rights and requires for its resolution a mode of thinking that is contextual and narrative rather than formal and abstract. This conception of morality as concerned with the activity of care centers moral development around the understanding of responsibility and relationships, just as the conception of morality as fairness ties moral development to the understanding of rights and rules.

This different construction of the moral problem by women may be seen as the critical reason for their failure to develop within the constraints of Kohlberg's system. Regarding all constructions of responsibility as evidence of a conventional moral understanding, Kohlberg defines the highest stages of moral development as deriving from a reflective understanding of human rights. That the morality of rights differs from the morality of responsibility in its emphasis on separation rather than connection, in its consideration of the individual rather than the relationship as primary, is illustrated by two responses to interview questions about the nature of morality. The first comes from a twenty-five-year-old man, one of the participants in Kohlberg's study:

> [*What does the word morality mean to you?*] Nobody in the world knows the answer. I think it is recognizing the right of the individual, the rights of other individuals, not interfering with those rights. Act as fairly as you would have them treat you. I think it is basically to preserve the human being's right to existence. I think that is the most important. Secondly, the human being's right to do as he pleases, again without interfering with somebody else's rights.

> [*How have your views on morality changed since the last interview?*] I think I am more aware of an individual's rights now. I used to be looking at it strictly from my point of view, just for me. Now I think I am more aware of what the individual has a right to.

Kohlberg cites this man's response as illustrative of the principled conception of human rights that exemplifies his fifth and sixth stages. Commenting on the response, Kohlberg says. "Moving to a perspective outside of that of his society, he identifies morality with justice (fairness, rights, the Golden Rule), with recognition of the rights of others as these are defined naturally or intrinsically. The human being's right to do as he pleases without interfering with somebody else's rights is a formula defining rights prior to social legislation."

The second response comes from a woman who participated in the rights and responsibilities study. She also was twenty-five and, at the time, a third-year law student:

> [*Is there really some correct solution to moral problems, or is everybody's opinion equally right?*] No, I don't think everybody's opinion is equally right. I think that in some situations there may be opinions that are equally valid, and one could conscientiously adopt one of several courses of action. But there are other situations in which I think there are right and wrong answers, that sort of inhere in the nature of existence, of all individuals here who need to live with each other to live. We need to depend on each other, and hopefully it is not only a physical need but a need of fulfillment in ourselves, that a person's life is enriched by cooperating with other people and striving to live in harmony with everybody else, and to that end, there are right and wrong, there are things which promote that end and that move away from it, and in that way it is possible to choose in certain cases among different courses of action that obviously promote or harm that goal.

> [*Is there a time in the past when you would have thought about these things differently?*] Oh, yeah, I think that I went through a time when I thought that things were pretty relative, that I can't tell you what to do and you can't tell me what to do, because you've got your conscience and I've got mine.

> [*When was that?*] When I was in high school. I guess that it just sort of dawned on me that my own ideas changed, and because my own judgment changed, I felt I couldn't judge another person's judgment. But now I think even when it is only the person himself who is going to be affected, I say it is wrong to the extent it doesn't cohere with what I know about human nature and what I know about you, and just from what I think is true about the operation of the universe, I could say I think you are making a mistake.

> [*What led you to change, do you think?*] Just seeing more of life, just recognizing that there are an awful lot of things that are common among people. There are certain things that you come to learn promote a better life and better relationships and more personal fulfillment than other things that in

general tend to do the opposite, and the things that promote these things, you would call morally right.

This response also represents a personal reconstruction of morality following a period of questioning and doubt, but the reconstruction of moral understanding is based not on the primacy and universality of individual rights, but rather on what she describes as a "very strong sense of being responsible to the world." Within this construction, the moral dilemma changes from how to exercise one's rights without interfering with the rights of others to how "to lead a moral life which includes obligations to myself and my family and people in general." The problem then becomes one of limiting responsibilities without abandoning moral concern. When asked to describe herself, this woman says that she values "having other people that I am tied to, and also having people that I am responsible to. I have a very strong sense of being responsible to the world, that I can't just live for my enjoyment, but just the fact of being in the world gives me an obligation to do what I can to make the world a better place to live in, no matter how small a scale that may be on." Thus while Kohlberg's subject worries about people interfering with each other's rights, this woman worries about "the possibility of omission, of your not helping others when you could help them."

The issue that this woman raises is addressed by Jane Loevinger's fifth "autonomous" stage of ego development, where autonomy, placed in the context of relationships, is defined as modulating an excessive sense of responsibility through the recognition that other people have responsibility for their own destiny. The autonomous stage in Loevinger's account witnesses a relinquishing of moral dichotomies and their replacement with "a feeling for the complexity and multifaceted character of real people and real situations." Whereas the rights conception of morality that informs Kohlberg's principled level (stages five and six) is geared to arriving at an objectively fair or just resolution to moral dilemmas upon which all rational persons could agree, the responsibility conception focuses instead on the limitations of any particular resolution and describes the conflicts that remain.

Thus it becomes clear why a morality of rights and noninterference may appear frightening to women in its potential justification of indifference and unconcern. At the same time, it becomes clear why, from a male perspective, a morality of responsibility appears inconclusive and diffuse, given its insistent contextual relativism. Women's moral judgments thus elucidate the pattern observed in the description of the developmental differences between the sexes, but they also provide an alternative conception of maturity by which these differences can be assessed and their implications traced. The psychology of women that has consistently been described as distinctive in its greater orientation toward relationships and interdependence implies a more contextual mode of judgment and a different moral understanding. Given the differences in women's conceptions of self and morality, women bring to the life cycle a different point of view and order human experience in terms of different priorities.

The myth of Demeter and Persephone, which McClelland cites as exemplifying the feminine attitude toward power, was associated with the Eleusinian Mysteries celebrated in ancient Greece for over two thousand years. As told in the Homeric *Hymn to Demeter,* the story of Persephone indicates the strengths of interdependence, building up resources and giving, that McClelland found in his research on power motivation to characterize the mature feminine style. Although, McClelland says, "it is fashionable to conclude that no one knows what went on in the Mysteries, it is known that they were probably the most important religious ceremonies, even partly on the historical record, which were organized by and for women, especially at the onset before men by means of the cult of Dionysos began to take them over." Thus McClelland regards the myth as "a special presentation of feminine psychology." It is, as well, a life-cycle story par excellence.

Persephone, the daughter of Demeter, while playing in a meadow with her girlfriends, sees a beautiful narcissus which she runs to pick. As she does so, the earth opens and she is snatched away by Hades, who takes her to his underworld kingdom. Demeter, goddess of the earth, so mourns the loss of her daughter that she refuses to allow anything to grow. The crops that sustain life on earth shrivel up, killing men and animals alike, until Zeus takes pity on man's suffering and persuades his brother to return Persephone to her mother. But before she leaves, Persephone eats some pomegranate seeds, which ensures that she will spend part of every year with Hades in the underworld.

The elusive mystery of women's development lies in its recognition of the continuing importance of attachment in the human life cycle. Woman's place in man's life cycle is to protect this recognition while the developmental litany intones the celebration of separation, autonomy, individuation, and natural rights. The myth of Persephone speaks directly to the distortion in this view by reminding us that narcissism leads to death, that the fertility of the earth is in some mysterious way tied to the continuation of the mother-daughter relationship, and that the life cycle itself arises from an alternation between the world of women and that of men. Only when life-cycle theorists divide their attention and begin to live with women as they have lived with men will their vision encompass the experience of both sexes and their theories become correspondingly more fertile.

THE NATURE OF BEAUTY

CONCEPTIONS OF BEAUTY: A SURVEY OF CONCEPTIONS OF BEAUTY IN THE HISTORY OF PHILOSOPHY

by John Cunningham & Mark Liederbach

> *If life is worth living, it is so in order that man may behold beauty.*

—Plato (5th Century BCE)

Why do we feel compelled to look when we see something beautiful? A beautiful face in a crowd draws our attention, reducing all other faces to background images. When we are struck by a beautiful sunset, we stop and enjoy the moment. A beautiful work of art grabs our attention and calls for appreciation. What is it about beautiful things that call for our attention?

The Greeks were aware of the apparent connection between beauty and calling. Their word for beauty, *kalon*, comes from the root word *kalein*, which means, "to call." They understood that those things that are beautiful call to us, stir something in us, move us. Beauty draws our attention as a candle lit in a dark room draws our eyes.

But what does it mean that a person, a sunset, a gesture, a sculpture, or an idea is *beautiful*? We have difficulty explaining ourselves when we try to define precisely what we mean by "beauty" or "the beautiful." Interestingly, there are no direct synonyms in English for the word "beauty." We may speak of that which is "lovely", "attractive", "good-looking", etc., but none of these cognates captures the essence of the word "beauty." It would seem that beauty is unique.

To further explore the difficulty in conceptualizing beauty consider the following questions. Many critics consider Picasso's *Guernica*—a huge work depicting the atrocities and horrors of war—to be one of his finest paintings. But is "beautiful" the right term for it? If one person considers Micheangelo's Sistine

Chapel ceiling to be beautiful and another does not, is one of them wrong? Does having "bad taste" make someone a less developed person? All of these questions point to deeper questions: How do we perceive? What is the nature of beauty? And how do we determine what is beautiful and what is not?

Over the centuries, these questions have occupied philosophers and resulted in differing (sometimes contrary) conceptions of beauty. What has remained a constant, however, is that in every age philosophers have tried to gain some understanding of beauty. In fact beauty has remained one of the "great ideas" in Western culture. This chapter will explore several influential ideas about beauty, beginning with the ancient Greeks and progressing to some modern thinkers.

I. Classical Aesthetics

The understanding of beauty developed by the classical Greek & Roman philosophers endured in one form or another for well over a thousand years and, in fact, many of their ideas still remain with us today.

The Classical view centers in the notion of *due proportion*: the idea that something is beautiful to the degree that the relationships of its various parts combine in a pleasing and harmonious way. The quest for perfect proportions became the hallmark of Greek aesthetics, and was similarly adopted by the Romans. For instance, Greek sculptors believed that the "ideal" human body had exact and measurable proportions that did not vary. Variety was seen as a deviation from perfection not, as we sometimes think today, an indication of unique value, or "specialness."

From the beginning of the classical tradition, beauty was conceived in terms of musical harmony. That concept was expanded almost immediately beyond the auditory however, to include symmetry—which was considered to be the visual or spatial equivalent of harmony. For many of the classical thinkers, then, something was beautiful if it was harmonious or symmetrical.

At core, the concept of proportion is rational and mathematical. This view of beauty was established by the Pythagoreans (6th century BCE), who were brilliant mathematicians. They conceived beauty in terms of the ordered relation of parts, which could be expressed *numerically*. They developed this view based on observations of the harmonies produced by shortening the strings of a musical instrument according to mathematical ratios. Pythagoras also observed that when a blacksmith struck an anvil with hammers of differing weights, different tones resounded. From this he realized that the connection between weight and pitch could be correlated mathematically. This numerical, so the Pythagoreans went on to claim, is observable in all beautiful things—whether audible, visual, or conceptual.

According to Pythagoras, however, not only is the beauty of the things that we can see and hear numeric, but even the cosmos itself is numerically ordered. He believed that the orbiting of the planets around the stationary earth produced a *musica mundana*, or a harmonious melody of the spheres. Pythagoras developed a theory that each planet produced a tone corresponding to notes on a scale—the furthest planets generating a higher pitch, and the closer ones a lower tone. Together, they produce a symphony of music that, although it cannot be heard by people, is beautiful beyond compare.[1]

Since the Pythagoreans thought that the very nature of the universe was mathematical, and because they believed that beauty also had a mathematical foundation, the conception of beauty became linked with metaphysical theories about the ultimate nature of reality. For many Greek theorists, a person's enjoyment of a beautifully composed painting or a melodious piece of music is identifiable in its symmetry or harmony, but the beauty present in the piece of art or music ultimately lies in the object's alignment with the order of the universe.

Of course, not all classical thinkers agreed on every point. For example, those conceptions of beauty that are linked to the nature of ultimate reality (like the Pythagoreans) lead to an *objective* understanding of beauty—something independent of, and unaffected by people's opinions about it. The Sophists, however, held a *subjective* understanding of beauty. They saw beauty as a matter of individual taste. For example, the

Dialexeis, an anonymous Sophist treatise, claims that everything is beautiful, and everything is ugly.[2] Similarly, Epicharm, who also was affiliated with the Sophists, contended that the most beautiful thing for a dog is a dog, and for an ox, another ox. It is an individual's own likes and dislikes, he claimed, that affect his or her view of what is beautiful.[3]

Another point of disagreement can be found in the work of Stoic philosophy. In general the Stoics agreed with the Pythagoreans that beauty is primarily constituted by due proportion (although they do add a criterion of pleasing color). They define beauty as "that which has fit proportion and alluring color."[4] However, Stoicism, which is a materialist philosophy (i.e., stoics believe that physical matter is all that exists), tended to restrict the concept of beauty to those things we can see with our eyes. Thus stoics rejected the metaphysical tendencies of the Pythagoreans and their assumptions of an otherworldly, immaterial order that lies "behind" the proportion and harmony we observe.

In addition, the Stoics introduced the lasting notion of "aptness," fittingness, or congruence. According to this view, beauty is understood in terms of *appropriateness*. A beautiful object is one that is ideally suited for a particular situation. Beauty has to do with the *purpose* of a thing. Therefore, a well-designed trashcan may be more beautiful than a golden shield, which due to its weight, would be very inappropriate for use in battle.[5]

So then, while a variety of conceptions of beauty emerged in classical thought, a consensus emerged that viewed beauty as a harmonious relation between various parts conceived in terms of due proportion. This idea has had an enduring legacy. Even today we often evaluate beauty in terms of proportion, harmony, and symmetry.

II. The Platonic Tradition

Plato (c. 427—c. 347 BCE) has had a profound impact on the history of philosophy. He touches on almost every major philosophical topic, and in many cases, frames the discussion of that topic for many generations to come. So, whether a thinker agrees or disagrees with Plato, almost invariably he or she must interact with his views. This is especially true for Plato's ideas about beauty. The importance of the concept of beauty for Plato is expressed in his statement that: "If life is worth living, it is so in order that man may behold beauty."

Plato's Symposium

Plato's *Symposium*, and the interpretations of it through the ages, has shaped the philosophy of beauty perhaps more than any other single text. Many commonly held Western notions about beauty may be traced to it.

Today a "symposium" is usually an academic or political conference in which a group of experts are assembled to present papers on a particular topic. In ancient Greece, however, a symposium was an upper-class drinking party at which part of the entertainment was an intellectual discussion among the guests.

In Plato's *Symposium* the topic of the discussion is the god *Eros*, who represents passionate love, or yearning desire. While the subject of the *Symposium* ostensibly is love, Plato also uses this dialogue to advance his ideas about beauty, several of which have had lasting influence.

Plato expresses his ideas through the speeches given by the various characters. The first guest to deliver his speech is Pausanius. He says, "we all know that Eros is inseparable from Aphrodite." (In Greek mythology *Eros* is the god of Love, and *Aphrodite* is the goddess of beauty). Plato, and the speakers at the dinner party, do not think of gods in the way that we do today. Gods and goddesses are more like symbols of ideas, in this case of love and beauty. Also, *Eros* is a particular kind of love. It is a desirous love, like one has for a lover. It is related to the feeling of being "in love." Our word "erotic" is derived from it. So when Pausanius says that Eros and Aphrodite are inseparable, he means that love is always connected with beauty.

And this is the first major theme: *Love is intrinsically oriented toward beauty*; our yearning desire is always for *the beautiful*. Said another way, we love beauty, and whatever we love is beautiful.

But this raises problems. For instance, is all desire a god-inspired love? Is everything we desire beautiful? What about base lust and raw desire? Can we rightly say that something like pornography is actually beautiful, not simply that which incites sordid passion?

This is one of the central questions of Plato's *Symposium*: Some of the speakers think that there are two different kinds of beauty, a better and worse, that appeal to two kinds of desire in us. Others think that "good" and "bad" love or desire is the same kind of thing, just in a better and worse form. Pausanius claims that there are two Aphrodites (Beauties) one "higher" which elicits a higher, more noble form of desirous love, and a "lower" or "Common Aphrodite." For Pausanius, the Common Aphrodite is more base. She represents a love that "has no discrimination," being "such as the meaner (i.e., base, degraded) sort of men feel." The lower Love is "of the body rather than of the soul." This kind of love is unconcerned with the person's heart or mind, as long as he or she is good looking. We might call this kind of "love" lust. It is seen as fleeting, chaotic, and salacious, being based in the passions.

The "Heavenly Aphrodite," though, according to Pausanias, has nothing to do with the wanton. It inspires a "Heavenly Love" that is pure and chaste, faithful and lasting. It values the soul over the body, is based in the order of divine reason (*logos*) and fosters true virtue (*arete*).

Another speaker in the *Symposium*, Eryximachus (who is a physician) does not separate the body from the soul, as did Pausanius. He considers Love as unitary, but existing in two forms, either healthy or diseased, just as the body does. Thus, a "healthy" person would be attracted to true beauty, whereas a pathological expression of desire will lead the person astray.

The second major issue about the nature of beauty introduced by Plato, then, is *whether beauty appeals to the same kind of love in us, or on the other hand, if some beauty appeals to true love, and another kind to lust*. This debate continues today. Think, for instance, of the variety of opinions about the boundary between art and pornography.

Another speaker in the *Symposium*, Aristophanes (a famous comedic playwright), delivers a very different type of address. The famous comic poet relates a poignant and amusing myth of the *Andrognoi*, (or hermaphrodites, or "circle-people"). The first human beings, according to Aristophanes' myth, had two heads, four arms, and four legs, and were complete in every way. They eventually became too proud, however, and after much debate Zeus devised a plan to deal with their arrogance. He decided to thwart the insolent humans by dividing them—literally. In the end, each four-legged, two headed circle-person was split, resulting in the two-legged, one headed form we are familiar with today. Thus, each human person is half of a whole. From that point on, humans have wandered the earth, searching longingly for the half that will complete them. From that point on, humans have been needy, rather than self-sufficient. According to Aristophanes, this searching is what we now experience as love; we want to be complete. "Human nature was originally one and we were a whole," says Aristophanes, "and the desire and pursuit of the whole is called love." He conceives love as the longing and quest for integration. We love, then, because we are not unified; we love because we lack.

And thus, a third major idea is introduced by Plato: *somehow the experience of the beautiful is understood to complete us, or fill us*. On this view, beauty is seen as a deep human good. We, by nature, lack and beauty meets us at the place of our neediness, completing us, making us whole.

After another speaker, Socrates (who is usually the hero of Plato's dialogues) finally speaks. He says that he learned everything he knows about beauty from a (fictitious) priestess named Diotima. In this famous "Diotima myth" Socrates puts forth the idea that that: 1) love is *a mean between* the beautiful or good and what is evil and foul; and 2) love is not a deity, but rather a mediating *daemon* between the gods and humans. In both cases the beautiful *links the divine or ultimate with the mundane and material*, bridging what would otherwise be an ultimate separation. He presents beauty as a passage to the transcendent, or a glimpse of something beyond the mud and muck of this world. This view, as we will see, becomes central to the tradition that follows in Plato's wake, and it is the fourth theme introduced by Plato: *our desire for true beauty is an essentially spiritual longing, and that the experience of the beautiful can transport us beyond this world.*

On this view, the soul should progress from contemplation of *sensible beauty* to the contemplation of *supra-sensible beauty*. In other words, the beauty that appeals to our senses is okay, but the best people will move beyond it to an appreciation of a higher, more intellectual and spiritual kind of beauty. The love of the physical beauty should awaken in us a desire for eternal beauty. We should become less and less satisfied with earthly, sensual pleasure. The love of the eternal, the absolute, or the immutable then, should lead us up into a timeless mystical contemplation of the Form of the Beautiful. The contemplative life "is that life above all others which man should live." Here we see yet another abiding platonic understanding of beauty: *beauty is directly associated with the highest end of human existence and should, therefore, be the object of contemplation.* Those who are satisfied with the merely physical are somehow less noble than those who contemplate the higher nature of true beauty. It is for this reason that the life of contemplation of the beautiful became the aspiration of many a saint and philosopher after Plato.

Plato's *Symposium* has had an enduring place in history. Like many established works in the canon of Western thought, the *Symposium* has yielded a variety of interpretations. Historically, however, when it comes to beauty, most of Plato's readers have valued the higher over the lower, reason over passion, and the soul over the body. A constellation of related views regarding beauty are traceable to this work. They include the following notions:

1. Beauty is a very broad and capacious concept. The term "beauty" is rightly applied to immaterial things such as ideas, souls, etc.
2. Beauty evokes in us a longing or yearning.
3. Human beings are, by nature, incomplete and lacking.
4. The experience of beauty makes us whole, integrates, or completes us in some way.
5. Because of #3 & #4, the desire for beauty is intrinsic to human nature.
6. Our innate desire for beauty may be manifested in a "higher" form (spiritual, intellectual, contemplative, noble, eternal), or
7. Our innate desire for beauty may be manifested in a "lower" form (earthly, passionate, lustful, base, temporal)
8. Material, physical beauty is of much less value than spiritual, intellectual beauty. A beautiful soul is better than a beautiful body.
9. Beauty itself serves as a mediator between ultimate reality and our earthbound existence.
10. The virtuous soul will seek and contemplate the higher beauties without being sidetracked by the lower ones.
11. The experience of beauty leads one higher and higher up—as if up the rungs of a spiritual ladder—from the "lower" to the "higher" beauties.
12. In each experience of desiring the beautiful, we ultimately long for the eternal Form of Beauty.

III. Neoplatonism

Platonism had a profound impact on the Hellenized world. As Greek ideas spread—especially through the conquests of Alexander the Great, and then the Romans—Platonism grew and evolved, often absorbing other strains of thought. By the second century CE, it had developed to such an extent that it is now referred to as *Neo*platonism. The most notable Neoplatonist was Plotinus (204-269 CE), who lived and taught in Alexandria, Egypt. Plotinus developed an intricate philosophical system that borrowed from many schools of thought but focused particularly on certain platonic ideas which he amplified to such a degree that they became something new. A lot could be said about Neoplatonism's influence on the philosophy of beauty, but the focus here will be on three of the most important aspects: 1) Metaphysical monism, 2) the affective character of Beauty, and 3) the Neoplatonic program of religious praxis, ascent of the soul.

Metaphysical Monism

Pythagoras and Plato had conceived Beauty as a connecting link to ultimate Reality. But it is important to remember that Plato is a metaphysical *dualist*, i.e., he thinks there is another "realm" besides the one in which we live. For him, that other domain of Forms is higher, better, and more real than our world because everything here is just an imperfect copy of a perfect Form located there. Things "down here" are real only to the degree that they accurately represent the eternal form. Therefore, according to Plato, everything that is beautiful is a *copy* in some sense of the Form or Essence of Beauty.

Plotinus, however, has a slightly different view. While Platonic dualism locates essences in a separate realm, Neoplatonism sees everything that exists *as a part of* an ultimate reality, or "*The One.*" In other words, his is a monistic view of reality in which some of the true Form of beauty exists in the object being observed, thus the beauty in an object is not merely a reflection or copy of true beauty, the object actually participates in Beauty.

In this perspective, both sensible beauty (e.g., an *object d'art*, beauty in nature, the human form, etc.) and intelligible beauty (e.g., a mathematical theorem, a beautiful moral choice, etc.) are part of the Ultimate beauty. Beauty is the source of the beautiful—and not merely as a pattern, but in its very presence. As Plotinus says, "We hold that all the loveliness of this world comes by *communion* in Ideal-Form."[6] (emphasis added) Here the word "communion" is employed quite literally to indicate a "union with" Ideal-Form, not merely a representation of it. The beautiful is no longer conceived merely as a model or blueprint that beautiful earthly objects imitate, represent, or reflect. Rather, the very *reality of beauty* is seen in the beautiful object. The beauty of the earthly thing is a physical "instant" of actual beauty. Beautiful things are understood to emanate from the source of ultimate beauty as if from a fountain, or as rays emanate from the sun. In Neoplatonism, then, vision of the beautiful is a vision of ultimate reality.

Also, since "The One" emanates both beauty and being, everything that exists (i.e., has being) is beautiful to some degree. Absolute ugliness is an impossibility; perceived "ugliness" is really just a lack of beauty. As Plotinus says, "Beauty *is* Authentic Existents and Ugliness is the Principal contrary to Existence."[7]

Based on this view of metaphysical monism Plotinus tenders the first significant criticism of the classical idea that beauty is based in a harmonious distribution of parts according to proper proportion. Plotinus acknowledges the importance of the role of symmetry, but seeks to press beyond it to something more essential. He says, "Can we doubt that beauty is something more than symmetry, that symmetry owes its beauty to a remoter principle?"[8] He bolsters his case by appealing to the beauty of things like gold, light, pure color, and the stars—which are not made up of parts. These things, by virtue of being indivisible, are not subject to laws of symmetry, which are dependent on the arrangement of parts.

For Plotinus, then, beauty is an expression of Ultimate Being, and whatever exists is therefore beautiful to the degree that it participates in it.

The Affective Nature of Beauty

"What do you feel in the presence of . . . [beauty]?"[9] This simple question, asked by Plotinus, represents a big shift in Platonic aesthetics. In Neoplatonism the affective nature becomes central. Much more emphasis is laid on the effect that beauty has on our feelings and emotions. Plotinus answers his own question with references to "pangs of desire" or "Dyonisiac exultation."[10] Observe the (italicized) emotional language in the following citation from Plotinus' Sixth *Ennead*:

> And the one that shall know this vision [of the beautiful]— with what *passion of love* shall he not *be seized*, with *pang of desire*, what *longing* to be molten into one with This, what *wondering delight*! If he that has never seen this Being must *hunger for it with all his welfare*, he that has known must *love and reverence* It as the very Beauty; he will be flooded with *awe and gladness, stricken by a salutary terror*; he *loves with a veritable love, with sharp* desire; all other loves than this he must *despise*, and *disdain* all that once seemed fair.[11]

In addition to describing beauty as an expression of Ultimate Reality, he also highlights the emotional impact of beauty in a new way, placing a special emphasis on desire and delight.

The Ascent of the Soul

Neoplatonism quickly came to have a religious flavor. Indeed, many versions of Neoplatonism were expressly religious, in some cases being presented as a conscious alternative to Christianity. By emphasizing the ethical strains in previous Platonism, Neoplatonism elevated the pursuit of the good through beauty to an unmistakably religious level.

The goal of Neoplatonism is reunion with "The One," which occurs through "the ascent of the soul." The goal of religious Neoplatonism is to ascend out of the material realm to reunite with the One. Vision of the beautiful draws the soul upward in its ascent. In earlier Platonism, emphasis was placed on the *rational* approach to beauty, in the Neoplatonic scheme, Beauty must be *mystically* apprehended. This mystical union with the Divinity is the goal of the ascent of the soul.

However, to be able to see this spiritual beauty, the seeker must cleanse him or herself of all bodily, material and earthly attachments and pleasures. Neoplatonism is inherently ascetic (Asceticism is a disciplined self-denial, and abstention from earthly attachments). This purging of the soul enables it to reflect divinity as if it were a mirror from which mud had been wiped. Finally, the soul is joined with the One in mystical union. The Neoplatonic religious program may be reduced to three stages: 1) moral purification, 2) introspection, and 3) mystical union; or, 1) 'turn away', 2) 'turn in', and 3) 'turn up'). These three stages correspond to the three divisions of Greek philosophy: Ethics (the purgative stage), Physics (the illuminative stage), and Anoptics or Metaphysics (the unitive stage).

So then, Neoplatonism contributed a number of themes to Platonic aesthetics, including:

1. The teaching that all of creation is permeated with beauty.
2. This beauty is a *direct* link to ultimate reality.
3. Beauty appeals to our affective (or emotional, passional) nature.
4. It does so primarily through desire and delight.
5. Beauty is invested with overtly religious significance.
6. Pursuit of the higher beauties requires an ascetic lifestyle.

IV. Christian Platonism

Almost from its inception, Christian theology was formulated in Platonic categories. Tertullian, an early Christian thinker from the 2nd century once protested, "What does Athens have to do with Jerusalem?" meaning that Christian theology should have nothing to do with 'pagan' philosophy. But even Tertullian held a lot of Platonic ideas. Other thinkers, like Origen, consciously tried to merge Platonic philosophy and Christian doctrine. Almost without exception early Christian thinking drew upon Late Middle Platonism and then Neoplatonism.

Gregory of Nyssa (c. 335-395 CE), a Christian philosopher and bishop from Cappadocia (in modern Turkey) is representative of this influence in Christian philosophy. Many other thinkers could be cited, but in the following quote we see many of the typical features of Christian Platonist aesthetics.

> Such an experience seems to me to belong to the soul which loves that which is beautiful. Hope always draws the soul from the beauty which is seen to what is beyond, always kindles the desire for the hidden through what is constantly perceived. Therefore, the ardent lover of beauty, although receiving what is always visible as an image of what he desires, yet longs to be filled with the very stamp of the archetype. And the bold request which goes up the mountain of desire asks this: to enjoy the Beauty not in mirrors and reflections, but face to face.[12]

Among other things, we see through this quote that 1) Beauty is conceived in higher and lower forms that correspond to the sensible (having to do with the senses) and the suprasensible (or *beyond* what we perceive with our senses), 2) that love is conceived as *Eros*, or desire, 3) that what we love is *beauty*, 4) that this love will lead to progressively higher beauties, and ultimately to Beauty itself, 5) that this archetype of beauty is identified with God.

While always attempting to be faithful to the Christian revelation, most early theologians saw substantial parallels between Christianity and the thinking of the day. Many Christian thinkers naturally identified the "ultimate beauty" that the philosophers talked about with the God of the Bible. Gregory of Nyssa, for instance, asserts that "The Deity is in very substance Beautiful."[13] Furthermore, Gregory agreed with his Platonic heritage that beauty is enticing to us. He says beauty "is essentially (i.e., in its very nature) capable of attracting in a certain way every being that looks toward it."[14]

Many early Christian thinkers found support for their views of beauty in the scriptures. Psalm 19 says that "the heavens are telling of the glory of God; And their expanse is declaring the work of His hands." Likewise, the Apostle Paul is read to be in agreement with the notion that all of creation is permeated with a divine beauty when he says "For since the creation of the world His (i.e., God's) invisible attributes, His eternal power and divine nature, have been clearly seen, being understood through what has been made."[15]

Platonic thinking heavily influenced Early Christian beliefs and lifestyle. Origen was just one Christian who adopted the Neoplatonic idea of the "ascent of the soul" as a model for spiritual growth. Origen identified three stages of spiritual development. He thought they were represented by the three books of the Bible written by Solomon: *Proverbs*, *Ecclesiastes*, and *The Song of Songs*. The first stage, symbolized by the book of Proverbs, is the *purgative* stage which is essentially concerned with ethical and moral purification of the soul. The second stage, typified by Ecclesiastes, is an *illuminative* stage, in which the soul contemplates reality. It is summarized by Solomon's cry "vanity, vanity, all is vanity,"[16] which reflects a realization that this world is not ultimate, and that we need God. The third, *unitive* stage follows from this and is summarized in the Song of Songs, or Canticles by the affirmation, "My Beloved is mine and I am His."[17] The hallmark of the final stage is union with God, the Divine Beauty.

These approaches to religion are integrally connected to aesthetics; the driving impetus of ascent was conceived as desire (i.e., *Eros*, love) for beauty. Reflecting ideas from Plato's *Symposium*, love, in its lowest form appears as the desire for physical beauty. In its highest form, however, love is a desire for a transcendent and immortal beauty.

Such thinking, however, reflects a low esteem for physical beauty which becomes problematic for many Christian theologians who want to affirm God's physical creation as good and beautiful (as the creation account in Genesis reports.) They also want to view Christ, who was incarnated in a *physical body* as truly beautiful. Gregory of Nyssa for instance is ambivalent about physical things, but feels compelled to affirm the Christian doctrine. He speaks almost disparagingly of physical beauty at times, but in the end affirms it as good. For him, though, physical beauty will never be enough for ultimate religious purposes: "As regards the inquiry into the nature of beauty," he says, "we see, again, that the man of half grown intelligence, when he observes an object which is bathed in a glow of a seeming beauty, thinks that the object is in its essence beautiful . . . But the other, whose mind's eye is clear, and who can inspect such appearances, will neglect the elements which are the material only upon which the Form of Beauty works . . ."[18]

So then, while at significant points, early Christianity modified the character of Platonic thinking, we witness a confluence between Neoplatonism philosophy and Christian theology which is particularly evident in the philosophy of beauty. As Christianity came to prominence, the Christian "take" on Platonic categories of thought that became dominant view. Some features of the aesthetics of Christian Platonism include:

1. The identification of ultimate beauty with the person of God.
2. An ambivalence with, softening, or mitigation of the categorical disdain for matter found in prior Platonism.

V. The Medieval Tradition

Augustine

Augustine (354-430 CE) is one of the most influential philosophers of all time. His early writings are squarely in the Christian Platonist tradition, but his thinking grew and developed into a unique and enduring theology. His views charted the course for much of what followed in medieval philosophy, and his conception of beauty prevailed for over a millennium. Augustine's theological aesthetics developed through a selective blending of three discrete influences, 1) Classical aesthetics, formulated primarily in terms of due proportion; 2) Neoplatonism as transmitted from the Plotinian school through the Christian Platonists; and 3) finally, Augustine's own experience interpreted through Christian scripture. The aesthetics of the mature Augustine may be conceived in terms of "incarnation," and center in his notion of Divine illumination.

Significantly, Augustine's first work, written at the age of 26 or 27—before entering the Church, was a book about beauty; questions regarding the nature of the beautiful endured throughout Augustine's long and prolific career. Although the book was lost during Augustine's lifetime, his brief recounting of its contents in Book IV of the *Confessions* places it squarely in the main-stream of Classical philosophical thought regarding beauty. Recall that classical views of beauty center in proportion and harmony. Augustine helped transmit these ideas to the medieval tradition. By Augustine's own account (in the *Confessions*), his reading "of the Platonists" sent him in a new philosophical direction that ultimately led to his Christian conversion. From the Neoplatonists Augustine borrowed a monistic view of metaphysics. Augustine co-opts a lot of Plotinus' ideas of "The One" as a description of God. As do other Christian Platonists, he identifies ultimate Beauty with the person of God. Referring to Christ he says: "Late have I loved you, Beauty so ancient and so new."[19] For Augustine, God is Beauty. Therefore, the experience of beauty is a spiritual experience.

Augustine also agrees with the Neoplatonic tradition's view on the emotional impact of beauty. He conceives love as worshipful longing for beauty. Love is a desire to see God and be like him, and only divine Beauty stirs this yearning. As this desire is properly ordered and rightly satisfied, it changes into delight.[20] So then, for Augustine beauty is the object of love, and love is desire for beauty. "What things can we love, if not the beautiful?"[21] he asks. "We love the beautiful,"[22] he says simply.

In his early works (e.g., *Soliloquies*), Augustine uses and develops the model of the ascent of the soul, i.e., the progression through stages of the rational soul's quest for union with God. According to this Neoplatonic idea, once the soul has been purified from worldly attachments, a person can look within his own soul to see divine beauty. To know the Supreme beauty, the person, it was taught, must turn within oneself. The early Augustine declares, "Wherever you turn, by certain traces with which wisdom has impressed on her works, she speaks to you, and *recalls you within*, gliding back into *interior things* by the very forms of exterior things."[23] In his early works, then, Augustine argues that because the soul is created in God's image, therefore one may see God by contemplating his own soul. Nothing else is more divine.[24]

As Augustine's thinking developed, however, he realized that this system of thought did not square with his personal experience. Augustine's restless heart and questioning mind led him to yet another major change in his thinking. In the early works, Augustine embraced, taught and defended the Christian Platonist platform he had inherited. However, driven by his own experience and his reading of the scriptures he significantly altered it. His way of reading the Bible changed everything.

A look into the soul was supposed to reveal divine beauty, but Augustine's introspective gaze revealed something very different: dark, inexplicable forces inclining him to sin. Even when he wasn't actually committing sin, Augustine suspected that it was just because he didn't have an opportunity. He noticed that a manure pile often doesn't stink until it's stirred up, and he feared that his seemingly moral life may only be due to a lack of temptation. Augustine's look within ultimately revealed to himself that he was profoundly, and helplessly sinful.

Part of what led Augustine to this conclusion was his focus on delight—which was so central in the Plotinian/Christian Platonist tradition. The role of delight grew in Augustine's thinking until it was viewed as the only possible source of action. He reasoned that we do things because we want some result that we delight in. Nothing besides delight was seen as able to direct the will.

Here we see the beginnings of the separation of the intellect and the will, which prior to Augustine were integrated in Greek thinking and Christian theology. To know the good was to do the good. The intellect, or reason, was to guide human action. In this view (propounded originally by Plato in the *Phaedrus*) the rational aspect of humankind is to guide and restrain the appetitive part (the part necessarily concerned with the gratification of bodily needs and desires) and the spirited (which is also driven by desire, albeit a desire for the non material). The role of the rational part is to guide the desire of the soul. However, Augustine began to see things in precisely inverse order. Rather than the intellect guiding the desires, and leading to a course of action, now desire is seen to be the sole guide to human action. In the end, realizes Augustine, we pursue whatever we delight in, not that which we think we ought to.

This cuts at the very foundation of the Christian Platonist program for spiritual growth, which assumed that people could do what they thought they should. Contrary to this idea, Augustine begins to develop the notion of Original Sin: that human nature is corrupt from birth and can't choose the good without help from God. After the first sin of humanity (The Fall), people are blind to divine beauty, and moral purification, the starting point of Neoplatonic project, is now beyond human control.

As a result of this Augustine abandoned the notion of the ascent of the soul in favor of a view requiring *Divine descent*. That is, if humans are to experience God and true Beauty, then they are dependent upon the grace of God to do so. This divine grace is extended to humans through Jesus Christ, the second person of the Trinity. For Augustine, beauty becomes God's *self-revelation*.

Beauty, then, as revelation, affects human knowledge. Augustine relates beauty to the idea of *illumination*. God "turns on the light," for those bound in darkness, and they subsequently may see, and be drawn to Beauty. "The will itself can have no motive unless something presents itself to delight and stir the mind. That this should happen is not by any man's power." Rather, when our delight is realigned toward God it is due to "the inspiration of God and to the grace he bestows,"[25] not to human works, reason, or effort.[26]

In short, the mature Augustine views beauty as God's gracious revelation in a fallen world. "You," says Augustine to Christ, the ultimate Beauty, "called, and cried out to me and broke open my deafness; you shone forth and you scattered my blindness."[27] God awakens the desire of the restless heart through beauty, descending to address it in this world, and calling it to find rest in Him.

Following this idea, then, Augustine comes to view beauty as *incarnation*. Not in a Neoplatonic sense in which "Reality" must be extirpated from the flesh into which it has fallen. But in the sense that

God—the perfection of beauty—was willing and gracious enough to "put on of flesh" and reveal himself to humankind.

And herein lies Augustine's watershed contribution to the philosophical question about the nature of beauty. Previous views tended to fall on one of two extremes. On the one hand Stoicism center on sensible, this-worldly, physical and rational views of beauty. Beauty is an immanent or this worldly-thing. On the other hand, the Neoplatonism (and the early Christian version of it) located beauty in the transcendent realm. Beauty was metaphysical, spiritual, and otherworldly. From the time of Plato the tension abided between the physical and the metaphysical, the intelligible and the mystical, the earthbound and the supernatural—in short, between immanentist and iranscendentist views of beauty. Augustine, however, forged a synthesis that embraced much in each view, and provided a bridge between them. His view emerged from the Christian doctrine of incarnation. In the person of Jesus Christ, beauty becomes the nexus of immanence and transcendence, linking the timeless eternal to the time-bound mortal, the immutable to the changing, and God to his creatures in grace.

So then, Augustine reconstructs many significant aspects of the Neoplatonic interpretation of Christianity. Metaphysical monism is qualified by a doctrine of creation. Emphasis on desire and delight is reconfigured. The program of ascent is undercut at the foundation, hamstringing human self-purification and flipping the intent of introspection on its head. Only an emphasis on mystical union conceived in terms of the *Visio Dei* (seeing God) is retained, and this becomes the cornerstone of Augustine's mature understanding of the nature of beauty.

So Augustine, the great synthesizer, accepts much that had been taught before him, but adds that:

1. Beholding beauty "illumines" us; when we see beauty, "the lights go on" in a new way.
2. Beauty is revelation from God.
3. We can only see true beauty by grace (i.e., God is helping us).

VI. High Medieval Views

Christian Platonism remained the dominant influence on medieval aesthetics up through the thirteenth century. At that time, however, a shift occurred that may be traced to the rise of Aristotelianism, culminating in the work of Thomas Aquinas (1225-74). This shift is marked by the emergence of a new metaphysical understanding of the nature of things.

The essence of Platonism is metaphysical *idealism*. "Reality" exists not in this realm, but in the transcendent realm of "ideas." During the thirteenth century a new metaphysical model was emerging, one which may be referred to as *hylomorphism*. In this reading of Aristotle the form, or essence of a thing is not in some other world, but in the *particular* matter itself. Hylomorphism agrees that things have a form, or essence, but sees it as existing *in* the particular matter.

While Platonic idealism does not ascribe much value to material beauty (because it is merely a distant copy of the more real thing), hylomorphism sees each particular instance of beauty as unique and important. For example, Thomas Aquinas says "Beauty of spirit is one thing, and beauty of the body another; *and yet another thing is the beauty of one body or another.*"[28] So each instance of material beauty becomes important in itself, not just because it represents the other world. The thirteenth century theologians, rather than disavowing the material, were more concerned with understanding its relation to form.

The difference is a matter of emphasis. Whereas earlier theologians reluctantly affirmed the value of this world, but considered it ultimately less real in the great chain of being, Thomas and others saw the great other world as very literally present in this one.

Aquinas' Definition of Beauty

Thomas Aquinas' definition of beauty became very influential. Reflecting the shifts in philosophy in the thirteenth century, his view makes two significant modifications to the traditional views of beauty. First, he centers the experience of beauty on *pleasure*, more than in *desire*. Second, while the former platonic tradition tended toward mysticism in the apprehension of beauty, Thomas places more emphasis on the *intellect*.

In the 4th century BCE Aristotle had included the notion of pleasure in his definition of beauty, defining beauty as: "That which, being good, is also *pleasant*." By the mid to late thirteenth century, Scholastic theologians begin to cast beauty as offering the end of desire, experienced as satisfaction, or *pleasure*. William of Auvergne, for instance, says, "We call a thing visually beautiful when of its own accord it *gives pleasure* to the spectators and delight to the vision."[29] Similar understandings may be found in Albert the Great and others, but Thomas is the most systematic. He offers a definition of beauty that locates its essence in the capacity to give pleasure. This definition is advanced in two essentially similar versions: 1) as "that which *pleases* when seen,"[30] and 2) as those things "the very perception of which *gives pleasure*."[31] The important feature here is Thomas' identification of the experience of the beautiful in its capacity to give *pleasure*, understood as the quenching of desire. In Aristotelian terms, pleasure is the coming to rest of desire. Thomas, referring to pleasure, says, "It pertains to the notion of the beautiful that in seeing or knowing it the appetite comes to rest."[32] By way of comparison, then, whereas Platonic views of beauty depict it as stirring up desire, Aristotelian models consider the experience of the beautiful as the ending of desire.

The second big shift involves centering the experience of the beautiful in the intellect. For Thomas, "seeing" beauty does not mean merely observing with our eyes, but rather with our minds. When someone says, "I see what you mean," she is using the concept of sight metaphorically in the way Thomas does.

In Thomas' definition of beauty as "that which pleases *when seen*," we find an intellectual emphasis, over a mystical one. Beauty is seen, not so much as a window into heaven, but as something the rational mind can ponder (which may indeed lead to spiritual insight). Thomas does think that reason leads to God, but gone is the more overt mysticism of the early medievals. For the Platonists, sight of the beautiful was sight of God. For Thomas, the beautiful is material for the mind, which is most capable of apprehending divinity.

So then, these emphases, while not exclusive to Thomas, are new in the thirteenth century and reveal a significant shift. While Platonic notions depicted beauty as the object of desire (*Eros*) and as an entree into the heavenly realms, the new Aristotelianism conceives beauty as that which gives intellectual pleasure.

VII. The Enlightenment

By the late Middle Ages stress fractures began to appear in the monolithic facade of Western culture. Everything was changing. Adventurous traders like Marco Polo traveled to far off lands bringing back, along with their exotic commodities, challenging thoughts. Scientists like Copernicus and Galileo were changing long held understandings of the universe. Religious reformers like Luther took their stand against the very core of cultural authority and unity. The unifying authority of the church in medieval culture eventually crumbled, giving way to a progressive process of disintegration. What had lasted for a millennium as a generally unified culture in pre-enlightenment Europe gave way to a breakdown of the societal authority. As many thinkers sought to regain some sure footing, the age of the Enlightenment emerged.

With so much difference of opinion, many philosophers wanted a basis of knowledge that was reliable, dependable, sure. Reason was seen as the answer, and was elevated to a preeminent status. The Enlightenment, then, is rightly known as the *Age of Reason*.

Prior to the Enlightenment, the beautiful was considered to be a mystery that could be apprehended, but not ultimately comprehended. Beauty was seen to be fundamentally and deeply mysterious. But something beyond comprehension was not likely to be of much interest to the new breed of Enlightenment philosophers who strove for absolute certainty.

Early Enlightenment philosophers did not consider beauty to be an essentially rational phenomenon. As Gottfried Leibnitz (1646-1716) says, "We have no *rational* knowledge of beauty."[33] He claims that we can recognize something as beautiful, but "cannot explain why it is so."[34] Following this, Christian Wolff (1679-1754) observed that our knowledge of *particulars* (actual things, not the mental concept of them) is never clear and distinct. Unlike abstractions, which *are* rational in their origin, particular existing things present themselves *to the senses*. Alexander Gottlieb Baumgarten (1714-1762), later coined the term "aesthetic" to designate that realm of sense-related human experience that is undeniable, but is not within the grasp of reason. For him, aesthetic images are *clear but confused*. That is, they are immediately self evident as beautiful, but not clearly explainable by ideas of *reason*.[35] In the Enlightenment, *beauty is primarily aligned with sense perception* rather than reason. Indeed, the etymology of the word "aesthetic" links it to the senses.

In Rationalistic thought, which makes a hard distinction between "understanding" and "sensibility," sensory perception is held in comparatively low esteem. Sense perceptions are often in error, and that which is apprehended by the senses can never yield complete knowledge. When we look at a tree for instance, we cannot see the back, or the molecules of which it is composed, or what is inside. But a rational concept, like the idea of a circle is clear and distinct. Everything is understood. Nothing is unclear. By aligning beauty with sense perception, beauty is dissociated from reason. Consequently, beauty is separated from truth. This is a significant departure, of course, from premodern views which linked beauty to truth, and to reason.

So then, while most Enlightenment thinkers don't place much emphasis on beauty, they do offer some significant modifications of the concept:

1. Beauty is seen to be beyond rational comprehension.
2. Beauty is seen to have more to do with the senses than the mind.
3. Beauty is dissociated from truth.

VIII. The Eighteenth Century

The eighteenth century was a period of decisive change in our views of the arts and beauty. That century gave birth to our modern concept of the *aesthetic*. During the eighteenth century, art took on a new *social* role. Before that time, art museums were pretty much unknown; people didn't plan their social calendars around the symphony, and poets were not held up as the paragons of high culture.

In fact, the very concept of "high culture" is largely a product of the eighteenth century. Two ideas that emerged in the 1700's are central to our notions of cultural refinement. The first is the concept of *Bildung*—a German word that is hard to translate but has to do with becoming a "cultured, " "polite" (in the sense of 'polished'), or "refined" person. The cultural elite came to view the arts and the appreciation of beauty as central to *Bildung*. A truly refined lady or gentleman would read novels and poetry, frequent concert halls and art galleries, and appreciate the beauty of nature. Even today art museums, poetry readings, the opera, and the like are considered the purview of the upper class. This idea is traceable to the eighteenth century concept of *Bildung*.

The second development that still influences us is the emergence of the concept of the *fine* arts. Before this time people didn't tend to distinguish between "high" and "low" arts, or "arts" and "crafts." Sculpture, painting, the theatre and the symphony were not seen as substantially different from pottery making, woodcarving, jewelry making, etc. This systematic ranking of the arts is new to the eighteenth century.[36]

But why were certain practices like sculpture, painting, poetry, and architecture grouped together? What do they have in common? Creativity? Lots of things involve creativity besides the arts (indeed, some criminals are very creative in their scheming). So why were these things combined together as the "fine arts?" The answer leads us to another significant idea that emerged in the eighteenth century, that of the *aesthetic*.

Alexander Baumgarten coined the word "aesthetic" during the Enlightenment, and the concept spread quickly and began to further develop. The eighteenth century view of the aesthetic emerges from the concept of beauty inherited from the Middle Ages: that beauty is "that which pleases when seen, or contemplated."

So what do the fine arts have in common? The eighteenth century theorists answer that we experience *the same special kind of pleasure* when we behold a beautiful painting that we do when we watch a beautiful ballet. Our experience is an *aesthetic* one and the common factor in each of the arts is beauty.

Many thinkers, particularly British and German theorists, helped develop these views. However they reach their most influential form in the German philosopher Immanuel Kant (1724-1804). Kant was a prolific and systematic thinker who advanced many influential opinions about aesthetics. His definition of beauty has had widespread impact throughout the eighteenth century even in modern ideas. He famously defines the experience of beauty as "disinterested pleasure." Undoubtedly, Kant's greatest impact on aesthetic theory has centered in the concept of *disinterest*. Disinterested appreciation of beauty does not mean a *lack* of interest, or boredom, but emphasizes instead that the person's appreciation must not motivated by *ulterior* interests. For Kant disinterested pleasure is a kind of pleasure that isn't dependent on anything besides the beauty in the object itself. Kant formulates his notion of "interest" in terms of *desire*. He says: "*Interest* is what we call the liking we connect with the presentation of an object's existence. Hence such a liking *always refers at once to our power of desire.*"[37] So *disinterested* liking is an appreciation of it that has nothing to do with wanting it.

Part of Kant's rationale for such a claim is fairly straightforward. If one enjoys a particular work of art because it is a sound financial investment, or because she may impress her friends as a cultured person, or because the artist was a dear friend, then such interests will cloud objective judgment. Her interests will bias the appreciation. Her pleasure will be interested in something besides the beauty of the art alone. "Everyone has to admit," asserts Kant, "that if a judgment about beauty is mingled with the least bit of interest then it is very partial and not a pure judgment of taste. In order to play the judge in matters of taste, we must not be in the least biased.

So we can see Kant's point. He goes well beyond battling bias, however. He opposes judgments of beauty not only to prejudice, but also to *desire*, and to concern for the *existence* of the object. This leads him to distinguish the realm of beauty from that of the *agreeable* (i.e., that which is sensually pleasing, e.g., the pleasure taken in warmth on a cold day, or food when we are hungry), and from that of the *good* (that which is pleasing morally which is discerned through reason). "Both the agreeable and the good refer to our power of desire . . ." he says,

> A judgment of taste, on the other hand, is merely *contemplative*, i.e., it is a judgment that is indifferent to the existence of the object: it [considers] the character of the object only by holding it up to our feeling of pleasure and displeasure.[38]

In other words the discernment of the beautiful stems not from a desire to posses or consume (in which case existence is necessary), but merely to behold (in which case only the image is necessary). Often times, Kant observes, we take greater aesthetic pleasure in, say, the reflection in a river of a building, than in the building itself. Unlike the case of desire, the actual object is irrelevant to aesthetic pleasure, which is concerned only with an image presented to our senses. The separation of beauty from existence or being is a big shift from the pre-modern tradition that thought that beauty showed us ultimate reality or the true existence of things.

Modern conceptions of the beautiful are so grounded in aesthetic *pleasure* that it is now difficult to conceive of beauty in any other terms. For Kant, the recognition of beauty is based on one thing: we identify "the character of the object," he says, "only by holding it up to our feeling of pleasure and displeasure."[39]

However, beauty has not always been conceived in this way. Prior to the thirteenth century, Western conceptions of beauty were primarily formulated in terms of *desire* more than of *pleasure*. Many thinkers *include* the phenomenon of pleasure in their ideas of beauty, but Kant's ideas are more radical. For him the experience of beauty is *determined* by it, and no other emotions (especially desire) can coexist. The innovation and radicality of his system is the *exclusive* primacy of pleasure and the absolute uncoupling of beauty and desire.

The influence of Kant's ideas have been enormous. His impact would be difficult to overstate. Some of Kant's ideas that have had a big influence include:

1. That aesthetic pleasure, or the appreciation of beauty, is disinterested.
2. That beauty is experienced as pleasure.
3. That beauty has little to do with the actual world, but is concerned with images.

IX. Romanticism

Romanticism is a cultural movement that defies precise definition. Perhaps it is best understood as a conglomeration of ideas that when considered individually are not unique in themselves, but when configured together are characteristic of the Romantic movement. In particular, to understand Romanticism one must keep in mind that it was a *reactionary* movement against the ideas of modernity. By "modernity" the authors mean the new age that began in the Enlightenment. That era was originally heralded as the dawning of a golden age. Technology and reason, it was assumed, would eventually solve all of our problems. Within a hundred years or so, however, this initial optimism soured.

The Romantics argued that by focusing exclusively on reason and rational problem solving, society had lost its soul. Romantic philosophers claimed that reason alone was insufficient to grasp a great many of the most important things in life. Love, passion, emotion and experience, are prime examples. Romanticists interpreted the goal of modernity to be a desire to control and managing reality in an attempt to harness it for practical gain. Utilizing reason to "build a better mouse trap" becomes the ultimate goal. Lost however, is the enjoyment of beauty, the mystery of religion, the passions of being human.

A particular complaint of the romantics was their claim that modernity exuded an overconfidence in the role of reason. The following poem by John Keats (1795-1821) typifies the romantic attitude toward over rationalization. While reading it remember that by "philosophy" he does not mean an academic discipline, rather, at that time, it meant what we mean by "science."

> Do not all charms fly
> At the mere touch of cold philosophy?
> There was once an awful rainbow in heaven:
> We know her woof, her texture; she is given
> in the dull catalogue of common things.
> Philosophy will clip an angel's wings,
> Conquer all mysteries by rule and by line,
> Empty the haunted air, and gnomed mine—
> Unweave a rainbow.[40]

For Keats science "unweaves the rainbow," "empties the haunted air," and " clips the angel's wings." He thought that trying to understand everything *completely*, and to think that truth only has to do with reason, guts reality of its true essence. Instead he prefers a rich, mysterious view of the world. Rather than attempting to prove the intelligibility of beauty through reason, the Romantics view "the aesthetic" as a way of life. Seeing Rationalism as heavy handed and lame-hearted, ignoring of transcendent mysteries, Romanticism sets itself in *opposition* to reason. Romantic conceptions of beauty, then, offered an escape from the paltry existence of the Industrial age, where reason led to specialization, and isolation in the work place. The experience of the beautiful, the romantics claimed, delivers us, at least for a moment, from the grubby cares of modern life. Beauty is cast as saving us from our soulless necessity to make a buck. It is seen as re-connecting us with ourselves, with nature, and with a transcendent reality. Beauty comes to be viewed as a savior, and poets and artists as prophets.

The view of aesthetic pleasure as a separate, higher experience than our normal daily experiences started in the eighteenth century. That opinion, however, both broadened and deepened in Romanticism which tended to equate the aesthetic with escape from the "real" world. The proper response to beauty, then, was not disinterested pleasure, as Kant claimed, but a *surrender* to it or an *absorption* by it. In either case, the beholder escapes or leaves world—a momentary release from the cares of the world.

Another feature of Romanticism is the emphasis placed on passion and human experience. In an essay entitled *On Immaculate Perception*, Friedrich Nietzsche (1844-1900), unleashes a vitriolic attack against those who see in the experience of the beautiful as a disinterested escape from desire. Neitzsche mocked such views. "How you soil noble names!" he thunders, claiming that the very name of "beauty" is dishonored by the idea of disinterest. According to Neitzsche, any assumption that a man might view an artistic depiction of a voluptuous nude without any desire, is either naive or disingenuous. From a distance, he argues, ideas of disinterest may they look like a "god's soul," but in actuality, they are nothing other than "snake's filth and bad odors."[41]

Further emphasis on experience may be seen in Nietzsche's view of beauty as a tension between the Appolonian (from Apollo, the god of order, restraint, and reason), and the Dyonisiac (from Dyonisius, the god of passion, chaos and revelry). As do most romantics, Nietzsche sways in the direction of Dyonisius.

A few of the features of Romantic views of beauty that we have noted are:

1. Beauty is seen to offer an escape from the ills of modern society.
2. The experience of beauty is set in distinction to the experience of reason.
3. Special human experiences, especially of beauty, become more important than mundane day-to-day experiences.
4. An elevation of the role of art and the artist to new heights of importance for the human soul and for society.

X. Recent Views of Beauty

For the most part, conceptions of beauty do not play a major role in modern aesthetics. When the idea is discussed it is generally thought of in terms of disinterested pleasure with some romantic features added. One interesting exception, however, is the thought of the German philosopher, Martin Heidegger (1889-1976) and some of those who borrow or adapt his ideas about beauty (including many "post modern" thinkers).

Heidegger starts by expanding the Romantic critique of modernity. He presents a stark account of Western culture. After having been misled by Plato, he says, western culture has gone from bad to worse. According to Heidegger, ever since Plato, we have tried to understand ultimate Reality in a way that ends up reducing it to proportions manageable by our finite minds. But when we try this, we necessarily distort reality by oversimplifying it, and by forcing it to fit into categories we can understand. The end result is a complete disconnection with reality—what Heidegger calls a "forgetfulness of Being."

The condition of modernity, then, is one of radical *crisis*. Whereas Nietzsche locates the crisis in the *loss of values* experienced in the "death of God," Heidegger traces this crisis to a *separation from "Being."* That is, the modern person has become so engulfed in the interests of "technology," that his or her capacity to hear, see, or recognize Being is diminished. The crisis centers in the *disposition* of the modern human, resulting in immense loss to both individual and society. Modern humans, according to this view, adopt a violent stance toward reality, seeking always to use it or to get something from it. Every part of reality is viewed from the perspective of usage—an attempt to plunder Being. Consequently, human are separated and alienated from Being, and ultimately and tragically, from him or herself.

And here is where beauty comes in. Heidegger believes that that the experience of beauty counters this pernicious tendency. Beauty is conceived as the "unconcealment" of Being. Heidegger calls the revelation of Being that happens in the experience of the beautiful a *phainesthetic* experience, meaning the "lighting-up" or "shining-forth" of Being in beauty. Truth, then, is an *epiphany* (from the Greek epi-faino, to shine upon); and beauty is a "dynamic disclosure" through which truth-beyond-appearance irrupts. In other words, the experience of beauty is "Reality" speaking "truth" to us.

But what *kind* of truth is unconcealed? For Heidegger the truth that Being communicates is non-rational, non-scientific, not deduced, not logical, not propositional, non-conceptual, inexact, non factual, uncertain, and not related to probability. In other words, it is diametrically opposed to Enlightenment conceptions of truth. This type of truth is "found", or revealed, not deduced logically. For him, beauty reveals a truth that has more to do meaningfulness than factualness.

While Heidegger seems to blend beauty and truth together in a way that blurs the distinction, and while the irrationalist notion of "conceptless knowledge" is hard to make sense of, nonetheless Heidegger's legacy has been profound. His views have not only influenced aesthetics, but also literary theory, theology, and broad strands of postmodernism.

Endnotes

[1] Eco, Umberto, translated by Hugh Bredin, *Art and Beauty in the Middle Ages.* New Haven: Yale University Press, 1986, p. 32

[2] Tatarkiewicz, p. 133

[3] Tatarkiewicz, p. 133

[4] Ibid., p. 122

[5] Ibid., p. 133.

[6] Plotinus *Ennead I*, V1.2

[7] Ibid., *I*, VI.6

[8] Ibid., *I*, VI. 1

[9] Ibid., *I*, VI. 5

[10] Ibid., *I*, VI. 5.

[11] Ibid., *I*, VI.5.

[12] Gregory of Nyssa, *The Life of Moses* (II, 231.232)

[13] On the Soul and the Resurrection. Schaff, Philip and Wace, Henry, eds. *A Select Library of Nicene and Post-Nicene Fathers of the Christian Church, Second Series, Volume V: Gregory of Nyssa: Dogmatic Treatises, Etc*. Grand Rapids, Michigan: Wm. B. Erdmans Publishing Company, 1978, p. 449

[14] On the soul and the Resurrection, Schaff p.449

[15] Romans 1:20

[16] Ecclesiastes 1:2

[17] Song of Songs 2:16

[18]On Virginity, XI, Schaff p. 355.

[19]Augustine, *Confessions* X, 38.

[20]Augustine *De Ordine*, II, XV

[21]Quoted in Tatarkiewicz, p. 132

[22]Augustine *De Musica* VI. xiii. 3 8

[23]Augustine *De Lib. Arb*. II. 16

[24]Augustine *De Q*. 77.

[25]Augustine *De Div. Q. ad Simplic*. 21

[26]Ibid.

[27]Augustine *Confessions* X.27

[28]In De div. nom. c. IV lecture 5 Quoted in Tatarkiewicz, p.260.

[29]Cited in Umberto Eco *Art and Beauty in the Middle Ages*, translated by Hugh Bredin (New Haven: Yale University Press, 1986), p. 67.

[30]Summa Theologiae. I q. 5 a 4 ad 1.

[31]Summa Theologiae, I-a II-ae. q. 27 a I ad 3.

[32]Ibid., I-II, 1 ad 3. Quoted in Eco. p. 72.

[33]Cited in Tatarkiewicz, *A History of Six Ideas*, p. 150.

[34]Ibid.

[35]Alexander Gottlieb Baumgarten, *Reflections on Poetry (Meditationes philosophicae de nonnullis ad poema pertinentibus)* translated by Karl Aschenbrenner and William B. Holther (Berkeley and Los Angeles: University of California Press, 19540, p. 42.

[36]See P. O. Kristeller's Our Modern System of the Arts.

[37]Immanuel Kant, *Critique of Judgment*, translated by Werner S. Pluhar, Indianapolis: Hackett Publishing Company, 1987, § 1, p. 204. [Hereafter cited as *Critique of Judgment*. Akadamie pagination.]

[38]*Critique of Judgment*. § 5. 209

[39]*Critique of Judgment*. § 5. p. 209.

[40]John Keats, *Lamia*, Part II. 11.229-237.

[41]Freidrich Nietzsche, *Thus Spake Zarathustra*, translated by Walter Kaufmann, Penguin Press, p. 13 1.

ART AND RELIGION—SOME MODERN VIEWS

by Ge Baas

Tillich on Art

Tillich argues that art arises out of the dialectic tension of human existence. Human beings are finite and yet belong to the infinite. It is this double awareness of belonging and exclusion which produces an ontological anxiety. For the artist, this anxiety becomes the urge to express the essential unity of that which we are in artistic symbols.

In his view, human beings are not only excluded from the infinite to which they belong; they are also excluded from everything finite that is other. Out of this fundamental loneliness human beings strive to participate in other beings and to take the world into themselves. Yet their participation is restricted by the appearance and structure of things in their relation to other things.

Tillich argues that this double awareness of belonging and exclusion leads to a double perception of reality. On the one hand, human beings perceive objects through their immediate functional context: a pen is a tool used for writing. Within this functional perception, a thing's identity is perceived by seeing it in relationship with something other—or, by seeing it through its opposite. For example, we perceive the meaning of "hot" as we contrast it with "cold." On the other hand, Tillich suggests, human beings may catch a glimpse of a thing's identity as fully realized in itself, without comparing or contrasting it with another. For a moment, we are struck by the deeper quality of an object, and we "forget" all that is associated with it as we come to consider it only for itself. This second kind of perception, Tillich argues, is that of the artist. Artists see the glimmer of the infinite within an object and are then inspired to lift that object out of its finite context and into the stream of the ultimate.

In order to differentiate between these two types of perception, Tillich uses the term "cognitive reception" to refer to seeing a thing in relation to other things. "Aesthetic perception" is Tillich's term for seeing a thing in itself. Art's power, then, lies in the fact that it gives us a unique insight: it reveals the finite world as the bearer of ultimate reality. Art frees objects from having an excessively finite identity. Tillich felt that Expressionism as an artistic style came especially close to the ideal of art as the breaker of the prison of forms. The expressionist painters, he felt, freed the object to

Be the bearer of ultimate Being. Tillich was also fascinated by the paintings of Rothko and Pollock, praised Munch's **The Scream** as the revelation of universal existential dread and admired Cezanne of whom he said that the artist restored things to their real metaphysical meaning.

While speaking at the Museum of Modern Art in 1950, Tillich said that he had come to the conclusion that "an apple of Cezanne has more presence of Ultimate Reality than a picture of Jesus by Hoffman" (Paul Tillich, *On Art and Architecture*, p. 69).

In conclusion, Tillich sees Art as alone capable of this unique contribution to our world: it reconnects the world in our perception to ultimate meaning and reality.

Sources

Paul Tillich, *On Art and Architecture*, Eds. John and Jane Dillenberger. Trans. Robert P. Scharlemann. New York: Crossroads, 1987.

William H. Willimon, "Tillich and Art: Pitfalls of a Theological Dialogue with Art," in *Religion in Life*, Spring 1976.

Charles W. Kegley, "Paul Tillich on the Philosophy of Art," in *Journal of Aesthetics and Art Criticism*, Winter 1969.

Martland on Art

Thomas R. Martland's work *Religion as Art: An Interpretation* is perhaps the most eloquent defense for art's compatibility with religion. He argues that religion and art detach and create: neither expresses what is already the case; both look beyond the here and now. They must necessarily detach in order to be freed to new understanding. They must suspend a habitual pattern to pay attention to things previously ignored. They impose a new understanding on old givens, thus changing them.

In Martland's view, Art consists of convention and innovation. Creativity cannot occur in a vacuum: it must make use of already established forms. Yet it does not merely copy them: it discloses and liberates them. Art and religion, then, are both home breakers; their calling is to create new relationships, not to service old ones. While his claim that art and religion share a similar "work" is valuable for a discussion of art's relationship to religion, it also provides a deeper insight into the nature of art itself. Art's work, then, is to "redeem" the world as we see it and know it from its "fallen state", namely its reduction to the mundane. Our ordinary, habitual seeing and knowing of the world longs for the disclosure of new meaning within it. This longing to participate more fully in the world is expressed and met by the artistic creativity: artists show us that which we have missed or, perhaps, have long ago stopped seeing. Artists turn an almost innocent, naive eye on the world, as if seeing it for the first time. Artists "rename" the world for us, through us, and through their art we "rename" ourselves. The great power of the poets, for example, lies in the fact that they describe us to ourselves. Poets describe the world as we find it in ourselves yet cannot describe: poets tell us the words we have long hoped to hear or have heard but could not speak. Poets lift ordinary words to extraordinary power to describe that which we all long to describe and know: a world that holds an extraordinary and sacred depth.

We may summarize Martland's findings on the nature of art as follows:

1. Art calls us to see what we have not yet seen.
2. What art calls us to see must relate to our previous seeing.
3. What art shows us must be distanced from our previous seeing.
4. The characteristic function of art is that it distances us from previous seeing.
5. Art is necessary to the process through which we come to a new understanding.
6. What we come to see and understand is a new time and space.
7. To know art's function is to stand in critical innocence and fascination before a work of art.

Source

Thomas R. Martland, *Religion as Art: An Interpretation* Albany: State University of New York Press, 1981.

THE NATURE OF ART, TRUTH, AND REALITY

PLATO AND THE MASS MEDIA

by Alexander Nehamas

Alexander Nehamas is professor of philosophy and humanities at Princeton University, and he works primarily in ancient philosophy, Nietzsche scholarship, and literary theory. He is author of Nietzsche: Life as Literature *and translator (with Paul Woodruff) of Plato's* Symposium. *Nehamas argues that recent complaints about the influence of television resemble Plato's complaints against the drama of his own time. This is appropriate, Nehamas contends, for Plato's allegations about poetry are attacks on the popular entertainment of the day, not on art in general.*

The metaphysics of Pygmalion is still in the center of our thinking about the arts. To see that this is so, and why, we must change subjects abruptly and recall Newton Minnow's famous address to the National Association of Broadcasters in 1961. Though Minnow admitted that some television was of high quality, he insisted that if his audience were to watch, from beginning to end, a full day's programming,

> I can assure you that you will observe a vast wasteland. You will see a procession of game shows, violence, audience participation shows, formula comedies about totally unbelievable families, blood and thunder, mayhem, violence, sadism, murder, western badmen, western goodmen, private eyes, gangsters, more violence, and cartoons.

This general view of the vulgarity of television has been given a less extreme expression, and a rationale, by George Gerbner and Larry Gross:

> Unlike the real world, where personalities are complex, motives unclear, and outcomes ambiguous, television presents a world of clarity and simplicity .... In order to complete a story entertainingly in only an hour or even half an hour conflicts on TV are usually personal and solved by action. Since violence is dramatic and relatively simple to produce, much of the action tends to be violent.

An extraordinary, almost hysterical version of such a view, but nevertheless a version that is uncannily close to Plato's attitude that the lowest part of the soul is the subject-matter of poetry, is given by Jerry Mander. Television, he writes, is inherently suited for

> expressing hate, fear, jealousy, winning, wanting, and violence ... hysteria or ebullience of the kind of one-dimensional joyfulness usually associated with some objective victory—the facial expressions and bodily movements of antisocial behavior.

Mander also duplicates, in connection with television, Plato's view that poetry directly influences our life for the worse: "We slowly evolve into the images we carry, we become what we see." This, of course, is the guiding premise of the almost universal debate concerning the portrayal of sex, violence, and other disapproved or antisocial behavior on television on the grounds that it tends to encourage television's audience to engage in such behavior in life. And a very sophisticated version of this Platonic point, making use of the distinction between form and content, has been accepted by Wayne Booth:

> The effects of the medium in shaping the primary experience of the viewer, and thus the quality of the self during the viewing, are radically resistant to any elevation of quality in the program content: as viewer, I become *how* I view, more than *what* I view.... Unless we change their characteristic forms, the new media will surely corrupt whatever global village they create; you cannot build a world community out of misshapen souls.

... Plato's reason for thinking that our reactions to life duplicate our reactions to poetry is that imitations are superficially identical with the objects of which they are imitations. Exactly this explanation is also given by Rudolph Arnheim, who wrote that television "is a mere instrument of transmission, which does not offer any new means for the artistic interpretation of reality." Television, that is, presents us the world just as it is or, rather, it simply duplicates its appearance. Imitations are substitutes for reality. In Mander's words,

> people were believing that an *image* of nature was equal ... to the experience of nature ... that images of historical events or news events were equal to the events ... the confusion of ... information with a wider, direct mode of experience was advancing rapidly.

Plato's argument against poetry is repeated in summary form, and without an awareness of its provenance, in connection with television by Neil Postman: "Television," he writes, "offers viewers a variety of subject-matter, requires minimal skills to comprehend it, and is largely aimed at emotional gratification." The inevitable result, strictly parallel to "the bad government in the soul" which Plato would go to all lengths to avert, is, according to Postman, an equally dangerous "spiritual devastation."

Parallels between Plato's view and contemporary attitudes such as that expressed in the statement that "daily consumption of 'Three's Company' is not likely to produce a citizenry concerned about, much less committed to, Madisonian self-government," are to be found wherever you look. Simply put, the greatest part of contemporary criticisms of television depends on a moral disapproval which is identical to Plato's attack on epic and tragic poetry in the fourth century B.C. In this respect, at least, we are most of us Platonists. We must therefore reexamine both our grounds for disapproving of Plato's attack on poetry and our reasons for disapproving of television ....

My effort to establish a parallel between Plato's deep, complex, and suspicious hostility toward Homer and Aeschylus on the one hand and the obviously well-deserved contempt with which many today regard *Dynasty* or *Dallas* may well appear simply ridiculous. Though classical Greek poetry still determines many of the criteria that underlie the literary canon of our culture, most of television hardly qualifies as entertainment. Yet my position does not amount to a trivialization of Plato's views. On the contrary, I believe, we are bound to miss (and have already missed) the real urgency of Plato's approach if we persist in taking it as an attack against art as such. Plato was neither insensitive to art nor inconsistent in his desire to produce, as he did, artworks of his own in his dialogues; he neither discerned a deep characteristic of art that pits it essentially against philosophy nor did he envisage a higher form of art which he would have allowed in his city. Plato's argument with poetry concerns a practice which is today paradigmatically a fine art, but it is not an argument directed at it as such a fine art. At this point, the history of art becomes essential for an understanding of its philosophy. Though Plato's attack against poetry in the *Republic* may be the originating text of the philosophy of art, his argument, without being any less profound or disturbing, dismisses poetry as what it was in his time: and poetry then was popular entertainment.

The audience of Attic drama, as far as we now know, was "a 'popular' audience in the sense that it was a body fully representative of the great mass of the Athenian people" and included a great number of foreign visitors as well. During the Greater Dionysia in classical times no fewer than 17,000 people, perhaps more, were packed into the god's theater. Pericles, according to Plutarch, established the *theorikon*, a subsidy to cover the price of admission and something more, which ended up being distributed to rich and poor alike, and made of the theater a free entertainment.

The plays were not produced in front of a well-behaved audience. The dense crowd was given to whistling . . . and the theater resounded with its "uneducated noise." . . . Plato expresses profound distaste for the tumult with which audiences, in the theater and elsewhere, voiced their approval or dissatisfaction (Rep. 492c). Their preferences were definitely pronounced if not often sophisticated. Since four plays were produced within a single day, the audience arrived at the theater with large quantities of food. Some of it they consumed themselves—hardly a silent activity in its own right, unlikely to produce the quasi-religious attention required of a fine-art audience today and more reminiscent of other sorts of mass entertainments. Some of their food was used to pelt those actors whom they did not like, and whom they often literally shouted off the stage. In particular, and though this may be difficult to imagine today, the drama was considered a realistic representation of the world: we are told, for example, that a number of women were frightened into having miscarriages or into giving premature birth by the entrance of the Furies in Aeschylus' *Eumenides*.

The realistic interpretation of Attic drama is crucial for our purposes. Simon Goldhill, expressing the recent suspiciousness toward certain native understandings of realism, has written that Electra's entrance as a peasant in the play Euripides named after her "is upsetting not because it represents reality but because it represents reality in a way which transgresses the conventions of dramatic representations, indeed the representations of reality constructed elsewhere in the play," In fact, he continues, "Euripides constantly forces awareness of theatre as theatre." This, along with the general contemporary claim that all art necessarily contains hints pointing toward its artificial nature and undermining whatever naturalistic pretensions it makes, may well be true. But it doesn't alter the fact that it is of the essence of popular entertainment that these hints are not, while the entertainment still remains popular, consciously perceived. Popular entertainment, in theory and practice, is generally taken to be inherently realistic.

To be inherently realistic is to seem to represent reality without artifice, without mediation and convention. Realistic art is, just in the sense in which Plato thought of imitation, transparent. This transparency, I believe, is not real. It is only the result of our often not being aware of the mediated and conventional nature of the representations to which we are most commonly exposed. As Barish writes in regard to the theater, "it has an unsettling way of being received by its audiences, at least for the moment and with whatever necessary mental reserves, as reality pure and simple." Whether or not we are aware of it, however, mediation and convention are absolutely essential to all representation. But since, in such cases, they cannot be attributed to the representation itself, which, transparent as it is, cannot be seen as an object with its own status and in its own right, they are instead attributed to the represented subject-matter: the slowmoving speech and action patterns of soap operas, for example, are considered (and criticized) as representations of a slow-moving world.

Attributed to subject-matter, mediation and convention appear, almost by necessity, as distortions. And accordingly . . . the reality the popular media [is] supposed to represent has always been considered, while the media in question are still popular, as a distorted, perverted, and dismal reality. And it has regularly involved campaigns to abolish or reform the popular arts or efforts on the part of the few to distance themselves from the arts as far as possible. And insofar as the audience of these media has been supposed, and has often supposed itself, to react directly to that reality, the audience's undisputed enjoyment of the popular arts has been interpreted as the enjoyment of this distorted, perverted, and dismal reality. It has therefore also been believed that this enjoyment both reflects and contributes to a distorted, perverted, and dismal life—a vast wasteland accurately reflected in the medium which mirrors it.

This is the essence of Plato's attack against poetry and, I believe, the essential idea behind a number of attacks against television today. Nothing in Plato's time answered to our concept of the fine arts, especially to the idea that the arts are a province of a small and enlightened part of the population (which may or may not be interested in attracting the rest of the people to them), and Plato holds no views about them. His quarrel with poetry is not disturbing because anyone seriously believes that Plato could have been right about Homer's pernicious influence. Plato's view is disturbing because we are still agreed with him that representation is transparent—at least in the case of those media which, like television, have not yet acquired the status of art and whose own nature, as opposed to what they depict, has not yet become in serious terms a subject in its own right. And because of this view, we may indeed react to life, or think that we do, as we react to its representations: what is often necessary for a similarity between our reactions to life and our reactions to art is not so much the fact that the two are actually similar but only the view that they are. Many do in fact enjoy things on television which, as Plato wrote in regard to poetry, some at least would be ashamed, even horrified, to enjoy in life.

The problem here is with the single word "things," which applies both to the contents of television shows and to the situations those represent. What this suggests is that what is presented on television is a duplicate of what occurs in the world. No interpretation seems to be needed in order to reveal and to understand the complex relations that actually obtain between them.

By contrast, no one believes that the fine arts produce such duplications. Though we are perfectly willing to learn about life from literature and painting (a willingness which, in my opinion, requires close scrutiny in its own right), no one would ever project directly the content of a work of fine art onto the world. The fine arts, we believe, bear an indirect, interpretative relationship to the world, and further interpretation on the part of audience and critics is necessary in order to understand it. It is precisely for this sort of interpretation that the popular arts do not seem to call.

Yet the case of the *Republic* suggests that the line between the popular and the fine arts is much less settled than is often supposed. If my approach has been right so far, Plato's quarrel with poetry is to a great extent, as much of the disdain against television today is, a quarrel with a popular form of entertainment. Greek drama, indeed, apart from the fact that it was addressed to a very broad audience, exhibits a number of features commonly associated with popular literature. One among them is the sheer volume of output required from any popular genre. "Throughout the fifth century B.C. and probably, apart from a few exceptional years, through the earlier part of the fourth century also," Pickard-Cambridge writes, "three tragic poets entered the contest for the prize in tragedy, and each presented four plays." If we add to these the plays produced by the comic poets, the plays produced at all the festivals other than the City Dionysia (with which Pickard-Cambridge is exclusively concerned), and the plays of the poets who were not chosen for the contest, we can see that the actual number of dramas must have been immense. The three great tragedians alone account for roughly three hundred works. And this is at least a partial explanation of the fact that so many plays were different treatments of the same stories. This practice is imposed on popular authors by the demands of their craft and is in itself a serious source of satisfaction for their audience.

The most important feature of popular art, however, is the transparency to which we have already referred. The idea is complex, and it is very difficult to say in general terms which of a popular work's features are projected directly onto reality since, obviously, not all are. A television audience knows very well that actors shot during a show are not really dead, but other aspects of the behavior of such fictional characters are actually considered as immediate transcriptions of reality. On a very simple level, for example, it is difficult to explain otherwise the fact that the heroines of *Cagney and Lacey* invariably buckle their seat belts when they enter their car, whether to chase a murderer or to go to lunch. And many aspects of their relationship are considered as perfectly accurate transcriptions of reality. Popular art is commonly perceived as literally incorporating parts of reality within it; hence the generally accepted, and mistaken, view that it requires little or no interpretation.

Arthur Danto has recently drawn attention to art which aims to incorporate reality directly within it, and has named it the "art of disturbation." This is not art which represents, as art has always represented, disturbing reality. It is art which aims to disturb precisely by eradicating the distance between it and reality, by placing reality squarely within it. Disturbational art aims to frustrate and unsettle its audience's aesthetic, distanced, and contemplative expectations: "Reality," Danto writes, "must in some way . . . be an actual component of disturbatory art and usually reality of a kind itself disturbing. . . . And these as components in the art, not simply collateral with its production and appreciation." "Happenings" or Chris Burden's viciously self-endangering projects fall within this category. And so did, until relatively recently, obscenity in the cinema and the theatre.

The purpose of disturbational art, according to Danto, is atavistic. It aims to reintroduce reality back into art, as was once supposedly the norm: "Once we perceive statues as merely designating what they resemble . . . rather than containing the reality through containing the form, a certain power is lost to art." But contemporary disturbational art, which Danto considers "pathetic and futile," utterly fails to recapture this lost "magic."

This failure is not an accident. The disturbational art with which Danto is concerned consists mainly of paintings, sculptures, and "happenings" that are essentially addressed to a sophisticated audience through the conventions of the fine arts: you dress to go see it. But part of what makes the fine arts fine is precisely the distance they have managed, over time, to insert between representation and reality; this distance can no longer be eliminated. Danto finds that disturbational art still poses some sort of vague threat: "Perhaps it is for this reason that the spontaneous response to disturbational art is to disarm it by cooptation, incorporating it instantaneously into the cool institutions of the artworld where it will be rendered harmless and distant from forms of life it meant to explode." My own explanation is that the cool institutions of the artworld are just where the art of disturbation, which is necessarily a fine art, has always belonged.

Disturbational art aims to restore "to art some of the magic purified out when art became *art.*" This, I believe, is not a reasonable goal: once a genre has become fine, it seldom if ever loses its status; too much is invested in it. And yet, I want to suggest, "the magic purified out when art became *art*" is all around us, and just for that reason almost totally invisible. The distinction between representation and reality is constantly and interestingly blurred by television—literally an art which has not yet become art—and which truly disturbs its audience: consider, as one instance among innumerable many, the intense debate over the influence on Soviet-American relations of the absurd mini-series *Amerika* in the spring of 1987.

As a medium, television is still highly transparent. Though, as I have admitted, I don't yet have a general account of which of its features are projected directly onto the world, television clearly convinces us on many occasions that what we see *in* it is precisely what we see *through* it. This is precisely why it presents such a challenge to our moral sensibility. The "magic" of television may be neither admirable nor even respectable. But it is, I am arguing, structurally identical to the magic Plato saw and denounced in Greek poetry, which also, of course, was not *art*.

Plato's attack on poetry is duplicated today even by those who think of him as their great enemy and the greatest opponent of art ever to have written. It is to be found not only in the various denunciations of television, many of which are reasonable and well-supported, but even more importantly in the total neglect of television on the part of our philosophy of art. Aesthetics defends the arts which can no longer do harm and against which Plato's strictures hardly make sense. His views are thus made incomprehensible and are not allowed to address their real target. Danto writes that every acknowledged literary work is "about the 'I' that reads the text . . . in such a way that each work becomes a metaphor for each reader." The key word here is "metaphor": we do not literally emulate our literary heroes, in the unfortunate manner of Don Quixote; we understand them through interpretation and transformation, finding their relevance to life, if anywhere, on a more abstract level. But such literal emulation was just what Plato was afraid of in the case of tragic poetry, and what so many today are afraid of in regard to television: "we become what we see." Plato's attack on "art" is still very much alive.

THE ETHICAL SIGNIFICANCE OF MODERN ART

by Karsten Harries

> *Karsten Harries is Mellon Professor of Philosophy at Yale University. His books include* The Meaning of Modern Art *and* The Bavarian Rococo Church: Between Faith and Aestheticism. *In the selection that follows, Harries argues that contemporary art serves an ethical function, not in the traditional sense of promoting specific moral values, but in the currently more important sense of disrupting our complacency about ethical matters.*

In a televised debate that was part of the discussion that preceded the establishment of the National Endowment for the Arts in 1965, John Kenneth Galbraith declared arts legislation to be the "final step now that recognizes that the artist is a first-class citizen, that he is worthy of being taken as seriously as the scientist, the businessman, or even the economist." Like many such declarations, this one asserted what is readily granted: do we really need the artist as much as we do the scientist, the businessman, and perhaps even, although here there is more reason for doubt, the economist? While I should like to agree with Galbraith, I do not find his claim easy to defend.

In *The Painted Word* Tom Wolfe claimed that art and the public today are linked mostly by mutual indifference: while the art world is self-contained and unconcerned about the public, the public in turn is not paying much attention to modern art and cares little whether it thrives or not. To be sure, Tom Wolfe's sketch of the art world, including the artists and a small well-to-do aesthetic elite, restricted to eight cities in five countries, offered only a caricature. But that caricature still has its point: an enormous gap separates modern art from the general public and its concerns. Only the most serious art seems to have a little public significance, less certainly than professional sports, soap operas, or popular music. Because so many value the latter and are willing to pay for what they enjoy, here there is neither need nor demand for federal funding. Why not entrust the future of art, too, to the forces of a free market? If there is an aesthetic elite that values and is willing to support modern art, fine—why not leave it at that? But does a democratic government have any more business supporting the arts than it does supporting baseball or gourmet cooking? And if widespread indifference should threaten the survival of modern art, who is to say that something essential would be lost? What today is the social significance of art?

We are given a hint by a response that goes beyond indifference: by the widespread hostility to modern art. Usually such hostility expresses itself in nothing more damaging than a cutting comment, directed perhaps at a curator unfortunate enough to have hung some work of abstract art upside down, or in the delight that tends to greet reports that yet another art expert has been taken in by the forger's skill or that a janitor inadvertently used a Duchamp ready-made as the simple snow shovel it once was. Tom Wolfe's clever barbs directed at what he calls Cultureburg betray more than a trace of such hostility.

Hostile reactions are not always as harmless. As a recent article in *Art News* pointed out, vandalism directed against works of modern art has become a serious problem. I will give just two examples.

What caused a 29-year-old student of veterinary medicine to punch holes into Barnett Newman's *Who's Afraid of Red, Yellow, and Blue?*, which Berlin's New National Gallery had just acquired for one million dollars? The vandal, one Josef Klein, claimed that the painting had made him afraid; also that the sum paid for it had scandalized him. Both claims must be taken seriously. How can such an expenditure be justified? Should money and time be spent on art as long as there are persons who go homeless, hungry, and lack adequate medical care? Such questions become more difficult to answer when the money is the taxpayer's.

Given the painting's title, Klein's assertion that it made him afraid is of special interest. I well understand reacting to a Barnett Newman with some nameless fear: given this modern version of the sublime, Klein's reaction can hardly be called altogether inappropriate, although Klein could be accused of a failure to preserve aesthetic distance. That Klein's attack on the Newman possessed a social significance is shown by the way the Berliners elevated him into a minor hero—if not quite into an Oliver North, at least into a Bernard Goetz. By punching holes into the canvas, Klein seemed to strike blows against forces threatening to unravel the social fabric. Reader's responses to Newman's painting were predictable: any house painter's apprentice could have created that sort of object at a fraction of the cost; visit any first- or second-grade classroom and you will find works of comparable quality; not the vandal is crazy, but those willing to pay one million dollars for the Newman.

Equally revealing is the decision of some local politicians in the Rhineland to use an enamel bathtub, which Josef Beuys, emulating Duchamp, had transformed into a readymade-aided, as a wine cooler. What provoked these representatives of the people to scrub and clean the tub, in which the artist as baby had been bathed and which was now awaiting exhibition in some German castle? What prompted them to thus "destroy and desecrate," as the art work's owner put it, a work of art? Once again public opinion tended to side with the vandals. Outrage was directed not so much against the deed, as against the court's subsequent award of DM 80,000 in damages, plus interest, to the owner.

It would be easy to go on. All I want to suggest here is that such acts of vandalism have an ethical significance. The perpetrators understand themselves as defenders of good sense that they see being mocked and threatened by art works that defy expectations of what art should be. That this threat is taken seriously suggests that the works, too, are perceived to possess ethical and political significance, albeit of a negative, subversive sort. Does that perception presuppose a more positive significance? What is the ethical significance of art? The following remarks attempt an answer.

I will begin with three statements, three voices from the not-too-distant past. Although they come from very different quarters, they yet agree in their condemnation of modern art. Each assumes the ethical significance of art; each accuses modern art of subversion.

The first belongs to Congressman George A. Dondero, who in 1949, when many feared Moscow's diabolically clever scheming, thought it his duty to awaken his presumably nodding colleagues in Congress to the dangers of modern art. Art, he proclaimed,

> is considered a weapon of communism, and the Communist doctrinaire names the artist as a soldier in the revolution against our form of government, and against any government or system other than communism.

Had the Russian revolution not used this weapon successfully against the Czarist government? And did the fact that this revolution, once it had become the new establishment, was quick to divorce itself from modern art not testify to this art's corrosive power? The Soviet leadership knew very well what it was doing when at home it enforced an edifying realism "extolling the imaginary wonders, benefits, and happiness of existence under the socialized state" while abroad it continued to use modern art against its adversaries, especially against the United States, resorting to a more subtle form of germ warfare. The congressman was particularly disturbed by the fact that this foreign pest had not only invaded but actually taken over this country's art education.

> We are now face to face with the intolerable situation, where public schools, colleges, and universities, art and technical schools, invaded by a horde of foreign art manglers, are selling to our young men and women a subversive doctrine of "isms," Communist-inspired and Communistconnected, which have one common goal— the destruction that awaits if this Marxist trail is not abandoned.

I do not know how many of those who heard the congressman were able to take his remarks seriously—were able to take art that seriously, for what power must art possess to be capable of seducing our young men and women, threatening our free society with destruction. Today Dondero's speech would seem to provide little more than an unpleasant footnote to the triumphant progress of modern art in this country. Have we not learned to take pride in the fact that New York has replaced Paris as the world's artistic capital? Who today would blame this country's ills on modern art? The very suggestion seems preposterous. Is not art by its very nature innocent, harmless, wonderfully irrelevant?

Given the congressman's assertion of a deep link between modern art and communism, it is interesting to note that at just about the same time communists saw in modern art the tool of decadent capitalism. The second voice belongs to Vladimir Kemenov, the former director of Moscow's Tretjakow Gallery. The passage is taken from an article published in 1947.

According to Kemenov, those who plead for the political innocence of modern art are mistaken. By assuming the mask of such innocence, by insisting that art be for art's sake and as such free of all ideological content, modern artists only hide the true political function of their work.

> As a matter of fact, this "pure" art actually disseminated reactionary ideas, ideas that were advantageous or useful to the capitalists. Formalistic artists ceased to be rebels and became the abject slaves of capital, even though from time to time they did assail capitalism, sometimes even sincerely.

But such professions of solidarity with the suffering masses are belied by an art that, born of narcissistic self-preoccupation, idealizes the individual. Instead of giving voice to the proletariat, art for art's sake cannot but subvert revolutionary fervor. To such decadent art, Kemenov opposed what he called "a vital Soviet art, ideologically forward-looking and artistically wholesome: socialist in content and national form; an art worthy of the great Stalin epoch."

The third voice is national and socialist with a vengeance. It belongs to Adolf Hitler, who, unable to forgive those who had twice denied the would-be artist a place in the Vienna Academy, vowed to make vandalism public policy, promising to unleash a tornado that would destroy modern art and to put its practitioners into asylums or prisons. The occasion for the following remarks was the inauguration of the Great Exhibition of German Art in 1937 in Munich's newly built House of German Art.

> I do not want anybody to have false illusions: National-Socialism has made it its primary task to rid the German Reich, and thus, the German people and its life of all those influences which are fatal and ruinous to its existence. And although this purge cannot be accomplished in one day, I do not want to leave the shadow of doubt as to the fact that sooner or later the hour of liquidation will strike for those phenomena which have participated in this corruption.

Different as they are, all three statements agree in attributing to art the power to subvert the health of the community. Modern art is judged by political criteria and found wanting. All three statements presuppose that art has an ethical function, even, and indeed especially, when it disavows this function and claims to exist only for art's sake; they presuppose that art helps to mold the ethos of those who come under its spell, the way individuals understand themselves and their place in society; and they presuppose that modern art does so irresponsibly. And regardless of our distaste for these particular advocates of political control of the arts, can the presupposition that art possesses an ethical function really be dismissed? If not, must we not insist that the guardians of the state make sure that art exercise this function responsibly?

Insistence that art be subject to political control is, of course, not at all a new phenomenon. The statements above are but three of countless variations on a theme first stated in Plato's *Republic*. Socrates there challenges poetry and her sister arts of imitation to prove their right to exist in a well-ordered state. Such a proof, he insists, would have to show, not only that art is pleasant, but that it is "useful to States and to human life." The primacy of the political is taken for granted. The rulers of the state would be negligent, did they not recognize and control the ethical function of art. To assume that responsibility is to assume also the responsibility of censorship.

Plato's critique of the arts would hardly have been so vigorous had it been directed only against the uselessness of art. Such uselessness is easily defended. As Aristotle knew, life would be hollow were it not for activities that we engage in for their own sake, for experiences that are their own justification. We would not delight in such experiences as we do, were it not for their uselessness.

But when Plato's Socrates questions the right of the poets to a place in his *Republic*, and we can extend his questioning to all the arts, he does so not because they give pleasure, but because, while giving pleasure, they also usurp, perhaps unwittingly, the role of the educator. That ancient quarrel between poetry and philosophy of which Socrates speaks is a quarrel about who should be entrusted with moral education. Is it not obvious that it should be entrusted to those who know best, because they have thought most responsibly about such matters? If Socrates considers expelling the poets from his Republic, this is first of all because although perhaps disguised as entertainers, they do shape, or rather misshape, the self-understanding of the citizens. Their work is measured by the philosophers' understanding of truth and found wanting. The poets lie too much, and they especially lie too much about the gods. Such tales of idealized human beings should guide and illuminate human existence; they should communicate edifying truths and thus reinforce what is good in us and make it more difficult for us to give in to selfish impulses. But what do poets like Homer tell us of the gods? That they fight, whine, despair, lie, commit adultery. The poets' gods are all too human, entertaining perhaps, but hardly edifying. Nor should this surprise us: Vice is more interesting and thus more entertaining than virtue. Consider the heroes of our own popular art, our movies, our soap operas.

Plato is convinced of the ethical power of poetry and, more generally, of art. He knows that even if philosophers may possess a better grasp of moral truths than poets or artists do, we do not change human behavior with clear reasons as much as with affecting images and words. Just because of this he insists that the philosopher's reason controls art, just as the doctor's reason should control the use of drugs.

In spite of familiar arguments for the autonomy of the aesthetic realm, it is not easy to dismiss claims that poetry, and more generally art, can have an ethical function. Think of Plato's own poetic portrayal of Socrates as a new kind of hero, whose calm reason, selfless love, and fearless courage are to replace the virtues of Homer's Achilles. Or think of the Gospels, which tell stories of a very different courage and love.

We do not have to limit ourselves to such extraordinary examples. Most art of the past has served a particular way of life, has called human beings to a particular ethos. It would be easy to be specific. I could discuss, for example, the educational function the Jesuits assigned to art; or the way art helped shape the ethos of Victorian gentlemen. Or the function of social realism.

But what of modern art? What is the ethical function of Frank Stella's protractor paintings or of Roy Lichtenstein's pop fantasies? Has modern art not lost or, if you prefer, shed its ethical function and become art for art's sake? I shall return to these questions. But regardless of how they are answered, can we deny an ethical function to today's popular art and entertainment? To give just the most obvious examples, must the endless hours so many spend before their television sets not shape their ethos, and not only because of what appears on the screen, but because of the nature of the medium? Can the casual way in which these screen heroes love and kill be a matter of indifference to society? And if such images and stories do indeed help shape the ethos of those exposed to them, would it not be irresponsible to entrust that power to artists and entertainers who may care little whether what is offered is a destructive lie, as long only as this lie finds its public and becomes a commercial success? In the *Republic* Plato reserves thus the privilege of lying for the rulers. They alone "may be allowed to lie for the public good. But nobody else should meddle with anything of the kind."

The rulers' monopoly on lying assumes that they know what is in the public's best interest. Do we have such confidence in our statesmen? Plato solves this problem by making the philosopher king. In him reason and political power are joined. Today we are likely to insist that there be no such state monopoly on lying; that free discussion and democratic practices, while no doubt imperfect, are yet better suited to bring about the desired union of reason and political power. But can we disagree with Plato when he insists that art be ruled by a thoughtful determination of what is in the public's best interest? This raised a more basic question: is unprejudiced reason capable of determining the public good? An affirmative answer is presupposed by all attempts to subject the arts to its control.

Like so many philosophers, Plato calls for the subjection of passion and emotion to reason, for a domestication of eros by the power of logos. Just because, as Plato reminds us, the point of art is not "to please or to affect the rational principle in the soul," but rather man's "passionate and fitful temper," we have to guard against its seductions.

Can we divorce reason and passion in this manner? I have suggested that Plato's own discourse owes its effectiveness to eros as much as to logos, to the siren charms of poetry as much as to the cooler voice of reason. The hold that Plato's Socrates still has on us today is due not only, perhaps not even primarily, to the arguments Plato presents in support of this way of life, but also to the story that he tells. That story communicates something of Socrates' quite distinctive ergs, which continues to affect us and invites us to follow Plato's example and to choose Socrates as our hero.

Could Plato the philosopher have dispensed with Plato the poet? One might answer that the telling of the story was not necessary to establish the truth that mattered to Plato, although it may well have been necessary to let that truth become effective in the world. But is Plato's poetry no more than a concession to those who will not heed the truth unless it appears dressed up in poetic garments? At issue is the more fundamental question: does reason have the power to determine the true ends of human existence, objectively and dispassionately, free from all personal or cultural prejudice? If that is granted, if we can indeed determine the truth and falsity of moral discourse just as we can determine the truth and falsity of the discourse of science, if there are such things as moral facts, then there is no need to quarrel with Plato's claim that the philosopher must be declared the winner in his contest with the poet. We should then call on philosophers as on society's experts in all moral matters. They would draw boundaries that human beings should not violate. The highest vocation of art would then be to become the handmaid of moral philosophy.

Philosophers, increasingly on the fringes of the academic establishment, may find it tempting to thus see themselves as the guardians of the spiritual health of the nation, at, or at least close to, the centers of power: the highly paid advisers of doctors, lawyers, and artists. It is a dream philosophers and society should resist.

Can reason be practical? Of course, if by practical reasoning we mean reasoning about means or reasoning that seeks to articulate and systematize individual or social preferences. But can unprejudiced reason discover the true ends of human action? From Plato to Kant and indeed right down to the present, philosophers have certainly tried to show that it can. That such attempts continue is itself a comment on what is being attempted. I cannot make sense of objective values or of categorical imperatives. Both seem to me contradictions in terms.

For what would be meant by objective values? Presumably that values are very much like facts. To be sure, these would not be ordinary facts; values do not exist as the things of this world do. But these ideal facts, too, would be what they are, regardless of what anyone would take them to be. Correspondence with these facts would make moral judgments true or false. Just as the pursuit of truth in science demands unprejudiced inquiry, so to gain proper access to values, one would first have to free oneself from all personal or cultural prejudice, rise beyond one's all too subjective interests and desires, transcend oneself as an engaged, embodied self.

But values must engage and claim us. To recognize an asserted value as a value, an individual must recognize it as an articulation of what more immediately affects him. To communicate values, discourse must touch this affective base, which cannot be divorced from our concrete biological and historical being in the world. A disinterested and, in this sense, truly objective knowing could never discover values.

Just as it makes no sense to speak of objective values, so it makes no sense to speak of a categorical imperative, an unconditional ought, with no regard to reward or punishment, to happiness or unhappiness. We may indeed feel that to be true to our own self we must respect the dignity of every human being or be convinced that we truly gain ourselves only when ready to sacrifice ourselves for a larger whole, a whole that may include only one other loved person or embrace all humanity. But such self-understanding rests on passion or faith rather than on the voice of pure reason.

Like the poets' tales of gods or heroes, the philosopher's moral speculations are born of his necessarily precarious attempt to articulate what he feels to matter. The philosopher may cast these feelings into a form that claims the agreement of all unprejudiced inquirers, but this is first of all a rhetorical appearance. Values are human creations. They have their ground in the affective life of individuals, who, while concerned with their own survival and welfare, also experience themselves as parts of larger social wholes, and are caught in the tensions this amphibian state brings with it. If we are to acknowledge the validity of such creations, we must recognize them as articulating what more immediately claims us. We must, as Plato would say, recollect their truth, but that truth should be sought, not above, in a timeless Platonic heaven, but below, in what Plato calls our "passionate and fitful temper." That is to say, to be effective, the communication of values must be sufficiently rhetorical, or poetic, or artistic to touch the hearts of those to whom it is addressed. Without this, asserted values will seem but arbitrary constructions. Similarly arbitrary will seem laws enacted to enforce obedience to values that have died, that is, lost their affective base. And as particular laws lose their authority, the authority of all law is threatened, as it comes to be understood as first of all a matter of mere power.

But must this suggestion that moral discourse inevitably objectifies subjective interests and desires not threaten that shared sense of values on which society depends? How can there be a responsible exercise of political power, if there is no practical reason to guide it?

Confident in the power of reason to determine what ought to be, Plato offers us his vision of a state where reason rules. Reasonable challenge to such rule would appear to be impossible. In such an ideal state individuals would have learned to understand themselves as parts of the political whole and to keep the place they have been assigned. Plato knew of course about the dangers of basing public policy on utopian thinking. The confusion of human beings with angels or gods has often proved disastrous and those in power have rarely been blessed with a particularly developed moral sense. All too often private passion has masked itself by claiming the authority of reason.

The problem is, however, not just a problem of the inevitable distance that separates every ideal from reality. The very assumption of a pure practical reason, capable of offering the one true determination of what ought to be, must be challenged. What fashions a multiplicity of persons into a community is not so much reason as common sense. This common sense is itself a historical product, precariously established out of countless individual feelings and desires, some selfish, some selfless. Attempts to ground this common sense in reason put the cart before the horse.

There will always be tension between private desires and common sense. Nor are desires and common sense constant. They can be expected to change as conditions change. Such change calls for an ongoing interpretation, reappropriation, and recasting of values that have come to be articulated, established, and accepted. Attempts to shore up and secure inherited values by appealing to supposedly timeless dictates of reason are likely to have the opposite effect. By freezing common sense, by covering up the affective base of values, such appeals prepare for the erosion of common sense and for the devaluation of old values.

To be sure, society needs stability. But we need not fear that by grounding values in necessarily subjective affects we surrender morality "to our random and changing appetite." The very existence of societies argues that human beings are sufficiently alike to share enough desires to allow for the emergence of a common sense. Even Hobbes takes for granted that, atomized as they are, human beings have certain interests in common: if human beings did not fear death, seek power, and love liberty, they could not arrive at a covenant that allows them to escape from the state of war. All effective government is supported by an already established common sense. Not that such a common sense is fixed once and for all. To live, common sense, too, must grow and change. Current discussions centering on equal rights or on the abortion issue are part of the ongoing evolution of this society's common sense. It would be a mistake to cut such discussions short by invoking the authority of some supposedly timeless truth.

But how does common sense get established? How do private feelings gain a public voice? Plato already points in this connection to art. Art awakens, communicates, reinforces, and shapes affective states. Thus it can help to establish and maintain, but also to subvert, a common ethos. It is precisely this power that gives art its ethical significance.

If this is right, no state can afford to neglect the aesthetic education of its future citizens, for at stake is the establishment and continuing support of that common sense without which the social order threatens to unravel. This, however, is not to say that government should prescribe to art what it is to say. For where would such prescription find its norms? In moral reasoning? But such reasoning must ground itself in common sense. In common sense then? But common sense does not furnish anything like a secure and stable ground. It is itself the changing product of changing personal convictions. Art is one instrument serving the evolution of common sense. The artist has his necessarily precarious place between the already established and what still struggles to gain voice. Art must dare venture beyond the boundaries of what has come to be judged acceptable; it must be a place of experimentation; it therefore cannot be justified by appeals to accepted criteria. Creative achievement and nonsense are uncomfortably close neighbors.

I have challenged the assumption that practical reason can ground political practice. Such reason must rather ground itself in and serve evolving common sense, recognizing the need for stability as well as the need for change, the right of the past as well as the right of the future. Nor can censorship invoke the authority of pure reason. Reason, too, is only an instrument of evolving common sense. That evolution cannot be determined in advance. The precariousness of censorship is thus the inverse of the precariousness of artistic creation. If one is conservative, the other counsels change. What has come to be established does not as such have authority, and what presents itself as new liberating insight may only be a willful and self-indulgent fancy. In their different ways censors and artists both make a significant contribution. The struggle between them is part of a healthy society . . . .

Often the mask of the fool has proved insufficient to protect the artist. The hostility that a good part of the public has so often felt when confronted with modern art is not altogether unlike the hostility that led the Athenians to condemn Socrates to death. Socrates was accused of being "a doer of evil, who corrupts the youth; and who does not believe in the gods of the state, but has other divinities of his own." Both charges had their point. By calling on the individual to think of himself, Socrates did shake further an already shaken confidence in the established and usually taken for granted. Thus Socrates made people uncomfortable. His questioning touched something that threatened the self-understanding that they had come to acquire as good Athenians. The deity that presided over Socrates' life and called him to his subversive life of questioning did not belong with the public deities, which always appear to give supernatural blessing to what is being done. This deity demanded of the individual that, instead of simply living as one lived, he step back from and examine inherited and taken-for-granted conventions.

Like Socrates, the modern artist dislocates and thereby liberates. If Socrates wanted to lead others to think for themselves, the artist lets us see, feel, and also think for ourselves. Kandinsky claimed that the task of art is to make things visible. That this should be a task presupposes that because we usually do not see or only half see the things that are closest to us, the clothes we wear, the room we live in, the street we cross every day, we take them for granted. We are too busy in the world, too accustomed to it, to open ourselves to its reality. That goes also for our own reality. Just as the mysterious presence of things is veiled by the established and the accepted, so are our own needs and desires. To open ourselves to our own selves and to the world around us, we must first free ourselves from the everyday, from its talk, from its cares and concerns; take leave from the familiar but only to return to it, now with clearer and more questioning eyes. In this sense art may be said to help us recover the affective base without which all talk of values rings hollow or false.

Earlier I suggested that one task of art is to make public affective states. Art furnishes shared metaphors of what is essentially private; thus it helps bridge the gap that separates individuals and society and contributes to the establishment of a genuinely common sense. But common sense loses its roots in the affective states of individuals, when shared commitments give way to the rule of what one says and does. When this happens art gains another function: its second task is to plough the crust of convention, to call individuals in danger of losing themselves to what has come to be taken for granted back to the affective ground in which all effective common sense must finally be rooted. There appears to be tension between these two tasks: while the first seems edifying and constructive, the second seems subversive and destructive. And yet such subversion is itself an essential part of the life of common sense. To be sure, the guardians of the established would rather see the artist serve the existing order, express what has already been approved. But a healthy society must allow for places where its presuppositions and commitments, its established ways of thinking and seeing, are challenged and new alternatives are hinted at, presented, and explored. Without such challenge, what has come to be taken for granted tends to be mistaken for what has to be. The achievements of the past threaten to become obstacles to new creation; the future is sacrificed to the past. Common sense offers no final security. It must be tested by a constant pushing toward its boundaries. Without such testing it becomes rigid and dies.

Especially today, in this rapidly changing world, art should be a place of challenge and experimentation. Its primary point should be not to amuse or titillate, nor to comfort. Art should both excite us and make us uneasy, even afraid. If it is to do so, if it is to lead us to and beyond the boundaries of established common sense, we must make sure that the distance that separates the fool and the king, art and politics, is preserved; we must recognize that there is a sense in which the artist must be left alone, just as the artist must preserve his distance from the community and protect the apolitical character of his art and his fool's freedom. But paradoxically, just this apolitical character gives genuine art its profoundly political and ethical significance. A society that possesses the courage to face an unknown future will support a free art, knowing full well that often the return for such support will be questions and provocations, or even nonsense.

ART AND THE MODAL IMPERATIVE: ANALYZING ACTIVIST ART

by Donald Kuspit

> Donald Kuspit is professor of art history and philosophy at the State University of New York at Stony Brook and Andrew Dixon White Professor at Large at Cornell University. In 1983 he received the Frank Jewett Mather Award for Distinction in Art Criticism, awarded by the College Art Association. His books include Louise Bourgeois and The New Subjectivism: Art of the 1980s. The following reading is an abbreviated version of the original article of the same title. Kuspit argues that the political art of our era is an aesthetic failure.

What is of interest to me is the cast of mind that leads the artist to attribute unique moral grandeur to himself. He is of course hardly the only member of society who does so. And, in his case, as in those of the others, moral pretentiousness serves an indispensable psychic function. But his case is different, for his emphasis on the moral purpose of art is at odds with the assumption that its essential purpose is aesthetic. Whatever else it might articulate, and as important as that may be, is secondary to its goal of achieving aesthetic importance. In other words, the moralizing artist uses art in a fundamentally inappropriate way. He misapplies it, as it were. No doubt art can and does have moral implications, but these are beside the point of its aesthetic intention. However, the moralizing artist thinks righteousness is more important than aesthetics. The latter, he believes, must serve the former, not vice versa. How does he come to believe this? Why does he perversely justify art in moral rather than aesthetic terms? Why, psychologically speaking, does he stand the meaning of art on its head, making a secondary meaning it might have primary and its primary meaning secondary? . . .

The social protest of the moralizing artist, and his general conception of art as inherently moral—which he thinks makes him a more authentic, authoritative artist than the aesthetically oriented artist—is necessary to his self-regard. This is especially so in the Modern situation of artistic decadence, so-called pluralism, indicative of stylistic insecurity and, even more fundamentally, basic uncertainty about the character and necessity of art. Nothing any longer seems innately artistic—perhaps the basic meaning of artistic decadence. Decadence is an ambiguous concept, traditionally having to do with the dialectic of decay and rejuvenation. But it can also be regarded positively: the splitting of art into a variety of conflicting factions, seemingly weakening it as a whole, in fact signals its healthy differentiation, that is, the discovery of new artistic possibilities. But the fragmentation of art is no doubt also an enfeeblement of it, and suggests general uncertainty about its effect on the individual and society—its impact. It is as though art must try out a variety of stylistic and conceptual strategies in the hopes that one will hit the psychosocial mark— take hold in human as well as art history.

The activist artist's moral intention is not simply the latest instance of the old belief, traceable to antiquity, that art must have a moral purpose to be socially credible, but the facile answer to a complex epistemological and narcissistic crisis—to art's seemingly unresolvable self-conflict and undefinability, inherent uncertainty and lack of self-identity, leading to its ambiguous fragmentation. Activist art is one subliminally anxious response to the modern inability to achieve a totally cohesive, seemingly self-adequate work of art, whose parts are decisively equilibrated—an art emblematic of ego strength and self-integration. In lieu of what increasingly looks like a modern incapacity to achieve a work of art that seems integral in itself—a seamlessly whole yet subtly differentiated work, ripe despite the incommensurateness of its parts— activist art offers a totalitarian conception of art as moralistic. That is, it totalizes art as morally responsible or dispenses with it as next to nothing at all. Activist art believes in effect that the only hope of putting the pieces of the Humpty Dumpty of art together again is by giving it an exclusively moral determination.

The artist's claim to moral authority has escalated in the last decade. He presents himself as though he alone was sufficiently fit to wear the mantle of moral authority. He in effect exhibits himself as society's superego—its most authentic moral force. Indeed, in the last decade we have seen the virtual institutionalization of moralizing activist art. In certain quarters it is assumed that an art without an overt moral mission is necessarily immoral. This is the current version of the artist-moralist's case against doggedly aesthetic art. So influential is this view, that art without an overt moral point feels compelled to insist that it has a covert one, as in the case of Richard Serra's steel plate sculpture. Supposedly a moral protest against capitalistic society, especially in the way the sculpture presumably "defeats" the capitalistic skyscraper, if Serra's work must have sociomoral meaning, it can in fact be said to epitomize rather than resist the social order. For its crudity and delusional grandiosity, and especially the contradiction between its heroic look and inner shakiness—bold, self-confident appearance and structural unsoundness, giving one the sense of its inner insecurity—are exactly the traits of capitalistic society.

Similarly, Ross Bleckner declares his black paintings memorials to people with AIDS, as though their aesthetic elegance was insufficient to give them artistic credibility. The need Bleckner feels to wrap his refined pictures in the cloak of moral concern suggests the defensive posture aesthetic artists must take to survive in today's self-righteous art world. Support for the victims of AIDS is without doubt an important moral, sociopolitical cause, and one is grateful for an artist's sensitivity to it. But to use it to justify an art that needs no justification is another matter. Bleckner feels compelled to apologize for producing an essentially aesthetic art, as though that is not good enough. In fact, he admits that the idea of associating his melancholy images with people who have died from AIDS occurred to him after he painted them. It was presumably a way of adding to their inherent gravity, and above all giving them a social weight and moral credential they did not originally have or need. No doubt if an artist says so his work can spontaneously acquire an overlay of moral meaning—a specious moral depth—at will. Such determination to give art moral meaning seems to allow for spurious superegoism, that is, conscience as an adaptational, art-politically judicious afterthought.

Moreover, it should be noted that in finding social targets the artist often avoids the most psychosocially consequent ones, e.g., the entertainment industry, with its mass production of false subjectivity. Perhaps this is because the contemporary artist unconsciously regards himself as an entertainer manque—the persona of Warhol seems to imply as much, seems to generalize itself over the scene like a blight. Is he envious of entertainment's mass appeal and enormous social effect? I suggest the art of Barbara Kruger and Jenny Holzer, among others, is the confused result of such emulative, even identificative envy, as well as the wish to make an explicitly public, socially influential, and communicative art. Similarly, ecologically concerned art, while intending to be socially catalytic, deals with an issue that has become not just an urgent matter of survival but entertaining, "popular." It seems that part of the motivation of moralizing activist art is its wish to be socially accepted—to belong—as though that, perhaps in and of itself, will make it credible.

The activist argument is that if art is not explicitly in the moral opposition, it finds itself naively in the service of the immoral status quo. Activist art has not only become a standard part of the art scene—mainstream rather than marginal—but ruthlessly passes judgment on it . . . .

In fact, contemporary activist art is a caricature of avant-garde art. For, while avant-garde art originates in antagonism to existing society and art, as Renato Poggioli remarks, its value ultimately resides in the stylistic innovation which is the aesthetic result of its antagonism—its answer to some sense of the questionableness of existing society and art. In contrast, contemporary activist art, however antagonistic, is more avant-gardistic than avant-garde, for it eschews aesthetic innovation—it is not stylistically challenging. Indeed, the activist artist cannot truly call his style his own. He uses conventionalized avant-garde styles, so simplified and stereotyped that they are no longer either a social threat or intellectual challenge—no longer provocative. He modifies them—with a shrewd sense of art world Realpolitik, so that his work will seem art historically credible—to his facile communicative purpose. He offers nothing artistically new, and indeed avoids stylistic experimentation as a threat to communication. This suggests that oppositionality and subversiveness—part of the standard expectation (catechism?) of avant-garde art, automatic guarantees of avant-gardeness—have become trendy cliches, very much in need of a critique. Activist art of course offers none, for it depends on the cliche of oppositionality and subversiveness. . . . The question is whether that is enough . . . .

The artist-moralist attempts to impose a moral limit or construction on art, as its most serious, ultimate meaning, in order to repress, even deny, its fundamental aestheticity, because that aestheticity is the emblem of desire. Aestheticity affords the illusion that desire can exist in a free, pure state—that there can be free passage of pure desire. It assumes that desire can be precipitated out of history by art, even as desire makes history happen, flow. This is an illusion, for desire always exists both constructively and subversively within the semiotics of events. But it is a necessary illusion, luring life on—indeed, justifying it to itself—with the belief that it can know its own depths, renew contact with what is most basic in itself, and as such revitalize itself.

The idea that one must perpetually renew desire to exist in the fullness of one's being—work with fresh desire, desire that has been liberated from its sedimentation in semiosis, and that can be a source of new semioticization of existence—is the motivation for art, or rather aestheticity, which at its best is experienced as desire rejuvenated and re-energizing life. Every aesthetic innovation is an attempt at the restoration of desire. The artist-moralist attempts to immobilize covert aesthetic desire—arrest its vital and vitalizing passage—by making stridently super-egotistic art. In doing so, he reveals the conflict of his own mental life—the conflict, already described, implicit in his experience of bad beautifulness of the lifeworld . . . .

Activist art, the latest version of moralistic art, is at bottom opposed to the free display and play of desire. Indeed, that is what oppositionality in general and opposition to the aesthetic in particular is fundamentally about. As such, activist art is inherently antiart, for the task of art is to find new ways of articulating desire, freeing it all of all ideological—that is, didactic—predetermination. Desire has neither social, moral, nor generally ideological meaning, however much it may fuel such meanings—which it will revolt against when they become reified, as they invariably do, when there is an attempt to indoctrinate people with them.